WINTER IN PRAGUE

Center for International Studies
Massachusetts Institute of Technology

Studies in Communism, Revisionism, and Revolution
(formerly *Studies in International Communism*)
William E. Griffith, general editor

1. Albania and the Sino-Soviet Rift
   William E. Griffith (1963)

2. Communism in North Vietnam
   P. J. Honey (1964)

3. The Sino-Soviet Rift
   William E. Griffith (1964)

4. Communism in Europe, Vol. 1
   William E. Griffith, ed. (1964)

5. Nationalism and Communism in Chile
   Ernst Halperin (1965)

6. Communism in Europe, Vol. 2
   William E. Griffith, ed. (1966)

7. Viet Cong: The Organization and Techniques of the
   National Liberation Front of South Vietnam
   Douglas Pike (1966)

8. Sino-Soviet Relations, 1964–1965
   William E. Griffith (1967)

9. The French Communist Party and The
   Crisis of International Communism
   François Fejtö (1967)

10. The New Rumania: From People's
    Democracy to Socialist Republic
    Stephen Fischer-Galati (1967)

11. Economic Development in Communist Rumania
    John Michael Montias (1967)

12. Cuba: Castroism and Communism, 1959–1966
    Andrés Suárez (1967)

13. Unity in Diversity: Italian Communism
    and the Communist World
    Donald L. M. Blackmer (1967)

14. Winter in Prague: Documents on
    Czechoslovak Communism in Crisis
    Robin Alison Remington, ed. (1969)

WINTER
IN
PRAGUE

*Documents on
Czechoslovak Communism
in Crisis*

Edited by ROBIN ALISON REMINGTON

with an introduction by William E. Griffith

Czech and Slovak translations revised by Michael Berman

The M.I.T. Press
Cambridge, Massachusetts, and London, England

CONTENTS

II. LIBERALIZATION IN PRAGUE AND ORTHODOX RESPONSE

III. PRESSURE AND NEGOTIATION

IV. INVASION OF CZECHOSLOVAKIA AND SPLIT IN WORLD COMMUNISM

V. NORMALIZATION

VI. EPILOGUE

PREFACE

IN 1968 PRAGUE ATTEMPTED to sweep the ashes of Stalinism from the Czecho-slovak road to socialism. This book is intended to document that experiment. It has been compiled for those who wish to learn the substance of change in Czechoslovakia in the words of the participants, to see the tension that process created in other Communist countries, and to develop a feeling for the depth of the shock to the Communist movement when Soviet troops invaded to cut off Prague's evolution toward socialist democracy by force. In addition to providing not easily accessible material in English, the text includes intro-ductory analyses to make the documents meaningful in context.

The book is neither exhaustive nor complete. Given space, I would have happily included twice as many documents. That was not possible. Therefore, I stuck to the highlights — that is, those documents I considered essential for understanding the internal crisis of the Czechoslovak Communist Party, Mos-cow's response, the near-panic of more orthodox East European Communist regimes, and the significance for other Communist parties. With respect to internal developments, this meant illustrating key themes such as the issue of Czech-Slovak federation, interest groups, the state of the economy, and the "leading role" of the Communist party. Documents were chosen to show the spectrum of opinion from the remaining conservatives in the Central Com-mittee to the Dubček supporters and radical intellectual dissenters. Finally, I selected material to indicate the content of "normalization."

Documents are arranged chronologically except in cases where they are in response to an earlier statement. The only exception is V. Mencl and F. Ouředník's account, "What Happened in January" (Document 4), which has been included in the time period it discusses rather than when it was pub-lished in November.

A book involving so many countries and languages is of necessity a collec-tive effort. It would not have been compiled without the enthusiasm and en-couragement of Professor William E. Griffith. I profited greatly from the comments of Donald L. M. Blackmer, Stanley Riveles, Rosemarie Rogers, Joan Barth Urban, and, most of all, visiting Czech and Slovak scholars, who due to the unhappy events of August 1968 must remain anonymous. The research assistance of Mary Patricia Grady and Natasha Cyker Lisman made my own work of editing much easier. The Center editor, Nancy C. Poling, contributed many helpful suggestions for the introductory notes.

Except in the case of Czechoslovak documents published in English and General Prchlík's radio press conference (Document 32) of which it was impossible to obtain a printed version, all translations have either been made from or revised from the original language. The bulk of this burden has fallen on Michael Berman who painstakingly revised translations of Czech and Slovak documents. When possible *Current Digest of the Soviet Press* (*CDSP*) translations have been used for Russian documents. When they were not available, Russian (and Polish) translations were checked by Mrs. Lisman. Rumanian and East German documents were revised by Miss Rodica Saidman, French and Italian by Miss Grady, Castro's speech by Ilda S. Aviles, the Albanian Declaration by Peter R. Prifti, the Hungarian document by László Urban, and the Yugoslav resolution by Gena M. Fine. The manuscript was typed by Mrs. Eileen Smith and Mrs. Lila Fernandez and prepared for press by Mrs. Elizabeth G. Whitney and Mrs. K. B. Inglee.

Finally I am grateful to the Center for International Studies and to its director Max F. Millikan for their support in this study. Its publication has been made possible by a generous grant to M.I.T. by the Ford Foundation for research and teaching in international affairs. However, neither the Center, the Foundation, nor any of those whose suggestions or assistance contributed to this documentary are responsible for the book's contents and errors. That responsibility is mine alone.

ROBIN ALISON REMINGTON

Cambridge, Massachusetts
April 18, 1969

INTRODUCTION

HISTORY HAS TAUGHT the Czechs to use cunning rather than defiance to survive.[1] Their last armed revolt was bloodily crushed in 1620, and for centuries thereafter the Czechs were ruled by Austria. T. G. Masaryk's First Republic, the only democracy east of Switzerland, lasted only twenty years. In 1938 the Czechs were abandoned by the West and enslaved by the Nazis. In 1945 Washington bowed to Moscow's demand that the Red Army take Prague. Small wonder that most Czechs and Slovaks, fearful of German imperialism and despairing of the West, in 1945 accepted Russian protection and in 1948 Communist rule.

Yet the nationalist, Western, and democratic traditions of Czech and Slovak history, and the survival of a large, trained intelligentsia, predisposed Czechoslovakia to resent foreign domination and domestic oppression. Moreover, the Czechoslovak Communist Party had a mass base, a major position in pre-1938 Czech intellectual life, and in the early 1920's a right-wing, Social Democratic tradition.

Thus liberalization in Czechoslovakia was only delayed. Five factors drove out Novotný and unleashed reform. First, de-Stalinization. The forced public revelations of his complicity in Stalinist crimes, and the end of massive police terror destroyed Novotný's authority and prestige. The second was economic. By 1963 the Czechoslovak economy had a negative rate of economic growth and Czechoslovak exports were not competitive on the world market. The disruption in the early 60's of Czechoslovak foreign trade patterns with China, Rumania, and even, in worsening of terms of trade, with the Soviet Union, the counter-productiveness of the centralized Stalinist economic model for a highly-developed economy, extensive Soviet-decreed credits to the Third World, and low agricultural productivity had resulted in an increasingly desperate economic situation. Incompetent, politically-appointed managers, the

[1] This introduction is a revised version of my "Eastern Europe After The Soviet Invasion of Czechoslovakia," pp. 11–19. For bibliography, see pp. 463–465. I am grateful for discussions with my friends Zbigniew Brzezinski, R. V. Burks, Melvin Croan, Fritz Ermarth, Nathan Leites, J. M. Montias, Robin Remington, Stanley Riveles, and Paul Zinner. I owe the most to many discussions with Czechs and Slovaks in and outside of Czechoslovakia, who because of the events of August 21, 1968, must remain nameless.

preference of a large part of the unskilled working class for security over incentives, wage egalitarianism, and declining work discipline made the problem seemingly insolvable, at least with Novotný's continuing centralized political repression. He and his associates *could* not themselves drastically reform the economy because they were too personally threatened by the reforms. They rightly perceived that the personnel changes required for rationalization and decentralization would imperil their political power. The resulting economic situation convinced the intelligentsia, many party cadres, and even most of the working class that Novotný must go.

The third factor was the recoalescence and return to influence of the large Czech and Slovak intelligentsias: writers, journalists, economists, and social scientists. For the Communist intellectuals, de-Stalinization and economic collapse had destroyed the authority of the Stalinist model, and indeed of Leninism as well. Under the influence of the young Marx, the great inter-war PCI theoretician Antonio Gramsci, and the ideas of Rosa Luxemburg, they began in the early 1960's to search for a new synthesis of democracy and socialism. Moreover, behind them, politically submerged since 1948 but active after Novotný's fall in January 1968, there was the mass of the non-Communist Czech intelligentsia, who, contrary to all other East Europeans, had another modern, democratic ideology available: that of the founder of Czechoslovakia, the great philosopher-statesman T. G. Masaryk. In 1968 Masaryk became increasingly important: symbolically to Communist intellectuals, ideologically to many others.

Thus from 1962 on the intelligentsia was cautiously preparing for the great turn, which finally came at the end of 1967. Much of this preparation was carried out by three working groups — on democratization, technological backwardness, and economics — in the Czechoslovak Academy of Sciences. These groups concluded that democratization required institutionalization of interest groups as genuine participants rather than transmission belts in the political process and that economic modernization would require massive inputs of Western technology and drastic economic reforms.

Moreover, a feeling developed that the party leadership was, at the least, ambiguous on how to handle dissent. At the June 1967 Writers' Congress a few writers defied Novotný's regime, and in October 1967 student demonstrations broke out in Prague. Both were hesitatingly and only partially crushed — a sure mark of the regime's weakness.

Fourth, the attitude of Czech intellectuals toward the Germans and the Russians began to change. (Slovak intellectuals had never been so anti-German or pro-Russian.) West European and West German economic progress had led to the realization by many liberal Communists in Prague and Bratislava that only massive West German credits and technology could make the Czechoslovak economy again competitive on the world market. Rising hatred of the pro-Novotný Ulbricht, combined with realization by many Czechs now allowed to travel there that West Germany was neither neo-Nazi nor militarist, led to a more favorable attitude toward Bonn. Conversely, continued Soviet support of Novotný and Ulbricht, plus growing Soviet technological inferiority to Western Europe and the United States, lowered Soviet prestige and authority.

The fifth, and at the end the precipating factor was the revolt of the Slovak Communists against domination from Prague. Slovakia, like Québec, is the poorer, less developed, strongly Catholic part of a multinational state, less democratic but deeply nationalist. Since 1919 the Czechs, Communists even more than non-Communists, have ruled Slovakia from Prague not wisely but too closely and too clumsily. Wartime "independence" and post-1948 domination from Prague coupled with rapid economic development led to strong but frustrated Slovak nationalism.

In 1963 Novotný reluctantly sacrificed the two leading pro-Prague Stalinist Slovak Communists, Široký and Bacílek. The latter was replaced as head of the Slovak Communist Party (KSS) by Alexander Dubček. Dubček had been raised in Soviet Central Asia, where his father, an early Slovak Communist, had settled after an unsuccessful stay in the United States. However, both father and son had been expelled from the Soviet Union in 1938, while some of their associates were shot or imprisoned there. Although Dubček rose in the KSS after 1945, went through the Moscow Party School, and enjoyed good relations with the Russians, he probably did not forget his earlier experiences. Once head of the KSS, he cultivated popularity, used academic experts, and worked toward a more rational, partially liberalized communism and equality for Slovakia with the Czech lands. A personal clash with Novotný in October 1967 made Dubček and the Slovaks ally with the Czech Communist progressives. Thus by the end of 1967 the anti-Novotný coalition in the top party leadership included Slovak nationalists, dogmatists (such as Hendrych, whom Novotný had personally antagonized, and Kolder), centrists, and progressives. It was a potentially conflict-ridden alliance. In an unprecedentedly free Central Committee plenum, and despite belated, halfhearted Soviet opposition, they got rid of Novotný, first as Party Secretary in January, then in April as President. But Dubček was a compromise candidate more acceptable to the Russians, Novotný, and the dogmatists as well as to the progressives than were the other possibilities. Moreover, he was known not to be a strong personality, an additional reason for his choice.

To get rid of Novotný, Dubček gave freedom to liberal Communists in the communication media. Once free, they led the massive thrust toward economic rationalization, free speech and press, equality ("symmetrical federation") for the Slovaks, improved political and economic relations with the West (especially with Bonn) alongside the primary alliance with Moscow, a reform of the Communist party and a degree of institutionalized political opposition which, many of them hoped and expected, would lead to a genuine multiparty system. For the Soviets perhaps the most serious threat was the guarantee of the right of Communist party members to try to change decisions once reached — i.e., the end of the Leninist party model. In short, this was a model of democratic socialism for a developed European country. With the Communist *apparat* discredited and demoralized, and given his own indecisiveness, Dubček did not attempt to lead or prevent the reform, only (albeit with partial success) to control it, thereby it seems becoming more liberal in the process.

The likelihood exists, however, that after removing his conservative opponents Dubček would have tried to push back liberalism as well. In any case, he wanted to rehabilitate communism by reforms but also to maintain what he saw as the three essentials of communism in Czechoslovakia: alliance with Moscow, continuing nationalization of industry, and a Communist party federalized but retaining control of the commanding heights of the society. Other interest groups would be consulted in the decision-making process but not allowed to form opposition parties. In short, the result would have been a kind of Communist corporative state. Neither he nor any of his associates anticipated the Soviet invasion; but even if they had, it seems doubtful that Dubček could have restrained the popular pressure for change.

Pushed by Ulbricht and Gomulka to intervene and by Tito, Ceauşescu, Longo, and Waldeck Rochet not to (and probably itself divided on the question), the Soviet leadership hesitated long before the invasion. Why did the Soviet Union finally march in? Moscow feared that Dubček would not or could not safeguard his essentials, that the conservatives would be purged, that opposition parties would be formed, that press freedom would bring rising criticism of Moscow, East Berlin, and Warsaw, and that East Germany, Poland, and indeed the Soviet Union itself would thus become infected. In part, such Soviet fears were probably justified: liberalization in Czechoslovakia would have encouraged liberalization among its neighbors. (Whether the Soviet solution, invasion, will in the long run allay these fears is another question; indeed, it may eventually bring them to pass.)

The Soviets expected that, in order to modernize and make his economy competitive, Dubček would accept even more massive West German credits than Rumania has. (Bucharest now has a near $400 million trade deficit with Bonn.) Thus West Germany would begin to replace Soviet economic influence in Czechoslovakia, thereby automatically contributing toward isolating and destabilizing East Germany and threatening vital Soviet interests. Finally, Dubček's emerging alliance with Tito and Ceauşescu, a revival of the interwar Little Entente, was seen by Moscow as anti-Soviet. In sum, Moscow was not prepared to allow its influence in Czechoslovakia to be eroded and the devolution of its empire in Eastern Europe to proceed; rather, it gave precedence to preserving its position by military force over relations with the West and with many other Communist parties.

Even so, Soviet action was slow, hesitant, and often contradictory. First, Moscow reluctantly let Novotný be replaced by Dubček. Second, thereafter underestimating the speed and extent of change in Czechoslovakia, the Russians still hesitated, thus losing in world opinion and in Warsaw and East Berlin by their hesitation to invade, and misleading Dubček as well. Third, when on August 21 they finally did invade, in large part to prevent the rout of the conservatives, their political planning, unlike their military moves, was based on two mistaken assumptions: that popular resistance would not be a major factor and that some conservatives would support them. They did have some basis for the latter belief. Reports indicate that three of the conservative leaders, Indra, Kolder, and the KSS First Secretary Bil'ak, were relatively pro-Soviet. But although in modern times Czechs did not resist Nazism or communism very strongly, this time the almost unanimous heroic passive resistance of Czechs and Slovaks so intimidated potential quislings that the Soviets could not find any to endorse them publicly. Moreover, Czechoslovak radio stations continued broadcasting and mobilized the whole country against the invaders while helping to prevent major clashes with Soviet troops. Conversely, the Soviets, hoping to get President Svoboda to collaborate, did not remove him.

Even after Dubček and his closest associates were arrested, however, Svoboda held firm. Thus Czechoslovakia and its leaders remained steadfast in passive resistance, storing up the kind of patriotism through sacrifice and suffering which the country never had had before and will profit from greatly in the future. The spirit to which its people so nobly responded was fittingly put into words in an August 22 KSS resolution:

> . . . Let us lift our heads against the raised gun barrels. With the calm and prudence of a dignified and free people . . . let us stand proudly as our fathers stood and so that our children will not be ashamed of us. We are adopting this standpoint to the sound of the occupation forces shooting, but we do so freely, and with an awareness of our historic responsibility. . . .[2]

So the Soviets again reversed their tactics. They decided to exact from Svoboda and Dubček in Moscow, by threat of indefinite military occupation, the concessions they had not gained by force in Prague: reimposition of censorship and banning of opposition parties or clubs; renewed security police activity; return of Soviet "advisers" to defense, intelligence, and political police areas; limitation of the purge of the conservatives and removal of some liberals; and, most importantly, continued Soviet military occupation until Moscow agrees that the situation is "normalized" — and thereafter the permanent stationing of Soviet troops in Czechoslovakia. The Moscow agreement was also a partial retreat for the Russians: after arresting them and publicly denouncing them as traitors, they returned Dubček and his associates to power. Such hesitant tactics are hardly the stuff of which empires are permanently maintained.

The Czechoslovak leadership agreed to these concessions to prevent indefinite military occupation and an eventual quisling regime and in the hope that the future, as National Assembly President Smrkovský put it, would allow "a renewal of the trend toward socialist democratization." [3] They seem to have left the degree to which they would implement their agreement an open question.

We are still far from knowing all that happened, and why, in the period before the Soviet invasion. We inevitably know much less of what has hap-

---

[2] "Proclamation to the Slovak People," Radio Czechoslovakia, August 22, 1968.
[3] *The New York Times*, August 30, 1968.

pened thereafter. Since the story is still unfolding, only the most tentative analytical conclusions should be drawn now.

It is difficult not to be pessimistic about the prospects in the near future for freedom and independence in Czechoslovakia. Since last August the Soviets have gained politically much, but as yet not all, of what they wanted from the invasion. They have done so by steady political and economic pressure, backed by the threat of ruthless military intervention. Moscow systematically exploited Dubček's weakness, divisions in the Czechoslovak leadership, and Husák's ambition, while lack of effective concern in the Communist and non-Communist world and the increasing weariness of popular opposition contributed to Soviet gains.

At first after the invasion this did not seem to be the case, but, then, neither did it in Poland in late 1956. The invasion and the unprecedented passive resistance to it released a tidal wave of nationalism in Czechoslovakia. This was particularly noticeable among the working class, which only after the invasion became strongly politicized against the Soviet Union and for Dubček and the reforms. Only then did much of the working class, led by the revitalized trade unions, form an effective alliance with the protesting students. Thus ironically the mass base of support for Dubček and his colleagues was much greater after the invasion than before. Such heroic events as the self-immolation of the student Jan Palach and the subsequent demonstrations seemed to bring Prague back to Hussite days.

But appearances were deceptive. The party élite and much of the intelligentsia became increasingly weary and also reluctantly convinced that Dubček was too weak to resist the Russians and that in any case his departure might well be the price of retaining some of the reforms. The April 1969 demonstrations throughout the country following the defeat of the Soviet hockey team by the Czechoslovaks took on anti-Soviet overtones, quite possibly as a result, at least in Prague, of Soviet-planned provocation. Thereupon Marshal Grechko and Semenov descended on Prague and made clear the Soviet insistence that Dubček go, effective censorship be restored, and anti-Soviet actions cease. Shortly thereafter a group of generals, headed by Novotný's Chief of Staff Otakar Rytíř, presumably with Soviet knowledge and quite likely with Soviet support (Rytíř subsequently became a liaison officer for "affairs concerning the troops temporarily stationed in Czechoslovakia"), attempted a military coup. President Svoboda again blocked it, but Dubček's doom was clear: Husák replaced him as First Secretary.

Gustav Husák may probably well be viewed, as the saying goes in Czechoslovakia, as a much more intelligent and educated Gomułka. A clever and energetic lawyer, a major figure in the KSS since the prewar period, jailed under Novotný, he has, like Gomułka, learned little and forgotten less. He appears to be taking up where he left off in the early 1950's. Personally authoritarian by temperament, and a strong Slovak nationalist, he has never cherished democratization, civil liberties, or opposition currents; rather, he is a Leninist by conviction. But he is also a Slovak patriot, and his coming to power does not represent, at least as yet, anything like a quisling government. As KSS First Secretary, he kept Bratislava far less liberal than Prague, giving ruthless priority to Slovak nationalism over democratization. He will probably do the same in Prague.

What, then, remains of the "Prague spring"? Slovak equality and autonomy, the lack, so far, of a restoration of mass police terror plus tourism and some foreign travel. What does not remain are oppositional political groups, liberals in significant power positions, freedom of communication media, or ties with the West. Some conservatives are returning, but all in all the Novotný group has not resumed power. In short, Czechoslovakia in mid-1969 was somewhere between Poland and Hungary at that time. Little enough, one may think; but anything more must await major changes in Soviet policy, which in the near future, given the cautious, divided oligarchy now ruling in Moscow, seem unlikely.

On the international scene, for the time being the Soviets have restored their domination in Czechoslovakia, thereby stifling any tendencies in Hungary, Poland, East Germany, or Bulgaria toward major liberalization or independence, and checking a major potential success for West Germany. On the other hand, Moscow has greatly worsened its relations with Yugoslavia, Rumania, and all West European Communist parties, who for the first time almost unanimously denounced the Soviet invasion, as have the Chinese and the New Left. Castro, dependent on Soviet aid, endorsed Moscow but only in order to try to push Soviet policy in a more militant, anti-American direction, and for the first time publicly asked for a Soviet military guarantee. The disintegration of NATO and unilateral withdrawal of U.S. troops from West Germany have been at least delayed. West Germany, more fearful of Moscow, is less likely, as is Japan, to move away from the United States. Bonn has also suspended its decision to begin ministerial-level discussions with East Berlin, a major Soviet and East German objective. The U.S. loss of international prestige and influence from its Vietnam policy was partially, but most likely temporarily, counterbalanced by the worldwide outcry against Moscow's occupation of Czechoslovakia. Finally, the blow to East-West détente slowed down U.S. ratification of the non-proliferation treaty and (much more important to Moscow) is still helping to delay West German ratification. It also postponed, but only temporarily, the initiation of and progress in the U.S.-U.S.S.R. strategic weapons negotiations.

In short, by restoring their control over Czechoslovakia, the Russians have blocked any potential deviations in Poland, East Germany, Hungary, and Bulgaria, but in the rest of the world their influence has suffered. Even in Czechoslovakia, where the Good Soldier Švejk's tradition of silent, concealed, but persistent opposition to foreign domination is long, the Czech and Slovak peoples will hardly soon forgive or forget. The Soviet invasion has probably ended the long tradition of pro-Russian feeling among the Czechs, who will now bide their time and husband their strength for the long, complex struggle ahead.

Much will depend on the skill and the persistence of the Czechoslovak leaders. As Smrkovský said, "We realized that our decision could be regarded by the Czechoslovak people and by history as a wise solution or as treason." [4]

William E. Griffith

Cambridge, Massachusetts
August 7, 1969

[4] *Ibid.*

BIOGRAPHICAL PROFILES OF
CZECH AND SLOVAK LEADERS*

Bil'ak, Vasil — Replaced Dubček as First Secretary of the Slovak Communist Party and became a member of KSČ Presidium in the post-January 1968 period. Born August 11, 1917 in Krajná Bystrá near Bardejov in eastern Slovakia. Father was a smallholder. Orphaned in childhood and worked as a part-time farm laborer. Took part in Slovak Uprising in 1944. Seems to have joined Communist party in 1945 or 1946. Graduated from Prague Party College 1952. 1954 became member of KSČ CC, 1955 of KSS CC. From 1958 to 1962 Commissioner and later Minister of Education and Culture in Slovakia. In 1962 joined Slovak Presidium, became a KSS CC secretary and head of CC ideological commission. Role analagous to Hendrych with Czech intellectuals. After the August 1968 invasion, Bil'ak, considered a pro-Soviet collaborator, was replaced as First Secretary of the KSS by Gustav Husák. He was formally cleared of such charges by the June 1969 KSČ Presidium meeting, after Husák had come to power. Subsequently appointed CC Secretary in charge of international affairs.

Černík, Oldřich — Premier, January 1968 to date, member of KSČ Presidium. Czech. Born October 27, 1921 in Ostrava region. Father was a miner. Elementary education. Worked in Vitkovice Iron Works until 1949. Joined Communist party in 1945. Member and secretary of the Central Committee KSČ from 1956-1960. June 1960 took seat in the National Assembly, then in July became Minister of Fuels and Energy (1960-1963). Named Deputy Prime Minister and Chairman of the State Planning Commission in September 1963. June 1966 replaced Z. Fierlinger in the KSČ Presidium. April 1968 became Premier in the post-January government. Continued as Premier after the invasion, in the Czech-Slovak federal government of January 1969, and after Husák became First Secretary.

Císař, Cestmír, Dr. — Secretary of the Central Committee in post-January government. Czech. Born January 2, 1920 in Hostimice-nad-Bilinou. Father was proprietor of a small printing house. Graduated as a doctor of philosophy from Charles University in Prague 1948. Joined the Communist party in 1945. From 1946 worked in party posts on the District Committee in Prague and on CC and District Committee in Plzeň. Between 1957 and 1961 assistant to the editor-in-chief of *Rudé*

* These profiles have been compiled from data of the Archive on Political Elites in Eastern Europe at the University of Pittsburgh, RFE Analysis, "East Europe's Communist Leaders — Czechoslovakia" (September 1, 1966) and *Rudé právo*, April 5, 1968 and January 9, 1969.

právo; from 1961 to 1962 editor-in-chief of *Nová mysl*. 1963–1965 Minister of Education and Culture, and a secretary of the KSČ CC Ideological Commission. 1964–1966 deputy to the National Assembly. 1965–1968 Czechoslovak Ambassador to Rumania. Returned to become a secretary of the KSČ CC in the post-January 1968 government. Resigned under pressure following the August 1968 invasion. Currently chairman of the Czech National Council.

Colotka, Peter, Dr. — Became Prime Minister of the Slovak government in April 1969. Slovak. Born January 10, 1925 in the village Sedliacka Dubová. Father was a peasant smallholder. Graduated from high school and studied law at university in Bratislava. Professor of Civil Law in Bratislava. Joined KSČ 1947. Leader of KSS student organization. Member of KSS CC and KSČ CC. Served as Vice Premier in Dubček government. Chairman of Federal National Assembly from January–April 1969, then became Premier of Slovakia.

David, Václav — Foreign Minister under Novotný. Czech. Born 1910. Father was a cartwright. Attended a Commercial Institute in Prague and worked in a heavy industry factory in Prague. Joined Communist party 1935. Worked with the Communist underground during World War II and fought in the Prague Uprising. Member of National Assembly and KSČ Presidium. Pro-Soviet; resigned in April 1968.

Dubček, Alexander — First Secretary of the KSČ CC, January 1968–April 1969. Member of Presidium. Slovak. Born November 27, 1921 in Uhrovec, western Slovakia. Father was a cabinetmaker and a Communist who, after pre-1914 emigration to the United States, lived in Soviet Union with his family from 1925 to 1938. Dubček became a locksmith. Joined KSČ in 1939. Fought in Slovak National Uprising. Party posts: Leader of Secretary of Regional Committees in Banská Bystrica (1953–1955) and Bratislava (1958–1960). 1958 member of KSČ CC and candidate member of KSS Presidium. 1960 replaced Černík as secretary of the KSČ CC. 1962 full member of KSS Presidium and secretary to KSS CC. May 1963 replaced Karel Bacílek in KSČ Presidium and also as First Secretary of the KSS. January 1968 replaced Antonín Novotný as First Secretary of the KSČ. Retained in this position after the occupation of Czechoslovakia by Soviet troops in August 1968 until replaced by Gustav Husák April 1969. Remained in Presidium in Husák regime and became Chairman of the Federal Assembly.

Erban, Evžen — Presidium member and Chairman of the National Front in the post-invasion government. Czech. Born in Prague June 19, 1912. Completed university but did not finish as a doctor of law. Joined Communist party in June 1948. Also in 1948 deputy chairman of the Social Democratic Party. Member of KSČ CC. At various times chairman of the State Commission for Pension Insurance, State Office for Social Security, and State Management of Material Reserves.

Hájek, Jiří, Dr. — Foreign Minister in the post-January government. Czech. Born June 6, 1913. Graduated from Charles University in Prague before 1939. Joined the KSČ in June 1948. Ambassador to Great Britain 1955–1958. Deputy Foreign Minister 1958–1962. Became head of Czechoslovak Mission to the United Nations 1962. 1966–1967 Minister of Education. Became Foreign Minister April 1968. Resigned under pressure September 1968.

Hendrych, Jiří — Member of the KSČ Presidium, Secretary of Central Committee and Chairman of the CC Ideological Commission under Novotný. Born December 1913 in Northwestern Bohemia. Father reportedly a miner. Went to high school and began to study law in Prague; however he was expelled and arrested for distributing Communist propaganda. Originally worked with the agitprop department of the Communist Youth League. Joined the Communist party in 1934. Rose in the party until 1952 when he suffered a setback because of his association with Slánskýites in the sphere of control over culture. Reinstated in 1954 as CC secretary responsible for ideology and culture. Political image even more conservative than Novotný; instrumental in attacking the writers following the Writers' Congress in June 1967. After Dubček replaced Novotný, Hendrych lost his positions as Secretary of the KSČ CC, member of the Presidium, and Chairman of the Ideological Commission, April 4, 1968. Role after August 1968 invasion unclear.

Husák, Gustav — Replaced Dubček as First Secretary of the KSČ in April 1969. Slovak. Born 1913 in Bratislava. A lawyer by training. Joined KSČ in early 1930's and was a leading member of the "DAV" group. After the Nazi occupation active in the underground and one of the organizers of the Slovak Uprising. Became Chairman of the Slovak Board of Commissioners, was purged as a "bourgeois nationalist" in the early 1950's and sentenced to life in prison. Released in 1960, rehabilitated in 1963. Did not return to political life until becoming Deputy Premier in the post-January 1968 government in charge of the commission on Federalization. After the August 1968 invasion took over Vasil Bil'ak's job as First Secretary of the Slovak Communist Party, instrumental in demanding that Josef Smrkovský be replaced by a Slovak as Chairman of the new Federal Assembly in 1969.

Indra, Alois — Member of KSČ CC under Novotný and a Secretary of the CC in the post-January 1968 government. Czech. Born March 17, 1921 in Medzev, district Košice in Slovakia. Father an industrial worker. Finished high school; then worked as a railroad functionary. Joined the Communist party in 1937. 1958–1962 candidate member of KSČ CC; 1962 full member of Communist party. 1962–1963 Minister-Chairman of State Planning Commission. 1963–1967 Minister of Transport. Leading dogmatist in post-January 1968 government at which time he was a secretary of the KSČ CC. Reported to have led the quisling government President Svoboda rejected immediately after the August 1968 invasion. Rehabilitated after Husák came to power, CC Secretary responsible for state organs and social organizations June 1969.

Kolder, Drahomír — Member of KSČ Presidium under both Novotný and in post-January 1968 government. Czech. Born December 29, 1925 in Ostrava. Father a coal miner. Began working in the mines at 15 years old. At 18 was active in the resistance movement. Joined Communist party in 1945. 1952–1954 attended and graduated from the two-year party political school. 1962 became member of KSČ Presidium and Secretary of the CC. 1963, Chairman of CC Economic Commission. Kolder was considered one of the dogmatists in the post-January 1968 government. After the August invasion, he became economic adviser to the Czechoslovak Embassy in Sofia. Began to rise again after Dubček fell in April 1969.

Kriegel, František — Member of KSČ Presidium and Chairman of the National Front in the post-January 1968 government. Born on April 10, 1908 in Poland. Graduated from Charles University Medical School in Prague in 1934. Between 1936 and 1939 fought as a volunteer in the Spanish Civil War with the Republican Army. 1939–1945 fought against Hitler in World War II. After the war, worked in the Regional Committee of the KSČ in Prague. 1949–1952 was Deputy Minister of Health. 1952–1960 worked as a doctor and appears to have had no official post. 1960–1963 was an adviser on matters of health in Cuba. 1964 Deputy and member of the Presidium of the National Assembly. From 1966 member of the CC of KSČ; became a member of the KSČ Presidium in April 1968. Removed from the

Presidium and as Chairman of the National Front after the August 1968 invasion. Expelled from the party on charges of being antiparty, antisocialist, and anti-Soviet at KSČ CC May 1969 Plenum.

Kudrna, Josef — Mnister of Interior under Novotný. Czech. Thought to have been born in 1920. 1957 to 1965 Security Colonel and Deputy Minister of Interior. 1965–1968 Minister of Interior. Candidate member of the KSČ CC. Replaced in post-January 1968 government by Josef Pavel.

Lenárt, Jozef — Premier under Novotný; became alternate member of the Presidium and Secretary of the CC in the post-January 1968 government. Slovak. Born April 3, 1923 in Liptovská Porúbka. First worked as a laboratory technician in the Baťa Shoe factory during which time he took a degree from a school of chemical studies. Worked in illegal Slovak CP from 1943 and took active part in the Slovak National Uprising of 1944. 1952 Deputy Minister of Light Industry. 1953–1956 attended higher party school in Moscow. May 1958 became Secretary of KSS CC in Bratislava; June 1958 elected to KSČ CC. April 1960, KSS politburo; two months later elected to National Assembly. 1962–1963 Chairman of Slovak National Council. 1962–1968 member of KSČ Presidium. 1963 replaced Vilém Široký as Premier. Held post until 1968.

Lomský, Bohumír — Defense Minister under Novotný. Czech. Born April 22, 1914 in České Budějovice, southern Bohemia. Father was a worker. Went to military school for reserve officers and from 1939 was an officer in Czech army. Attended military academy in Moscow 1945–1947. Joined the KSČ in 1950. 1954–1956, Deputy Minister of National Defense. 1956–April 1968 Minister of National Defense. 1958 became member of KSČ CC.

Marko, Ján — Foreign Minister in the post-invasion period 1968 to date. Slovak. Born October 25, 1903. Member of KSS. December 1954–March 13, 1959 Slovak Commissioner for Finance. 1956–1960 Deputy Chairman of the Board of Slovak Commissioners. June 1961 became Slovak Commissioner for Capital Construction. 1966 Minister without Portfolio.

Novotný, Antonín — First Secretary of the KSČ Central Committee, President of the Republic 1953–1968, Member of the KSČ Presidium and Chairman of the National Front. Czech. Born December 1904 in Letňany near Prague. Father was a bricklayer. Eight years of elementary education; then became a mechanic. Joined KSČ in 1921 at 17 years old. Since 1929 has been a full-time party functionary except during World War II (when he was in the Mauthausen concentration camp) and a few months in 1953 when he was Deputy Prime Minister. Party Posts: Chairman of Prague District Communist Party Committee 1930–1935; went underground from 1938 to 1941 when he was arrested. In concentration camp until 1945; then became leading Communist party secretary in Prague region, played important role in 1948 *coup d'état*. Improved his position during Stalinist purges. 1951 became Secretary of KSČ Central Committee and member of the Political Secretariat (now the Presidium). Klement Gottwald shifted Novotný to Deputy Prime Minister in 1953 but then Gottwald died and in September 1953 Novotný became First Secretary of the KSČ. He was simultaneously President of the Republic and Chairman of the National Front. Replaced by Dubček as First Secretary in January 1968.

Pavel, Josef — Minister of Interior in post-January 1968 government. Czech. Born September 18, 1908 in Novosedly in Bohemia. Joined Communist party in 1932. Attended Marx-Lenin Institute. 1948–1951 Deputy Minister of Interior. 1949–1951 member of KSČ CC. 1951 expelled from party and jailed for anti-Communist activities. Date of rehabilitation unknown. Became Minister of Interior with Dubček regime in April 1968. Replaced after August invasion.

Pelnář, Jan — Minister of Interior in the 1968 post-invasion government to date. Czech. Born 1911 in Mrákov, Bohemia. Father was a worker. Elementary school education; worked as a mason. Joined the Communist party in 1945. Specialized in agriculture and worked with regional CP Committee. In 1964 became member of the Commission for Agriculture of the Regional CP Committee in Plzeň.

Šik, Ota, Dr. — Vice Premier in the post-January 1968 government; architect of the economic reforms. Czech. Born September 11, 1919. Graduated as Doctor of Economics from Charles University in Prague 1946. Thought to have joined the Communist party in 1945. 1945–1948 Professor of Political Economy in the Party School in Prague. 1957–1962 Professor of Political and Economic Science in the KSČ CC Institute of Social Science in Prague. Since March 1964 member of CC Economic Commission. Became Vice Premier in April 1968. Was out of the country at the time of the August 1968 invasion and has remained in Switzerland. Expelled from the Central Committee at KSČ CC May 1969 Plenum.

Smrkovský, Josef — Member of Presidium and Chairman of National Assembly in the post-January government. Czech. Born February 26, 1911 in Velenka, central Bohemia. Worked as a baker and was active in the Communist Youth League after 1930. Joined Communist party in 1933. After a year of party training in Moscow became Secretary of the Communist Youth League in Prague, 1933–1935. Went underground during World War II and headed illegal KSČ CC in 1944 until May 1945. Important figure in May 1945 Prague Uprising. 1948–1951 Deputy Minister of Agriculture, also member of party presidium. Arrested in 1951 in connection with Slánský trial and sentenced to life in prison. Released in 1955, but not re-habilitated publicly until 1963. 1963–1965 returned to political activity as Deputy Chairman of the Central Commission of Control and Statistics. Reelected to KSČ CC in 1966. January 1967, Minister of Forestry and Water Conservation. April 1968 became member of KSČ Presidium and Chairman of the National Assembly. After the August 1968 invasion remained in government and party posts until replaced as Chairman of the new Federal Assembly by Peter Colotka in January 1969. Lost Presidium post when Husák took over as First Secretary in April 1969.

Strougal, Lubomír — Currently member of KSČ Presidium and Chairman of the Bureau of Czech Lands. Czech. Date and place of birth unknown. Thought to be in early 40's and from southern Bohemia. Father reputed to be a cement factory worker. Trained as a lawyer. Elected to the KSČ CC in 1958; became Minister of Agriculture in 1959. Replaced Rudolf Barak as Minister of the Interior in 1961; left this post in 1965 and became a secretary of the Central Committee and Chairman of the Central Committee Agricultural Commission. 1968 became a Vice Premier in post-January government and head of the Economic Council. At November 1968 CC Plenum replaced Z. Mlynář in Secretariat, became Chairman of the Bureau of the Czech Lands (established as a parallel to the Slovak Communist Party) and member of the Presidium. Appointed deputy to KSČ First Secretary Gustav Husák in June 1969.

Svoboda, Ludvík — President of Czechoslovakia April 1968 to date. Czech. Born November 1895. A career army officer who escaped to Poland in 1939 and commanded the Czechoslovak contingent there. After the German invasion captured by the Russian Army. Commanded Czechoslovak troops in Russia 1941–1945. Became Minister of Defense under President Beneš in 1945 and did not resist the

Communist takeover in 1948, after which joined the Communist party. Also served in the National Assembly after 1948. During the Stalinist period in the early 1950's left the army. Dismissed as Minister of Defense and appears to have been arrested between January and June 1952. Full rehabilitation occurred only in 1965 when he was awarded the titles of Hero of the Soviet Union and Hero of the Czechoslovak Socialist Republic on his 70th birthday. Took over Novotný's office of President in April 1968. Negotiated the return of Dubček and other leaders arrested by the Soviets during the August 1968 invasion and has continued as President in the post-invasion period to date.

ABBREVIATIONS

APL	Partia e Punës së Shqipërisë (Albanian Party of Labor)
APR	Albanian People's Republic
BCP	Bulgarian Communist Party
CC	Central Committee
CCP	Communist Party of Czechoslovakia; also KSČ
CDSP	Current Digest of the Soviet Press
CDU	Christliche Demokratische Union (Christian Democratic Union — a West German political party)
CEMA CMEA	Council for Mutual Economic Aid
CPSL	Slovak Communist Party; also KSS
CPSU	Communist Party of the Soviet Union
CSPD	Czechoslovak Social Democratic Party
ČSR ČSSR	Československá socialistická republika (Czechoslovak Socialist Republic)
CSU	Christliche Sozialistische Union (Christian Socialist Union — a West German political party)
ČTK	Czechoslovak News Agency
FRG	Federal Republic of Germany
GDR	Deutsche Demokratische Republik (German Democratic Republic — East Germany)
GMT	Greenwich Mean Time
HSWP	Hungarian Socialist Workers' Party
JPRS	Joint Publications Research Service (U.S. government translation service)
KAN	Club of Committed non-Party Members
KSČ	Komunistická strana Československa (Communist Party of Czechoslovakia)
KSS	Komunistická strana Slovenska (Communist Party of Slovakia)
LCY	League of Communists of Yugoslavia
MTI	Hungarian News Agency
NATO	North Atlantic Treaty Organization

NTS	Narodno-trudovoy Soyuz (People's Labor Alliance)
PCC	Political Consultative Committee (of the Warsaw Pact)
PCF	Parti communiste français (French Communist Party)
PCI	Partito comunista italiano (Italian Communist Party)
PPR	People's Republic of Poland
PRB	People's Republic of Bulgaria
PUWP	Polska Zjednoczona Partia Robotnicza (Polish United Workers' [Communist] Party)
RFE	Radio Free Europe
RSR	Rumanian Socialist Republic
SED SUPG	Sozialistische Einheitspartei Deutschlands (Socialist Unity Party — Communist Party of East Germany)
TASS	Soviet News Agency
USSR	Soyuz Sovetskikh Sotsialisticheskikh Respublik (Union of Soviet Socialist Republics)
UN	United Nations

I. Prelude to January

Kresba Jaroslava Maláka

"Mommy, what will happen to me in the framework of the separation of functions?"

Literární listy, No. 9, April 25, 1968.

DEMANDS FOR SOCIALISM WITH
A HUMAN FACE: VACULÍK AND RICHTA

THE PRAGUE SPRING of 1968 was deeply rooted in many winters of economic discontent. Stalinist methods of centralized planning, bureaucratic bottlenecks, forced investments in heavy industry, and especially a foreign trade crisis had resulted in an economic depression. By August of that year, the third Five-Year Plan was abandoned. As the economy limped to a halt, the Novotný regime reluctantly agreed to extensive economic reforms. Theoretically, an improved system of management based on a watered-down version of Professor Ota Šik's principles of decentralization came into force January 1, 1967. However, belief by many Communist *apparatchiki* in the superiority of a centrally planned economy coupled with fears that they would lose their jobs if managerial rather than political criteria were applied acted as a brake. Indeed, the party hung paralyzed between the actions necessary to improve the economy and the social consequences that would undeniably be the first results of reform — greater differentiation in wage scales, higher prices, the specter of unemployment.[1]

Yet it was not dissatisfied workers (in part because even in the worst periods the regime had subsidized wages) but the intellectuals who began the revolt of Czechoslovakia. At the Fourth Congress of Czechoslovak Writers in June 1967,[2] dissatisfaction with Novotný's token de-Stalinization and the party's rigid control of all cultural activity (increasingly insistent since 1963) became articulate criticism of the regime. The young novelist Ludvík Vaculík flatly

---

[1] Michael Gamarnikow, *Economic Reforms in Eastern Europe* (Detroit: Wayne State University Press, 1968), pp. 43 ff. For the theory behind the reforms, see John M. Montias, "A Plan for All Seasons," *Survey*, No. 51 (April 1964), pp. 63–76, and Ota Šik, *Plan and Market Under Socialism* (New York: International Arts and Sciences Press, Inc., 1969).

[2] For the most detailed analysis of events leading up to the fall of Novotný and the "regeneration" of the Czechoslovak Communist Party, see Pavel Tigrid, *Le Printemps de Prague* (Paris: Seuil, 1968). The section on the Fourth Writers' Congress, pp. 141–171, quotes extensively from Vaculík. Also H. Gordon Skilling, "Crisis and Change in Czechoslovakia," *International Journal*, Vol. XXIII, No. 3 (Summer 1968), pp. 456–465, and Edward Táborský, "The New Era in Czechoslovakia," *East Europe*, Vol. 17, No. 11 (November 1968), pp. 19–30.

charged that "no human problem has been solved in our country for 20 years" (Document 1).[3]

The regime's cultural spokesman, Jiří Hendrych delivered a violent counter-attack at the Congress. *Kulturní tvorba,* the cultural weekly of the KSČ Central Committee, immediately accused Vaculík and other speakers such as Pavel Kohout, Alexander Kliment, and Václav Havel of demagoguery and anarchy.[4] Nonetheless, the Congress' concluding resolution echoed some of the sentiments of the rebels:

> The great opportunity of socialism is that it can . . . defend itself . . . against dehumanizing tendencies. Socialist culture in its widest sense, as a collection of experience gained in the course of creating material and spiritual values, is therefore connected with democratization of human relations and the acquisition of a larger freedom. . . .[5]

The party responded by expelling Vaculík and a number of other writers.[6] To ensure future acquiescence, the Writers' Union weekly, *Literární noviny,* was taken over by the Ministry of Culture and plans made to disperse the Writers' Union into regional units. Considering the extent of attack, however, the regime's response was both hesitant and divided. At the same plenum where Vaculík was expelled, *Rudé právo* ideologist Jan Fojtík warned against the danger of "Leftist sectarianism and dogmatism."[7] Nor were party attempts at control implemented in full. Many writers defiantly refused to contribute to the government-controlled journal, and Hendrych appeared unable to pack the Writers' Union.[8]

The revolt of the writers was only the first of many voices demanding

---

[3] Details of the proceedings reported by Andreas Razumovsky, *Frankfurter Allgemeine Zeitung,* July 3, 1967. For some of the speeches *Reden zum IV. Kongress des tschechoslowakischen Schriftstellerverbandes — Prag, Juni 1967* (Frankfurt: Suhrkamp Verlag, 1968). Vaculík also began a chain of demands for historical rehabilitation of Tomáš G. Masaryk, President of the First Czechoslovak Republic, that would be picked up by the post-January party leadership. In April 1968 the new President Ludvík Svoboda put flowers on Masaryk's grave, the first gesture of respect for the Czechoslovak national hero to come from a top Communist leader. Moscow bitterly resented this upgrading of Masaryk; see M. Shiryamov, "Whose Interests Did President Masaryk Defend?", *Sovetskaya Rossia* (May 4, 1968), *Current Digest of the Soviet Press (CDSP),* Vol. XX, No. 19 (May 29, 1968), pp. 8–9.

[4] *Kulturní tvorba,* July 6, 1968.

[5] *Literární noviny,* July 8, 1967. Reportedly, the resolution was passed after the official delegation led by Hendrych left the Congress in a rage.

[6] See coverage by Michel Tatu in *Le Monde,* September 29, October 2, and Octboer 10, 1967.

[7] *Rudé právo,* October 3, 1967.

[8] Although the response of the Communist Party of Czechoslovakia (KSČ) to the writers' Congress was neither immediate nor completely ruthless, that is not to say it was not harsh. In addition to the expulsions, Milan Kundera, Pavel Kohout, and Jan Procházka received "party punishment." For Procházka this meant loss of his position as a candidate member of the Central Committee. The party-subsidized Writers' Fund was abolished, and many writers felt reprisals in the form of refusals to publish their works. Shortly after the plenum, the KSČ Presidium was able to pressure the National Assembly into condemning the writers. Moreover, the party strongly condemned KSČ officials who had in any way supported or protected the writers.

socialism with a human face. Since 1965, a working group attached to the Institute of Philosophy, Czechoslovak Academy of Sciences, and headed by Dr. Radovan Richta had been probing the implications of the scientific and technological revolution for socialism. Richta's work played a large role in convincing the Czechoslovak political elite that economic recovery was impossible without major steps to overcome the technology gap. Document 2 is from the epilogue of that voluminous study.

DOCUMENT 1
Speech by Ludvík Vaculík to the Fourth Congress of Czechoslovak Writers
June 1967
Excerpts
[*From the protocol of the Fourth Czechoslovak Writers' Congress*
(Československý spisovatel, Prague, 1968), pp. 141–151]

❦

. . . I am speaking as the citizen of a state which I will never renounce, but in which I cannot lead a satisfactory life. Although my mind is full of issues relevant to all citizens, I find myself in a delicate situation: I am also a member of the Communist party, and I should not and do not want to talk about party matters.

Nonetheless it seems we have practically nothing left which does not become a party issue at a certain stage of debate. What can I do when my party and my government have done all they can to merge?

I would like to return to what I feel holds true for all kinds of power: its development and conduct are determined by its inner laws, which neither the individual in power nor the class in power can change because they regularly characterize human behavior in a given situation — when they hold power. The first law of power is that it tries to maintain itself by reproducing itself more and more precisely. Secondly, it becomes more and more homogeneous, purging everything foreign to it until each part is a replica of the whole and all parts are mutually interchangeable.

Then it enters a new phase, which I designate as the dynastization phase. Power convokes its legislature at a favorable moment and has its independent position incorporated into the constitution. Anything it does from that time on is constitutional. And since it does not bring this point up for discussion for 10, 12, or 15 years (since no one *can* bring it up or convoke another constitutional legislature power), power founds its own constitutional dynasty, a dynasty completely new to history in that it preserves one important democratic principle: anyone who wants to can join. It is not, therefore, subject to extinction. . . .

In setting forth my ideas on the nature, development, and behavior of power, I have tried to show how the mechanisms of controlling power break down, causing the citizen to lose his self-respect and his rights as a citizen. If this situation exists as long as it has in our country, it becomes engraved into the thinking of many people, and the younger generation is liable to accept it as a philosophy of life as a result of their not having learned at school or from practical experience that there is a certain continuity in the human struggle for a perfect democracy. Should this situation continue (and a natural defensive reaction against it fail to develop), the character of our peoples will change in the course of the coming generation. A civilized society will give way to an easily controlled populace which a foreigner would find a real pleasure to rule. What was the point of putting up such a fight these thousand years, if things have come to such a pass?

If we all agree that none of us was born to be easily controlled, I propose that the Union of Writers, in cooperation with the Union of Journalists and other professional groups with problems similar to ours, take the initiative of requesting that the Czechoslovak Academy of Sciences make a study of the Constitution and, if necessary, suggest changes.

Art cannot renounce the subject of government because governing means making direct or indirect administrative decisions which affect the lives of men, their joys and disappointments, what they think about but cannot decide on. The act of power and the act of art merge in what cannot be but somehow is decided on. Art must continue to criticize governments because it is culture which makes governments what they are. . . .

I see a persistent trend: the danger that the bad old days will return. Otherwise, what is the meaning of the words that we have received a Union, literary fund, publishing house, and newspapers? A threat that they will take it all away if we don't behave. . . . But are they really masters over everything? If not, what do they delegate to others? Nothing? Then we have no business sticking around. Why don't they come out and admit that in essence a handful of people want to determine everything's right to be or not to be, what is to be done, thought, felt? Then we would have a fair picture of the state of culture in our country, a far cry from the individual works of art which have cornered the publicity market.

Last year we often had occasion to hear that the ruling circles were beginning to recognize a degree of autonomy for culture in its own field. But culture must not take offense at being reprimanded when it crosses over into the field of politics. The standard argument runs that we are contradicting our own slogan, namely, that each type of work should be done by its own experts. It is true that politics, too, should be run by experts, but what makes them so sure that they are experts? . . . Autonomy for art and culture? This is just a slogan and familiar tactics. . . .

Just as I don't feel safe in a cultural situation that the ruling power can throw into turmoil, I don't feel sure of myself as a citizen outside the walls of this hall, that is, of this "playground." I am not being hurt, and I have not been hurt. Things like that don't happen any more. Should I be grateful? Somehow I do not feel any gratefulness. I'm afraid. I have no firm guarantees.

I see the courts working better, but even the judges lack sound guarantees. I see state prosecutors working better, but do they have any guarantees? Do they feel safe? With their consent, I would like to interview some of them for the papers. Do you believe the interview would be printed? I would not be afraid to ask the head prosecutor why people who were innocently convicted and [then] rehabilitated do not get back their original rights, why national committees do not want to give back their apartments or houses — but it would not be printed. Why haven't these people received a decent apology? Why don't they enjoy the privileges of the politically persecuted? Why do authorities haggle with them over money? Why aren't we allowed to live where we wish? Why can't tailors go to Vienna for three years? Why can't painters go to Paris for thirty years with the foreknowledge that they can return without being branded as criminals? . . . Why shouldn't people who have decided they don't like it here be allowed to go to hell? . . .

True, some new and better laws have been passed. True, more are in the works. True, the new press law is making a clean sweep. True, an amendment to the law on civil liberties that will guarantee freedom of assembly and association is in preparation. But while the Ministry of Interior is drawing up the proposal, an article about it which *Literární noviny* had already set is withdrawn. I simply cannot see any guarantees. What kind of guarantees? I don't know. I must stop here because I have reached my last, overwhelming doubt. Do the ruling circles themselves, the government and its individual members, enjoy any guarantee of their civil liberties? Without that, no creative work is thinkable, not even the creation of government policies. . . .

It must be admitted that not one human problem has been solved in the last twenty years — from such elementary needs as housing, schools, and economic prosperity to more subtle needs which the undemocratic systems of the world cannot provide: a feeling of one's full worth in society, a feeling that politics is subordinate to ethics, a belief in the meaning of humble work, the need for confidence among people, the advancement of education for the people. And I'm afraid we have not taken our proper place in the world arena. I have the feeling that our republic has lost its good name. . . .

In conclusion, I would like to state explicitly what is surely implicit in my entire speech: In criticizing Czechoslovakia's power system, I do not place the blame on socialism, because I am not convinced these developments were necessary in our country and because I do not identify this power with the concept of socialism, although that is just what the power structure tries to do. Not even their destinies need be identical. And if the people who exercise this power — I would charm them out of their power for a time and address them as individuals with the feelings and thoughts of individuals — were to come here and ask whether this dream can be achieved, they would have to accept my answer as an expression of my good will and highest civic loyalty if I were to say, "I do not know."

DOCUMENT 2

"PRACTICAL ASPECTS — SOME IDEAS FOR CONSIDERATION"

Excerpts

[From the Epilogue of *Civilization at the Crossroads: Social and Human Implications of the Scientific and Technological Revolution, II,* by Radovan Richta and a research team, Prague, 1967, pp. 1–14]

❦

The study undertaken by the authors of this book has been concerned with theoretical concepts; we have moved in the realm of basic research. The scientific and technological revolution, including its social and human implications, is so radical a movement that at the present stage and with the knowledge at our disposal we cannot lay down detailed measures to be applied in practice and certainly not prescribe any ready-made recipes; any such steps will have to be independently conceived and handled by the responsible authorities. Nevertheless, we would like here to call attention to some general aspects, without giving them any absolute significance. They have a bearing on the approach that will be taken to the whole question. We are not concerned with the actual course to be taken, but with suggesting the main lines on which the ground may be prepared.

A) A country that has traversed the stage of industrialization and socialist reconstruction finds itself face to face with the beginnings of the scientific and technological revolution — as an organic component and vital condition of further profound social transformations. The scientific and technological revolution is by its nature a universal, continuous transformation of all the productive forces in society and human life, involving their entire structure; consequently, it is a profoundly revolutionary social process with far-reaching implications for the position of man in producing his own life and for all social relationships; it impinges on the structure and nature of work, the levels of skills, extent and type of education, the configuration of life and wants, the breadth and intensity of human contacts, the nature of the environment, the relation between man and nature, the laws and forms of historical development, the position of the individual in society, the type of management and modes of thinking.

While the scientific and technological revolution carries forward the fruits of the industrial revolution (industrialization), it differs in its substance and its implications and in many respects produces completely opposite effects. The need therefore arises:

a) to adopt [throughout] the whole range of undertakings (whether programmes or economic prognoses, practical decisions or theoretical schemes) the methodological principle that it is now impossible to formulate any concepts concerning the development of society without reference to the new conditions and demands engendered by the scientific and technological revolution;

b) to arrange for integrated investigation, interdisciplinary investigation of the scientific and technological revolution, its social and human implications, at the level of basic research (involving philosophy, economics, sociology, "science of science", psychology, pedagogy, aesthetics, law and history, theory of architecture, hygiene, political science, anthropology, ergonomics, cybernetics, the natural sciences, technology, medicine), to be followed by applied research. It will be necessary in this connection to see how far new branches are prepared and fill any gaps in the system of the sciences of man;

c) to acquaint the public with the true facts and the perspectives offered by the scientific and technological revolution, so that they may be prepared for the scale of future changes in the basis of civilization, in the style of human life and for unaccustomed lines of advance — and particularly, so that they may grasp the vital necessity of such happenings from the standpoint of socialism and communism and be able to play a really effective part.

B) In an advanced socialist country such as Czechoslovakia, the main barrier in approaching the scientific and technological revolution is provided by some elements of immaturity in the economic structure, in the impulses and means linking the ordinary man with the advances of science and technology and with progress in the productivity of social labour in the mass. In these circumstances, socialism cannot conclusively manifest its essential nature or achieve effective scientific and technological development (and ultimately human development, too). Consequently, full implementation of fundamental measures underlying a new system of economic management is the main step in a decisive turn to intensive growth of the productive forces and the precondition for an approach to the scientific and technological revolution. In this connection it is of crucial importance for the stimulation of scientific and technological advance that incentives to fostering a spirit of socialist enterprise be freely used and categories of value adjusted in practice as essential groundwork for guiding the objective and subjective elements in the processes of civilization.

C) The vital question for coming decades will be the extent to which science — as the leading agent in the dynamic civilization of our day — will permeate and be operative in the life of society. This requires:

a) rapid development of research capacities at a level adequate to the present trends in the world and geared to the long-range perspectives of economic growth. This implies eliminating some unhealthy symptoms of purely formal growth (inadequately qualified personnel in applied research and development) and envisaging science and research growing into a significant sector of the national economy (about 15 per cent of the industrial work force by 1980), on a scale bearing no comparison with the era of industrialization;

  b) elaboration of a strategy for science in a small, advanced country, rely-
     ing on an increased share of basic research in the distribution of scien-
     tific and technological resources, concentrating applied research in
     selected fields, drawing on work in other countries (cooperation within
     the socialist group and purchase of licences), expanding information
     services to provide comprehensive surveys of the state of science in the
     world;
  c) organization of the media and channels by which scientific findings
     may flow into all sectors of the community: employing to this end
     primarily economic means; further, through scientific advisory bodies
     attached to all top institutions, and insistence on expertise or competitive
     selection preparatory to every fundamental decision by leading authori-
     ties on fundamental projects; finally, through building up an atmosphere
     of scientific progress based on confidence, recognition for creative effort,
     free and friendly discussion on disputable problems, etc.

  D) The scientific and technological revolution is an intricate social process
in which advance of science and technology is intimately connected with
various social and human preconditions and implications. An effective approach can be made only if all new trends in science and technology (drawing
on various lines of work hitherto undertaken to complete industrialization,
aggregate production, etc.) are judiciously combined with the prospects offered
by integration within the socialist system and with the special circumstances
of the country concerned. An important point is to make the maximum use
of favourable factors, such as the tradition of a labour force with expert knowledge and skills, and to compensate some drawbacks such as restricted raw-
material resources. With this in mind, it is essential to project the course of
the scientific and technological revolution, embracing the whole body of innovations in technology, raw materials, power, and in skills and organization,
into long-range technico-economic concepts, always linked with considerations
of the social and human implications of the respective intents (impact on
structure of work, skills, development of human powers, working and living
environments, etc.). This should not be a system of allocating directive assign-
ments, but a social and technological programme, outlining the substance of
the process and the measures available (a programme of comprehensive
mechanization and automation, application of chemical processes, computer
techniques, biological processes, handling of the power problem, modernization
of machine-building, reform of agricultural techniques, treatment of urbaniza-
tion problems, etc.), which should be followed up by the state plan and would
provide scope for initiative by economic interests.
  A vital factor in the success of this dynamic orientation of growth in Czechoslovakia will be the ability to integrate and to achieve division of labour within
the socialist system, to engage in close international cooperation in science and
technology along the lines envisaged for the course of the scientific and technological revolution.
  E) The scientific and technological revolution inverts the elementary tech-

nological, economic, social and anthropological conditions of civilization's progress. In contrast to industrialization, we find that gradually, in more and more areas, science and its technical application, and through this medium man and the development of his creative powers, are providing the crucial dimension of growth of the productive forces. In these circumstances there is no use in automatically applying the growth patterns and the proportions of reproduction inherited from the age of industrialization. Effective growth is less and less dependent on multiplying labour inputs and industrial plants. The gap between the growth rate of groups I and II is gradually narrowing. The new basic growth pattern (intensive growth) now implies science being ahead of technology, and technology ahead of industry. We can no longer insist that the growth of production proper be the most rapid — that is, insofar as its effect can be equalled or outdone by more effective generation of productive powers in the pre-production stages (science and research), and also in care for people and the development of human powers (the "quarternary sector"). Division into a "productive" (production proper) and "non-productive" area loses its value for delimiting proportions in the national economy (investments, etc.) and has to be subordinated to a higher division deduced from the new logic of generating productive powers, in whatever sector the process may take place. In view of the multidimensional dynamics of the productive powers today, a progressive orientation (optimalization) of intentions can only be ensured if it stems from a well-planned and functioning economic system of interests, geared to absolute growth in the productivity of all social labour, and if it is combined with a scientific system of time economy drawing on modern economic growth theories, including the economics of human resources, mathematic modelling, an efficient computer network, etc. Elaboration of such a system makes it possible to determine at any given time the area (be it production, science, education, services, care for people, etc.) which, under the given conditions, affords the maximum preparation of the productive powers of human life. . . .

I) The scientific and technological revolution brings into play a new, independent growth factor — human development on a broad front. Far more is expected of individual activity, the fullness of man's inner life, the ability to surpass oneself and to cultivate one's own capacities — and growth of the individual acquires a wider social significance. Hitherto individual social endeavour has tended to be put at a disadvantage, the horizons of "reproduction life" have been hard and fast — in short, individual initiative has been curbed by a mass of directives. We now face the necessity to supplement economic instruments with socio-political and anthropological instruments that will shape the contours of human life, evoke new wants, model the structure of man's motivation, while enlarging, not interfering with, freedom of choice, in fact relying on a system of opportunities and potentialities in human development. Otherwise, instead of progressively providing scope for new wants (due to be felt with full force when present consumption has something like trebled), the approaching transition phase of "mass consumption" will revolve in a closed circle. An urgent task in this field, in which scientific and technological advance can make an especially hopeful contribution, is to bring into operation a variety of ways by which the individual can share in directing all controllable processes of contemporary civilization and to do away with some of the restricting, dehumanizing effects of the traditional industrial system. . . .

We must bear in mind that if the apparatus of management is not equipped with substantially higher training it will be unable to keep pace with the dynamics of the scientific and technological revolution. Experience shows that unskilled management drives society along the old paths of extensive industrialization.

L) The growing role of subjective agencies in the context of the scientific and technological revolution will call for diverse forms of management:

a) it is necessary to take into account all the implications of changes in the social structure that allow socialism to approach the scientific and technological revolution with an effective deployment of forces (specialists, technologists and scientists become a component part of the working class and the significance of the skilled sections of the workers grows);

b) the Communist Party's leadership will increasingly rely on science and on ways of promoting scientific advance. In this connection it will be of the utmost importance to elaborate and stabilize means, rules and forms whereby new scientific concepts and progressive projects can be realized without the lengthy period of gestation customary with traditional methods and without the delays and waste occasioned by mistrust of or failure to understand unorthodox departures;

c) in the context of the scientific and technological revolution, the Communist Party, as the leading force, will find it necessary to look beyond the horizon of patterns solely directed to tackling issues arising from class struggle (and the structure of political power as such); it will have to evolve a diversity of new approaches and more effective means, taking in technology, the economy, social policies, psychical and anthropological factors, by which to adjust conditions for socialist endeavour. . . .

SLOVAK ECONOMIC COMPLAINTS

THE SEPTEMBER 1967 PLENUM of the Communist Party of Czechoslovakia (KSČ) Central Committee moved to suppress the intellectual dissent of the Fourth Writers' Congress. Yet just as the writers were taken in hand, Alexander Dubček, First Secretary of the Slovak Communist Party and KSČ Presidium member since May 1963, demanded a radical overhaul of government practices in Slovakia. In retrospect, his September speech (Document 3), focusing on the need to promote socioeconomic goals from a territorial viewpoint, appears to have opened the challenge to Novotný along a second front.[1] The anti-Novotný coalition was growing.

DOCUMENT 3

DUBČEK SEPTEMBER 1967 CC PLENUM SPEECH

Excerpts

[*Rudé právo,* September 29, 1967]

. . . It is no secret, however, that voices and signals are emerging which testify to the existence and growth of distrust and doubt as to whether or not we shall be able to hold to the road embarked upon in this direction and overcome old obstacles and habits. These apprehensions are based on findings that economic tools do not always operate in the required direction. This is no surprise, since the economic management system is still in its infancy, and we anticipated that its design would have to be directly verified by practice.

Such distrust, however, is voiced mainly because loopholes and shortcomings in economic tools cannot be repaired by the revival of administrative guidance methods which not only fail to produce the required initiative but breed speculation and undermine the cohesion of interests of individuals, enter-

---

[1] See Stanley Riveles, "Slovakia: Catalyst of Crisis," *Problems of Communism,* Vol. XVII, No. 3 (May–June 1968), pp. 1–9.

prises, and society. It is primarily we, the party and Central Committee, who must react to these problems. The economy will not automatically of its own internal forces implement the required social changes and desired development — and, primarily, it will not do so at the proper time. It is all well and good that at today's plenum we are once more stressing the extension of economic tools and the refinement of prices as a basis of making these tools more effective, but I feel that the emphasis placed on extending economic tools toward thrift and profitability and the proper relation between productivity and wages constitutes only one aspect of the matter, even though a very important one.

By their design our economic tools must affect not only the needs of the moment but also the scope opened for the development of progressive production, for structural changes and technical advancement. Last but not least, they must promote the implementation of our socioeconomic goals from a territorial viewpoint. . . .

Such economic tools cannot be devised through compromise or by means of amendments and exceptions: they must be an organic component of the managerial system and of its principles, which stem from the main goals of the whole society.

Ensuring optimum territorial development of productive forces for the purpose of creating the prerequisites for the implementation of the interests of all our society constitutes a very important sector in which the economic tools should and will have to show greater effect.

The documentary material submitted to the plenum shows convincingly how unequally — I should even say antagonistically — manpower resources are distributed, and how they contrast with the placement of investments.

Now this certainly is an important socioeconomic factor, which it is impossible to underrate or to disregard since it plays a very important role. A society which fails to use its population productively — and this concerns to a decisive extent the young prospective labor force — cannot say that it has an intensive economy and is taking full advantage of its possibilities. These problems are already topical. For all practical purposes we are failing to solve the problem of the growth in employment of women in Slovakia, and as far as youth problems are concerned we only have shelved this problem for the next three years.

The argument would be incomplete, however, if limited to labor forces and their absolute increase in Slovakia. This is not the only reason why we must strive for better distribution of the production forces. It is a fact that the prevalence of labor resources in Slovakia would present no problems if the productive forces were correctly located. It is a positive feature that in the eastern part of the state, where other sources for industrial growth exist, additional manpower resources also are available. A decisive share of the imported raw materials and exported products passes — and will do so even more in the future — through Slovakia to the Soviet Union and other socialist countries. The Danube plays an important role here, and so forth.

Progressive power resources are rapidly growing in Slovakia; imported gas, oil, and relatively extensive resources of raw materials, which we must exploit more fully, are available in Slovakia. All this creates the prerequisites for a more marked strengthening of the processing industry. There are new capacities in Slovakia which must be fully developed; their exploitation must be stepped up to open a wider area for employment.

These problems are well known at the center. Nor does the problem lie in willingness or unwillingness, or in politico-economic directives — those are quite clear. The 13th Czechoslovak Communist Party Congress directed that as a component of the consolidation and dynamic development of the national economy, we must also in the future deepen the prerequisites for the harmonious development of the provinces of our country, and in this connection, it prescribed better exploitation of the possibilities for an intensification of the economy of Slovakia and the solution of problems concerning industrial agglomerations. These Congress guidelines must be respected more and must be more consistently complied with in practice.

It appears, however, that when it comes to realizing these clear and especially urgent goals as well as the directives pertaining to regional development we are lacking in well-devised and legally finalized tools which correspond to the new managerial system, particularly for the distribution of new investments. The government tried to bring about optimal placement by the resolution on the verification and transfer of newly initiated investments into provinces where labor resources were available. But this resolution failed to produce the desired result. . . .

An urgent and important demand has arisen: Economic tools must be extended to affect various regions, and economic pressure must be applied to influence narrow enterprise viewpoints and lead them toward the interests of the entire society in this area.

It is also necessary before such an assessment of efficiency factors from a territorial viewpoint is undertaken that the center assume this task with all its authority. Economic tools must be created for this purpose. The need is becoming evident for rather serious consideration of the establishment of an appropriate central fund to ensure the advancement of progressive sectors, which will serve to implement correct placement and at the same time economic structural changes.

In Slovakia, for example, this would involve full utilization of lumber and other raw materials, the solution of urgent microregional problems, etc. Each state in the world today is establishing and maintaining such funds and rights, since the development and advancement of the productive forces objectively demand it. When the new managerial principles were prepared, this task of the center was also considered. But it has now fallen into oblivion.

I deem it quite necessary to make it clear that when an economically necessary and practicable plant is built in one or another region where labor is abundant, this is no policy of salvage or sacrifice. What matters is distributing investments in such a manner as to take advantage of our economic conditions in the most rational manner. Thus I should say that it is impossible to counter-pose these things, and I believe that, on the contrary, if the resources and reserves that the Slovak economy offers are not exploited rationally and effectively it will be detrimental to the Czechoslovak economy as a whole.

KSČ LEADERSHIP STRUGGLE

IN OCTOBER, police brutality in breaking up a peaceful student demonstration against miserable dormitory conditions abruptly escalated the volatile political situation.[1] Student mass meetings protested the police action and passed resolutions against the "unhealthy situation in the country," providing a recognizable link between student spokesmen and the rebels of the June Writers' Congress.[2] Even the National Assembly condemned the police action and demanded an investigation. It was the first time that the majority of the deputies had supported an antiregime activity.

Obviously, the divisions at the highest level of the party were no longer over the issue of how to handle the dissatisfied intellectuals. Successive sessions of the Central Committee in late October and mid-December now revealed a leadership struggle in which the party was divided against itself (see Document 4).[3]

After Brezhnev's quick trip to Prague on December 8 (reportedly at the personal invitation of Novotný, although perhaps with the knowledge of the Czechoslovak Presidium), the Soviets appear to have opted for neutrality, leaving the extent of the crisis to become public when Dubček replaced Novotný as First Secretary of the Communist Party of Czechoslovakia on January 5, 1968. For the first time in Czechoslovakia's history, a Slovak had become the most powerful figure in the state.[4] In his speech to the February 1 Congress of Agricultural Cooperatives (Document 5), the new First Secretary made his first public commitment to party and social reform, setting forth a platform of political participation involving all strata of society.

[1] Andreas Razumovsky reports in *Frankfurter Allgemeine Zeitung,* November 10 and 22, 1967.

[2] The connection was made explicit in condemnations by one of the regime's spokesmen against the writers, František Kolár (*Kulturní tvorba,* November 16, 1967).

[3] This remarkable document appeared in November 1968, well after the Soviet invasion of Czechoslovakia. For an earlier, less complete account see O. Šik, "How the Battle Was Joined," *Kulturní noviny* (March 29, 1968), translated in *Studies in Comparative Communism,* Vol. 1, Nos. 1 and 2 (July and October 1968), pp. 171–178.

[4] A detailed analysis of the early relationship of the KSČ and the Communist Party of Slovakia may be found in Zdeněk Eliáš and Jaromír Netík's section on Czechoslovakia in William E. Griffith (ed.), *Communism in Europe,* Vol. 2 (Cambridge, Mass.: The M.I.T. Press, 1966).

DOCUMENT 4
"WHAT HAPPENED IN JANUARY"
Vojtěch Mencl and František Ouředník

Excerpts

[*Život strany*, Nos. 16, 17, 18 August–September 1968; translation revised from RFE Czechoslovak Press Survey No. 2133 (November 13, 1968) and No. 2142 (November 29, 1968)]

❦

. . . Reform of the Political System

Certain suggestions to this end were made, for example, during debates in the KSČ CC in January 1965, and although these proposals met with strong resistance on the part of Novotný's political leadership, the conflict showed signs of a possibility for differentiation within the forces on which, up to then, Novotný's concentration of power had mainly depended. The incipient conflict between Novotný and Hendrych was the first indication of crisis in the hitherto homogeneous leadership of the KSČ. And it soon became evident that tensions would be increasing in another sphere as well.

It is fairly characteristic — and not for the first time in our history — for the pressure of social opposition to first become apparent in the sphere of literary and artistic creation. Especially artists of the word — writers and journalists — can note and express fairly quickly any social dissonance and deformed elements in the life of the people. They have many sensitive ways of portraying social conflicts as fictitious human stories, which can sometimes be violently accurate expressions of reality. Besides, the sphere of artistic creation is always relatively free; especially when it employs metaphor and allegory, which help it to get across ideas that, under conditions of preliminary censorship, would be difficult to express as political, historical, or other conclusions. This is in fact what happened.

Ever since 1956, little flames of nonconformist journalism have been burning in Czech and Slovak cultural magazines. A number of articles were suppressed by press supervisors, but some had to be passed. Novotný's leadership attempted from time to time, rather clumsily, to carry out a so-called policy of differentiation between the cultural and the scientific front. Thanks to the attempts to initiate such a policy, there were alternating waves of greater liberality and refreezing. After such oscillations, especially within the machinery of the KSČ CC, the officials in the forefront of policymaking in these sectors were the political losers; they were called to account after periods of more liberal policy and removed from office (for example, Císař, Auersperg, Slavík, and others).

This form of social criticism was particularly annoying to Novotný's leadership. It responded more and more nervously and began resorting to administrative intervention. There was an attempt to reduce the leeway of artistic, and especially literary, creation to assure that permanent criticism and fundamental social dissatisfaction could not flame up. This, however, drew the attention of the cultural front back to the development and state of political conditions and politics. This front began increasingly to turn to direct and open political criticism, especially through the media of the press, radio, and television. Starting from the beginning of the 1960s, another focal point for action aimed at breaking down the barriers of the concentrated power system had developed.

A serious source of dissatisfaction was certain changes in the position of Slovakia within the state, especially the constitutional changes introduced in 1960. The increasingly asymmetric constitutional arrangement of Czech and Slovak relations and the further deepening of centralism — above all the abolishment of the Slovak Board of Commissioners — considerably limited the opportunities for the Slovak national and party agencies to adopt a policy which would solve the pressing problems of the Slovak nation. Direct management of Slovak regions from the center, frequently without any knowledge or understanding of Slovak problems, gave rise to difficulties and serious dissatisfaction in Slovakia. The centralization of management with respect to Slovakia sometimes went to silly and insulting extremes. The Central Committee of the Slovak Communist Party, for example, was not permitted to settle its own cadre problems without previous consent, even though regional committees were permitted to do so. It could not even appoint the editors of its own newspaper. What with all the economic failures and difficulties, dissatisfaction with the excessive centralization became treated as "dissatisfaction with Prague." This resulted in a situation which was liable to activate serious discord between the Czech and Slovak peoples and between the KSČ and the Slovak Communist Party.

Communists in Slovakia watched this state of affairs with growing anxiety. They began to realize with increasing clarity that improvement could be achieved only by a radical change in the working methods of the party center, together with corresponding changes in the whole system of political and economic management appropriate to the conditions of the period. This gave rise to a constantly increasing desire for changes in the constitutional arrangement of the Czech and Slovak national relations. It should be emphasized that Novotný's political line showed extreme indifference to and took a "grand-Czech attitude" toward Slovak problems.

Another serious problem, which became steadily more acute, was the cooling attitude of the younger generation to the party and to socialism. František Kriegel, for instance, stated at the October 1967 session of the KSČ CC, that according to information from the north Moravian region, in nearly a third of the basic organizations there was not one member under the age of twenty-five. In the Přerov district there were no members under twenty-five in 44 percent of the party organizations. There were a number of signs that the ability of the Czechoslovak Union of Youth and the Pioneer organization to attract members and to take action had radically decreased. The drop in political activity and youth involvement was naturally only an indication of the general decrease in the political involvement of Czechoslovak citizens.

A considerable degree of social dissatisfaction was also apparent in the mood of the broad masses of the KSČ membership. Serious changes took place in the attitude of a considerable number of party members toward party activities and toward participation in political activity in general. For instance, at KSČ membership meetings attendance was scanty, frequently as low as 30 to 40 percent. Discussions at party meetings were purely formal. Resolutions were not implemented. As far back as 1964, there were increasing signs that party members accepted their functions with reluctance.

During this period a number of profound changes took place in the development of party work in the highest offices of the KSČ. The party leadership, concentrated in the hands of a very narrow circle of people, began to suffer increasingly from a sort of "defensive reflex." The party center, led by Novotný, expended an enormous amount of political energy not only on making centralized decisions on a great number of problems, but on an increasing effort to suppress any demonstration of criticism. As criticism and dissatisfaction grew, efforts to suppress them became the focus of its activity, the real essence of governing.

This also resulted in "new looks" at cadre policy. More and more people — willing and "capable of anything" — began to take over the higher positions. People with no opinions or ideas of their own, but always loyal to the chief representatives of centralized power, they were always willing to stamp out any kind of criticism.

To the same degree that dissatisfaction grew and party work was disrupted, the clear-cut unambiguous concentration of power at the summit of the party organism increased. Enormous power was more and more concentrated in the hands of a very small circle of people, especially the First Secretary of the KSČ CC, Antonín Novotný.

Cabinet Politics

The whole mechanism with Novotný at its head developed according to the specific ideas of its creator. It was, in fact, an apparatus for "cabinet politics." It created the opportunity to settle even ideological disputes by cabinet methods. In this situation not much room was left for differences of opinion, not even among members of the highest most exclusive KSČ leadership. At the same time, it was precisely the top party leadership that was in fact managing the affairs of the party and all society.

The excessive concentration of social management in the hands of the KSČ — which actually meant in the hands of the apparatus — naturally overwhelmed the directing center with an enormous burden of state and economic duties. This avalanche of tasks completely excluded the possibility of any real political action. Problems were shelved and remained unsolved, resolutions were passed and decisions were made which had no bearing either on the fast developing situation or on the context of other resolutions and decisions. This way of working excluded from management first state and economic agencies, and in the course of time also party agencies. Decision-making, and consequently actual governing, were thus transferred to individuals, frequently not even those in the most responsible positions. Responsibility and any realistic possibility of control disappeared. Political and other issues were settled by "opinions," by individual decisions, by instructions from anyone who had enough power to impose his "opinion" on the others. At the summit of the whole system stood the "personality" of the First Secretary of the KSČ CC, Antonín Novotný.

In this situation the function and role of the highest elected body of the KSČ — the CC Plenum — became purely formal. Though the Central Committee of the KSČ held fairly regular sessions, the members of the CC were presented with the individual questions of the program in a way that made it impossible for them to make political decisions regarding them. Alternative solutions were not even offered. It is characteristic that in the period between the beginning of 1965 and October 1967 the party CC did not even once discuss the political situation in the country, did not examine the working methods of its organs and apparatus, did not discuss the party budget, etc. Consequently, in the Plenums of the KSČ CC unconsidered approval rather than real discussion of proposed resolutions was the order of the day.

This atmosphere was further reinforced by the prevailing ideas about the unity of the party. Unanimous agreement was promoted in order to demonstrate "party strength." If any criticisms or objections were voiced, they were characterized as willful disruptions of unity.

In the KSČ CC Plenum there was direct suppression of criticism. For instance, the order in which speakers were called on during discussions in the CC Plenum was frequently determined on a purely subjective basis, not according to order of application, and potential critics were usually unable to take part in the discussion. Piller, who had criticized Novotný before the second presidential election, had from that time kept applying in vain for permission to speak. That similar procedures were followed at the 13th KSČ Congress is demonstrated by the fact that the Presidium of the Congress was against Šik's being allowed to join the discussion. Novotný finally did allow him to speak at the very end of the debate. Direct pressure was exercised with increasing frequency even on members of the Central Committee known to want to voice a critical attitude.

The key problem of essential changes in the existing political system and above all the assertion of the leading role of the party was systematically suppressed in the KSČ CC Plenum discussions. To this end, the discussions at the 13th KSČ Congress were subjected to preliminary "streamlining." Although they had to make a number of concessions during the preparations for the 13th Party Congress, Novotný and those who stage-managed the Congress opposed with the utmost vigor any mention of these issues. By 1966, however, the Czechoslovak socialist community had reached a stage of development in which any delay in setting forth basic economic and political reforms acted as an appreciable brake on the creative forces of our society and of the KSČ and hindered taking advantage of opportunities which had arisen during the twenty-year period of socialist development.

The fact that as a result of resistance on the part of the conservatives in the

Presidium and the Party CC the 13th KSČ Congress was unable to solve the basic problems of our society or even outline them in sufficient depth was the spark that set off a political crisis in the country and in the KSČ. Considering the conditions within the KSČ, it was obvious that efforts to achieve a structural reform of the political and economic system of Czechoslovak socialism would take the form of a sharp internal political conflict in the KSČ, and that the first event in this conflict would be the battle to destroy the regime's personal power in the party. This opened the road to the events of 1967 and to January 1968.

The first indications of open encounter had already become evident at the session of the KSČ CC in February 1967. It had been planned that the Plenum would discuss questions of social unity and the unity of the party, differentiation of interests, and especially problems of the younger generation. During such debates any thorough analysis was bound to end in criticism of the whole political system of the KSČ, and at this meeting a number of CC members did speak very critically. One speech in particular had an extraordinary impact — that of Marie Sedláková, who, in an allegorical story about a village, hinted at the real state of affairs in the party. She concluded that it was incorrect to say that the masses in the party were passive, that they were losing interest in politics. She asked whether it was correct to blame failures on workers, farmers, and the intelligentsia. She emphasized that in such a situation the greatest share of blame rested with "the managers, who are responsible for directing the destiny of society, who create the general political conditions for the activity of the masses, and on the basis of this experience it would be correct to start thinking about the past and present work of the party."

Černík also spoke critically at this plenum. From the old Leninist thesis that the attitude of the party toward its own mistakes is the basic criterion of its social responsibility, he deduced that it was necessary to overcome the sectarian opinions which made it impossible for the party to see reality clearly. A number of other persons spoke in a similar vein.

When the February Plenum was over, there was a lively discussion in the KSČ CC Presidium. Novotný expressed his dissatisfaction with the conduct of the Plenum and even declared categorically that "the February Plenum must never be repeated."

But of course he did not prevent the conflict from growing. The spring and summer of 1967 produced an increasing number of new signs of dissatisfaction. The situation became acute at the Fourth Congress of Czechoslovak Writers. Novotný's political clique was nothing less than shocked by the Writers' Congress. The sharpness in individual speeches, unusual for the period, the outspoken and natural manner in which some of those taking part violated all the formerly recognized taboos, caused a political fever in the circles around Novotný. Face to face with this ideological revolt, which in a number of discussions even reached a wholesale criticism of the political system, there was nothing they could do but engage in open political warfare.

They had no other choice but to resort to repression. In his campaign against the Writers' Congress, Novotný achieved only one political victory.

He managed to set back Hendrych and his growing group of followers in the KSČ leadership which had been waiting around for something to break ever since it gradually began to disassociate itself from his policy after the February 1967 Plenum. The position of this group had strengthened when the department of political organization of the KSC CC came under its influence. Especially after the Writers' Congress, Hendrych was forced to endorse the spirit of Novotný's sharp policy vis-à-vis the writers and the whole cultural front, all of which weakened his position.

The September Plenum

An evaluation of the Writers' Congress was made at the conference of the KSČ CC in September 1967, though originally the Plenum was not scheduled to deal with this question. At the same time, proposals were made that sharp measures be taken against the Union of Czechoslovak Writers, their publication *Literární noviny,* and certain Communist writers. The Plenum proceedings and its attitude to the Writers' Congress were influenced by biased and distorted information supplied by Novotný and Hendrych and by the Central Control and Revision Commission.

A different position was adopted by Vodsloň, who suggested that the KSČ stand on the cultural front should also include a certain amount of self-criticism. Novotný reacted sharply to this proposal: "I am surprised at his statement, and I understand the motive behind it. I prefer not to discuss it." Such probings for hidden "motives and intentions" behind critical statements created an atmosphere in which more thought was given to "how shall I say it," than to "what shall I say." In other respects, too, the atmosphere at the conference on the questions of the Fourth Writers' Congress was very nervous and tense. The Plenum finally approved the proposals that had been submitted to it, but only after Novotný had declared at the end of the discussion that he had proof that the "Writers' Congress had been prepared in Paris." To date he has not supplied any proof of this, although he was requested to do so several times at later plenums. As a result of all this a resolution was passed which most unfortunately sharpened the conflict between the KSČ and the writers, who were united in a solid bloc. A conflict also developed between the party and the intelligentsia, who sympathized with the writers.

It was in this atmosphere that in the summer of 1967 certain phenomena began to appear in Czechoslovak political life signaling a further escalation of Novotný's political methods and policies. There was an obvious endeavor to initiate a sharp offensive against the ever growing surge of criticism inside as well as outside the party.

The whole summer of 1967 was a time of extraordinary personal political activity on the part of Novotný, who undertook a number of visits to various regions of the Republic. On September 1, 1967, in his speech at the graduation exercises of the Higher Military Schools, he disregarded to a great extent the spirit and letter of the resolutions of the 13th KSČ Congress. He declared, for instance, "Our democracy is a class democracy, our freedom is a class freedom," even though the resolution of the 13th Congress on this subject reads: "Since the 12th Party Congress the socialist social relations in our countries have been characterized by the elimination of class antagonism. Socialist classes and strata have developed internally and have gradually come closer together, despite the existing differences, which were due primarily to different economic and social positions." The 13th KSČ Congress also made clear that the future development of our society was directly linked to the spread of socialist democracy and the active participation of all working people in government and management. Novotný, however, asserted in his speech that "only the Communist party, and not just any group which feels itself authorized to do so, can oversee and direct the social process, and where necessary set right shortcomings and mistakes which may arise during its development." That was a signal for the return of the kind of politics that existed before the 13th KSČ Congress, or even in the 1950s.

At conferences of the KSČ CC Presidium, which was drafting the program of the October Plenum of the party CC, Novotný also voiced ideas which indicated his decision to take a sharp line against any endeavor to democratize the party. At the meeting of the Presidium of the KSČ CC on September 5 he said, "We have allowed Šik to write and even to speak at the 13th party Congress; he was allowed, as the last speaker, to give a stormy speech about democracy. Naturally, when this was discussed at the Congress, the writers climbed on the bandwagon too, storming 'Democracy, democracy!' " In the same speech the First Secretary of the KSČ CC gave his warm support to the political purges taking place in other parties and countries. That too was disquieting.

But that was not all. For instance, the Eighth Department of the KSČ CC issued a special internal directive called "The Concept of Work," with a report by Comrade Novotný concerning the sector of the Eighth Department of the KSČ CC and suggestions for measures to be taken in the near future. Ideological and political questions were discussed in almost military language, using specialized military terms. Further, ideological and theoretical problems were confused with political problems and presented as signs of ideological diversion. The need to analyze and establish which positions "ideological enemies have occupied or intend to occupy, where their blow will fall, and what they intend to use in their support" was also discussed in the directive.

At the same time at some party assemblies (especially at the conference of the leading KSČ district and regional committee secretaries on September 17–19 and later in Novotný's report), certain viewpoints were expressed which very decisively reacted to demands made by a number of officials and some regional organizations for more serious changes in party working methods. Novotný again defended the centralistic concept of party work, even going as far as to say that the KSČ must maintain its leading role everywhere and by whatever means it feels suited to the particular time and place.

The clash between Novotný and the representatives of some regional organizations was a product of conflicting acts derived from the strict centralistic decisions made in the highest party center. The state of crisis in the work of the central party agencies, which we have already mentioned, caused considerable delay in deciding on a number of burning questions which could not be delayed down in the districts and regions. The districts and regions were forced to await a number of decisions and had to work according to their own judgment. The Presidium of the KSČ CC, which had centralized decision-making on an enormous number of issues, was in fact losing control of the lower organs in the party system by doing so. In time, this independence of procedure in some district and regional organizations (undesirable from higher authority's point of view, but essential) caused the officials at all these levels to begin to appreciate the necessity for very radical changes in the style and methods of party work from top to bottom. This sharpened the conflict inside the party organization itself between the regime of personal power in the party and some of the regions (north Moravian, south Moravian, partly the north Bohemian and some of the Slovak regions, with the Slovak CP CC in the lead). This discord with the center was of varying intensity and frequently could be traced to diverse motives, but potentially it existed nearly everywhere. It was this factor which ignited the chain reaction that finished with the fall of Novotný's leadership.

It Started at the October Conference of the KSČ CC

The plenary session was opened on October 30, 1967. A number of CC members who had come to discuss the question of the KSČ role in the present stage of development of Czechoslovak socialist society were fully aware of the necessity to introduce profound changes in the work of the party. Even the preparation of the Plenum was fairly extensive. A number of suggestive papers from scientific centers, party organizations and organs, and the party apparatus as well as the results of some research and proposals of party commissions were assembled to help with the preparation of theses which were to be submitted for discussion. Unfortunately, all this rich source material remained in the final draft virtually untapped. The originally proposed variant of the theses seemed to the majority of the KSČ CC Presidium members too "daring," and so nearly overnight a new proposal was prepared, written by people who had not had the opportunity to make use of the flood of materials and proposals from the regions and districts. The result was that the proposal submitted to the October Plenum far from satisfied those who expected that from this infrequent opportunity, when the Central Committee was discussing the most basic questions of life and party activities, there would come a deeper, if not fundamental, change.

The discussions on the proposed theses about the role of the party soon showed, however, that the roots of some problems would be examined after all. In their speeches Comrades Kostelanský, Rigo, and others said that it was necessary to improve the cadre composition of the leading links in party management and take a position which would save the Central Committee from losing authority inside as well as outside the party. Rigo spoke of the aversion to and fear of criticism and said that it was impossible to identify political leadership with economic management and that at present criticism downwards outweighed criticism upwards. He also said, "It is wrong to keep people in office who do not belong there."

The key factor was, however, the speech by Alexander Dubček, because this started a discussion which gradually turned to the fundamental problems connected with the existing method of asserting the leading role of the KSČ. Dubček began with the assumption that

> Before us lies in all its urgency the job of characterizing the new stage we have reached and its new qualities from all sides. The well-known statement that the whole epoch from capitalism to communism is a "class epoch" will not help one bit towards understanding the internal divisions of that epoch. Such generalizations, however, can become a smokescreen for conservatism and political sectarianism if we fail to seek out the qualitative steps appropriate to this stage and the main tasks which correspond to them. Everything of value from the past must be incorporated into the future, but we must keep our distance from all that is incompatible with the new conditions and has failed to help the party in the past.

Let us take a good look at these words. They expressed a view diametrically opposed to the one uttered a few days before by Novotný. Dubček's words express what our times demand: a well-thought-out political system appropriate to the *new* stage of development of the Czechoslovak socialist community.

The gauntlet had been thrown to political conservatives in the leadership of the KSČ. The conflict could now start; it could not help but start.

Dubček went on to say that this type of change in conditions is accompanied by inevitable political and ideological conflict. "The danger of conservatism and sectarianism is no less acute for the party, especially during a time of change — and I would like to underline the words 'during a time of change' — than are liberal tendencies." Here for the first time in such a straightforward form Dubček drew attention to the serious danger of conservatism in the party which the existing leadership underrated and about which no one was even permitted to speak. "I intend to support this opinion," he continued,

> by citing the views of the Presidium of the south Moravian region. They warn that in the opinion of both members and officials, as well as in party practice, an attitude to questions about the leading role of the party which is unsuited to the new conditions is still prevalent and that these conditions call for an open analysis and the same fundamental approach to conservative, as well as to liberal, opinions. . . .
>
> Defending our society against capitalistic influences and the remains of class relations should clearly be among our basic duties. We cannot, however, be content with a defensive attitude, because it may only be hiding the seeds of stagnation and conservatism. We can best strengthen the achievements of socialism, if we combine them with economic, social, and cultural victories. . . . It would also be a serious mistake to confuse results with causes. Neither emigrés nor imperialist agents can cause us major problems, and therefore we should not devote such powerful, undeserved, and for us damaging propaganda to them. In this idea we should find a considerable contribution to strengthening the unity of our people.

As soon as Dubček raised the question of the changes essential to the "new stage" of the political system, he also had to consider the question of the party role in this new system. Among other things he said,

A new stage and new jobs require basically new, more accurate and more adequate methods of political leadership and management and more clearly defined relations between them. We will, we must make a fundamental change and undertake considerable shifts in the work of the party. Following these theses, we must make the basic transition from doing all the work ourselves to true leadership toward the development and building of socialism. All serious thinking about the tasks and methods of political leadership emphasizes the principle that the party should not manage society, but lead it.

In conclusion Dubček said, "It is natural for conflicts to occur between the old and the new, inside and outside the party between the new and progressive and the conservative and customary. The supporters of the one and of the other are always individuals." He emphasized, therefore, that it is necessary to clarify the responsibilities of the central organs, to examine new demands on the Central Committee, and to take a stand on the accumulation of functions.

Dubček's speech made a deep impression on the KSČ CC Plenum. It was in fact the first systematic criticism and confrontation of the present leading role of the party from the new stage of socialist development in Czechoslovakia. At the same time, it was a specific criticism of those opinions of First Secretary Novotný which had deviated in the past from the resolution and line of the 13th KSČ Congress.

M. Vaculík reacted immediately to Dubček's speech. He said that he considered it his party duty to comment on it. He declared ". . . never before has Comrade Dubček expressed his attitude in the form he has used today. He spoke differently, for instance, when we were discussing the comments of the Presidiums of the regional and district committees of the party or the viewpoints of the basic organizations." He described the speech as "tendentious and unstable" and concluded, "I don't think that Communists' private affairs should be settled from the tribune of the Central Committee even if they are members of the highest party agencies."

H. Leflerová and M. Chudík, who followed immediately, did not react to the growing conflict. Then, however, came Sedláková. She called the situation in the party serious: "In the whole party, not excepting the Central Committee, there is a certain stuffiness and nervousness." She demanded that proof should be supplied for Novotný's assertion at the September Plenum that the Congress of Czechoslovak Writers was prepared in Paris. Then she started to criticize Novotný on specific points. "Comrade Novotný, as we heard at the previous CC Conference, said that our government does not govern as a government and that it is necessary to draw conclusions from that fact. If this new government does not govern either, there must be some reason for it." The cause, she said, was the system of replacing state and economic agencies with the party and its apparat. Finally, she protested against the manner in which Vaculík had commented on Dubček's speech. She said that his words confirmed her opinion that relations in the Presidium were not quite what they should be.

Nothing else of significance was said until Kriegel's speech stirred up new excitement. Kriegel turned his attention to internal party conditions, labeling them unpleasant. "This 1,700,000-member giant is insufficiently active or efficient. A great number of its agencies are rarely active or else entirely inactive." As a result, within the party organism proper there arises "dissatisfaction with itself, as well as dissatisfaction with the brain that is supposed to be managing it." He demanded internal democratization of the party, proposed the introduction of a secret ballot, and rejected Vaculík's attack on Dubček.

The conflict, which was fundamentally a conflict over basic views of KSČ policy, began to take on the appearance of a personal dispute. A number of other speakers (Slavík, Sabolčík, and Kadlec) also deplored Vaculík's attack on Dubček, and it was demanded that he should clarify the matter. Finally Vaculík did so: "In my opinion the solid partisan approach is this: when a member of a specific organ — the party Presidium in this instance — discusses his problem within that body, it may happen that a majority of members of the CC Presidium do not agree. Then it is obviously the normal duty of that comrade to bring these problems to the party Central Committee." This was rather a strange argument, echoing as it did the habit of demanding a certain "fractional discipline" in the Presidium and a certain confusion and shift in understanding the problem of unity within the party. Vaculík did not give enough consideration to the fact that the highest party organ between Congresses is the Central Committee.

Špaček, the leading secretary of the south Moravian KSČ CC, spoke next. He expressed his opinion of the situation in the party and society in terms similar to those which Dubček had used before him. Then Dubček asked if he could make a factual comment. He read a passage in the minutes from the conference of the Presidium of the KSČ CC which showed that the accusation that he had not spoken in the same vein at that meeting was groundless.

The progress of the Plenum was reaching a critical state of tension when Kolder, the chairman, suddenly declared, "I ask all comrades who are not members or candidates of the CC to leave the conference room. Comrade Novotný has made a request to this effect."

In the closed part of the discussions of the KSČ CC October Plenum, Novotný was the first to speak. He talked extemporaneously, very excitedly and sharply. He expressed a number of ideas with which it was very difficult to agree. In reaction to demands for further democratization of the party and society he came out with the statement that "we have had more than enough of democracy in life." He did not comment on the content of Dubček's contribution to the discussion but declared that he had already disagreed with it in the form in which it was put forward in the KSČ CC Presidium. He also said that in personal discussions he had told Dubček that as First Secretary of the Slovak CP CC he was not following a valid and responsible policy, that he was too much influenced by local interests, that he did not deal firmly with incorrect opinions, and even that he was influenced by "narrow and national interests." This was tantamount to an accusation of nationalism. Novotný went on to speak negatively about the advancement of demands for federalization, which he called a "political mistake" for which not only the Slovak people would pay, but working people in general.

Novotný's speech was accepted by the Plenum with considerable embarrassment and mixed feelings. The leading secretary of the north Moravian KSČ CC, Voleník, expressed his disquiet at Novotný's slighting approach to such serious questions. A number of others spoke in similar vein, e.g., Málek and Borůvka, who said among other things that the question of the relations of the two fraternal nations of our Republic was a very serious matter. "I feel personally responsible to the next Congress, and even more to the party as a whole. And because the matter at hand is so complicated and of such import, I propose — in accordance with the saying that it is better to sleep on it — that we do not close today's discussion of the Central Committee." He proposed that the Plenum should adjourn for two or three weeks and discuss very seriously "where and what are the causes of the problems which emerged so sharply yesterday."

Later on, following Kladivo, Bil'ak made a very serious statement: "I do not intend to lecture, only to remind. In the fifties we denounced the Slovak Communists as nationalists. Four years ago here, we carried out rehabilitation and the Central Committee engaged in self-criticism. We have admitted the terrible damage which we caused to our party, to the relations between Czechs and Slovaks. The practice of describing even justified national demands as nationalism has been deplored. Now again we hear the view that what the Slovak Communists say here — *en bloc* — is in conflict with the line of the party, and the First Secretary of the Slovak CP CC, Comrade Dubček, is even described as a nationalist. Where is the proof of all this?" He noted that when one of the Czech members of the KSČ CC Plenum criticizes something, he is not accused of nationalist motives. He supported the proposal that the discussion should not be closed and that it should be adjourned for two to three weeks.

These proposals were put to the vote, but before that Novotný put forward the view that the next (i.e., December) Plenum had such a full program that it would be proper to close all questions connected with the October Plenum forthwith by passing the proposed resolution. Only a few hands were shown in support of the proposal not to close the discussion and continue it in the next Plenum — Kriegel, Borůvka, Sedláčková, Jankovcová, and Jirásková. The great majority favored terminating the proceedings and passing the resolution on the question of the KSČ role at the present stage of development of the socialist community.

At the close of the October Plenum it appeared that the attempt had foundered to put an end to the existing state of affairs in the party and to establish the political bases for changes in the assertion of the leading role of the party and the whole political system in the new stage of the developement of socialism. But the conflict inside the KSČ CC Presidium had not been settled either. Had the situation of the KSČ and all society been generally more stable, it is possible that the conflict of opinions which came to light at the October

Plenum would have been fairly quickly evened out and resolved. But the situation was developing into one of deeper and more fundamental conflict. From the crack, which to a superficial observer would have appeared minute and perhaps insignificant, a gap started to open which gradually divided the members of the Presidium, and later the members of the Plenum of the KSČ CC, into two basic groups. One group was of the opinion that affairs were in such good order that it was not necessary to introduce any serious changes in the working methods of the KSČ or to accompany them by corresponding cadre changes. The other group was becoming more and more convinced that the road ahead demanded a hard and ruthlessly fair criticism of the existing state of affairs along with essential changes in leading party offices.

Excerpts

[*Život strany,* No. 19, September 11, 1968; translation revised from RFE Czechoslovak Press Survey, No. 2133 (November 13, 1968)]

Authors Vojtěch Mencl and František Ouředník explained in Nos. 14 to 17 of this biweekly the political and historical connections which led to the January Plenum of the KSČ CC. In the present issue we publish a further installment. It was written before the unhappy events of these days. Nevertheless, nothing need be changed.

The December Plenum

Because of the events which took place in the Presidium of the KSČ CC, the session of the Central Committee was postponed until the second half of December. It finally opened on December 19, 1967. After J. Lenárt's report on the scheduled item of the program, economic expansion and the standard of living, Novotný took the microphone. He was obviously aware of the extraordinarily complicated nature and delicacy of his position and of the fact that, in his speech at the October Plenum, he had committed some unpleasant and dangerous errors. He said that he wished to take a self-critical stand in connection with his October speech, stressing that he had prepared it hastily and as a result used some unfelicitous formulations, "particularly with respect to the work of our comrades in the leadership of the Slovak Communist Party."

He continued to defend the political essence of his October speech, however, saying, "I should like you to understand that a number of reasons and factors influenced my speech, especially some of the problems which are presently confronting us." He concluded by saying that he was "disturbed by the fact that our enemies rejoice in our difficulties and exploit them for their own aims." In spite of the serious criticism of his own work and the methods of the KSČ as a whole, the "activities of the enemy" in exploiting current difficulties appeared to him to be the number-one political problem. Of course, a fight against the "enemy" follows its own rules and uses its own methods and resources; therefore the question arose as to whether these same methods and resources would again be employed as the main way of solving difficulties in the party's policy.

He also touched upon the question of the accumulation of functions, declaring ". . . that if we are to work on the problem of accumulation of functions with a view to its gradual solution, we will also have to return to the question of combining these two highest posts." He argued that because of the lack of clarity on this matter and the need for elaborating it further the whole matter should be referred to the KSČ CC session in February or March of 1968. However, he emphasized at the same time, "Naturally, this is a question which will demand, in its internal as well as its international ramifications, a concrete and thorough examination from many angles so that we may select the most suitable way of settling it for our conditions without jeopardizing our traditions." This, too, is evidence of his desire to shelve the solution of this touchy problem, posed by the October Plenum, into the distant future.

Novotný informed the session briefly about Brezhnev's visit, saying that "during his visit, as reported in the press, Comrade Brezhnev met with Comrade Lenárt, several Presidium members, secretaries of the party Central Committee, and me. Mutual party relations and some of our internal problems were discussed at these meetings." However, he did not expand on these discussions of "some of our internal problems" to the Plenum of the KSČ CC.

The reaction was immediate. After the speech F. Vodsloň took the floor at once and said with visible excitement:

Comrades, what do you take us for? We have heard reports by Comrades Lenárt and Novotoný. I do not know whether the report expresses the collective stand of the Presidium but, whatever the case may be, comrades, I should like to ask why we have to hear about controversies within the Presidium from other sources than the Presidium itself. I feel that the comrades should state their viewpoints to the Central Committee. I read in the papers that Comrade Brezhnev was invited by the Central Committee; the next day I read that the invitation was extended by the Presidium. These are very important points. Do you really think we are blind to the way things are now among the people, among the party members? It is time for us to stand up to all this because this way all we are doing is losing the people's confidence.

Although B. Laštovička, who was presiding, made an attempt to play down Vodsloň's words and the justification for his stand, the spark had already ignited the tension-heavy atmosphere. From that moment the discussion turned back to the problems discussed by the October Plenum of the KSČ CC on which the Presidium could not reach an agreement in the period between the October and December plenary sessions.

The next speaker, Zdeněk Fierlinger, expressed very serious alarm about the party's situation. In an evaluation of party conditions and policies, he said that "since the 12th Congress, for over six years now, we have been marking time." And he concluded: "This moment, therefore, had to come. It was inevitable in view of the quality and quantity of our shortcomings. We have reached a point of extreme crisis in our party, and we cannot in good faith solve it by the method proposed by Comrade Novotný, that is, by another postponement, by renaming the ministries." He also criticized very severely the policy pursued with respect to the Slovak question.

Next O. Šik delivered a long speech. He posed two fundamental questions: Why is there increasing dissatisfaction in the party and society and why does the party cling to methods which cause this dissatisfaction? He declared that this state of affairs produces the differences of opinion which have come to the surface in the highest party organs. He emphasized that "in every period the party faces the problem of how to organize itself to be the instrument best able to achieve the necessary goals." Because, according to Šik, we have now passed the period when working methods of the KSČ were dictated by the need for leading and controlling, for watching vigilantly over every organ of power and leadership, the survival of the old concept of the party's role has become a brake on the progress of society. He continued by requesting that "new conditions bring about changes in the party, the part it is to play, its organization and methods of work." At this new stage, Šik said, it is of primary importance for "the party to provide true leadership in the field of politics and to unite all social groups, not only ideologically but also with respect to their special interests. The party must work to overcome all the increasing social conflicts and to ensure the unity of the people as they move toward realizing their aims, those aims which correspond to the fundamental progressive interests of all the working people and in the final analysis to the progressive international interests of the workers of the whole world." If, in Šik's opinion, instead of fulfilling this basic duty, which nobody will fulfill on its behalf, the party continues to do the jobs of all the other bodies of power and authority, including the government, if it continues to direct and control life in every detail instead of providing true political leadership for society, it will begin to overlook the fundamental political problems in the country. It will fail to provide solutions to society's basic conflicts and will find itself lagging behind swiftly moving events.

According to Šik, there were four fundamental reasons why the KSČ found itself in its present state and was unable to overcome it. First of all, there was the policy of intimidation which eliminated all criticism; second, there was the undemocratic suppression of discussion; third, there were the many methods of rendering both critics and their criticism ineffective, mainly through cadre manipulations; and finally, there was the detailed direction of and close watch on all important agencies, which ensured that nothing would "leak out" and no truth would be revealed.

He made suggestions as to how to start overcoming the problems without delay. "First, the enormous accumulation of power in the hands of certain comrades, especially those of Comrade Novotný, should be reviewed; this accumulation I see to be the greatest obstacle in the way of a rapid cure for the party." He proposed that Comrade Novotný should be asked to lay down immediately the office of First Secretary of the Central Committee of the KSČ.

As the second step, he proposed the immediate election of a commission which would submit to the December Plenum the names of at least two candidates for the office of First Secretary. The voting for this office would then proceed by secret ballot.

His third suggestion was that "after the above-mentioned election the Presidium should immediately be charged with drafting the fundamental measures for democratization within the party, the main points of which would still have to be discussed." In this respect, several proposals were made which, even when seen through today's eyes, hold up as a thorough appraisal of the existing situation and as an indication of the point of departure for the revival of the competence of the KSČ.

Šik's speech was the final breakthrough in the development of the Plenum. From that moment each of the participants in the debate reacted to Šik's opinions in one way or another.

While the first day of the KSČ CC session ended with substantial opposition to Novotný's stand and a spirit of criticism toward the state of affairs in which the party found itself, discussion assumed a somewhat different character on the second day when a number of speakers argued against radical changes in the situation within the party.

J. Lenárt, the very first speaker, defended the opinion that it was "necessary to approach this issue" — the separation of functions issue — with a clear goal in view and make definite plans in advance to ensure that our society will profit and avoid extremes." In the name of the Presidium, he rejected "the fantastic rumors" which dramatize its discussions. He said that as far as Šik's proposals were concerned, "it is our opinion that in view of the fact that this proposal goes beyond the framework of the Statutes," neither the Presidium nor the Central Committee "is entitled to decide on changes of so far-reaching a nature." He also pointed out international political considerations and proposed that discussion be resumed as planned for the agenda of the KSČ CC Plenum.

V. Slavík reacted to this speech by protesting that "the discussion at the Plenum has hardly started" and yet "a value judgment has already been expressed in the statement that Šik's proposal goes beyond the framework of the Statutes." Next, L. Hrdinová asked for an explanation of the circumstances connected with Brezhnev's visit, and Való spoke about several problems concerning Slovakia and expressed support for "all proposals which endeavor to deal with the shortcomings in our lives."

Next came M. Chudík's speech attacking the ideas expressed in Šik's report. Chudík accused Šik of "failing to take the proposed resolution into consideration," disregarding the reports which had been made and setting forth his own Proposal for Further Democratization Measures Within the Party. He rejected Šik's standpoint as being at variance to the decisions approved by the Presidium in October and the resolution submitted to the December Plenum. He recommended that Šik's proposals be rejected and treated in the same manner as the other contributions to the discussion.

Piller, however, who spoke of questions involved in the work of the Presidium which, in his opinion, "does not work as a collective," went so far as to declare: "If we really want to call a spade a spade, we must state that the consequences of the personality cult have survived to a great extent in our country. They continue to harm our party and ruin many people's lives. Many people do not say aloud what they think and feel." He criticized Novotný personally but added that an immediate division of powers at the December Plenum would in his opinion be a "rash step."

Following a line similar to that of Chudík, O. Šimůnek criticized Šik's proposals and pointed out that the merging of powers had been based on a decision made by the KSČ CC in 1957 "as an important political principle, corresponding to the leading role of the party in every sphere of our country." He alluded to the fact that this principle was also embodied in the Constitution and that therefore, "We must not treat principles of this kind in a reckless manner."

Vasil Bil'ak's speech amounted to a detailed chronological exposition of the relationship between Novotný and the Slovak Communist Party (CPSL) Central Committee. His main point was that "what happened at the October Plenum was not accidental. Comrade Novotný merely expounded more concretely on what he has been saying in a more covert form for a number of years. His reservations vis-à-vis the CPSL CC, aimed chiefly against Comrade Dubček, have been sensed by many members of the CPSL CC from the time when Comrade Bacílek had to be dismissed from his post as First Secretary of the CPSL CC and member of the Presidium of the CPSL CC. From that time it appeared as if all of a sudden Comrade Novotný regarded Slovakia as the weak spot in the Republic." Bil'ak then described how the powers of the CPSL CC had been gradually curtailed and its political influence reduced until it was practically on the level of a regional party agency.

He criticized the way in which the rehabilitation of those comrades who had been condemned in 1954 on trumped-up charges had been carried out. He emphasized that the atmosphere of suspicion had not yet disappeared from the party and said, "Many members of the CPSL cannot understand why Comrade Novotný, who attended the Plenum of the CPSL at which Comrade Bacílek was removed from his post of First Secretary and Comrade Dubček nominated to replace him, went to such great lengths to exculpate and even justify Comrade Bacílek and left the meeting before Comrade Dubček was elected. The fact that Comrade Dubček had been elected First Secretary of the CPSL CC could not be published for several months."

Although Bil'ak's arguments came as a surprise to the majority of the members of the KSČ CC, they reaffirmed their opinion that there were tensions in the relations between Novotný and the CPSL CC, tensions which did not work to the advantage of the party. In conclusion, Bil'ak advocated "an immediate settlement of the separation of functions issue."

A. Indra's speech had a marked influence on the views of the members of the KSČ CC. He alluded to several difficulties which had come up in the relations between the Presidium of the KSČ CC and the government, saying that the latter was being pushed into the position of an outsider which was not entitled to have its say in serious and important matters. He quoted a few concrete examples which cast a new light on the much criticized work of the government.

One might say that the December 20 session of the KSČ CC, which began with a counteroffensive by those speaking on behalf of the conservative wing, ended in their complete rout.

On the evening of December 20, 1967, the Presidium of the KSČ CC met to appraise the situation which had arisen at the Plenum. It seems that it was at this meeting that Novotný came to the conclusion that his position was too badly shaken for an easy defense.

On the third day of the session, Novotný spoke first and made a brief statement in which he said, "I am putting the post of First Secretary of the Central Committee of the KSČ at the disposal of the plenary session. It was by the will of the Central Committee of the party that I was entrusted with this post and therefore, it is now up to the Central Committee of the party to consider whether I am to continue to hold this post. I shall accept any decision which the Central Committee deems fit to make."

After Novotný's speech, Dubček, who was in the chair, acquainted the Plenum with the Presidium's proposals. The Presidium moved that discussion of Point One on the agenda, i.e., the plan for 1968 which had been hardly mentioned up to then, be concluded. Next the Presidium recommended that the draft resolution of the KSČ CC supporting the convocation of a consultative meeting of Communist and Workers' Parties be approved. And thirdly, the Presidium proposed that the discussion on the problems of party work be continued at another session of the KSČ CC to be called for January 3, 1968.

It became evident, however, that there was a group within the KSČ CC which harbored the hope that if the proposal for Novotný's resignation were to be debated immediately, it would be possible to keep Novotný in his post by seeing to it that the KSČ CC decided against dismissing him. Since at this stage no alternative candidate existed, this hope did not seem unrealistic.

The floor was then opened to a debate revolving around the question of whether discussion should be closed and the proposals of the Presidium accepted or whether discussion should continue and decision be once more deferred.

The course of the discussion then changed and the Presidium's proposal was adopted. Subsequent discussion concerned the draft resolution referred to in Lenárt's report. This resolution was quickly approved, as was the resolution on the convocation of a consultative meeting of Communist parties.

After an interval, the discussion returned to the question of separating functions. As requested by the Plenum, the secretaries of the KSČ CC and the members of the Presidium expressed their opinions one after another in detailed statements. D. Kolder was in favor of the separation of functions. B. Laštovička advocated a deferment. J. Hendrych was in favor of a settlement of the problem of the accumulation of functions and suggested that Comrade Novotný's proposal, to "put the post of First Secretary at the disposal . . . ," be accepted. M. Vaculík spoke in a self-critical vein about the allegations that he had made against Dubček in October; he also supported the proposal for a separation of functions, adding that he requested it be done in "a suitable manner." J. L. Štrougal, Š. Sádovský, and V. Koucký spoke in favor of a separation. Supporting the proposed separation of functions, A. Kapek asked Novotný to understand that even if only 10 percent of the members of the Central Committee opposed his tenure of the post of First Secretary, this would be sufficient to cause a rift in the party. Others who favored a separation were: M. Sabolčík, O. Černík, J. Dolanský, and Dubček. O. Šimůnek, P. Hron, and M. Pastyřík, however, supported Novotný, although they did not openly oppose a separation of functions. At the conclusion of this part of the discussion, Novotný declared that he could not reach a decision with regard to these statements of his colleagues immediately but that he would return to the matter at the January Plenum.

Then Dubček presented V. Nový's proposal, which was backed by the Presidium of the KSČ CC, that proceedings be broken off and that the Presidium and nominated regional representatives be charged with drafting a new proposal for the next Plenum based on the resolution and discussion and dealing with the accumulation of functions issue. It was further proposed that the next Plenum be called in the first days of January 1968. After a short discussion this proposal was passed and the Plenum's session closed.

Elected to the consultative group, which, in cooperation with the Presidium of the Central Committee, was to draft the proposals to be laid before the January session of the Plenum were: J. Piller, F. Červenka, F. Samec, J. Černý, O. Paul, J. Borůvka, J. Špaček, O. Voleník, A. Perkovič, E. Rigo, and M. Hladký.

January 1968

The session of the Plenum of the Central Committee of the KSČ, which had been broken off on December 21, 1967, started at 0900 hours on January 3, 1968. Prior to its opening the consultative group was, on Dubček's proposal, augmented by F. Barbírek, representing the KSČ CC, and by M. Čapek, a replacement for O. Voleník, who had been taken ill.

The chairman gave the floor to J. Lenárt who, in a long speech, reported on the ministerial discussion of the proposed changes in the scope and organization of work of the central government bodies. He acquainted the KSČ CC Plenum with his own opinion regarding the present situation in the party. Referring to the separation of functions, he defended the principle that no action should be taken without thorough reflection.

A very comprehensive report by Novotný followed Lenárt's speech. It was clear that the former was still determined to fight for his position and especially for a postponement of the separation of his two functions. He spoke about himself and about his work. Although he admitted to some errors and shortcomings, he rejected in principle the criticism of his work as First Secretary. He reiterated his negative standpoint with respect to the proposals made by O. Šik.

At the end of his speech he acquainted the Plenum with the proposal of the Presidium of the KSČ CC which had been agreed on after a conference with the consultative body. The Presidium proposed: (1) to continue the discussion of pending problems; (2) to accept as the basis for discussion (a) the draft resolution submitted by the Presidium to the December Plenum of the Central Committee, (b) Novotný's December 21 stand placing the office of First Secretary at the disposal of the Central Committee, and (c) the proposal made by V. Nový and approved the same day; (3) to charge the Presidium of the KSČ CC to submit at the conclusion of the January Plenum, in cooperation with the consultative group, a draft resolution to determine as concretely as possible the role of the Presidium in preparing the next session of the Central Committee — in the spirit of the Central Committee's discussions — for the activities of the central agencies and their relations with one another and the issues under discussion at the Plenum.

It was clear that neither the Presidium nor the consultative body had been able to take a definite stand since the end of the December Plenum concerning the fundamental questions which constituted the essence of the December discussions. Thus, the decision remained with the KSČ CC Plenum.

Concerning the amalgamation of the posts of First Secretary of the KSČ CC and President of the Republic, Novotný said: "It is agreed that it is desirable to separate these two functions. Once we have arrived at this agreement, we must decide when and how the matter should be resolved, taking into consideration all side issues, so that the party benefits politically and that its unity, its ability to act, and its authority at home and abroad are strengthened."

Novotný's viewpoint shows quite clearly that his followers in the leadership of the KSČ had succeeded in pushing through a compromise solution which nurtured the hope that the separation of these offices would be postponed. Such a postponement could ultimately have led to a situation in which the question of separating functions might appear as far less necessary or even quite impossible.

On the whole, this compromise reflected the general situation and the existing views at the December Plenum of the KSČ CC. The further course taken by events at the January Plenum demonstrated that a considerable shift had taken place in the mood and attitude of most members of the Plenum since December. Even those members who in the face of the surprising and dramatic development had hesitated in December now took a more determined stand.

Very firm was the speech delivered by V. Mináč, who declared inter alia: "Contrary to several other speakers, I believe that — among other causes of our present difficulties — Comrade Novotný is a cause which is of decisive importance and should not be overlooked."

The next speaker, K. Mestek, defended Novotný, recommending "for the sake of continuity" a postponement of the settlement "by a month or two or three."

J. Smrkovský's speech was of particular importance. He said, "I have the feeling we are witnessing one of the critical moments in the history of our party and are about to determine for a long time to come its progress or its standstill." He sharply criticized signs of onesidedness and stressed that no individual or group in the KSČ must be permitted "to claim the right to be the sole guarantors of our relations with the Soviet Union." The same may be said, he emphasized, on the subject of "anyone who speaks for or represents the interests of our working class." At the end of his speech he said something that clearly reflected the atmosphere of the Plenum's session:

> Among our comrades prevails a feeling of uncertainty as to what would happen if, after all the criticism that has been expressed, everything remained as it was. I say openly — and I feel that someone has to say it without mincing matters — that many comrades are afraid — and in view of certain experiences they may not be entirely wrong — that there could be, to some extent at least, a return to the fifties, to harsh repression of opponents within the party, and that such a struggle might lead to the use of the instruments of power, especially those of the security organs, to resolve internal party problems. Of course, this would be of the most serious danger for the whole republic. All this has convinced me that it is imperative for the decision about the office of First Secretary to be made at this Plenum.

Smrkovský strongly condemned the course taken by Antonín Novotný who by placing his post at the disposal of the Plenum had forced a discussion which could mean the division of the KSČ CC into two camps. In this connection he said: "Comrade Novotný took upon himself the responsibility for a solution in the manner we are now witnessing, which is a very serious affair."

On the morning of January 4, 1968, when the session opened, the list of those wishing to speak was already 60 names long. The course of the discussion had substantially influenced the opinion of the Presidium and the consultative body which O. Černík introduced to the Plenum. He announced that the consultative group had come to the conclusion that "the problems relevant to the item on the agenda submitted to it should be solved at this session of the party's Central Committee." He further announced that the Presidium had charged Antonín Novotný together with the consultative body to prepare proposals for the evening session of the Presidium so that on the morning of January 5 he would be in a position to submit suggestions for further action.

On January 4, 19 members of the KSČ CC took part in the debate. In essence, all the speeches can be divided into two groups; the majority was for an immediate solution, J. Hečko and O. Rytíř being the only exceptions. The question as to whether or not there should be a separation of the two functions did not arise at all; it was now only a question of when it should take place.

The discussion was drawing to a close. The Presidium of the KSČ CC together with the consultative group were already discussing how to deal with the party's internal crisis. Many head-on clashes took place during the debate, and a number of suggestions were raised. As the balance of views and forces within the Central Committee became clearer, however, it became more and more obvious that the Plenum would settle for nothing less than an immediate separation of functions and that for the office of First Secretary it would not accept a candidate unless he carried an overwhelming majority of the KSČ CC Plenum. At the same time, the opinion that changes would also have to take place in the structure of the Presidium of the KSČ CC was gaining ground.

On the morning of January 5, as a result of these discussions, Antonín Novotný submitted the proposal of the consultative group and the Presidium that he be released from the office of First Secretary, and that Alexander Dubček, the present First Secretary of the CPSL CC, be elected in his place.

On the occasion of his laying down the office of First Secretary, Novotný declared, "I state frankly that I am doing this in the interest of party unity, and it is my desire that this decision be interpreted in this light." These words may be said to have expressed Novotný's personal attitude to the criticism of both his political and personal errors and indicated the line of his future political actions. He made it quite clear that he was leaving but not capitulating.

Another 51 members of the KSČ CC were to speak in the debate. If voting on the submitted draft was to take place and democratic order complied with, all those who put their names down had to be heard. Under these circumstances a number of prospective speakers withdrew, while most of the remaining ones cut their speeches supporting the proposal to the minimum.

When the voting finally took place, Alexander Dubček was elected unanimously as First Secretary of the KSČ CC. The Presidium of the Central Committee of the KSČ was augmented by E. Rigo, J. Špaček, J. Piller, and J. Borůvka. The session concluded with the approval of the resolution of the Plenum of the KSČ CC.

Thus on January 5 ended a session of the KSČ CC which in the history of the Czech and Slovak nations and of the Communist Party of Czechoslovakia will be recorded as one of the most important for the development of the party since 1921. The January 1968 Plenum cleared the way to establishing a Czechoslovak democratic model of socialism corresponding to its own specific conditions. The door was opened to a new current, new ideas, new people, and new trends in party work. A time for historic changes, for a general reworking of the concept of the party's role, of the National Front, and of the socialist state had arrived. Socialism in Czechoslovakia had entered the stage of its democratic and humanistic revival.

DOCUMENT 5

DUBČEK SPEECH AT AGRICULTURAL CONGRESS
February 1, 1968
Excerpts
[*Rudé právo*, February 2, 1968]

❧

. . . We are proceeding from our historical experience and from everything which has proven its worth in past practice. We are not changing the general line of internal and foreign policy. But we must give serious thought to ways of contributing to faster socialist development in our country, new methods and approaches for our new stage which is characterized by a new social structure, the rapid advance of the scientific and technical revolution, and the corresponding urgent jobs to be done in science, culture, and economics, all of which create their own special problems. The point of departure — I might even say the key — to settling these problems lies in the field of politics, in the development of socialist democracy, in the activization and unification of social forces in all sectors of our society's life. You well know how many concrete problems and new jobs lie before us in every sector. The basic job of our activities as a society is to make room for the participation of all groups of our society without dividing them up according to generation or nationality. The importance of this political and social change today stems from the principle that the bearer of socialism and its further development does and must include the widest possible strata of working people, and that the leading political force — the Communist Party of Czechoslovakia, its organs and representatives — wishes to do all it can to promote social development as the vanguard — the organizational force — of the growth of the public's commitment to social progress. Among the decisive criteria of successful political work we must include the growth of activity among the people, a feeling of the usefulness of one's work, the willingness to commit oneself to trying to solve the economic, scientific, and cultural problems of our society in the interests of international progressive forces. Another criterion is pride in everything positive we have achieved — and that is quite a bit — and respect for our peoples' revolutionary history.

When we succeed in the spirit of the conclusions of the October and January party Central Committee Plenums in deepening socialist democracy through our future work, making room for all types of participation by the people, removing the barriers which stand in the way, and literally setting in motion the creative efforts of our people and all the physical and moral forces of society, and when every honest citizen who has socialism, his country, and the unity of our peoples and nations at heart feels he is useful, and has a job to do, we will be well on our way. It is difficult to assess today what great energies this will let loose toward the full self-realization of the individual, more spirited action, and the further development of our socialist society. . . . We are preparing an action program to implement the great wealth of ideas which have emerged recently and were discussed at the latest plenums of the party Central Committee.

Its substance is to be the development of a concentrated effort by all healthy and progressive forces in our society to realize the tasks and objectives which follow from the line of the Thirteenth Party Congress and to make this line more concrete.

At the same time, we hope to develop a resolute approach to overcoming everything outdated without resorting to the distortions and deformations which hampered our progress forward in the political, economic, and ideological spheres. This criticism of everything outdated and ossified will direct us toward the near future when we will want to emphasize a more long-term concept in the work of the Central Committee of our party and of the government of the Republic and a programmatic view of the development of our socialist society. For that reason we want our action program — which will underline the most immediate jobs to be done — to be linked with a purposeful approach to the detailed elaboration of the key problems of socialist progress, so as to enable us to do a good and prompt job of preparing the agenda of the Fourteenth Congress of our Communist Party of Czechoslovakia. . . .

ON INTEREST GROUPS: MLYNÁŘ

AS EARLY AS 1965, Zdenek Mlynář (at that time secretary of the legal commission of the Central Committee) had been the most influential, albeit initially tentative, spokesman on the importance of interest groups within socialist society.[1] From 1966 at the Institute of State and Law, Czechoslovak Academy of Sciences, he headed a research team investigating the best forms of social political systems. In analyzing the conclusions of the January 1968 CC Plenum unseating Novotný, Mlynář frankly advocated a pluralist political system in which interest groups act as a "first fundamental guarantee against a harmful concentration of power." His view that the minority has the right to maintain its own identity as a political agent moved closer to justifying factionalism both within the Communist party and society as a whole. These formulations were expressed somewhat more cautiously within the Action Program under Dubček (April 10, Document 16); their implications for the party were spelled out by the draft KSČ Statutes (August 10, Document 43). To Moscow, they signaled an impermissible departure from the orthodox Leninist canon of democratic centralism.

[1] Z. Mlynář, "Problems of Political Leadership and the New Economic System," *World Marxist Review,* Vol. 8, No. 12 (December 1965), pp. 75–82. In 1965 Mlynář was, in fact, far less outspoken than the Slovak legal scholar Michal Lakatos, who considered conflicts of interests as the motive force of society. See M. Lakatos, "On Certain Problems of the Structure of Our Political System," *Právny obzor,* No. 1 (1965). For analysis and relevant quotations from Lakatos, see Stanley Riveles, "Interest Groups in Czechoslovakia: Form and Theory," RFE Research Analysis, March 5, 1966. Also H. Gordon Skilling, "Interest Groups and Communist Politics," *World Politics,* Vol. XVIII, No. 3 (April 1966), pp. 435–451.

DOCUMENT 6

"OUR POLITICAL SYSTEM AND THE DIVISION OF POWER"

Z. Mlynář

Excerpts

[*Rudé právo,* February 13, 1968; translation revised from RFE Czechoslovak Press Survey No. 2019 (37, 40, 41) February 27, 1968]

The conclusions reached by the December and January plenums of the KSČ CC have paved the way toward a solution of many fundamental problems connected with the development of our political system. The problem of an excessive concentration of power in the hands of an individual, an agency, or the apparatus assumes an important place among these problems, but it cannot be understood or settled as an isolated problem; what is involved is the development of our whole political system, its basic structure, and its relationship to society. . . .

The Logic of the Existing System

The basic problem of our present political system lies in the fact that it was established as an instrument for the solution of other problems than those which our society is facing today. In the past 20 years, the entire structure and all relationships of the political system in this country were established under the influence of two factors: the political system was to render it possible to enforce, without resistance, the class interest of the working class against the bourgeoisie for the liquidation of private ownership relations; and at the same time, it was to consolidate the centralist directive system of management of the socialist economy. Moreover, particularly in the fifties, the political system was directly and decisively influenced by the deformations collectively and inaccurately defined as the "personality cult."

This means that, for many years, the political system in this country was deliberately adjusted to conform to the demand that a single interest, embodied in the form of directives issued by the center, should be made to prevail without any resistance. Thus, the logic of this whole system was based on demands for directives to be carried out rather than on demands for decisions to be made in a democratic manner. For many years, the slogan "participation of the people in governing" merely meant participation in the execution of directives (instead of democratic participation in the process of decision-making), and therefore control chiefly meant a control which was to ensure that directives were executed in every detail (and not a control designed to examine whether the directives themselves were correct). Of course, this characterization is oversimplified, and a number of attempts made in the past decade to bring about a reform have gone beyond it; but essentially it defines the logic of the whole system.

A political system whose structure and operation is based on a logic of this kind is bound to support tendencies toward a concentration of power and decision-making within a small number of closely interconnected parts of the whole mechanism, i.e., in the hands of a few people and of one person. In principle, therefore, every relationship or structure which would establish mutual control of individual parts of the political system, as well as the fundamental rights of the citizens to express their own interests, needs, and opinions over and beyond the bounds "foreseen" in the directive concerned, appears as an obstacle to effective government aiming at the execution of directives "without obstacles." A political system based on this logic undermines the entire atmosphere created by democratic freedom of speech as a part of political life. This must necessarily affect the internal relationships of the individual components of the political system and, in particular, the internal relationships within the party.

Therefore, a harmful concentration of power cannot be explained by certain character traits of individuals alone, and replacement of individuals cannot be regarded as a solution reaching down to the roots of this problem. The fundamental problem facing our whole society, state, and party, does not lie in how we can "perfect" the existing political system, but in how we can ensure its qualitative reform.

What Must Be Changed?

Of course, the point at issue is not that we ought to change its socialist quality. . . . First of all, it must be recognized that, not only can "society as a whole" be accorded the *status of an independent political agent,* but that this status must also be accorded its individual components, social groups and strata, common-interest groups, and last but not least every citizen as an individual. Every institutional component of the political system must also be an independent political agent: the state (its agencies), the party, and many social organizations which represent various interests (the interests of producers and consumers, various professional groups, various types of labor, the interests of specific generations, cultural interests, etc.). The status of all these components, as independent political agents, must be safeguarded in such a manner that none of them can assume the place of another or control it and regard it as a "lever of transmission," as an instrument and not as an independent political agent.

Every citizen, as an individual, is also a political agent and not merely an "object of government" or of political care. This status must be guaranteed by the legal order, which must specifically safeguard all political rights as the rights and liberties of every citizen (and not reduce them, as frequently occurs, to the rights of institutions and of "workers' organizations"); it is the concern of politics to ensure and guarantee in practice that these civil rights can actually be exercised. . . .

As soon as we really recognize the independent identity of the various components in our political system and begin gradually to put the corresponding reforms of basic political relationships into actual practice, we shall have created *the first fundamental guarantee against a harmful concentration of power* and against a misuse of this concentration for subjective decisions. Opportunities will exist permitting those components (and people's interests) which would be adversely affected by this decision-making monopoly to resist independently. Naturally, this principle will have to be injected into the entire logic of the political system: into the relationships among institutions themselves as well as between institutions and individual citizens, into the relationship of politics to public opinion, into the selection of persons for political posts, etc.

In the further development of our political system, however, we must also resolve the no less important question of principle of how to arrange the relationship of individuals to political institutions within the basic components (agents) of the whole system. After all, it is in these relationships that the problem of harmful concentration of power and of the deformation of human interests and needs begins. It is essential to build a mechanism into these relationships permitting the prompt correction of mistakes and errors before they accumulate.

First of all, guarantees must be furnished ensuring that within the individual political organisms (the party, social organizations, representative agencies of the state, etc.) the "whole" or majority not be recognized as the sole agent; the minority must also have a chance to put forward its opinions, its interests, or proposals and maintain its own identity (down to the individual). A number of complicated problems is connected with this, arising from the fact that the decision of the majority will always be adopted and must be executed. In general, however, there must be some way of guaranteeing that the duty to execute the decision of the majority does not mean that the minority can be suppressed, eliminated, or liquidated as an agent of political activity.

Another important principle demands mutual control and a degree of equilibrium among the different components of the governing systems within every component of the political system: that is to say, the state, the party, and every social organization. The division of powers and responsibility, the real possibility of mutual control of one component (such as the executive branch) by another component (such as an elected body) of the same organization — all this is an important precondition for the development of the whole system. All these relationships must be formed in logical unity right down to the basic agent in every organizational system — right down to the citizen in the state, to the individual member in the party and in social organizations.

As far as internal party relationships are concerned, the last plenum of the KSČ CC has clearly shown a way out; the party's internal relationships have already become the subject of discussions, and in practice suggestions for new solutions are being prepared. *Gradually, however, the same critical job must also be tackled in the life of all social organizations and, in particular, in the structure of the state mechanism itself.*

The limited space provided for this article does not permit a more specific analysis of these problems. It is beyond dispute that such arrangements as, for instance, the concentration of all types of security agencies and of a large part of enforcement posts, practically in a single apparatus, no longer conform to the general principles of the development of our political system. In this sector, in particular, it will be necessary to establish a better conceived and more thorough system of mutual control and equilibrium of independent state mechanism, a system in which independent courts, subject to no one but the law, will play the decisive role. Many other problems arise concerning the relationship of the National Assembly and the government, the development of the election system, guarantees of legality with respect to the citizens and their rights, the regulation of the expression of public opinion, freedom of the press, etc.

What Kind of System Do We Require?

Of course, we have disregarded other highly important questions here, particularly those concerning the relationship between economic and political management (or, more accurately, concerning the set of problems connected with the fact that political direction as such cannot replace the nonpolitical activity of people — whether productive, scientific, or artistic activity — and that to direct this activity and the working process itself in society requires a number of additional measures and theoretical concepts). However, from the point of view of the question which we have asked here — how to counter a harmful concentration of power in the political system — the problems with which we have dealt are obviously the fundamental ones. That is to say, if these problems are solved, a political system based on a new logic would be established: a system oriented toward making decisions which express the objective requirements of the whole of socialist society, and not toward the execution of directives which are, *a priori,* regarded as correct.

Naturally, it is exactly this type of system which socialism needs once it has passed the phase in which it was really "*a priori* known" that, in the class struggle, it was in the interest of the workers to liquidate class relationships based on private ownership and to replace them by new ones. If today we are to find the correct answer to the question of what really benefits the interests of the workers in various solutions suggested for untangling economic, scientific, social, and cultural problems, we must choose the path which leads us to a creative search for common interests, although it may involve disputes and conflicts. The ruling political ideology must also adopt a truthful recognition of these new, more complicated facts to permit it to become the necessary "unifying element" of the political system's new logic.

Even if we were rapidly and successfully to solve the problems which we have discussed, our whole political system would still be left with a number of other tasks to be tackled. In the first place, there is the necessity of rationalization and of effective structures and relationships in the whole directive system, based on firm scientific foundations. These structures and relationships do not spring into being automatically after political questions have been resolved. They require the development and support of scientific expertise in all methods of political work, and they require people who possess the necessary qualifications.

However, scientific, rational direction cannot be implemented in a political system without specific political preconditions. Otherwise we might come up with an effectively working, rational "machine," without being able to recognize or control the social and human effects of its operation. Therefore, a scientific analysis of the political system cannot be carried out as an analysis of the mere rationality of the governing system "in general." It must result from the cooperation of a number of branches of science, particularly in the sphere of the social sciences.

Of late, our political system has become the subject of a systematic study initiated by a number of political scientists, lawyers, sociologists, historians, economists, and management theory experts. The chief ideas in this article are drawn from the conclusions and concepts of this collective effort. There are sufficient creative intellectual forces in our party to contribute to the solution of our political problems, unless they are prevented from doing so by the subjective arbitrariness which the last plenum of the KSČ has tried to prevent from asserting itself in the life of the party.

THE ROLE OF THE ARMY: PEPICH

THE EXTENT OF potential military support for Novotný is far from clear. Rumors that Novotný attempted to stage a coup with the help of Defense Minister Bouhumír Lomský (an attempt reportedly thwarted by the former head of the army's Political Administration, Václav Prchlík) remain unsubstantiated, and there is some reason to think that Novotný's support came from Lomský's subordinates rather than from the Defense Minister himself. However, the defection of Major General Jan Šejna, the suicide of Deputy Minister of Defense General Vladimír Janko, and the eventual removal of Lomský show that the army was much more than casually involved in the political struggle. General Šejna, who had been deprived of his parliamentary immunity and accused of embezzlement, defected to the West in late February 1968. His defection, coupled with the belief that he had offered Novotný military support,[1] provided an excuse for subsequent upheavals within the party leadership.[2]

The first official indication of the role of the military with respect to the Central Committee debates came in an interview given by Major General Egyd Pepich[3] on February 23 (Document 7). The new Head of Political Administration in the army spoke of friction between the Eighth Department and army political headquarters. He mentioned only "some functionaries" responsible for attempts to influence the Central Committee. The implication was subsequently expanded by Prchlík in an interview[4] where he referred more openly to the role of Šejna.

---

[1] See H. Gordon Skilling, "Crisis and Change in Czechoslovakia," *International Journal*, Vol. XXIII, No. 3 (Summer 1968) and Václav Holešovský, "The Revolution Begins in Czechoslovakia," *Dissent* (May–June 1968).

[2] Novotný resigned the presidency March 22, and was removed from the Central Committee in June. He was followed out of office by other staunch dogmatists, including Minister of the Interior Josef Kudrna and Jiří Hendrych, the Secretary of the Central Committee who had directed party suppression of the writers at the September 1967 CC Plenum.

[3] Pepich had recently replaced Prchlík, who in turn took over the job of Miroslav Mamula as head of the CC State Administrative Department (referred to as the Eighth Department) in charge of the army, security, justice, and the militia.

[4] *Rudé právo*, March 19, 1968.

DOCUMENT 7

"WE HAVE NOTHING TO HIDE"

Interview with Major General Egyd Pepich

Excerpts

[*Obrana lidu,* February 24, 1968; translation revised from RFE Czechoslovak Press Survey No. 2040 (March 19, 1968)]

❧

. . . *Question:* Some time has passed since the plenum of the KSČ CC. Although this period is not so very great, practical steps ought to be considered to implement the decisions of the KSČ CC regarding the army. What do you feel must gradually be done in the army's party agencies and organizations and especially in the Main Political Administration?

Answer: . . . We are exposed to constant pressure from two sides: Life demands us to act expeditiously, especially in those spheres which have been troubling us for some time. On the other hand, experience has taught us that it is unwise to exceed our range. Rash action has never helped in anything; well considered and systematic measures alone can lead us to our goal. . . .

The relationship between the Main Political Administration and the collective of Communists at the Ministry of Defense has been, and still is very ill-defined. To mention only one aspect: We have very often said at various meetings and conferences that the Communists at the Ministry are a great asset to the party. We have all said this, confirmed it; we have all agreed it is so. But if we take a closer look at this beautiful idea, we must admit that everything is not exactly as it should be.

It is no secret that the attitudes of the former Eighth Department of the KSČ CC and the Chief Committee of the KSČ at the Defense Ministry isolated the Main Political Administration from party work at the Ministry. We wish to state quite clearly: the Main Political Administration wants to demonstrate its sincere confidence in the Communists at the Defense Ministry and relies on the latter's active participation in the formation of the party's military policies.

Question: You have said, Comrade Pepich, that the proceedings at the last plenary sessions of the CC met with full approval in the army. However, it is rumored that the Ministry of Defense was once again forced to "capitulate." Allegedly it has become a refuge for those who were quite happy about this uneasy relationship. Is this true, and what do you think about it?

Answer: If we want to evaluate the attitude of the army, the attitude of the army's party organization is the most important factor involved. As early as during the December and January Plenums, its leadership expressed the opinion of the Communists through the statement made by Comrade Prchlík, member of the KSČ CC. It must be said that this standpoint was clearly supported throughout the army. It is quite true that in spite of an express warning by Comrade Prchlík, some officials of the Main Committee of the Ministry of Defense furnished one-sided information about the course of the CC plenum to the Presidium of the Main Committee and to the party activists. Under the influence of this inaccurate information the activists approved their resolution. It seems to me — and I am not alone in this opinion — that we must learn a lesson from this case. Now is the right time to find out about motivations and who is after what.

Certain individuals, claiming to speak "in the name of all the Communists" at the Ministry, tried to make others believe they had the right to do so. I want to express my conviction that the overwhelming majority of Communists in this Ministry are upright people, loyal to the party. Indeed, their attitude was most clearly demonstrated during the proceedings at the CC plenum. Attempts to interfere with and to influence the deliberations of the CC cannot be laid at the door of the Communists at the Ministry; they may be connected with the names of only a few officials.

To put it frankly: The army, as an instrument of power designed to serve the defense of the country, is not meant to be used to interfere with discussions within the party. On the other hand, each member of the army's party organization is entitled to participate actively in discussions and debates within the party. The matters discussed at the CC meetings were primarily the CC's affair, the party's affair. The Main Political Administration strictly observed this principle. . . .

II. Liberalization in Prague and Orthodox Response

MELODIE BUDOU OVŠEM SPECIFICKY NAŠE!

"The melody, of course, will be our own."

Literární listy, No. 10, May 2, 1968.

DRESDEN MEETING

INITIALLY, MOSCOW RESPONDED to changes in Czechoslovakia with an almost studied version of noninterference in the internal affairs of fraternal countries.[1] The Soviets showed little regret at Novotný's passing. Indeed, *Pravda* printed a long biographical article on Dubček along with Brezhnev's telegram of warm congratulations to the new First Secretary.[2] Dubček's visit to the Soviet Union at the end of January was seen as an assurance that no major changes in Prague's foreign policy would be forthcoming. Economic reforms were acceptable. No word appeared on Czechoslovakia's domestic political developments until mid-March when *Pravda* reprinted a series of favorable excerpts from *Rudé právo* stressing the need to "further consolidate the leading role of the Communist party in the development of socialist society."[3] Subsequently, Radio Moscow duly broadcast the text of Novotný's letter resigning the Presidency.

Yet there was growing cause for Russian concern. Voices could be heard in Czechoslovakia demanding investigation of the mysterious death of Jan Masaryk, the first Czechoslovak Minister of Foreign Affairs after the war.[4] Mlynář's theory of interest groups had un-Marxist implications, and there was the unheard-of call of the censors for an end to censorship (Document 8). The East Germans and Poles were increasingly jittery at the possibility of Czechoslovakia legitimizing freedom of press and, from their point of

[1] Detailed chronological treatment of Soviet and East European reactions to events following the January Plenum may be found in William F. Robinson, "Czechoslovakia and Its Allies," *Studies in Comparative Communism*, Vol. 1, Nos. 1 and 2 (July/October 1968), pp. 141–170.

[2] *Pravda*, January 6, 1968.

[3] *Pravda*, March 14, 1968. There was no comment actually originating from Moscow until the end of April (*Pravda*, April 30, 1968).

[4] See analysis of Czechoslovak press response to the anniversary of Masaryk's death, *Le Monde*, March 13, 1968. In April, the case was officially reopened with Dr. Jiří Kotlář put in charge of the investigation. TASS objected that speculations concerning the death of the former Czechoslovak Minister of Foreign Affairs were being circulated by "enemies of Socialist Czechoslovakia" obviously intent on stirring "anti-Soviet sentiments among politically unstable people" (*Pravda*, May 8, 1968). From Prague, a *Lidová demokracie* editorial defended the investigation and elaborated charges against Soviet advisers in connection with trials of Czechoslovak citizens (*Lidová demokracie*, May 8, 1968).

view, an intolerable brand of inner-party democracy. Moreover, although the Czechoslovak representative Vladimír Koucký had condemned the Rumanian walkout from the Budapest Consultative Conference at the end of February, he substantively supported some of Bucharest's views, reserved the right to return to the matter at a "suitable" occasion, and openly criticized the documents of earlier international Communist meetings as out of date, especially with respect to Yugoslavia.[5]

The Dresden meeting was a time of accounting for Prague, a warning, perhaps even an attempt by Moscow and more orthodox East European regimes to define the limits of independent action (Document 9). The Rumanians, who have consistently opposed meetings devoted to the internal affairs of any socialist country, were not invited. (For Ceaușescu's objections, see Document 10.)

DOCUMENT 8

CZECHOSLOVAK CENSORS CALL FOR AN END TO CENSORSHIP

Complete Text

[Czechoslovak News Agency, ČTK, in English, March 14, 1968]

❧

The Communist party members on the board are deeply distressed that Interior Minister Josef Kudrna, Chairman of the Publication Board Eduard Kovařík, and his Deputy Jan Kovář have not yet responded to the public criticism of censorship.

During a reappraisal of the practical activities of censorship in Czechoslovakia we have come to the conclusion that preventive political censorship should be abolished, the statement says, blaming at the same time Jiří Hendrych, Secretary of the Communist Party Central Committee, for the existence of censorship in Czechoslovakia. By his political directives, decisions and public statements, he has led us astray on several occasions. Such was especially the case of judging (The Writers' Union Weekly) *Literární noviny*.

The Central Publication Board and the office which preceded it — The Main Board of Press Supervision — which were established entirely without any legal basis in 1953 by a mere government decree, were headed by senior security officials who ran the boards by a system of order.

This has created an atmosphere unbreathable even for the censors, the statement implies, and in conclusion again stresses the responsibility of Interior Minister Josef Kudrna.

[5] Vladimír Koucký's statement to Prague radio correspondent, Prague Domestic Service, March 1, 1968 and Michel Tatu in *Le Monde*, March 3, 1968.

DOCUMENT 9

DRESDEN COMMUNIQUÉ

March 25, 1968

Complete Text

[*Pravda,* March 25, 1968, quoted from *CDSP,* Vol. XX, No. 12 (April 16, 1968), pp. 16–17]

❧

A meeting was held in Dresden on March 23, 1968, of leading figures of the Communist and Workers' Parties and governments of the People's Republic of Bulgaria, the Hungarian People's Republic, the German Democratic Republic, the Polish People's Republic, the Union of Soviet Socialist Republics and the Czechoslovak Socialist Republic. The following persons took part in the meeting:

S. Todorov, member of the Politburo and Secretary of the Bulgarian Communist Party Central Committee; Zh. Zhivkov, member of the Politburo of the B.C.P. Central Committee and First Vice-Chairman of the Council of Ministers of the People's Republic of Bulgaria; and A. Pashev, member of the B.C.P. Central Committee and Chairman of the P.R.B. State Planning Committee;

J. Kádár, First Secretary of the Hungarian Socialist Worker's Party Central Committee; J. Fock, member of the Politburo of the H.S.W.P. Central Committee and Chairman of the Hungarian Revolutionary Workers' and Peasants' Government; and I. Pardi, member of the H.S.W.P. Central Committee and Chairman of the Hungarian People's Republic State Planning Committee;

W. Ulbricht, First Secretary of the Central Committee of the Socialist Unity Party of Germany and Chairman of the State Council of the German Democratic Republic; W. Stoph, member of the Politburo of the S.U.P.G. Central Committee and Chairman of the G.D.R. Council of Ministers; E. Honecker, member of the Politburo and Secretary of the S.U.P.G. Central Committee; and W. Krolikowski, member of the S.U.P.G. Central Committee;

W. Gomułka, First Secretary of the Polish United Workers' Party Central Committee; J. Cyrankiewicz, member of the Politburo of the P.U.W.P. Central Committee and Chairman of the Polish People's Republic Council of Ministers; S. Jędrychowski, member of the Politburo of the P.U.W.P. Central Committee and Chairman of the P.P.R. State Planning Committee; and E. Gierek, member of the Politburo of the P.U.W.P. Central Committee;

L. I. Brezhnev, General Secretary of the C.P.S.U. Central Committee; A. N. Kosygin, member of the Politburo of the C.P.S.U. Central Committee and Chairman of the U.S.S.R. Council of Ministers; A. P. Kirilenko, member of the Politburo and Secretary of the C.P.S.U. Central Committee; P. Ye. Shelest, member of the Politburo of the C.P.S.U. Central Committee and First Secretary of the Ukraine Communist Party Central Committee; N. K. Baibakov, member of the C.P.S.U. Central Committee, Vice-Chairman of the U.S.S.R. Council of Ministers and Chairman of the U.S.S.R. State Planning Committee; and K. V. Rusakov, member of the C.P.S.U. Central Inspection Commission;

A. Dubček, First Secretary of the Czechoslovak Communist Party Central Committee; J. Lenárt, member of the Presidium of the C.C.P. Central Committee and Chairman of the Government of the Czechoslovak Socialist Republic; O. Černík, member of the Presidium of the C.C.P. Central Committee, Vice-Chairman of the C.S.R. Government and Chairman of the C.S.R. State Planning Committee; D. Kolder, member of the Presidium and Secretary of the C.C.P. Central Committee; and V. Bil'ak, First Secretary of the Slovak Communist Party Central Committee.

The party and government leaders exchanged opinions on highly important problems of political and economic development and cooperation. It was noted with satisfaction that while the economies of the U.S.A. and a number of other capitalist countries are experiencing serious convulsions, the national economies of the countries of socialism, which are developing on a planned scientific basis, are in a state of continuous upswing. The participants in the meeting expressed their views on prospects for the further growth of the socialist economy on the basis of the utilization of economic ties within the framework of the Council for Mutual Economic Aid (CEMA) and on a bilateral basis.

The participants in the meeting exchanged opinions on international problems of interest to them. In the course of this exchange, they reaffirmed the coincidence of their views on the questions discussed and the unity of their positions as set forth at the Sofia conference of the Political Consultative Committee of Warsaw Pact States. During the exchange of opinions on questions of European security, special attention was paid to the growth of militarist and neo-Nazi activity in the Federal Republic of Germany (F.R.G.) and to the latest steps of the Kiesinger-Brandt government, which are directed against the interests of the German Democratic Republic and the other socialist countries.

The representatives of the fraternal parties expressed the unanimous opinion that in the present international situation it is especially important to increase vigilance with respect to the aggressive intentions and subversive actions that the imperialist forces are attempting to carry out against the countries of the socialist commonwealth. The delegations stated their determination to take the necessary steps for the further consolidation of the socialist countries on the basis of Marxism-Leninism and proletarian internationalism. They unanimously reaffirmed their determination in the near future to effect concrete measures for strengthening the Warsaw Treaty and its armed forces, as well as for cooperation in achieving a further upswing in the economies of the countries of the socialist commonwealth.

For the purpose of considering common economic problems, the parties agreed to hold an economic conference on the highest level in the near future.

An exchange of opinions and information on the state of affairs in the socialist countries took place. The representatives of the C.C.P. and the C.S.R. government provided information on progress in the realization of the decisions of the January plenary session of the C.C.P. Central Committee, which are aimed at the implementation of the line of the 13th C.C.P. Congress. Confidence was expressed that the working class and all the working people of the C.S.R., under the leadership of the Czechoslovak Communist Party, will ensure the further development of socialist construction in the country.

The Dresden meeting of leaders of the Communist and Workers' Parties and governments of the socialist countries proceeded in a friendly atmosphere.

RUMANIA OBJECTS TO DRESDEN

WHEN THE Rumanian Party Secretary Nicolae Ceausescu objected (Document 10) that decisions concerning the Warsaw Pact were taken at a meeting to which Bucharest had not been invited, he was protesting an isolation of Rumania that actually had begun early in March. Rumania had attended the Sofia Warsaw Pact Political Consultative Committee (PCC) meeting on March 6 and 7. At the end of that session, Moscow and the other East European members issued a declaration endorsing the draft nonproliferation treaty.[1] Rumania refused to sign. And for the first time a document not unanimously agreed upon was issued at a PCC meeting. It was a move clearly limiting Bucharest's room for organizational maneuvering within the Warsaw Pact.[2]

DOCUMENT 10

Speech by Nicolae Ceausescu to the Bucharest Party Aktiv

April 26, 1968

Excerpts

[*Scînteia,* April 28, 1968]

. . . Esteemed comrades, I shall conclude by referring to some international problems discussed at the plenary session of the party Central Committee. The

---

[1] *Pravda*, March 9, 1968; *CDSP*, Vol. XX, No. 10 (March 27, 1968), pp. 5–6. Significantly an *Izvestia* editorial stopped just short of calling the Declaration a Warsaw Pact document. However, the implication was clear and the editorial was at pains to give the Declaration on the nonproliferation treaty and the PCC communiqué equal weight (*Izvestia,* March 12, 1968).

[2] For an analysis of earlier Rumanian maneuvering, see Robin Alison Remington, "The Changing Soviet Perception of the Warsaw Pact" (Cambridge, Mass.: Center for International Studies, M.I.T., C/67–24, November 1967), pp. 36–91.

foreign policy of our country is known. At its center is many-sided collaboration with the countries of the socialist world system. Rumania is developing its relations of collaboration with all countries regardless of their system, and is paying outstanding attention to broadening its relations with countries fighting to consolidate their national independence and for economic and social progress. At the basis of its relations with all states our country sets the principles of equality of rights, noninterference in internal affairs, respect for national sovereignty and for the right of each people to decide themselves on their own fate. These principles are affirming themselves to a growing extent as a sure basis for lasting collaboration among all the peoples and for peace in the world.

I shall refer briefly to the session of the Political Consultative Committee of the Warsaw Pact member countries, a session which took place in March in Sofia. The session was convened at Rumania's request, in order to carry out an exchange of opinions in connection with the treaty for nonproliferation of nuclear weapons. Other states also proposed other problems for the agenda. The session unanimously adopted a declaration of solidarity with the struggle of the Vietnamese people.

In this connection I would like to stress that our country holds it necessary for all air raids and other acts of war against the Democratic Republic of Vietnam (DRV) to stop. The United States must stop procrastinating and meet halfway the position adopted by the DRV with a view to getting down to negotiations.

As regards the nonproliferation of nuclear weapons, the participating countries made their positions known. The position of our country is known to you, and I shall, therefore, not refer to it. The delegation of our country was not empowered to decide in Sofia on approving the treaty in its present form; this matter is to be decided on by the Central Committee and the government at the proper moment. In this spirit the proceedings of the Political Consultative Committee closed.

In the evening, at the end of the reception, Comrade Zhivkov informed me that some delegations wanted to sign a separate declaration affirming their decision to sign the nonproliferation treaty. I told him that it was the right of each party to proceed as it thought best, but that in my opinion it was not good to have a separate declaration signed in Sofia. As you know, on the evening of the second day, a separate declaration signed by six countries participating in the Sofia meeting of the Political Consultative Committee was published.

Rumania has been and is in favor of a nonproliferation treaty. We think, however, that further efforts must be made to obtain improvements to this treaty, particularly the pledge to take measures regarding nuclear disarmament and the giving of guarantees to countries renouncing nuclear weapons that those weapons would not be used against them and that they would not be subjected to blackmail with this weapon, and ensuring for all states the possibility of unlimited utilization of nuclear energy for peaceful purposes. The activity carried out for over a year in Geneva in the framework of the Disarmament Commission has shown that actions undertaken along those lines

can still obtain improvements. Let us do all in our power for the nonproliferation treaty to correspond in the best possible conditions to the interests of
all the peoples, to the cause of socialism, security, and peace in the world.

Our country was not invited to the Dresden meeting. We do not reproach
anyone for that. But what struck our attention is the fact that at this meeting
problems of CEMA activity and of the high command of the united armed
forces of the Warsaw Pact were discussed. We hold that the discussion of
such problems, referring to international bodies in whose founding Rumania
took part, cannot be carried out by only some member countries. We are
astonished that the military command of the Warsaw Pact member states
was discussed, because it was decided in Sofia by all delegations that the
ministers of the armed forces should draw up within 6 months proposals for
improving the activity of this command. It is also not understandable why
CEMA activity should have been discussed at Dresden, since the CEMA
bodies meet with what one might call mathematical regularity. As experience to date has proven, such actions and procedures are not likely to contribute to strengthening those bodies, to increasing the trust, collaboration,
and unity of the socialist countries.

As is known, at the Bucharest meeting of July 1966 all states came out in
favor of the abolition of NATO concomitantly with that of the Warsaw Pact.
At the same time the determination of all participating states was affirmed
that as long as NATO existed the Warsaw Pact should be maintained, too.
In the spirit of the joint declaration of the states participating in the Bucharest meeting, our country is determined to make its direct contribution to
the activity of the Political Consultative Committee of the Warsaw Pact, including the activity of the military high command of the states participating
in this pact.

As a socialist country, Rumania, whether or not the Warsaw Pact exists,
will continue militating undeviatingly to strengthen collaboration with the
socialist countries in all fields, including the military field. Our country is
also in favor of developing collaboration with the CEMA member countries
in the spirit of the statute and of the fundamental principles adopted by the
member states. At the same time we are militating for the comprehensive
development of economic and scientific collaboration with all the countries
of the socialist world system, because we think that in this fashion we are
fulfilling our duty both toward our people and toward the cause of socialism
throughout the world. . . .

EAST GERMAN ATTACK: HAGER

EXCEPT FOR THE pointed suggestion that Czech General Jan Šejna had been "obviously recalled by his bosses," [1] the East Germans virtually ignored events in Czechoslovakia until party ideologist Kurt Hager openly attacked Josef Smrkovský (then Minister of Forestry) for giving encouragement to Bonn (Document 11). This was the first shot in a running battle between the East German and Czechoslovak press that became more and more acrimonious throughout the spring. It made explicit the implications of the Dresden communiqué's hard line on West Germany for domestic politics in Czechoslovakia. Nor was the attack taken lightly by Prague. Czechoslovak Foreign Minister Václav David (subsequently replaced) formally protested to the East German Ambassador on the following day.

DOCUMENT 11
"THE PHILOSOPHICAL TEACHING OF KARL MARX AND ITS CURRENT MEANING"

Speech by Kurt Hager, Member of SED Politburo and Central Committee, to the Philosophy Congress

March 26, 1968

Excerpts

[*Neues Deutschland,* March 27, 1968]

The Springer Publications and the "Heart of the Czechs"

. . . In this connection comrade Hager made a blunt statement.

In their campaign against our socialist constitution the West German propaganda centers are relying on the developments in the ČSSR. They are eagerly quoting the statements of Minister of Forestry Smrkovský; they give an ex-

[1] *Neues Deutschland,* March 12, 1968.

tensive account of the writers' and journalists' attacks on the role of the party, of the CC and its apparat and leading members of the government.

They often express their sympathy with these statements and phenomena in the ČSSR. Typical and revealing in this respect is today's editorial of the Springer newspaper *Die Welt* (March 26, 1968). It states that Federal Ministers and members of Parliament are watching developments in the ČSSR with the greatest attention, that "their heart urges them" to speak to reassure the Czechs and the Slovaks that we Germans are favorably impressed by the change they are struggling for. Finally *Die Welt* writes: "The Central European heart is beating again in the chest of responsible Czechs," and "Beyond the ideologies, the systems and political crust, the peoples will surge to the surface." Federal Ministers and members of Parliament regret that they cannot express their sympathy even more clearly; however, *Die Welt* informs us that they still place their hopes in "Evolution," "Liberalization," and "Sturm und Drang" days in Prague. . . .

The appearance of Smrkovský and others fills them with the hope that the ČSSR will be drawn into the "turmoil of evolution" in the sense of the Springer Press.

RADICAL INTELLECTUAL DISSENT:
HAVEL AND SVITÁK

CZECHOSLOVAK RADICAL INTELLECTUALS were not slow to go beyond the theory of interest groups to demands for opposition parties. Early in April, the young and internationally famous Czech playwright Václav Havel, the author of *The Garden Party* and *The Memorandum,* published a biting indictment of proposed reforms. He dismissed as "illusory" the assumption that willingness of the leading (Communist) party to allow internal party opposition would ensure democracy and rejected the existing non-Communist parties of the National Front as discredited by twenty years of slavish docility to the Communist line (V. Havel, "On the Subject of Opposition," Document 12). One of the dissidents at the Writers' Congress in June 1967, Havel had coauthored the statement of the program of the Club of Independent Writers.[1] Not surprisingly his political theories found little enthusiasm in Moscow (N. Vladimirov, "The 'Political Instincts' of Václav Havel," Document 13).

Moreover, if Havel's political instincts were dubious from the Soviet view, those of the Czech philosopher Professor Ivan Sviták were outright counterrevolutionary to Moscow. Sviták wrote of the "sausage realism" of Czechoslovak political life in the Novotný era (I. Sviták, "With Your Head Against the Wall," Document 14). He helped to found the Club of Committed Non-Party Members (KAN), contending to still another such group that "Today we are a club. Tomorrow we are a force, and the day after tomorrow we shall be equal to the Communists." [2]

Within Czechoslovakia, Sviták was reprimanded by Drahomír Kolder, a conservative member of the KSČ Presidium and Central Committee, for preaching the psychology of Munich — a psychology that according to Kolder could lead only to severing Prague's alliance with the socialist camp (D. Kolder, "On the Margin of Certain Political Reflections," Document 15).

---

[1] For a description of the founding of this club, see Bohuslav Hlinka and Alexander Kliment, "Political Commitment for All," *Lidová demokracie* (April 12, 1968); RFE Czechoslovak Press Survey, No. 2071, May 15, 1968. Perhaps most important among the other political groups to spring up in Prague that April was Club K 231. Its members were former political prisoners who had been deprived of their freedom under Law No. 231 on the protection of the Republic. For the chronology, see *ČSSR: The Road to Democratic Socialism: Facts from January to May 1968* (Prague: Prago Press, 1968).

[2] Quoted by Richard Eder in *The New York Times,* April 28, 1968.

The most detailed Soviet attack on Sviták came not before but after the invasion of Czechoslovakia (Soviet "White Book" on Czechoslovakia, Document 63, pp. 32–85).

DOCUMENT 12

"ON THE SUBJECT OF OPPOSITION"

Václav Havel

Complete Text

[*Literární listy*, April 4, 1968; translation revised from RFE Czechoslovak Press Survey No. 2055 (98), April 11, 1968]

If some of the ideas about the possible form of a political opposition in present-day Czechoslovakia which have so far appeared in the various official speeches sometimes give the impression of a desire "to have your cake and eat it too," we cannot be surprised. The fact that the more progressive and democratically minded people within the Communist party can, in the course of a few weeks, win over the conservatives by no means signifies that within the same short period the members of the movement — in whose whole history not a single attempt has been made to change the system once the movement was victorious — are capable of seriously facing up to the idea of opposition, which until recently has been anathema to them. If they nevertheless go so far as to permit public discussion of this subject, until recently taboo, it would seem that all those who have anything to say about it should seize this opportunity as a challenge to discuss the matter.

To begin with, what is it that makes the ideas advanced so far sound so half-hearted?

We hear quite often that as a result of our present and future freedom of speech (which is said to be the essence of democracy) the natural function of opposition will be exercised simply by public opinion kept well-informed by mass communications media. Such a concept assumes *faith* that the government will draw from public criticism all the necessary inferences. However, democracy is a matter not of faith but of *guarantees*. Even if we admit that the public "competition of views" is the first condition, the most important means to and the natural result of democracy, its very essence — and the true source of our guarantees — is something else, namely public and legal *"competition for power."* At the same time public opinion (e.g., the press) can effectively control and thus influence the quality of the ruling power only if it too has recourse to effective means of control — in other words if it can lead to public decision-making (e.g., in elections). When all has been said it is a fact that power respects power, and a government can be made to improve itself only when its existence is at stake, not just its good name! As a matter of fact, the ability of a government to use its authority to influence public opinion by a "free" limitation of its freedom (either illegally or by changing the laws) grows in proportion to the loss of the ability of public opinion to exert authority over the government. Not only that. If "competition of views" is substituted for "competition of power" the door is, in fact, open to undemocratic processes (for instance, if ministers were dismissed not by parliament but by television or public meetings, the citizen would have no legal control over power, and thus would have no preventive protection against its misuse).

I also consider as illusory the assumption that internal democratization of the leading party (willingness to tolerate something like internal party opposition) offers a sufficient guarantee of democracy. I hold this position not only because, in principle, the only true democracy is one which applies equally to everybody, but also because it has been the bitter experience of every revolution that if the political group which takes over does not restore *control from outside* in time, it must sooner or later also lose its *own internal control* and begin, slowly but surely, to degenerate. A group's internal control pressures, which improve the quality of its leadership, necessarily die out unless they are fed by control pressures from without, which improve the quality of the group as a whole. The group, instead of continually and naturally regenerating itself, suffers from progressive sclerosis, and alienates itself increasingly from reality. The consequences of this process are well known. When the situation becomes uncontrollable, the first expected disturbance causes an explosion and ushers in a period of bloody palace revolutions, coups, lobby conspiracies, nonsensical trials, counterrevolutions, and suicides. The "competition for power," which had disappeared as an overt phenomenon some time ago, suddenly reappears and strikes in every direction, all the more insidiously because it is hidden. The absence of legal guarantees, which the group failed to renew in time, returns to it now like a boomerang. The group liquidates itself. In other words, if the Communist party does not make possible rapid development of strong outside control, it will have no guarantee that it will not soon enter into a gradual degeneration all over again. It is clear that internal party democracy cannot survive for any length of time without democracy in the whole of society. It is not the former which guarantees the latter, but vice versa.

Another idea which has sprung up — that independent individuals might take the part of the opposition in elections and in various agencies — is to my mind a classic example of how to cut the ground from under the opposition's feet before it has had a chance to form. A handful of private individuals — without any political background, lacking any possibility of collective agreement on procedures, candidates, coordination, and a broad concept of political work, and given only a few local communal rights and duties — would have to stand up against a perfectly organized and disciplined political party with an ideology, an apparatus, press and propaganda organs, and a program for society as a whole. In elections, these independent candidates

would not have the support resulting from general knowledge of the activities of the society as a whole, a program, and the advantages of a group which
proposes them and to which they belong; thus — unlike the candidates of
the leading party — they would be deprived of the classic, time-tested means
of guiding the electorate, an overwhelming majority of which neither can
nor will make distinctions between individual candidates but can always be
counted on to distinguish between familiar political concepts. Also, this
atomized "opposition" would not have the slightest chance of developing any
effective and coordinated political activity that could compete with that of
Communists. What it boils down to is that the leading party cannot take seriously any "competition for power" that is not, by reason of its organization,
a real political force, nor can it believe that its monopolistic position is put
to any serious test of quality by such opposition.

Another type of potential control or actual opposition is sometimes apparent
in social and special-interest organizations. Even this is not a fundamental,
sound solution, though some of these organizations may in time acquire a
certain amount of political influence. Based on principles other than those of
political conviction, and designed for a purpose other than that of sharing the
political power of the state, these organizations can never play the role of an
organ that controls the exercise of power, simply because they do not fulfill
the fundamental condition — that of independence of the controlling element
from what it controls. Membership in these organizations not only does not
exclude membership in a leading or other party, but as a matter of fact at
the highest level the functionaries of these organizations are almost exclusively members of the party, subordinated to its higher bodies and responsible to it for their guidance of the special-interest organizations. If we
add to this the well known system of party groups, party lists of candidates,
and the party-disciplined system of voting (plus the election rules which make
it practically impossible for even a majority of non-Communist voters to elect
an opposition candidate), we can understand that true control from without
is difficult to imagine, even if the practice of ballot manipulating should
undergo certain changes, as it certainly will. Since it seems certain that there
will now be a trend toward dividing up many of the artificially united and
unwieldy colossi, and toward greater differentiation among organizations, any
attempt at the political integration or coalition of these organizations into some
"political-control" bloc would have a counteractive effect on our development
and would lead to no worthwhile end.

The most logical and easiest solution would be to constitute an opposition
in the manner most often proposed by official sources: through regeneration
of the existing non-Communist parties of the National Front. It is not *a priori*
out of the question that forces capable of leading such an opposition might
come out on top in these parties, but I personally do not put too much faith in
this type of solution. I am afraid that in the course of the past twenty years,
during which time these parties and their representatives were authorized
only to agree slavishly with everything the leading party did, they have compromised themselves so much that their advantages (their existing organiza-

tions, press, etc.) cannot outweigh their main disadvantage — the difficulty of regaining lost confidence. Not to mention the fact that it would be quite easy, and not unjustified, to call this "a return to outmoded and obsolete forms of bourgeois democracy," a criticism often heard in official sources when the idea of opposition is broached. Essentially, it would be only an attempt to bring back the mummified remnants of pre-February political forces — which were even then very questionable.

That all these concepts are so spiritless seems to be due to one fact — none of them makes a true choice possible. Let's be frank. One can talk about democracy seriously only when people occasionally have an opportunity to elect freely those who are to govern them. This again assumes the existence of at least *two comparable alternatives*. That is to say, two equal and mutually independent political forces, both of which have the same chance of becoming the leading force in the country, if the people so decide.

In other words, as long as it is modern in our country to recognize the existence of the Communist party as a party, the demand for a *second political party* as its full-fledged and dignified partner in the "competition for power," and as the full guarantee of its control from without, will also be modern. To my mind the only truly logical, and indeed, in our circumstances, effective way (only until someone can convince me of a better way, of course) to reach the ideal of democratic socialism is a regenerated and socialist social structure patterned on the *two-party model*. As these, obviously, would not be parties based on class, with different economic and social programs dictated by class, and thus conflicting ideas of how to run the country's economy and organize its society, their relationship could be based on a historically new type of *coalition cooperation*. While preserving full political independence in the enforcing of mutual control, these parties could at the same time be bound by agreement on the fundamental common aim — humane, socially just, and civilized self-realization on the part of the nation via democratic socialism. This principle could be anchored and laid down in detail in a "national program" (which would, for example, also formulate the basics of foreign policy, etc.) accepted by and binding on both parties (and possibly other social organizations as well). The manner and extent to which this program is or is not fulfilled, as well as possible future modifications, would be evaluated by the population in general elections, which would reflect their confidence in both parties in the coalition and in each of them separately.

Although it would amuse me as a writer — that is, one working in the sphere of fiction and fantasy — to invent a so-called "positive" program for a so-far nonexistent party, and to project it onto various spheres of social life, I am too sensible to do so; one cannot plan strategy without an army. Political programs do not spring from the desks of writers; they evolve from the daily political activities of those who implement them, from their continuous reflections on the interests the movement is dedicated to, from their continuous confrontation with social reality, public opinion, expert analyses, etc. Therefore I shall confine myself to general remarks.

Today the need for a strong and specifically Czechoslovak democratic and humanistic tradition is frequently stressed. However, at the same time we tend to forget what this means in concrete terms: that many really democratic-minded and humanistic-minded people exist in this country who have refrained from participating in political life (within the framework of the KSČ) because of their beliefs or simply because they did not regard the practices of the Communist party as sufficiently democratic and humanistic. These potential grass roots of a new party also suggest its possible conceptual outline, which could be based on a traditional democratic and humanistic spirit and, therefore, form a kind of *democratic party*. This, of course, does not mean that such a party ought to claim to be the sole legitimate partisan of democracy, just as the Communist party cannot claim to be the only really socialist force: democracy and socialism can only be categories in society as a whole, categories whose development concerns everyone. And if the Communist party and the democratic party were to be the two main partners, this would only mean that their names would symbolically guarantee the two poles of a common "coalition" task: democratic socialism. At the same time I would regard the moral basis for a democratic party being formed in this manner as a kind of — I don't mean to sound pompous — *national moral revival*. That is to say, emphasis on suprapersonal categories and general social ideals in whose name the right of the individual to have a destiny of his own was suppressed during the years of dictatorship, has led this nation — as is often pointed out today — to the brink of a moral crisis. This was particularly true during the period of the system's progressive degeneration, in which the government-by-command of a dehumanized party bureaucracy with its all-embracing phraseological ritual, completely divorced from reality, was characteristic; the general decline in working morale is nothing more than the natural result of this demoralizing system in the area of economics. Unhampered by the premises and consequences of this process — with which the Communist party will have to cope within its own ranks for a long time to come — this new party could restore fundamental human individuality to its place at the center of attention much more rapidly, and re-establish the individual as *the yardstick for society and for the system*. However, such a party would not adopt the abstract term "individual" as the basis for a new phraseological ritual. Rather it would have a simple and practical attitude, expressed through its interest in specific human destinies, an interest which would not be filtered through various *a priori* ideological barriers separating it from the individual's immediate and exclusive concerns. The new party would express its interest by fighting for specific human rights, demands, and interests; by concretely, actively, and unconditionally rehabilitating those values which until recently were regarded as "metaphysical," like conscience, love of one's neighbor, sincerity, compassion, confidence, understanding, etc.; by adopting a new attitude toward human dignity and respect for the individual; by taking into consideration the moral caliber of leaders, etc. It seems to me that as a result opportunities would be offered not only to persons of various age groups, social position, faiths, and viewpoints who, because of their concrete humanism, had been unjustly prevented from making themselves felt politically; the same opportunities would also be open to a great degree to the younger generation. From what I have gleaned about the efforts of this generation to find itself (for instance, from the various statements of the students' movement — which, incidentally, I regard as one of the few social forces today that is actually working toward real political independence), I hold that such a conceptual climate might be particularly attractive to this generation. However, I do not have in mind an attempt to "recruit" the young for political work (the KSČ failed to recruit them because it spent its efforts entirely on recruiting), but an attempt to make it possible for them to once again become principals in political activity, instead of mere objects, an attempt to make it possible for their will and concepts to be accepted instead of their being forced to accept the will and concepts of others.

So much, then, for the subject of a "second party." In conclusion I would like to mention something I consider highly important: I am afraid that in the non-Communist majority of the nation broader and more active political force will never be formed unless it becomes possible to win a certain degree of basic *moral and political recognition* for the non-Communist viewpoint, a recognition which must come from the acceptance of certain evident truths and manifest its validity in certain unequivocal political actions aimed at the righting of wrongs which no one has so far attempted to put right. It seems to me that without this recognition — as an explicit moral basis for any further activity — the non-Communists can never be fully confident in the significance and possibility of success of their further undertakings. This should not surprise you; it is very difficult to commit oneself earnestly and in one's own way without a minimal guarantee that a Communist error is not, once and for all and fundamentally, worth more than a non-Communist truth. And if many a non-Communist recognized Communist error even when the Communists did not have the slightest inkling that a fallacy existed, then those non-Communists must be given belated credit, however unpalatable this may be; if this is not possible, it means that Communists are a special type of supermen who — in principle — are always right even when they have made a mistake, while the non-Communists — in principle — are always in error, even when they are right. In such circumstances non-Communists would be really foolish to commit themselves on any point. If Communists have a right to err from time to time, non-Communists must be guaranteed the right to be right sometimes; otherwise no useful purpose can be served.

What is specifically involved? Nothing more than the demand for complete rehabilitation of all non-Communists who have had to suffer for many years (and who to this day bear traces of the stigma of Cain) for the fact that they recognized certain things before the Communists arrived at the same conclusions. This is a highly relevant point nowadays when those who were punished in the past for their conviction that a socialism which was ready to sacrifice democracy and liberty (allegedly to aid its own development) could not be good — when such people are rightfully bitter because after all these years our order has arrived at exactly the same conclusions. This means that they were right, but our order is not prepared to admit it or draw certain practical conclusions in their case.

Just one example: in 1949 and 1950 tens of thousands of talented students were forced to give up their university studies because of the purges, although they had not been guilty of anything but disagreeing (or being liable to disagree — according to their fanatical colleagues in the political check-up commissions) with the then political practice of the Communist party. Some were guilty simply of not being Communists. (It is hardly necessary to point out the damage these and similar actions have done to the nation; those who stayed in this country and were dispersed in various occupations were in most instances unable to return to their original calling and are to this day dogged by a dubious personnel record; those who emigrated are also lost to us, although by now many of them are professors at various American and West European universities.) What I am concerned about in this regard is the conviction that those who carried out these purges in the past and who today — full of a resurrected youth-movement euphoria — thunder at students' meetings about the "times of darkness," about liberty, democracy, and justice, should make a gesture, which might not appeal to them but which would strongly confirm their progressive spirit; they should support the rights of their erstwhile "ideological opponents," who, thanks to the irony of history, must still pay for having believed in these rights 20 years ago. There are things which can never be corrected. However, there are many other things which can be corrected. Analogously, one could give a number of other examples of more drastic wrongs, affecting every social group from farmers to small tradesmen, from university professors and writers to village priests. (In this connection the roughly 80,000 political prisoners of the fifties can be regarded as a particularly important and to date virtually untapped force: they came from a variety of social strata who passed so hard a test of their moral strength and spirit of fellowship that it would be unforgivable if this force were not actively integrated into the political life of the nation.)

There is something else here which might appear to be of no concern to us: the problem of the post-February political and nonpolitical Czechoslovak exiles. All these people are still, in most cases, regarded as enemies of the country and of the people, in spite of the fact that most of them have done nothing worse than become convinced 20 years ago that democracy ought not to be sacrificed to the socialist system. Moreover, many of them emigrated for the sole reason that they were in danger of being imprisoned or persecuted, or had no opportunity to work at their occupation or profession in this country; though some may have left the country illegally, it is doubtful whether — in the light of the Declaration of Human Rights — this can be regarded as a crime under conditions in which legal opportunities to emigrate did not exist. Unless the relationship of the state to these exiles is revised in a spirit of magnanimity, the situation here, among ourselves, can not be fully normalized. After all, every democratic state takes pride in keeping its international account free from the stigma of having forced people into exile.

In a word, I believe it is no longer acceptable or possible to continue to

look at this nation exclusively from the point of view of the February conflict — which, of course, applies to both the opposing camps of that time. I do
not say this because I would like to see a return of the pre-February situation
(although we are now laboriously trying to achieve a number of things which
then were taken as a matter of course). On the contrary, I say so simply
because such a return is no longer possible.

Full political and moral recognition of the non-Communist position is by no
means a simple matter, and the rights regained under this recognition will not
fall from the heavens. It is chiefly up to the non-Communists themselves to
take the initiative and win these fights gradually. It is also possible that various
non-Communist forces may form even without this recognition. However, it
seems to me that without it the ensuing activity will always be half-hearted and
beset with reservations and alienation, that it will not be entirely authentic
and, therefore, that it will lack the necessary drive. It is difficult to enter the
arena of political life when one feels like an outsider who does not enjoy full
rights — a feeling which has been hardening for a full 20 years.

DOCUMENT 13

"THE 'POLITICAL INSTINCTS' OF VÁCLAV HAVEL"

N. Vladimirov

May 15, 1968

Complete Text

[*Literaturnaya Gazeta*, No. 20 (May 15, 1968), quoted from *CDSP*, Vol. XX,
No. 20 (June 5, 1968), p. 10]

❧

The Voice of America has a keen ear that enables it to detect instantly when
anyone begins to proclaim truths akin to those the Voice itself tries to drum
into the heads of its listeners.

Recently the Voice of America has been listening carefully to what is going
on in Prague. In a broadcast on April 29 the Voice reported that "clubs of
independent political thought" have sprung up there and that the leaders of
these clubs "hope to establish a movement that would make it possible to develop political instincts among those who, because of hostility to the Communist Party, used to keep such instincts to themselves."

Among the "prominent Prague figures" endowed with these "political instincts" the Voice of America singled out the playwright Václav Havel. To
the American propagandists this person seemed quite akin to them in a
symptom they cherish: "hostility to the Communist Party." Havel's writings
in the weekly *Literární listy*, which were detected by the "ears of America,"
clearly echo the "program" that bourgeois "well-wishers," seeking to under-

mine the people's-democratic system, have been foisting upon the socialist countries for decades now.

Soon after Havel was presented by the Voice of America as a "public figure," he himself crossed the ocean for the premiere of his play "The Memorandum" and overjoyed *The New York Times* with a whole series of confidences, in which this representative of "independent political thought" demonstrated how "independently and freely" he can repeat slogans formulated by the enemies of communism long before the author of "The Memorandum" appeared on this earth (Václav Havel is now 31 years old).

Havel declared that "swift political actions by the liberals are now necessary" in Czechoslovakia. He stands for neither more nor less than the creation of an opposition party, which would be particularly convenient for those who seek to bring Czechoslovakia into conflict with the socialist path of development.

Though Havel has as yet advanced the slogan "Overthrow the leadership of the Communists!" only with respect to creative organizations such as the Czechoslovak Writers' Union, everyone realizes that this is nothing but a mask. Havel and "liberals" like him are trying for the time being to "restrain their instincts." The essence of the matter here is that an attack is being made on the socialist system in Czechoslovakia.

As for the creative organizations, the election of a substantial number of Communist Party members to their executive bodies is, as Havel himself of course knows, first and foremost merely a sign of the well-deserved trust and respect that Communists enjoy among their colleagues.

It was not without bitterness that the Voice of America noted in its broadcast on "independent political thought" in Czechoslovakia: "Although the new political clubs in Czechoslovakia maintain contact among themselves, there is no organizational bond among them. The organizational structure of the clubs themselves is diffuse."

This of course pains the overseas "observers." But they hopefully quote the words of an associate of Havel's: "Today we are a club; tomorrow we shall be a force! And the day after tomorrow we shall be equal to the Communists."

In reproducing these words, however, the Voice of America was forced to say that in these clubs so dear to its heart "workers merely meet," thereby showing that "liberals" of Havel's type have no support among those to whom the present and the future of socialist Czechoslovakia really belong.

DOCUMENT 14

"WITH YOUR HEAD AGAINST THE WALL"

Lecture by I. Sviták at the Philosophical Faculty of Charles University in Prague

March 20, 1968

Complete Text

[*Student,* No. 15, April 10, 1968; translation revised from RFE Czechoslovak Press Survey No. 2075 (108), May 24, 1968]

Chaos' friends owed many of their successes to him and wished to show their gratitude. They took counsel and came to a decision. They ascertained that Chaos had no sense organs to assess the external world, and so one day they gave him eyes, the next day a nose and in a week's time they had finished transforming Chaos into the type of sentient being they themselves were. While they were congratulating one another on their success, Chaos died.

— Huang-tzu, 3rd century B.C.

I. Paradoxes of Reality

1. The friends of chaos who humanize chaos destroy it. Hence, it is not the enemies of chaos who bring about its demise, but its friends, its loyal friends, its most devoted friends.

2. This paradoxical oddity in an old Chinese riddle represents the harsh truth of the political spring in Czechoslovakia 1968. It is not chaos' enemies who lead the efforts to liquidate the chaos in economic and political life — even though they want to. It is its former friends who destroy it in their desire to do something for it. The enemies of chaos support them, although they know full well that its friends will abandon their own efforts as soon as they realize what they are doing.

3. Reality is paradoxical, and "to expose oneself to paradoxes means to expose oneself to truth." Without an understanding of the paradoxical character of the current changes one cannot grasp the meaning of current events nor their inexorable further development which is hardly something one can look forward to. The friends of chaos, apparent apostles of democracy who make Masaryk seem like a second-rate bungler, have their limitations which will soon begin to prevail over questions of principle.

4. This paradoxical reality will, during the next two years, turn the present leaders of the revival process into ministers, ambassadors, and secretaries of the Czechoslovak state, who will then have an immediate and direct interest in maintaining the status quo, the same interest as they have today in going beyond the bounds of the existing totalitarian dictatorship. We support the new team that wants to supersede the previous team in the Communist party, but we must clearly realize that we support the program of this new team

and not its members and that their maximal program is our minimal program.

5. The agreement of critical intellectuals with the high officials of party and state bureaucracy is a passing expression of identity of interests; this agreement will end as soon as the new team has taken firm hold of state power and begins to regard democratization as complete at the stage already reached when it assumed power. Democratization will come to an end and democracy will not begin.

6. Intellectuals who can see what is happening behind the scenes and who understand historical processes must provide the nation with something more than a political program which roughly states: We want democracy, not democratization. Democratization is merely the minimal program of the road toward democracy.

7. Democratization may be the road toward democracy, and in this sense we support everything that leads to a greater measure of civil and human rights and we shall not be impatient; however, we do not really know what democratization is. During the three months since the critical events occurred we have not been told what actually happened. Is this democratization?

8. On the other hand, we know exactly what democracy is, and two hundred years of experience with this form of government permit us to establish safely that — with the exception of the temporary halt of censorship, which can be recalled at any time — none of the attributes of this form of government are present in this country. No program demands whatsoever exist in this respect, nor have they even been raised by our seemingly so perspicacious writers.

9. The slogan of democratization is an improvisation bred from exceptional circumstances involving personal conflicts within the Politburo; it is the fruit of empirical policies and the accidental product of the efforts made to channel civil dissatisfaction into a desirable direction. Democratization has never been, and still is not the political aim of the new team striving for power; at the most, it is a by-product which cannot be immediately prevented. Therefore, it is tolerated and used against individuals in leading posts.

10. The bizarre character of this democratization at once becomes apparent when we realize that the defection of a major general and the suicide of a colonel general have been explained away with alfalfa seeds and that no justifiable grounds have been given for the resignation of certain leading officials. We need these explanations to enable us to understand what they are criticized for and why they resign, since those who criticize them are of the same ilk. In other words, we do not need lessons on democratization in order to make us democrats. The protagonists of totalitarian dictatorship who do need such lessons are superfluous in a socialist democracy. Any attempt to democratize the cultural terrorists of totalitarian dictatorship would be tantamount to attempting to square a circle. Round squares do not exist.

II. Totalitarian Dictatorships

1. Dictatorships are as old as mankind. The essence of dictatorship consists in unrestricted rule over the state by a single person, clique, or power group,

and it is of merely secondary importance whether or not parliaments exist, elections are held, or various forms of state agencies and posts are established. Moreover, modern dictatorships do not merely represent a tighter form of the old features of autocracy, despotism, and tyranny; they also have certain novel features. Modern dictatorships — that is to say, totalitarian dictatorships — are the government monopoly of a ruling minority. But in contrast and in addition to the historical forms of dictatorship, they have at their disposal a mass movement and a mass ideology, they govern the whole state by commands, and they intervene in every sphere of the life of the citizens, including their private lives. Not only do the totalitarian dictatorships and their ideology offer their citizens a higher standard of living or a better form of government but they also offer solutions for all sorts of problems in the life of the individual and thus become a secular substitute for religion, a message of redemption through a new faith in ideology, the party, and the leader.

2. Totalitarian dictatorship is a new form of absolutism, a modern type of despotism. The essence of totalitarian dictatorship is the reduction of the individual to a target for the power apparatus. Every totalitarian dictatorship must destroy personality and individuality, not because the leading politicians are sadists (although there are sadists too), but because the totalitarian orientation arises from the character of absolute, centralized, and unrestricted power. Propaganda and terror, the control of the mass information media, and the secret police are the most important instruments for the functionalization of the individual.

3. Totalitarian dictatorship does not know the methods of indirect government; it rules by terror, fear, and indirect action. Because of this, the common-interest organizations originally formed in the interest of those who formed them, become bureaucratic mechanisms for the purpose of ruling over broad sections of the population, the workers, the young, etc. This power is exercised under the assumption that everything is permitted in the interest of the race, class, or nation, and that humanistic considerations are a mere sign of weakness. Dictatorships of the Metternich or Bach* type of emperors and tsars were regimes far more humane than the modern dictatorships.

4. A totalitarian dictatorship is a closed and uncontrollable system of power which is led by people who are convinced that they understand progress and mankind's best interests, that they know what is good for their race, nation, or class — in fact, what is good for the whole world — and who, in their fanaticism, believe that they have the right to impose their program on the masses. Conflicts within the ruling elite are settled by means of the dialectics of orthodoxy and heresy, periodic purges and tricks, since where there is no control they cannot be dealt with in any other manner. The people, the masses, the classes do not participate in decision-making, but they are encouraged to offer their thanks to the party and government.

5. Totalitarian dictatorship is based on terror and cannot retain power without it. This terror is not a temporary expedient resorted to only in ex-

* Austrian prime minister in the first years of the reign of Emperor Francis Joseph I. Translator.

ceptional circumstances in order to attain specific ends; it is the specific form of government of totalitarian dictatorships. The basic function of terror consists in ensuring the functionalization of the citizen and in turning him into a pliable political tool of the power elite. Even when a totalitarian dictatorship is tottering, its secret police — the chief instrument of terror — continues to function reliably. The result is the complete subjugation of life to politics and the military.

6. A totalitarian dictatorship derives its support from the emotionalism of the masses and the disintegration of rational attitudes and value standards in modern times. It must be able to deal with crises. It ensures its efficiency through absolute control over the opinions and attitudes of the population and through propaganda spread by its mass information media. Clichés and stereotyped oversimplifications, which become the generally accepted truth through constant repetition, are not subject to verification nor to criticism.

7. Totalitarian dictatorships operate with the *a priori* assumption of unity of the people, nation, party, bloc, that is, with the postulate of moral and political unity, although this unity does not exist. Therefore, differences of opinion are regarded as heresy and those holding them are regarded as enemies and traitors. Not only are the liberties of the individual and civil rights thrown overboard; this very suppression of freedom is extolled as a triumph of progress and the hallmark of a higher social order.

8. The functionalization of the individual in a totalitarian dictatorship is ensured chiefly by means of propaganda in its mass information media and secondarily by terror. Constantly repeated allegations regarding a fictitious enemy create a psychosis about a constant threat to the achievements of the revolution, race, nation, or class, a danger which justifies the permanent state of martial law, affecting ideas and people. If the citizen is to be permanently confused, it is necessary to operate with the fiction of an enemy (the Jews, the imperialists, another nation, the whites, the blacks, the Chinese, the Europeans, etc.) who constitute a threat to the citizen from which the dictatorship protects him.

9. Totalitarian dictatorships arise from the internal weakness of democratic orders, whose disintegration is a precondition for the rise of dictatorships just as the establishment of democracy is the precondition for the fall of a dictatorship. Totalitarian dictatorships, mass movements, and the party apparatus undergo substantial functional changes after assuming power. In the struggle for power, the movement usually turns into the bureaucratic machinery of government, power is institutionalized, and a separate totalitarian organization is established. The spontaneous movement and its motives are replaced by the monopolistic system of party views, a party surrounded by a system of satellite organizations. The state turns into an instrument of the totalitarian elite, which preserves through its own political institution — the party — a decisive influence; this is the origin of the dual government of state and party, so typical of every dictatorship.

10. As soon as the ruling elite constitutes itself after the take-over of power, it begins to govern autocratically and to influence public opinion in its own

interest, which is presented as the interest of the masses. The trend toward an accumulation of power leads inevitably to loss of control over power, which then becomes an apparatus of suppression, turned also against those very classes which enthroned the new elite. In practice, the totalitarian state is based on violence against both people and ideas and on actively functioning, effective violence. Totalitarian states have been, and remain, the biggest threat to humanity throughout its history; they constitute a total threat to human values, to European culture, and to the meaning of human freedom.

III. The Nature of the Czechoslovak Dictatorship

1. The nature of the totalitarian dictatorship under which we have lived for the past twenty years had certain national characteristics. An outstanding advantage of the regime was the fact that it was headed by full-blooded Czechs, combining their Austrian tradition of joviality with the muddled inefficiency of a concierge (for which the Czechs use that good old German word "Schlamperei" *) in a three to one proportion. A more detailed definition of this specific quality would require a team of geniuses familiar with the great thoughts of N. C. Parkinson on the natural growth of inefficiency.

2. The Czechoslovak type of totalitarian dictatorship was totalitarian above all in the measure of its chaos. This dictatorship was rather a comic paradox. Apart from some murders, the government was as helpless in the handling of absolute power as a baby with a slide rule. The occasional fits of democracy, periodically installed and dethroned, never succeeded in bringing about fundamental changes, and the foundations of this system were undermined again and again by aggressive stupidity.

3. The spontaneously spouting geyser of this stupidity, tirelessly gushing for twenty years in the official press and in tolerated culture, in declarations made by statesmen and pioneer leaders, has not in spite of all the extreme efforts been able to undermine the foundations of the socialist order. The natural intelligence of these good-hearted Slovak, Moravian, and to some extent also, Czech people, always reduced the worst excesses to a tolerable measure.

4. Thus our history of the last twenty years may be likened to a strenuous march, but a march in place, marking time, which nonetheless switched back and forth into trots, doubletimes, and at eases. Under such circumstances, one must ask one's compatriots what the purpose of the "march" might be? It is like the question which a naughty girlfriend of mine used to put to soldiers confined to barracks over the weekend, when she asked them over the fence whether they liked the service. When they said "no" she asked them why they did not leave? To voice this kind of question has now become one of our duties.

5. A second characteristic of this totalitarian dictatorship was that for twenty years it kept itself free of any internal political shocks because in the critical year 1956–1957 it was able to reduce the price of Hungarian sausage and blacken its critics as intellectuals. It repeated this method in every critical situation before and after. The political philosophy of the statesmen

* Slovenliness. Translator.

of this period was based on scapegoats — capitalists, kulaks, Jews, and intellectuals — and Hungarian sausage. Therefore if a politician had been unable to reduce the price of Hungarian sausage it might have had fatal consequences for him.

6. Sausage realism in politics was effective as long as there was something whose price could be reduced. It must be admitted that both our nations were satisfied with this state of affairs. This realism was pursued at the expense of economic efficiency, for it made possible less work for more money, and ensured actual, legal, and economic equality between the laborer and the university professor. Thanks to this *consensus gentium* there has never been any political opposition to speak of in Czechoslovakia, not even in the past ten years, marked as they were by growing economic difficulties. The country has been ushered toward collapse with the tacit discipline of subjugated but thrifty citizens whose hopes have not been pinned to freedom but to an MB.*

7. The cemeterylike quiet of this dictatorship and its well functioning, truncheon-assured respectability seemed to be unassailable from within. Suddenly, the resources, which made possible the grand policy of bribing the nation by a higher standard of living, failed. Actually it was the economics of the high consumer standard that failed. The sudden failure of the economic structure — by no means incurable — was sufficient to bring about a state of insecurity and to provoke a remarkable change in political orientation.

8. A third fundamental feature of the Czechoslovak totalitarian dictatorship was its extraordinarily conservative character, conflicting with the ineradicable tradition of elementary freedoms in European states. In Poland, they did not execute their Gomułka, in Bulgaria and Hungary they executed one minister each, but the crop of Czechoslovak Stalinism was the richest of all.

9. In every important question concerning the socialist bloc, the Czechoslovak foreign policy has stuck most persistently to the hard line. The gradual emancipation of Yugoslavia, Poland, Hungary, Albania, China, Rumania, and Cuba from the Soviet example was followed grudgingly, and any attempt at copying these examples condemned. The reason given was always the same — the lower standard of living in these countries, in other words the pocket of Mr. Čehona.†

10. Our conservative foreign policy was by no means platonic, and sincere statements of support for the fascistlike Arab regimes of the Nasser type were no empty words. The supplies of war material, financed so readily by irretrievable credits, directly served Arab imperialist policies. The characteristic features of dictatorship, i.e., its Czech realistic and conservative nature, must be taken into consideration when we attempt to understand the possible further development of this totalitarian dictatorship.

IV. The Nature of the Present Changes

1. Are we experiencing a revolution or a revolt? A revolution means structural social changes in class relations, in the relations between economy and

* Recent model of "Škoda" car. Translator.
† The model of Czech petit bourgeois respectability. Translator.

policy, and in the structure of the mechanisms of power. A revolt (*putsch*) is an exchange of teams and does not affect structural relations and questions. It is up to us to decide which of the two we are experiencing — the game is open in both directions.

2. We are profoundly indifferent to the latter possibility. We have no reason to be enthusiastic about an exchange of persons. The sociologists and philosophers know that "institutions are stronger than people," and that without the control mechanism of public opinion every member of the elite must degenerate. There is no exception to this rule. Antonín Novotný started as an exponent of the liberalizing trend. Today young people must barricade themselves at the university against the Polish national hero of 1956.

3. The possibility of structural changes is, on the contrary, of the greatest interest to us because it opens the way to an open socialist society, i.e., to socialist democracy. This stage is still far off, although it appears at the moment to be an illusion embracing the whole nation, based on the resignation of a few persons. The students have little reason to support this illusion; on the contrary, they have every reason to be on the lookout for false cards which may yet appear on the table in the course of the game and decide the nature of the state in which we are to live.

4. If we observe with a realistic and critical eye the results of the three-months-old process of regeneration so far, we must come to the conclusion that there have been no structural changes in the mechanisms of totalitarian dictatorship, with the sole exception of the temporary nonexistence of censorship. The monopoly of a single party has been unaffected and there is no machinery for forming the political will of the people.

5. The hierarchic concept of state bodies and social organizations, directed from a single center, remains unchanged. It is incompatible with democracy, of which an essential ingredient is a political will formed of certain social processes where various factors play relatively independent roles. On the ideological level, ideological values and political programs compete with each other, while on the level of state power the legislative, the executive, and the judiciary (i.e., parliament, government, and the independent judiciary) check one another, and finally on the level of the economic and civic activities of the citizenry, the special interest groups, the bureaucracy, and public opinion play their independent roles.

6. There is only one factor at the present time which justifies hopes in the process of democratization — the free expression of public opinion. It is therefore in this area that the counterattacks of the conservative forces must be expected in the near future. These forces will call for restraint; they will offer new economic programs and new persons instead of fundamental political changes. We, on the other hand, must attempt to make the best use of the freedom tolerated thus far and set up democratic elections as the next step on our way toward establishing a European socialist state.

7. This process is possible only if the fundamental conflict of the present Czechoslovak state is solved. This conflict is by no means limited to the relationship between our two peoples. It festers within the mechanism of the

totalitarian dictatorship. The bureaucracy of this dictatorship did do away with the Stalinist cult, but it has kept without change the power structure of Stalinism, including bureaucratic apparatus and its policy of using a cultural whip. We must liquidate this dictatorship or it will liquidate us.

8. Our achieving democratic socialism is contingent upon the liquidation of the mechanisms of totalitarian dictatorship and the totalitarian way of thinking. Totalitarian dictatorship is our enemy Number One. We have enough brains and hands for the program of socialist freedom, but we also have a large number of resistant elements. The reply to the question "From where, with whom, and where to," is brief: "From Asia to Europe, on our own."

9. This means, from totalitarian dictatorship to an open society, to the liquidation of the monopoly of power, and to an effective control of the elite in power by a free press and public opinion. From the bureaucratic management of society and culture by "the cutthroats of the official line" (an expression used by Wright Mills) to the realization of basic human and civil rights, at least to the extent known in bourgeois democratic Czechoslovakia. With the workers' movement minus its *apparatchiks,* with the middle class minus its groups of willing collaborators, and with the intelligentsia in the forefront. The intellectuals of this country must stake their claim to the leadership of an open socialist society moving toward democracy and humanism if there is to be an end to the irrational dialectic of abuse and tyranny.

10. The peculiar character of the present changes lies in the fact that until now no substantial changes have taken place; the mechanisms of totalitarian dictatorship have remained untouched. All we really have gained is freedom of the press and the hope that there may be democratic elections and some rearrangement in the functions of state power. We are not interested in a change-over of cadres appointed by a grossly undemocratic system. What does interest us is a lasting process of democratization, in other words a permanent transformation of totalitarian dictatorship into a European system with a democratic form of government.

DOCUMENT 15

"IN THE MARGIN OF CERTAIN POLITICAL REFLECTIONS"

Drahomír Kolder

Excerpts

[*Rudé právo,* June 21, 1968]

❦

A number of articles by Ivan Sviták continue to call forth many responses. Polemical articles and letters expressing basic objections and sharp disagreement with many of Sviták's conclusions are piling up in our editorial office. We are convinced that matter-of-fact polemics are all that is important, and this is why last week we published an article by Zdislav Šulc in *Rudé právo*. Below we print Comrade D. Kolder's contribution to questions causing conflicts of opinion — conflicts that take place not only on the pages of *Rudé právo*. . . .

Critical comments about certain articles in the press and speeches on radio and television — comments made at the latest party Central Committee meeting, in the resolutions of certain organizations, and by ordinary citizens — are causing unrest and fear among journalists. They are causing fear that this criticism might mean the start of a limitation of free speech and a return to attitudes held before January, toward the old practices when criticism "from above" resulted in further political and legal sanctions against the author of opinions that deviated from the accepted line.

At the same time, critical reservations toward the journalists' work are being reproached for their universality and for their indiscriminateness, and it is asked whether there isn't a certain amount of "crying wolf" going on, when accustomed views and speeches are designated as antisocialist and anti-Communist. It is even said that such designations are old ammunition, such as comes from the cold-war arsenal.

I understand the journalists' unrest and fears. Therefore I should like to say first of all, in agreement with the conclusions of the party Central Committee, that workers in the press, radio, and television have been playing an important role in our development since January and emerging as an effective, public control over all sections of the management of our society. They have a significant share in bringing to light controversial and insufficiently clear questions and differences of opinions, in exposing past errors, offenses, and damage. In this manner they contribute to the search for points of departure and to the elimination of pernicious deformations. They should continue this mission.

However, despite this unquestionably positive contribution of the information media, I cannot fail to notice certain demagogic voices that have nothing in common with the socialist revival process and that are emanating from anti-Communist positions. (I do not think at all that anticommunism is dead and thrown away with the old rubbish; if only it were! In spite of the speeches of certain debaters, the times have not yet come for universal embraces, and the world today bears graphic witness to the sharp battle, sword in hand, not only against communism and socialism but also against much lesser signs of progress.)

I agree with the journalists' claim that it is impossible to condemn universally; it is necessary to cite concrete examples, names, articles, and broadcasts. I want now to cite a concrete example and to try my hand at matter-of-fact polemics, above all with the articles "With Your Head Against the Wall" and "Your Present Crisis," printed in issues 15 and 18 of the periodical *Student,* in which Ivan Sviták appears as a philosophizing politician.

Since we have accepted the principle of a free exchange of views, I should like to give several of my own comments on these articles — not for the sake of challenging certain points of view, but above all because it is precisely from such sources that they are drawing water for the mill of the leftist sectarian tendency condemned by the January Plenum and discredited by past developments.

I favor isolating all leftist conservative attempts and influences, and therefore I am taking a stand against everything that can put them back on their feet and in any way further their type of viewpoint: "You see, we told you so; you see where this is leading." Their aspirations are well known from various "leaflets" written by would-be genuine Communists, written in a primitive style and playing on backwardness of the lowest level. The May Plenum of the Czechoslovak Communist Party Central Committee condemned these actions which bring out the powerlessness, bitterness, and fury of yesterday's obdurate people. It is clear that we must also take a stand against everything that adds fuel to these people's fire and resist their attempts to interfere with those honest party members and other citizens who are justly anxious and disturbed by attacks from the right which, unfortunately, were not answered decisively and in time, for fear of admonition.

And now let us turn to certain "concepts and deliberations" of I. Sviták. In the above-mentioned articles in *Student* and elsewhere, Sviták's exposition represents a varied jumble of views by means of which the author wants to attach his individual ideas and intentions to the course of the present democratization process and to the attainment of its aims.

The total upheaval of political attitudes contained in his comments is aimed at completely negating and writing off our entire twenty years of work, our political institutions, the sources of our ideas, and the results we have achieved. He has only a cynical grimace for them; for him, they are merely an expression of an admission of failure of the totalitarian dictatorship with which he identifies our whole political system. Its external and internal characteristics, as set forth by I. Sviták, will not lead to the rejection of the deformations of socialism, but to the negation of socialism itself, whose course in Czechoslovakia he compares to the qualities and power orientation of fascist systems. Our past allegedly has much in common with these. (See Sviták's article "With Your Head Against the Wall" in issue 15 of *Student*.)

This has not yet been thrown in the face of those millions of people who carry all the difficulties, victories, and losses of socialist construction on their shoulders. However, Ivan Sviták is thorough; he offers an unambiguous prescription for the future: Do not reform the present system. Sweep it away to the last vestige by a "democratic coup" aimed at creating a new political structure similar to the bourgeois-democratic type, with the requisite domestic and foreign orientation to create new laws for the Czechoslovakia of the future.

In the article "With Your Head Against the Wall," Sviták resolutely announces: "The reply to the question 'From where, with whom, and where to,' is brief: From Asia to Europe, on our own." This statement contains substantially everything — from rejection of our foreign political orientation toward the Soviet Union and extrication from these alliances, to association with all sorts of European projects on the basis of active or passive neutrality.

There is nothing new under the sun; he introduces to us and offers us a well-known point of view that forcefully calls to mind the Munich psychology and mentality and that would also logically lead to the results of Munich.

Sviták's concept is nothing original; it is essentially a plagiarism and copy of well-known essays from the rich literature and miscellany of modern anti-Communist doctrines about how to act when the expected crisis occurs to best transform a Communist system into a "free, open society" — doctrines that Sviták has clearly thoroughly studied and assimilated. He elaborates on the bitter experiences of counterrevolution, drawn from the failures in Poland and Hungary in 1956, and places the main emphasis on "democratic methods" and on a "democratic" concept of socialism that has lately been formed in the West as the most acceptable and least discredited variant of anticommunism.

The instructiveness and uncompromising nature of Sviták's article speak for themselves. This is how Sviták describes the results of the democratization process up to now: "The totalitarian dictatorship effected a change in personnel; it publicly announced its crisis and intentions according to the new form of political life . . . apart from people, nothing has so far been changed in the mechanism of the totalitarian dictatorship and its heritage" ("Your Present Crisis," *Student,* issue 18).

According to Sviták, totalitarian dictatorship clearly means the power of the working class as such, without its known deformations; it is socialism and socialist relations against which he declares war. The logic of an approach reaching toward a structural transformation of our society, toward something whose faint outline can only be the pre-Munich republic, is set forth here with unbelievable openness and a complete lack of ambiguity. "We shall live either in a sovereign European state with a polycentric political system or in a form of state that is not sovereign and in which the leading representatives fear most of all the tank divisions of their allies."

In his theses Sviták openly declares his resolve to undertake a hazardous risk, partly to bring public attention to his ideas and partly counting on using extreme means to carry them through. It is impossible to shrug off as some sort of literary embellishment the opening allusion in this article to the situation of Hamlet, who was forced to act without regard to the tragic results of his decision. Those voices we hear in the dark, hidden from the public and claiming we must not fear even sharp conflict or the greatest possible sacrifices, are surely no secret.

Just as Sviták begins his political program with a threat, his concluding remarks bear a similar tone, one that is in the nature of a challenge to action. We may now pose a further question: Does this mean that before it is too late there may be recourse to some sort of preventive action — or, to be more exact, action designed to anticipate the situation — if the progressive political reversal that Sviták concedes without recourse to all the sneers against democratization and that our society has been following since January does not develop according to the ideas of Sviták the "strategist?" It is possible to exclude this possibility from the general context of Sviták's declaration and his exposition of socialist democracy, which contradicts the concept of the action program. He says at the top of his voice: "If people's political activity is not incorporated into the establishment of a socialist democracy" (that is, Sviták's concept of socialist democracy) "then we shall inevitably create many more thorny problems liable to threaten the state and both its peoples." It is essential to refute these points with great precision because they somewhat water down the unambiguous nature of other political standpoints which demand a peaceful "democratic" transformation of our present political setup. It is obviously not possible to lose sight of them in connection with the general line set forth in Sviták's challenge.

As far as the general concept behind Sviták's ideas goes, we can say for certain that it goes even further than a restoration of pre-February attitudes: "A return to the pre-February structure of the National Front and to the political configuration of those days is not a step forward, while the creation of at least two new parties on a Christian and social democratic basis is indispensable." He is therefore striving for a plurality structure of political parties in which he wishes to oppose the Communists with a Christian–social and reformist political doctrine which is newly formed along party lines, given the role of political opponents, and placed outside the framework of the National Front.

Let us stick to realities and facts. In Sviták's articles there is much talk about respecting specific Czechoslovak conditions, but in fact he has something else in mind; various political coalitions and combinations in Western political life are marked by various internal conflicts but united in their anti-Communist views. It is not by chance that Sviták talks about the model of a democratic contest for power, but leaves the economic sphere completely to one side. It is difficult for him to put his cards on the table; any proposed political structure is unthinkable without a viable economic arrangement if it is to be of any significance at all. This can only be a system of some sort of free market economy with "democratic competition" among various proprietary sectors. Obviously, this is quite different from the existence of socialist production relations and a socialist economic policy. And in the present situation even Sviták cannot beat the drums about this.

However, what is absolutely unbelievable is the self-confident attitude with which Sviták also reveals the details of an approach meant to ensure the realization of a new sort of inverted February. I have in mind the answer to the question why the concept of the Club of Committed non-Party People should be taken into account today and how the polarization of views within its framework should be developed so that in the future they will change into new political parties striving for power. . . .

There is justification in asking the question: To what extent is Sviták's concept feasible, and what chance does it have of being put into practice? It is possible to say that his concept is speculation to a considerable degree, that it does not take into account the actual movement of social forces, especially of the working class, farmers and intelligentsia, and that it mainly speculates on the power of attracting politically immature and unstable groups of our population.

Sviták's prescription also programmatically overlooks such a vitally important requirement, in the present democratization movement, as the question of the federative arrangement of national relations; he is unwilling and incapable of somehow organically squeezing national relations into his scheme. This is the Achilles heel of Sviták's concept; he writes off the Slovak question in his pontifical way of looking at things.

On the other hand, Sviták's concept is the most expressive combination of views and requirements promulgated so far that aim at founding and developing within our democratization movement elements that are alien to socialism. It should not be overlooked that certain designs of this concept can take cover in the present situation, which is marked by several chaotic and disintegrating tendencies, and can be enhanced in certain internal and international circumstances. If the democratization movement is not stimulated by the purposeful Communist policy laid down by the May Plenum of the Czechoslovak Communist Party Central Committee, if it does not rely on the purposeful development of the progressive attitudes of the working class, the farmers, and the intelligentsia, and if it is not formed in collaboration with a dynamic policy of the National Front, it is quite possible that topsy-turvy deformations like Sviták's will come into force. . . .

A mere confrontation of the Communist approach with Sviták's concept graphically shows who is really concerned with the working class fulfilling its revolutionary and historical mission, and who is only out for himself.

However, what plays most into the hands of Sviták's proposals are certain tendencies among Communists themselves — on one hand, depression and passivity stemming from the bitter knowledge of past deformations; and on the other hand, reflections that are polemically and problematically opposed to the concept of the National Front, set out in the action program and shared by its partners.

We quote at random one of the opinions printed in *Rudé právo* May 4, 1968, which considered the main shortcoming of the democratization of the political system to be that the important thing was "the discussion of pressure groups, rather than competition among genuinely political groupings." In the same issue of *Rudé právo* another author says that "a system of a number of viable political parties inevitably creates competition in political life." That is, not partnership, collaboration and agreement, but political competition with all its negative results.

In this connection certain other tendencies appear that have also been expressed in the press, in *Literární listy,* to the effect that the present Czechoslovak Communist Party should form two parties: one that would represent democratic socialism and another that would be a Bolshevist party of the classic type. Similar tendencies are really the most important danger allowing intentions and attempts set out with such clarity and openness in the theses of Ivan Sviták to gain a footing.

This disunity is the rift by which certain people like Sviták, without any sort of authority, try to pass themselves off as the spokesmen of "6 million nonparty members." And if this antagonism of views grows, there is no doubt that the demands of these "tribunes of the people" will inevitably intensify and increase. This is the way one should understand Sviták's cheap comparison about the mongoose and the snake in which, in language typical of a fable, he gives directions on how to attack the party, how to destroy its influence, and how to upset its standing in our society. On the other hand the author shows by this comparison how seriously we may take his declaration about dissociating himself from the policy of anticommunism.

A dynamic party policy with all signs of vigor is therefore the main way of safeguarding the aims we are following at present and will lead to the paralysis of attempts to impose the model of yesteryear. What Ivan Sviták himself fears is shown by a quotation from his essay where, in terminology typical of his approach, he says: "Intelligent and able politicians in the forefront" [here Sviták has in mind the role of the Communist party correctly and democratically implemented] "of a monopolistic apparatus of power are far more dangerous than the simple-minded grandpas who are even incapable of choosing able generals for their revolution." Yes, they are dangerous for self-appointed restorers of yesteryear's attitudes and for hardcore leftwingers, but they also guarantee the socialist character of the democratization movement, the brain and soul of which was, is, and will be the Czechoslovak Communist Party.

It is impossible to imagine us continuing without protest, to close our eyes as though we did not know anything about the fact that certain Communists are taking part in formulating demands for setting up opposition parties, that Communists themselves are talking about this in the press, that certain other views are being tolerated and voices interfering with our alliance with the USSR are not being shouted down, and that the main criterion is to oppose the party at any cost, even when it is a question of the vital interests of our society. . . .

ACTION PROGRAM AND SOVIET RESPONSE

IN ITS ACTION PROGRAM (Document 16), the Communist Party of Czechoslovakia epitomized the art of the possible.[1] In principle, the program defended the right of the minority to maintain its views while sustaining the leading role of the party. Obviously influenced both by Richta's work on the implications of the scientific and technical revolution for socialism and by Mlynář's theory of interest groups, the program attempted to institutionalize a division of power within a Communist system. It projected economic reform but avoided any mention of the inevitable painful economic reallocations necessary for change. As to foreign affairs, the KSČ went out of its way to assure the Soviet Union that fraternal alliance within the Warsaw Pact was fundamental to the Czechoslovak road to socialism.

However, Moscow (and far less Ulbricht) could not have been particularly pleased to see recognition of East Germany juxtaposed to "the necessity for giving support to realistic forces in the German Federal Republic," especially within the context of a marked drop in Prague's anti-West German propaganda[2] and an increasing exchange of high-level visitors with Bonn. The German issue was central. Neither the Soviets nor the East Germans felt that they could afford to have Prague follow Bucharest's example in this respect.[3] The Dresden meeting had been called in part to underline how seriously Moscow viewed the prospects of East European Communist regimes contributing to further isolation of Pankow.

If any doubts remained, they were eliminated when the CPSU CC April Plenum Resolution (Document 17), published one day after the Czechoslovak Action Program, insisted on the solidarity of all socialist countries in the "struggle against West German imperialism." Indeed, the April Plenum signaled hardening of the Soviet line across the board. The United States, West Germany, and Israel were all painted blacker than before. The CPSU,

---

[1] See Michel Tatu in *Le Monde,* April 11, 1968.

[2] Stanley Riveles, "The Czechoslovak Action Program," RFE Analysis, April 26, 1968. Interestingly enough the paragraph on Germany was one of the few reproduced in full by the TASS version of the program, *Pravda,* April 17, 1968.

[3] For an East German comment on Rumanian recognition of West Germany, see *Neues Deutschland,* February 3, 1967.

87

by implication Prague, was warned against imperialist attempts to subvert socialist society from within. Soviet writers were forbidden "to sneak alien views" into their works. On April 22, V. V. Grishin, First Secretary of the Moscow city party organization and a candidate member of the Soviet Polit-buro, sharpened the warning (speech on the anniversary of Lenin's birth, Document 18) in a violent attack on imperialist bridge building to socialist countries. Thus, although ideological saboteurs might rely on "revisionist, nationalist, and politically immature elements," Moscow was determined that no erosion of socialism would be permitted.

DOCUMENT 16

THE ACTION PROGRAM OF THE COMMUNIST PARTY
OF CZECHOSLOVAKIA

Adopted at the Plenary Session of the Central Committee of the Communist Party of Czechoslovakia, April 5, 1968.

Complete Text

[*Rudé právo*, April 10, 1968; translation revised from ČTK, Prague, April 1968]

The Czechoslovak Road to Socialism

The social movement in the Czech lands and Slovakia during the 20th century has been carried along by two great currents — the national liberation movement and socialism.

The national liberation struggle of both nations culminated in the emergence of an independent state in which for the first time in history Czechs and Slovaks were united in a single state. The founding of the Czechoslovak Republic marked an important step forward in the national and social development of both nations. The democratic order eliminated old monarchist remnants and created favorable conditions for fast progress in all spheres of national life.

The pre-war bourgeois order, however, did not settle the onerous class antagonisms and was not able to lay reliable foundations for the lasting prosperity of the new economic entity or guarantee workers and employees full employment and a secure existence. Its nationalist regime, though liberal towards the minorities, ignored the individuality of the Slovak nation and did not succeed in eliminating the influence of extreme nationalism and in introducing harmony among all nationalities of the Republic. Under the conditions prevailing at that time in capitalist Europe, not even the independence of the Czechoslovak Republic could be permanently safeguarded.

The progressive forces tried to respond to these shortcomings. Their most energetic component was the Communist Party of Czechoslovakia which was striving for a socialist conception of Czechoslovak society.

As a consequence of the anti-Fascist movement — which originated in connection with the breakup of prewar Czechoslovakia — and even more of the national liberation struggle, the integration of socialism with the national and democratic movement began to take shape.

During the national and democratic revolution of 1944–45 the national and democratic values of socialism were united for the first time. The democratic and national movement began to be socialized and socialism became truly national and democratic. Czechoslovakia's road to socialism, which began with the Slovak National Uprising and the Prague Uprising in 1944–45, is the source of the most progressive traditions of modern Czech and Slovak history.

The Republic, whose liberation was the result of the heroic fighting of the Soviet Army and the national liberation struggle of the Czechoslovak people, was restored on new foundations which facilitated the solving of the most acute national problems. The existence of the Republic as a state was ensured by close alliance with the Soviet Union. By nationalization the Republic gained an economic system providing conditions for rapid restoration and for the further development of the economy toward socialism. The considerable expansion of informal political freedoms was the true culmination of the whole democratic tradition of Czechoslovakia's development. Socialism became the embodiment of the modern national program of the Czechs and Slovaks.

Czechoslovakia was the first industrial country to put socialist reconstruction into practice. The policy of Czechoslovakia's road to socialism from 1945 to 1948 was an expression of the attempt to respect the complexity of the specific internal and international conditions of Czechoslovakia. It contained many elements which can contribute toward achieving our present aim of democratizing the socialist order.

We identify ourselves with traditions of the liberation struggle in which patriots participated at home and in various parts of Europe and the world. 375,000 men and women gave their lives for these ideals. We will support a scientific examination of the history of both nations, the conclusions of which cannot be decreed by anyone, but can only be the result of the study of history itself. The February victory of the working people was an important milestone in the socialist development of post-war Czechoslovakia; it created the conditions necessary for accelerating the advance to socialism. After February 1948 the Party took a new road of socialist construction backed by confidence and support of the broadest strata of the population.

It was a difficult road. In a divided world in the grips of the cold war, our nations had to increase their efforts to safeguard their hard-won national existence and therefore concentrate on reinforcing their own defense system and that of all the other socialist states. Building the new Republic, which lacked many of the internal resources essential for developing the economy, was closely connected with the progress and problems of the whole socialist camp. The inclusion of the Republic in the system of socialist states brought substantial changes in the direction of development of the national economy and also in its internal structure, in the character of the state and the social order. We therefore respected the common tasks of those countries in which combating problems of economic and cultural retardation and creating new forms of ownership played a leading role.

All this influenced the speed, form, and content of the profound economic, social, and political reconstruction which the Republic experienced during the building of socialism. They called for an exceptional exertion of energy from the working class and the whole people, great sacrifices from Communists and the dedicated work of tens of thousands of functionaries.

The unusual size, quality and challenge of the changes, however, gave rise to the contradictions, grave shortcomings, unsolved problems, and deformations of socialist principles which are known as the personality cult.

The construction of the new social system was marked by insufficient experience, lack of knowledge, by dogmatism and subjectivism. Many signs of the times, conditioned by heightened international tension and compulsory acceleration in building industry, were understood as the generally valid forms of life and development in a socialist society. The stage of development of the socialist states at the beginning of the fifties and the arrest of the creative development of knowledge concomitant with the personality cult, conditioned a mechanical acceptance and spreading of ideas, customs, and political conceptions which were at variance with Czechoslovak conditions and traditions. The leading bodies and institutes of the Party and the state of that time are fully responsible. The centralist and directive-administrative methods used during the fight against the remnants of the bourgeoisie and during the consolidation of power under conditions of heightening international tension after February 1948 were, in this situation, unjustifiably carried over into the next stage of development and gradually grew into a bureaucratic system. Sectarianism, suppression of the democratic rights and freedoms of the people, violation of laws, signs of licentiousness, and misuse of power became apparent in the internal life of the Republic, undermined the initiative of the people and, what is more, gravely and unjustly afflicted many citizens — Communists and non-Communists alike. The irreparable losses suffered by our movement at that time will forever remain a warning against similar methods.

The extraordinary strength of our people led to great historic successes. Basic socialist social changes have been accomplished and the socialist order has sunk its roots deeply and firmly into our land. Our society, in which the means of production are mainly in the hands of the socialist state or of workers' cooperatives, has got rid of capitalist exploitation and the social wrongs connected with it. Every citizen of the Czechoslovak Socialist Republic has the right to work and enjoys basic social security. Our society has emerged from a period of industrialization with an extensive industrial base. We have achieved noteworthy successes in the advancement of science and culture. The broadest strata of the people have unprecedented opportunities for gaining a suitable education. The international status of the Republic among the socialist countries is firmly secured.

At the end of the fifties our society entered another stage of development. The political line which we wish to apply and develop began to take shape at that time. The following features are characteristic of the present stage:

• antagonistic classes no longer exist and the main feature of internal development has become the process of bringing all social groups closer together;

• methods of direction and organization hitherto used in the economy are outdated and demand urgent changes, i.e., an economic system of management able to enforce a turn toward intensive growth;

• the country must be made ready to join the world scientific-technical revolution. This calls for especially intensive cooperation of workers and agricultural workers with the technical and specialized intelligentsia and will place high demands upon knowledge and qualifications and the application of science;

• a broad scope for social initiative, a frank exchange of views, and the democratization of the whole social and political system have literally become a necessity if socialist society is to remain dynamic. They are also a condition for being able to hold our own in world competition and fulfill our obligations toward the international workers' movement honorably.

Surmounting the Causes of Profound Social Crisis

Even when this Party line was in the formation stage and just starting to be applied, it ran up against a lack of understanding for the new tasks, a relapse into methods of work from the time of sharp class struggle and the opposition of those who in one way or another found the deformations of socialist reality convenient.

We need a frank statement of what these mistakes and deformations were and what caused them so as to remedy them as soon as possible and concentrate all forces *on the fundamental structural change in our lives* which we are facing at the present time.

After the 20th Congress of the Communist Party of the USSR, which was an impulse for revival of the development of socialist democracy, the Party adopted several measures which were intended to overcome bureaucratic-centralist sectarian methods of management or its remnants, to prevent the instruments of the class struggle from being used against the working people. Many Communists and whole working collectives tried to open the way for a progressive development of the economy, the standard of living, science and culture. The clearer it was that class antagonism had been overcome and foundations for socialism laid, the greater was the stress placed upon promoting cooperation among all working people, social strata, groups, and nationalities in Czechoslovakia and on making fundamental changes in methods employed during the time of acute class struggle. They rightly judged the development of socialist democracy to be the main social condition for realizing the humanistic aims characteristic of socialism. However, they met with a lack of understanding, various obstacles and, in some cases, even direct suppression. The survival of methods from the time of the class struggle caused artificial tension among social groups, nations, and nationalities, different generations, Communists and nonparty people. Dogmatic approaches impeded a full and timely re-evaluation of the character of socialist construction.

The measures adopted did not therefore bring the anticipated results. On the contrary, over the years, difficulties piled up until they closed in a vicious circle. Subjective conceptions which held that construction of the new society was dependent only upon an accelerated and extensive development of production were not overridden in time. This led to a precipitate expansion of heavy industry, to a disproportionate demand on labor power and raw materials, and to costly investments. Such an economic policy, enforced through directive administrative methods, no longer corresponded to the economic requirements and possibilities of the country and led to exhaustion of its material and human resources. Unrealistic tasks were allotted to the economy, illusory promises were made to the workers. All these factors intensified the unfavorable structure of production, which fell out of step with national conditions: skilled labor could not be put to sufficient advantage, production suffered considerable technical retardation, the development of public services was slowed down, the equilibrium of the market upset, the international status of the economy worsened (especially in foreign trade). The result was stagnation and, in certain cases, a reduction in the living standard of the people.

These shortcomings were directly caused by the maintenance and constant restoration of the old directive system of management. Economic tools of supply and demand, and marketing ties were replaced by directives from the center. Socialist enterprise did not expand. In economic life, independence, diligence, expertise, and initiative were not appreciated, whereas subservience, obedience, and even kowtowing to higher ups were.

A more profound reason for keeping up the outlived methods of economic management was deformations in the political system. Socialist democracy was not spread in time. Methods of revolutionary dictatorship deteriorated into bureaucracy and became an impediment to progress in all spheres of life. Political mistakes were added to economic difficulties and a mechanism created which resulted in helplessness, conflict between theory and practice. Many of the efforts, activities, and much of the energy of workers of the Party, the state, the economy, science, and culture were squandered. The adverse external circumstances of the early sixties brought things to a head, and a serious economic crisis followed. This period saw the start of the difficulties with which the workers are still confronted daily: the slow increase in wages after many years, stagnation of the living standard and especially the constantly increasing retardation of the infrastructure in comparison with advanced industrial countries, the catastrophic state of housing and insufficient construction of houses and apartments, the precarious state of the transportation system, poor quality goods and public services, a low quality living environment and, in general, conditions which tangibly affect the human factor, opportunities for developing human energy and activities, which are decisive for a socialist society. The people grew bitter. They began to feel that despite all the successes which had been achieved and all the efforts exerted, socialist society was making headway with great difficulty, with fateful delay and with moral and political defects in human relations. Quite naturally, apprehensions arose about socialism, about its human mission, about its human features. Some people became demoralized, others lost perspective.

The main link in this circle was that of remnants or revivers of the bureaucratic, sectarian approach in the Party itself. The insufficient development of socialist democracy within the Party, an unfavorable atmosphere for the promotion of activity, the silencing or even suppression of criticism — all of this thwarted a fast, timely, and thorough rectification. Party bodies took over tasks of state and economic bodies and social organizations. This led to an incorrect merging of the Party and state management, the monopolized power-position of some sections, unqualified interference, the undermining of initiative at all levels, indifference, a cult of mediocrity, and unhealthy anonymity. Irresponsibility and lack of discipline consequently gained ground. Many correct resolutions were never fulfilled. This adversely affected theoretical thinking, making it impossible to recognize in time the shortcomings and danger connected with the outdated system of management. Reform in the economy and politics was held up.

All of these questions became a focus for clashes between forces insisting upon fundamental changes and the bearers of the old conception. The situation was clarified, and essential social progress pushed ahead. At the December and January sessions of the Central Committee, thorough, concrete criticism was made of the main causes of the aforementioned shortcomings and their backers, and corrective measures were instigated in the leading bodies of the Party themselves. One of the immediate causes was said to be that inside the Party there was too great a concentration of decision-making power, that certain individuals, and above all A. Novotný held exceptional positions. This criticism allowed the whole Party and society to start overcoming old approaches and sectarian bureaucratic practices on the basis of self-critical evaluation of the work to date, from top to bottom, so as to create real unity of Czechoslovak society on the basis of social democratism, to implement thoroughly the principles of the new system of economic management, to modernize and rationalize life in Czechoslovakia, to open up long-term perspectives of gradually including Czechoslovakia in the scientific-technological revolution — so that in all spheres of society the strength of socialism might be revived and start out along a new road of socialist development.

A Policy of Unity and Confidence

Decisive for the socialist development of this country was the creation of a broad alliance of progressive forces of the town and country headed by the working class and the combined Czech and Slovak nations.

The resolution of the 13th Congress of the Communist Party of Czechoslovakia set the task of "continuing to strengthen the unity of the working class, which is the leading force in the society, with agricultural cooperative workers and the socialist intelligentsia as the political base of the state, helping the mutual rapprochement of classes and strata of the nations and nationalities in Czechoslovakia, and consolidating their unity." The sense of the present policy is to provide continuous stimulation for democratic relations of co-operation and confidence among the various social groups without differentiation, to harmonize their efforts, to unite their forces on the basis of the development of the whole society.

All social classes, strata, groups, both peoples and all nationalities of the society agree with the fundamental interests and aims of socialism. One of the great advantages of socialist development to date is that a decisive factor in assessing the standing and activity of the people in this society is what they accomplish at work and their progressive social activity, not their membership in this class or that stratum. The Party resolutely condemns attempts to oppose the various classes, strata and groups of the socialist society to each other and will eliminate everything that creates tension among them.

On behalf of unity and the interests of the whole society, there can be no overlooking the various needs and interests of individual people and social groups according to their work, qualification, age, sex, nationality and so on. In the past we have often made such mistakes.

Socialism can flourish only if enough scope is given to the various interests of the people. It is on this basis that the unity of all workers will be brought about democratically. This is the main source of free social activity and development of the socialist system.

The Party is backed, and will continue to be backed, by the *working class,* which has shown that it is able to carry the main weight of socialist endeavor. Under prevailing conditions, we rely especially upon those, who, with their awareness, i.e., profound understanding of the real interests and tasks of the working class in the revolutionary reconstruction of the whole society, with their qualifications, and their cohesion with modern technology, with the high effectiveness of their work and their social activity, contribute markedly to the further progress of Czechoslovak production and to the society as a whole. The working class began the revolutionary struggle so as to abolish every sort of exploitation, erase all class barriers, facilitate the liberation of all people, and transform the conditions of human life and the character of human labor, make way for the full self-realization of man, and by all this to change even itself. These long-term interests of the working class have not yet been fully realized. The workers, however, now have in their hands new technical, social and cultural means which allow them to continue changing their working and living conditions and developing elements of purposeful creative endeavor in their work. We are determined to develop all the creative and by far not fully utilized energy which the working class possesses for these tasks.

In the past, workers did not always have an opportunity to develop their own interests. Therefore the Party will strive to activize the social life of the workers, to provide scope for profiting from all their political and social rights through political organizations and trade unions and to strengthen the democratic influence of collective teams of workers in the management of production. It will strive for the alleviation of extremely tiring jobs, the humanization of work, and the improvement of working conditions.

One of the most significant results of the transformation of the social structure was the creation of social groups which organically coalesce with the workers — *agricultural cooperative workers*. This fact must be appreciated politically. The Party will strive for the absolute economic equalization of agriculture with industry and appreciation for the social importance of agricultural work. In accordance with the conclusions of the 7th Congress of Agricultural Cooperatives we shall support the setting up of all-state agricultural cooperative organizations and increase their political authority; we want to abolish all administrative, bureaucratic obstructions which impede the independent initiative of agricultural enterprises, everything that endangers the security of cooperative enterprise and results from a lack of confidence in the ability of agricultural cooperative workers to act independently and in a socialist way.

Likewise it will be necessary to understand that the character of our *intelligentsia* has gradually changed; it has become an intelligentsia of the people, a socialist intelligentsia. It represents a force which takes a creative part in the development of society and makes the wealth of science and culture available to all people. Today, workers will find in the intelligentsia an integral part of their own inner strength. The constantly closer collaboration of the technical intelligentsia with workers in productive collectives is further proof of how we have been surmounting former class barriers. The Party will support the growing unity between the intelligentsia and the rest of the working people. It will combat the recent under-estimation of the role of the intelligentsia in our society. It will combat everything that upsets relations between the intelligentsia and the workers. It will strive for just remuneration of complex and creative mental labor.

Just as with the working class, so with the agricultural workers and the intelligentsia, the Party will rely mainly upon those who best understand and most actively further social interests and who, by effective work, most markedly contribute to social progress. Cooperation among all groups of socialist society will be effective and possible only when everyone has become aware of his responsibility to everyone else and does not give preference to narrow professional interests.

Czechoslovak statehood is founded on the voluntary and equal co-existence of *Czechs and Slovaks*. The establishment of socialist relations will provide for the strengthening of the fraternal co-existence of our nations. Our Republic can be strong only if there are no sparks of tension or signs of nervousness and suspicion in relations between the Czech and Slovak nations and among all our nationalities. We must therefore resolutely condemn everything which has occurred in the past which might undermine the principles of the equality and sovereignty of both socialist nations. The unity of the Czechs and Slovaks can be strengthened only on the basis of an unhampered development of their national individuality in harmony with economic progress and objective changes in the social structure of both nations, and on the basis of absolute equality and voluntariness. The more developed the two nations, and the greater use made of the enormous economic and cultural resources in Slovakia, the stronger our Republic will be. Indifference to national interests or even endeavors to suppress them is considered by the Party to be a gross distortion of its program and political course. The Party will consistently defend the Leninist principle that overlooking the interests of a smaller nation by a larger is incompatible with socialist relations between nations. It will oppose any kind of endeavor to denigrate the continuous search for the best methods of developing the constitutional relations between our nations on the basis of equal rights and voluntariness. Communists of both nations and all nationalities in this country defend the principles of internationalism; the Communists of each nation and nationality are themselves surmounting nationalistic relics in their own surroundings.

Under socialist conditions, each of the national minorities — Hungarian, Polish, Ukrainian, German, etc. — has a right to its own national life and a thorough realization of all other constitutional rights.

The Party stresses it will oppose all expressions of anti-Semitism, racism and any antihumanistic ideology, tending to set people against one another.

Various *generations* of our society have grown up under different conditions and naturally vary in their outlook on many questions pertaining to our life. The Party strongly renounces endeavors to play off the interests of these generations against one another and will devote special care to harmonizing and satisfying the needs of the different age groups.

It is true that thanks to the dedicated work of the older generation, our system has provided better conditions for the young people than the pre-Munich Republic. Nevertheless, we still owe much to our youth. Shortcomings and mistakes in political, economic and cultural life, just as in human relations, make an especially strong impression on the young. Contradictions between words and deeds, a lack of frankness, a phrase-mongering bureaucracy, attempts to settle everything from a position of power — these deformations of socialist life must painfully affect students, young workers and agricultural workers and give them the feeling that it is not they, their work, their efforts which are decisive for their own future life. Restoring contact with young people everywhere and making them responsible (socialism gives them this responsibility) for their independent work is an urgent task.

This especially applies to improving working conditions and opportunities for young people to be active in social and cultural life and thoroughly erasing everything that evokes a lack of confidence in socialism among young people. We are all glad about youths' enthusiasm and their positive and critical initiative, necessary conditions if they are to see their cause and future in socialism and communism.

Neither should we overlook the material conditions and social esteem, which give the older generation a dignified and well-merited retirement. This society should pay great attention to ensuring adequate security for the active members of the resistance movement, to whom everyone owes respect.

To deformations of Party and state policy belongs blame for the fact that in the past the problem of women, especially those in employment, was not considered a serious political matter. In state, economic and cultural policy, women should have access to positions which comply with principles of socialist democracy and the significant role taken by women in creating material and spiritual values of the society.

In the further development of our society we must count on the activity of all strata of the population in public life and constructive endeavor. We can say quite openly that we are also reckoning with believers, who, on the basis of their faith, wish, as equals, as builders of a socialist society, to take their part in helping to fulfill all our exacting tasks.

Developing Democracy and Eliminating Equalitarianism

Using and unifying the manifold interests of social groups and individuals calls for the elaboration and implementation of a new political system in our lives, a new model of *socialist democracy*. The Party will strive to develop a state and social order that corresponds to the actual interests of the various strata and groups of this society and gives them a chance to express their interests in their organizations and voice their views in public life. We expect that in an atmosphere of mutual confidence between people and their institutions civic responsibility will grow and the norms of human relations will be respected.

Meanwhile, the Party will strive to link the democratic principles of the social system with expert and scientific management and decision-making. In order to be able to judge responsibly what is in the interest of the whole society, we must always have before us several alternatives for appraisal and expertly drawn-up proposals for solving all disputable matters, and we must ensure that the people get a greater amount of candid information.

Today, when class differences are being erased, the main criterion for evaluating the status of people in society is how the individual contributes toward social progress. The Party has often criticized equalitarian views, but in practice leveling has spread to an unheard of extent and become one of the impediments to an intensive development of the economy and raising the living standard. The harmfulness of equalitarianism lies in the fact that it gives careless, idle, and irresponsible people an advantage over dedicated and diligent workers, the unqualified over the qualified, the technically backward over the talented and initiative-oriented.

Though attempting to replace equalitarianism with the principle of appraising actual achievements, we have no intention of forming a new privileged stratum. We want the remuneration of people in all spheres of social life to depend upon the social importance and effectiveness of their work, upon the development of initiative and upon the degree of responsibility and risk. This is in the interest of the development of the whole society. The principle of appraising actual achievements raises the technical standard, profitability and productivity of labor and the respect and authority of the managers responsible.

It stresses the principle of material incentive and the growing importance of high qualifications for all workers.

One of the key conditions of the present and future scientific, technical and social development is to bring about a substantial increase in the qualifications of managers and experts at all levels of economic and social life. If the leading posts are not filled by capable, educated socialist cadre experts, socialism will be unable to hold its own in competition with capitalism.

This fact will call for a basic change in the existing cadre policy, in which education, qualifications and ability have been underrated for years.

To apply the principle of remuneration according to the quantity, quality and social usefulness of work we must put an end to income leveling. This is not to be understood as an excuse to neglect the interests of citizens in the lowest income group, the interests of families with many children, citizens with reduced working ability, pensioners and certain categories of women and youth. On the contrary, a thorough application of the principle of differentiated remuneration according to actual work achievement is the only effective means for developing resources which enable the standard of living to rise and, according to the spirit of socialist humanism, determine and ensure good living conditions for all strata of the society. We want to make it quite clear that honest work for the society and efforts to improve qualifications are not only duly remunerated but must also enjoy due respect. A socialist society respects those who achieve exceptional results, who are active and show initiative in advancing production, technical, cultural and social progress; it respects talented people and creates favorable conditions for them to make themselves felt.

The Leading Role of the Party — A Guarantee of Socialist Progress

At present it is most important that the Party practice a policy fully justifying its leading role in society. We believe that this is a condition for the socialist development of the country.

The Communist Party, as a party of the working class, won the struggle with capitalism and the struggle to carry out revolutionary class changes. With the victory of socialism it became the vanguard of the entire socialist society. During the present development the Party has proven its ability to lead this society; from its own initiative it launched the process of democratization and ensured its socialist character. In its political activity the Party intends to depend particularly on those who have an understanding of the requirements of the society as a whole, who do not see their own personal and group interests as opposed to those of socialism, who use and improve their abilities for the benefit of all, who have a sense for everything new and progressive and are willing to help advance it.

The Communist Party enjoys the voluntary support of the people. It does not practice its leading role by ruling society but by most devotedly serving its free, progressive socialist development. The Party cannot enforce its authority. Authority must be won again and again by Party activity. It cannot force its line through directives. It must depend on the work of its members, on the veracity of its ideals.

In the past, the leading role of the Party was often conceived as a monopolistic concentration of power in the hands of Party bodies. This concept corresponded to the false thesis that the Party is the instrument of the dictatorship of the proletariat. This harmful conception weakened the initiative and responsibility of state, economic and social institutions, damaged the Party's authority, and prevented it from carrying out its real functions. The Party's goal is not to become a universal "caretaker" of the society, to bind all organizations and every step taken in life by its directives. Its mission lies primarily in arousing socialist initiative, showing the ways and real possibilities of Communist perspectives, and in winning over all workers to them through systematic persuasion and the personal examples of Communists. This determines the conceptional character of Party activity. Party bodies do not deal with all problems; they should encourage activity and suggest solutions to the most important ones. At the same time the Party cannot turn into an organization which influences society only by its ideas and program. Through its members and bodies it must develop the practical organizational methods of a political force in society. Political and organizational Party activity coordinates the practical efforts of the people to turn the Party line and program into reality in the social, economic, and cultural life of the society.

As a representative of the interests of the most progressive part of all strata — and thus the representative of the perspective aims of the society — the Party cannot represent the entire scale of social interests. The political expression of the many-sided interests of the society is the National Front, which expresses the unity of the social strata, interest groups, and of the nations and nationalities of this society. The Party does not want to and will not take the place of social organizations; on the contrary, it must take care that their initiative and political responsibility for the unity of society is revived and flourishes. The role of the Party is to seek a way of satisfying the various interests which does not jeopardize the interests of the society as a whole, but promotes them and creates new progressive ones. The Party policy must not lead non-Communists to feel that their rights and freedom are limited by the role of the Party. On the contrary, they must interpret the activity of the Party as a guarantee of their rights, freedom, and interests. We want to, we must achieve a state of affairs where the Party at the basic organizational level will have informal, natural authority based upon its ability to manage and the moral qualities of Communist functionaries.

Within the framework of democratic rules of a socialist state, Communists must continually strive for the voluntary support of the majority of the people for the Party line. Party resolutions and directives must be modified if they fail to express the needs and possibilities of the whole society. The Party must try to ensure for its members — the most active workers in their spheres of work — suitable weight and influence in the whole society and posts in state, economic and social bodies. This, however, must not lead to the practice of appointing Party members to posts, without regard to the principle that leading representatives of institutions of the whole society are chosen by the society itself and by its individual components and that functionaries of these components are responsible to all citizens or to all members of social organizations. We must abolish discrimination and "cadre ceilings" for non-Party members.

The basis for the Party's ability to act is its ideological and organizational unity based upon broad inner-Party democracy. The most effective weapon against methods of bureaucratic centralism in the Party is the consolidation of the influence of Party members in forming the political line and the reinforcement of the role of really democratically elected bodies. Elected bodies of the Party must first of all guarantee all rights of its members, collective decision-making and ensure that all power will not be concentrated in a single pair of hands.

Only down-to-earth discussion and an exchange of views can lead to responsible decision-making by collective bodies. The confrontation of views is an essential manifestation of a responsible multilateral attempt to find the best solution, to advance the new against the obsolete. Each member of the Party and Party bodies has not only the right, but the duty to act according to his conscience, with initiative, criticism, and different views on the matter in question, to oppose any functionary. This practice must become deeply rooted if the Party is to avoid subjectivism in its activity. It is impermissible to restrict Communists in these rights, to create an atmosphere of distrust and suspicion of those who voice different opinions, to persecute the minority under any pretext — as has happened in the past. The Party, however, cannot abandon the principle of requiring that resolutions be put into practice once they are approved. Within the Party, all its members are equal regardless of whether they hold any post in Party bodies or in the bodies of state and economic organizations. Nevertheless, anyone who occupies a higher position also carries greater responsibility. The Party realizes that a deeper democracy will not take hold in this society if democratic principles are not consistently applied in the internal life and work of the Party and among Communists. Decisions on all important questions and on filling cadre posts must be backed by democratic rules and secret ballot. The democratization of Party life also means the strengthening of work contacts between the Party and science. In this line we shall make use of consultations and exchanges of opposing and contrary views, since the role of science does not end with the preparation of analyses and documents. It should continue on Party grounds by observing the innovations produced by various resolutions and by contributing to their materialization and control in practice.

The Central Committee of the Communist Party of Czechoslovakia set out on this road at its December and January sessions and will make sure that in the months to come questions of the content and democratic methods of Party life and relations between elected bodies and the Party apparatus are clarified throughout the Party and that rules will be elaborated to define the authority and responsibilities of the individual bodies and links of the Party mechanism, as well as the principles of the Party's cadre policy, which will ensure an effective, regular change of leading officials, guarantee to keep its members well informed and regulate relations between Party bodies and Party members in general. In preparing the 14th Party Congress the Party will ensure that Party statutes correspond to the present state of its development.

For the Development of Socialist Democracy and a New System of the Political Management of Society

In the past decade, the Party has often put forward the demand for the development of socialist democracy. Measures taken by the Party were aimed at enhancing the role of elected representative bodies in the state. They emphasized the importance of voluntary social organizations and of all forms of popular activities. Party policy initiated a number of laws which increased the protection of rights of every citizen. It was clearly stated in the theses of the Central Committee of the Communist Party of Czechoslovakia prepared for the 13th Party Congress that "the dictatorship of the working class has fulfilled its main historical mission in our country" and guidelines for further development of our democracy were given no less clearly — "the system of socialist democracy — the state, social organizations, and the Party as the leading force — endeavors to bring out the different interests and attitudes of working people to social problems in a democratic way and to settle them within social organizations with regard to nationwide needs and goals. The development of democracy must proceed hand in hand with strengthening the scientific and professional approach to social management."

Nevertheless, *the harmful characteristics of centralized directive decision-making and management have survived to the present.* In relations among the Party, the state, and social organizations, in internal relations and methods among these components, in the relations of state and other institutions to individuals, in the interpretation of the importance of public opinion and of keeping the people informed, in the practice of cadre policy — in all these fields there are too many elements embittering the life of the people, obstructing professionally competent and scientific decision-making, and encouraging highhandedness. The reason may be sought, first and foremost, in the fact that the relations among these bodies in our political system have been built up for years to serve as the instrument for carrying out the orders of the center, and hardly ever made it at all possible for the decision itself to be the outcome of a democratic procedure.

The different interests and needs of people not foreseen by the system of directive decision-making were taken as an undesirable obstacle and not as new needs to be respected by politics. The often well-meant words of "an increase in the people's participation in management" were of no avail, because in time "participation of the people" came to mean chiefly help in carrying out orders, not in making the decisions. Thus it was possible that views, measures and interventions were enforced even though they were arbitrary and did not comply either with scientific knowledge, or with the interests of the various strata of the people and individual citizens. Centralized decision-making put into effect in this way could not be effective. It led to a number of resolutions not being fulfilled and a weakening of goal-oriented management of social development. This, in turn, has in many cases kept positions occupied by people who were incapable of any other type of "management," who consistently revive old methods and habits and surround themselves with people who humor them and not with people whose capacities and character would guarantee the successful filling of their posts. Although we consistently condemn the "personality cult," we are still unable to eradicate certain characteristics of our society which were typical of that period. This undermines the people's confidence in whether the Party can change the situation, and old tensions and political nervous strain are revived.

The Central Committee is firmly determined to overcome this state of affairs. As noted above, for the 14th Congress we must cast the fundamental issues of the development of the political system into a concept meeting the demands of life, just as we have established the fundamental concept of the new economic system.

We must reform the whole political system so that it will permit the dynamic development of socialist social relations, combine broad democracy with scientific, highly qualified management, strengthen the social order, stabilize socialist relations and maintain social discipline. The basic structure of the political system must, at the same time, *provide firm guarantees against a return to the old methods of subjectivism and highhandedness from a position of power.* Party activity has not been directed systematically to that end, and in fact, obstacles have frequently been put in the way of such efforts. All these changes necessarily call for the *commencement of work on a new Czechoslovak Constitution* so that a draft may be thoroughly discussed among professionals and in public and submitted to the National Assembly shortly after the Party Congress.

But we consider it indispensable to change the present state of things immediately, even before the 14th Congress, so that the development of socialism and its inner dynamics will not be hampered by outdated factors in the political system. Our democracy must provide more leeway for the activity of every individual, every collective, every link in management, at lower and higher levels and in the center too. People must have more opportunity to think for themselves and express their opinions. We must radically change the practices that allow the people's initiative and critical comments and suggestions from below to meet with the proverbial deaf ear. We must see to it that the incompetent but readily adaptable people are replaced by those who strive for socialism, who are concerned with its fate and progress and the interests and needs of others, not with their own power or privilege. This holds for people both "above" and "below." It is going to be a complicated process, and it will take some time. At all levels of management, in the Party, in state and economic bodies and in social organizations, we must ascertain which body, which official, or which worker is really responsible, where to look for guarantees of improvement, where to change institutions, where to introduce new working methods, and where to replace individuals. The attitude of individual Party officials to new tasks and methods, their capability of carrying the new policy into practice, must be the basic political criterion.

No Responsibility Without Rights

Which body and which official are responsible for what, and the rights and duties involved, must be perfectly clear in our system of management in the future. It is the basic prerequisite for proper development. To this end, each component part should have its own independent position. Substitution and interchanging of state bodies and agencies of economic and social organization by Party bodies must be stopped. Party resolutions are binding for the Communists working in these bodies, but the policy, managerial activities, and responsibility of the state, economic, and social organizations are independent. The Communists active in these bodies and organizations must take the initiative to see to it that the state and economic bodies as well as social organizations (notably the Trade Unions, the Czechoslovak Union of Youth, etc.) take the problem of their activities and responsibilities into their own hands.

The whole *National Front,* the political parties which form it, and the social organizations will take part in the creation of state policy. *The political parties* of the National Front are partners whose political work is based on the joint political program of the National Front and is naturally bound by the Constitution of the Czechoslovak Socialist Republic. It stems from the socialist character of social relations in our country. The Communist Party of Czechoslovakia considers the National Front to be a political platform which does not separate political parties into government and opposition factions. It does not create opposition to state policy — the policy of the whole National Front — or lead struggles for political power. Possible differences in the viewpoints of individual component parts of the National Front or divergency of views as to a state policy is to be settled on the basis of the common socialist conception of National Front policy by way of political agreement and unification of all component parts of the National Front. The organization of political forces to negate this concept of the National Front, to remove the National Front as a whole from political power, was ruled out as long ago as 1945 after the tragic experience of both our nations with the prewar political development of the Czechoslovak government; it is naturally unacceptable for our present republic.

The Communist Party of Czechoslovakia considers the *political leadership* of the Marxist-Leninist concept of the development of socialism as a precondition for the proper development of our socialist society. It will assert the Marxist-Leninist concept as the leading political principle in the National Front and in all our political system by seeking, through the means of political work, such support in all the component parts of our system and *directly among the masses of workers and all working people* that will ensure its leading role in a democratic way.

Voluntary social organizations of the working people cannot replace political parties, *but the contrary is also true. Political parties in our country cannot exclude common-interest organizations of workers and other working people from directly influencing state policy,* its creation and application. Socialist state power cannot be monopolized either by a single party, or by a coalition of parties. It must be open to all political organizations of the people. *The Communist Party of Czechoslovakia will use every means at its disposal to develop such forms of political life that will ensure the expression of the direct voice and will of the working class and all working people in political decision-making in our country.*

The whole existing organization, its activities, and incorporation of various organizations into the National Front must be revised and restructured under the new conditions and built up so that the National Front may carry out its qualitatively new tasks. *The National Front as a whole and all its component parts must be granted independent rights and its own responsibility for the management of our country and society.*

Voluntary social organizations must be based on truly voluntary membership and activity. People join these organizations hoping they will express their interests, and they therefore have the right to choose their own officials and representatives, who must not be appointed from outside. These principles should form the foundation of our unified mass organizations. Although their activities are still indispensable, their structure, their working methods, and ties with their members must respect the new social conditions.

The implementation of the *constitutional freedoms of assembly and association* must be ensured this year so that the possibility of setting up voluntary organizations, special-interest associations, societies, etc., is guaranteed by law and the present interests and needs of various strata and categories of our citizens are tended to without bureaucratic interference and without a monopoly by any individual organization. Any restrictions in this respect can be imposed only by law and only the law can stipulate what is antisocial, forbidden, or punishable. Freedoms guaranteed by law and in compliance with the constitution also apply fully to citizens of various creeds and religious denominations.

The effective influence of views and opinions of the working people on the policies and a firm opposition to all tendencies to suppress the criticism and initiative of the people cannot be guaranteed if we do not ensure constitution-based freedom of speech and political and personal rights to all citizens, systematically and consistently, by all legal means available. *Socialism cannot mean only liberation of the working people from the domination of exploiting class relations, but must provide for a greater degree of self-fulfillment than any bourgeois democracy.* The working people, who are no longer ordered about by a class of exploiters, can no longer be dictated to by any arbitrary interpretation from a position of power as to what information they may or may not be given, which of their opinions can or cannot be expressed publicly, where public opinion may play a role and where it may not. Public opinion polls must be systematically used in preparing important decisions and the main results of such research published. Any restriction may be imposed only on the basis of a law stipulating what is antisocial — which in our country is mainly determined by the criminal code. The Central Committee of the Communist Party of Czechoslovakia considers it urgently necessary to define in a press law and more exactly than hitherto in the shortest possible time when a state body can forbid the propagation of certain information (in the press, radio, television, etc.) and exclude the possibility of preliminary factual censorship. It is necessary to overcome the holding up, distortion, and incompleteness of information, to remove any unwarranted secrecy of political and economic facts, to publish the annual balance sheets of enterprises, to publish even alternatives to various suggestions and measures, and to increase the import and sale of foreign newspapers and periodicals. Leading representatives of state, social, and cultural organizations are obliged to organize regular press conferences and give their views on topical issues on television, radio, and in the press. In the press, it is necessary to make a distinction between official standpoints of the state, Party organs and journalists. The Party press especially must express the Party's life and development along with criticisms of various opinions among the Communists, etc., and cannot be made to coincide fully with the official viewpoints of the state.

The Party realizes that ideological antagonists of socialism may try to abuse the process of democratization. At the present stage of development and under the conditions of our country, we insist on the principle that bourgeois ideology can be challenged only in open ideological struggle before all of the people. We can win people over to the ideas and policy of the Party only by a struggle based on the practical activities of Communists for the benefit of the people, on truthful and complete information, and on scientific analysis. We trust that in such a struggle, all sections of our society will contribute actively towards the victory of truth, which is on the side of socialism.

At present the activity and responsibility of publishing houses and editors-in-chief, of all Party members and progressive staff members of the mass communication media, must be to push through socialist ideals and implement the policy of the Party, of the National Front, and of the state.

Legal norms must provide a more precise guarantee *of the freedom of speech for minority interests and opinions* also (again within the framework of socialist laws and in harmony with the principle that decisions are taken in accordance with the will of the majority). The *constitutional freedom of movement,* particularly that of travel abroad for our citizens, *must be precisely guaranteed by law.* In particular, this means that a citizen should have the legal right to long-term or permanent sojourn abroad and that people should not be groundlessly placed in the position of emigrants; at the same time it is necessary to protect by law the interests of the state, for example, as regards the drain of some categories of specialists, etc.

Our entire legal code must gradually solve the problem of how *to protect in a better and more consistent way the personal rights and property of citizens,* and we must especially remove those stipulations that virtually put individual citizens at a disadvantage against the state and other institutions. We must in the future prevent various institutions from disregarding personal rights and the interests of individual citizens as far as personal ownership of family houses, gardens, etc. is concerned. It will be necessary to adopt, in the shortest possible time, the long-prepared law on compensation for any damage caused to any individual or to an organization by an unlawful decision of a state organ.

It is a serious fact *that hitherto the rehabilitation of people* — both Communists and non-Communists — who were the victims of legal violations in the past years, *has not been always carried out in all its political and civic consequences.* On the initiative of the Communist Party Central Committee bodies, an investigation is under way as to why the respective Party resolutions have not been fully carried out, and measures are being taken to ensure that the wrongs of the past are made good wherever it has not been done yet. No one having the slightest personal reason from his own past activity for slowing down the rectification process may serve in the political bodies or prosecutor's and court offices that are to rectify unlawful deeds of the past.

The Party realizes that people unlawfully condemned and persecuted cannot regain the lost years of their life. It will, however, do its best to remove any shadow of the mistrust and humiliation to which the families and relatives of those affected were often subjected, and will resolutely ensure that such persecuted people have every opportunity of showing their worth in work, in public life, and in political activities. It goes without saying that even in carrying out full rehabilitation of people, we cannot change the consequences of revolutionary measures made in the past years in accordance with the spirit of class law aimed against the bourgeoisie, its property, economic, and social supports. The whole problem of the rectification of past repressions must be approached with the full responsibility of the state bodies concerned and based on legal regulations. The Central Committee of the Communist Party of Czechoslovakia supports the proposal that the procedure in these questions and the problems of legal consequences be incorporated in a *special law.*

A broad democratic concept of the *political and personal rights of citizens,* their legal and political safeguards, is considered by the Party to be a prerequisite for the necessary strengthening of social discipline and order, for a stabilization of socialist social relations. A selfish understanding of civil rights, an "I'm all right, Jack" attitude toward social property, the policy of placing one's particular interests over those of the whole society — all these are features which Communists will oppose with all their might.

The real purpose of democratization must be the achievement of better results in day to day work due to wider possibilities of purposeful activity and a concern for the interests and needs of the people. Democracy cannot be identified with empty speechmaking. It cannot stand in opposition to discipline, professionalism, and effectiveness of management. But arbitrariness and an obscure definition of rights and duties make such a development impossible. They lead to irresponsibility, to a feeling of uncertainty, and hence also to indifference towards public interests and needs. A more profound democracy and greater measure of civic freedoms will help socialism prove its superiority over limited bourgeois democracy and make it an attractive example for progressive movements even in industrially advanced countries with democratic traditions.

The Equality of Czechs and Slovaks Is the Basis for the Strength of the Republic

Our republic, as a joint state of two equal nations — Czechs and Slovaks — must continually check to be sure that the constitutional arrangement of relations between our fraternal nations and the status of all other nationalities of Czechoslovakia develop as required to strengthen the unity of the state, foster the development of the nations and nationalities themselves, and correspond to the needs of socialism. It cannot be denied that even in socialist Czechoslovakia, in spite of outstanding progress in solving the problem of nationalities, *there are serious faults and fundamental deformations* in the constitutional arrangement of relations between the Czechs and Slovaks.

Let it be stressed that the very asymmetrical arrangement was unsuited by its very character to express the relations between two independent nations, because it expressed the standings of the two nations differently. The difference was mainly in the fact that the Czech national bodies were identical with the central ones which, having jurisdiction over all the state, were superior to the Slovak national bodies. This prevented the Slovak nation, to all intents and purposes, from taking an equal share in the creation and realization of a country-wide policy. The objective shortcomings of such a solution were underlined by the existing political atmosphere and practice, which adversely affected the standing and activity of Slovak national bodies. Under such conditions, the activities of Slovak national bodies were weakened, both in the fifties and in the fundamental conception of the 1960 Constitution of the Czechoslovak Socialist Republic. Thus the Slovak national bodies found themselves in a position from which their influence on the state machinery could be only of peripheral importance. These shortcomings, especially in view of the unsound elements of the political atmosphere of the recent past could not be overcome even by the 1964 joint document of the Central Committee of the Communist Party of Czechoslovakia and the Central Committee of the Communist Party of Slovakia on a strengthening of the role of the Slovak National Council.

This development necessarily caused misunderstandings to arise between our two nations. In the Czech lands lack of national bodies made the Slovak national bodies seem superfluous. In Slovakia the people were convinced that it was not the Slovaks who governed their own house but that everything was decided in Prague.

In the interest of the development of our socialist society it is therefore absolutely necessary to strengthen the unity of the Czechoslovak people and their confidence in the policy of the Communist Party of Czechoslovakia, *to effect a crucial change in the constitutional arrangement of the relations between Czechs and Slovaks* and to carry out the necessary constitutional changes. It is essential to respect the advantage of a *socialist federal arrangement* as a recognized and well-tested legal state form of the coexistence of two equal nations in a common socialist state.

For reasons of organization, the final federative arrangement must be preceded, as an integral part and its developmental stage, by *the removal of the most flagrant shortcomings in the present unsatisfactory state of things* in the legal relations between the Czech and Slovak nations. It is therefore necessary *to draw up and pass a constitutional law* to embody the principle of a symmetrical arrangement as the goal to work toward after the 14th Congress. On the basis of full equality, this law will settle the status of Slovak national bodies in our constitutional system in the nearest future — before the elections to the National Assembly and the Slovak National Council. It will have to

• constitute *the Slovak National Council as a legislative body, the Slovak Council of Ministers as a collective executive body,* and ministries as individual executive organs of the Slovak National Council, widening the real powers of all these organs so that the division of legislative and executive powers between statewide and the Slovak bodies may essentially comply with the principles of the Košice government program;

• *entrust the management of national committees in Slovakia to Slovak national bodies* and, in connection with an efficient arrangement between the state center and the Slovak national bodies, set up a full-scale Slovak ministerial office for internal affairs and public security;

• *adjust the competence of Slovak national bodies so that they may draw up and approve an economic plan and budget for Slovakia* in all its items including the relevant economic tools. Set up a suitable structure of ministerial economic executive bodies in the Slovak National Council and modify the organizational pattern of the material and manufacturing base in Slovakia accordingly;

• *renew the institution of state secretaries* in central departments, especially in the ministries of foreign affairs, foreign trade and national defence, and make the secretaries members of the government;

• *exclude, politically and constitutionally, the possibility of outvoting the Slovak nation* in legal issues concerning relations between the Czechs and Slovaks and the constitutional status of Slovakia;

• in addition, outside the scope of the constitutional law, *effect in terms of concrete political practice the principle of equal rights of both nations in appointments to central bodies, diplomatic service, etc.*

In preparing the 14th Congress of the Party and the new constitution, it is necessary to submit a professionally and politically backed proposal for a constitutional arrangement of relations between our two nations that will fully express and guarantee their equality and right of self-determination. The same principles shall be applied to the pattern of the Party and social organizations.

In the interests of strengthening the unity, coherence and *national individuality of all nationalities in Czechoslovakia — of Hungarians, Poles, Ukrainians, and Germans —* it is indispensable to work out a statute stipulating the status and rights of the various nationalities, guaranteeing the future of their national life and the development of their national individuality. The Central Committee of the Communist Party of Czechoslovakia realizes that, in spite of indisputable achievements in solving the problems of nationalities, serious shortcomings exist. We deem it necessary to stress that the principles of our program with respect to our two nations extend also to other nationalities. To that end, it is necessary to stipulate constitutional and legal guarantees of a complete and real political, economic, and cultural equality. The interests of nationalities will also have to be safeguarded from the point of view of the pattern of state, regional, district, municipal, and local organs of state power and administration. It is necessary to see that the nationalities are represented, in proportion to their numbers, in our political, economic, cultural, and public life, in elected and executive bodies. Active participation of the nationalities in public life must be ensured in the spirit of equality of rights and according to the principle that the nationalities have the right to independence and self-administration in provinces that concern them.

The Power of Elected Bodies Emanates from the Will of the Voters

With the coming *elections* begins the onset of implementation of the principles of this Action Program in the work of the elected bodies of the state.

Although efforts were made in the past few months to improve the preparation for elections, it proved to be impossible to have the elections organized by the originally proposed deadline if we wished to meet the requirements of the principles of an advanced socialist democracy. It is therefore necessary to work out an electoral system that will take the changes in our political life into account. An electoral law must lay down exactly and clearly democratic principles for the preparation of the elections, the proposal of candidates and the method of their election. The changes in the electoral system must be based, in particular, on the new political status of the National Front and the elected bodies themselves.

The *national committees* make up the backbone of the whole network of representative bodies in our country, the democratic organs of state power. It must be in the national committees that state policy is formed, especially in districts and regions. In their work the principle of socialist democracy is to be fully applied. The various interests and requirements of the people must be expressed and united in the general, public interest of communities, townships, districts, and regions.

The Party regards the national committees as bodies that have to carry on *the progressive traditions of local government and people's self-administration*. They must not be taken for local bureaucratic offices supervising local enterprises. The essential political mission of national committees is to protect the rights and needs of the people, to simplify the process of settling all matters with which the people turn to the national committee, to pursue public interest and oppose efforts of some institutions to dupe the people and ignore their requirements.

The Party regards the National Assembly as a socialist parliament with all the scope for activities the parliament of a democratic republic must have. The Communist deputies must see to it that the National Assembly draws up a number of concrete measures before the new electoral period, measures that will put into actual practice the constitutional status of the National Assembly as the supreme organ of state power in the Czechoslovak Socialist Republic. It is necessary to overcome formalism in negotiations and the unconvincing unanimity concealing factual differences in opinions and attitudes of the deputies. From this point of view it is necessary to settle, as soon as possible, the relations between the National Assembly and Party bodies and a number of problems regarding internal activities of the National Assembly, particularly those of organization and competence. The result must be a National Assembly which actually decides on laws and important political issues, and not only approves proposals submitted. The Party supports a strengthening of the controlling function of the National Assembly in our entire public life and, more concretely, with respect to the government. The controlling machinery must be in the hands of the National Assembly, which will establish it as its own body. Together with closer bonds between the National Assembly and our public opinion, all of this may, in a short time, increase the role and the prestige of the National Assembly in our society.

Separation and Control of Power: Guarantee against Highhandedness

The Communists in the government, too, must ensure as soon as possible that the principle of responsibility of the government towards the National Assembly covering all its activities is worked out in detail. Even under the existing practice of political management, the opportunity afforded for independent activity of the government and of individual ministers was not sufficiently made use of; there was a tendency to shift responsibility on to the Party bodies and to evade independence in decision-making. The government is not only an organ of economic policy. As the supreme executive organ of the state it must, as a whole, deal systematically with the whole scope of political and administrative problems of the state. It is also up to the government to take care of the rational development of the whole state machinery. The state administration machinery was often underrated in the past. This machinery must consist of highly qualified people, professionally competent and rationally organized, it must be subject to systematic, democratic supervision; and it must be effective. The oversimplified idea that these could be attained by underrating and decrying the administrative machinery in general has done more harm than good.

Within the whole state and political system, it is necessary for us to create such relations and rules that would, on the one hand, provide *the necessary safeguards to professional officials* in their functions and, on the other hand, enable *the necessary replacement of officials* who can no longer cope with their work by professionally and politically more competent people. This means establishing legal conditions for the recall of responsible officials and providing legal guarantees of decent conditions for those who are leaving their posts through the normal way of replacement, so that their departure does not amount to a "drop" in their material and moral-political standing.

The Party policy is based on the principle that no undue concentration of power must occur, throughout the state machinery, in one sector, one body, or in a single individual. It is necessary to provide for such a division of power and a system of mutual supervision that can rectify the faults or encroachments of any of its links with the activities of another link. This principle must be applied not only to relations between the elected and executive bodies, but also to the inner relations of the state administration machinery and to the standing and activities of courts of law.

These principles have been infringed mainly by undue concentration of duties in the existing ministry of the interior. The Party thinks it necessary to turn it into a department for internal state administration, to which the administration of public security also belongs. All those areas in our state which were traditionally within the jurisdiction of other bodies and with the passage of time have been incorporated into the ministry of the interior must be withdrawn from it. It is necessary to elaborate proposals as soon as possible to transfer the main responsibility for investigation to the courts of law, separating prison administration from the security force, and hand over the administration of press law, archives, etc., to other state bodies.

The Party considers the problem of a correct incorporation of the security force in the state as politically very important. The security of our lives will only benefit, if everything is eliminated that helps to maintain a public view of the security force marred in the past period by violations of law and by the privileged position of the security force in the political system. That past period impaired the progressive traditions of our security force as a force advancing side by side with our people. These traditions must be renewed. The Central Committee of the Communist Party of Czechoslovakia deems it necessary *to change the organization of the security force* and to split the joint organization into two mutually independent parts — State Security and Public Security. *The State Security* service must have the status, organizational structure, men, equipment, methods, and qualifications which are in keeping with its work of defending the state from the activities of enemy centers abroad. Every citizen who has not been culpable in this respect must know with certainty that his political convictions and opinions, his personal beliefs and activities, cannot be the object of attention of the bodies of the State Security service. The Party declares clearly that this apparatus *should not be directed toward or used to solve internal political questions* and controversies in socialist society.

The Public Security service will combat crime and keep public order. It is to this end its organization, men, and methods must be adapted. The Public Security force must be better equipped and strengthened; its precise functions in the defense of public order must be laid down by law and will be directed by the national committees. Legal norms must create clearer relations of control over the security force by the government as a whole and by the National Assembly.

It is necessary to devote the appropriate care to carrying out *the defense policy in our state.* In this connection it is necessary to work for our active share in the conception of the military doctrine of the Warsaw Treaty countries, strengthening the defense potential of our country in harmony with its needs and possibilities, a uniform complex understanding of the problems of defense and all problems of the building of socialism in all our policy, including defense training.

The legal policy of the Party is based on the principle that in a dispute over rights (including administrative decisions of state bodies) the basic guarantee of legality is proceedings in court which are independent of political factors and are bound only by law. The application of this principle requires a strengthening of the whole social and political role and importance of courts of law in our society. The Central Committee of the Communist Party of

Czechoslovakia will see to it that work on the complex of the required proposals and measures proceeds so as to find the answer to all the necessary problems before the next election of judges. In harmony with and parallel to that, it is also necessary to settle the status and duties of the public prosecutor's office so that it may not be put above the courts of law, and to guarantee full independance of lawyers from state bodies.

Youth and Its Organization

We regard young people as those who are to continue the socialist transformation of society. Present political activity and the part young people are taking in the revival process prove that the reproaches often leveled against them are without any foundation. A decisive part of the working and student youth is, thanks to its energy, critical approach, matter-of-factness, and initiation, a natural ally and important factor in the creation and implementation of the program aims of the Party. For this reason, it is indispensable *to open wide and confidently the doors of our Party to young people.*

At the same time it is necessary to give young people of all social categories, according to their age and abilities, the opportunity to have a voice in all their own and public matters in elected bodies; their organizations should be recognized as partners of Party and social organizations, economic bodies, national committees, and administration of schools in solving social, working, study, and other urgent problems of youth and children. Young people must be given an opportunity to apply their knowledge, qualifications, and talents in appropriate places — including leading positions. Cultural, sporting and recreation facilities must be built with their cooperation so that they may spend their leisure time in a healthy and effective way. The work of voluntary and professional trainers, coaches, instructors, and other workers who sacrifice their time and devote their abilities to children and youth must be regarded as socially highly beneficial and praiseworthy.

In this connection, let us say *a few words of self-criticism on the relations of the Party and the Czechoslovak Union of Youth.* Until recently, we expected the latter or its representatives to pass on to the young people more or less ready-made instructions, often the result of subjective opinions, which tactlessly interfered with the internal affairs of the youth organization. We did not sufficiently encourage young Communists to take part in the creation of Party policies by making them consistently defend, develop, and express the interests, needs, requirements, and viewpoints of the youth as a whole and of its individual categories. Thus the initiative of the youth and the role of its organization were impaired in public and political life. This tendency was exacerbated by the incorrect principle of direct Party control of the Czechoslovak Union of Youth.

However, the independence of the youth and children's movement does not eliminate, but in fact presupposes ideological guiding, a systematic interest of the whole Party in the problems of youth and of children's education, the practical assistance of Communists in children's and young people's collectives and tactful attention to young people in everyday life.

The multiformity of needs, interests and frequently changing inclinations of young people, increased many times over by variations in age, social strata, qualifications, etc., require *a diversified and well-differentiated organization of children and young people.* Apart from partial interests and inclinations of the moment among various categories of young people, there are pressing immediate and prospective needs and interests affecting the whole younger generation, which can be expressed and pushed through only by *joint action of all the important youth categories; this calls for a suitable form of organization and social representation of young people.* We are of the opinion, without, of course, wanting to prescribe any pattern of youth organization, that a form of federation would be most fitting for the present needs and situation of youth and children's movements.

To a great extent it is up to the present officials of the Czechoslovak Union of Youth and of other social organizations to assist in this process, to prevent both the suppression and unnecessary diversification of the sound initiative of young people, to make good use of all their experience and all possible opportunities in the search for the optimum development of our socialist youth and children's movement.

The National Economy and the Standard of Living

The 13th Congress approved conclusions stating that the improvement of our economy and the transition to intensive economic development cannot be achieved by traditional approaches or partial improvements of the directive system of management and planning, that a basic change of the machinery of socialist economy would be necessary. The idea which prevailed was the idea of an economic reform based on a new economic system, the revival of the positive functions of the socialist market, necessary structural changes of the economy and a profound change in the role of the economic plan which would cease to be an instrument for issuing orders and would become an instrument enabling society to find the most suitable long-range trends of its development by scientific methods; a change from an instrument designed to enforce subjectively determined material proportions to a program of economic policy, ensuring an effective development of the economy and the growth of the standard of living. The implementation of the first important steps of the economic reform has met with the active support of the working people, experts and the broad public.

Certain features of the economic development over the past two years, better utilization of production factors, a drop in the share of material costs in the social product, the growing demands placed by consumers on the technical level and the quality of products, etc., fully confirm the validity of the conclusions adopted by the 13th Congress. These positive features of economic development have not yet begun to better satisfy the needs of society or reduce the tension in the internal market because former tendencies are still strongly apparent, the old structure of production and foreign trade still survives, and adaptation of production to the changes and growing demands of the market is moving forward very slowly. This is connected with many inconsistencies and gaps in implementing the program of economic reform.

Instead of a consistent effort to establish more objective market criteria which would expose the economic backwardness and old deformations of the economic structure and gradually eliminate their existence, there are still considerable efforts to deform these criteria, to adapt them to the given conditions and thus create a situation in which the backwardness and the deformations would remain concealed, could survive and thrive at the expense of us all.

The system of protectionism — furthering economic backwardness, and maintained by our policy of prices, subsidies, and grants and by the system of surcharges in foreign trade — continues to prevail in our economic policy. This confused system of protectionism creates conditions under which ineffective, poorly managed, backward enterprises may not only exist but are often given preferences. *It is not possible to blunt the economic policy for ever by taking from those who work well and giving to those who work badly.* It is therefore necessary to be objective about value relations. Differences in income between enterprises should reflect actual differences in the level of their economic activities. *Nor is it politically correct for the consumer to pay indefinitely for inefficiency either directly in high prices and taxes or indirectly by different forms of siphoning off material from efficient enterprises.*

Enterprises facing a demanding market must be given a free hand in making decisions on all questions directly concerning the management of the enterprise and its economy and must be allowed to react in a creative way to the needs of the market. A demanding market, together with sound economic policy, will thus put pressure on production to become more effective and to introduce healthy structural changes. Economic competition, especially with advanced foreign firms, must be the basic stimulus for improving production and reducing costs. This competition cannot be replaced by subjective adjustments of economic conditions and by directive orders of superior bodies.

Socialism Cannot Do Without Enterprising

The democratization program in economy links economic reform more closely with the processes facing us in the sphere of politics and the general management of society, and stimulates the determination and application of new elements to develop the economic reform even further. *The democratization program of the economy places special emphasis on ensuring the independence of enterprises and enterprise groupings and their relative independence from state bodies, the full implementation of the right of the consumer to determine his consumption and his style of life, the right of a free choice of working activity, the right and real possibility of various groups of the working people and different social groups to formulate and defend their economic interests in shaping the economic policy.*

In developing democratic relations in the economy we at present consider as the most important task the final formulation of the economic position of enterprises, their authority and responsibility.

The economic reform will increasingly push whole working teams of socialist enterprises into positions in which they will directly feel the consequences of both good and bad management. The Party therefore deems it necessary that the whole working team which bears the consequences should be allowed to influence the management of the enterprise. We must set up democratic bodies in enterprises and vest them with limited rights with respect to the management of the enterprise. Managers and head executives of the enterprises, which would also appoint them to their functions, would be accountable to them for the overall results of their work. These bodies must become a direct part of the managing mechanism of enterprises, and not a social organization (they cannot therefore be identified with trade unions). They would be made up of elected representatives of the working team and representatives of certain components outside the enterprise, thereby ensuring the influence of the interests of the entire society and an expert and qualified level of decision-making; the representation of these components must also be subordinated to democratic forms of control. It is likewise necessary for us to define the degree of responsibility of these bodies for the results of the management of socialist property. These principles raise many concrete questions; at the same time it will be necessary to propose a set of by-laws to cover them, using certain traditions of our factory councils from the years 1945–48 and experiences in modern enterprising.

This naturally in no way reduces the indivisible authority and responsibility of the leading executives in managing the enterprise which, together with their qualifications and managing abilities, is the basic precondition of successful enterprising.

In this connection it is also necessary to reassess the present role of trade unions. In the centralized system, their function of supporting directive management coincided with defending the interests of the working people. Moreover, they also performed certain state functions (e.g., labor legislation). The resulting situation was that on the one hand they took inadequate care of the interests of the working people and on the other they were accused of "protectionism." Even a socialist economy places working people in a position in which it is necessary to defend human, social and other interests in an organized way. The central function of trade unions should be to defend the professional interests of the workers and the working people, and act as an important partner in solving all questions of economic management; on this platform, the trade unions would be more effective in developing their function of organizing workers and employees for a positive solution of the problems of socialist construction and their educational function connected therewith. Communists in trade unions will take these principles into account and take the initiative to ensure that the trade unions themselves analyze their position and the functions and activities of the central and union bodies on the basis of the whole Action Program of the Party, that they evaluate the internal life of trade unions as an independent democratic organization and work out their own political line in solving these questions.

The enterprise must have the right to choose its organizational pattern. Supra-enterprise bodies (like the present general and branch managements) cannot be imbued with State administrative power. The individual branches, with due regard to their conditions, must be transformed into voluntary associations, on the basis of the economic interest and enterprise requirements. Enterprises must have the right to decide the activities of these associations, the right to leave them and become independent and to join associations which will better ensure the functions resulting from the concentration and specialization of production and integration processes.

The withdrawal of enterprises from the existing supra-enterprise agglomerations and their free association cannot begin before the rules for this process are outlined by the government. During the transition period it will be necessary to ensure that even after becoming independent the enterprises will fulfill precisely predetermined financial and cooperation obligations which result from their previous membership in the supra-enterprise body.

It is necessary to put an end to the previous simplified, schematic approach to formulating the organizational structure of production and trade. The structure of enterprises must be varied, just as are the demands of our market. It is therefore necessary to take into account the development of small and medium-sized socialist enterprises, whose importance lies first and foremost in competitive production, a fast supply of new items to the market and in a flexible reaction to different customer demands. In the development of the organizational structure of production and trade it is necessary to open up scope for economic competition among enterprises of all sorts and forms of enterprising, above all in the production and supply of consumer goods and foodstuffs.

Agricultural production contributes to a great extent to the consolidation of our national economy. The latest period and particularly the future needs of the economy clearly emphasize this positive role of agriculture. Agriculture should develop in such a way as to gradually ensure a rational structure of nutrition to the population. This is why the Party considers it necessary to raise and concentrate the aid of the State and of all branches, especially the chemical and engineering industry, in ensuring the growth of crop and animal production. This is and continues to be the foremost task of our economic policy.

Cooperative enterprises in agricultural production are of exceptional importance for the development of our economy. The Party supports the conclusions of the Seventh Congress of Unified Agricultural Cooperatives, particularly the creation of a national organization of cooperative farmers, the right of unified agricultural cooperatives to do business also in other branches and the possibility of selling part of farm products directly to the population and to retailers. The State bodies will help to ensure all-year employment for the farming population.

The Party considers the development of agricultural production in cooperatives and in State farms to be the decisive line of large-scale production in agriculture. It would be expedient for Communists to prepare proposals which will develop new forms of closer contact between agricultural producers and supply and sales organizations of agricultural products so that these new forms may ensure direct contact of agricultural production with suppliers and the market and would be to a certain extent similar to the former farm cooperatives.

We shall support the development of different forms of credit for farming and recommend that the whole credit system in the agricultural economy be reexamined. At the same time, the Central Committee recommends that agricultural and other State managing bodies seek and support other forms of enterprise in utilizing land in mountainous, hilly and border regions. In the border regions it is necessary to strive for the creation of further suitable conditions designed to intensify economic activities, i.e., to make better use of existing small workshops, to extend recreation possibilities and engage in further capital construction. This should help stabilize the settlement of the border regions and normalize their life. Even though the production of individual farmers constitutes a relatively small part of overall production, it is important to facilitate their work, improve their economic conditions and aid their cooperation with cooperative and State enterprises.

In keeping with the proposals made at the 13th Congress of the Communist Party of Czechoslovakia, it is also necessary to create possibilities for cooperative enterprising wherever cooperatives earn the money for their activity. It will be expedient to make individual cooperatives independent economic and social organizations with full rights, abolish the impractical administrative centralization of cooperatives and create only such bodies over cooperative enterprises whose economic activity is advantageous for them. In connection with the development of cooperative enterprises, it appears to be expedient to elaborate more thoroughly the co-ownership relations between cooperative farmers and cooperative property.

A serious shortcoming in our economic life has long been the low standard and shortage of services of all sorts which reduces the standard of living and arouses justified discontent among the population. The improvement of communal services (water, gas, sewerage, municipal transportation, road cleaning, etc.) will require considerable investments and can be achieved only gradually if their profitability is to be ensured. The unsatisfactory state existing in other services is caused by the way they are organized and administered, by low interest of the workers in their economic result, by the fact that certain services are unprofitable, by bad supplies of material, and low and poor investments.

Neither the standard of productive forces, nor the character of work in services, repairs and artisan production warrants the present high degree of centralization in their management and organization which involves quite unnecessary administration and burdens the services with inexpedient costs. This is why it is necessary to take immediate measures for improving and extending all existing forms of services (cooperatives, communal enterprises) and simplify their management and organization in the spirit of the principles of the new system. In the sphere of services it is particularly justified to make individual shops independent and to remove unnecessary administrative links of management. Small-scale individual enterprising is also justified in the sphere of services. In this respect it is necessary to work out legal provisions concerning small-scale enterprises, which would help fill the existing gap in our market.

The Role of the State in Economy

Spreading social wealth is the concern of our entire society. The actual tasks and responsibility fall both on enterprises and on managing bodies, particularly on the government. It is therefore in their common interest to make use of the growing political activity of the working people, which has been taking place since the December and January plenums of the Central Committee, and to win them over to the path leading toward the consolidation of the national economy.

To achieve this it is necessary to recast the entire organism which implements the economic policy of the State. The appropriate organizational questions must be solved by State and economic bodies. The Party considers it desirable that the final setup should correspond to the following principles:

Decision-making about the plan and the economic policy of the State must be both a process of mutual confrontation and harmonization of different interests — i.e., the interests of enterprises, consumers, employees, different social groups of the population, nations, etc. — and a process of a suitable combination of the long-term development of the economy and its immediate prosperity. Effective measures protecting the consumer against the abuse of the monopoly position and economic power of production and trading enterprises must be considered as a necessary part of the economic activity of the State.

The drafting of the national economic plan and the national economic policy must be subject to democratic control of the National Assembly and specialized control of scientific institutions. The supreme body implementing the economic policy of the State is the government. This presupposes an institutional setup of central management which enables the decision-making process to express and unify special interests and views and to harmonize the operation of individual economic instruments and measures of the State in the implementation of the economic policy. At the same time, the institutional setup of the bodies of economic management must not allow opportunities for the assertion of departmental and monopoly interests and must ensure a marked superiority of the interests of citizens as consumers and sovereign bearers of the economic movement. In all central economic bodies it is indispensable to ensure a high level of specialization, rationalization and modernization of managerial work, even if changes in cadres are required to do so. All this must be the concern of the government bodies which analyze the national economy, work on alternative solutions of its development and that of the national economic plan, compare planned development with actual market development, and proceeding from these findings, take effective economic measures etc., and thus consistently and purposefully influence the real course of economic development (i.e., the activity of enterprises and their associations) in the direction outlined by the economic policy of the State. State bodies approach enterprises and their associations and integrated groups in the same way as they approach other independent legal subjects. The means at the disposal of the State are the result of the work of all the people and must be used for satisfying the needs of the entire society in a way which society recognizes to be reasonable and useful.

An important part of economic management must be a well-conceived technical policy based on an analysis of world-wide technical progress and its own conceptions of economic development. The purpose of this policy will be to regulate the technical level of the production base and to create economic conditions which would arouse strong interest in seeking out and using the most up-to-date technology.

In this connection it would be useful for the State bodies concerned to examine all kinds of public expenditures and for the government to work out a program of State and public measures designed to reduce them. The State budget must become an instrument for restoring the equilibrium and not for its weakening. The Central Committee considers it necessary and possible to reveal and reasonably utilize extraordinary internal and external resources for achieving a speedy restoration of the economic equilibrium.

At the same time, the Central Committee appeals to all enterprises, their associations, plants and workshops to work out and implement, using their enhanced economic authority, a program for rationalizing all managing, production and business activity, in order to ensure their smooth running and reduce production costs. Such a program is the precondition for an economic evaluation of existing capacities and for technical modernization of production.

We are putting great hope into reviving the positive functions of the market as a necessary mechanism of the functioning of socialist economy and for checking whether the work in enterprises has been expended in a socially useful way. However, we have in mind not the capitalist, but the socialist market, and not its uncontrolled but its regulated utilization. The plan and the national economic policy must appear as a positive force contributing to the normalization of the market and directed against tendencies of economic imbalance and against monopolistic control of the market. Society must plan with due insight and perspective, it must use science to work out the possibilities of its future development and choose its most reasonable orientation. This, however, cannot be achieved by suppressing the independence of other subjects of the market (enterprises and the population), since this would on the one hand undermine the interest ensuring economic rationality and on the other deform information and decision-making processes which are indispensably necessary for the functioning of the economy.

The economic structure of Czechoslovakia, its technical standard, concentration and specialization must be developed in a way enabling it to react quickly to economic changes at home and in the world.

The level of the adaptability and flexibility of the national economy is also the result of the skill and the technical and cultural standard of the working people, their ability to adapt themselves quickly to the changing technical and economic conditions of production. From the point of view of the resources for economic growth in Czechoslovakia, manpower, its abilities and quality, technical and cultural standard as well as its adaptability and mobility, are of quite exceptional importance. Even from the point of view of future economic growth, the Czechoslovak economy does not possess more promising resources than its great human resources. Czech and Slovak workers and farmers have always been known for their know-how, their skill and creative approach to work. As a result of the directive method of management, the new generation has only partly taken over these qualities from the older generation. Instead of a feeling of satisfaction from well done work, this directive system encouraged indifference, mechanical fulfillment of tasks, and resignation to situations caused by management incompetent and without initiative. The Party believes that the prime condition for eliminating these losses is to give leading positions to people who are really capable and who are able to secure natural authority in working teams by their professional and human level.

More Effective Participation in International Division of Labor

Experience resulting from our economic units' many years of isolation from the competitive pressure of the world market has clearly shown that such isolation creates exceptional conditions for the activity of economic units, conditions causing a relative lagging behind in rate of technical progress and in structural economic changes that this progress creates, a loss in competitiveness of our products on the world market and undue tension in external trade and payment relations. The limited raw material base of our economy and the limited size of the home market make it impossible to implement the changes in the material base of production brought about by the scientific and technical revolution without widely integrating our economy into the developing international division of labor.

The development of international economic relations will continue to be based on economic cooperation with the Soviet Union and the other socialist countries, particularly those aligned in the Council of Mutual Economic Assistance. It should be understood, however, that the success of this cooperation will increasingly depend on the competitiveness of our products. The position of our country in the development of the international division of labor will strengthen with the more general convertibility of our products. In our relations with the CMEA countries we shall strive for the fuller application of criteria of economic calculations and mutual advantage of exchange.

We shall also actively support the development of economic relations with all other countries in the world which show interest in such relations on the basis of equality, mutual advantages and without discrimination. We support the development of progressive forms of international collaboration, especially cooperation in production and in the pre-production stage, the exchange of scientific and technical know-how, business in licenses and suitable forms of credit and capital cooperation with interested countries.

Opening our economy to the pressure of the world market makes it continually necessary to rid the foreign trade monopoly of administrative conceptions and methods and to eliminate directive management in foreign trade transactions. In this sphere, the Central Committee considers it necessary to carry on an effective State commercial and currency policy, based on economic rules and instruments of indirect management.

The Central Committee considers it indispensable to raise the authority and responsibility of enterprises in the concrete implementation of international economic relations. Production and trading enterprises must have the right to choose their export and import organizations. At the same time it is necessary to formulate conditions which would entitle enterprises to act independently on foreign markets.

Our economy's many years of isolation from world markets has divorced home trade price relations from price relations in the world market. Because of this situation, we consider it necessary to enforce a policy of bringing the home and world market prices gradually closer together. In practice this means a more energetic policy of removing various surcharges and subsidies from prices of the foreign market. Enterprises must be aware that it is only temporary protection they are receiving from the State and that they cannot count on it indefinitely. They must therefore work out a program of changes in production which will enable them in the next few years to do without subsidies and surcharges. Another side of this policy of eliminating price surcharges and subsidies must be a more broad-minded approach to those branches and enterprises in the national economy which from the point of view of the national economy are capable of selling their products effectively in foreign markets. The Party considers it expedient to speed up the necessary changes in the present system of price relations and put them gradually in order both by the pressure of the market forces and by creating a proper rational price system based on a well-conceived state economic policy. This policy must be accompanied by energetic measures designed to ensure the internal stability of the currency. This presupposes the production of effective and good-quality stocks of products marketable in foreign markets, achievement of equilibrium in the internal market of commodities, money and labor, an effective restrictive investment policy, achievement of equilibrium in our balance of payments and creation of necessary currency reserves.

The phased opening of our economy to the world market, the final aim of which is to create conditions for the convertibility of our currency, must be carried out to an extent that would not cause too many social problems nor endanger the growth of the standard of living. However, it must be realized that we are living in conditions of sharp competition and that every concession today will worsen the prerequisites of effective economic development and of the growth of the standard of living in the future.

Problems of the Standard of Living — An Urgent Task of the Economic Policy

The basic aim of the Party in developing the economic policy is the steady growth of the standard of living. However, the development of the economy in the past has been one-sidedly focused on the growth of heavy industry with long-term returnability of investments. This was done to a considerable extent at the expense of the development of agriculture and consumer goods industries, the development of the production of building materials, trade, services and non-productive basic assets, particularly in housing construction. This one-sided character of our economic development cannot be changed overnight. If, however, we take advantage of the great reserve existing in the organization of production and work, as well as in the technical and economic standard of production and products, if we consider the possibilities offered by a skillful utilization of the new system of management, we can substantially speed up the creation of resources and on this basis raise the growth of nominal wages and the general standard of living.

As far as the growth of the standard of living, special emphasis must be placed on the growth of wages and salaries. However, the growth of average wages and salaries cannot be speeded up in such a way that enterprises will raise wages regardless of the real economic results. It will be continually necessary to apply the principle that the development of wages depends on finished products which have proven their social value. The methods of influencing the development of wages will have to take this into account. In keeping with the growth of wages in production, it is at the same time necessary to ensure the growth of wages in education, health services, and other non-productive branches.

The present system of retail prices is markedly divorced from the costs of production, gives an incorrect orientation to the structure of personal consumption of the population — including the consumption of food — and reduces the possible degree of satisfying their requirements. Under these conditions, we must do much more to remove existing disproportions in prices so as to create prerequisites for a faster growth of the standard of living. The solution of these questions will require shifts in prices of individual products and their groups — the prices of some articles will have to be raised; the prices of others will have to be reduced. Rational price relations cannot be fixed and proclaimed by a State authority; it is necessary to enable market forces to influence their creation. This naturally involves a certain risk that changes in price relations will occur with a certain growth in the level of prices, because in the situation we have taken over from the directive system of management over-all demand is greater than supply. While opening up the required scope to internal price shifts, the central bodies must therefore regulate general economic relations so as to ensure an excessive growth of the price level and prevent the growth of real wages by at least 2.5–3 per cent per year.

It is impossible in the near future to effect a substantial raise in claims for appropriations from social funds, since this could not be done without substantially weakening remunerations for work. However, in the spirit of the resolution adopted by the plenary meeting of the Central Committee of the Communist Party of Czechoslovakia in December 1967, it is possible to solve the most urgent problems of social policy, such as the raising of low pensions, the extension of paid maternity leave and aid to families with children. It is also possible to outline the principle that social pensions will grow in keeping with the growth of the cost of living. The Central Committee demands that State bodies ensure the removal of obstacles which weaken the interest of citizens in permanently continuing active work after qualifying for old age pensions. We also want to examine the justification of certain measures carried out in connection with the reorganization of the social security system in 1964 (e.g., taxation of pensions and the possibility of its gradual removal, introduction of a higher base for granting scholarships, etc.). We consider it necessary to raise the social security allowances of those who participated in the national struggle for liberation. We shall also elaborate the conception and the further course of improving the wage tax system so that after 1970 we can make fairer decisions concerning the taxation of women, mothers, and persons who have brought up children and further strengthen measures promoting a more favorable population development.

An important factor in determining standard of living and style of life is health care. In our society, we have introduced a number of measures in health care which capitalism was unable to develop. However, there are still many untapped possibilities, both in the organization of health care and of spa services as well as in the working conditions of doctors and health personnel. The Central Committee appeals to Communists in the health services and to other health workers to take the initiative and submit proposals designed to solve the problems which unnecessarily embitter citizens and health workers and which are the result of bureaucratic methods in medical care.

From the point of view of preventive care designed to strengthen the health of the people — particularly children and youth — and the effective use of spare time, we consider it indispensable to duly appreciate the social importance of all forms of physical and military training and recreation. We are in this respect expecting a principled stand from the government and the educational administration as well as initiative from social organizations.

An important qualitative aspect of the standard of living will be the general introduction of a five-day working week, for which it is necessary to create technological, organizational, economic and political conditions in order to enable its operation by the end of 1968.

It is a serious shortcoming that the housing construction program was not carried out in past years. At present we regard the solution of housing construction problems as essential for the standard of living. We consider it necessary to concentrate forces in this sphere and secure the necessary support of the government and of State bodies for substantially raising the annual number of flats built by building organizations and for utilizing the initiative of the population in building family houses. At the same time, we must work out a long-term housing policy to correspond to changing social conditions, which will gain the confidence and support of the population, promote the interest of citizens in building and modernizing flats, and influence the development of the material basis and capacity of the building industry. For a transitional period it also will be expedient to endeavor to employ building organizations and manpower of other countries and concentrate construction in places where the need is most urgent.

It is characteristic of the bureaucratic and centralist tendencies applied over and over again in our life in the past that one of the places most affected by insensibility toward people is the center of our Republic—Prague. The capital city, with its experienced and highly qualified cadres of workers, technicians, scientists, artists, organizers of socialist construction and which boasts an immense wealth of monuments and cultural values, has paid dearly for sectarianism in economy and politics, for the low standard of responsible officials. Its facilities and amenities are not in keeping with its social functions, growing tourism and the requirements of the life of its inhabitants. It is indisputably necessary to speed up housing construction in the capital and, in addition, to concentrate efforts on at least some of the other problems which annoy the people in Prague most: municipal and suburban transportation facilities and keeping the city clean. We must also solve the problems of the capital city of Slovakia–Bratislava. We must see to it that as many children as possible from these cities spend their holidays outside the capital in view of the present lack of adequate recreation facilities in Prague.

The Central Committee is of the opinion that despite the faster growth of the standard of living, neither present results nor even these measures meet existing needs. Nor do they correspond to our real economic possibilities; however, the low effectiveness of our economy is creating barriers which in the process of the further satisfaction of personal and social needs can be overcome only by efforts to mobilize the reserves and to develop resources in production. The elimination of the shortcomings in economy will require time. But we are convinced that consistent implementation of the economic reform and activation of all Communists and nonparty members will enable our country to embark upon the road of a fast, modern development of the economy.

Rational Utilization of Resources in Slovakia
Will Lead to the Prosperity of the Republic

The economy of the Czechoslovak Socialist Republic is the integration of two national economies which makes it possible to multiply the economic potential of our entire society. This is contingent on a rational utilization of the resources and growth of the reserves of both our national political regions in the interest of an effective development of the Czechoslovak national economy as well as on the creation of a social and economic balance between the various regions. The new constitutional setup must firmly rely on the integration base and further integration tendencies in the economy of the entire State.

The past development of Slovakia within the unified Czechoslovak economy was marked by major changes in the economic and living standard. Slovakia has become an industrially advanced, agriculturally developed part of the Republic. For further development of an integrated Czechoslovak economy it is not important to make partial adjustments. We must work out the rational integration of the national political regions into the economic complex of the entire State.

However, the undeniable achievements were accompanied by the emergence of serious problems. Although Slovakia's share in the creation of the national income increased from 14.2 per cent in 1948 to 24.4 per cent in 1965, it is not adequate when compared with the possibilities of growth which exist in Slovakia: favorable geographic position, qualitative changes in the fund of manpower, possibilities of space concentration, new basis of chemistry, metallurgy, fuels and power, agriculture, natural resources.

The process of creating a balanced social and economic level between Slovakia and the Czech lands is characterized by internal contradictions. An undeniable success of Party policy has been elimination of social and economic backwardness and a decrease of relative per capita differences. However, the faster rate of growth has not been sufficient to reduce absolute differences. The process of creating a balanced level was not based on the conception of the economic effectiveness of the development of the Czechoslovak economy.

The existing problems are caused mainly by the fact that the extensive economic growth of the Czechoslovak Socialist Republic was also enforced in the economic development of Slovakia. A potential source of growth was not used rationally, either in industry or in agriculture. The tertiary sphere, particularly the build-up of scientific research and development bases, has lagged greatly behind. Slovakia's development was not sufficiently coordinated; it proceeded along departmental lines, without the internal integration relations of modern entities.

The intensive development of Slovakia's economy is contingent on a complex of measures connected with the solution of short-term factual problems, the clarification of conceptual questions of long-term development, the effective operation of the new system of management and the definition of the competence and authority of the Slovak national bodies.

The measures designed to speed up Slovakia's economic development by 1970 constitute the starting point for a fundamental change in Slovakia's integration into the process of transition of the Czechoslovak economy to the road of intensive growth. At the same time it is necessary to seek possibilities of solving acute problems: employment, the lagging behind of micro-regions with special regard to those which are inhabited by Hungarian and Ukrainian fellow-citizens, specific problems of the standard of living, particularly the housing problem, etc.

It is of decisive importance for Slovakia's long term economic development to raise substantially Slovakia's participation in the creation and the utilization of the national income and to solve the task of creating a balanced economic level by 1980.

This necessitates faster economic development in Slovakia than the national average, and we must therefore give strong support to progressive structural changes, intensify agricultural production and the interconnected processing industry, develop the tertiary sector in all spheres, purposefully concentrate production and the infra-structure.

The development of Slovakia is taking place within the new system of management. However, this system in its present form has not created scope for the development policy of national political regions. Past adjustments of the plan and of economic instruments are not sufficient. It is therefore necessary to elaborate the system of management in such a way as to ensure that territorial and national aspects of development also become equal organic components of the system of management of the entire economy.

The Development of Science, Education, and Culture

At the present stage we must base the development of our society to a much greater extent on the progress and application of science, education, and culture. Their wealth must be used fully and completely to the benefit of socialism, and our people should understand the complicated claims connected with creative work in these spheres.

The Importance of Science in Our Society Is Growing

Socialism originates, holds out and wins by combining the working movement with science. There is no relationship of subordination and compromise between these forces. The more resolute and impartial the advancement of science, the more it is in harmony with the interests of socialism; the greater the achievements of the working people, the bigger is the scope opened to science. The development and application of science to the life of socialist society shows how much the working people are aware of their historical tasks, to what extent they really enforce them. Socialism stands and falls with science, just as it stands and falls with the power of the working people.

Just now, at the beginning of the scientific-technological revolution in the world, the social position of science is changing considerably. Its application to the entire life of society is becoming the basic condition for the intensive development of the economy, care for man and his living environment, culture of the society and growth of the personality, modern methods of management and administration, the development of relations between people and the solving of various problems raised by the current period. It is in the field of science and technology where the victory of socialism over capitalism is decided in long-term perspective.

Therefore the Party regards it as one of its primary tasks to provide an ever greater scope for the promotion of creative scientific work and for a timely and more efficient application of its results in social practice.

Relatively complete foundations of basic, applied research and development unprecedented in extent and importance have been built up in this country together with the construction of socialism. A number of qualified scientific workers who are respected throughout the world have made important contributions to building up this country. In spite of this, the opportunities offered by socialism for development of science and especially for application of its results to the benefit of society are, for the time being, far from being fully used, partly because of the still existing branch barriers between science, technological development, and production. The inflexibility of the system of management by directives, connected with the low-level qualifications of managing personnel is one reason for this. In the sphere of research the reasons are mainly differences in the levels of applied research institutes due to a lack of scientifically trained staff.

To improve existing conditions we shall continue making substantial improvements particularly in the *material conditions of our basic research* so that in the decisive branches it can permanently remain at a world level. The development of science must take into consideration the real possibilities of Czechoslovakia as a middle-size country, which can ensure top-level scientific research only by efficient specialization and concentration of energy plus extensive international cooperation and exploitation of the results of world science. Therefore it is also necessary to develop a system of evaluating scientific workers in such a way that selected progressive, scientific and socially important directions of research can be supported more fully by a system of moral and material incentives.

If the social sciences are really to become an official instrument of scientific self-knowledge in socialist society, we must respect their internal life and ensure them a position and conditions that will enable them to achieve a high scientific level. Party organs will take the initiative in encouraging the development of social sciences and contributing to their orientation toward important social problems; but they will not interfere with the process of creative scientific work and in this respect will rely on the initiative and social responsibility of scientists themselves.

In addition to creating favorable conditions for the development of science *we must strive to surmount all obstacles between science on the one hand and social practice on the other.* Even though the full and consistent application of the new system of management is expected to bring the fundamental solution, we shall help further this process with new measures at the level of central management. The Party will especially support the development of feasible stimuli for applying the results of science in production and other social practices and for a rapid improvement of the qualifications of slowly developing applied research institutes. At the same time we shall also support a more profound examination of the social function of science, especially the problem of its effectiveness and the relationship between science and economy in Czechoslovak conditions.

The development of socialist society is at the same time a process of constant increase of the social involvement and responsibility of science and its application in managing and shaping the entire society. We shall strive on a broader scale than hitherto for the participation of scientists in the work of representative bodies and in the activities of other bodies of social management. We shall intensify the active participation of scientific institutions and scientific workers in drawing up proposals for political and economic measures. We shall encourage the broadest possible placement of scientific workers in social management and the educational system and create favorable social and economic conditions for their activity in these fields. We shall prepare without delay to introduce a binding system of scientific expertise and opposition on important proposals. This will contribute to qualified decisions at all levels of management.

Quality of Education — The Aim of Our Educational System

The progress of socialist society is contingent upon the growth in education of the people. This is a precondition for solving initial tasks of the scientific-technological revolution, promoting the relations and institutions of socialist democracy and further asserting the cultural and humanistic character of socialism and the development and employment of every man in it.

Therefore we regard further progress in education as a primary task. In this respect we proceed from the traditions of the education of our nations and from the good results by which the socialist stage of development has improved our school system, especially by its broad democratization and the introduction of coeducation. It is still necessary to surmount the consequences of past shortcomings, when the quantitative development of education was frequently achieved at the expense of the quality of teaching. Nor was sufficient care given to the qualitative training of teachers. The frequent reorganization in the past did not contribute to the desirable improvement of the standard of education. On the contrary, this was the reason why, in many respects, it was lagging behind the existing needs and future demands. Therefore it is a foremost task today to concentrate the main attention and strength on a purposeful improvement of the standard, demands, and value of education and especially on improving and raising the standard of general education, expanding the base for more efficient ways of finding and training special talents, and modernizing the content, forms and means of education.

The dynamic development of our economy and of the whole society requires an end to the underevaluation of education and of the needs of schools and teachers; it requires that a much bigger proportion be set aside from social resources for the development of education. We shall ensure that educational bodies in cooperation with the broad masses devote much thought to developing projects which will enable our economy to keep pace with the dynamics of the development of science and technology and with the needs of the time. We consider the following tasks as the most urgent ones:

a) To draw up a draft hypothesis on the long-term development of the educational system which will make it possible to stabilize the development of the educational system at all levels, and design its personnel and material base in advance so as to gradually eliminate the uneven development of education in individual regions of the country.

To prepare a new concept in harmony with the long-term project of basic polytechnic education, which would be based on a logical grasping of the subject, take advantage of the independence and initiative of students and make it possible to fully apply the principle of differentiation according to interests and talents, solve the urgent problems of secondary general education schools by extending the base and time of secondary general education, and thereby improve preparations for later university studies while preparing those secondary school students who will not study at universities to take practical jobs.

To form and gradually introduce a system of additional education for young people who start working at 15 years, to increase the thoroughness of the preparation of young skilled workers in harmony with the technological and structural changes in our economy by improving the theoretical, specialized and general education of young apprentices, to take advantage to a greater extent of the resources of plants and enterprises for the construction and equipment of apprentice centers of the new system of management of the national economy and in justified cases also to grant state subsidies, and not to allow a further decrease of material investments in these establishments. The same criteria should also be applied by National Committees in the construction and equipment of apprentice schools.

b) To create material and personnel conditions at secondary schools and universities for all young people who fulfill the necessary requirements and have proven themselves in the course of their earlier education eligible to be enrolled for studies. Therefore the system of enrollment at secondary schools and universities should be made more flexible. Administrative methods should be replaced by economic and moral stimuli, a sufficient amount of information and improved educational advice, which will help regulate sensitively the influx of students to particular branches and bring closer together the abilities and interests of individuals and the needs of society. Meanwhile secondary and university education should not be understood only as training for a certain profession, but as a means of improving the extent of education, the cultural level of man and his ability to solve new situations in the production process as well as in the economic, social and qualification structure of society. This requires simultaneously an increase in the social responsibility of economic, cultural and political institutions and of every individual for the application of education in practice.

c) In the management of universities, democratic principles and methods should be consistently applied. The prerequisites of scientific work, unity of teaching and research, should be continually strengthened; the authority and autonomy of university scientific councils should be increased. Universities should be given preference regarding modern equipment, the possibilities of scientific work should be improved, all-round cooperation between research, universities and secondary schools should be intensified, expensive equipment should be taken advantage of jointly by research institutes and universities. Universities should be given broader access to foreign literature and more opportunities for study and training visits abroad in view of their pedagogical and scientific work, while understanding correctly the importance of acquiring knowledge for the development of science and flexibly applying the principles of profitability of foreign currency resources.

d) The structural changes in the national economy will also require retraining and complementing of the general or specialized education of adults. Therefore it will be necessary for schools, enterprises, social organizations and mass information media (press, radio, television) to cooperate in order to improve and intensify the system of education for adults.

e) The complexity of education management should be safeguarded by legal arrangements so as to raise the role of school administration. In this connection it will be desirable to ascertain the effectiveness of university law so as to strengthen the democratic relations in the internal and external management and the social position of universities. The authority of Slovak National Council bodies in education in Slovakia should be applied fully in view of the importance of education as a basic element of national culture.

f) Equal study and development conditions should be consistently ensured for young people of all nationalities. An end should be put to the belittling approach towards solving problems of nationality education, and legal and institutional preconditions should be created to allow the nationalities to have something to say on the specific issues of nationality education.

The Party appreciates the work of our teachers in educating the young generation. Teachers belong above all to the school and young people, and their work must not be disturbed. Educational work is of nation-wide and society-wide importance. Therefore the social position of teachers must be safeguarded in the first place by the respective state bodies and National Committees. Efforts to provide conditions essential for their work must also follow this pattern. This means ensuring a high standard of training of teachers, developing wage relations of teachers and other school staff in harmony with the growth of real wages of workers in other branches, and also solving other urgent material needs of teachers so that they can perform their responsible profession with full concentration. In projects and the materialization of school capital construction, it is essential to ensure its complex character, including flats for teachers. The Party regards this as part of its policy to increase the prestige, authority, and social importance of the educators of the young generation.

The Humanistic Mission of Culture

The development of culture in the broadest sense is one of the basic conditions for the dynamic and harmonious development of socialist society. The culture of socialist Czechoslovakia consists of independent and equal Czech and Slovak cultures, together with the cultures of the other nationalities. The arts and culture are not a mere decoration of economic and political life; they are vital for the socialist system. If culture lags behind, it retards the progress of policy and economy, democracy and freedom, development of man and human relations. *Care for culture, material and spiritual, is not only the concern of the cultural front; it must become an affair of the entire society.*

It was an important tradition of the Communist Party from the start that it was able to unite the best men of culture and art around itself. This is proved not only by the socialist orientation of our pre-war artistic vanguard, but also by the fact that most of the cultural intelligentsia sided with the left or were in the ranks of the Party after the liberation in 1945. Later, especially in the early fifties, certain representatives of culture were discriminated against, some were subjected to unjustified political repression, and the cultural policy of the Party was deformed.

The documents of the 13th Congress should have been a starting point of a new cultural policy, which would proceed from the best traditions of the past and from much positive experience acquired after 1956 and after the 12th Congress of the Communist Party of Czechoslovakia. However, the surviving bureaucratic attitudes and old methods of management prevented the impetus of the Congress from developing. The contradictions between proclaimed and practiced policies created tension and restricted the involvement and development of socialist culture. The Central Committee will investigate all the reasons for these conflicts and will create favorable conditions to normalize the situation.

We reject administrative and bureaucratic methods of implementing cultural policy, we dissociate ourselves from them, and we shall oppose them. Artistic work must not be subjected to censorship. We have full confidence in men of culture and we expect their responsibility, understanding and support. We appreciate the way in which cultural workers helped instate and create the humanistic and democratic character of socialism and how actively they participated in eliminating the retarding factors of its development.

It is necessary to overcome a narrow understanding of the social and human function of culture and art, overestimation of their ideological and political role and underestimation of their basic general cultural and aesthetic tasks in the transformation of man and his world.

The Party will guard and safeguard both the freedom of artistic work and the right to make works of art accessible.

To administer culture socially means, first of all, to create favorable conditions for its development. Disputes, which will naturally arise, will be solved by discussion and democratic decisions. *Independent decisions* of cultural workers in the spheres of their activity must also be an expression of the necessary autonomy of culture and art. They must be indispensable partners for state bodies. We are convinced that Communist intellectuals and all other leading workers in the sphere of culture and art are capable of cooperating in the formation and responsible, independent implementation of the policy of the Party in state, social, cultural, and interest group institutions, that they are a guarantee of the socialist, humanistic orientation of our culture.

Of course, the social effect of culture does not occur outside the political context. We shall ensure that the freedom of different views, guaranteed by the Constitution, is fully respected. However, the Communist Party cannot give up its inspiring role, its efforts to make art, too, efficiently help form socialist man in the struggle for the transformation of the world. The Party will apply consistently its political program; it will stimulate the development of Marxist thinking.

Socialist culture is one of the primary agents of the penetration of socialist and humanistic ideas in the world. *It helps unite the humanistic streams of world culture. It has the capacity of bringing closer the socialist nations and of strengthening the cooperation and fraternal relations of nations and nationalities.* Culture is a traditionally important value for our nations; it has always been of service to us in proving our vitality and individuality to the world. But the interpretation of the national traditions of the culture of the Czechs and Slovaks was one-sided in many respects, and whole important periods were artificially omitted from it. We give our full backing to the humanistic traditions of national cultures, and we shall support all efforts to endorse this heritage in the present psychology of Czechs and Slovaks.

We are supporters of both internationalism and national uniqueness of culture. We think it inevitable to take efficient measures without delay so that culture in Slovakia has the same conditions and possibilities as those in Bohemia, so that disproportions do not grow, but disappear. *The equal position of national cultures* also requires an equal position of national institutions. The competence of national bodies in Slovakia includes the management of the decisive instruments of national culture, such as radio, television, film, scientific institutes, artists' unions, book publishing, care for historical monuments, etc. It is necessary to secure the representation of Slovak national culture abroad; to increase the exchange of information and cultural values between the Czech and Slovak nations; to ensure the cultural life of the Slovaks in the Czech lands and of the Czechs in Slovakia in their native tongue.

Similar principles must be applied also towards the cultures of all the nationalities in Czechoslovakia, while realizing that they are specific cultures and not Czech and Slovak culture translated into another language. *The culture of nationalities* is an organic part of Czechoslovak socialist culture, but it is also in context with the general culture of its own nation, with which it is inseparably linked. Material conditions and personnel problems of the further development of national cultures must be guaranteed institutionally; scientific and cultural institutions and offices must be established with a view to nationality needs. The decisive role and care for the material base of national cultures pertains to state bodies, National Committees, together with the cultural unions of the various nationalities.

We shall take care not only of cultural work, but also of the system of *communication of cultural values*. We shall strive for the active participation of citizens in the development of socialist culture and in their *cultural education,* in the closest possible cooperation and complex influence of mass and local culture. We consider it urgent to examine the reasons for the catastrophic shortcomings of cultural and aesthetic education and to take measures to rectify them; — to create sufficient material, organizations, and other conditions of cultural activity, *to permit more flexibility in organizational forms;* — to allow the establishment of various cultural and hobby groups as well as their regional and national associations; — to complete an efficient network of cultural establishments with an active participation of National Committees, enterprises, social and group-interest organizations; — to purposefully build up new important *regional cultural centers* outside the capitals.

The entire sphere of culture must be responsibly safeguarded economically, in view of its importance, and protected from the uncontrolled nature of the market and from commercialism. We shall recommend, in the spirit of the 13th Congress resolution, that the government complete without delay the projected *revamping of the economics of culture*. Planned expenditures on culture must be stabilized and must increase progressively in harmony with the trend of the national income. We shall also support voluntary combination of the means of industrial and agricultural enterprises, national committees, and social organizations for culture. The means invested in culture can become an important instrument of its development if whoever makes use of them becomes a modern socialist customer.

Because they are dependent upon new distribution of the means for culture on a national scale the *following problems are most urgent:* to guarantee material care for the creators of important cultural values; — to eliminate discrepancies in the royalties, wages, incomes, and tax system in culture; — to cover the whole territory of the Republic with a good quality radio and television signal as soon as possible, to introduce a second television channel in 1970; — to overcome without delay the disastrous state of the printing industry; — to secure more paper in desirable assortments for the press and publishing houses; — to improve care of historical objects of art and save handicraft among other things by making way for cooperative or private enterprise in this sphere.

The planned expenditure on culture must *be concentrated in culture directing bodies* which must distribute it to cultural institutions. To increase the economic independence and responsibility of cultural establishments, enterprises, and groups is a prerequisite of the functioning economy of culture. Independent control will lead to a more rational exploitation of means and possibilities, to increasing the spirit of enterprise.

The International Status and Foreign Policy of the Czechoslovak Socialist Republic

We shall be putting the Action Program into practice during a complicated international situation, and its further development will influence the realization of certain important principles of the program. On the other hand, the process of the revival of socialism in Czechoslovakia will make it possible for our Republic to influence this international development more actively. *We stand resolutely on the side of progress, democracy and socialism in the struggle of the socialist and democratic forces against the aggressive attempts of world imperialism. It is from this point of view that we determine our attitude toward the most acute international problems of the present and our share in the world-wide struggle against the forces of imperialist reaction.*

Proceeding from the real relationship of international forces and from the awareness that Czechoslovakia is an active component of the revolutionary process in the world, the Czechoslovak people will formulate its own attitude towards the fundamental problems of world policy.

The basic orientation of Czechoslovak foreign policy was born and verified at the time of the struggle for national liberation and in the process of the socialist reconstruction of the country. *It is alliance and cooperation with the Soviet Union and the other socialist states. We shall strive for friendly relations with our allies — the countries of the world socialist community — to continue, on the basis of mutual respect, to intensify sovereignty and equality, and international solidarity.* In this sense we shall contribute more actively and with a more elaborated concept to the joint activities of the Council of Mutual Economic Aid and the Warsaw Treaty.

In the relationship to the developing countries, socialist Czechoslovakia will be contributing to the strengthening of the anti-imperialist front and supporting within its power and possibilities all the nations opposing imperialism, colonialism, and neocolonialism and striving for the strengthening of their sovereignty and national independence and for economic development. Therefore we shall continue supporting the courageous struggle of the Vietnamese people against American aggression. We shall also be in favor of enforcing a political settlement of the Middle East crisis.

We shall actively pursue the policy of peaceful coexistence towards advanced capitalist countries. Our geographical position, as well as the needs and capacities of an industrial country, require us to carry out a more active European policy aimed at the promotion of mutually advantageous relations with all states and international organizations and at safeguarding collective security of the European continent. *We shall consistently proceed from the existence of two German states, from the fact that the German Democratic Republic, as the first socialist state on German territory, is an important peace element in Europe, from the necessity of giving support to the realistic forces in the German Federal Republic, while resisting neo-nazi and revanchist tendencies in that country. The Czechoslovak people want to live in peace with all nations.* They want to develop good relations and cooperate with all states in the interests of strengthening international peace and security as well as mutual confidence in the economic, cultural, scientific and technological fields. We shall also take more active advantage than we have done so far of our Republic's membership in international organizations, especially in the United Nations and its agencies.

Our science, culture, and art can do much more to strengthen and increase the international authority of socialist Czechoslovakia in the world. Czechoslovak foreign policy must provide conditions and extend the scope for the international application of our culture abroad. A broad application of our science and art abroad helps to prove efficiently the advantages of socialism and the possibilities of an active policy of peaceful co-existence.

Our foreign policy has not taken advantage of all opportunities for active work; it did not take the initiative in advancing its own views on many important international problems. The Central Committee of the Communist Party of Czechoslovakia, the National Assembly, the government and the respective ministry must overcome these shortcomings without delay and consistently ensure that our foreign policy should express fully both the national and international interests of socialist Czechoslovakia.

A full development of the international role of socialist Czechoslovakia is inseparable from the education of citizens in the spirit of internationalism, which comprises both the grasping of common interests and aims of the world progressive forces and understanding of specific national needs. This is linked with the necessity of making prompt and detailed information on international problems and the course of our foreign policy available to the public and thus creating conditions for an active participation of Czechoslovak citizens in the shaping of foreign political attitudes.

The Communist Party of Czechoslovakia will be more active in the sphere of the international Communist and workers' movement. *We shall put special emphasis on friendly ties, mutual consultations and exchange of experiences with the Communist Party of the Soviet Union, with the Communist and workers' parties of the socialist community, with all the other fraternal Communist parties.*

The Communist Party of Czechoslovakia will continue taking an active part in the struggle for the unity of the international Communist movement, for strengthening the active cooperation of Communist parties with all the progressive forces while regarding a resolute struggle against the aggressive policy of American imperialism as the most important task. The Communist Party of Czechoslovakia will take full advantage of its specific possibilities of establishing contacts with the socialist, peaceful and democratic forces in the capitalist and developing countries. It will contribute to expanding the forms of cooperation and coordinating the work of Communist parties, while attaching great importance to international party consultative meetings. From this point of view it welcomes and supports the outcomes of the Consultative Meeting of Communist and Workers' Parties in Budapest. With dozens of fraternal parties the Communist Party of Czechoslovakia supports the proposal for convening an international Communist consultative meeting in Moscow late in 1968.

Comrades,

We are submitting to you quite openly all the main ideas which have guided us and which we want to adhere to at the present time. Everyone will understand that the proposals comprised in this Action Program are far-reaching and their realization will profoundly influence the life of this country. We are not changing our fundamental orientation. In the spirit of our traditions and former decisions we want to develop to the utmost in this country an advanced socialist society, rid of class antagonisms, economically, technologically and culturally highly advanced, socially and nationally just, democratically organized, with a qualified management, by the wealth of its resources giving the possibility of dignified human life, characterized by comradely relations of mutual cooperation among people and free scope for the development of the human personality. We want to start building up a new intensely democratic model of a socialist society which will fully correspond to Czechoslovak conditions. But our own experiences and Marxist scientific knowledge lead us jointly to the conclusion that these aims cannot be achieved along the old paths or by using means which have long been obsolete and harsh methods which are always dragging us back. We declare with full responsibility that our society has entered a difficult period when we can no longer rely on traditional schemes. We cannot squeeze life into patterns, no matter how well-intended. It is up to us to make our way through unknown conditions, to experiment, to give the socialist development a new look, while leaning upon creative

Marxist thinking and the experiences of the international workers' movement, relying on a true understanding of the conditions of the socialist development of Czechoslovakia as a country which assumes responsibility to the international Communist movement for improving and taking advantage of the relatively advanced material base, unusually high standards of education and culture of the people, and undeniable democratic traditions to the benefit of socialism and communism. No one could forgive us were we to waste this chance, were we to give up our opportunities.

We are not taking the outlined measures to make any concessions to our ideals — let alone to our opponents. On the contrary. We are convinced that they will help us to get rid of the burden which for years provided many advantages for the opponent by restricting, reducing, and paralyzing the efficiency of the socialist idea, the attractiveness of the socialist example. We want to set new penetrating forces of socialist life in motion in this country to give them the possibility of a much more efficient confrontation of social systems and world outlooks and allowing a fuller application of the advantages of socialism.

Our Action Program comprises tasks, intentions, and aims for the immediate future, up to the 14th Party Congress. We are aware that many of the shortcomings and difficulties which have accumulated over recent years cannot be fully overcome in a short time. *However, the fulfillment of this program can open up the way to solving other, more complicated and important problems of the organization and dynamic development of our socialist society in directions which could be only indicated until now; in the coming years, we want to start working out a long-term program, which will give form to and elaborate in detail the concept of the over-all development of our socialist society in the stage we are entering, make clear the conditions and open up prospects of its Communist future.* After everything we have lived through over the past years we are obliged to give a reply to all our workers and ourselves as to how the Party imagines its aims can be achieved, how it wants to materialize the expectations and desires which are being invested by workers in their lives and in their participation in the Communist movement. We believe that our Marxist science has gathered and will gather now and in the future more than enough strength to enable it to prepare responsibly scientific preconditions for such a program.

We are not concealing the fact that difficult moments and extraordinarily exacting and responsible work face us in the coming months and years. For the fulfillment of the forthcoming progressive tasks it will be necessary to unite as many citizens of our Republic as possible, all who are concerned with the welfare of this country, with its peace efforts, with a flourishing socialism. The confidence, mutual understanding, and harmonious work of all who really want to devote their energy to this great human experiment will be needed. But the work and initiative of every Communist, every worker will be needed above all. We want to responsibly, consistently, and without reservations make room for this, remove all the barriers which stand in its way, set the creative capacities of our citizens, all the physical and moral capacities of society in motion. We want to create conditions so that every honest citizen who concerns himself with the cause of socialism, the cause of our nations, should feel that he is the very designer of the fate of this country, his homeland, that he is needed, that he is reckoned with. Therefore let the Action Program become a program of the revival of socialist efforts in this country. There is no force which can resist people who know what they want and how to pursue their aim.

The Central Committee of the
Communist Party of Czechoslovakia

DOCUMENT 17

"ON CURRENT PROBLEMS OF THE INTERNATIONAL SITUATION
AND THE CPSU'S STRUGGLE FOR THE SOLIDARITY
OF THE WORLD COMMUNIST MOVEMENT"

Resolution of Plenary Session of CPSU Central Committee
Adopted April 10, 1968

Excerpts

[*Pravda,* April 11, 1968, quoted from *CDSP,* Vol. XX, No. 15 (May 1, 1968),
pp. 3–4]

. . . The plenary session fully approves the Politburo's active and comprehensive work in further development of ties with the fraternal socialist countries. The plenary session places special emphasis on the importance of the Dresden meeting of Party and government leaders from six socialist countries. The plenary session reaffirms our party's readiness to do everything necessary for the steady political, economic and defensive consolidation of the socialist commonwealth.

In noting the continuing seriousness of the situation in the Near East as a result of the aggressive actions of Israel's ruling circles, which are backed by U.S. imperialism, the plenary session fully approves the measures of the Politburo and the Soviet government aimed at elimination of the consequences of Israeli aggression and liberation of the occupied Arab territories, as well as at comprehensive support for the progressive forces in the Arab countries.

The Central Committee plenary session confirms the correctness of the policy of exposing revanchism and militarism in West Germany and emphasizes the importance of joint action by the C.P.S.U. and the fraternal countries to increase the solidarity of the socialist countries, other peace-loving states and all anti-imperialist forces for the struggle against West German imperialism.

The plenary session notes that the present stage of historical development is characterized by sharp exacerbation of the ideological struggle between capitalism and socialism. The entire huge apparatus of anticommunist propaganda is now aimed at weakening the unity of the socialist countries and the international Communist movement, dividing the progressive forces of our time and attempting to undermine socialist society from within. While experiencing serious upheavals and encountering major setbacks in domestic and foreign policy, imperialism, primarily U.S. imperialism, in addition to undertaking adventures in the military-political domain, is directing increasingly greater efforts at subversive political and ideological struggle against the socialist countries, the Communist movement and the entire democratic movement.

In these conditions implacable struggle against enemy ideology, resolute exposure of the schemes of imperialism, Communist upbringing of C.P.S.U. members and all the working people, and intensification of all the Party's ideological activities acquire special significance and are among the most important obligations of all Party organizations. It is their duty to wage an offensive struggle against bourgeois ideology and to oppose actively any attempts to sneak views alien to Soviet society's socialist ideology into individual works of literature, art or other works. Party organizations must direct all available means of ideological upbringing at strengthening, in every Communist and every Soviet citizen, communist conviction and a sense of Soviet patriotism and proletarian internationalism, as well as ideological fortitude and the ability to resist all forms of bourgeois influence. . . .

The Central Committee plenary session holds that the present-day international situation insistently requires vigorous and united action by all the forces of socialism, democracy and national liberation. The C.P.S.U., for its part, will continue to pursue a policy of dealing a resolute rebuff to imperialism and of preventing world war, a policy of strengthening the commonwealth of socialist countries and increasing the solidarity of the Communist movement and all anti-imperialist forces.

DOCUMENT 18
"UNDER THE LEADERSHIP OF THE CPSU, ALONG THE LENINIST PATH—TOWARD COMMUNISM"

Speech by V. V. Grishin on the Anniversary of Lenin's Birth
April 22, 1968
Excerpts
[*Pravda*, April 23, 1968]

. . . It is only necessary to reduce the onslaught or relax revolutionary vigilance in this or that sector of the anti-imperialist front for a real threat of a reactionary counteroffensive to arise. Facts of recent years convincingly show that imperialism does not want to surrender its positions. Now here, now there it carries out a "trial of strength" and seeks to discover "a weak point" in our ranks.

Having lost hope of gaining the upper hand over socialism by frontal attack, by carrying out the so-called strategy of rolling back communism, imperialists have not renounced their aims but have only changed their methods. They disdain no means to weaken individual revolutionary detachments. This is proven by the U.S. aggression in Vietnam, the Israeli attack on Arab countries, the counterrevolutionary coup in Greece, the encouragement of Bonn revanchists, and the intensification of intrigues by imperialism in Asia and Africa. Not of the least importance in the designs of imperialist strategists are plans for the so-called erection of bridges to socialist countries. This is the name given by defenders of imperialism to plans for the ideological subversion of world socialism.

In this they rely most on revisionist, nationalist, and politically immature elements. Bourgeois propaganda highly lauds elements of this kind, praises them, and represents them as heroes. Anti-Communist ideologists do not conceal that the aim of all this advertising is to encourage activity which might lead toward "erosion" of socialism, permit its decomposition from within, and finally lead to restoration of capitalism in socialist countries. There is no doubt that this move by imperialism will be defeated just like all the previous ones. The Soviet people and the peoples of other socialist countries have joined their fates firmly and forever with socialism and communism; they will allow no one to divert them from this road. . . .

Comrades, the present policy of imperialism aimed at separation and division of various detachments of the world liberation movement and at dealing localized blows at certain sections of the anti-imperialist front raises as the central task the problems of uniting and coordinating the actions of the revolutionary forces. This is a great problem. Various revolutionary detachments act in different conditions and differ from each other both in the composition of social forces and in many practical tasks.

For this reason the forms of unity and cooperation of actions should possess sufficient flexibility. The Communist and workers' parties of the world, which possess the mighty weapon of the scientific analysis of reality, Marxist-Leninist theory, today are capable of providing an answer to the vital question of the century, helping other detachments of the world liberation movement find a correct orientation, and finding the most effective forms and methods of struggle. This is why strengthening the unity and cohesion of the international Communist movement, the vanguard of mankind's liberation struggle, is the most important and decisive condition for successful counteraction to imperialism's counterattacks and for further extension of the offensive of all revolutionary forces. . . .

Faced with the historic successes of the new system, anticommunism does not always venture to act in the open. It works in cunning and adroit ways, attempting to poison the consciousness of people while wearing the mask of a defender of freedom and democracy. We must act energetically, comrades, against any manifestations of bourgeois ideology, give a firm rebuff to its machinations, and expose its falsity. As Vladimir Ilich Lenin taught us, "It is our task to overcome all the resistance of the capitalists, not only military and political resistance but also ideological resistance, which is the most profound and the mightiest. . . ."

REHABILITATION AND SLOVAKIA

AFTER THE January 1968 Plenum ousting Novotný, the question of rehabilitations surfaced as one of the most sensitive issues in Prague.[1] As an indicator of the party's good faith in correcting past mistakes, the extent of rehabilitation was a measure of progress toward democratization. Gustav Husák spoke forcefully on the subject from personal knowledge (Document 19). One of the key figures in the Slovak Uprising of 1944 and a former Chairman of the Slovak Board of Commissioners, he had been purged as a "bourgeois nationalist" in the early 1950s and sentenced in 1954 to life imprisonment. He was released in 1960. By 1963 he was officially rehabilitated and readmitted to the party.

Until he became deputy prime minister of the post-January regime,[2] Husák had refused to return to political life, in spite of some offers, and worked at the Historical Institute of the Slovak Academy of Sciences. In this speech to the regional Slovak Communist Party in Bratislava, he both documented earlier excesses and balanced support for rehabilitation with a warning that party welfare imposed limits.

[1] The most comprehensive treatment of the political trials in the 1950s appeared almost a year later, after the occupation of Czechoslovakia. At that time, the historian Karel Kaplan systematically analyzed and documented the trials (see K. Kaplan, "Thoughts About the Political Trials," *Nová mysl*, Nos. 6, 7, and 8 (1968) and RFE Czechoslovak Press Survey Nos. 2147, 2148, 2149 (December 9, 10, and 11, 1968). Also K. Kaplan, "The Iron Logic of the Trials," *Život strany*, No. 29 (November 27, 1968) and RFE Czechoslovak Press Survey No. 2157 (December 19, 1968).

[2] Although Husák was not noted for tolerance prior to his arrest, he became, at least temporarily, an advocate of democratization after returning from jail. See his article demanding legal guarantees, "Old Anniversaries and New Hopes," *Kultúrny život*, January 12, 1968

DOCUMENT 19

"WE ARE GETTING RID OF BAD METHODS"

Gustav Husák Speech at Regional Conference of the Slovak Communist Party
in Bratislava
April 21, 1968
Excerpts
[Bratislava *Pravda,* April 23, 1968]

❧

If after years of suppression the possibility for freedom suddenly appears, a
great number of different opinions and views emerge. At such a time we must
not even be astonished when people express false views, because it is under
democratic conditions that better views have a chance to emerge victorious
in a confrontation and struggle with others. Since we presume that people
are wise and experienced and that they understand and sense who is struggling
for the better views we believe that in this discussion the views advocated by
our party with its new leadership and by the action program will prevail and
that the party will be capable of democratically convincing the majority of
our people of its validity. . . .

Rehabilitations Without Scandals

The interpretation of the rehabilitation issue is so broad among the public
today that some people imagine that we are going to annul February 1948,
some think that we will go back as far as 1945, and others perhaps think
that we will even rehabilitate Tiso and the Slovak state or the most various groups and individuals. We Communists must hold firm views on this
issue. We are not out to abolish the revolution which was victorious in
Czechoslovakia, destroyed the capitalist order, brought the working class
to power, and made the idea of communism victorious in our country. We are
not out to abolish socialism. We wish to abolish invalid methods and the
wrongs they caused.

These are two different things. At present, when the rehabilitation law is
being formulated and prepared, the main problem (among politicians and
experts) concerns formulating, that is, finding that subtle border between
ensuring the redress of wrongs and violating the principles of socialism. Because this is our goal.

Let me give an example: Do we regard the principle of collectivization and
the idea of placing farming on a cooperative basis as correct? I do. Do we
regard the methods which were used in many cases and by which some people
were unjustly victimized as correct? In many cases these methods were certainly incorrect. Thus, when redressing wrongs, we must find this subtle line,
that is, we must eliminate the wrongs but keep the result, that is, cooperative
farming as the progressive basis for further agricultural production. This

subtle differentiation must also be observed in all other sectors. This is a political principle.

It is true that at present people try to coin small change out of the idea of rehabilitation. This is what the discussion of yesterday and the day before yesterday was about. In many cases comrades and even nonparty people come up with concrete cases, but they are reasoning backwards. They do not search for the authors — the people who were politically or in some other manner responsible for the arrest, investigation, and condemnation of an innocent person. Instead they pick on persons who made themselves conspicuous during this procedure — the prosecutor or the judge, anyone that was visible. One comrade here spoke about this very well. I will briefly recall a few points pertinent to my own case so you may understand what I am trying to get at.

Clementis, Novomeský, and I held high party and state functions in 1949, and with the consent of certain highly placed people and the security organs a secret investigation was initiated against us because of such and such crimes. Comrade Löbl is here. He had been in jail since 1949; he knows the whole affair very well. I repeat: It was an agreement between leading comrades in the party and the security organs. Then about six months later, as a result of these secret investigations, it was decided to recall us from our functions and criticize us politically. A secret investigation continued in the meantime run by the same people: a group of politicians and a group of leading workers of the security service. Six or seven months after we had been criticized and recalled from our functions, we were arrested, and after another thirty-nine months of investigation we had a trial in which the prosecutor and judge figured prominently. I have been asked at many political meetings about who sentenced me and who was the prosecutor.

If I have chosen not to mention these names, it is not because I want to protect these people, because, after all, they had consciously violated the law in my case since they knew what was going on. I told them quite clearly what the problem was, refuted their accusations, and offered them evidence. However, the prosecutor and judge were actually insignificant, minor figures when compared with the directors who made all the top-level decisions and had even determined in advance the sentences and punishments.

Why then should I malign small, insignificant people even if they violated the law and behaved without character? After all, their directors and chiefs have sat and, in some cases, still sit on the party Central Committee.

I bring up this matter, comrades, so that in our search we will look for the real culprits and not for those people most easily accessible to us. I think that in this respect the Central Committee should speed up its review of the political and possibly also the legal responsibility for all the trials which took place in those years. A political commission exists, and it should accelerate its work. I am glad that the Central Committee Presidium adopted a resolution, at its most recent session, I believe, to investigate Comrade Novotný's case. These problems should be investigated and the public should be clearly informed as to what functionaries and what people are concretely responsible for the deformations in the entire area of rehabilitation. This is necessary to satisfy the people's sense of justice but, comrades, also for another reason — for cleansing the whole party.

The "Directors" Are Mainly Responsible

There is another curious aspect to this issue. Today all of us are speaking of our difficult political and economic situation and the problems we must solve in coming years, but nobody assumes responsibility for the past and for the political and economic errors in our country. I specifically have in mind Comrade A. Novotný's speech at the Central Committee Plenum. His assertion that in essence he acted correctly all those years must be refuted as brazen demagoguery. Yesterday Comrade Ervin Polák spoke here about Comrade Novotný's share only as far as the problem of the trials is concerned, and this could be supplemented endlessly on the basis of concrete facts concerning the direct responsibility of Comrade Novotný.

Comrades, if we do not settle such problems as, for example, the case of Comrade Novotný, we will not win confidence from among the masses of citizens. Yesterday a comrade here told me, "Today many honest people are not joining the party and say they will not join as long as we have Novotnýs, Bacíleks and their like in our ranks." I mention these things because sometimes a proper sense of proportion is not maintained when seeking culprits and we arrive at a point where people are maligned and subjected to vexations who in essence are not responsible for these deformations.

I heard on television that in connection with the Zinger trial Comrades Falťan and Rasla, whose names were mentioned in the trial, were maligned. In other contexts additional persons are being maligned. I do not know whether this is done out of naïveté or whether some people think they can malign Communist functionaries one after another, "shooting them down" in a row. What a good way of subverting and weakening our party.

We will not prevent anyone from freely stating his views. However, presenting a view at a meeting where one speaks for oneself and presenting a subjective view on radio, television, etc. where one addresses millions of people, are two different things. I believe that all of us here and all the millions of people besides us — not merely the person who at the moment stands at the microphone or has access to it — should speak on radio and television or in the pages of the press. I think that this is also a problem of public control and responsibility. But in this connection, as I say, we must bear in mind that there exist trends to malign certain honest people and remove them from public life.

I want resolutely to reject the tendency toward holding our whole party responsible for the deformations even though I see it in the villages and districts where minor functionaries are being attacked.

Two days ago in Nitra I was asked quite a few questions of this sort: How can a person say one thing or another when just before Christmas he was a loyal partisan of Novotný; how can he hold a post today? But who among those who previously worked in politics and held minor or intermediate positions could before this new year criticize or oppose Comrade Novotný?

Some may have been able to, some perhaps dared, but how could a minor functionary do so? Therefore we cannot "shoot down" our small functionaries on this account. We must not permit these attacks on honest people to spread. They would dissolve our party altogether, and I think some people would welcome them. . .

Nobody Can Retard Federalization

And now a few ideas about federalization. Today the idea of a federalized Czechoslovakia is generally accepted. Not even in Bohemia, as far as one can observe from meetings, papers, and contacts with people, are there any serious objections. At present we are faced with the task of elaborating this question concretely in specialized and political circles and preparing the federalization law.

The unanimous trend in Bratislava and Prague is to speed up these preparations and submit the federalization law as soon as possible to the public. Then it will go to the government and parliament, who will discuss it and put it into practice as quickly as possible. Nobody can fix a precise deadline now for the simple reason that this issue involves an extremely large number of political, economic, and administrative problems. Of course, when undertaking such a project, we wish to do it seriously and honestly. I do not say this in order to lull the public. I merely do not want anyone to think that the federalization law — which will regulate relations between Czechs and Slovaks and which will involve the whole range of national councils and the entire economic sphere — is a question that can be formulated by some twenty people during one evening over a glass of wine. Comrades, things never were and never will be that simple.

From 1945 to 1948 we struggled for three full years with these problems. As you know, at that time political circumstances were less favorable and hence there were no results. But even today an honest piece of work will take several months, and I can responsibly say that nowhere is there a tendency to hold up, delay, or impede this work in any way. I wish to stress in particular that even among the Czech comrades there is no such tendency. In fact, they even say: Let us speed up this work so that we may have stability in our state administration as soon as possible. Budgets and plans are being prepared, and everyone wants to know where it is all leading. Thus there is no tendency toward procrastination. Everything depends on the ability of a broad, well-trained group of people who must solve the problems of how soon we will be able to appear before the public with this law.

Let me also remark in this connection that uncertainty has been voiced in Slovakia over relations with the Czech nation. I know that there is much bitterness from the past. This bitterness has accumulated and sometimes it explodes. However, we should bear in mind one thing: Today, among leading Czech party people, there is understanding for solving this problem, that is, understanding for the federal solution. Positive trends in relations with the Slovak nation are becoming prevalent. Therefore, we Slovaks — and I include those of us who hold public office — should at times moderate the somewhat fiery and wild and sometimes even unnecessary tendencies which can offend the Czechs. . .

Slovakia Is Not Lagging Behind

One last remark about the process of democratization in Slovakia. It is true that there are various interpretations of what we call the democratization process. I have heard or read views that Slovakia is lagging behind in the democratization process. I wonder whether it is out of inertia that some people always come back to this idea of Slovak backwardness or whether it suits somebody's game. On the other hand, Prague Czechs will tell you about the role played by the Slovaks in the struggle against conservatism and dogmatism, not only now but in 1963–1964.

The Czechs highly value the role of Comrade Dubček and other Slovak comrades who carried out this recent attack, and Slovakia's position in December, January, and February was a very important factor, if we are to give credit where credit is due. Thus Slovakia as a whole and the Slovak Communist Party as a whole played a progressive role. And now, allegedly, we are lagging behind and things are better over there. I suppose people will again say that Slovakia is reactionary, conservative, and so forth. Some people judge the situation by the number of people replaced or by who knows what other yardsticks. Nobody wants to prevent criticism, but one should think more sensibly. What happens in Prague must not be mechanically copied in Bratislava. I think that in statewide ratios Slovakia is not lagging behind in the democratization process and that there is no discrepancy between democratization and the struggle for the federalization of the state. After all, federalization means nothing more than applying democratic principles in the field of nationality policy — principles that cannot be asserted without general conditions for the democratization of the whole society.

Sometimes the way things have been looking has caused people to ask whether in this democratization process a party functionary has the right to state his view without people accusing him of raising his finger, prohibiting, or commanding. I don't think, comrades, that things are so bad in our party and in this state that no one may state his view, that Communists must keep silent and be forbidden to polemicize against incorrect views or have their say on behalf of the party.

This is the old antidemocratic spirit, only turned upside down. If we accord, say, journalists or other comrades the right to some criticism, we must also accord the right to criticize and to take up a standpoint to the party as a whole, to its agencies, and to Communists as individuals. Democracy is not only freedom or a demand for freedom. It goes hand in hand with responsibility. This is an idea which must penetrate to the very heart of our people.

ČSSR GOVERNMENT PROGRAM

THE GOVERNMENT DECLARATION presented to the National Assembly on April 24 (Document 20) closely paralleled the party Action Program. However, it was more concrete. Whereas the Action Program had implied that although changes could not be made overnight economic reorganization would substantially speed conditions favoring a rise in the standard of living, this statement was absolutely blunt about Czechoslovakia's economic plight. It made clear that for the present even justified demands would have to wait.

As to foreign policy, the Declaration went beyond the Action Program's position on West Germany. It detailed contacts, recognized "democratic" (instead of merely "realistic") trends in the German Federal Republic, and favored normalization of relations. Viewed in the perspective of Dubček's speech at the 20th Anniversary celebration two months before, this formulation showed a marked increase in receptivity to Bonn's desire for rapprochement with Eastern Europe. Dubček had referred only to the revanchist forces in West Germany, orthodoxly pledging Czechoslovak support to "Comrade Ulbricht" and the East German workers in their struggle against a new variety of fascism taking root in the Federal Republic.[1]

DOCUMENT 20
Program Declaration of the ČSSR Government, April 24, 1968
Excerpts
[*Rudé právo*, April 25, 1968]

. . . II. Economy

In our economy, which is the fruit of the work of many generations and the result of a considerable effort by the entire populace in the past twenty

---

[1] *Rudé právo*, February 23, 1968.

years, there exist a number of contradictions. On the one hand, we have achieved certain unquestionable successes; on the other hand difficulties have accumulated which cannot be overcome by past methods.

We have developed comparatively powerful productive forces. For instance, in the past twenty years basic production funds have increased by 400 billion crowns. We have full employment, we have trained over one million specialists with higher or specialized secondary education, we have allocated large resources for developing scientific research in which at present some 139,000 workers are employed. Our place in the world, according to the per capita national income, is comparatively good. But we still lag some 30–40 percent behind advanced Western countries. We have increased personal consumption twofold. We have put into operation a wide network of educational, cultural, and health facilities. Our nations have done a good, honest job during the past twenty years. But it is clear to everybody that despite the successes we can exhibit, the state of our economy does not correspond to the situation of an industrially advanced country more than twenty years after the war. There is still a shortage of some types of goods, both retail goods and those for the supply of enterprises. Production is not smooth; there are difficulties in investment building — its time limits in our country are two to three times longer than in other nations. The volume of unfinished projects is growing, and the environment in which the working people are living, working, doing their purchasing, commuting to work, and so forth is getting worse or is improving only slowly.

Because of all this, the working people are justifiably asking what our real economic situation is like and why serious difficulties persist when in the course of twenty years we have increased the national income threefold and industrial production as much as sixfold, when we have attained an exceptionally high per capita output of steel, coal, cement, and of fabrics and footwear so that in these respects we are in leading positions in the world?

The problem lies above all in the unsuitable structure of our economy.

A small landlocked state has under today's conditions an objectively difficult situation to contend with, and more urgently than large states it is faced with the imperative need of evolving its economic structure in such a way as to be able to effectively assert itself in the world market.

Yet we have failed to take advantage of the superiority of socialist development. Following the first postwar years when we began to further progressive forms of management and attained certain successes in consolidating the economy, we later failed to orient development in the right direction.

The problem had already arisen in the fifties from two fundamental causes: on the one hand, there was a tense international situation, a policy of embargo conducted by the Western states, the cold war; on the other, the rigid concept of the priority development of heavy industry, the attempt to direct socialist economy's expansion toward autarky, as well as a failure to understand the role of foreign trade. All this determined our further development for a number of years.

A considerable change in orientation of foreign economic relations with socialist countries brought into the national economy certain assuring factors in the safeguarding of basic needs and markets. However, we failed to put into effective and broad operation a deeper and more efficient division of labor in the manufacturing industries.

Thus, we built up an industry which at present is to a large extent incapable of effectively insuring our needs in foreign trade or of satisfying our domestic market requirements.

The extent and influence of this uneconomic structure may be characterized for instance by the fact that each year it is necessary to allot thirty billion crowns from the state budget to grants and subsidies. Much of this goes for agriculture, transport, housing construction, and similar purposes; but a comparatively substantial part pays for uneconomical production, the constantly growing volume of unused stocks, etc. Moreover, by exporting our goods in foreign trade, we are gaining the hard currency that is indispensable for the import of raw materials and machinery at considerably higher cost than would correspond to their actual earning potential. As a result, these costs are constantly increasing. Our national income makes roughly twice the demand on the consumption of primary sources of power and steel than is the case in highly developed countries.

Under these conditions, it in increasingly difficult for our economy to balance our payment relations with capitalist states without loss of effectiveness. This is also why we are in debt in the free currencies (for not quite $400 million). The extent of this indebtedness is comparatively small and far less than the debts incurred by a number of highly developed countries which to a far greater extent than we have utilized external resources for developing their economies. It is, however, disagreeable since our debts have been unfavorable, short-term payment obligations, while our far more substantial assets are to a large extent repayable on a long-term basis, or are in nonconvertible currencies.

Our state is on the whole in the position of a creditor. The fact that the present structural disharmony is causing difficulties with respect to our balance of payments is evidence of the inadequate adaptability of our economy. At the same time, our foreign trade exchange does not nearly measure up to the level of countries at a similar level of development, nor does it ensure an efficient division of labor. A situation is thus created in which we cannot keep abreast of technology, product quality, or living standards.

The second considerable problem is a high degree of tension in all economic relations. Our economy has for many years been developing extensively. The policy of bringing about economic equilibrium was not sufficiently mastered. This is why in a whole series of spheres, we suffer serious trends toward demand outrunning supply which strengthen the position of suppliers vis-à-vis consumers, impair the quality and technological standards of products and of investment construction, as well as labor discipline, and have a detrimental influence on the whole community.

The third basic problem springs from insufficient inner dynamism and effectiveness of our productive forces. Much of the extensive capital equipment we have built up does not measure up to the highest technological standard; it is not fully built up or is based on obsolete technology or small scale mass production techniques. Poor organization, incompetent management, low social weight given to qualifications, and widespread leveling often act as a brake on the efficacy of skilled work. Scientific research is too widely dispersed, and its results are little reflected in production. The over-all management of society has failed to provide enough stimulation for the advancement of initiative and enterprise.

As a result, we have been unable to satisfy without difficulty the ever-growing and real economic demands of the populace and to ensure at the same time the indispensable growth of quality.

These shortcomings were long fostered and even aggravated by the directive system of management, in that it made production for production's sake possible, divorced production from the market, operated with artificial prices, encouraged extensive development at the expense of quality, failed to insist on standards of expertise, and gave no leeway to initiative. This is why the introduction of an economic system of management is exceptionally important.

At the same time, the government declares that our economy is far from being in a state of crisis.

The problem does not so much lie in the rate of growth or level of the national economy, nor in our economy being indebted to any very large extent. The problem is that its internal structure, the nature of its work, its technical standard, profitability, production quality, and overall efficiency are not such as to enable us to hold our own in the scientific and technological revolution which is in progress all over the world.

As a result of this development, which began in the fifties, we missed a whole series of opportunities and failed to create conditions that would enable the ample capabilities and creative forces of our working people to function properly.

In the sixties, the external situation has changed; a certain relaxation of relations with capitalist states has begun, and the needs and orientations of the socialist economies have changed. Nevertheless, the tendencies to plan development in the old manner have survived. This was chiefly demonstrated in the third Five-Year Plan, which in fact further aggravated the structural problems of our economy by piling up tasks in an unrealistic fashion. The total collapse of this concept in 1962 and mainly in 1963 created an exceptionally complex situation in the economy, in which it was possible to prevent a further decline in the living standards only with great effort and with certain sacrifices.

Thus began the extensive analytical studies which became the basis for a new concept of economic development, mainly as concerns preparations for the new system of management and an analysis of the situation and the fourth Five-Year Plan.

Practical economic policy had to struggle with concrete disproportions caused by the preceding development. It worked in a narrow space which was delimited by a stagnating national income, the amortization of extensive funds, low efficiency of the economy, and declining initiative on the part of working people.

Under these difficult conditions the first steps leading to an economic system of management and to the necessary structural changes could not be implemented consistently. During the past two years, the national income has grown by roughly one sixth, so that although a certain measure of revival has occurred, it may by no means be regarded as a fundamental turning point. This complex task is still ahead of us, nor is it any easier than it was three years ago. In fact it will even be harder. Today's government is thus placed in a situation which is objectively speaking more difficult. . . .

The government proceeds from the fact that at present, an era characterized by the advance of the scientific and technical revolution throughout the world, more than ever before the development of science and technology is of primary importance because it is the basic and permanent resource which ensures the growth of the social productivity of labor and national income. Scientific knowledge and its free and independent development constitute one of the principal forces of social development and the decisive factor in its progress.

The effectiveness of scientific and technological development on the further development of our society will increase, provided there is a consistent and systematic implementation of the modern achievements of science and technology in industry and in social practice. Much will depend on the extent to which this knowledge permeates actual decision-making at all levels of management and how well working people understand the importance and tasks of mental work.

If science and technology are to accomplish their tasks, the program of the development of science and technology must be incorporated in the plan of the long-term development of the economy. We must make it the concrete subject matter of long-term plans in factories and enterprises and ensure that a high technical and organizational standard becomes the fundamental criterion in evaluating and judging the progressiveness of individual enterprises, branches, and the entire national economy.

The economic policy of the government will proceed from this realization and an appreciation of the role of science and technology in the further development of society and will create the necessary public, social, and economic conditions for its further development. We consider it to be of particular importance that further development of the economic system of management be oriented in this direction, that conditions be created for apprehending technical backwardness, and the first preference be given to progressive technology.

The government proceeds from the fact that the present development of the national economy, some of the institutions, principles, and plans of the new system of management have created for the development of science and technology some indispensable prerequisites but that, on the other hand, it is necessary to increase the role of science and technology in our economy. This will depend on how science and technology assist production in acquiring a better position in the world and the home market and how, conversely, production realizes in good time that it needs science and technology.

The government also plans to continue to provide the required financial and material means from state-wide resources to facilitate further reinforcement of pure research and will speed up the solution of some of the basic research and development programs which are decisive for the entire economy. At the same time, the government must necessarily bear in mind the realistic possibilities and strategic conditions of our state which can secure the highest level of science and technology only by a purposeful and well-thought-out specialization and utilization of the results of science of the entire world. In scientific research, the government will strive to prevent splintering and ensure that research utilizes with the greatest effectiveness the scientific potential of workers in research institutes and universities.

Attention will also be paid to the further perfection of the system of management, research, and development which must completely do away with administrative forms, fully implement the economic principles between the central and enterprise spheres, and raise the authority and responsibility of research institutes with regard to the results of their management.

In view of the importance of the role of further scientific and technological development, the government intends to deal, in the near future, with the problems of the development of the sciences and technology from many points of view.

The achievements of science and technology can permeate everyday life only through the daily activities of millions of people who know their work and have adequate abilities, knowledge, skill, and a broad enough overview so they will be able to master their tasks with the application of strict world-standard criteria.

Therefore, the government thinks it necessary to put an end to the underestimation of qualifications, to dilettantism, and the placing of average abilities above creative forces and abilities. If creative and qualified work is to regain the place to which it belongs, the first prerequisite is the correct stressing of this work in everyday organizational work. In the sphere of economic policy, the government will ensure that differences in skilled work are correctly reflected in salary and wage regulations and that able, skilled, and progressive-minded workers can advance democratically throughout the entire process of management.

A basic change will also be required to take care of institutional problems. The old methods of management, which enterprises are justified in criticizing, have survived because economic changes were not accompanied by the desired and necessary changes in the organizational structure. We approached the new system of management with the old structure of a central management apparatus which was created and set up as an apparatus of directive management of the national economy and was only partially amended. There was no consistent final solution to relations between enterprises and central organs, and there remained strong elements of a superior to inferior sort of relationship. Even the changes in the organizational pattern of enterprises implemented in 1965 brought no change, because they manifested trends of their own directive administration methods of management. . . .

The government is fully aware of its responsibility to maintain healthy economic development. In all its activities, including those involving the policy on state expenditures, it will look after the economic efficiency and consistently enforce regulations dealing with the needs and interests of society as against particular interests.

The new government starts its work in a situation when our economy is seriously affected because a whole series of clear problems in the economy and in the entire society have been overlooked for a long time.

Frankly speaking, a big debit has been built up as regards housing development, communications, and other nonproductive investments, and also regarding the renovation of obsolete factories.

In a number of cases it cannot be said that wages correctly reflect economic merit. The transition to the management system and the revival process through which we are now passing have contributed to the fact that a number of justified demands and needs have begun to be openly discussed.

Even though a great number of the demands are justified, it is not possible to satisfy them immediately. The government therefore asks all citizens to understand that fresh demands cannot be presented until new resources exist. Otherwise an open inflationary development and weakening of the currency would take place, dragging with them all the usual consequences.

The government feels it is its duty to stress, first, that compared with the past, when the government accumulated and distributed almost all the resources of the society as an administrator, it will now be necessary gradually to create a situation in which the resources of the society will to a larger degree be distributed on the spot and the enterprise will take care of management itself.

Therefore we must understand that at the present time wages cannot increase until production is made substantially more economical. All workers can participate in this with their full initiative. The reserves in this respect are large: unutilized results of research and technical development, unused capacities and qualifications, possible improvements in the organization of production and labor, work morale and greater production flexibility.

All these reserves have one thing in common: they can be put into practice only by honest and conscientious work. Hence, the government expresses its support and recognition for all responsible and conscientious organizers of production, functionaries, senior officials in industry, foremen, technicians, and workers who have realized this need and are opposing unjustified demands and striving to improve the efficiency of production.

Second, the over-all situation of the national economy is characterized by an absolute lack of resources to meet legitimate demands for wages and investments and for the time being does not permit anything but the temporary postponement of the largest part of these demands. They will be satisfied only if there is an increase in the creation of these resources in the future period.

The government therefore turns to all working people of our country and asks them to understand that an accelerated consolidation of the economy can be fostered only by the elimination of all uneconomical measures. Unrealistic wage demands only interfere seriously with such a consolidation. The present situation is not, however, completely deadlocked. How we succeed — through a concerted effort of all citizens and of the government — in changing this situation depends entirely upon us.

Third, today's economic criteria, still very highly distorted and on the whole not very exacting, do not permit our severely closed-in economy to make a responsible assessment of and adopt certain long-term investment projects in industry despite the fact that in certain aspects they seem very urgent. We must therefore delay their definitive assessment.

The government emphasizes that a gradual and carefully considered settlement of cadre and organization structure problems is also necessary. It will have to be treated entirely naturally — predominantly from below — without administrative intervention by government or state agencies. Yet it would not be sensible in the present situation to conduct a campaign for the exchange of economic executives, or the disbanding of enterprises and the like regardless of whether new enterprises can hold their ground under the future market's exacting conditions or whether today's prices and other conditions correctly gauge an enterprise's efficiency. At the same time, we cannot rule out the immediate execution of urgent changes which are rightly being demanded. Procedure in these questions will be regulated by the government with rules which it will issue in the immediate future.

All the aforementioned questions add up to an exacting and difficult program. In harmony with the action program of the Czechoslovak Communist Party, they provide the government with a point of departure for its work in the coming period. Today it would be irresponsible to promise more.

The government wishes to stress explicitly that we must not look upon the future as an easy development without conflicts in which, in one blow and without great effort, a substantial improvement can be made. It is to be expected that settling complex matters will involve a constant conflict between progressive and backward-looking elements and that it will be braked by the limited possibilities we possess. Further steps and a more concrete elaboration of the program will be possible only after a thorough consideration of the needs and resources of our economy along with the initiative of working people in rendering production more efficient. For this purpose we will need to conduct profound analyses and call for expert scientific opinions. To effect these exacting measures, the government has prepared its own concrete program of work. In addition, the government will also prepare a long-term program of economic policy as soon as the basic starting positions have been clarified. In these endeavors the government expects understanding from the members of the National Assembly as well as support for the steps it will have to take. . . .

IV. Foreign Policy

In the sphere of foreign policy, the government considers its basic tasks to be the safeguarding of peaceful conditions for the expansion of a prosperous democratic socialist society and the independence and security of the country.

We are putting exacting internal state policies into effect in a period of increased international tension brought about by the aggressive policies of imperialist circles. The Czechoslovak Socialist Republic stands unequivocally on the side of those who fight for social progress in the world and for international peace. Czechoslovakia is in a good position to take active part in creating international conditions in which the interests of all nations will be safeguarded under conditions of peace and cooperation, not only for the vital interest of our country but also on the basis of the social order and principles of international solidarity which we acknowledge.

The Czechoslovak Socialist Republic is a socialist country. The permanent foundation of Czechoslovak foreign policy is friendship and close cooperation with the Soviet Union and the other socialist countries. Our alliance with the Soviet Union belongs to those permanent, firm values whose purity has been fully confirmed by the critical examination of all values in our current revival process. This is so because our friendship with the Soviet Union arises organically from a number of experiences paid for so dearly by our nations, because we were brought to it by the very logic of historical development, the vital interests and needs of our homeland, because it is supported by the will, needs, and feelings of our people.

In consistent consolidation of international solidarity with the socialist countries, based on the democratic principles of equality and independence, noninterference, and mutual respect, we see a guarantee that ties between the socialist countries will strengthen and conditions for a foreign policy with initiative will develop favorably. In this spirit, the Czechoslovak Socialist Republic will actively fulfill the tasks arising from the Warsaw Pact. It will support its defense power and in so doing implement the democratic principles of cooperation and the interests of the republic within the framework of the treaty.

Economic and scientific technological cooperation with the socialist countries will also be further expanded by us on a bilateral and multilateral basis. We regard the current state of the social division of labor within the CMEA framework as insufficient, and because of this we shall contribute our proposals toward its improvement.

An important factor in the deepening of sincere friendships among all nations of the socialist countries is the maximum expansion of cultural, scientific, and other relations.

In its foreign policy, the government will continue to emphasize eliminating the threat of nuclear war. It therefore supports all measures designed to reduce the dangers of a nuclear conflict and favors a speedy conclusion of the treaty on the nonproliferation of nuclear weapons.

Our policy is guided by the principle of the indivisibility of peace and collective security as expressed in the UN Charter. We support the aims of this world organization, and we strive for the full application of its peaceful role and its further expansion.

In harmony with the humane and democratic character of the socialist system, we claim full participation in the International Year of Human Rights which the year 1968 has become in accordance with a UN resolution.

As far as capitalist states are concerned, we will strive for peaceful coexistence. In view of our position in Europe and our economic and cultural links with all parts of the continent, we are in a good position to effect an active European policy. We favor the development of good relations and cooperation with our neighbors and with the other European states on the basis of the principles of independence and sovereignity, equality of rights, noninterference in internal affairs, and mutual advantage. We regard the main factor in the stabilization of conditions in Europe as the recognition of the present state in Europe by all countries. We will strive for the extension of pan-European cooperation in all spheres so that a basis may thus be created for mutual understanding among European nations and for the strengthening of their security. We are convinced that the time has come for taking measures toward a lessening of tension in Europe, such measures as would permit the enormous amount of European material and manpower potential which has been expended for military purposes to be progressively applied toward improving the material and spiritual conditions of the life of nations.

We see great possibilities for expanding our bilateral contacts with France, Italy, Great Britain, and the Benelux countries. The same holds true for the Nordic states, some of whose foreign policy positions we are following with sympathy. We will also devote attention to an all-round expansion of good neighborly relations with neutral Austria.

As far as relations with United States are concerned, it is above all up to the U.S. Government to remove the obstacles which stand in their way. For instance, there are still the issues of returning the Czechoslovak gold reserve — which was looted by Hitler and which since the end of World War II has been frozen by the U.S. Government — as well as the issue of removing discriminatory measures from the time of the cold war.

The fundamental problem of Czechoslovak policy has been and remains the German question, one of the key aspects of European security. The Czechoslovak Socialist Republic consistently bases its policy on the existence of two German states. The German Democratic Republic is an important factor in promoting peace and the balance of forces in Europe, and it enjoys our full support in the building of socialism and consolidation of its international position.

It is with the greatest interest that we are following developments in the neighboring German Federal Republic. We decisively reject revanchist, antidemocratic, neo-Nazi, and militarist tendencies in the German Federal Republic. On the other hand, we note with satisfaction that in the public and among some political representatives realistic and democratic views and currents are beginning to appear. Today we have certain contacts in the economic, cultural, and scientific spheres with West Germany. The prerequisite for normalizing political relations, which would correspond to good neighbor principles, is a recognition of existing realities and the settlement of certain questions which are of fundamental importance to us.

The Czechoslovak Socialist Republic wishes, to the full extent of its possibilities, to share in the peaceful settlement of conflict situations and the most pressing problems of contemporary international relations presently exacerbating the atmosphere of world understanding. . . .

MAY PRESS CAMPAIGN: USSR

BY MAY, pressure on Prague was building up. Dubček flew unexpectedly to Moscow on May 4 for the first in a series of high-level exchanges that month.[1] Although the First Secretary reportedly reassured the Soviets that the process of Czechoslovak democratization would not be allowed to turn against socialism,[2] Soviet and other East European party leaders (once again minus Rumania) met in Moscow on May 8 to reassess the situation.[3] Simultaneously, Soviet and Polish troops maneuvered on Czechoslovak borders. In the context of the rumored remarks by the Head of the Main Political Administration of the Soviet Armed Forces, General Alexander Yepishev, that the Red Army would be willing to do its duty should a group of "loyal Communists" appeal to the Soviet Union and other socialist countries to help save socialism in Czechoslovakia,[4] the maneuvers set off a spiral of speculation. The Czechoslovak Foreign Ministry responded that Prague had been informed in advance of Warsaw Pact maneuvers in Southern Poland.

Whether that was true or not, the fact of these maneuvers heightened the tensions created by Soviet press attacks throughout May. Moscow objected to

---

[1] On May 8, Soviet Marshal I. S. Konev, former Commander of the Warsaw Pact Forces, arrived in Prague to celebrate Czechoslovakia's liberation day, May 17. Kosygin came for a ten-day "rest cure" at Karlovy Vary; an eight-man military delegation led by Defense Minister Grechko and including the chief political officer, General Yepishev, also arrived on the 17th for a week's visit. From the Czech side, Foreign Minister Jiří Hájek held discussions with Gromyko in Moscow May 6–8.

[2] Dubček interview, *Rudé právo*, May 7, 1968; reprinted in *Pravda*, May 8, 1968. Considering former Czechoslovak Minister of National Security Karel Bacílek's implication of Mikoyan in the Slánský trial (*Smena*, April 28, 1968; reported in *The New York Times* April 29, 1968), Moscow may well have needed assurances from Prague.

[3] A brief and totally uninformative communiqué appeared in *Pravda*, May 9, 1968.

[4] *Le Monde*, May 5, 1968. Prague radio immediately condemned the statement as a "trumped-up provocation" and called on the Soviet Union to renounce it. (Prague ČTK International Service in English 1050 GMT May 7, 1968). Yepishev issued a denial but only two weeks later at the airport in Prague.

157

rehabilitation of Tomáš G. Masaryk,[5] attacked Czechoslovak writers[6] (see "On the Political Instincts of Václav Havel," Document 13), and strongly defended the leading role of the Communist party. V. Stepanov's *Izvestia* article expanding the ideological implications of Grishin's speech of April 22 was among the most authoritative of these polemics (Document 21). Speaking to domestic as well as foreign Communists, the editor-in-chief of *Kommunist* rejected the possibility of "noninterference" of a Communist party in the state, economic, or ideological life of a socialist country. His emphasis on the CPSU Party Program and the resolutions of the CPSU 23rd Congress showed increased Soviet concern that demands for liberalization in Prague could infect the Soviet Union itself. The worry was real in that Moscow already had felt it necessary to forbid subscriptions to Czechoslovak Ukrainian-language publications[7] — and realistic!

DOCUMENT 21

"THE LEADING FORCE IN THE CONSTRUCTION
OF COMMUNISM"

V. Stepanov
May 11, 1968
Condensed Text

[*Izvestia*, May 11, 1968, quoted from *CDSP*, Vol. XX, No. 20 (June 5, 1968),
pp. 10–12]

. . . *The Marxist Party Is the Vanguard of the People.* — The Western press, especially recently, has been giving currency to the idea of the possibility of "noninterference" by a Communist or Workers' Party in a given socialist country's state, economic and ideological life. But this idea is born of bourgeois ideology and is dangerous for the future of socialism and communism. It is well known in the imperialist camp that the invincible might of socialism lies in its leading force — the Marxist-Leninist Communist and Workers' Parties.

---

[5] *Pravda*, April 30, 1968 quoted a conservative secretary of the KSC CC Alois Indra referring to "unhealthy phenomena" in Czechoslovak communications media such as "exhalting the role of T. G. Masaryk." See also *Sovetskya rossia* attack on Masaryk, May 14, 1968.

[6] One interesting exchange centered about the Czech writer Jan Procházka; see "The Train Jan Procházka Missed," *Literaturnaya gazeta*, May 8, 1968; his response, "To the Comrades," *Literární listy*, May 16, 1968; and the comment of Eduard Goldstücker, chairman of the Czechoslovak Writers' Union, "Let Us Talk About It, Friends," *Literární listy*, May 16, 1968. Translations of the three documents have been reprinted in *Studies in Comparative Communism*, Vol. 1, Nos. 1 and 2 (July and October 1968).

[7] Paul Wohl, *The Christian Science Monitor*, November 5, 1968.

Therefore in the urge to undermine or weaken the unity of the working people in the socialist countries, our enemies in the imperialist camp aim their blows first and foremost against the chief foundation of this unity, against the leading role played in socialist society by the working class and its vanguard — the Communist parties.

These attacks are made under the artful slogan of "democratization" or "liberalization" of public life in the socialist countries. In this sense it is instructive to note the suspicious interest that representatives of U.S. ruling circles have manifested in so-called "liberalization ideas" in the Central and Southeast European countries. For example, Averell Harriman, a special representative of the U.S. President, recently let it be clearly understood that all manifestations of "liberalization" are in U.S. interests insofar as they "undermine communism." And this, if you please, is one of the U.S.A.'s chief goals.

The imperialist circles themselves, which personify the blackest reaction in their own countries and organize counterrevolutionary coups in other states — these circles and their paid ideologists have suddenly begun to show a touching "concern" for the socialist countries. They are displeased by the fact that Communist parties occupy the leading position in these countries. Our opponents, for the purpose of "perfecting" democracy, would even like to see "opposition parties" there that could not exactly create a socialist society jointly with the people, but could take the position of critics of this creative activity, be loud-mouthed back-benchers in the socialist parliament and, if a suitable opportunity were to arise, oppose socialism outright. What is the program of such an "opposition party"? None at all. It is not to deal with concrete problems. Criticize everyone and take responsibility for nothing — in essence, obstruct things as much as possible, get underfoot and fish in muddy waters. This is a program of a sort, but a program that is antipopular, antisocialist, dear to the hearts of our enemies and good camouflage for the real objectives of the "opposition party." After all, if such a party were to declare that it is dedicated to the cause of socialism, it could no longer be an "opposition party" but would have to build a socialist society hand in hand with the Communist Party and all the people. If that party were to declare openly that it rejected socialism, the people would naturally turn away from it, and it would disappear from the arena of public activity. Now some zealots of the development of democracy have also advanced the thesis of giving the "opposition party" the same rights as the Communist Party has, but without a program, without responsibility to the people for its actions. The clear purpose here is to shatter unity, sow doubts and leave the antisocialist, antipopular elements free to attack socialism.

Genuine Marxist-Leninist parties are political organizations of the working class that are called on to lead it in implementing its world-historic mission of overturning the capitalist system and building a communist society. They cannot confine their activity merely to the benevolent function of "enlightening" the public and the passive statement of their views, and they cannot expect society to restructure itself under the influence of ideas alone. The parties of the working class are revolutionary, actively functioning political organizations, and they understand quite well that ideas have force when they are backed by people who are making them a practical reality, when ideology and policy are one.

What the Experience of History Teaches. — History itself has brought the Communist and workers' parties to leadership in the socialist states. They are the ruling parties and cannot, without betraying Marxist-Leninst views, abandon their role as political leader of the working people; they cannot "scruple" at delving deeply into all spheres of the life and development of society and state or at exerting an active influence on them. A weakening of the Party's leading role in the socialist state would be a compromise of socialism's class positions and would signify backsliding toward bourgeois liberalism, which merely serves the purpose of world imperialist reaction.

Continuous growth of the proletarian party's leading role is an extremely important societal pattern that necessarily emerges and develops in the proletariat's class struggle against the bourgeoisie and during socialist and communist construction. . . .

The socialist society is a complex system of various production collectives, state agencies and public organizations that interact with one another and constitute a single social organism. A central guiding force is necessary if all the component parts of this organism are to function harmoniously, purposefully and rhythmically, while helping one another. This force is the Communist party, the vanguard party, which has no connection with sectionalist, group or departmental considerations, which examines all questions from the statewide, nationwide point of view and as political leader possesses higher authority than all other organizations.

In present conditions theory has become especially important. The practical solution of highly complex problems of Communist construction depends largely on creative development of Marist-Leninist theory, scientific generalization of the very rich experience accumulated by the Soviet people, the possession of profound theoretical knowledge and the ideological and political upbringing of the working people. This work can be done only under the leadership of the Communist Party, which has mastered to perfection the theory and method of Marxism-Leninism.

Thus, the necessity of enhancing the Communist Party's leading role in socialist society arises from objective conditions and the requirements of further developing society itself along the path to communism.

Achievements in the construction of communism in our country depend not only on internal conditions and prerequisites. We are building communism in a very complex international situation, in conditions of acute struggle between two world systems — socialism and capitalism. The imperialists have not abandoned their hopes of undermining socialism and weakening its forces. They are waging a criminal war against Vietnam, organizing reactionary conspiracies wherever possible, actively supporting the West German revanchists and militarists, encouraging the Israeli aggressors and intensifying ideological warfare against the U.S.S.R. and the other socialist countries, and have used chiefly nationalist and revisionist elements for these purposes.

Given the various zigzags of history, in these complex conditions the correct line of development for a socialist state can be found only by the Communist Party, the party that is faithful to Marxism-Leninism, capable of correctly analyzing all the peripeteia in the struggle of the classes and their parties in the world arena and implacable toward bourgeois ideology, ruling out any compromise with it, the party that consistently defends the purity of Marxism-Leninism in the struggle against all its enemies and misinterpreters, has broad international ties and can take advantage of the experience of Communist movements in other countries. . . .

In organizing the ideological struggle against the U.S.S.R. and the other socialist countries, the imperialist ideologists and politicians make use of lies, slander and misinformation and juggle the facts. They count on influencing some people in the socialist countries who are insufficiently steadfast in their moral, ideological and political attitudes and on finding among them allies and helpers through whom they can exert their corrupting influence from within. It must be said that individuals susceptible to bourgeois praise do sometimes fall into the propaganda snares cleverly set by the imperialists' ideologists. Lacking firm ideological convictions, they become yesmen and peddlers of bourgeois ideology hostile to socialism.

Proceeding on the basis of profound objective analysis of the present international situation and the struggle between socialism and capitalism in the world arena, the April plenary session of the C.P.S.U. Central Committee gave instructions on intensifying all Party ideological work. The Central Committee plenary session emphasized that implacable struggle against reactionary bourgeois ideology, resolute exposure of all imperialism's intrigues, and Communist upbringing of Party members and all working people are among the chief obligations of all Party organizations. Party and Soviet organizations, Communists and all workers in ideological institutions are called upon to wage an offensive against bourgeois ideology, to oppose actively any attempts to drag into literary or artistic works views alien to the socialist ideology of Soviet society and to make skillful use of existing means of ideological steadfastness and feelings of Soviet patriotism and proletarian internationalism.

MAY PRESS CAMPAIGN: POLAND

DURING THE FIRST part of May, the Poles certainly equaled, perhaps surpassed, Soviet and East German condemnation of antisocialist tendencies in Czechoslovakia. Warsaw had reason for pique. Not only had the Prague press and radio freely criticized Warsaw's anti-Zionist campaign and faculty dismissals following the March student protests in Poland but Professors Leszek Kołakowski and Bronisław Baczko were thereafter invited to lecture at Charles University in Prague.[1] Letters of protest had been presented by members of the Czechoslovak Academy of Sciences to the Polish Embassy.[2]

The Polish Ambassador in Prague on May 6 formally protested against this "anti-Polish campaign." According to the Deputy Editor-in-Chief of *Trybuna ludu,* Jozef Barecki (Document 22), such criticism was inspired by "antisocialist, Zionist elements" — a charge made more ominous by his favorable quotation of orthodox statements by one of the remaining conservatives in the Czechoslovak Central Committee, Alois Indra.

DOCUMENT 22

TELEVISION INTERVIEW WITH JÓZEF BARECKI
DEPUTY EDITOR-IN-CHIEF OF "TRYBUNA LUDU"
May 11, 1968
Excerpts
[Special translation from Polish Monitoring; RFE Polish Press Survey, No. 2133 (May 22, 1968)]

. . . I would now like to pass to a matter which you have already mentioned, namely, to what you have called attacks on socialist states in the Czechoslovak

[1] William F. Robinson, "Czechoslovakia and Its Allies," *Studies in Comparative Communism,* Vol. 1, Nos. 1 and 2 (July/October 1968), pp. 144–147.

[2] *Práce,* March 29, 1968.

press. About a week ago, our press carried a very brief item on the protest note submitted by our ambassador in Prague, protesting against the anti-Polish campaign, as it was called, conducted by the Czechoslovak press and TV. . . .

Here again it must be said that antisocialist elements, Zionist elements, are also trying to foster this kind of anti-Polish campaign. A few examples at hand — the paper *Práce* published a letter from three writers on May 4, accusing us of an anti-Semitic policy, and defending antisocialist, antistate elements in Poland. On April 23, Lustig came out on Prague TV with insults against the Polish people, going so far as to compare us with the Nazis. . . .

We Poles can be expected to trust the Czechoslovak Party or the Communist leaders to realize these dangers and will take steps to counteract this incorrect, dangerous development in the situation. One can enumerate the voices of the First Secretary Dubček, of President Svoboda and many other Czechoslovak leaders.

If only in Cieszyn.

Indeed, a few days ago — I was just going to talk about that — a great Polish-Czechoslovak rally took place in Cieszyn, a rally which has had a wide response and at which Edward Gierek spoke for us, while a secretary of the CC of the Czechoslovak Party, Alois Indra, spoke for the Czechoslovak side. He stated clearly that there can be no question of the creation of an opposition bourgeois party in Czechoslovakia, of leading the republic away from the road of socialist construction and alliance with the Soviet Union and with other socialist countries.

Let us not forget, said Indra, that we live in a world full of conflict and disquiet, that there are still forces which would like to carry out their revisionist program. . . .

MAY PRESS CAMPAIGN: EAST GERMANY

LIKE POLAND, East Germany had its own reasons for participating enthusiastically in the May press campaign against Czechoslovakia. Not only was the tentative thaw in Prague's attitude toward West Germany anathema to the Ulbricht regime but on May 3 *Rudé právo* had printed an article "distorting" East German tightening of access to Berlin.[1] Pankow continued to attack after the intensity of the Soviet polemics had temporarily subsided with the visits of Kosygin and Grechko. The diatribe against Prague (Document 23) of Dr. Hajo Herbell, deputy chief editor of *Neues Deutschland,* appeared on the same day that the Czechoslovak press agency ČTK announced Warsaw Pact maneuvers would be held on Czechoslovak territory in June. The question of such joint maneuvers had become an issue of Prague's good faith[2] and, conceivably, represented a compromise between Soviet desire for Warsaw Pact troops on the Czechoslovak–West Germany border and Czechoslovak lack of enthusiasm for any joint military activity in the country until the political situation was more stable. Herbell forcefully reminded Prague, and perhaps Moscow, that members of the socialist community had other obligations as well.

---

[1] The East German ambassador to Prague, Peter Florin, officially protested the *Rudé právo* article (*Berliner Zeitung,* May 11, 1968).

[2] Reportedly, joint maneuvers scheduled for March had been postponed because of political tensions. However, at Dresden the Czechoslovaks pledged "concrete" measures to strengthen the Warsaw Pact (see the Dresden communiqué, Document 9). May 4, the same day that Dubček unexpectedly visited Moscow, the new Czechoslovak Defense Minister Martin Dzúr announced joint exercises would be held in the country later in 1968. On his return, Dubček described joint military exercises in individual countries as a practical part of military cooperation under the Warsaw Pact (Dubček interview, *Pravda,* May 8, 1968). In sum, Prague had agreed, but only in principle.

DOCUMENT 23

"BONN BETWEEN FEAR AND HOPE"

Dr. Hajo Herbell
May 24, 1968
Excerpts
[*Neues Deutschland*, May 24, 1968]

❧

In a recent meeting with workers from Czechoslovakia, workers of our republic emphasized the great importance attached to the successful development of
friendship ties between the GDR and the Czechoslovak Socialist Republic.
Our relations are good, indeed this is proved by the great understanding displayed by the GDR for current problems in Czechoslovakia, as demonstrated
by the various meetings of the party and state leaderships of both countries.

Regarding the different aspects of the building of socialism in Czechoslovakia, which is taking place under conditions somewhat different from ours,
our party and state leadership is guided by the principle of proletarian internationalism; that is, the problems are the concern of the Czechoslovak working
class and the Czechoslovak Communist Party and its Central Committee under the leadership of First Secretary Comrade Alexander Dubček. In this connection, the successful socialist development of the Czechoslovak neighbor state
is naturally of great importance to our party, our republic, and the entire socialist community. Varied and deep relations exist between us in all spheres.
Our states are members of the Warsaw Pact. They are linked by bilateral
treaties of friendship, cooperation, and mutual assistance. Our schoolchildren
have already learned that the Czechoslovak Socialist Republic plays an important political and geographical role in Europe; and, like the GDR, it plays
the role of an outpost in the socialist community of states.

Our party and the GDR Government act in accordance with the need
to consolidate the common fighting traditions and solidarity with the Czechoslovak working class and the friendship and alliance with our fraternal neighboring state. Together with it, we stand guard for peace at the western border
of the socialist camp where we are facing a common enemy — revanchist West
German imperialism.

What is at stake in the Czechoslovak Socialist Republic? The working people of Czechoslovakia, led by the Czechoslovak Communist Party and in close
cooperation with the Soviet Union and other socialist countries, have made
great achievements in building socialist society in the historically short period
since February 1948. For example, since that time industrial production
has increased by more than 450 percent and the national income by 200
percent. The author of this article has been able to visit Slovakia several times.
Its image, in particular, has completely changed.

However, during the great upsurge, which we in the GDR have followed with warm sympathy as members of one and the same family, difficulties have also occurred, just as they have occurred in every country faced with the complicated task of building socialism and with the profound changes in social forms resulting from the implementation of this historic process. On the complicated road forward into unexplored social spheres, as our Czechoslovak friends have found, a number of serious mistakes have been made. Urgent questions have not been taken up in time. Thus, much resentment has been created at a time when the Czechoslovak Socialist Republic, just like the GDR and other fraternal countries, is faced with a new complicated task: to create a well-developed socialist society amid an aggravated class struggle in the international arena and the conditions of the scientific-technical revolution.

Thus, in the Czechoslovak Socialist Republic it is now important to new and complicated problems, to build socialist democracy in accordance with the new stage of development, and to continue to consolidate the foundations of socialism. It is the concern of our fraternal Czechoslovak people, of the working class of the Czechoslovak Socialist Republic, and of the Czechoslovak Communist Party how these tasks will be fulfilled. We are confident that they will fulfill the tasks successfully.

Enemy Intentions

We have mentioned the fact of an intensified class struggle in the international arena. Everyone can see this struggle daily. Imperialism and its inhuman system of exploitation, oppression, neocolonialism, and war is already being fought in its own strongholds. In France, more than ten million people are waging a powerful struggle against the state monopoly system. In the United States, the movement in support of civil rights and against the Johnson clique's crimes against the Vietnamese people is mounting. In Italy, the Communist party emerged victorious and even stronger from the elections. At the same time, socialism's appeal is being increasingly enhanced because of the successes scored by the Soviet Union and its fraternal countries.

Thus, we can see that imperialism has not grown stronger; nor will it grow stronger. On the contrary, its power has been thoroughly shaken. But this is precisely why its aggressiveness is increasing. Evidence of this is present in all its barbaric frightfuless: American napalm is devastating the cities and the fields of the Vietnamese people. Israel — the aggressor supported by the United States and Bonn — impudently refuses to release the territory it usurped in the summer of 1967 and is fanning a new war. In West Germany, the Kiesinger-Strauss government is proceeding to establish an unmitigated emergency dictatorship — an act of internal aggression in preparation for external aggression.

So that no one will misunderstand us, we repeat in this connection: The events in the Czechoslovak Socialist Republic to which we refer are the affair of the people of the Czechoslovak Socialist Republic. But these events are not taking place in isolation from the world. And this world is not one world — there is socialism and there is imperialism.

In view of the world balance of power, imperialism is not in a position to mount a frontal attack against socialism. However, this does not mean that it has abandoned its objectives. It merely seeks to apply more effective, intelligent variants of aggression — so-called psychological warfare, covert propaganda, infiltration of anti-Communist theories, economic enticement with a view to exerting political blackmail, and so forth. One would have to be divorced from reality not to see through this scheme. And everyone can easily see that, in view of the difficulties besetting it, the imperialist enemy is attempting to take advantage of the difficult situation of our Czechoslovak comrade. It now appears that he is vacillating between fear and hope: fear that socialism in the Czechoslovak Socialist Republic may become stronger as a result of current developments, and hope that this can be prevented and that the tide of events can be turned against socialism.

We want to examine in detail only one of the methods employed by the enemy. This is a method which he is employing against the Czechoslovak Socialist Republic and that country's Communist party and also against the GDR — part and parcel of the so-called new Eastern policy which is aimed at the socialist community in general.

At the very beginning of this examination, we come across a noteworthy fact. In their nonfrontal, covert attack, the imperialists are currently refraining from openly spreading their antisocialist slogans. Rather, they are couching them in reports and "on the scene" reportages. They let others do the job. With their help, they are composing a picture which is to serve as a guide for the "renewal of socialism." They are disseminating certain calculated news items which counterrevolutionary elements use as a guide. Thus, we see that this is a method which does not represent strength but which is insidious and dangerous.

The example we shall use to demonstrate this method is a single article from a single West German journal, Der Spiegel, a special psychological warfare organ which is financed by various imperialist intelligence services. We want to scrutinize this journal's "arguments" point by point.

Slander of the Czechoslovak Communist Party

1. The main thrust is directed against the Czechoslovak Communist Party. With obvious glee, Der Spiegel quotes from an article published in the magazine of the Czechoslovak Writers' Union in which an author named Jiří Hanak writes: "If the majority of the people no longer want Communist party leadership, will they nevertheless declare succinctly that the revolution is unassailable, that every country which has been won over to communism once must forever remain communist? This seems absurd."

To begin with, it should be admitted that Hanak and Der Spiegel see one thing quite correctly: Revolution and leadership by the Communist party are inseparable. Then the argument really becomes absurd, for a country where the socialist revolution has been victorious and which "has been won over to communism" must, after all, be considered a country which has been freed from imperialism. In such a country, there is no longer any capitalist exploitation. In such a country, the road to democracy, in the actual sense of the word, has been opened for the first time in that country's history: the road to worker-peasant power, to socialist ownership as the economic basis of the working people's real freedom, and to increasing participation of all the people in the affairs of the economy and the state.

Beginning with the Great October Revolution, the Soviet Union was the first country in the world to embark on this road. Everything which has been built on this fifty-year road by titanic efforts, heroism, and sacrifices shows that without socialism there is no freedom for the working people. Socialism and democracy are one. Socialism is the highest form of democracy; under it the citizens own the state. All political power is exercised by the working people. Man is the object of all endeavors of the socialist society and its state. What the people create by their labor belongs to them.

Thus, when *Der Spiegel* asks through Hanak whether this state of affairs must last forever, this question absurdly implies that history may go backward instead of forward: imperialist power again instead of the worker-peasant power; imperialist monopolies again instead of socialist property; exploitation again instead of freedom from exploitation; the role of humiliated, insulted, and oppressed people again instead of independence and dignity. History does not go backward. The West German imperialist journal's shady formula is not improved in any way by the fact that it proceeds from the "assumption" that the "majority of the people" would want such a development.

We do not know of a single example in world history where the majority of a people that had been liberated from imperialism would have wanted to undo its own power and freedom. Such wishes exist only in the minds of the representatives of monopoly capital.

Bucketfuls of Dirt

2. With the typical perceptiveness of a covert warfare agent, *Der Spiegel* has an idea of how the thrust against the Communist party could be mounted. It declares — again citing another source — "We are digging up so much dirt from the past that even the most convinced Communists must be disgusted." Dirt, of course, refers to the mistakes which we mentioned.

Each of us understands the desire and efforts of the Czechoslovak comrades to correct these mistakes. However, what the imperialists want is something totally different from an objective rectification of mistakes made while marching forward, in the struggle against the enemy. They would like to have an unlimited seditious discussion of mistakes, exclusively backward oriented. They want to have all socialist achievements obfuscated and slandered.

At this point let us raise a question: Who in history and who in the world of today has, after all, piled up so much dirt? Who is stained with so much dirt and blood that even the most credulous worshipers of this system should be disgusted and frightened? Again we recommend a look at the American theater of war in Vietnam. We advise people to recall German fascist imperialism and the crimes it committed against its own people in the east and west, north and south. We refer to the Greek terrorist regime, to Spain and Portugal, to the new genocidal plans being hatched by the Bonn general staff.

We recall the bloodshed caused by imperialism, ranging from the murder of Karl Liebknecht and Rosa Luxemburg to the shots fired at Dr. Martin Luther King and Rudi Dutschke. . . .

The Counterrevolutionary Slogan

3. After it has waged a blow against the Communist party and believes that the socialist order is sufficiently soiled, *Der Spiegel* tackles the question of who is to lead the "reformed" society. According to the writing of a man named Ivan Sviták, who calls himself a "Marxist philosopher," the leadership should include "the workers' movement without its apparatchiks, the middle classes without collaborators, and the intelligentsia as the top leader." One need not necessarily be a historian to know the origin of this. In 1919, the counterrevolutionaries in Kronstadt had the following slogan: With the Soviets, but without "their" Communists. Today the Communists, particularly officials of the Communist party, are described as "apparatchiks." These officials, however, as the shop stewards of the working class and the working people, are the most experienced cadres of every Marxist-Leninist party, its Central Committee, the other elected organs, and their staff members: department heads, instructors, editors, and so forth. If one were to take these cadres away from the party, it would become weak enough for the counterrevolution to make progress.

Let us consider the other elements in the "leadership model" of *Der Spiegel*: middle classes "without collaborators." In plain language this means the dissolution of the alliance of all strata of the working people with the working class and replacement of socialist cooperation with the old destructive antagonism. And the intelligentsia as the top leader? We socialists certainly do not need anyone to teach us about the great creative role of the intelligentsia. We socialists do not need anyone to enlighten us about the performances of our socialist intelligentsia in science and technology, literature and art, in public education, and so forth.

However, only the class that represents the majority of the people, that has made the greatest sacrifices in the struggle against the old order, that has registered the greatest performances in building the new order, that is the best organized, and that is equipped with a scientific ideology is qualified to lead the entire society on the unexplored road to the building of socialism. This is the working class.

It must also be realized what the people at *Der Spiegel* mean by the intelligentsia: every monopolist, every crazy petit bourgeois who dabbles in "art," every artistocratic dandy. This would be a fine leadership for a socialist society! And here is something else to think about: Of all people, those who as representatives of the late capitalist society in West Germany are strengthening the state machinery by the transition to open dictatorship and who wish to manipulate all the people and induce them to support their ideology through the mass media, recommend that the socialist countries abolish the state, worker-peasant power, "open" themselves [to capitalist influence], and abandon their political-moral unity and cohesion. Do they seriously believe that we do not know who would benefit from this and whom it would harm?

Convergence Theory

If someone should seek to find a common denominator for the three hostile methods which we have discussed up to this point, he will find it in the so-called convergence theory. Thus, it is no surprise when *Der Spiegel* supplies it on the spot — this time it cites the Yugoslav revisionist Milovan Djilas. This man, who was ousted by the Yugoslav League of Communists many years ago and sentenced to prison a number of times for his antisocialist activities, writes — and this suits *Der Spiegel* because it fits into the complex of its counterrevolutionary recipes — "We are living in a world which tends to become an entity. . . . Socialism is becoming ever more liberal, capitalism ever more socialist. This is one of the most elementary phenomena of our time."

We are convinced that our readers will personally take issue with this incredible nonsense, and that we do not need to make a thorough explanation. Perhaps only one: Anyone who looks at the United States, Great Britain, France, or West Germany will hardly believe that modern capitalism is becoming "ever more socialist," and that, vice versa, socialism is becoming "ever more liberal." This can be recognized as demagogic humbug, at least by those who know a little about the course of history. After all, the line of social progress leads from the bourgeois revolution via early, progressive bourgeois liberalism and petit bourgeois democracy — which of course could not overcome the exploiter system — to the revolutionary workers' movement. By its struggle, and only by it, are the progressive aims and ideals of freedom of all previous progressive forces being fulfilled. This struggle and the world historic victories of the working class are the "most elementary event," the fundamental law of the motion of our time. In them, and only in them, lies the reason for the powerful attractiveness which socialism, embodied in and led to victory by the Marxist-Leninist parties, holds for everyone in today's world who thinks in a humanist, democratic, peace-loving, and progressive manner.

Horsetrader Manners

4. Although it is a futile undertaking, the enemy seeks to undermine cooperation among the socialist states. In this connection, *Der Spiegel* feels it can invoke statements by Czechoslovak Deputy Premier Ota Šik. The paper writes that the Czechoslovak Socialist Republic needs a half billion dollars worth of credit and, for that matter, "in hard foreign exchange because the required machines are obtainable only in the West." The Hamburg news magazine attributes such obvious plans to a country which itself has a highly developed machine-building industry. Moreover, this country has socialist partners whose industrial power cannot be disregarded even by imperialists such as those of the United States. Thus, we are dealing with a case of traditional imperialist impudence and arrogance, to which must be added the following crude attempt: As the competition among the principal imperialist

countries becomes increasingly intense, they seek to direct economic expansion at the socialist countries, control their markets, and thus make them "compliant," as Bonn Foreign Minister Brandt and newly appointed World Bank President McNamara recently put it. As we said, these are plans which the imperialists have expressed out loud, not assumptions on our part.

Let there be no misunderstanding. Socialist countries can of course buy machines, licenses, and complete installations in capitalist states. This, as is well known, is also done by the GDR, which favors worldwide trade and wants such trade to serve peace. But as all economic and political experiences show, this is not the main road to economic strengthening pursued by the community of socialist states. Anyone who wants to pursue a socialist policy must himself be economically strong; this is demonstrated in particular by the history of the Soviet Union. Anyone who wants to pursue a successful socialist policy must, together with the fraternal countries, strive to attain and seek to determine the top world standard.

Let us refrain from discussing how questionable *Der Spiegel*'s economic baits are at this juncture, when the dollar and pound sterling are suffering from chronic consumption and their stability has become a doubtful factor. Let us also refrain from discussing the adversary's obvious tactics of counseling the socialist states to engage in economic disintegration at the very moment when the principal capitalist countries are seeking, in the class interests of the monopolies, to integrate their economies one way or another.

Anti-Soviet Orgies

5. To promote its divisive and seditious tactics, *Der Spiegel* dishes up a variety of anti-Soviet slander. The people of Europe are to forget that they were liberated from Hitlerite barbarism by the Soviet Union. The people are to forget that it is primarily because of the Soviet Union's power that it has been possible to restrain the American imperialists and Hitler's successors in Bonn and to prevent them from unleashing a third world war. The people of the Czechoslovak Socialist Republic are to forget that the remains of 150,000 Soviet soldiers who fell for the liberation of the Czech and Slovak peoples are buried between Košice and Ústí. They are to forget the assistance the Soviet Union has given and continues to give the Czechoslovak Socialist Republic and the other fraternal countries in building the new society. To this end lies are spread such as the one about the alleged murder of former Czechoslovak Foreign Minister Jan Masaryk who, in actual fact, committed suicide in 1948, and whose "murder" was invented by a creature named Veigl, who is notorious in the Czechoslovak Socialist Republic. It is necessary to descend from politics to the gutters of imperialism to recall that this Veigl started his career as a crook, as a "Spanish prince," and that later he sold nothing less than the Prague Hradcany Castle to a rich but unsuspecting Arab sheik. . . .

Our Standpoint

People who wage a struggle against socialism with such methods as those used by Veigl pass judgment upon themselves. At the same time, they also reckon without the host, without the nations which are building socialism and to which the building of communism in the Soviet Union is a shining beacon in their struggle. They reckon without us, whose confidence in the Czechoslovak working class and their party they wish to undermine. They are barking up the wrong tree. We have confidence in the Czechoslovak Communist Party, the working class, and the people of Czechoslovakia. We have good reason for this confidence, not only by virtue of the more than twenty years of the joint building of socialism, but also because of the avowed determination of the Czechoslovak Communists to further develop the socialist society and protect it from hostile attacks.

In Czechoslovakia the workers' militia has taken a stand against "the slander campaign abroad and a few secret efforts of the extremists to divert our socialist democratization process from the socialist road." It has condemned all statements belittling the work performed by the party to date. It has supported the firm alliance with the Soviet Union as the basis of Czechoslovak foreign policy. The League of Antifascist Resistance Fighters has called for undeviating friendship with the USSR.

At a conference with party secretaries in Prague, Comrade Alexander Dubček, First Secretary of the Czechoslovak Communist Party Central Committee, stated that the Central Committee decisions on the further building of socialism were being implemented and that the party must resist hostile tendencies directed against the leading role of the working class and the Czechoslovak Communist Party, against the socialist state. The conference concluded that the Communists would under all circumstances defend, consolidate, and develop the results achieved by the working class and all the people under the leadership of the Czechoslovak Communist Party in February 1948 and in the further building of socialism.

Bonn will certainly continue to hover between fear and hope. Hoping that the current events in the Czechoslovak Socialist Republic could still be channeled against socialism, Der Spiegel wrote that "The gentle spring in Prague will be followed by a hot Prague summer." We certainly also hope for a beautiful sunny summer for the people of Prague and also for us. However, as far as the political temperature is concerned, the summer will become ice cold for the people in Bonn. The Czechoslovak working class and its party, with which we are fraternally linked, will resolutely rebuff the antisocialist forces who feel encouraged and sense their opportunity. The Czechoslovak working class and its party will lead the socialist development forward. In this advance we will firmly stand by their side.

"DRAFT PROPOSAL" OF THE ECONOMISTS

ALTHOUGH OBVIOUSLY a working paper, the "Draft Proposal" of Czech and Slovak Economists (Document 24) was a detailed projection of the demands raised by Dubček in his September 1967 Plenum Speech (Document 3). The draft carefully outlined what was to be done ideally. Yet the question of putting equality into practice subsequently voiced by the Slovak Leader Gustav Husák with respect to a constitutional settlement, obviously applied to assemblies and budgets alike: "There are to be Czech national organs as well as Slovak national organs, but who is to lead and how are decisions to be made in the central organs?" [1] In short, the Czechs' insistence on majority rule in the central organs was potentially irreconcilable with the Slovak demand for parity — that is, equality — in decision-making.

DOCUMENT 24
"DRAFT PROPOSAL BY A GROUP OF ECONOMISTS: THE
PRINCIPLES OF FEDERATION OF THE ECONOMY OF THE
CZECHOSLOVAK PEOPLE"
Complete Text
[*Rudé právo,* May 18, 1968]

At the initiative of the ideological sections of the central committees of the Czechoslovak and Slovak Communist Parties, Czech and Slovak economists met at a joint conference in Bratislava on April 29 this year to discuss fundamental problems resulting from the federation of the economy of the Czechoslovak socialist republic. They have agreed on the principles which will become the basis for further discussions and for the working out of problems by pertinent commissions formed by the republican government. At the same time

---

[1] *Rudé právo,* July 6, 1968.

they expect discussion in the specialized press will help to explain and elaborate the most sensitive and decisive sphere of the new regulation concerning the relations between our peoples.

I. The Self-Realization of Peoples in an Integrated Czechoslovak Socialist Economy

The socialist settlement of the nationality problem in all fields and hence also in the economic field proceeds from the fundamental conclusions of Marxist-Leninist doctrine.

1. In its ultimate consequences social development tends toward equal conditions for the self-realization of all members of society. Under socialism relatively equal conditions for this self-expression are being created.

2. Socialism is marked by differences in the quality of labor expended and hence by natural differences in the position of the labor force. At the same time, however, socialism implies the economic equality of the position of the entire national labor force with respect to the labor force of another people.

3. The right of peoples to self-determination is associated with the prerogative of peoples to enter a higher state synthesis. The principle of acting according to one's own will, the mutual benefits of a settlement, and the right to actual participation in state policy eliminate any form of endowing a greater share of power on any people.

4. Czechoslovakia is a state of two peoples with equal rights. Its economy is an integrated synthesis of two national economies. These national economies — the Czech and the Slovak — constitute an open system of a material production base and an economic base which serve the self-realization of the peoples in their work and in their lives.

The integrated economy of the Czechoslovak Socialist Republic is a higher, fully justified economic synthesis and an expression of the dynamic, economic, interdependence of the Czechs and Slovaks which makes it possible to utilize the national wealth of both peoples more economically than if the economic peaks of their national development were simply added up. This is why an integrated economy makes it possible not to scatter economic potential but to raise it to a higher power and thus satisfy present and future needs in a more comprehensive manner. The self-determination of the peoples of the Czechoslovak Socialist Republic is being realized in all fields of social life: political, economic, cultural, legal, and so forth.

5. The right to self-determination presupposes economic independence on the part of the peoples of the Czechoslovak Socialist Republic. Sovereignty among peoples requires their economic aptitude for the management and utilization of the wealth created by them as well as, on the other hand, national responsibility for results achieved. The national economy energizes the important motive force of the people's initiative.

6. The choice of each people to incorporate its economy into a higher state synthesis is its own exclusive right. In practice, however, this right has objective limitations which result from the very nature of the socialist economy and from the principles of the mutual advantage of the solutions.

7. We regard incorporation of the national political regions as a whole into the state-wide economy as the most advantageous principle. The development of the Czechoslovak economy requires a principled elaboration of the all-round incorporation of national political regions into an integrated Czechoslovak economy.

II. Characteristics of the Integration of the National Economies

1. Previous development of the Czechoslovak economy prevented a rational economic integration. Integration of the two national economies was brought about authoritatively and administratively, from above. The specific economic interests of the Czech and Slovak peoples were only solved incidentally without a considered plan in mind. Previous development has negatively affected the development of the entire economy of the Czechoslovak Socialist Republic. Its final consequences have acted against the economic interests of both national political regions.

2. The vital interests of the two national economies and of the Czechoslovak economy as a whole fairly cries out for progressive economic integration to be brought about on the basis of natural economic processes — from below — in harmony with the thorough implementation of an economic management system.

3. Partnership between the economic factors of both our national economies is the first step toward progressive economic integration. Advancement of creative national forces is opposed to national isolation. In fact, at the present level of Czechoslovak productive forces and with a modern investment policy, advances in the emerging scientific-technical revolution must lead to a more rational utilization of resources of national wealth. To achieve this, multifaceted forms of integration will be implemented.

4. Particularly in Slovakia, accelerated implementation of progressive forms of economic integration is necessary because of the greater deformations of previous development and the clearer impact of unsolved problems related to the new managerial system. It is necessary to eliminate the one-sided nature of departmental and branch structure, weaknesses in the composition of production programs, lack of rationality in investment policy mainly with respect to the labor force, and critical lags in the tertiary sector, as well as the social underrating of Slovak agriculture.

5. Economic integration must create a more dependable basis for the social and economic equalization of Slovakia with the Czech lands, eliminate discriminatory conditions in Slovakia and ensure, in accordance with the action program of the Czechoslovak Communist Party, equalization by 1980.

6. Internal economic integration which is thus conceived will not weaken the position of the Czechoslovak Socialist Republic in the context of international division of labor. On the contrary, by incorporating the national economies in this process in an optimum manner it will multiply the effect of linking the republic with the world economy, especially the European economy. It can be particularly helpful for a more effective utilization of the opportunities of cooperation among socialist countries, mainly with the USSR.

7. A unified integrated economy of the Czechoslovak Socialist Republic requires a unified market which in turn presupposes the following features: (a) a unified currency; (b) free movement of labor; (c) free flow of funds; (d) unified principles in the managerial system and in economic policy (agreed upon by the national organs).

8. A unified currency reflects the unity of the state at home and abroad. It represents the most comprehensive instrument for influencing the state's economic policy and a manifestation of the national convertibility of the work of the two economies. A unified currency is distinguished by the following features: (a) a single monetary unit (the crown [koruna]); (b) a single rate of exchange with respect to foreign currencies; (c) unified principles of banknote issue.

9. A joint market makes it possible to buy and sell anywhere throughout the state without any customs barriers, at approximately identical prices, with standard prices for the basic necessary articles and services and with a roughly identical over-all price level. It also creates equal conditions for effectiveness in business activity even though the economic tools may vary.

10. The free movement of labor results from the free choice of trade and employment on the territory of the Czechoslovak Socialist Republic. The price of labor as a production factor must be calculated rationally, keeping in mind the location of labor resources as it is today and as it will be in the future. This price also comprises a compensation for the transfer of the labor force migrating from one national political region into another. Socioeconomic preferential measures are required for the free movement of labor forces in the process of interregional economic equalization.

11. The free flow of funds promotes progressive forms of founding, expanding, and combining enterprises throughout the republic. It makes it possible to invest, to build branches, to utilize foreign capital participation, and so forth according to the principles of economic rationality. It prompts an active loan policy in Slovakia and social elimination of the backward infrastructure of Slovakia while solving Slovakia's economic priorities problem and using economic instruments for stimulating economic activity.

12. The nature of the market and the processes of this market in a modern society are influenced and formed in a basic manner by the state's economic policy and by the overall managerial system (which comprises the financial and credit system, the price and wage system, the fundamental norms of economic law, and so forth). This is why uniformity of the market requires uniformity of the basic principles of economic policy and of the management system, which must be ensured by joint actions of the two national organs.

13. Common principles in compiling socioeconomic data will enable both national economies to carry out comparative analyses of the effectiveness of development of integrated groupings in the individual regions.

14. Stimulating, integrating, and protecting functions promote progressive integration: (a) development (stimulating) functions foster progressive structural changes in the two national economies which conform with scientific-technical development, a balanced development of microregions, and so forth;

(b) integrating functions bear weight on the creation of rational territorial production and urban units characterized by conditions of optimum working and living conditions; (c) protective functions protect the national enterprises from unfavorable, discriminatory influences. Economic integration must not harm the economic interests of the peoples or discriminate where utilization of their natural, technical, or human resources is concerned.

15. The delineated principles, features, and functions which promote progressive forms of integration of the national economies create the framework for the federal organization of economic relations in the Czechoslovak Socialist Republic at all stages of the substantive and institutional settlement of problems.

III. Economic Principles of Federal Organization

The economic principles of the federal reorganization of the relations between the peoples of the Czechoslovak Socialist Republic proceed from respect for national sovereignty and from the need for a thorough implementation of the economic management system in both national economic regions. Such an approach excludes misunderstandings concerning a possible "big political" and "small economic" federation, and it unequivocally leads to a politicoeconomic federation.

1. Macrodevelopment considerations, comprising basic national economic relations, will constitute the basis for the long-term development of the economy of the Czechoslovak Socialist Republic and of the national economies. The Czech and Slovak national organs will draft independent concepts and plans for the optimum development of the national economies. The central plan will develop and coordinate independent concepts and plans for the optimum development of the national economies in the interest of the optimum advancement of the Czechoslovak economy.

2. Budgeting will be carried out through a central (federal) budget and two national budgets. The national budgets will contribute to the central budget in accordance with a key previously agreed upon, for example, in conformity with the relations between the budgetary receipts of both economies. Cost of individual state-wide activities (national defense, foreign service, federal administration) will also be paid for from this budget.

Independent national budgets will be formed of all the budgetary receipts (taxes and deductions), according to the local production principle. The national budgets will encompass all economic organizations (if necessary, even individual plants), budgetary, subsidized, and other organizations which have their seats in the national political regions with the exception of activities financed centrally as per previous agreement.

The national organs have the power to regulate and execute the national budgets. The relations between the national budgets and the central budget will be fixed for prolonged periods of time. National organs will discuss national budgets and their closing balances and will then approve them.

3. Price policy will proceed from the following principles: (a) a common price pattern, identical price regions, and identical relations with world prices will constitute a basic principle throughout the republic; (b) basically standard

prices for basic foodstuffs and raw materials will apply throughout the Czechoslovak Socialist Republic; (c) the extraordinary economic and political significance of prices for both the Czech and Slovak economies calls for the full participation of the national organs in the shaping of the concepts of price policy as well as for power on their part to implement the policy; (d) the power of the federal government with respect to price policies will be defined by an agreement between the two national organs.

4. Wage policy: (a) in the Czechoslovak Socialist Republic there apply uniform principles of compensation which are dependent on the results of individual and collective work. As a result of this there exist common wage regulations; (b) the system of common wage-policy principles does not preclude under special statewide or national conditions the possible existence of economically justified wage differences; (c) in view of the free movement of labor the national organs also pursue a wage policy in the national political regions.

5. The realization of the tax and deduction policy requires — in view of the joint market and free movement of labor and funds — that essentially identical demands be made on effectiveness in the field of enterprises, and hence it requires essentially uniform basic principles for the tax and deduction system. National organs which act on the basis of previously agreed upon obligations toward the federal government have the power to fix taxes and deductions and to determine their rates, as well as lay down principles for the creation of enterprise funds (reserve funds, enterprise funds, the working people's fund, and other funds).

6. A banking system in which the issuing of currency is objectively and organizationally separated from commercial activities is consonant with the conditions of an economic managerial system and federal arrangement. Commercial banks and national banknote-issuing centers will operate independently in the national political regions. The rules regulating the operations of the federal currency organ must be laid down in detail.

7. The concept of foreign policy relationships (territorial and structural trends in trade, outline-type international agreements, and so forth) are formulated by the federal organ in agreement with the national organs or producers and buyers. The national organs ensure the realization of foreign trade activities on the territories of the national political region and directly participate in the preparation and conclusion of trade agreements which concern their national economies. The banking organs of the national political regions will conduct foreign currency operations. Additional and no less important aspects of the federal arrangement (investment policy, economic interest, and so forth) which today are regulated by blanket schematic methods will have to be worked out by the national organs of the two national political regions.

IV. The Position of Economic Managerial Organs

1. The position of the enterprises is being treated in a basically new manner in the spirit of the action program of the Czechoslovak Communist Party. The enterprises cease to be operational administrators of state funds. They be-

come active factors in the market. These axioms apply throughout the republic to both Czech and Slovak enterprises and require additional institutional changes.

2. The creation of enterprise organization relations which agree with territorial principles is connected with federal organization. The federation will create broad possibilities for supra-enterprise integration on the basis of the new leeway in decision-making and within the framework of the whole state, irrespective of the territory of the national political regions and in accordance with the economic needs of the enterprises. Associations of this type can also be formed at many echelons. It is likewise possible to form joint research, development, design and trade organizations and working places with a statewide field of activities, joint scientific research centers (atomic research, electronics, etc.), and to establish joint activity in the field of patents, and establishing norms and measures.

3. Under the conditions of a federal arrangement the retention of the present ministerial institutional management system of the economy created by the system of centralized directives would render impossible a thoroughgoing introduction of the economic system of management. Not even supplementing the presently existing institutional system by establishing new organs at the level of the state and national centers would qualitatively change the situation. The federal arrangement requires the elimination of the institutional relics of directive centralized administration of the economy at all management levels.

4. The division of power between the national and federal organs proceeds from the principle that the national organs are the entities in which resides the original state-forming sovereignty. Their authority is original and general. The federal organs have that power which the national organs voluntarily vest in them. The authority of the central organs is derived from the national organs and is limited to exhaustively determined spheres of activity. The task of the national organs in economic management is to achieve optimum development of the national economies. Central federal organs are to strive for the optimum development of the integrated Czechoslovak national economy.

5. The national organs are responsible for development of the national economies. They work out macroconcepts, blueprints, long-term and short-term plans, etc., administer the national budgets, create and change economic instruments and rules of economic policy, provide a beneficial macroclimate for the economic activities of enterprises and organizations, organize the inventory of resources of national wealth, ensure the flow of information, and take care of personnel policy and all the other activities of the given national entity.

From the original authority it is clear that the national organs will pursue price, wage pension, tax and currency policies among others. But these aspects of the economic life call for the implementation of unified principles, criteria, and methods wherever joint action is necessary on the basis of agreements between the national organs as well as in delegating certain activities to the federal organs.

6. The central government should be charged with state-wide activities in the field of state defense, foreign affairs, and in establishing principles of eco-

nomic policy, chiefly foreign trade policy; currency policy; the comprehensive promotion of integrating the two national economies; the economic management system and uniform socioeconomic data system; and the policy of the economic equalization of the national political regions.

7. National and federal economic management organs must conform to the economic managerial system, the present system or general organs must be reorganized as soon as possible and in the spirit of the economic management system Czech and Slovak national organs must be created.

We regard the principles of a federation of the economy of the peoples of the Czechoslovak Socialist Republic as the basis for a concrete draft of a Czechoslovak federation. They will make it possible to prepare a constitutional law concerning a symmetrical federal constitutional law arrangement. These principles were worked out at a joint conference of Czech and Slovak economists in Bratislava on April 20, 1968.

Signed: Ivan Angelis, Michal Baraník, František Boreš, Václav Čáp, Ondrej Capo, Antonín Červinka, Ján Ferlanc, Peter Gallo, Dalibor Haneš, Štefan Heretík, Filip Hronský, Ján Janovic, Hvezdon Kočtuch, Miloslav Kohoutek, Bohumil Komenda, Jozef Kosnár, Pavol Kováč, Čestmír Kožušník, Ján Krajčí, Eugen Löbl, František Miseje, Zdeněk Nekola, Viktor Pavlenda, Ignác Rendek, Jozef Rosa, Jiří Řezníček, Ladislay Říha, Nikulas Sedlák, Jozef Sojka, Anton Strucka, Zdislav Šulc, Gustav Thomas, Josef Toman, Pavol Turčan, Bohumil Urban, Ladislav Veltruský, Václav Zabalka, Vlastimil Zeman.

HUNGARIAN EQUIVOCATION

THE KÁDÁR REGIME reacted to democratization in Czechoslovakia much more favorably than either the East Germans or Poles. Despite warnings by Budapest in March that "misdirected, antisocialist elements" might precipitate a repetition of 1956,[1] political developments in Prague received comparatively extensive coverage in the Hungarian press.[2] Rumors that Kádár played a conciliatory role at the five-party meeting in Moscow May 8 were not denied.[3] Moreover, although the Soviet attack on the Czech writer Jan Procházka was reported on by the Hungarian news agency MTI, it was not picked up by either press or radio.

That favorable articles continued to appear even after *Literární listy* published its blunt commentary on the execution of Imre Nagy (Document 25)[4] indicated the extent of Budapest's sympathy for Czechoslovakia. Tamas Zala's reports from Prague[5] in late June (see Document 26) show that the Hungarian journalist's concern extended beyond simply identifying the mood of that city.

---

[1] *Népszabadság*, March 19, 1968; a television interview with Politburo member and secretary for interparty affairs Zoltán Komocsin, March 26, referred to by William F. Robinson, "Czechoslovakia and Its Allies," *Studies in Comparative Communism*, Vol. 1, Nos. 1 and 2 (July and October 1968), p. 152.

[2] Articles honoring the twenty-third anniversary of Czechoslovak liberation in *Népszabadság, Magyar nemzet, Népszava,* and *Esti hírlap* on May 8 and 9 strongly praised the "revival" in Prague. Also see roundup of events in Czechoslovakia in the party journal *Tarsadalmi szemle*, Vol. 23, No. 5 (May 1968).

[3] Eric Bourne, *The Christian Science Monitor*, May 15, 1968.

[4] Machatka's article appeared the same day that Dubček headed a delegation to Budapest to renew the 1949 Czechoslovak-Hungarian Treaty of Friendship, Cooperation and Mutual Aid. That it seriously concerned the Hungarians is confirmed by Lt. General Václav Prchlík's press conference in July (Document 32).

[5] A series of articles printed in the official newspaper of the Hungarian People's Front, *Magyar nemzet*, June 23, 25, and 30, 1968.

DOCUMENT 25

"ANOTHER ANNIVERSARY"

Osvald Machatka

Excerpts

[*Literární listy,* June 13, 1968]

. . . Since his forced departure to Rumania (where he was reportedly taken by the Soviet police after he had left the Yugoslav embassy in Budapest) until the trial, Nagy was a target of fire meant for Yugoslavia. He was declared to be an ideologue of national communism, and national communism was declared to be treason against the fatherland and an instrument designed to break up the unity of the socialist camp. National communism also became the principal motif of the trial.

The report on the trial reminds us much too vividly of our own well-known court documents. But in contrast to them, it is an anonymous report. It does not mention the names of those who conducted the trial, nor does it mention the time or place where the trial was held and the sentence executed. The report states that the trial proved Nagy's leading role in the preparation of a counterrevolutionary uprising. He was charged with having contacts with the most reactionary domestic and international forces. The style of the sentence reminds us of the Cominform resolution of 1949, "On Tito and his Band of Spies and Assassins." Facts were replaced by political phraseology and insults (for example, the charge that Imre Nagy and his group acted under the coward's flag of national communism, and so forth). Some experts on Hungarian law point out that the report lacked the so-called *stylus curialis* of Hungarian jurisprudence and that it is a poorly camouflaged act of the Soviet and Hungarian state security.

Nagy's death further discredited the socialist world, and anti-Communists exploited it for their own use. The news of his death was received with enthusiasm in socialist countries, while the democratic public of the world protested. The Yugoslav government sent a protest note expressing its doubt as to the legality of the process and rejecting the charge that Nagy had betrayed socialism. It expressed the view that his death was the liquidation of an ideological opponent.

The execution of Imre Nagy was a signal to launch a campaign against Yugoslav revisionism by drastically criticizing the program of the League of Communists of Yugoslavia of April 1958. It was an act of revenge for failing to force Yugoslavia to return to the "socialist camp" and a preventive warning to all "revisionists" in other socialist countries meant to quell efforts to bring about national communism. For example, the leadership of the Polish United Workers' Party, which up to that time had a somewhat different view of the Hungarian events and did not consider them so completely counterrevolutionary as did the other Communist parties in the socialist countries, spoke up. Gomułka agreed with the sentence and denied reports that he had protested the execution. The Yugoslav *Politika* of June 23 wrote that the execution of Imre Nagy was a dreadful warning to opponents of the revival of the Stalinist policy, a factor which caused a deterioration in the relations between Yugoslavia and the other social states. Those days were characterized by rejection of specific roads to socialism and by a hysterical campaign against national communism.

Nagy's concepts of socialism were published in English and French. The French edition appeared under the appropriate title "Communism Which Does Not Forget Man." Ideas which anticipated so much and apparently are no longer so frightening today should not remain unknown in our country.

DOCUMENT 26

"IT IS NECESSARY TO GO THROUGH THE FOREST"

Tamas Zala

Excerpts

[*Magyar nemzet,* June 23, 1968]

The process set in motion by the party plenum in January of this year in Czechoslovakia is even linked with the 150th anniversary of Marx's birth and is regarded as practical proof of the renaissance of Marxism. A reinterpretation of Marx's life work makes it crystal clear that the basic characteristic of Marxist theses and Marxist practice is concern for human beings and that it is profoundly humanitarian. It shows that Marxist theory is in essence a philosophy of happiness, and that the mission of a political movement embracing Marxism is to realize this philosophy of happiness for individuals and to their advantage.

I must apologize to my readers for this apparently irrelevant and excessively general meditation. It will emerge later, however, that these thoughts are indeed related to the inner essence of the current processes in Czechoslovakia. I have referred to the reinterpretation of Marxism for another reason. I am encouraged by the theoretical work accompanying it and its results to approach the Czechoslovak events "from the viewpoint of the national character" of Czechs, Slovaks, and other nationalities.

On the occasion of a visit in Rome, Professor Goldstücker, too, noted the awareness of Czechoslovaks and the historical experience shaping it. When he described — with great optimism — the prospects "of democratic revival" to a correspondent of *l'Unità,* by virtue of its historical experience, he said, "Czechoslovakia virtually condenses the problems of Europe as a whole, and the citizens of the Czechoslovak state have in a generation lived through almost everything that has been experienced by mankind over centuries: national oppression and liberation, a bourgeois republic and a socialist revolution, Hitlerite racial persecution, foreign occupation and anti-Fascist resistance, a People's Front, and a period briefly characterized by Professor Goldstücker as Stalinism."

Let us not be taken aback by the unusual sharpness of his expression, for one cannot enter today into exchanges of views with Czechoslovaks and convey their concepts in any other way than by sharp terms. To render the meaning of Goldstücker's assertions even more tangible, let us cite from a public opinion poll. The Public Opinion Research Institute of the Czechoslovak Academy of Sciences between May 24 and 26 raised the question as to what kind of dangers lay in store as a result of the changes. Seventy percent of those interviewed answered that antisocialist forces would not dare to attempt to overthrow the regime and only seventeen percent said that such a danger seriously existed.

One could argue whether it is not too naive to underestimate this danger. The forms in which it manifests itself and its representatives we will deal with in another article later. It is certain, however, that the process in question can only be correctly interpreted through the Czechoslovaks' human makeup and moral, ideological, and political disposition.

As for the name Goldstücker, it would be well to remember it not only because of his remarks cited above, but also because, as has been noted by *l'Unità,* the attitude of the chairman of the Czechoslovak Writers' Union vividly expresses the essence of the Prague events.

Let us return to our original starting point. The people of Prague bear with discipline, patience, and even good humor the annoyances caused them by the breakdown of public transportation. A bourgeois commentator has noted that the most cheerful revolution of all time is taking place in Prague. One can hardly concur with the appraisal of the essence of the changes as a revolution. His characterization of the mood, however, is quite acceptable.

It is a fact that the Czechoslovaks are beginning to awake from their nightmare, and their gloomy mood is being replaced by a cheerful optimism. That might also be the reason why they do not take offense at the quite frequent references to Hašek's Švejk in the columns of foreign newspapers. In any case, a regular little game has developed between foreigners, who are given a friendly welcome, and the people of Prague. Each time he walks toward the main railway station from the direction of Wenceslas Square in the company of a resident the question is invariably raised: Do you see this old building with the towering crane above it? It is almost mandatory to answer in the negative, at which point the following explanation is made with an impish smile: that is the Parliament, but you need not think that it is only the exterior, only the building that is being modernized.

III. Pressure and Negotiation

ZIONISM AND ANTI-SEMITISM

CONFORMITY to the Soviet line on Israel provided still another index of Communist orthodoxy in Eastern Europe. To Moscow, Israel represented a tentacle of imperialism stretching into the Midde East, and Zionism, an insidious form of ideological subversion. This view was put forth most energetically by the Poles, but K. Ivanov's attack on "Israel, Zionism, and World Imperialism" (Document 27) showed that Warsaw was not alone in raising the specter of a Jewish fifth column. Moreover, the Soviet polemicist's approval of a Polish statement by I. Loga-Sowinski (one of Gomułka's closest associates), coupling Zionism with "any manifestations of chauvinism and nationalism," had obvious relevance to Czechoslovakia.[1]

Already by early spring, Prague's attitude toward Israel had become equivocal. The Action Program referred only briefly to favoring a political settlement of the Middle East crisis. There were growing demands that the Slovak writer Ladislav Mňačko, who had left Czechoslovakia in protest against the government's anti-Israeli policy following the June 1967 war, be allowed to return home.[2] Polish anti-Semitism in the form of reprisals against Jewish students and faculty of Warsaw University had been openly condemned. Conversely, forces opposed to the post-January reforms within Czechoslovakia hewed closely to a violent anti-Zionist position. The open reply of Professor Eduard Goldstücker, Chairman of the Czechoslovak Writers' Union, to an anonymous poison pen letter (Document 28) revealed much of the tone of such attacks.

[1] It was a recurring theme. Following the invasion of Czechoslovakia, an East German editorial charging that Zionist forces had taken over the leadership of the KSČ made explicit the sinister implications of Ivanov's article (*Neues Deutschland,* August 25, 1968). Also see the Soviet "White Book" on Czechoslovakia (Document 63), p. 80.

[2] Gustav Husák referred to a press, radio, and television campaign raising the issue of Mňačko as early as mid-March (Husák's address to a Bratislava Youth Meeting, Bratislava Domestic Television Service in Slovak, 1900 GMT 20 March 1968). In Bratislava, the attitude toward Israel had become a touchstone of whether one was for or against liberalization. The writer did, in fact, return to Czechoslovakia May 17, 1968. For his own explanation both of his original departure and the decision to return, see Rudolf Olšinský, "Interview with Ladislav Mňačko," *Kultúrny život,* No. 21 (May 24, 1968), pp. 1–7; JPRS No. 45815 (June 28, 1968), pp. 48–67.

DOCUMENT 27
"ISRAEL, ZIONISM AND INTERNATIONAL IMPERIALISM"

K. Ivanov

Excerpts

[*International Affairs,* No. 6 (June 1968), p. 19]

. . . Zionist leaders are trying to instill into the minds of Jews in various countries, including the Socialist countries, that they have a "dual citizenship" — one, a secondary one, in the country of actual domicile, and the other, the basic spiritual and religious one, in Israel. Those were the very tricks used by the leaders of Third Reich in the interests of German imperialism. In this way the Nazis set up their "fifth column" in other countries, and in the same way modern Zionism tries to secure international support for Israel and its aggressive expansionist policy.

Only people who are politically blind can fail to see the danger lurking in this concept of "dual citizenship." The imperialist intelligence services and psychological warfare agencies have been spending hundreds of millions of dollars to subvert and corrupt the international working class and anti-imperialist movement as a whole, and especially the fraternal militant community of the Socialist countries. In this context, the "dual citizenship" concept and the "bridge-building" policy are two sides of ideological and political subversion and indirect aggression designed for the ultimate restoration of capitalism.

The April Plenary Meeting of the C.P.S.U. Central Committee emphasized that, being incapable of a head-on trial of strength with the main forces of Socialism, imperialism has now placed its main stake on the penetration and internal, especially ideological, corruption of the Socialist countries. This is well illustrated by the recent events in Poland. Chairman of the Central Council of Trade Unions of Poland, I. Loga-Sowinski was right when he said that "danger of Zionism for Polish state interests lies above all in the fact that Polish citizens of Jewish origin who feel themselves Jewish by nationality and who adopt the ideology of Zionism also serve imperialism through their ties with Israel in the present concrete international situation. . . .

"International Zionism is an enemy of Socialist ideas. It is waging a campaign of hatred against the Soviet Union, Poland and other Socialist countries. We are fighting against Zionism and anti-Semitism, as against any manifestations of chauvinism and nationalism, which have always been used by the forces of reaction and the bourgeoisie in their defense of the capitalist monopolies, in their struggle against the working class, and the forces of progress and democracy". . . .

DOCUMENT 28

"BE CAREFUL, CITIZENS"

Eduard Goldstücker

Complete Text

[*Rudé právo,* June 23, 1968]

The anonymous letter I received several days ago seems to me to call for an answer, which can reach its author only through this public medium. The author (or authors) of this distressing document, however, is not nearly as important as the extent to which it is indicative of issues of urgent public concern on which all citizens of our country should take a stand. For this purpose, or rather with this request I lay before them its full text as mailed from Brno on May 28 with the false return address of *Lidová demokracie.**

Mr. Goldstücker — Zionist hyena bastard,

Please accept several million curses for your birthday from the working classes of both our country and the other socialist countries. All honest members of the KSČ despise you, you subversive despot bastard. Recent events have all the more opened the eyes of the honest Czech people, workers and KSČ members to the fact that you deserved the noose not life for your part in the Slánský affair. As an agent of the West you are not recognized as a KSČ member no matter what clever mask you hide behind. Why don't you set up some other party, an ISRAELI party? The workers don't want a hyena like you in their party. We didn't pick our convictions up off the roadside, in England or Israel. The road to our convictions as Communists was filled with want, hunger, suffering, unemployment, and imprisonment during the First Republic and during the occupation in concentration camps where we lost our nearest and dearest and the times when we couldn't give our own children dry bread for lunch during the period of Masaryk's humanism. At a time when our workers were at their lowest point and our children and KSČ members, a dangerous hyena like you could study at universities. At that time a Communist couldn't even get work as a day laborer. And when Communists were thrown in jail during the occupation, you were in good with the London Czechoslovak government probably because you called yourself a Communist like you do. We know who you kept company with and what kind of friends you had in England, Israel, and elsewhere and that they are representatives of central spy agencies and we have photographs and other materials which we will hand over to the proper authorities in the near future and mainly the Soviet Union and others who will take the necessary steps to unveil your personality in the international arena. We will also supply them with the necessary materials deal-

---

* The daily organ of the Czech People's Party. Translator.

ing with your financial capital, etc., which you own and have tucked away abroad so the people, workers, and members of the KSČ will know what you are really like when they find out and you get what's coming to you and disappear like steam — write your last will and testament to the one you're leaving it all to. You despot, you. You are the cause of all the recent events, which you and company have been setting up for a long time. But the working class has not had its last word. Now that it's all over our goal is clear. You are such a philosopher, egotist, and despot that you talk as if Czechoslovakia didn't even have a working class. You are such a wretch of a philosopher you don't even know that the KSČ is first and foremost a workers' party with other allies. Of course you despot, you've turned it upside down. Why don't you go set up a new party of Jewish intellectuals with Mňačko, that lily-livered follower of Israeli aggressors and Jews. Workers and honest KSČ members hate him as much as you and Slánský's wife. Jews used to try to claim to be part of the Germanic race. You and your Jewish followers didn't even want to speak Czech, you preferred German — the language of Hitler the hyena. And our people remember it well. You don't just want to rule in Israel, your Zionist cravings make you want to rule the whole world, wherever possible, so you and Hitler might just as well shake hands on that. That's why we in Czechoslovakia know that the instigators of recent events and also in Poland and elsewhere are Zionists who have instigated everything within the framework of fulfilling the conquest-crazy plans of international Zionism. That is why honest KSČ members, workers and our Militia have their own plan and will put an end to all this excitement. Television, radio, and the press will again be expropriated from the Jews and will again belong to the workers. Your propaganda and public opinion is based on selected individuals and bastards chosen by yourself. Even though you say you are a Communist, we never heard you talk so hotly for the workers as you did for Mňačko or those students from bourgeois families, the ones you organized Strahov* with. That's not over with yet. You have been known to say that the police handled the students on Strahov like an enemy class. What about the students, did they act friendly? And those slogans the students were carrying "February — a 1948 period of darkness." † You can't tell me that was a friendly challenge to the working class, and other slogans. Just like a real philosopher you couldn't find words to express and evaluate what a friendly attitude they have to the working class. And you call yourself a Communist and try to make fools of our ranks and honest workers with your cheap arrogance, and their salary is peanuts and pocket money for you. The Strahov event was falsely interpreted by you and the other Jews with you, they leaned to one side without the same chance being given to the other side to defend itself. Jews and Zionists are also behind the events in Poland. You are known to have said you would be willing to let Jewish students rightly thrown out of school there come and study in Czechoslovakia.

---

* Strahov, a complex of student dormitories in Prague, was the scene of a peaceful demonstration late in 1967 for better living conditions. Translator.

† "Period of darkness" refers to the period following the defeat at White Mountain in 1620. Translator.

What are we supposed to think of that, family and Party members from its founding, when members of our families couldn't study during the period of Masaryk's humanism in the First Republic and during the occupation they were sent to concentration camps and our children who we have left after us did not get to go to universities in spite of this great sacrifice. But for Jews from Poland there's plenty of room. Who will rehabilitate our children for the damage this will do them — how do you as a philosopher propose to make amends for that? Nobody has ever given us anything for our sacrifices in concentration camps during the occupation, and on top of it all children of Communists aren't admitted to universities. And while our republic is being pillaged by you and your kind, your salary runs up into the hundreds and thousands and you still go on attacking our country and republic and once more who will pay with their toil? Honest workers. That's just like Jews and you yourself. Like Jews and Zionists you know how to turn lies into the truth. We don't blame the party for our children not getting to go to school, we blame people like you who went to a lot of trouble to harm us intentionally and consciously — it is no coincidence that Strahov and similar events were run by a carefully selected caste of students. Even though you invented excuses about how all the students in Prague wanted was light and that they had no bad intentions, they were all lies, which is obvious from other student events in other places where all they care about is getting a conflict started off in a definite direction. If all they wanted was light, there are places they could have gone to fix it up and what kind of contact did you have with the students anyway if you didn't realize that or maybe the students were afraid to trust you to try to fix things up the right way??????

But your time will come you despot — your days are numbered. You dirty Jew.

This type of literary genre used to be called the formal challenge. It served the author to declare war on the addressee for a wrong he had either suffered or imagined. In the name of "the working classes of both our country and the other socialist countries" and "the honest Czech people, workers, and KSČ members" the anonymous author of this letter expresses sorrow over my not being hanged for my "part in the Slánský affair" and announces his intention of setting right this oversight in the near future. At a time when the National Assembly is fulfilling the will of our entire society by preparing a law to rehabilitate those who were prosecuted without reason, he proclaims exactly the opposite intention, thereby demonstrating how far removed he is from the thoughts, feelings, and moral qualities of the nation, class, and party he cites with so much hullabaloo.

It might seem as if the letter had been written by a madman, but although we cannot discount this possibility, the method in his madness argues against it. The letter points more to a man who has undergone a strange kind of ethical perversion, to a kind of criminal nature. It may be objected that he is the product of the pathological periphery of political life existent in every society. That is all well and good, except for the fact that people of my generation cannot forget that the Nazi Party grew up on the same sort of pathological periphery. Which is my way of intimating that it would be an unpardonable oversight to make light of these phenomena and ignore their substance and the conditions from which they stem. To me — and doubtless to a good number of my readers as well — this "formal challenge" seems all too familiar.

I know its vocabulary, phraseology; I know how it is constructed. For quite some time I was forced to live in daily contact with people who thought and talked this way and apparently do not wish to think or talk any differently today (or perhaps are no longer able to). It is the speech of my Ruzyně investigators in 1951–1953, of my Pankrác, Leopoldov, and Jáchymov prison guards from 1953 to 1955, of my indictment and the introductory statement by the counsel for the prosecution (or his representative) which ended with a demand for the death penalty. Ever since those years, whose burden cannot be put into words, I have been battling with myself to be just to my investigators and guards. I feel that in their thought and speech patterns they followed a schematic system which determined their ideas and trained them to carry them out, a system calculated to conform to the level of understanding of primitive brains and develop their initiative. The result was meant to overwhelm the masses whom they disdained but in whose interests they pretended to act.

I would therefore be willing to bet a thousand to one that this letter was not written by a worker. Even though he might have been a worker to begin with, he had long since given it up. From his perverted way of thinking and expressing himself I am certain that he was connected with the State Secret Security Agency of the fifties and that having been a cog in the Agency's machinery during the days of Kopřiva and Bacílek, he is apparently still turning the way he did after his first winding.

No, this pack of scurrilities was not compiled by a worker. It is the work of a creature dehumanized by wielding uncontrollable power for a long period of time, one of those who were hoisted into posts they occupied for years through pull. Now, when they see that their time has come, that they will no longer be able to hide their lack of ability or illegal activities, they try to keep their privileged status by means of demagogical witch hunts and conspiracies, by opposing everything which those among their fellow citizens who have retained some semblance of human feeling welcome with all their hearts: freedom's promise of a more worthy life. The author of my letter is one of those who became so accustomed to speaking in the name of the working class, the people, or the KSČ that they never thought of asking them whether they regarded them as their spokesmen.

One of the tenets of democratization must ensure that this type of ruined imposter disappears from our public life. We must also put an end to speeches and actions in the name of the working class or any other stratum of the population without its express mandate, and demand that every accusation be thoroughly and publicly substantiated. I therefore call upon my anonymous correspondent to make public immediately the name of the assembly of people's representatives or workers, the name of the party organization that gave him the authority to write his letter. If he does not respond, it will be clear that he was unjustified in citing them and is therefore guilty of fraud. I call upon the author of these coarse affronts to display publicly his evidence that I committed the heinous crimes he has attributed to me. His letter is a crystal-clear example of the mentality that came up with the wild accusations that sent innocent people to prison, torture, and death. I call upon him to present his case to the public because I feel that all honest people in our country must insist that such serious indictments never again be fabricated behind the backs of the working class or any other stratum of the population to make certain that their name will never be sullied by such awful crimes against truth, justice, and humanity.

It is a matter for serious reflection that as we set about righting the old wrongs of a secret cabal that tried to deceive the people of this country and the entire world, in some dark corner of our society there is a band of criminals at work that believes it can put something over on decent people again by creating a smoke screen of false propaganda to nip in the bud the promise of freedom and a worthy life in this country. Come out of the sewers that hide you into the light of day. Hand over the fruits of your criminal imagination to the judgment of the people in whose name you are unjustly operating. Tell them the proofs you have of the "Zionist plot," which is always brought up when an attack on freedom is in the offing because it is felt that this atavistic bogy is enough to make people abandon their ability to reason and give up the fruits of the long and difficult struggle toward a freer life and toward becoming a more worthy human being. People in the category of my anonymous correspondent go through the motions of standing firmly behind the interests of the working class, nation, and KSČ while actually manifesting an abysmally deep scorn for them; they think they can forever lead the working class and the nation around by the nose like an amorphous, easily manipulated mass which can neither think nor feel like humans and are easily taken in by those who make their living out of demagoguery.

In this instance the situation is all the worse because my correspondent and his followers dare to use the name of the KSČ. It is high time they be told in no uncertain terms that they have confused the Communist party with a fascist organization which would better suit their views and criminal mentality and that the time has come to purge the Communist party of people who have smuggled in Nazi demagoguery and the flag-waver's perverted ideas. It is high time that the KSČ in its own vital interest rid itself of those elements which discredit it in the eyes of all decent people, that it free itself from those fossils which will not shrink from fraud, underhanded dealings or criminal actions to hold onto the privileged position they acquired in times of the worst deformations and which are terrified of independent thought and the possibility of a democratic community of workers, farmers, intelligentsia, and youth making its own decisions.

The main reason I am making this anonymous letter public is to show what profound perversions of human values socialism's falsifiers have sunk to and to appeal to all my fellow citizens who respect these values to keep in mind that as we all contribute what we can toward making our public life worthwhile, there are evil forces among us just waiting for the right moment to stick their knives in our backs for fear of losing an undeserved sinecure or meeting with retribution for unpunished crimes. I ask all of you who read these lines to be vocal in your opposition to this type of machinations. We've had enough; any more could well be fatal for the existence of the nation.

Workers should once and for all prohibit individuals whose only concern is to keep the working masses in their sway from speaking in their name. They should elect representatives who will respond to the voice and interests of the working class. I ask Communists to see to cleaning out their ranks of smugglers of fascism. I ask members of the People's Militia to work vigorously at stamping out propaganda efforts which make them look like a *putsch* organization, and members of the State Police to rehabilitate their reputation among the public at large by clearly and consistently keeping their distance from elements which tend to throw on them a shadow of suspicion that they have retained followers of the reprehensible methods of the fifties in their ranks. We will not allow them to turn our republic into a village of toughs.

My anonymous letter tells me that someone is fantasizing about the possibility of hatching another trial in our country against the supposed Zionist plot and that he has his eyes on me for the role of prize defendant. That is why my influence is so exaggerated and I am attributed almost superhuman qualities. For everything that has gone on here which does not please the author I am held primarily responsible. I've heard that song before; I know its composer and I know its lyricist.

I realize my life is at stake. Putting myself in the hands of my fellow citizens is surely my best protection.

Eduard Goldstücker

"2,000 WORDS": STATEMENT AND RESPONSE

AT THE END of June, Ludvík Vaculík's statement "2,000 Words to Workers, Farmers, Scientists, Artists, and Everyone" (Document 29) shattered the uneasy calm maintained while Warsaw Pact forces maneuvered in Czechoslovakia.[1] Vaculík charged that after the war the Communist party had bartered away popular trust in return for public office. Post-January reforms had not gone far enough, nor would they if people waited for the party to implement from above. Rather, spontaneous initiatives were needed at the district level — resolutions, demonstrations, strikes, and boycotts — to force out the remaining conservatives who misused their power. Spring in Prague had ended. A hot summer began.

Immediately the Statement became a *cause célèbre*. A flood of supporting and dissenting articles appeared in Czechoslovakia. Josef Smrkovský, Chairman of the National Assembly, wrote an amazingly moderate "1000-word" reply suggesting that it was time to transfer such discussions from the pages of newspapers to closed rooms.[2] Premier Černík qualified his expression of faith in the motives of the signers with blunt regret that the proclamation had incited extremists from both sides.[3]

In truth, the statement was no political asset for Dubček in Moscow. The Soviets publicly condemned it as a counterrevolutionary platform designed to tear Czechoslovakia from the community of socialist nations (see I. Alexandrov's *Pravda* attack, July 11; Document 30). Despite the KSČ May Plenum condemning anti-Communist forces, the Dubček regime was in the Soviet view unable to control the situation. According to Alexandrov, the foundations of socialism in Czechoslovakia were under attack and Moscow was not indifferent.[4]

---

[1] Polemics had continued, but at a lower level than throughout May. In particular see the exchange between Academician F. Konstantinov and KSČ CC secretary Čestmír Císař in mid-June (*Pravda*, June 14, 1968 and *Rudé právo*, June 22, 1968).

[2] *Rudé právo*, July 5, 1968. Smrkovský was sharply criticized by Radoslav Selucký in an editorial commenting that policy had been made in closed rooms for much too long (*Práce*, July 10, 1968).

[3] Černík speech to the National Assembly, *Rudé právo*, June 29, 1968.

[4] A fact underlined by Brezhnev at the Soviet-Hungarian friendship rally even before Alexandrov's article in *Pravda*, July 4, 1968.

In CPSU theoretical journal *Kommunist,* P. N. Demichev seconded Alexandrov's pointed analogy between developments in Czechoslovakia and counterrevolutionary conditions in Hungary in 1956 (Document 31). A candidate member of the Politburo and Secretary of the CPSU Central Committee, Demichev lumped the schismatic activities of Mao Tse-tung and company together with "nationalistic tendencies of revisionists." He called for a "decisive rebuff" to attempts by "imperialist apologists to slander the socialist state." Clearly, Moscow was in no mood to accept the Czechoslovak leadership's moderate condemnation of Vaculík's statement as sufficient.

DOCUMENT 29
"2,000 WORDS TO WORKERS, FARMERS, SCIENTISTS, ARTISTS, AND EVERYONE"
Ludvík Vaculík
Complete Text
[*Literární listy,* June 27, 1968]

The life of our nation was first threatened by the war. Then followed another bad time with events which threatened the nation's spiritual health and character. The majority of the nation hopefully accepted the program of socialism. Its direction got into the hands of the wrong people, however. It would not have mattered so much that they did not have sufficient experience as statesmen, practical knowledge, or philosophical education, if they had at least possessed more common sense and decency, if they had been able to listen to the opinion of others, and if they had allowed themselves to be gradually replaced by more capable people.

The Communist party, which after the war possessed the great trust of the people, gradually exchanged this trust for offices, until it had all the offices and nothing else. We must put it this way; those Communists among us know it to be so, and their disappointment over the results is as great as the disappointment of the others. The leadership's incorrect line turned the party from a political party and ideological alliance into a power organization which became very attractive to egotists avid for rule, calculating cowards, and people with bad consciences. Their influx into the party affected its nature and its conduct. Its internal organization was such that honest people who could have magnified it to keep up with the modern world could not wield any influence without shameful accidents. Many Communists fought this decline, but they did not succeed in preventing what happened.

The situation in the Communist party was the pattern and cause of a similar situation in the state. Because the party became linked with the state it lost the advantage of keeping its distance from executive power. There was no criticism of the activity of the state and economic organizations. Parliament forgot how to proceed; the government forgot how to rule and the directors how to direct. Elections had no significance and the laws lost their weight. We could not trust our representatives in any committee, and even if we did, we could not ask them to do anything because they could accomplish nothing. What was still worse was that we had almost lost our trust in one another. Personal and collective honor declined. Honesty led nowhere, and there was no appreciation for ability. Therefore, most people lost interest in public affairs; they were concerned only with themselves and with money. Moreover, as a result of these bad conditions now one cannot even rely on the money. Relations among people were spoiled, joy in one's work lost. To sum up, the country reached a point where its spiritual health and character were threatened.

We are all responsible for the present state of affairs, and the Communists among us are more responsible than others. The main responsibility, however, rests with those who were component parts or instruments of uncontrolled power. It was the power of a tenacious group spread, with the help of the party apparatus, everywhere from Prague to each district and community. The apparatus decided what one might or might not do; it directed the cooperatives for the cooperative members, the factories for the workers, and the national committees for the citizens. No organization actually belonged to its members, not even the Communist organization.

The main guilt and the greatest deception perpetrated by these rulers was that they presented their arbitrary rule as the will of the workers. If we were willing to believe this deception, we would now have to blame the workers for the decline of our economy, for the crimes against innocent people, for the introduction of censorship which made it impossible for all this to be written about. The workers were to blame for the mistaken investments, for the losses in trade, for the shortage of apartments. Naturally, no sensible person believes in such guilt on the part of the workers. We all know and, in particular, each worker knows that in practice the workers did not decide anything. It was someone else who controlled the workers' representatives' vote. While many workers thought that they ruled, the rule was executed in their name by a specially educated group of officials of the party and state apparatus. In effect, they took the place of the overthrown class and themselves became the new authority.

For the sake of justice, we must say that some of them long ago realized this bad game of history. We can recognize them now by the fact that they are redressing wrongs, correcting mistakes, returning decision-making power to the membership and the citizens, and limiting the authority and numbers of *apparatchiks*. They are with us against the obsolete views in the party membership. But many officials are still opposing change, and they still carry weight! They still hold instruments of power, especially in the districts and in the communities, where they may use these instruments secretly and unimpeachably.

From the beginning of the current year, we have been taking part in a revival process of democratization. That it began in the Communist party must be acknowledged. Even people among us outside the party who until recently expected no good to come from us recognize this fact. We must add, however, that this process could not begin elsewhere. After a full twenty years, only the Communists could live something like a political life; only Communist criticism was in a position to see things as they really were; only the opposition within the Communist party had the privilege of being in contact with the enemy. The initiative and efforts of the democratic Communists therefore is only an installment in the repayment of the debt the entire party has incurred with the people outside the party, whom it kept in a position without equal rights. Therefore, no gratitude is due the Communist party, although it should probably be acknowledged that it is honestly striving to use this last opportunity to save its own and the nation's honor.

The revival process is not contributing any very new things. It is producing ideas and suggestions many of which are older than the errors of our socialism and others of which emerged under the surface of visible events. They should have been expressed long ago; however, they were suppressed. Let us not cherish the illusion that these ideas are now victorious because they wield the force of truth. Their victory was decided rather by the weakness of the old leadership which, obviously, first had to be weakened by a rule of twenty years in which no one hampered it. Obviously, all the defective elements hidden in the very foundations and ideology of this system had to mature before they gained their full form.

Therefore, let us not overestimate the significance of criticism from the ranks of writers and students. The source of social change is the economy. The right word carries significance only if it is spoken under conditions which have already been duly prepared. By duly prepared conditions in our country, unfortunately, we must understand our general poverty and the complete disintegration of the old system of rule, in which politicians of a certain type calmly and peacefully compromised themselves at our expense. Thus, truth is not victorious; truth simply remains when everything else goes to pot! There is no cause for a national celebration of victory; there is merely cause for new hope.

We turn to you in this moment of hope, which, however, is still threatened. It took several months for many of us to believe that we could speak out, and many still do not yet believe it. Nevertheless, we *have* spoken out, and such a great number of things have been revealed that somehow we must complete our aim of humanizing this regime. Otherwise, the revenge of the old forces will be cruel. We turn mainly to those who have so far only waited. The time which will be decisive for many years.

The time which is coming is summer, with its vacations and holidays, when, according to old habit, we will want to drop everything and relax. We can be certain, however, that our dear adversaries will not indulge in summer recreation, that they will mobilize all those who are obliged to them, and that even now they are trying to arrange for calm Christmas holidays! Let us be careful, therefore, of what happens; let us try to understand it and respond to it. Let us renounce the impossible demand that someone higher up must always give us the only possible interpretation of things, one simple conclusion. Each of us will have to be responsible for drawing his own conclusions. Commonly agreed-upon conclusions can be reached only by discussion, and this requires the freedom of expression which actually is our only democratic achievement of the current year.

In the coming days we will have to display our own personal initiative and determination.

Above all, we will oppose the view, should it arise, that it is possible to conduct some sort of democratic revival without the Communists or possibly against them. This would be both unjust and unreasonable. The Communists have well-structured organizations, and we should support the progressive wing within them. They have experienced officials and, last but not least, they also have in their hands the decisive levers and buttons. Their action program has been submitted to the public; it is a program for the initial adjustment of the greatest inequalities, and no one else has any similarly concrete program. We must demand that local action programs be submitted to the public in each district and each community. By doing so, we shall have suddenly taken very ordinary and long-expected correct steps. The Czechoslovak Communist Party is preparing for the congress which will elect a new Central Committee. Let us demand that it be better than the current one. If the Communist Party now says that in the future it wants to base its leading position on the citizens' confidence and not on force, let us believe it as long as we can believe in the people whom it is now sending as delegates to the district and regional conferences.

Fears have recently been expressed that the process of democratization has stopped. This feeling is partly a manifestation of fatigue caused by troubled times and is partly due to the fact that the season of surprising revelations, resignations from high places, and intoxicating speeches of unprecedented verbal boldness is past. However, the struggle of forces has merely become less evident to a certain extent. The fight is now being waged over the content and implementation of laws, over the scope of practical steps to be taken. In addition, we must give the new people, the ministers, prosecutors, chairmen, and secretaries time to work. They have the right to this time so that they can either prove their worth or lack of it. Apart from this, one cannot presently expect more of the central political organs. They have, after all, given spontaneous evidence of admirable virtues.

The practical quality of the future democracy depends on what becomes of the enterprises and what will happen in them. After all is said and done, it is the economists who control things. One must seek out good managers and see to it that they get good positions. It is true that, compared to the well-developed countries, we are all badly paid, and some are worse off than others.

We can demand more money — but although it can be printed, its value will diminish. Let us rather demand that directors and chairmen explain to us the nature and extent of expenditures they want for production, to whom they want to sell their products and at what price, the profit they can expect, the percentage of this profit to be invested in the modernization of production and the percentage to be divided up.

Under apparently boring headlines, a very hard struggle is going on in the press relating to democracy and graft. As contractors, workers can intervene in this struggle through the people whom they elect to enterprise administrations and councils. As employees, they can do what is best for themselves by electing as their representatives to trade union organs their natural leaders, capable and honest people, regardless of party affiliation.

If at this time we cannot expect more from the present central political organs, we must achieve more in the districts and communities. Let us demand the resignation of people who have misused their power, who have damaged public property, or who have acted dishonestly or brutally. We must find ways and means to induce them to resign, for instance, through public criticism, resolutions, demonstrations, demonstration work brigades, collection drives for gifts to them when they retire, strikes, and boycotts of their doors. However, we must reject methods which are illegitimate, improper, or coarse since they might use them to influence Alexander Dubček.

We must so generally decry the writing of insulting letters that any letter of this kind which they may yet receive could be considered a letter they had sent to themselves. Let us revive the activity of the National Front. Let us demand public meetings of the national committees. To deal with questions which no one wants to know anything about let us set up special citizens' committees and commissions. It is simple: a few people convene, they elect a chairman, keep regular minutes, publish their finding, demand a solution, and do not let themselves be intimidated.

Let us turn the district and local press, which has degenerated to a mouthpiece of official views, into a platform of all the positive political forces. Let us demand the establishment of editorial councils composed of representatives of the National Front, or let us found newspapers. Let us establish committees for the defense of the freedom of expression. Let us organize our own monitoring service at meetings. If we hear strange news, let us check on it, let us send delegations to the people concerned, and nail their replies to the gates if need be. Let us support the security organs when they persecute genuine criminal activity. We do not mean to cause anarchy and a state of general insecurity. Let us avoid disputes among neighbors. Let us renounce spitefulness in political affairs. Let us reveal informers.

The heavy vacation traffic throughout the republic will arouse interest in the constitutional arrangement of the Czechs and Slovaks. We consider the federation a method of solving the nationality question; aside from this, it is only one of the important measures aimed at democratizing conditions. This measure alone cannot by itself ensure better living conditions for the Slovaks. The problem of the regime — in the Czech regions and in Slovakia individually — is not solved by this. The rule of the party-state bureaucracy may still survive — in Slovakia even more so, because it has "won greater freedom."

The recent great apprehension results from the possibility that foreign forces may interfere with our internal development.

Faced with all these superior forces the only thing we can do is decently hold our own and not start anything. We can assure our government that we will back it — with weapons if necessary — as long as it does what we give it the mandate to do, and we can assure our allies that we will observe our alliance, friendship, and trade agreements. Excited reproaches and ungrounded suspicions must necessarily make the position of our government more difficult and cannot be of any help to us. At any rate, we can ensure equal relations only by improving our internal conditions and by carrying the process of revival so far that one day at elections we will elect statesmen who will have sufficient courage, honor, and political wisdom to establish and maintain such relations. This, by the way, is a problem of the governments of all small countries in the world.

This spring, as after the war, a great chance has been given us. Again we have the possibility of taking into our own hands a common cause, which has the working title of socialism, and giving it a shape which will better correspond to our once good reputaton and the relatively good opinion we once had of ourselves. The spring has now ended and will never return. By winter we will know everything.

With this we conclude our statement to the workers, farmers, officials, artists, scholars, scientists, technicians — everybody. It was written at the suggestion of the scholars and scientists.

The following signatures are not a complete collection of all those who agree with us. It is merely a selection from various groups of the populace and includes only those whom we were able to reach at home: National Artist Beno Blachut, member of the National Theater Opera in Prague; Doctor of Medicine and Science Jan Brod, professor and director of the Prague Institute for Blood Circulation Diseases; Marie Buzková, sow breeder in Chotěbuz; Academician Bohumil Bydžovský, mathematician; Associate Professor Dr. Jiří Cvekl, philosopher; Věra Čáslavská, Olympic champion; Zdeněk Čechrák, ČKD worker; Zdeněk Fiala, ČKD technician; Milan Hanuš, ČKD worker; Engineer Jiří Hanzelka, writer; Doctor of Medicine Miroslav Holub, scientific worker of the Microbiological Institute of the Czechoslovak Academy of Science; Zdeněk Holec, ČKD worker; Rudolf Hrušínský, actor and director; Dušan Hruza, ČKD worker; Jan Chocena, private farmer in Chotěbuz; Jaromil Jireš, film director; Doctor of Medicine and Science Vilo Jurkovic, Professor and Chief of the Second Internal Polyclinic of the Medical Faculty of Charles University in Hradec Králové; Doctor of Medicine and Science Věra Kadlecová, chief of the Ophthalmic Clinic of the Faculty Hospital of Charles University in Prague; Associate Professor A. Knop of the Pedagogical Institute in Ostrava; Karel Kosík, philosopher; Academician Jaromír Koutek, geologist; Otomar Krejča, director; Doctor of Medicine and Science Jiří Král, professor and chief of the Prague Institute for Sports Medicine; Engineer and Candidate of Science Miroslav Král of the Higher Political School of the Czechoslovak Communist Party Central Committee; Karel Krautgartner, conductor of the Czechoslovak Radio Dance Orchestra; Doctor of Medicine and Science Vladislav Krůta, professor and chief of the Physiological Institute of J. E. Purkyně University in Brno; Academician Vilém Laufberger, chief of the Laboratory for Graphic Research Methods in Prague; Doctor of Medicine Pavel Lukl, professor, chief of the Internal Clinic of Palacký University of Olomouc, chairman of the Cardiological Society and vice president of the European Cardiological Society; Zuzana Marysová, Chotěbuz state farm; Jiří Menzel, director.

Vladimír Mostecký, ČKD technician; Josef Neversil, ČKD worker; Jaroslav Němec, ČKD worker; Doctor of Law Božena Patková, lawyer in Prague; Engineer Emil Petýrek, corresponding member of the Czechoslovak Academy of Science and director of the Mining Institute of the Czechoslovak Academy of Science; Professor and Doctor of Medicine and Science Otakar Poupa, corresponding member and chief of the third department of the Physiological Institute of the Czechoslovak Academy of Science in Prague; Doctor of Medicine and Science Jaroslav Procházka, professor and chief of the Surgical Clinic of the Faculty Hospital in Hradec Králové; Yvonna Přenosilová, singer; National Artist Alfréd Radok, stage manager; Emil Radok, film producer; Jiří Raška, Olympic champion; National Artist Jaroslav Seifert; Doctor of Medicine B. Sekla, professor and chief of the Biological Institute of Charles University in Prague; Academician and Doctor of Medicine and Science Zdeněk Servít, director of the Physiological Institute of the Czechoslovak Academy of Science in Prague; Associate Professor Engineer Jiří Sláma, Candidate of Science, Economic Research Institute of Industry and Building in Prague; Doctor of Medicine and Science Oldřich Starý, corresponding member of the Czechoslovak Academy of Science, professor and rector of Charles University in Prague; Jiří Snížek, ČKD technician; Jiří Suchý, poet; Doctor of Medicine Vojmír Ševčík, associate professor and traumatologist in the North Moravian region, Ostrava; Dr. Jiří Šlitr, composer.

Karel Šilha, ČKD worker; Václav Šroub, ČKD worker; Jan Svankmajer, film director; Marie Tomášová, actress; Doctor of Philosophy and Science Ladislav Tondl, professor in the Department of Scientific Theory and Methodology of the Czechoslovak Academy of Science in Prague; Josef Topol, writer; National Artist Jiří Trnka, director and cartoonist; Jan Tříska, actor; Ludvík Vaculík, journalist — the author of this text; Karel Vojíř, ČKD worker; Doctor of Medicine and Science Jan Vanýsek, professor and vice rector of Purkyně University in Brno; Associate Professor and Doctor of Medicine Jiří Velemínský, regional internist of the North Moravian Region, Ostrava; Doctor of Medicine and Science V. Vejdovský, professor and chief of the Ophthalmic Clinic of Palacký University in Olomouc; Viktor Voros, ČKD worker; Academician Otto Vichterle, director of the Institute for Macromolecular Chemistry of the Czechoslovak Academy of Science in Prague; National Artist Jaroslav Vojta, member of the National Theater; National Artist Jan Werich; Colonel Emil Zátopek, Olympic champion; Dana Zátopková, Olympic champion; and Engineer Jindřich Zogata, agronomist in Chotěbuz.

DOCUMENT 30

"ATTACK ON THE SOCIALIST FOUNDATIONS OF CZECHOSLOVAKIA"

I. Alexandrov

July 11, 1968

Complete Text

[*Pravda,* July 11, 1968, quoted from *CDSP,* Vol. XX, No. 25 (July 31, 1968), pp. 3–7]

The Czechoslovak Communist Party is working on the solution of complex and important tasks of socialist construction.

As is known, the January plenary session and subsequent plenary sessions of the C.C.P. Central Committee criticized the errors and shortcomings in the management of economic development and in the activity of party and state bodies related to violations of Leninist principles of socialist construction.

The C.C.P. Central Committee stressed the necessity of overcoming these errors and shortcomings in the interests of strengthening and further developing socialist society in the Czechoslovak Socialist Republic. The plenary sessions set the tasks of strengthening the economy, developing socialist democracy, enhancing the Communist Party's guiding role in the life of society and further developing the C.S.R.'s friendship with the Soviet Union and other socialist countries.

The period since the January plenary session demonstrated that solution of the problems confronting the party and the country involves considerable difficulties, related chiefly to the increased activity and growing subversive doings of rightist, antisocialist forces.

Forces in Czechoslovakia hostile to socialism are seeking to denigrate and discredit the C.C.P. as the vanguard of the working class and the guiding force in society and to undermine the foundations of the socialist state with the view of ultimately returning Czechoslovakia to the path of a restoration of capitalism. Enemies are trying to undermine the C.S.R.'s friendship with the Soviet Union and other socialist countries.

The May plenary session of the C.C.P. Central Committee stressed that in the present situation the party regards its basic task as prevention of the threats to the socialist character of the government and the social system posed by antisocialist and outright anticommunist forces.

The plenary session called for "ensuring the political leadership of society by the Communist Party and for effectively repulsing all attempts at discrediting the party as a whole, as well as attempts at sowing a lack of faith in the party and at denying its moral and political right to lead society and be the decisive political force of socialist rule."

Developments in the C.S.R. since the May plenary session have demonstrated that the session's warning was entirely justified; rightist, antisocialist forces continue to mount malicious and fierce attacks against the Communist Party and the socialist system. And many of these subversive actions are conducted openly, with the use of the Czechoslovak press, radio and television.

Not so long ago, for example, four Czechoslovak newspapers — Literarni Listy, Prace, Zemedelske Noviny and Mlada Fronta — simultaneously published a so-called open letter from a group of persons; it was entitled "2,000 Words to Workers, Peasants, Employees, Scientists, People in the Arts, to All Citizens."

The document is a sort of platform representing the forces in Czechoslovakia and abroad that are endeavoring, under the guise of talk about "liberalization," "democratization," etc., to strike out the entire history of Czechoslovakia since 1948 and the socialist achievements of the Czechoslovak working people, to discredit the Czechoslovak Communist Party and its leading role, to undermine the friendship between the Czechoslovak people and the peoples of fraternal socialist states and to pave the way for counterrevolution.

The authors of the document slander the C.C.P. and the socialist system in alleging that the "leadership's erroneous line turned the party from a political party and an ideological alliance into a great-power organization"; that "Parliament has forgotten how to discuss problems, the government how to govern, and the directors how to direct"; that "not a single organization actually belonged to its members, not even the Communist organization"; and that "the Communist Party deserves no gratitude." In essence the statement praises bourgeois Czechoslovakia and does not conceal its sympathies for the capitalist system.

Moreover, in attempting to activate antisocialist elements, the authors of the appeal and those who back them declare that the "ensuing period will be decisive for many years to come" and demand the right to present "their own decisions." They call for the use of such means as demonstrations, strikes and boycotts in order to get rid of party personnel and leaders, devoted to the cause of socialism, who do not suit them. They demand the "establishment of their own civic committees and commissions" in the localities, i.e., the seizure of power. They promise to act "with arms in hand" in favor of the leadership to which they will give their "mandate."

"The 2,000 Words," despite hypocritical phrases about "defending" the interests of the Czechoslovak people, leaves no doubt as to the authors' real objectives. They speak on behalf of the rightist, antisocialist forces in the country that are attacking the C.C.P. and the working class. Every day brings new facts to confirm that these forces are by no means concerned with correcting errors or with further developing Czechoslovakia along the road of socialism, but have taken the course of overthrowing the existing system and restoring capitalism. They do not say this openly; more often than not, they cover up their true objectives with phrases about "democratization" and declare their support for socialism. But in actual fact they are seeking to undermine the very foundations of the socialist state.

Such tactics are not new. They were resorted to by the counterrevolutionary elements in Hungary that in 1956 sought to undermine the socialist achievements of the Hungarian people. Now, 12 years later, the tactics of those who would like to undermine the foundations of socialism in Czechoslovakia are even more subtle and insidious. And the Czechoslovak working people, as well as all who hold dear the achievements of socialism, cannot fail to see the danger concealed behind the incitive, provocational activity urged by "The 2,000 Words."

The healthy forces in the party and in the country view this document as an overt attack on the socialist system, on the C.C.P.'s guiding role and on Czechoslovakia's friendship with the Soviet Union and other socialist countries.

The Presidium of the C.C.P. Central Committee, after discussing the statement, reached the conclusion that this political platform "opens the way to anticommunist tendencies" and "constitutes an attack on the present leadership of the C.C.P. and the state, requiring recourse to a struggle against the offensive of disorganizing, antisocialist forces."

In connection with the appearance of "The 2,000 Words," the Central Committee of the Slovak Communist Party declared: "Our people do not conceal their apprehensions over the fate of the Czechoslovak Socialist Republic. They want political and juridical guarantees. The appeal found no support or social base in Slovakia. It was characterized as inciting attacks against the republic since it calls for the creation of new agencies of rule and the use of illegal levers of administration. It calls for the seizure of power in this way and by people whose interests and goals remain unknown."

The publication of "The 2,000 Words" aroused much reaction in the country. The majority of the C.C.P. party organizations, as well as Communists who spoke at recent district conferences, condemned this counterrevolutionary platform. The Czechoslovak government and the National Front also spoke of it in negative terms.

At the National Assembly session, Deputy S. Kodaj justifiably called "The 2,000 Words" a "call for counterrevolution." Public organizations and the collectives of enterprises and institutions have also expressed sharp criticism.

At the same time as the party conferences and groups of working people, guided by the interests of strengthening socialism in the country and consolidating the Czechoslovak people's fraternal friendship with the peoples of the Soviet Union and other socialist countries, are rebuffing the new attack on Czechoslovakia's socialist foundations; some press and information organs in Czechoslovakia have taken a "special" position. The newspapers Prace, Zemedelske Noviny and Mlada Fronta and Prague radio and television are endeavoring to influence public opinion toward supporting "The 2,000 Words." In doing this they attempt to make it seem as if they speak on behalf of the people.

Judging from the Czechoslovak press, some reactionary journalists and writers have been expressing support for this position. These are the same people who have more than once called for putting an end to the C.C.P.'s guiding role and for returning to a "democracy" that would in fact mean the restoration of capitalism. It is precisely these people who are defending the "2,000 Words" statement, who are seeking to present it as the last word of some sort of unprecedented "socialist democracy" and who are quick to label as "conservatives" those who speak out against the counterrevolutionary statement "2,000 Words."

Unfortunately, some Czechoslovak leaders have made ambiguous statements attempting to minimize the danger of the "2,000 Words" statement and declaring that the fact of its promulgation "need not be dramatized."

Rightist forces hostile to socialism hastened to exploit the fact that some people found it necessary both to conceal the incitive character of the document and to gloss over the criticism by the Czechoslovak working people. In the last few days these forces, with the help of certain press organs, have been giving wide publicity to "The 2,000 Words."

It has now become more obvious than ever that the appearance of "The 2,000 Words" is not an isolated phenomenon, but evidence of the increasing activity in Czechoslovakia of rightist and overtly counterrevolutionary forces obviously linked with imperialist reaction. They have gone on to make fierce attacks against the foundations of socialist statehood. Evidently, forces hostile to the Czechoslovak people are hastening to take advantage of the unstable situation in the country in order to achieve their counterrevolutionary goals. The support that these forces have found among imperialists in the West is playing a considerable role in all this, as can be distinctly seen in connection with the publication of "The 2,000 Words."

If there are perhaps some people in Czechoslovakia who still harbor illusions about the real meaning of this statement, articles in the American bourgeois press, as well as in the bourgeois press of Western Europe, put an end to such illusions. The enemies of socialism view the document as another desirable step along the path that might lead to a "softening up" of the socialist system in Czechoslovakia and the restoration of capitalism. And, it should be stated outright, people are unlikely to be so simple-minded as to believe that The New York Times, Die Welt, Le Figaro or the Daily Telegraph are so concerned about the success of "liberalization" in Czechoslovakia because they dream of strengthening the socialist system there.

The Soviet people are linked to the Czechoslovak people by close ties of friendship and brotherhood, sealed by the blood shed in their joint struggle against the Hitlerite invaders. We are united by common aims in the struggle for the triumph of socialism and communism, for the strengthening of peace and security in Europe and throughout the world.

It was no accident that the letter to the Soviet people from members of the nationwide *aktiv* of the C.S.R. people's militia,* received such a broad response in the Soviet Union. The working people of our country saw in this letter an expression both of the serious responsibility felt by the Czechoslovak working people for the fate of their socialist homeland and of their firm resolve to defend the people's achievements against any encroachments, to rebuff firmly any antisocialist and anti-Soviet schemes and to strengthen the fraternal unity of the Soviet and Czechoslovak peoples. The working people of Moscow, Leningrad, Kiev and many other cities of our homeland, understanding and sharing

* Current Digest of the Soviet Press, Vol. XX, No. 26, p. 6.

the concern of the Czechoslovak Communists and the working class of the C.S.R., replied to the letter of the Czechoslovak comrades with expressions of sincere friendship and proletarian solidarity.

The peoples of other socialist countries are also attentively following the events in Czechoslovakia. In commenting on the "2,000 Words" statement, the newspaper Rabotnichesko Delo, organ of the Central Committee of the Bulgarian Communist Party, notes: "Attempts to undermine the party's authority and eliminate its leading role and to destroy the people's unity as embodied in the National Front have now become fashionable and widespread phenomena in Czechoslovakia. In point of fact, these attempts are designed to strike at the existing social system and push the country onto a dangerous, adventurist path. Our public cannot remain indifferent when the foundations of socialism are under attack in a friendly, fraternal country, when reactionary forces are engaged in incitive activities and when appeals are made for anarchy and reprisals against loyal sons and daughters of socialism."

The newspaper Nepszabadsag, organ of the Central Committee of the Hungarian Socialist Workers' Party, writes: "We too lived through periods that were similar in many ways and know from our own experience the thoughts and intentions concealed behind the formulations of 'The 2,000 Words'. Those who are speaking out against the people's rule, against the socialist system and its legal order must be fought by the most effective means required in the present situation."

The peoples of the Soviet Union and other socialist countries realize that the actions of certain antisocialist forces may do serious damage to the further successful development of fraternal Czechoslovakia. They view "The 2,000 Words" as an overt attack on the C.C.P. and the socialist state, against the socialist achievements of the Czechoslovak people. They express confidence that the Czechoslovak Communists and all the working people in the C.S.R., being deeply interested in strengthening the country's socialist foundations, will succeed in dealing a decisive rebuff to the reactionary antisocialist forces, in defending the republic's achievements, obtained through great labor by millions of people, and in ensuring the development of their homeland along the path of socialism, friendship and fraternal cooperation with all socialist states.

In the struggle for strengthening socialism in Czechoslovakia and for friendship among the peoples of the socialist states, the working class and all the Czechoslovak working people can always count on the understanding and complete support of the people of the Soviet land.

DOCUMENT 31

"BUILDING OF COMMUNISM AND THE TASKS OF
THE SOCIAL SCIENCES"

P. N. Demichev

Excerpts

[*Kommunist*, No. 10 (July 1968), pp. 14–35]

❦

. . . Imperialism is intensifying its pressure on the countries of socialism and the peoples who have been liberated from colonial oppression, unleashing "local" wars against progressive regimes and attempting to change the balance of world forces in their favor and, at the same time, the course of historical development. A special role in carrying out aggressive policy is played by American imperialism and the revanchists of West Germany.

If one were to define briefly the essence of the global political strategy of the imperialist bourgeoisie, it would consist of the following: the use of all ways and means to undermine the positions of socialism, weaken its influences and authority, and inflict losses on it. For these purposes the bourgeoisie is undertaking tremendous efforts to completely utilize the schismatic activities of the Mao Tse-tung group and the nationalistic tendencies of the revisionists of various colorations; turning socialist countries against one another, and especially against the Soviet Union — the embodiment of the power and unity of the entire worldwide system of socialism; and attempting to force a wedge between the socialist countries and the worldwide Communist movement on the one hand and the national liberation movement on the other.

A very important peculiarity of the tactics of imperialism at the present stage consists of the fact that it is counting on undermining the socialist countries from within. The imperialist bourgeoisie understands that an open attack upon socialism at the present time is too risky. Therefore, instead of open summonses to overthrow the authority of the working class, to liquidate socialism, and to restore capitalist orders, the opponents of the new system, more and more frequently, are given the advice to "modernize" socialism, speak out against the leading role of the Communist party, and effect a gradual substitution of socialist democracy by bourgeois-parliamentarian democracy. With that aim, there has been a popularization of the slogan for a kind of "liberalization" of socialism and the creation of equal opportunities for various, including nonsocialist, parties; and there has been a propagandizing of a nonclass interpretation of freedom and humanitarianism.

It is necessary to understand correctly the new tactic of imperialist reaction, which is changing, more and more frequently, from frontal attacks on socialism to a tactic of maneuvering, to a search for circuitous routes, and it is necessary to know how to combat it.

We are opposed by an entire industry of "psychological warfare." In the leading imperialist countries, especially in the United States and West Germany, hundreds of centers, well equipped with modern technology, have been created, including "scientific" centers which have collected together the most experienced forces of anticommunism and which are developing the strategy and tactics of ideological subversion. The scientific organization and the modern technical facilities are utilized to propagandize obviously pseudoscientific theories.

Anticommunism is being elevated more and more to the level of state policy. At the same time a very important peculiarity of the ideological struggle under present-day conditions is a certain "transformation" of anticommunism. It has been forced to change its tactics, to sense the moods of the masses, to adapt to conditions, and to regroup its forces in conformity with the new goals and tasks of the class struggle.

Present-day anti-Communists do not limit themselves simply to crude anti-Sovietism. They would like to represent themselves as some sort of expressers of "yearnings that are common to all mankind," of strivings for peace and material prosperity. The bourgeoisie cannot fail to take into consideration the tremendous moral and political authority of socialism in the eyes of the peoples of the entire world, including the peoples of the bourgeoisie's own countries. Singing the praises of capitalism, which has allegedly undergone a fundamental change in its nature and "come closer" to socialism, the bourgeoisie, for purposes of giving their arguments the appearance of objectivity, is ready even to acknowledge certain successes that have been achieved by socialism. Bourgeois propaganda widely advertises the theory of a "single industrial society," the bringing of capitalism and socialism closer together, and the "convergence" of the two social systems. These theories serve a definite ideological goal: the goal of suggesting to the workers the illusion that capitalism has already ceased to be capitalism and has become some kind of new order.

As a result, one comes to the conclusion: if capitalism and socialism are both moving in the same direction, there is no reason to fight for socialism, there is no need for a class struggle or for revolutions. As a logical consequence of the theory of the "convergence" of capitalism and socialism, there is proclaimed the thesis of the necessity of allowing, in the countries of socialism, the peaceful coexistence of opposing ideologies — the bourgeois and the socialist. The propagandists of that thesis state that peaceful coexistence of ideologies is an indispensable component and practically a prerequisite for the peaceful coexistence of states with different social and political systems.

The falseness of such statements was unmasked long ago. The peaceful coexistence of countries with opposing socioeconomic systems means the renunciation of war as a means of resolving points of dispute between states, but by no means the absence of a struggle — economic, social, political, ideological. The peaceful coexistence of two systems is a specific form of the class struggle between them. Compromise in ideological principles is unacceptable for the working class, for the Marxist-Leninist parties. Peaceful coexistence, that is, the elimination of war from the relations between states, by no means reduces, but on the contrary increases, the importance of our ideological struggle.

Specialists in the field of social science have been called upon to render effective assistance to our propaganda organizations in unmasking the goals and methods of anti-Communist propaganda. They must participate directly in the determination of the long-term task of ideological activity, its strategy and tactics, and the most effective forms and organization.

In this regard, the question of a "dialogue" between Marxists and non-Marxists deserves attention. Our opponents are attempting to force such a dialogue which would be accompanied by allowing "ideological pluralism" within Marxism, and by renouncing the principle of Communist party solidarity. They state that the scientific conclusions of Marxist-Leninist theory are an "ideological framework" which is allegedly too narrow for successful discussion.

What attitude should we have toward the problem of the dialogue? We must not occupy a sectarian position. Any discussion, any argument, should be utilized in the interests of the struggle against bourgeois ideology, in the interests of expanding the unification of the forces fighting against imperialism and for democracy, social progress, and socialism. Thus we cannot make any concessions in matters pertaining to the principles of our political philosophy, or waive our Marxist conscience.

The West has set in motion the concept of "de-ideologizing" science, which has received acknowledgement in bourgeois literature and among revisionists. It has also captivated certain progressive scientists who are protesting the reactionary bourgeois ideology and the self-seeking dictates of the monopolies and agencies of the bourgeois state in the field of scientific knowledge and culture. The conception of "de-ideologizing" in this form, as it was created by R. Aron in France and D. Bell in the United States, is directed against Marxist-Leninist ideology.

The theory of "de-ideologizing" sows the illusion that the path to truth lies in renouncing every class position. And yet the entire historical experience in the development of social thought has proven that for objective understanding it is necessary to take the position of the advanced class, which has a self-interest in the progressive transformation of society, in truth and historical justice.

"De-ideologizing" in no way means, in practice, the renunciation of ideology. That goal is infeasible in a class society. It ideologically demoralizes workers by attempting to paralyze the revolutionizing influence of Marxism-Leninism.

The imperialist bourgeoisie combine direct attacks upon socialism and the worldwide Communist movement with attempts to cause the "erosion" of Marxism. They praise to the skies the modern revisionists who, under the guise of combating dogmatism and eliminating the "deformation" of Marxism, are attacking the fundamental principles of scientific communism, and primarily the theory concerning the universal historical role of the working class and the dictatorship of the proletariat, and concerning the party and the party monopoly of ideology. . . .

A characteristic feature of the revisionism of our day consists of the fact that in many instances, not only on the basis of substance, but also on the basis of their argumentation and the formulation of their initial policy premises, the "leftists" not only stand right alongside the rightists, but frequently are simply indistinguishable from them. For example, anti-Sovietism, slander directed against the Soviet Union and the CPSU, constitute the common platform of all the revisionists and unite them with professional anti-Communists.

Nationalism is taking greater and greater form as a serious danger. As a rule, nationalism, intertwining with revisionist tendencies of all trends, constitutes the common feature that is typical of opportunistic conceptions that replace Marxism-Leninism as an international theory by its "national" versions. . . .

Our enemies cast aspersions on the socialist state, attempting to discredit and undermine the leading role of the Communist party in the system of the political organization of the socialist society, to belittle the importance and value of the civil and political rights of man under socialism, and to besmirch the Soviet social and state system. They attempt to poison the consciousness of the workers with counterrevolutionary ideas of "democracy without Communists," of "pure" democracy, and "absolute freedom."

Historical experience has shown that expatiations concerning democracy and "liberalization" are used by counterrevolutions as a smoke screen for attempts to liquidate the conquests of socialism and socialist democracy. We can recall how, during the Hungarian events of 1956, it was under those slogans that counterrevolution meted out bloody drumhead justice to Communists.

Therefore, it is necessary to give a prompt and decisive rebuff to all attempts by imperialist apologists to slander the socialist state and socialist democracy; it is necessary to carry the truth about our social and state system to the workers of other countries. At the same time we must speak out against the erroneous understanding of the nature of democratic freedoms under socialism.

The gage of real democratism is not abstract freedom for all — not only for friends, but also for enemies of socialism. The main thing in socialist democracy is the complete freedom of the individual from exploitation, the growth of the activity and consciousness of the masses, who, by their activity, infuse new blood into all the democratic establishments and institutions. . . .

National problems are presently the object of especially acute ideological warfare. Nationalism is emerging as one of the most dangerous weapons of the imperialists for causing a schism in the ranks of the workers' liberation movement.

In our time, numerous liberation movements of oppressed peoples are developing under the banner of nationalism. In this form one finds expressions of the progressive desires of broad segments of the people which oppose the reactionary nationalism of the imperialist bourgeoisie. But the nationalism of the democratic liberation movements reveals also its narrowness, it can, under certain circumstances turn into feeble reactionary impulses with regard to other peoples, and can also infect some of the Communists with a narrow nationalistic approach.

It should be taken into consideration that the development of the so-called "third world" has been the economic, political, and ideological influence not only of the Soviet Union and the worldwide socialist system, but also of imperialism, with all its economic might, and well-developed apparatus for spreading propaganda, including the propaganda of nationalist ideas.

The struggle against the intensification of reactionary nationalism in the liberated countries is seriously hampered by the demagogic propaganda of the Mao Tse-tung group, with its efforts to incite the economically less developed countries — the "poor" countries — against the highly developed countries, the "rich" countries, to use the Maoist terminology. In so doing, the Maoists do not make any distinction between the imperialist and the socialist countries.

At the basis of proletarian, socialist internationalism lies the acknowledgement not only of the equal rights of nations, but also the unity of international and national interests. That was repeatedly indicated by V. I. Lenin. It has been proven by life that it is precisely the fraternal collaboration of the socialist countries on the basis of the principles of proletarian internationalism that assures, and most solidly guarantees, the national interests of each individual country.

The capitalist countries, especially the United States and West Germany, court in every way individual socialist countries, offering economic "aid," and privileges for the probationary work of scientists at the expense of special funds — the Ford, Rockefeller, Carnegie, and other foundations. Everything is done to weaken or to break the connections between the countries of the socialist community. . . .

DIALOGUE ON THE WARSAW PACT:
PRCHLÍK AND *KRASNAYA ZVEZDA*

HEAD OF THE KSČ CC Military Department, Lt. General Václav Prchlík's press conference calling for basic revisions in the Warsaw Pact (Document 32) added a new dimension to Prague's increasingly tense relations with Moscow and Soviet supporters in East Europe. Prchlík was responding both to delays in the departure of Warsaw Pact forces from Czechoslovak territory following the June maneuvers[1] and the meeting of five Pact members in session in Warsaw July 14. Between July 4–6, the leaderships of the Soviet Union, Poland, Bulgaria, Hungary, and the GDR had sent letters to the Dubček regime proposing a summit conference to discuss the situation in Czechoslovakia.[2] Prague countered with a suggestion for bilateral meetings.[3] But the Soviets and other East European regimes proceeded with the original plan. Prchlík's concern at "fractionist" activities within the framework of the Warsaw Pact clearly alluded to that meeting.

On July 21, Moscow protested Prchlík's interview in a diplomatic note to the Prague leadership. Subsequently, an editorial in the Soviet military newspaper *Krasnaya zvezda* attacked the Lt. General's "antisocialist, counterrevolutionary" distortion of the Warsaw Pact (Document 33). Two days later Prchlík's party post was eliminated by a reorganization of the KSČ Presidium and he was reassigned to army duties. The incident brought a flurry of support for Prchlík within Czechoslovakia.[4] He himself expressed astonishment at the Soviet "irresponsible reaction" to his views.[5]

The unusual way of dealing with his case created confusion in that the

---

[1] *Pravda*, July 1, 1968, announced the end of the maneuvers. TASS almost immediately rescinded the announcement and on July 10 Prchlík admitted on Czechoslovak television that he could not say when Soviet troops would leave. At the time of his press interview, the last Soviet contingents were not expected to depart before July 21 (*The New York Times*, July 16, 1968).

[2] These letters were not published. They were mentioned on Radio Prague July 8, 1968, alluded to in the Warsaw Letter (Document 34), and discussed explicitly in Dubček's July 19th speech (Document 37) explaining the circumstances preceding the Five-Party condemnation of Prague.

[3] Jonathan Randal interview with Jiří Hájek, *The New York Times*, July 13, 1968.

[4] Prague party organizations went so far as to nominate Prchlík as a Candidate to the Central Committee, *Práce*, August 8, 1968.

[5] In an interview with *Práce*, July 25, 1968.

general was not immediately repudiated. Rather his post was ostensibly eliminated because its duties "overlapped" with other government agencies. On July 27, the Czechoslovak press agency ČTK said that Prchlík's statements were unauthorized and did not "express the official viewpoint." [6]

DOCUMENT 32

REPORT ON PRESS CONFERENCE WITH LIEUTENANT GENERAL VÁCLAV PRCHLÍK, HEAD OF THE STATE ADMINISTRATIVE SECTION OF THE CZECHOSLOVAK COMMUNIST PARTY CENTRAL COMMITTEE

July 15, 1968

Excerpts

[Prague Domestic Radio Service in Czech 1930 GMT 15 July 1968]

Esteemed listeners: As we have already announced in the newscast, a press conference was held in Prague today by Lt. General Václav Prchlík, head of the State-Administrative Section of the Czechoslovak Communist Party Central Committee, and his colleagues. The theme of the press conference was questions of our military and defense policy. In the first part of the press conference General Prchlík said among other things:

I think that when I say that the past period was characterized by a marked monopolization of information in general, this was doubly so as far as the field of military and defense policy was concerned. In this field one made use of the well-known magic word [? "top secret"], that is, of the veil of state and military secrets, while consistently one did not make or did not want to make a distinction between what was really a secret military subject and what, on the contrary, should be a public matter, known to all citizens. Precisely in this field of party activity all the negative consequences of the system of personal power markedly manifested themselves during the past period. During the whole past period the party enforced the system of direct army and security management. What is more, in the concept of the past model of the party this principle of direct management was very narrow, so that questions of military and defense policy were basically decided merely by a narrow group

---

[6] Quoted by *The New York Times,* July 28, 1968. There is some question as to whose viewpoint ČTK represented. Some two weeks later the Military Council of the Defense Ministry insisted that, although the Council identified with the content of the news agency's statement, it "did not know why the statement had been handed to ČTK anonymously" (Prague ČTK International Service in English 1746 GMT August 15, 1968). In conjunction with the purge of liberals in the KSČ leadership following Dubček's fall in April 1969, the central party apparatus reportedly began an investigation of General Prchlík's activities before and after the August invasion. *The New York Times,* June 2, 1969.

of the party and state bureaucracy at the very center and often in important questions even by one single person.

In recent years it appeared more and more clearly that this concept of direct management of the army and security, that is, the concept of the political management of these institutions, did not permit solving matters [? of concept] in all implications; the stiff bureaucratic centralism of the management did not make it possible to improve the process of cognition and decision-making. On the contrary, it was a very fertile soil for dilettantism and subjectivism. The system of management and command in these power institutions was not only characterized by all the ailments of which we are speaking today when we make a critical analysis of our political system; on the contrary, these ailments were even more marked in view of the specific principles governing the construction of these institutions.

The same thing applies to the party political system. As a result, serious conflict situations and contradictions emerged in the past in these institutions, that is, in the army and security, situations and contradictions that were unsolvable in the past system. The growing criticism of these phenomena by members of the above-mentioned institutions, by political party organs, and by party organizations, was frustrated by the overwhelming resistance and bureaucratic inability of the political leadership at the time to solve these questions. A [? sufficiently] solid analysis of the existing contradictions in the construction of the army was submitted by us in a report on the conditions and further development of party work in the Czechoslovak People's Army. All these and other reports, suggestions, and proposals were nothing but calls of a thirsty man in a desert.

The situation in the security sector could be characterized in a similar way. During the whole past period, basically since 1948, when the party was engaged in solving the basic problems of political power, until recently, no necessary qualitative changes took place in the function, substance, and working methods of this corps or in the qualitative structure of the members of security. It can be shown how dilettantish interference weakened the action ability of our public security organs which today suffer from a catastrophic shortage of both qualified people and necessary material and technical means so that they often work in a primitive way.

This was manifested even more markedly in the field of the work of the state security which often did not and could not perform with sufficient effectiveness its main and decisive tasks particularly in the field of counterespionage, that is, in the struggle against the real intelligence services of the enemy. On the other hand, it was very purposefully oriented toward watching the internal political problems. This was shown, for instance, by the meeting of Antonín Novotný with leading persons of the Ministry of Interior in December 1966 at which Novotný criticized the leadership of the Ministry of Interior for being insufficiently informed about the development of the internal political situation and at which he oriented the state security particularly toward strengthening the so-called internal bases, which are working in society [? to this day], directing them particularly against the workers of the scientific-theoretical front, the workers of the artistic and cultural front, university students, and secondary school teachers. This orientation [? as far as the secondary school teachers were concerned] was caused by Novotný's idea that university students were disobedient particularly because of the fact that evidently their secondary school education had been insufficient, a fact for which the secondary school teachers were responsible, and so forth.

This list could be continued [words indistinct] the first analyses made by us in the field of the military and defense policy show that, for instance, in the sector of the state security there have been some very progressively oriented workers, capable people who even in the past came out with criticism and certain proposals and suggestions which, of course, remained unheeded in the old system.

With regard to ensuring the internal security of the state we think that the party must relinquish the principle of direct management of the armed forces and security corps, that it must redraft the concept of political leadership and include these institutions of power in the structure of the state. We further think that in the forthcoming period the party, particularly its supreme organs, that is, the congress and the Central Committee, should work out the concepts of military and defense policy, develop them in a creative way, and implement them. In view of the significance of this sector of party activity we are trying to ensure that the congress adopt a special independent resolution on the problem of military and security policy or that at least one of the next plenums after the congress deal with the state of affairs of these institutions and give concrete shape to the general resolution of the congress.

Why do we make this request? We do so because so far the congress has dealt with the problem of military security policy only on the most general level. If you look at the individual congress decisions, you know that the congresses have adopted only a few short sentences, formulated in the most general way, which without any changes might have been adopted as well by the 9th, the 13th or the 14th congresses.

The Central Committee and its plenum did not deal with these questions at all. In the new model of the Central Committee — and this should be laid down in the statutes — one should precisely shape the duty of the plenum and its right to occupy itself with the basic questions of the military and security policy.

In view of this we must reorganize also the subdepartment of military and security policy, whose substance must be qualitatively different from the concept and function of the notorious eighth department. Further, in the spirit of the action program, we are preparing plans for the inclusion of the army and security in the structure of the state so that the National Assembly and the government on the basis of the line of military and security policy of the party may independently lay down the program of state policy and realize it in the activity of the institutions concerned, thus also discharging the function of public control.

In the National Assembly a military and security affairs committee has been set up. Currently the comrades concerned are working out the statute of this commission, of this committee. They are working out the basic functions to be fulfilled in this respect also by the plenum of the National Assembly. We are aware of the fact that this is a very necessary job; however, it will not help us to settle anything so long as the qualification structure of the plenum of the National Assembly is not changed, too. This is a question connected with the quality of the deputies and with the preparation of the forthcoming elections to the National Assembly which should provide safeguards that people are elected to the National Assembly who will be able to implement these functions.

We are preparing a proposal on the creation of a state defense council. We are still discussing its relation to the government and the question of the work and function of the secretariat of this council. We hold the view that the state defense council should be an organ of the government and that it should not be above the government or exercise government functions but that, on the contrary, it should serve the government as an expert organ in this field. Its primary task will be to discuss the necessity, possibilities, and necessary conditions for working out a Czechoslovak military doctrine. We suppose that the 14th congress will also express its view on this problem.

This is connected with the problem of further improving our military coalition and of the Warsaw Pact itself. We hold the view that necessary qualitative changes should be made in the Warsaw Pact with respect to the concept of its functions and to relationships within the pact. In the first place, in our opinion, one should strengthen the role of the political advisory committee which should become a regularly, purposefully, and systematically working organ and which should not be entirely dependent on being occasionally convoked; the committee has so far worked very sporadically, thus failing to implement its function. If the committee worked as we imagine it should, it would create objective conditions insuring that in the system of allied command, too, military aspects cannot take precedence over the political ones.

As far as relations within this coalition are concerned, we hold the view that they should be improved particularly in such a way as to emphasize the real equality of the individual members of this coalition, to emphasize real equality, so that every member of this coalition can really assert itself and have its share in the programmatic work of the whole coalition.

We further hold the view that clear guarantees should be created preventing the creation of individual groupings of members, that is, if we may say so, preventing fractionist activities within the framework of this coalition, activities which, whatever the interests of their protagonists may be, would lead in the last analysis to violating the basic items of this pact, particularly the items concerning the state sovereignty of the members and the principle of noninterference in the internal affairs of the individual members of this pact.

It stands to reason that in our preparations of congress materials we will also deal with a number of other problems, such as the structure of the party and other institutions in the army and security, the system of their management, and many other problems.

In an extensive question and answer session at the press conference, Lt. Gen.

Václav Prchlík . . . answered several questions. . . . The convening of this conference [the Warsaw conference] in my opinion is a lamentable act, all the more because our allies knew the positions of our Presidium and government about the convocation of this meeting. We know that the Presidium and the government rejected the meeting. We know that the Presidium and the government refused to participate in the joint conference, that they adopted a negative view toward convening it, but that they manifested an absolute willingness to open bilateral talks immediately with the representatives of the individual member states.

It is lamentable that a major grouping is taking place of individual states which have not respected our view. I myself have taken interest in the problem as to whether there are any provisions in the Warsaw Pact which would entitle the other partners to arbitrarily station or place their units on the territory of the other member states. I have studied all the available materials, but I have not found such a section in any one of them. On the contrary, the treaty of friendship, collaboration, and mutual assistance aims at further strengthening and developing collaboration and mutual assistance, and in both the preamble and in Section 8 it stresses, on the contrary, the need for respecting the sovereignty of states as well as the principle of noninterference in their internal affairs and matters.

On the basis of Article 5 of this treaty a document was drawn up, in 1956, which is called "Protocol on the Establishment of a Joint Command of the Armed Forces of the Warsaw Pact Member States." And this protocol respected the basic sections of the Warsaw Pact and emphasized that basic measures, particularly those measures which concern the stationing of forces, will always be carried out exclusively according to the requirements of mutual defense against the danger of an external enemy and after an agreement with the participating states in this treaty. I stress — after an agreement. Similar provisions are also contained in the statutes of the joint command of the armed forces.

During my visit to the general staff I asked responsible functionaries whether any secret supplements to these three aforementioned documents exist. These comrades stated in a responsible manner that, although they had participated in all the talks, they knew nothing about the existence of such secret supplements.

To the group of questions which concern the joint command of the Warsaw Pact itself: So far the situation is that this command is formed by marshals, generals, and officers of the Soviet Army and that the other member armies have only their representatives in this joint command.

These representatives, however, have so far held no responsibilities nor had a hand in making decisions, but rather played the role of liaison organs. This is why our party presented proposals in the past for the creation of the required prerequisites for the joint command to competently discharge its functions. One of these prerequisites is the demand that the allied command also be composed of appropriate specialists of the individual armies and that their incorporation in this command be of such a nature as to enable them to cocreate and to participate in the whole process of learning and deciding, in the whole command system. So far the proper conclusions have not been made.

From the viewpoint of the further work of this joint command, we believe that it also will be necessary to clarify the position of the ministers of the individual countries who have been holding so far the functions of deputy commanders of the joint command. I think that this relation does not fully express their representation on the basis of equal rights. . . .

[Another speaker, apparently Prchlík — recorded] This is why, in my opinion, we only have one way out and that is the way out which our government and the Presidium are realizing now, that is, to insist on the characteristic traits and tendency of our internal policy development, to insist that we shall not permit a violation of our state sovereignty or an interference in our internal affairs, and to insist on the view that we are capable of solving our own problems with our own forces.

What guarantees exist? In my opinion the guarantees lie in that we shall truly consistently insist on the position to which I referred and that we shall uncompromisingly demand that all pertinent provisions of our treaties are respected.

Furthermore, we shall influence the development of our internal policy situation so as to prevent the dogmatist-sectarian forces in our country, which are considerable, from becoming particularly active in a more ostensible manner and gambling on the situation which now has been created.

We have further guarantees in the fact that a differentiation of viewpoints is emerging within the Warsaw Pact itself and, in my opinion, we must know how to take advantage of these viewpoints, and we must also know how to exploit the viewpoints of those fraternal parties which are not members of the Warsaw Pact.

First of all, here are a few remarks on the viewpoint of the Hungarian comrades. The Hungarian comrades, particularly Comrade Kádár, at the recent talks which comrades Dubček and Černík had with him, have shown that the Hungarian comrades in essence sympathize with our policy, that they very positively assess the whole content of our social process even though they harbor certain apprehensions about the intensity of certain antisocialist manifestations of which, in their opinion, the most important was the material which was published in *Literární listy* on the day of the visit of our party-government delegation and which refers to the case of Nagy. This article has exasperated and worried them. After the explanation and clarification of the view of our Presidium, the Hungarian comrades are resolved to act in Warsaw in such a manner that nothing is adopted there which would further aggravate the dispute as well as nothing which would involve a violation of our state sovereignty.

Waldeck Rochet also is resolved to act in favor of our view. If there is a need to support our view, the Italian comrades also are resolved to do this, including Luigi Longo.

I think that in view of our firm standpoint, in view of the increasing pressure and influence of additional Communist parties, among which we also must list the Rumanian party and the Yugoslav League of Communists, it may be assumed that all the problems will be solved in a reasonable way. The French and Italian Communists are pointing out to the Soviet leadership the immensely harmful results it could have for the prestige of the Soviet Union if they should attempt to solve matters contrary to the viewpoint of our government and party. Naturally above all we are interested in seeing reason prevail in this whole tense period and that the contradictions do not increase further. And we on our side will not take any steps which would contribute to this. On the other hand, however, we do not intend doing this by means of concessions, by means of compromises which are unacceptable to us, but on the contrary we shall do it by means of consistently insisting on and implementing those principles which were adopted in several documents, no matter whether these are Warsaw Pact documents or those of the international Communist movement which have been adopted and implemented.

DOCUMENT 33

"WHOSE FAVOR IS GEN. V. PRCHLÍK CURRYING?"

July 23, 1968

Excerpts

[Editorial, *Krasnaya zvezda,* July 23, 1968, quoted from *CDSP,* Vol. XX, No. 30 (August 14, 1968), pp. 3–4]

❧

. . . Thanks to the indefatigable concern and consideration shown by the Communist and Workers' Parties and the governments of the fraternal socialist countries, the Joint Armed Forces of the Warsaw Pact possess invincible combat strength and are in a constant state of combat readiness. This has been demonstrated time and again at joint exercises, including the recently concluded joint staff exercises held in the Polish People's Republic, the German Democratic Republic, the Czechoslovak Socialist Republic and the Soviet Union and at the Sever [North] staff exercises. Even some bourgeois military and political leaders were forced to admit that the Warsaw Pact's armed forces possess not only formidable combat equipment and weapons but also comradeship-in-arms, solidarity and unity.

The Communist and Workers' Parties and the governments of the fraternal socialist countries are doing everything necessary to increase and strengthen the might of the Warsaw Pact's Joint Armed Forces and to improve in every way their comradeship-in-arms and their readiness to provide resolute defense of the peoples' socialist gains.

We have no doubt that both the Czechoslovak Communist Party and the

C.S.R.'s working people seek the same aim. But is it possible to look with indifference and equanimity at Czechoslovak press, radio and television statements attempting to misrepresent the aims and purposes of the Warsaw Pact and sow suspicion and mistrust among its members? After all, matters recently reached the point where the joint staff exercises of Warsaw Pact forces, so usual in the socialist countries' military cooperation, were used as a pretext for slanderous statements, for charges of "violation of the sovereignty" of Czechoslovakia and for fanning malicious fabrications about the allied armies.

One would think that any attempt to cast aspersions on the socialist countries' comradeship-in-arms and on the Soviet Army — which, at the price of such colossal sacrifice, delivered the peoples of Europe from the nightmare of fascist bondage — would be resolutely rebuffed by Czechoslovakia's party and military leadership.

To our great regret, it is necessary to report on circumstances of a totally different order. For some time the aims, purpose and very essence of the Warsaw Pact and its Joint Armed Forces have been grossly distorted by antisocialist, counterrevolutionary elements in Czechoslovakia. But now certain persons holding highly responsible posts have become involved in this unsavory business.

We have in mind the recent speech that Gen. V. Prchlik, chief of the C.C.P. Central Committee's Department for State and Administrative Affairs, made at a press conference given in Prague.

First Gen. Prchlik assured his audience at the press conference that "Czechoslovakia supports efforts aimed at further strengthening and improving the Warsaw Pact." But he immediately followed this with arguments whose meaning belies this. How can V. Prchlik's allegations, which so grossly distort the aims and purpose of the Warsaw Pact's Joint Armed Forces Command, serve to strengthen this pact? And, frankly speaking, how can this task be served by the outright slander with which he assailed the organizational principles of the Joint Command and the relations among the commanders and staffs of the Warsaw Pact Armed Forces? In doing so Prchlik thought nothing of denigrating Soviet officers and generals. At the same time he told an insulting lie about the officers and generals of the Czechoslovak and other fraternal armies, who, if Prchlik is to be believed, allegedly have "no powers whatever."

But everyone, including Prchlik, is well aware that the Quartet maneuvers, for example, were supervised by the G.D.R. Minister of National Defense. The operations of the allied forces participating in the Rhodope exercises were directed by the Bulgarian Minister of People's Defense. The Vltava maneuvers were supervised by the Czechoslovak Minister of National Defense, etc., etc. Soviet marshals, generals and officers share with their comrades-in-arms, as equals among equals, their experience in directing troop combat operations and training and educating personnel and participate, on an equal footing, in every measure taken to strengthen the Warsaw Pact Armed Forces.

Gen. Prchlik "is dissatisfied," we learn, with the activity of such a high and responsible body as the Political Consultative Committee. But may we ask who authorized Prchlik to pass judgment on a body whose practical activity, by virtue of objective conditions, can be discussed only by the socialist countries' governments and supreme party bodies? Has not Gen. Prchlik taken too much upon himself? Are not his eyes blinded by that selfsame "liberalization" under the pretext of which and behind which some people are even prepared to debate in the streets the most confidential state and military matters?

Everything Prchlik said about the Warsaw Pact armies has provided a convenient pretext for the masterminds of an invidious campaign aimed at discrediting this pact and separating Czechoslovakia from the socialist camp. Literally the next instant the paper Zemedelske Noviny, which from the very outset displayed an especially intense interest in the press conference, published an article claiming with simulated gravity that "Gen. Prchlik's statement has acquainted the public" supposedly "with amazing facts" concerning the Warsaw Pact that are of "exceptional interest" from the standpoint of "Czechoslovakia's sovereignty."

On the basis of these "amazing" (it would be more accurate to call them completely invented and slanderous) facts, the paper draws conclusions that completely expose those who are not averse to drawing Czechoslovakia straightaway into the fold of the "free" Western world. We learn that the writer of the Zemedelske Noviny article referring to Prchlik likes the North Atlantic bloc better. Indeed, he spares no colors in extolling the way this bloc does things. Is Zemedelske Noviny perhaps worried by the fact that at this very moment the North Atlantic bloc is rattling the saber at the borders of socialist Czechoslovakia after launching major new maneuvers there? Nothing of the sort. The paper and the writer of the article published in it are as far removed as their inspirer Prchlik from a consideration of NATO's social, class, aggressive essence.

Nor need we wonder that imperialist newspapers and magazines immediately took up Prchlik's line of reasoning and irresponsible utterances about the Warsaw Pact. Why not? This statement worked against the interests of socialism and the socialist camp. So why not exploit it for anti-Communist propaganda and slander against the U.S.S.R. and other socialist countries?

And the bourgeois press and radio are exploiting it, bestowing generous praise on Prchlik. Not without glee the Reuters correspondent says: "A prominent Czechoslovak general makes an extremely strong public attack on the Warsaw Pact." (Here we see how quickly one can become a "prominent general.") With equal enthusiasm the Reuters correspondent tells his compatriots: Look, a department chief of the C.C.P. Central Committee has "denounced the organizational structure" of the Warsaw Pact. What else do you need?

The New York Times depicts Prchlik as a kind of "hero." After all he has called for neither more nor less than "fundamental revision of the Warsaw Pact." Referring to Prchlik's statement, the newspaper provides "advice" on how the structure of the Warsaw Pact "should be changed."

Generally speaking, V. Prchlik has done a good job of currying the favor of both anti-Communist elements within Czechoslovakia and the anti-Communist, aggressive forces of the capitalist West, which have the same aim; pushing

Czechoslovakia off the socialist road and tearing the country away from the socialist camp.

We are far from thinking that V. Prchlik's idle fabrications about the Warsaw Pact and its Joint Armed Forces are shared by Czechoslovakia's working people or army personnel. We are firmly convinced that the reverse is true and that their opinion is diametrically opposed to such ideas. They have not forgotten the lessons of history. . . .

In Europe, where enormous amounts of weapons of mass destruction have been stockpiled, peace and the security of the peoples are maintained primarily thanks to the strength, solidarity, and peace-loving policy of the socialist states. The fraternal Marxist-Leninist parties bear full responsibility for this strength and unity of the socialist countries and for the destinies of peace. Let no one ever, for one moment, forget this responsibility.

THE WARSAW LETTER CONTROVERSY

THE FIVE-PARTY LETTER sent to Prague from Warsaw ("To the Czechoslovak Communist Party Central Committee," Document 34) was in effect an ultimatum outlining the rationale for invasion: (1) A counterrevolutionary situation existed; (2) Dubček had lost control over the course of events; (3) Czechoslovakia was being pushed off the path of socialism, thereby creating a threat to the frontiers of the socialist commonwealth in Europe; (4) "Healthy forces" [1] in Czechoslovakia must be rallied and could count on assistance of fraternal socialist countries. The Warsaw Letter specified a concrete program for getting the situation back in hand: complete repression of antisocialist, rightist forces, the banning of the political clubs, reimposition of censorship, and reorganization of the Communist party along "fundamental Marxist-Leninist lines."

With respect to foreign policy, Prague's increasingly less hostile policy toward West Germany was the issue. The passage on West German revanchist attempts to isolate East Germany strongly echoed *Neues Deutschland* charges[2] of the day before ("Massive Interference by Bonn with Internal Affairs of the Czechoslovak Socialist Republic," Document 35). Unidentified members of the Czechoslovak leadership were accused of flirting with Bonn against the interests of socialism.

Prague's reply ("The Point of View of the Presidium of the KSČ Central Committee on the Joint Letter of the Five Communist and Workers' Parties," Document 36) answered the charges and pointedly recalled the pledge of the Soviet Government Declaration of October 30, 1956, to base socialist relations on equality, respect of territorial integrity, national independence, sovereignty, and mutual noninterference in internal affairs. When Dubček went before a special session of the KSČ Central Committee to explain rejection of the Warsaw Letter (Document 37), the Presidium's stand was endorsed by acclamation. Czechoslovakia stood united.

Moscow's response ("Concerning the Point of View of the CCP Central Committee," Document 38) did not differ much from Stalin's reply to Tito in

---

[1] The analogy to 1956 became ever more explicit. See *Pravda,* November 4, 1956.
[2] Summarized in *Pravda,* July 19, 1968.

1948 — "We regard your answer as incorrect and therefore completely unsatisfactory." [3] Nor was Prague unaware of the similarities to 1948. For example, one of the editors of *Obrana lidu*, L. Svoboda, ranked the Warsaw Letter with the Cominform resolution in Yugoslavia as "one of the darkest aspects of the history of the international workers' movement" (L. Svoboda, "Czechoslovakia Is Not Going to Commit Suicide," Document 39).

DOCUMENT 34

"TO THE CZECHOSLOVAK COMMUNIST PARTY CENTRAL
COMMITTEE"

July 15, 1968
Complete Text

[*Pravda*, July 18, 1968, quoted from *CDSP*, Vol. XX, No. 29 (August 7, 1968), pp. 4–6]

Dear comrades!

On behalf of the Central Committees of the Communist and Workers' Parties of Bulgaria, Hungary, the G.D.R., Poland and the Soviet Union, we send you this letter, which is dictated by sincere friendship based on the principles of Marxism-Leninism and proletarian internationalism and by concern for our common tasks and for strengthening the positions of socialism and the security and socialist commonwealth of the peoples.

The developments in your country have aroused profound anxiety among us. The reactionaries' offensive, supported by imperialism, against your party and the foundations of the Czechoslovak Socialist Republic's social system, we are deeply convinced, threatens to push your country off the path of socialism and, consequently, imperils the interests of the entire socialist system.

We expressed these fears at a meeting in Dresden, during several bilateral meetings and in the letters that our parties recently sent to the Presidium of the Czechoslovak Communist Party Central Committee.

A short time ago we proposed to the Presidium of the C.C.P. Central Committee that a new joint meeting be held on July 14, 1968, to exchange information and opinions on the situation in our countries, including developments in Czechoslovakia. Unfortunately, the Presidium of the C.C.P. Central Committee did not take part in this meeting and did not take advantage of the opportunity for a collective comradely discussion of the situation that has taken shape.

[3] "Letter from the Central Committee of the Communist Party of the Soviet Union to Comrade Tito and Other Members of the Central Committee of the Communist Party of Yugoslavia" (March 27, 1948), in Robert Bass and Elizabeth Marbury, eds., *The Soviet-Yugoslav Controversy, 1948–1958: A Documentary Record* (New York: Prospect Books. 1959), pp. 6–12.

Therefore we deemed it necessary to set forth our common opinion to you in this letter with all sincerity and candor. We want you to understand us well and assess our intentions correctly.

We have not had and do not have any intention of interfering in affairs that are purely the internal affairs of your party and your state or of violating the principles of respect, autonomy and equality in relations among Communist Parties and socialist countries.

We do not appear before you as representatives of yesterday who would like to hinder your rectification of errors and shortcomings, including the violations of socialist legality that took place.

We do not interfere with the methods of planning and administration of Czechoslovakia's socialist national economy or with your actions aimed at perfecting the economic structure and developing socialist democracy.

We shall welcome adjustment of the relations between Czechs and Slovaks on the healthy foundations of fraternal cooperation within the framework of the Czechoslovak Socialist Republic.

At the same time, we cannot assent to hostile forces pushing your country off the path of socialism and creating the threat that Czechoslovakia may break away from the socialist commonwealth. This is no longer your affair alone. It is the common affair of all Communist and Workers' Parties and states that are united by alliance, cooperation and friendship. It is the common affair of our countries, which have united in the Warsaw Pact to safeguard their independence, peace, and security in Europe and to place an insurmountable barrier in front of the schemes of imperialist forces, aggression and revanche.

At the cost of enormous sacrifices, the peoples of our countries achieved victory over Hitlerian fascism and won freedom and independence and the opportunity to advance along the path of progress and socialism. The frontiers of the socialist world have shifted to the center of Europe, to the Elbe and the Bohemian Forest. And never will we consent to allow these historic gains of socialism and the independence and security of all our peoples to be jeopardized. Never will we consent to allow imperialism, by peaceful or nonpeaceful means, from within or without, to make a breach in the socialist system and change the balance of power in Europe in its favor.

The might and solidity of our alliances depend on the internal strength of the socialist system in each of our fraternal countries and on the Marxist-Leninist policies of our parties, which perform a guiding role in the political and social life of their peoples and states. Subversion of the Communist Parties' guiding role leads to liquidation of socialist democracy and the socialist system. This creates a threat to the foundations of our alliance and to the security of our countries' commonwealth.

You know that the fraternal parties showed understanding for the decisions of the C.C.P. Central Committee's January plenary session; they assumed that your party, keeping a firm hold on the levers of power, would direct the whole process in the interests of socialism without allowing anti-Communist reactionaries to exploit it for their own purposes. We were convinced that you would defend the Leninist principle of democratic centralism as the apple of your eye.

Disregard for any aspect of this principle both of democracy and of centralism inevitably leads to a weakening of the party and its guiding role and to transformation of the party into either a bureaucratic organization or a discussion club. We have repeatedly spoken about all these questions at our meetings, and we received assurances from you that you were aware of all the dangers and were fully resolved to repulse them.

Unfortunately, events moved along a different channel.

The forces of reaction, taking advantage of the weakening of party leadership in the country and demagogically abusing the slogan of "democratization," unleashed a campaign against the C.C.P. and its honest and devoted cadres, with the clear intention of liquidating the party's guiding role, undermining the socialist system and pitting Czechoslovakia against the other socialist countries.

The political organizations and clubs that have cropped up lately outside the framework of the National Front have in essence become headquarters for the forces of reaction. The social democrats persistently seek to create their own party, are organizing underground committees and are attempting to split the workers' movement in Czechoslovakia and to secure leadership of the country so as to restore the bourgeois system. Antisocialist and revisionist forces have taken over the press, radio and television and have turned them into platforms for attacking the Communist Party, for disorienting the working class and all the working people, for carrying out unchecked antisocialist demagoguery and for subverting the friendly relations between the C.S.R. and the other socialist countries. A number of mass news organs are systematically conducting genuine moral terrorism with respect to people who speak out against the forces of reaction or express their anxiety over the course of events.

Despite the decisions of the May plenary sessions of the C.C.P. Central Committee, which pointed out the threat from rightist and anti-Communist forces as the chief danger, the intensified attacks by the reactionaries have met no rebuff. It was precisely this that enabled the reactionaries to appear publicly before the whole country and publish their political platform, entitled "The 2,000 Words," which contains an open appeal for struggle against the Communist Party and against constitutional rule, an appeal for strikes and disorders. This appeal constitutes a serious threat to the party, the National Front and the socialist state and is an attempt to implant anarchy. In essence, this statement is an organizational-political platform of counterrevolution. Let no one be deluded by its authors' assertions that they do not want to overthrow the socialist system, that they do not want to act without Communists, that they do not want to sever the alliances with the socialist countries. These are empty phrases whose aim is to legitimize the platform of counterrevolution and lull the vigilance of the party, the working class and all the working people.

This platform, which was widely circulated in the crucial period prior to the extraordinary congress of the C.C.P., not only was not rejected but even found outright champions within the party and its leadership, champions who support the antisocialist appeals.

Antisocialist and revisionist forces are defaming the entire activity of the

Communist Party, waging a slander campaign against its cadres and discrediting honest Communists who are devoted to the party.

Thus, a situation has arisen that is absolutely unacceptable for a socialist country.

In this atmosphere attacks are also being made on the C.S.R.'s socialist foreign policy, and the alliance and friendship with socialist countries is being assailed. Voices are heard demanding a revision of our common coordinated policy with respect to the F.R.G., despite the fact that the West German government invariably pursues a course hostile to the interests of our countries' security. The attempts at flirtation by the F.R.G. authorities and the revanchists have found a response in ruling circles of your country.

The whole course of events in recent months in your country indicates that the forces of counterrevolution, supported by imperialist centers, have launched a broad offensive against the socialist system without encountering the requisite opposition from the party or the people's role. There is no doubt that the centers of international imperialist reaction, which are doing everything possible to inflame and complicate the situation by inspiring antisocialist forces to take action in this direction, have taken a hand in these Czechoslovak developments. Under the guise of extolling the "democratization" and "liberalization" in the C.S.R., the bourgeois press is conducting an incitive campaign against the fraternal socialist countries. F.R.G. ruling circles, which seek to make use of the events in Czechoslovakia to sow discord between the socialist countries, to isolate the G.D.R., and to implement their revanchist schemes, have been especially active in this.

Is it possible, comrades, that you fail to see these dangers? Is it possible to remain passive in this situation and to confine oneself merely to declarations and assurances of fidelity to the cause of socialism and alliance commitments? Is it possible that you fail to see that the counterrevolutionaries have taken one position after another from you and that the party is losing control over the course of events and is retreating more and more under the pressure of anti-Communist forces?

Was it not to sow distrust and hostility toward the Soviet Union and other socialist countries that your country's press, radio and television unleashed a campaign over the staff exercises of the Warsaw Pact Armed Forces? Matters have reached the point where a joint exercise of our troops with the participation of several Soviet army units, something customary for military cooperation, is being used for unfounded charges that the C.S.R.'s sovereignty has been violated. And this is happening in Czechoslovakia, whose people hold sacred the memory of the Soviet soldiers who gave their lives for the freedom and sovereignty of that country. At the same time, near your country's western borders the military forces of the aggressive NATO bloc are conducting maneuvers in which the army of revanchist West Germany is participating. But not a word is said about this.

As is obvious, the inspirers of this invidious campaign want to confuse the minds of the Czechoslovak people, disorient them and undermine the truism that Czechoslovakia can preserve its independence and sovereignty only as a socialist country, as a member of the socialist commonwealth. And only the enemies of socialism could today exploit the slogan of "defending the sovereignty" of the C.S.R. against the socialist countries, against the countries with which alliance and fraternal cooperation create the most reliable groundwork for the independence and free development of each of our peoples.

We are convinced that a situation has arisen in which the threat to the foundations of socialism in Czechoslovakia jeopardizes the common vital interests of the rest of the socialist countries. The peoples of our countries would never forgive us for indifference and unconcern before such danger.

We live in a time when peace and the security and freedom of peoples more than ever demand unity among the forces of socialism. International tension is not waning. American imperialism has not renounced its policy of force and open intervention against peoples fighting for their freedom. It continues to wage a criminal war in Vietnam, support the Israeli aggressors in the Near East and hampers a peaceful settlement of the conflict. The arms race has by no means slowed down. The Federal Republic of Germany, in which the forces of neofascism have swelled, attacks the status quo by demanding a revision of the borders, refuses to renounce its aspirations either to seize the G.D.R. or to secure access to nuclear weapons and opposes disarmament proposals. In Europe, where enormous means of mass destruction have been stockpiled, peace and the security of peoples are maintained primarily thanks to the strength, solidarity and peace-loving policies of the socialist states. We all bear responsibility for this strength and unity of the socialist countries and for the fate of peace.

Our countries are bound to one another by treaties and agreements. These important mutual commitments of states and peoples are founded on a common desire to defend socialism and safeguard the collective security of the socialist countries. Our parties and peoples are entrusted with the historical responsibility of seeing that the revolutionary gains achieved are not forfeited.

Each of our parties bears a responsibility not only to its own working class and its own people but also to the international working class and the world Communist movement and cannot evade the obligations deriving from this. Therefore we must have solidarity and unity in defense of the gains of socialism, our security and the international positions of the entire socialist commonwealth.

This is why we believe that it is not only your task but ours too to deal a resolute rebuff to the anticommunist forces and to wage a resolute struggle for the preservation of the socialist system in Czechoslovakia.

The cause of defending the rule of the working class and all the working people and the socialist gains in Czechoslovakia requires:

a resolute and bold offensive against rightist and antisocialist forces and the mobilization of all means of defense created by the socialist state;

a cessation of the activities of all political organizations that oppose socialism;

the party's assumption of control over the mass news media — the press, radio, and television — and utilization of them in the interests of the working class, all the working people and socialism;

solidarity in the ranks of the party itself on the fundamental basis of Marxism-Leninism, steadfast observance of the principles of democratic centralism and struggle against those who through their activities assist hostile forces.

We know there are forces in Czechoslovakia that are capable of upholding the socialist system and dealing a defeat to the antisocialist elements. The working class, the laboring peasantry and the advanced intelligentsia — the overwhelming majority of the republic's working people — are prepared to do everything necessary in the name of the further development of socialist society. The tasks today are to give these healthy forces a clear perspective, rally them to action and mobilize their energy for a struggle against the forces of counterrevolution in order to preserve and strengthen socialism in Czechoslovakia.

In the face of the threat of counterrevolution, the voice of the working class must resound with full strength to the call of the Communist Party. The working class, together with the laboring peasantry, made enormous efforts in the name of the triumph of the socialist revolution. It is precisely these forces that most cherish the preservation of the gains of socialism.

We express the conviction that the Czechoslovak Communist Party, realizing its responsibility, will take the necessary measures to block the path of reaction. In this struggle you may count on the solidarity and comprehensive assistance of the fraternal socialist countries.

[Signed:] On the instructions of the Bulgarian Communist Party Central Committee: Todor Zhivkov, First Secretary of the B.C.P. Central Committee and Chairman of the Council of Ministers of the People's Republic of Bulgaria; Stanko Todorov, member of the Politburo and Secretary of the Central Committee; Boris Velchev, member of the Politburo and Secretary of the Central Committee; Pencho Kubadinsky, member of the Politburo and Vice-Chairman of the P.R.B. Council of Ministers.

On the instructions of the Hungarian Socialist Workers' Party Central Committee: Janos Kadar, First Secretary of H.S.W.P. Central Committee; Jeno Fock, member of the Politburo of the H.S.W.P. Central Committee and Chairman of the Hungarian Revolutionary Workers' and Peasants' Government.

On the instructions of the Central Committee of the Socialist Unity Party of Germany: Walter Ulbricht, First Secretary of the S.U.P.G. Central Committee and Chairman of the G.D.R. State Council; Willi Stoph, member of the Politburo of the Central Committee and Chairman of the G.D.R. Council of Ministers; Hermann Axen, candidate member of the Politburo and Secretary of the Central Committee.

On the instructions of the Central Committee of the Polish United Workers' Party: Wladyslaw Gomulka, First Secretary of the P.U.W.P. Central Committee; Marian Spychalski, member of the Politburo of the Central Committee and Chairman of the Polish People's Republic State Council; Josef Cyrankiewicz, member of the Politburo and Chairman of the P.P.R. Council of Ministers; Zenon Kliszko, member of the Politburo and Secretary of the Central Committee.

On the instructions of the Central Committee of the Communist Party of the Soviet Union: L. I. Brezhnev, General Secretary of the C.P.S.U. Central Com-

mittee; N. V. Podgorny, member of the Politburo of the Central Committee and Chairman of the Presidium of the U.S.S.R. Supreme Soviet; A. N. Kosygin, member of the Politburo and Chairman of the U.S.S.R. Council of Ministers; P. Ye. Shelest, member of the Politburo of the C.P.S.U. Central Committee and First Secretary of the Ukraine Communist Party Central Committee; K. F. Katushev, Secretary of the C.P.S.U. Central Committee.
Warsaw, July 15, 1968.

DOCUMENT 35

"MASSIVE INTERFERENCE BY BONN WITH THE INTERNAL AFFAIRS OF THE CZECHOSLOVAK SOCIALIST REPUBLIC"

Dispatch from Bonn

Excerpts

[*Neues Deutschland,* July 17, 1968]

Despite strict secrecy by the Foreign Ministry, various details have been learned in Bonn political circles concerning measures taken by the Kiesinger government to influence developments in the Czechoslovak Socialist Republic in a proimperialist direction. It has been learned from the Foreign Ministry that the head of Bonn's trade mission in Prague, Heipertz, stressed the favorable repercussions of the measures he recommended in his recent report to the Foreign Ministry.

Illuminating details of a conversation between Heipertz and the official in charge of Section 2-A-2 — "German Eastern Questions," — Dr. Turnwald, were mentioned in Bonn journalistic circles. Turnwald deals in the Foreign Ministry with fundamental aspects of the "new Eastern policy." He qualified for his post through his doctorate thesis on "Documents Concerning the Expulsion of the Sudeten Germans."

Faster Than Expected

According to information circulating in Bonn, Heipertz told Turnwald that the hoped-for development in the Czechoslovak Socialist Republic is making progress more quickly than he himself originally expected. The pressure by certain pro-Western circles, especially some intellectuals who do not agree to the working class and its party playing the leading role, has increased appreciably. These circles are inspiring the efforts to disassociate the Czechoslovak Socialist Republic from the Soviet Union and the other socialist countries. In his report, Heipertz referred to a conversation with the writer Procházka, who, over a meal in the Dutch diplomatic mission in Prague, told him that the developments in Czechoslovakia would progress much faster if the present Czechoslovak Communist Party Central Committee and Government did not have to bear in mind the commitments under the alliance with the Soviet Union and other Warsaw Pact states.

Recommendations for the Press

Events within Czechoslovakia prompted the Bonn Foreign Ministry to recommend to the press, radio, and television in West Germany to refrain from all too open demonstrations of sympathy for the pro-Western groups in the Czechoslovak Socialist Republic. Their intention is to support the so-called reformers in the Czechoslovak Socialist Republic all the more strenuously behind the scenes while "officially displaying restraint." The Foreign Ministry is of the opinion that this attitude is in keeping with the wishes of the circles behind the "2,000 Words" manifesto. These circles, through the offices of a leading member of the Prague Economic Institute, conveyed the request as early as April for Bonn's official restraint so as not to complicate the situation of the pro-Western groups. For instance, the middleman from Prague has asked that the trip to Czechoslovakia by parliamentary SPD Chairman Schmidt be canceled and that Deputy Eppler be sent instead, since his visit could be arranged more discreetly. As we all know, as a consequence of this, a delegation of the lower house Foreign Affairs Committee traveled to Prague early in June. The delegation included, apart from Eppler, the CDU/CSU deputies Mueller-Hermann and Marx. Eppler is the SPD deputy who has since moved up to a minister's post in Bonn.

Brandt for Cautious Steps

After the above-mentioned conversations of the Czechoslovak economist with authorities in Bonn, Foreign Minister Brandt ordered that contacts with Czechoslovak groups friendly to Bonn be treated in the matter of a conspiracy, and that journeys to Czechoslovakia be allocated mainly to economists and persons not holding official government posts.

It was stated that a reference to the lessons learned from the 1956 events in Hungary is to be explicitly attached to the instruction. This is also the background of the so-called private journey of FDP Chairman Scheel, who is at present in Prague.

Brandt further pointed out that relations with the Czechoslovak Republic are to be developed on a gradual basis. For the time being the government does not insist on the resumption of diplomatic relations. It would be an important step forward if an appreciation of German policies deviating from that of the other socialist countries would be initiated and the polemics against Bonn suspended.

In Bonn, various statements by Kiesinger and Brandt are recalled to the effect that it is the federal government's aim to create new realities in Europe. The Foreign Ministry includes in these new realities a Czechoslovak foreign policy that detaches itself from the common views of the Warsaw Pact states and does not adhere to the jointly agreed policy. It is hoped that this process will be concluded with the establishment of diplomatic relations between the Czechoslovak Socialist Republic and the Federal Republic. This hope is based on remarks made by some Czechoslovak politicians on the need for a "European foreign policy" on the part of Czechoslovakia. . . .

Bonn's Offer of Credits

The Foreign Ministry [in Bonn] attaches particular importance to the establishment and expansion of economic relations with Czechoslovakia. The above-mentioned Heipertz, head of Bonn's trade mission in Prague, referred in his report to the Foreign Ministry to various conversations with "pro-Western reformers," from which it allegedly emerged that developments in Czechoslovakia would progress all the more favorably, the more quickly "the reformers" succeeded in showing economic successes.

Heipertz reported, among other things, a conversation with the Prague economist Selucký, who, after gossiping about internal aspects of negotiations between Czechoslovakia and the Soviet Union, allegedly told Heipertz that, by procuring a loan from the West, Czechoslovakia would be able to free itself from "economic dependence" on the Soviet Union. Selucký is of the opinion that in the coming months as many business transactions as possible must be concluded with Western firms so as to face the leading authorities in Czechoslovakia with accomplished facts and to prove that close economic links with the West are developing advantageously.

In his report, Heipertz hailed as successful the complete agreement between him and Selucký to grant needed guarantees to the West that it would not lose the invested money in the Czechoslovak Republic.

War Criminal Blessing in Prague

On the basis of the Heipertz report, relations have been established between a number of Czechoslovak State Banks and some West German Bank. Bonn evinced surprise and satisfaction when the so-called private visit in Prague was made possible for the West German President of the West German bank.

It was at first believed that Blessing would be rejected because of his criminal past. Investigations by the so-called Council of Research for German Reunification at the disposal of the Foreign Ministry in Bonn, dealing with the situation in Czechoslovakia, reached the conclusion that it would further West German foreign policy to give loans to the Czechoslovak Republic through a bank trust.

According to rumors, research is under way and proposals are being drafted in order to find out to what extent should foreign aid projects be reduced or cancelled, in order to release financial means for credits in favor of Czechoslovakia.

DOCUMENT 36

CZECHOSLOVAK REPLY TO THE WARSAW LETTER

July 18, 1968

Complete Text

[Revised from *The New York Times,* July 19, 1968]

❧

The Presidium of the Central Committee of the Communist Party of Czecho-slovakia has thoroughly studied the letter it has received from the meeting of the representatives of the parties of five Socialist countries in Warsaw.

The letter stresses that it is motivated by anxiety over our common cause and the strengthening of socialism.

On the basis of this fact and led by the same strivings, we wish to openly state our own attitude to the issues mentioned in the letter.

We are at the same time fully aware that an exchange of letters cannot fully explain such a complex problem, and our statement does not aim to do so; in fact, it presumes direct mutual talks between parties.

A number of fears expressed in the letter were also expressed in the resolu-tion of our May plenary session of the Central Committee of the Communist Party of Czechoslovakia.

However, we see the causes of the antagonistic political situation mainly in the fact that these conflicts accumulated over the years preceding the January plenary session of the Central Committee of the Communist Party of Czecho-slovakia. These conflicts cannot be satisfactorily solved suddenly in a short time.

In the process of the realization of the political line of the action program of our party it is, therefore, unavoidable that healthy socialist activities are accompanied by extremist tendencies, that the remnants of antisocialist forces in our society are trying to hang on and that at the same time the dogmatic-sectarian forces connected with the faulty policy of the pre-January period are also spreading their activities.

Party Affected by Disputes

Not even the party itself can remain untouched by internal disputes which accompany this process of unification on the line of the action program.

One of the negative aspects of this process is also the violation of the prin-ciples of democratic centralism in the dealings of some Communists, which is mainly one caused by the fact that for many long years the old party leadership governed according to the principle of bureaucratic centralism and suppressed internal party democracy.

All these factors prevent us from achieving the results in our political work which we ourselves wish.

We do not wish to hide these facts, nor do we hide them from our own party and people.

For this reason also the May plenum of the Central Committee stated clearly that it is necessary to mobilize all forces to prevent a conflict situation in the country and the endangering of socialist power in the Czechoslovak Socialist Republic. Our party has also unequivocally stated that if any such danger occurred it would use all means to protect the Socialist system.

We ourselves have seen the possibility of such danger. We understand that the fraternal parties of the socialist countries cannot be indifferent to this. We do not, however, see any realistic reasons for calling the present situation counterrevolutionary, invoking a direct threat to the basis of the socialist system or claiming that Czechoslovakia is preparing a change in the orientation of our socialist foreign policy and that there is concrete danger of our country breaking away from the Socialist community.

Our alliance and friendship with the U.S.S.R. and other socialist countries is deeply rooted in the social system, the historical traditions and experience of our peoples, in their interests, their thoughts and feelings. The liberation from Nazi occupation and the entry onto the path of a new life is forever connected in the consciousness of our people with the historical victory of the U.S.S.R. in the Second World War and with respect for the heroes who laid down their lives in this battle.

This is also the basis of the action program of our party which proclaims this tradition to be its starting point:

The basic orientation of Czechoslovakia's foreign policy was conceived and confirmed during the period of national liberation and Socialist reconstruction in our country; it is alliance and cooperation with the Soviet Union and the other Socialist countries. We shall strive to deepen friendly relations between our allies — the countries of the world socialist system — on the basis of mutual respect, sovereignty and equality, mutual esteem and international solidarity. To this end we shall contribute more actively and rationally to the common activities of the Council of Mutual Economic Assistance and the Warsaw Treaty.

Surprise Is Expressed

In the letter there is mention of attacks against socialist foreign policy, assaults against alliance and friendship with Socialist countries, and voices calling for the revision of our common and coordinated policy in relation to the G.F.R. and it is even stated that attempts at making advances on the part of the authorities of the G.F.R. and revanchists are enjoying favorable response in the leading circles of our country.

We are surprised at such statements because it is well known that the Czechoslovak Socialist Republic is following a thoroughly socialist foreign policy, the principles of which were formulated in the action program of the Communist Party of Czechoslovakia and the program statement of the Government. These documents and the statements made by leading Czechoslovak representatives and also our further actions are consistently based on the principles of Socialist internationalism, alliance and the development of friendly relations with the Soviet Union and the other Socialist states.

We are of the opinion that these facts are decisive and not the irresponsible voices of the individuals which are sometimes heard.

With regard to the bitter historical experiences of our nations with German imperialism and militarism it is inconceivable that any Czechoslovak government, no less a *socialist* government, could ignore these experiences and foolhardedly hazard the fate of our country, and we must refute any suspicion in this direction.

As regards our relations with the G.F.R., it is universally known that although Czechoslovakia is the immediate neighbor of the G.F.R., it was the last to take definite steps toward the partial regulation of mutual relations, particularly in the economic field, while other socialist countries adapted their relations to one or another extent much earlier without it causing any fears.

At the same time, we thoroughly respect and protect the interests of the G.D.R., our socialist ally, and do all in our power to strengthen its international position and authority. This is definitely proved by all the speeches of the leading representatives of our party and state in the entire period after January, 1968.

Commitments Are Respected

The agreements and treaties which connect the socialist countries are an important factor of mutual cooperation, peace and collective security. Czechoslovakia fully respects its contractual commitments and further develops the system of treaties with socialist countries. This is proved by the new friendship treaties which we recently concluded with the Bulgarian People's Republic and the Hungarian People's Republic, and also the prepared treaty on friendship and cooperation with the Rumanian Socialist Republic.

Like the authors of the letter we shall not allow the historic achievements of socialism and the safety of the nations of our country to be threatened. We cannot consent to imperialism — either by peaceful or forceful means — breaking down the socialist system and changing the balance of power in Europe to its advantage. The main tenor of our development after January lies in the attempt to increase our internal strength and the stability of the socialist system, and thus also our bonds of alliance.

Staff maneuvers of the allied forces of the Warsaw Treaty on the territory of Czechoslovakia are a concrete proof of our faithful fulfillment of our alliance commitments.

In order to ensure its smooth course we took the necessary measures on our side. Our people and the members of the army gave a friendly welcome to the Soviet and other allied soldiers on the territory of Czechoslovakia, the top representatives of the party and Government by their participation proved what importance we attach to it and the interest we have in it.

The confusion and doubts in the minds of our public occurred only after the repeated changes of the time of the departure of the allies' armies from the territory of Czechoslovakia after the maneuvers were over.

The letter of the five parties also deals with some internal problems of the present. We accept the assurance that the aim of this interest is not to interfere with the "methods of planning and management of the socialist national economy in Czechoslovakia" and with our "measures aimed at perfecting the structure of the economy and the development of socialist democracy" and that the "settlement of the relations between Czechs and Slovaks on the healthy principles of fraternal cooperation within the framework of the Czechoslovak Socialist Republic" are welcomed.

Inner Strength Vital

We agree with the opinion that the strength and firmness of our ties — which are undoubtedly the common vital interest of us all — depends on the inner strength of the socialist system of each of our fraternal countries.

We do not doubt that the undermining of the leading role of the Communist party would threaten the liquidation of socialist society. Just for this reason it is essential that we should understand each other on the question of what is the condition for the strength of the socialist system and the strengthening of the leading role of the Communist party.

In the action program of our party we set down the following on the basis of our previous experience:

"At the present time it is especially essential for the party to carry out a policy that makes it worthy of the leading role in our society. We are convinced that under the present circumstances it is a condition for the socialist development of the country . . ."

The Communist party depends on the voluntary support of the people. It is not implementing its leading role by ruling over society but by faithfully serving its free, progressive socialist development. It cannot impel its authority, but must constantly acquire it by its actions. It cannot force its line by orders, but by the work of its members and the veracity of its ideals.

We do not hide the fact — and we stated this plainly at the May plenum of the Central Committee — that there exist today tendencies aimed at discrediting the party, attempts to deny it its moral and political right to lead the society. But if we ask the question whether similar phenomena can be correctly judged as a threat to the socialist system, as a decline of the political role of the Communist Party of Czechoslovakia under the pressure of reactionary, counterrevolutionary forces — then we come to the conclusion that this is not so.

The leading role of our party gravely suffered in the past by the distortions of the fifties and the policy of their inconsistent removal by the leadership headed by A. Novotný. He is responsible for deepening the social conflicts between the Czechs and Slovaks, between the intelligentsia and workers, between the young generation and the older generations.

The inconsistent solution of economic problems has left us in a condition in which we cannot tend to a number of justified economic demands by our workers and in which the effectiveness of the entire national economy is gravely disrupted.

Further Mistakes Accumulate

Under that leadership the confidence of the masses in the party dropped and there were expressions of criticism and resistance, but all this was "solved" by interference from a position of power against justified dissatisfaction, against criticism, and against attempts to solve social problems in the interests of the party and in the interests of its leading role.

Instead of the gradual and well-considered removal of errors, further mistakes and conflicts accumulated as a result of subjective decision-making. In the years when socialist democracy could have been objectively developed gradually and scientific management applied, the subjective deficiencies sharpened the social conflicts and difficulties.

On the outside it seemed that everything was in order in Czechoslovakia and it was made to appear that developments were without conflict. In actual fact the decline in the confidence in the party was masked by exterior forms of directive party control. Although this regime was made to seem a firm guarantee of the interests of the entire socialist camp, inside problems were growing, and a genuine solution was suppressed by forceful measures taken against those advocates of new and creative approaches.

Any indication of a return to these methods would evoke the resistance of the overwhelming majority of party members, the resistance of the working class, the workers, cooperative farmers and intelligentsia.

The party would by such a step imperil its political leading role and would create a situation in which a power conflict would really arise. This would truly threaten the socialist advantages in the anti-imperialist front of the socialist community.

We agree that one of the primary tasks of the party is to thwart the aims of right-wing and antisocialist forces. Our party has worked out its tactical political plan and is solving its problems according to it. This plan is based on a system of measures which can be successful only if we have the conditions to gradually implement them over the course of several months.

Main Aims Specified

If we are to succeed in this endeavor, the realization of the action program and the preparations of the party congress must take their course without any false step which could cause a struggle for political power in our country. The May plenum stated this quite plainly in its resolution:

"The party considers the basic problem of the current situation is to prevent the threatening of the socialist character of power and social system from either side — either from the side of right-wing anti-Communist tendencies, or from the side of conservative forces, who were unable to ensure the development of socialism but who would wish for a return to the conditions before January, 1968."

Our party has laid down the following main aims and stages of political work:

1. To consistently separate the party as a whole from the distortions of the past for which specific persons of the old party leadership are responsible. These specific people are justifiably being called to task.

2. To prepare the fourteenth extraordinary congress of the party which will evaluate the development and political situation during the January plenum and in accordance with the principles of democratic centralism will lay down the compulsory line for the entire party, will adopt an attitude to the federal arrangement of Czechoslovakia, will approve the new party statutes and elect a new Central Committee so that it has the full authority and confidence of the party and the entire society.

3. After the fourteenth congress to launch the offensive for the solution of all the fundamental internal political questions: the construction of a political system based on the socialist platform of the National Front and social self government, the solution of the federal constitutional arrangement, the elections to the representative bodies of the state (federal, national and local) and the preparation of a new constitution.

At present we are at the stage of the political fight to implement the line of the May plenum of the Central Committee of the Communist Party of Czechoslovakia. It is a real fight, and therefore we both move ahead and suffer drawbacks.

According to the results of the individual battles, it is never correct to judge the outcome of the whole war. Despite this we think that we have managed to consolidate the political situation since the May plenum.

In the past days the extraordinary district and regional conferences have plainly shown that the party is becoming unified along the line of the action program.

Delegates have been elected to the congress, and their composition is a guarantee that the future fate of the party will not be decided by representatives of extremist opinions, but the democratically appointed progressive core of our party.

The representatives of the new leadership of the Communist Party of Czechoslovakia who are associated with the line of the action program and the May plenum of the Central Committee, were all proposed by the regional conferences to the new Central Committee. Therefore, a certain stabilization is going on in the party and the basic steps for the preparations of the congress have taken place with success.

Platform Being Created

In accordance with the resolution of the May plenum of the Central Committee of the Communist party of Czechoslovakia, a binding political Socialist platform of the National Front is being created on the initiative of Communists. All the political components of the National Front adopted the program statement made on June 15, 1968, which clearly accepts the historically-won leading role of the Communist party of Czechoslovakia and which expresses the principles of a socialist system and socialist internal and foreign policy.

The National Front is now discussing the proposal for its statute which is a binding form of organization ensuring the socialist political orientation of all parties and organizations.

We consider all these steps to be important results arising from the fulfillment of the line adopted at the plenary session of the Central Committee of the Communist Party of Czechoslovakia and important features for the consolidation of political conditions and the strengthening not only of the declared but the genuinely leading influence of the party in our country.

In spite of this we see and do not want to conceal the fact that not all conclusions drawn at the May plenary session are being carried out satisfactorily. Now, too, it happens that voices and tendencies appear in the press and the radio and in public meetings which do not coincide with the positive endeavors of the party, the state bodies and the National Front.

We consider the solution of these questions to be a long-term task and are guided by the resolutions of the May plenary session of the Central Committee according to which "political leadership cannot be imposed by the old, administrative and power structures." The Presidium of the Central Committee of the Communist Party of Czechoslovakia, the Government and the National Front clearly rejected the appeal of the proclamation, "two-thousand words," which urges people to engage in anarchist acts and violate the constitutional character of our political reform. It should be noted that, following these negative positions, similar campaigns in fact did not occur in our country and that the consequences of the appeal of "two-thousand words" did not threaten the party, the National Front and the socialist state.

The campaigns and unjustified slander against various functionaries and public officials — including members of the new leadership of the Communist Party of Czechoslovakia — which are conducted from extremist positions both left and right, are still a negative aspect of our situation.

Secretariat Opposes Methods

The Secretariat of the Communist Party Central Committee and leading officials have unequivocally come out against these methods in specific cases.

We know that this situation is facilitated by the abolition of censorship in our country and the enactment of freedom of expression and of the press. What had been spread in the form of "whispered propaganda" before can now be expressed openly.

By the law of judiciary rehabilitations we basically solved the painful problem of the illegal reprisals against innocent people which took place in the past years. This step has clearly helped, and now the attention of the public and the mass communications media no longer concentrates on these questions.

In September — immediately after the party congress — other new important laws will be discussed: the constitutional law on the National Front, which is to confirm the permanent existence of the system of political parties the National Front, and, further, a law on the right assembly and association which sets forth the legal regulations for the establishment and activities of various voluntary organizations, associations, clubs, etc.

This will give us an opportunity to put up effective opposition to anti-Communist forces to gain an organizational basis for public activities.

The Communists have also taken the initiative, according to the resolution of the May plenary session of the Central Committee, to solve the important questions of the work of the trade unions and enterprise workers councils. In general, the party has been able to overcome political demagogy which attempted to utilize the justified demands of the workers to disorganize our system and which fanned an impromptu movement in the name of "workers' demands" in order to make the economic and political situation in the country more difficult.

At the same time, however, according to the means at our disposal, we are solving some urgent social-political problems such as the increase of low pensions and urgent wage increases.

The Government is gradually dealing with the fundamental economic problems of the country in order to provide a new impulse for the development of production and prepare itself to move on to the further improvement of the living standard of our people.

We have taken the necessary measures to ensure the safety of our state borders. The party fully supports the consolidation of the army, security forces, prosecutors and judiciary of the workers' militia whose statewide *aktiv* gave full support to the new leadership of the Communist Party of Czechoslovakia and the action program. The importance of this step, as is known, was welcomed by the workers not only in this country, but also in the U.S.S.R.

Only a Part of Situation

If we ask ourselves though whether it is correct to consider such phenomena as a forfeit of the leading political role of the Communist Party of Czechoslovakia under pressure of reactionary counterrevolutionary forces, we reach the conclusion that this is not so. For all this is only part of our present political situation.

There is also another and, in our opinion, decisive aspect to this situation: the rise of the authority of the new, democratic policy of the party in the eyes of the broadest masses of the workers, the growth of the activity of the overwhelming majority of the people. The overwhelming majority of the people of all classes and sectors of our society favor the abolition of censorship and are for freedom of expression.   ˙

The Communist Party of Czechoslovakia is trying to show that it is capable of a different political leadership and management than the discredited bureaucratic-police methods, mainly by the strength of its Marxist-Leninist ideas, by the strength of its program, its just policy supported by the majority of the people.

Our party can prevail in the difficult political struggle only if it has an opportunity to implement the tactical line of the May plenary meetings of the Central Committee and to settle basic political questions at the extraordinary fourteenth congress in the spirit of the action program.

We, therefore, consider all pressure directed at forcing the party onto another path, that is to settle basic questions of its policy elsewhere and at another time than at the fourteenth congress, the principal danger to the successful consolidation of the leading role of the party in the Czechoslovak Socialist Republic.

Pressure of this sort is being brought to bear by domestic extremist forces on the right as well as from the positions of the conservatives, the dogmatists and sectarians, endeavoring for a return to conditions before January, 1968.

The evaluation of the situation as contained in the letter of the five parties and the no doubt sincerely intended advice for our further activities do not take into account the entire intricacy of the dynamic social movement as it was analyzed by the May plenary meeting of the Central Committee of the Communist Party of Czechoslovakia or the complexity of the conclusions that were adopted by this plenum.

Our policy, if it hopes to remain a Marxist-Leninist policy, cannot be based only on superficial phenomena which do not always reflect the precise and profound causes of social development but must determine the substance of development and be guided by it.

At the given time the interests of socialism in our country can be served best by a show of confidence in the leadership of the Communist Party of Czechoslovakia and full support for its policy by our fraternal parties. For this reason we have proposed, as a prerequisite of successful joint discussions, bilateral meetings of the representatives of our parties so that the joint talks may proceed from deep mutual consultations and factual information.

We sincerely regret that these proposals put forward by us were not implemented. It is not our fault that the meeting in Warsaw was held without us. We discussed the proposals of the five parties for holding this meeting at the Presidium of the Central Committee of the Communist Party of Czechoslovakia twice — on July 8 and 12 — and each time we immediately conveyed our view on the method of how this meeting was to be prepared as we believed to be most correct.

Unfortunately, our meeting of July 12 was already superfluous because, notwithstanding its outcome, the meeting had already been convened for July 14, a fact we learned only through ČTK in the afternoon of July 13, at the time when the representatives of the five parties were already on their way to Warsaw.

In no statement that we sent to the five parties did we refuse on principle to take part in joint conferences. We only voiced our view concerning their suitability at the present time and on the method in which they were prepared so that they could really be to the point and based on more profound information about our complex problems.

From the contents of the letters of the five parties, sent to us between July 4 and 6, 1968, we had the impression that such information is absolutely vital if the success of the meeting was not to be threatened by a preponderance of one-sided and sparse information of the large majority of the participants in the conference concerning the real situation in Czechoslovakia.

Purpose of Proposal Explained

This is the purpose of our proposal for preliminary bilateral meetings. We were motivated not by an effort to isolate ourselves from the community of our fraternal parties and countries, but on the contrary, by a desire to contribute to their consolidation and development.

We think that the common cause of socialism is not advanced by the holding of conferences at which the policy and activity of one of the fraternal parties is judged without the presence of their representatives.

We consider valid the principle expressed in the declaration of the Government of the Soviet Union of Oct. 30, 1956, which says: "The countries of the great community of socialist nations, united by the common ideals of the building of a socialist society and the principles of proletarian internationalism, can build their mutual relations only on the basis of complete equality, respect of territorial integrity, national independence and sovereignty and mutual non-interference in their internal affairs."

This principle, as is generally known, was confirmed at the conference of the representatives of Communist parties in Moscow in November, 1957, and generally adopted. In our activity we wish to continue to strengthen and promote the deep internationalist tradition which, according to our conception, must include both an understanding of the common interests and goals of the progressive forces of the world and an understanding of each nation's specific requirements.

We do not want our relationships to continue worsening and we are willing on our side to contribute to the calming of the situation in the interests of socialism and the unity of the socialist countries. On our side, we shall do nothing which would be against this aim. We expect, however, that the other parties will aid these efforts of ours and will express understanding for our situation.

We see an important task in implementing the bilateral talks which we have proposed as soon as possible assess the possibility of a common meeting of the socialist countries at which it would be possible to agree on its program and composition, the time and the place of its convening.

We consider it to be decisive for us to agree on positive steps in the near future, which would ensure the continuation of our current friendly cooperation and which would convincingly demonstrate our common will to develop and strengthen mutual friendly relations.

This is in the interest of our common fight against imperialism, for peace and the security of nations, for democracy and socialism.

DOCUMENT 37

"MANIFEST VICTORY FOR THE SOVEREIGNTY PRINCIPLE"

DUBČEK ADDRESSES SPECIAL KSČ CC PLENUM

July 19, 1968

Excerpts

[*Rudé právo* and *Svobodné slovo*, July 20, 1968]

❧

. . . You have acquainted yourselves with two documents of extraordinary political importance: the letter from five Communist and workers' parties sent to our Central Committee and the position which the Presidium of the Czechoslovak Communist Party Central Committee adopted toward this letter on July 17 this year. You also have before you the original letters from the five Communist parties and our draft proposals for action which we have sent to the representatives of the five Communist parties for discussion by the Presidiums of these five Communist parties.

Above all I want to inform you of how the events developed and what steps the Presidium of the Czechoslovak Communist Party Central Committee has taken. After January many fraternal countries showed an interest in talks with our representatives. As is known, we have realized some of these talks; many others (e.g., with Comrades Ulbricht, Tito, Ceauşescu, Rochet) could not take place, despite an agreement in principle, because of the shortage of time and the complexity and dynamic nature of our internal development.

In connection with the great demands caused by preparations for the extraordinary 14th Congress of the Czechoslovak Communist Party, the Central Committee Pesidium decided to postpone as many as possible of these as well as other meetings until a later time.

Moreover, this followed from the expectation that the fraternal parties would accept our sincere invitation to the congress and that this would be the most convenient occasion for an exchange of views.

On July 4 and 6, 1968, the Presidium of the Czechoslovak Communist Party Central Committee received letters from five fraternal parties which contained an appraisal of developments in the Czechoslovak Socialist Republic and a proposal for a joint conference at which the situation of the Czechoslovak Communist Party and of the Czechoslovak Socialist Republic would be reviewed. In the opinion of the CPSU and of other parties, such a gathering was to take place at summit level on Sunday, July 7, in Warsaw. The members of the Czechoslovak Communist Party Central Committee Presidium had been delegated to the regional conferences, which took place on July 4, 5, 6, and 7, and it would have been politically incorrect to recall them from the conferences. Thus, the Presidium of the Czechoslovak Communist Party Central Committee could not meet until July 8.

At this session, the Presidium of the Czechoslovak Communist Party Central

Committee unanimously welcomed the possibility of talks with the other Communist parties. It recommended to the representatives of the five Communist and workers' parties not to hold a short-term joint conference which would have on its agenda only the review of the situation in the Czechoslovak Socialist Republic and in the Czechoslovak Communist Party. The Presidium of the Czechoslovak Communist Party Central Committee proposed that within the shortest possible time bilateral talks be conducted with representatives of the fraternal countries, including the Rumanian Communist Party and the Yugoslav League of Communists, to inform one another about the situations in their respective countries and parties and to examine the possibility of convening a conference of the Communist and workers' parties of some socialist countries at a suitable time. At the same time, we talked with the Soviet comrades about the possibility of holding bilateral talks on July 14 or 17, or on some other date which would suit them.

We submitted similar proposals to the Polish, Hungarian, German, and Bulgarian comrades.

In reply to its recommendations the Presidium of the Czechoslovak Communist Party Central Committee received on Thursday, July 11, in the late evening hours, a joint letter from all five parties which once again urged the Presidium of the Czechoslovak Communist Party Central Committee to participate in the Warsaw conference. A new day for this conference was not mentioned in the letter. After another discussion of the situation on Friday, July 12, the Czechoslovak Communist Party Central Committee Presidium decided once more to ask the fraternal parties for understanding and for bilateral meetings, above all with the Soviet comrades.

On Saturday, July 13, 1968, we distributed a statement of our position to the other Communist parties, and on the same day news agencies were already reporting the arrival of the CPSU delegation in Warsaw.

On the night of Saturday to Sunday, that is, July 13-14, we sent a cable to Comrade Brezhnev in Warsaw with the request that in the interest of the international relations which link our Communist parties no steps be taken which might have an unfavorable impact on the complex situation in the Czechoslovak Socialist Republic. The extraordinary session of the Presidium of the Czechoslovak Communist Party Central Committee on July 15 once more addressed the request to the participants in the Warsaw gathering not to adopt any conclusions on the situation in Czechoslovakia. In reply, regret was expressed that the Czechoslovak Communist Party had not participated in the meeting.

From the course of our talks with the fraternal parties, it is obvious that the Presidium consistently proceeded from an endeavor to prevent misunderstandings and to contribute to the clarification of controversial questions and various appraisals of the political situation in Czechoslovakia.

We believe from the bottom of our hearts, comrades, that it is possible to solve all the emerging problems and possible misunderstandings through frank, comradely talks. . . .

The ties of our party with the CPSU and with the fraternal parties, the alliances and friendship between our peoples and the peoples of the Soviet Union and of the socialist countries are of basic vital interest to our people. We cannot imagine that the building of socialism and our state and national independence and security could be based on foundations other than the fraternal alliances and deep friendship between our states and Communist parties. This historically proven attitude today authorizes us to stress that another inseparable component part of proletarian internationalism is the principle that each party, in deciding how to go about building socialism, must proceed from the conditions in its own country. Socialism would be an empty abstraction if it were not to include the traditions, historical experiences, and ideological atmosphere of the people who are building the new, just socialist order.

We bear a great responsibility to our whole party, the working class, to all working people in our fatherland, and to our peoples to remain faithful to these international principles in our policy in this difficult situation, when we are discussing important problems with other fraternal parties.

We are resolved to continue the policy begun by the January session of the Central Committee. We have paid too dearly and still are paying for the practice of the past few years. This is why we are thoroughly implementing the measures which we have adopted in the action program.

We have created the conditions for completely frank discussion. We have abolished and eliminated censorship. We have expanded opportunities to implement the right of assembly and association. In the work of the party, government, parliament, National Front, and public organizations, we have changed a great deal, and we have created the proper prerequisites for the thorough rehabilitation of the victims of violations of legality and for the elimination of wrongs committed against them.

Naturally, the implementation of these changes could not take place nor will it take place in the future without difficulties, errors, or possibly extremes. It has not taken place without conflicts, changes in the original prerequisites, or attempts to misuse the temporary difficulties by anti-Communist and conservative forces; but these difficulties and the need for a flexible reaction to the political situation cannot be the decisive factors in appraising our entire situation and the party. . . .

We must also think about certain problems which might arise within our party. As for the Presidium's position regarding the letter of the five parties, we clearly state that we are aware of the problems and discrepancies which have appeared in the party since the Central Committee's January plenum. We hold the view that this is an understandable and inevitable state of affairs in solving such complicated questions. In the resolution of the Central Committee's May plenum, we pointed out the danger posed to the party's policy and leadership not only by antisocialist tendencies but also by conservative, sectarian tendencies. In the current complex situation, we cannot even dismiss the possibility that these conservative, sectarian forces might try to abuse the letter of the five parties to cause a rupture in the party and frustrate the adopted procedures and political aims contained in the resolution of the May plenum

of the Czechoslovak Communist Party Central Committee, in which we unequivocally condemned any attempts to divide our party, regardless of their
origin.

We must take an unequivocal position on this matter today, too. Just as we
must take very solemn and effective measures against any attempts to misuse
the present situation for rightist aims, we must have sufficient courage and
determination to take measures against attempts from leftist sectarian positions to upset the line of the Central Committee May plenum. The directives
of the Central Committee May plenum on preparations for the 14th Party
Congress must not be violated by any provocations or actions that abuse the
current discussions with the fraternal parties with the aim of returning the
party to the pre-January situation. . . .

The approach of the Central Committee Presidium has found unanimous
support not only in the ranks of our party, as expressed in the great number
of resolutions and letters received, but also in the international Communist
movement. We are convinced that the Central Committee will unanimously
approve our position. Our determined common approach is the guarantee that
we will overcome past discrepancies and that we shall approach the extraordinary party congress of the Czechoslovak Communist Party united as never
before. . . .

We explained this to the fraternal parties in the spirit of the May plenum.
The party's leading role now depends on the success of preparations for the
14th Congress — on how we will be able to ensure the necessary upsurge in
party activity during the complicated period facing us. We proceed on the
basis that the complicated and varied activities which mark our development
can best be recognized and purposefully led only by the party, which lives
on the soil of this development, which itself inspired it, and which makes
suggestions for continuing it.

We do not want to pose as infallible. The Presidium has tried to indicate
the nature of our difficulties as objectively as possible. Here, too, two things
are stressed: We are following a path along which we are seeking new
approaches, and we are not succeeding in all respects as we would like to. We
have absolutely no desire to represent our approach as a model for anyone else.

It is merely in line with our own conditions. In pursuing it, we are guided
by these conditions and by the will of our party and people.

Differences in conditions necessarily result in different approaches by other
parties and countries — approaches which correspond to their own people.
These are our guiding principles, and we wish to firmly abide by them. We
want friendly relations among the fraternal parties and socialist states to develop on the basis of strengthening the socialist order in each country according to its own conditions, historical prerequisites, and traditions. . . .

On one point, however, we must say something else and something more
fundamental here. We, the members of the party Presidium, realize in our
daily activities that we could not lead our people were we not essentially one
with them and if we did not intimately know their wishes and ways or how
to link them to the interests of the international Communist movement.

Within our society, we do not consider it abnormal if throughout the community of socialist countries there are different approaches and views on individual questions. Therefore, we do not consider our discussion a threat to the unity of or a sign of the breakup of the socialist community. Such tragic results might ensue only from wrong methods of coming to grips with various positions, not from different viewpoints in themselves. The historical experience of us all in the socialist community has taught us that the results of such wrong methods are profoundly harmful to both individual parties and countries and to the socialist community as a whole. We therefore want from the very beginning to make our practical contribution toward preventing such results.

We determinedly reject and will continue to reject any efforts to misuse our position for anti-Soviet sentiments and hysteria. We again declare that we will do everything possible to ensure that friendly relations between our party and the CPSU, as well as between our people and the Soviet people, are developed and strengthened on the basis of equality and respect for the profound, friendly feelings of our peoples. We will strive with all our energy to develop economic, state, military, and political cooperation with all countries and parties of the socialist camp within the framework of CEMA and the Warsaw Pact. Our party has stood behind these positions in the past and continues to stand behind them today.

As internationalists, we are vitally interested in fraternal cooperation with all socialist countries. Not even the recent meeting of the five fraternal parties in Warsaw can divert us from this principle.

We again wish to declare, aware of our great responsibility to the entire Communist and workers' movement and our people, that we will respect and defend our sovereignty, but that at the same time we will strive not only passively but actively for full, informal, comprehensive cooperation among our fraternal socialist countries and with the international Communist movement. Marxist-Leninists cannot act differently. . . .

DOCUMENT 38

"CONCERNING THE 'POINT OF VIEW' OF THE CCP CENTRAL COMMITTEE"

CPSU COMMENT ON CZECHOSLOVAK REPLY

July 22, 1968

Complete Text

[*Pravda,* July 22, 1968, quoted from *CDSP,* Vol. XX, No. 29 (August 7, 1968), pp. 10–11]

The ČTK news service has transmitted a document headed "The Point of View of the Presidium of the C.C.P. Central Committee on the Joint Letter of the Five Communist and Workers' Parties." It reports that this document was approved by the plenary session of the C.C.P. Central Committee held on July 19 with the participation of a group of delegates elected to the forthcoming extraordinary congress of the C.C.P.

The document reaffirms the political line adopted by the C.C.P. Central Committee at the January and subsequent plenary sessions. It notes that the misgivings over developments in Czechoslovakia expressed in the letter adopted by the participants in the Warsaw meeting of delegations of Communist and Workers' Parties were also expressed by the C.C.P. Central Committee in the resolution of its May plenary session. It admits that the present process in the C.S.R. "is accompanied by extremist tendencies" from which "the remnants of antisocialist forces in our society also are trying to gain advantage." It further points out that "in this complicated situation the party itself cannot avoid internal differences" and that "the negative phenomena of this process include violation of the principles of democratic centralism in the conduct of some Communists."

The document contains admissions that "not all the conclusions of the May plenary session of the C.C.P. Central Committee" are being satisfactorily followed and that "voices and tendencies discordant with the constructive efforts of the party, state agenices and the National Front are encountered from time to time at public meetings and in the mass news media." The document also admits that the appeals contained in "The 2,000 Words" incite "anarchistic actions and violation of the constitutional nature of our political reform." Finally, the document admits that there is now going on in Czechoslovakia "a campaign and groundless instigation against individual officials and public figures, including members of the new leadership of the C.C.P."

But what conclusions does the document draw from these admissions?

Avoiding a thorough political analysis of the actual situation in the country, the Presidium of the C.C.P. Central Committee has taken a step backward from the decisions of the May plenary session of the C.C.P. Central Committee, which said outright that the antisocialist forces operating in Czechoslovakia represent the chief danger at the present stage. The following statement in the document of the C.C.P. Central Committee Presidium testifies to the obvious change in political appraisals:

"We do not see real reasons that would justify describing the present situation as counterrevolutionary, proclaiming a direct threat to the foundations of the socialist system, or asserting that a change in the orientation of our socialist foreign policy is being prepared in Czechoslovakia and that a concrete threat of separating our country from the socialist commonwealth exists."

The document of the Presidium of the C.C.P. Central Committee turns out to have ignored the fundamental questions raised in the letter of the fraternal parties to the Central Committee of the C.C.P. and at the same time expresses disagreement with the estimate of the dimensions of the threat to the socialist system in Czechoslovakia.

Yet today's situation in the C.S.R. is such that hostile forces are pushing the country off the path of socialism and creating a threat of tearing Czechoslovakia away from the socialist commonwealth.

The rightist, antisocialist forces in Czechoslovakia, encouraged and supported by imperialist reaction, are bringing matters to the point of eliminating the Communist Party's guiding role in society, undermining the socialist state system and the socialist social system, and restoring the capitalist order. They have taken over the mass media — press, radio and television — and are using them for antisocialist propaganda, trying to inflame hostility to the Soviet Union and other socialist countries.

The letter of the fraternal parties formulated urgent tasks which it is necessary to carry out for the cause of defending the rule of the working class and the socialist gains of the working people of Czechoslovakia. The fraternal parties emphasized the urgent necessity of a resolute and bold offensive against rightist and antisocialist forces; the mobilization of all means of defense created by the socialist state; the cessation of the activities of all political organizations opposing socialism; party assumption of control over the mass news media and their utilization in the interests of the working class and of all the working people and socialism; solidarity in the ranks of the party itself on the fundamental basis of Marxism-Leninism; steadfast observance of the principle of democratic centralism, and the struggle against those whose activity helps hostile forces.

These proposals, dictated by sincere concern for the preservation and strengthening of the socialist gains of fraternal Czechoslovakia and prompted by the experience of the struggle of the international Communist movement against the forces of imperialism and reaction, are essentially being ignored.

This shows lack of understanding or lack of a desire to understand the full depth of the danger engendered by the offensive of the rightist, antisocialist forces against the revolutionary gains of the working class and all the working people of the C.S.R. Can it be that one should wait until the counterrevolutionary forces become master of the situation in Czechoslovakia before giving battle to them?

The Marxist-Leninist theory of proletarian revolution, confirmed by a half century of experience, places in the hands of the Communist and Workers' Parties a tested weapon in the struggle to hold and strengthen the positions of socialism. Success in this struggle depends on the internal forces of the socialist system in each of the fraternal countries of socialism, on the Marxist-Leninist policy of our parties, which perform the guiding role in the political and public life of their peoples and states. At the same time, undermining of the guiding role of the Communist Party inevitably leads to the elimination of socialist democracy and the socialist system. Any attempt to place the guiding role of the Communist Party in doubt, no matter what references to the special nature of the situation may be used to justify it, inevitably creates a threat to the socialist system and also endangers the common vital interests of the socialist commonwealth.

The fact that the antisocialist forces are continuing the offensive, although sometimes they resort to camouflage, has not escaped the attention of all who are following the development of the political situation in Czechoslovakia. For instance, the authors of the notorious "2,000 Words" have come forth with "explanations" that, if you please, they did not mean to undermine the foundations of socialism in Czechoslovakia. But these and similar tactical dodges are no less dangerous and cannot delude anyone, for the substance of the antisocialist elements' activity remains the same. We are reminded of this once more, incidentally, by the publication on July 20, the same day that the materials of the plenary session of the C.C.P. Central Committee were issued, of an article in Prace* containing a direct hint at the desirability of reconsidering Czechoslovakia's foreign policy. This article claims that the C.C.P. leadership may be obliged "to review certain basic aspects of foreign policy" because of "the resistance and disagreement of Communist and Workers' Parties." It emphasizes that "a conflict with certain socialist allies is beginning in Czechoslovakia against her will"(?).

Of course we do not regard the Prace article as on a par with the Party documents, but the appearance in this paper of such provocational reasoning at a moment when the C.C.P. leadership is assuring the fraternal parties of loyalty to allied obligations cannot fail to arouse concern.

The document of the Presidium of the C.C.P. Central Committee says that the leadership of the Czechoslovak Communist Party is interested in keeping "our relations from deteriorating further" and that it is prepared to help "cool the situation in favor of socialism and unity of the socialist countries." This declaration has its significance, of course. But one cannot fail to perceive that the very important fundamental questions raised in the letter of the participants of the Warsaw meeting to the Central Committee of the C.C.P. essentially remain open.

Soviet Communists and all the working people of the U.S.S.R., vitally interested in strengthening the socialist commonwealth and supporting the cause of peace and security in Europe, ardently back the letter that the participants in the Warsaw meeting addressed to the Central Committee of the C.C.P. Testifying to this are the resolutions adopted at meetings of the Party *aktiv* and the numerous letters from the working people which are being received by the Party Central Committee and newspaper offices.

The Communists of the U.S.S.R. and all Soviet people are convinced that the letter adopted by the fraternal parties in Warsaw will find understanding and support among the Communists and the peoples of Czechoslovakia as an expression of sincere, friendly international aid and will help to strengthen friendship between the peoples of Czechoslovakia, the Soviet Union and the entire socialist commonwealth.

As is known, on July 19 the Politburo of the Central Committee of the C.P.S.U. sent the Presidium of the C.C.P. Central Committee a letter proposing that a bilateral comradely meeting be held. The letter speaks of the great importance that the Central Committee of the C.P.S.U. attaches to this meeting and proposes that it be held at the highest level. Concrete proposals regarding the place and time of the meeting have been made. The Central

* Refers to V. Kotyk, "International Responsibility," *Práce,* July 20, 1968. Editor.

Committee of our party repeatedly proposed in June and in the first half of July that such a bilateral meeting of delegations of our parties be held, but it has not been held, since each time the Czechoslovakian comrades put it off indefinitely.

The new proposal of the Politburo of the C.P.S.U. Central Committee was dictated by the desire to strengthen the positions of socialism, unity of the socialist commonwealth, and fraternal relations between the Communist Parties and peoples of the Soviet Union and Czechoslovakia.

As the letter of the fraternal parties to the C.C.P. Central Committee rightly emphasizes, "each of our parties bears a responsibility not only to its own working class and its own people, but also to the international working class and the world Communist movement, and cannot evade the obligations deriving from this. Therefore we must have solidarity and unity in defense of the gains of socialism, our security and the international positions of the entire socialist commonwealth."

DOCUMENT 39

"THE ČSSR IS NOT GOING TO COMMIT SUICIDE"

Ludvík Svoboda

Complete Text

[*Obrana lidu,* July 27, 1968; translation revised from RFE Czechoslovak Press Survey No. 2107 (August 1, 1968)]

The time has come to call a spade a spade. We might tax the signatories of the Warsaw ultimatum and the initiators of the slander campaign — it cannot be called anything else any longer — against post-January developments in Czechoslovakia with illiteracy, if we still believed that all that is involved on their side is a misconception or a lack of understanding. It is only the ordinary citizens of these countries who are insufficiently informed or, more accurately, deliberately misinformed. We reciprocate their feelings of friendship toward us, but we are aware these feelings are being misused. Everything that happened before the Warsaw council and everything that has happened since tends to confirm this. The leading representatives of the five socialist countries who without proof or jurisdiction have decided to play the roles of prosecutor and judge know full well what issues are at stake in Czechoslovakia.

In spite of this, they delivered a verdict gift-wrapped in hypocritical phrases which is nothing less than a categorical imperative for socialist Czechoslovakia to commit moral suicide. One day, the letter from Warsaw will rank next to the infamous Cominform resolution on Yugoslavia as one of the darkest aspects of the history of the international workers' movement. It will stand as a document demonstrating how in a part of this movement as late as the middle of 1968 words contrasted with deeds, theory with practice, and solemn obligations with everyday facts. We hope that it will all become a part of history as soon as possible and cease to be a painful political reality, casting its shadow over good relations among fraternal countries.

Not through any fault of our own has our internal struggle against dogmatic and sectarian interpreters of socialism and its uniform Stalinist model overstepped the frontiers of Czechoslovakia. We ourselves have done nothing to cause the five allies to doubt our loyalty to proletarian internationalism and to all the obligations which we have taken upon ourselves, nothing that could motivate the commentator of *Krasnaya zvezda* to offer us the "help" of the Soviet army to assist us in settling our internal affairs. Our only sin — one, it seems, which is difficult to forgive — is our desire to rid socialism of all its former distortions, to return to it its humane content and its liberating mission, to cleanse the Communist party of bureaucratic-political procedures, to respect our own national tradition, and to fulfill the words of the constitution which says that the only source of power in this state is the people. *Our* people, *our* two nations, in *our* independent and sovereign state.

The ČSSR will not commit suicide. Its people have given its representatives a mandate of confidence which has, perhaps, no analogy in the fifty years of our republican history. We stand at this historical crossroad united as never before. Regardless of all difficulties and obstacles, we shall persevere on the path which we took in January 1968, no longer *under,* but *together with* the Communist party. For us, it is not a matter of prestige; it is a matter of vital necessity, without which we could no longer breathe in this country. It is our debt to ourselves and to the international workers' movement. We are not isolated in the family of socialist countries and Communist parties, and we have no doubt as to whom the future will prove correct. The history of the past twenty years makes us sure that we will not be the ones to review their present stand.

ČIERNÁ AND BRATISLAVA MEETINGS

IN REPLYING to the Warsaw Letter, the KSČ CC had agreed to bilateral meetings in principle. After some dickering as to whether the negotiations should be held in the Soviet Union or Czechoslovakia,[1] practically the entire Soviet Politburo (minus two members left in Moscow for housekeeping chores) went to Čierná-nad-Tisou. The circumstances were hardly favorable. Massive Soviet maneuvers on the Soviet-Czechoslovak border coincided with the Čierná talks, and Soviet troops in East Germany were reported moving toward Czechoslovakia.[2] Four days of reportedly heated discussion produced a totally bland communiqué (Document 40), shifting the discussion to Bratislava and inviting the other signers of the Warsaw Letter to take part.[3]

Substantively the Bratislava Statement (Document 41) was a web of orthodox platitudes that did not mention the specific problems of Czechoslovakia at all.[4] It tied Prague to such general laws of socialist construction as the leading role of the Communist party, emphasizing even closer cooperation within CEMA and the Warsaw Pact. "Implacable struggle against bourgeois ideology and all antisocialist forces" was considered necessary to guarantee the positions of socialism. The "fraternal parties" pledged "constant concern" for developing socialist democracy and "perfecting" party work based on the principles of democratic centralism. Rumanian objections (*Scînteia* editorial, Document 42) — reiterated even more sharply than after the Dresden meeting in March — were ignored.

Although most Western observers chalked up those negotiations as a sign

---

[1] The CPSU Politburo sent a letter to the KSČ Presidium July 19 suggesting a bilateral meeting in Moscow, Kiev, or Lvov for July 22 or 23 (*Pravda*, July 20, 1968). Simultaneously the Soviets detailed evidence of counterrevolution, repeating the pledge of aid to socialist Czechoslovakia. *Pravda* reported that a secret arms cache of foreign weapons had been discovered at the Czechoslovak–West German border (*Pravda*, July 19, 1968). An editorial in the military newspaper called on the people of socialist countries to fulfill their international duty (*Krasnaya zvezda*, July 20, 1968).

[2] *Pravda*, July 31, 1968 and *The New York Times*, August 1, 1968.

[3] Michel Tatu in *Le Monde*, August 2, 1968.

[4] For analysis see Richard Lowenthal, "The Sparrow in the Cage," *Problems of Communism*, Vol. XVII, No. 6 (November–December 1968), pp. 2–28.

that Dubček was winning in his war of nerves, both Moscow and Prague officially treated Čierná and Bratislava as a victory for socialist unity.[5]

DOCUMENT 40

JOINT COMMUNIQUÉ ON MEETING OF POLITBURO OF CPSU
CENTRAL COMMITTEE AND PRESIDIUM OF CCP CENTRAL
COMMITTEE

August 2, 1968

Complete Text

[*Pravda,* August 2, 1968, quoted from *CDSP,* Vol. XX, No. 31 (August 21, 1968), p. 3]

The meeting of the Politburo of the C.P.S.U. Central Committee and the Presidium of the C.C.P. Central Committee took place in Cierna-on-Tisa from July 29 to Aug. 1, 1968.

The following took part in the meeting [all the participants' names and titles follow].

A broad, comradely exchange of opinions on questions of interest to both sides took place at the meeting.

The participants in the meeting exchanged detailed information about the situation in their countries.

The meeting of the Politburo of the C.P.S.U. Central Committee and the Presidium of the C.C.P. Central Committee proceeded in an atmosphere of complete frankness, sincerity and mutual understanding and was aimed at seeking ways of further developing and strengthening the traditionally friendly relations between our parties and peoples, based on the principles of Marxism-Leninism and proletarian internationalism. During the talks the two delegations decided by mutual consent to propose to the Central Committees of the Communist and Workers' Parties of Bulgaria, Hungary, the G.D.R. and Poland that a multilateral comradely meeting be held. These fraternal parties agreed to this proposal.

The meeting of representatives of the Bulgarian Communist Party, the Hungarian Socialist Workers' Party, the Socialist Unity Party of Germany, the Polish United Workers' Party, the C.P.S.U. and the C.C.P. will take place on Aug. 3, 1968, in the city of Bratislava.

[5] See interviews with Dubček and Černík in *Rudé právo,* August 2, 1968; Dubček, *Rudé právo,* August 4, 1968; Zhukov in *Pravda,* August 5, 1968; *Pravda* editorial, August 8, 1968; and *Krasnaya zvezda* editorials August 6 and 8, 1968.

DOCUMENT 41

STATEMENT OF COMMUNIST AND WORKERS' PARTIES OF
SOCIALIST COUNTRIES
August 4, 1968
Complete Text
[*Pravda,* August 4, 1968, quoted from *CDSP,* Vol. XX, No. 31 (August 21,
1968), pp. 4–5]

❦

A conference of representatives of the Communist and Workers' Parties of
the People's Republic of Bulgaria, the Hungarian People's Republic, the German Democratic Republic, the Polish People's Republic, the Union of Soviet
Socialist Republics and the Czechoslovak Socialist Republic was held on Aug.
3, 1968, in Bratislava. The following took part in the conference:

On behalf of the Bulgarian Communist Party — T. Zhivkov, First Secretary
of the B.C.P. Central Committee and Chairman of the P.R.B. Council of
Ministers; S. Todorov, member of the Politburo and Secretary of the B.C.P.
Central Committee; and P. Kubadinsky, member of the Politburo of the B.C.P.
Central Committee and Vice-Chairman of the P.R.B. Council of Ministers.

On behalf of the Hungarian Socialist Workers' Party — J. Kadar, First Secretary of the H.S.W.P. Central Committee; J. Fock, member of the Politburo
of the H.S.W.P. Central Committee and Chairman of the Hungarian Revolutionary Workers' and Peasants' Government; and Z. Komocsin, member
of the Politburo and Secretary of the H.S.W.P. Central Committee.

On behalf of the Socialist Unity Party of Germany — W. Ulbricht, First
Secretary of the S.U.P.G. Central Committee and Chairman of the G.D.R.
State Council; W. Stoph, member of the Politburo of the S.U.P.G. Central
Committee and Chairman of the G.D.R. Council of Ministers; E. Honecker,
member of the Politburo and Secretary of the S.U.P.G. Central Committee;
H. Matern, member of the Politburo of the S.U.P.G. Central Committee
and Chairman of the S.U.P.G. Central Party Control Commission; G. Mittag,
member of the Politburo and Secretary of the S.U.P.G. Central Committee;
and H. Axen, candidate member of the Politburo and Secretary of the S.U.P.G.
Central Committee.

On behalf of the Polish United Workers' Party — W. Gomulka, First Secre-
tary of the P.U.W.P. Central Committee; J. Cyrankiewicz, member of the
Politburo of the P.U.W.P. Central Committee and Chairman of the P.P.R.
Council of Ministers; Z. Kliszko, member of the Politburo and Secretary of the
P.U.W.P. Central Committee; and A. Starewicz, Secretary of the P.U.W.P.
Central Committee.

On behalf of the Communist Party of the Soviet Union — L. I. Brezhnev,
General Secretary of the C.P.S.U. Central Committee; N. V. Podgorny, member of the Politburo of the C.P.S.U. Central Committee and Chairman of the

Presidium of the U.S.S.R. Supreme Soviet; A. N. Kosygin, member of the Politburo of the C.P.S.U. Central Committee and Chairman of the U.S.S.R. Council of Ministers; M. A. Suslov, member of the Politburo and Secretary of the C.P.S.U. Central Committee; P. Ye. Shelest, member of the Politburo of the C.P.S.U. Central Committee and First Secretary of the Ukraine Communist Party Central Committee; K. F. Katushev, Secretary of the C.P.S.U. Central Committee; and B. N. Ponomarev, Secretary of the C.P.S.U. Central Committee.

On behalf of the Czechoslovak Communist Party — A. Dubcek, First Secretary of the C.C.P. Central Committee; O. Cernik, member of the Presidium of the C.C.P. Central Committee and Chairman of the C.S.R. Government; J. Smrkovsky, member of the Presidium of the C.C.P. Central Committee and Speaker of the C.S.R. National Assembly; V. Bilak, member of the Presidium of the C.C.P. Central Committee and First Secretary of the Slovak Communist Party Central Committee; and J. Lenart, candidate member of the Presidium and Secretary of the C.C.P. Central Committee. L. Svoboda, President of the C.S.R., also attended for the Czechoslovak side.

Proceeding on the premise that the complicated international situation and the subversive actions of imperialism, which are directed against peace and the security of peoples and against the cause of socialism, demand further unity among the countries in the socialist system, and also taking into account the fact that the development of socialism advances new tasks whose solution necessitates a further unification of the socialist states' efforts, the representatives of the Communist and Workers' Parties of the socialist countries considered it necessary to convene this conference in Bratislava.

In the spirit of traditions that have taken shape and in an atmosphere of complete frankness, adherence to principle, and friendship the fraternal parties discussed urgent questions of the struggle for socialism, of the further strengthening of the socialist commonwealth and of the solidarity of the world Communist movement. Opinions were exchanged on problems of the present-day international situation and intensification of the struggle against imperialism.

The representatives of the Communist and Workers' Parties discussed ways of strengthening and developing the fraternal cooperation of the socialist states.

In the years since fascism was defeated and the working class came to power, the peoples of the European countries that embarked on the path of socialism have achieved victories in all spheres of societal life. During these years the parties, surmounting difficulties and constantly perfecting their work, have ensured in every socialist country both the creation of a mighty industry and the transformation of life in the countryside and have achieved a steady increase in the people's well-being and the flourishing of national culture. Millions of working people have been elevated to politically conscious lives. The Soviet Union has achieved especially great successes in the construction of socialism and communism. The international influence of the socialist states and their role in deciding major questions of world politics have grown immeasurably.

It is the common international duty of all socialist countries to support, strengthen and defend these gains, which were achieved at the cost of every people's heroic efforts and selfless labor. This is the unanimous opinion of all the conference participants, who expressed unswerving determination to develop and defend the socialist gains in their countries and to achieve new successes in the construction of socialism.

The fraternal parties have become convinced on the basis of historical experience that it is possible to advance along the path of socialism and communism only by strictly and consistently following the general laws governing the construction of a socialist society and primarily by strengthening the guiding role of the working class and its vanguard — the Communist Parties. At the same time, in creatively deciding questions of further socialist development, each fraternal party takes into account national characteristics and conditions.

Unshakable fidelity to Marxism-Leninism, indoctrination of the popular masses in the spirit of the ideas of socialism and proletarian internationalism, and an implacable struggle against bourgeois ideology and all antisocialist forces constitute the guarantee of success in strengthening the positions of socialism and repulsing the intrigues of imperialism.

The fraternal parties firmly and resolutely counterpose their inviolable solidarity and high level of vigilance to all attempts by imperialism and all other anti-Communist forces to weaken the guiding role of the working class and the Communist Parties. They will never allow anyone to drive a wedge between the socialist states or to undermine the foundations of the socialist social system. Fraternal friendship and solidarity in this direction are in the vital interests of all peoples and constitute a reliable basis for solving the social-economic and political tasks on which our countries' Communist Parties are working.

The fraternal parties consider it their duty to show constant concern for increasing the political activeness of the working class, the peasantry, the intelligentsia and all working people; for achieving all-round progress for the socialist social system; and for further developing socialist democracy and perfecting the style and methods of party and state work on principles of democratic centralism.

The diverse tasks of creating a socialist society in each of our countries is substantially easier to solve with mutual aid and support.

Fraternal ties expand and increase every socialist country's potential. The conference participants expressed the firm desire to do everything in their power to intensify all-round cooperation among their countries, based on the principles of equality, respect for sovereignty and national independence, territorial integrity and fraternal mutual aid and solidarity.

The Communist and Workers' Parties assign paramount importance to achieving further economic development and an increase in the working people's material well-being through making effective use of our countries' immense natural resources, through using the latest scientific and technical achievements, and through perfecting the forms and methods of socialist economic management. An effective way to achieve these noble aims is to develop economic cooperation among the socialist countries on a bilateral and a multilateral basis. Improvement of the work done by the Council for Mutual Economic Aid and development of production coordination and specialization among the socialist countries are becoming increasingly important: this makes it possible to make fuller use of the advantages of the international socialist division of labor.

In this connection the urgency of holding an economic conference at the highest level in the very near future was reaffirmed.

The participants in the conference consider it their duty to call the attention of the peoples to the fact that as a result of imperialism's aggressive policy the recent international situation has remained complicated and dangerous. In these conditions the fraternal parties of the socialist countries, guided by the interests of the struggle for strengthening universal peace and the security of peoples, for organizing a resolute rebuff to imperialism's aggressive policy and for affirming the principles of peaceful coexistence of states with different social systems, reaffirm their readiness to agree on and coordinate their actions in the international arena.

The working class, the peasantry, the intelligentsia and all working people crave peace and tranquillity for their countries and for all people on earth. The socialist countries have done, are doing and will do everything possible to see that these innermost hopes of the peoples are realized. Our parties declare that in solving this noble task they will continue to cooperate with all the Communist and Workers' Parties and all the world's progressive forces in the struggle for universal peace, freedom, independence and social progress.

The Communist and Workers' Parties of Bulgaria, Hungary, the German Democratic Republic, Poland, the Soviet Union and Czechoslovakia again solemnly declare their unswerving determination to continue supporting the heroic Vietnam people and giving them the necessary assistance in the just struggle against the American interventionists.

We are also concerned over the fact that as a result of the aggressive policy pursued by Israel's ruling circles, the Near East situation remains tense. Our parties will do everything possible to eliminate the consequences of Israeli aggression on the basis of the Nov. 22, 1967, resolution of the U.N. Security Council and the withdrawal of Israeli troops from the occupied Arab territories.

Having reviewed the situation in Europe, the participants in the conference note that activation of the forces of revanchism, militarism and neo-Nazism in West Germany directly affects the security of the socialist states and creates a threat to the cause of universal peace. In European affairs we shall continue to follow consistently a concerted policy that meets the common interests of the socialist countries and the interests of European security and to repulse all attempts at revising the results of the second world war and violating the frontiers that have taken shape in Europe; we shall continue to insist that the Munich agreement was invalid from the very beginning; we shall resolutely support the German Democratic Republic, a socialist state of German working people that is defending the cause of peace; we shall give constant support to the Communist Party of Germany and to all forces fighting against imperialism and revanchism and for democratic progress.

The Communist Parties of the socialist countries express determination to ensure European security and to affirm the principles of the Bucharest Declaration and the Statement of the Conference of European Communist and Workers' Parties in Karlovy Vary. They are prepared to do everything necessary to convoke a congress of the peoples of Europe in defense of peace on our continent. Preventing violation of the peace in Europe is of decisive importance for preserving peace throughout the world. Our joint efforts will be aimed at achieving this goal, which affects the interests of all peoples.

Today, when the imperialist forces of the U.S.A., the F.R.G. and other countries are demonstrating their aggressive activity and stubbornly attempting to weaken the socialist commonwealth, the representatives of the fraternal parties deem it necessary to emphasize once more the special importance of the Warsaw Pact. This pact, concluded by the socialist states in answer to revanchist West Germany's entry into the aggressive, imperialist NATO bloc, has been and continues to be a powerful factor of peace and security for the peoples of Europe. It serves as an invincible barrier to all who would like to revise the results of the second world war. It reliably defends the gains of socialism and the sovereignty and independence of the fraternal states. It is aimed at consolidating European security and preserving universal peace.

The present situation requires our unremitting efforts to raise the defense capability of every socialist state and the whole socialist commonwealth and to strengthen political and military cooperation in the Warsaw Treaty Organization.

The participants in the conference consider it their duty to struggle consistently to strengthen the solidarity of the international Communist movement. They note that recently a good deal of work has been done in preparing for a new international conference of Communist and Workers' Parties. The fraternal parties value this work highly and express the conviction that the forthcoming conference will proceed successfully and will make an important contribution to the cause of consolidating all the revolutionary forces of the present day.

We are fully confident that a unified Marxist-Leninist world view, the role of the Communist and Workers' Parties as the vanguard and leader of society and the socialist principles of our states' national economies will continue to serve as effective factors of further solidarity among the socialist countries and of their unity of action in the struggle for the great common goals.

The parties participating in the Bratislava conference issue this statement in the profound conviction that the positions and views expressed in it meet the interests of all the fraternal countries and parties, the cause of inviolable friendship among the peoples of our countries and the interests of peace, democracy, national independence and socialism. [Signed:] On behalf of the B.C.P. — T. Zhivkov, S. Todorov, P. Kubadinsky; on behalf of the H.S.W.P.

— J. Kadar, J. Fock, Z. Komocsin; on behalf of the S.U.P.G. — W. Ulbricht, W. Stoph, E. Honecker, H. Matern, G. Mittag, H. Axen; on behalf of the P.U.W.P. — W. Gomulka, J. Cyrankiewicz, Z. Kliszko, A. Starewicz; on behalf of the C.P.S.U. — L. Brezhnev, N. Podgorny, A. Kosygin, M. Suslov, P. Shelest, K. Katushev, B. Ponomarev; on behalf of the C.C.P. — A. Dubcek, O. Cernik, J. Smrkovsky, V. Bilak, J. Lenart.

DOCUMENT 42

"ALL EFFORTS TO STRENGTHEN THE UNITY OF THE SOCIALIST COUNTRIES"

Excerpts

[*Scînteia,* editorial, August 8, 1968]

The whole unfolding of international life and the very complex problems created by contemporary social development acutely demonstrate the need to strengthen the unity of the socialist countries and of the Communist and Workers' parties. The strengthening of unity, the development of reciprocal cooperation have an important significance for the achievement of the new system in each socialist country. At the same time, the close brotherly solidarity between the socialist countries is the source of the force of the world socialist system, of its growth as a decisive factor in the evolution of history, of the influence of socialist ideas in the world, for the achievement of the peoples' fundamental aspirations — liberty, democracy, independence, and peace. Proceeding from the basic interests of the Rumanian people and of socialism, the Rumanian Communist Party has worked for and is consistently working for the development of the friendship, alliance, and collaboration between Rumania and the socialist countries and for the strengthening of the ties of solidarity with all the Communist parties.

Certainly, the unity of the socialist countries is based on the common ideology — Marxism-Leninism — on socialist internationalism, the community of systems, the common goals — socialism and communism — on the interests of the struggle for peace against the common enemy — imperialism.

However, for this unity to develop and become stronger, it is imperatively necessary to respect unwaveringly the basic norms of the relations between the fraternal parties and countries and the principles of equality in rights, independence and sovereignty, noninterference in internal affairs, comradely mutual aid, and mutual advantage. These principles give the relations between the socialist countries deep and rich contents and make them durable and more fruitful and bring them to the fore as a new type of relations which are superior to the relations fostered in the capitalist world. . . .

The development and the strengthening of the unity of the socialist countries depend to a large extent on creating a climate of complete trust in and mutual respect for the Communist parties. An essential contribution to this is made by the final elimination of the practice of presenting the policy of a fraternal party in a distorted way, of branding and denigrating its activity, and of erroneously and tendentiously swaying public opinion regarding the situation in a fraternal country. Only correct information from direct sources, that is, on the basis of the documents and decisions of the respective party, corresponds to the principles of the relations between the parties and to the interests of unity.

The differences of opinion which naturally occur under the conditions of the great diversity in which the new system is being forged in the respective countries must be discussed with patience, between party and party and between leadership and leadership and must take into account the opinions of all and show understanding and receptiveness for the various opinions, aiming at eliminating misunderstandings, at establishing common points of view, and at finding common paths to strengthen the friendship between the socialist countries, between the Communist parties, and between their leaders.

Our party and country know the significance bilateral and multilateral contacts have for the strengthening of the ties of friendship between the fraternal countries. Naturally, it is the right of the party and of the government of every socialist country to meet, when they deem it necessary, when life demands it, with parties and governments of other socialist countries within either a bilateral or multilateral framework and to discuss the problems of mutual relations or other problems concerning the common interests of the participants, just as every party can sovereignly decide whether it will or will not participate in such meetings.

However, our party deems that when problems concerning the vital interests of all the socialist countries are dealt with, when analyses are made and conclusions are reached concerning countries between whom there are relations consecrated by treaties and pacts, and when decisions engaging the respective countries are made, it is an elementary and essential requirement that the discussions take place with the agreement and in the presence of the interested parties and countries. To discuss and make decisions on matters directly concerning other parties and countries which were not invited and are not present at conferences and which have not given the participants any mandate in this respect is utterly incompatible with the norms of relations between the fraternal parties and with the principles of equality between parties and countries.

The practice of following such a line, of bringing other parties before an accomplished fact, simply leaving them the alternative of agreeing or not to the conclusions of a meeting they did not attend is a deeply harmful practice that can only continue to generate resentment and dissent, encourage disruption of the socialist forces, and flagrantly violate the interests of unity — the interests of socialism. The road to unity, the strengthening of socialist solidarity is that of unrelenting consistent efforts for the normalization of relations based on the foundations of reciprocal confidence and respect.

Public opinion in our country, which watched the worsening of relations between some socialist countries and the People's Republic of Czechoslovakia, welcomes with satisfaction the easing of tension, the cessation of polemics, and the solving of divergencies by discretion and understanding resulting from talks between the leadership of the CPSU, the Czechoslovak Communist Party, and other parties.

This proves that when open discussions are being carried on in a comradely spirit of mutual understanding, solutions can be found for controversial problems and that it is necessary to have confidence in the Czechoslovak Communist Party and in the Czech people in carrying out the complex tasks set by the improvement of the socialist system, corresponding to [Czechoslovak] national aspirations and particular conditions in the interests of socialism. The fact cannot be ignored, however, that the Bratislava declaration of certain Communist and Workers' parties deals with a number of problems of great political importance directly affecting other socialist countries which were not invited and did not attend this conference.

In this connection, it is to be noted that, among other things, the activity of CEMA was discussed and it was recommended to hold a summit economic conference in the very near future. Problems concerning the Warsaw Pact were discussed. Rumania, as a member of these international bodies since their establishment, deems that the discussion of all the problems linked with the carrying out of their activities and with perfecting them must be done in common by all the member countries, which is the only way to solve the respective problems and to strengthen unity.

Our country's party and state leadership has already formulated its opinion in this respect. "We deem," Comrade Nicolae Ceaușescu said on April 26, 1968, after the Dresden meeting, "that the discussion of such problems pertaining to international bodies in whose founding Rumania participated cannot be carried out by only some member countries."

As proved by experience so far, such actions and procedures are not of a nature to contribute to the strengthening of these bodies and to increasing the trust, collaboration, and unity of the socialist countries.

That is why the greatest interests of the peoples of the socialist countries demand that such practices be avoided and that the line of bringing the socialist countries closer to one another be followed unwaveringly. . . .

All socialist countries which participated in the Bucharest conference solemnly reaffirmed that they are ready for the concomitant liquidation of the Atlantic alliance and of the Warsaw Pact.

The advisability of such a move is emphasized by the fact that during the period that has elapsed since [that conference] the forces hostile to military blocs and favoring the easing of tension and general European cooperation have increased.

Our party and the Rumanian Government have constantly expressed their view that, as long as NATO exists, there is need for the existence of the Warsaw Pact. Faithful to its alliances, Rumania is determined — whether the Warsaw Pact exists or not — to make its full contribution, together with the other socialist countries, to the defense of the peaceful work of the peoples of these countries and to the strengthening of general security. . . .

KSČ DRAFT STATUTES

FOR A FEW DAYS following the Bratislava Statement, overt hostility between Prague, Moscow, and the orthodox East European regimes ceased. Then on August 10, the new Draft Statutes of the Czechoslovak Communist Party (Document 43) appeared.[1] Although democratic centralism ostensibly remained the guiding principle of party life, the minority was guaranteed the right to formulate its point of view, to demand that it be recorded, and thereafter to continue to hold those views despite their rejection by a majority. It could also demand periodic reassessments on the basis of new knowledge. This would have meant the end of the Leninist party as defined at the 10th CPSU in 1921.[2] The Czechoslovak Draft Statutes could not conceivably have fitted into the common principles of socialism hurriedly reformulated by Moscow's ideological spokesman, I. Pomelov.[3] Not surprisingly they were subsequently attacked by the Soviet "White Book" on Czechoslovakia (Document 62) as an attempt to legalize factionalism.

[1] Information from Soviet military personnel in Prague indicates that actual preparations for a military move against Prague may have been under way when their units went on alert on August 11 (*The New York Times*, August 24, 1968).

[2] The 10th Congress resolution on party unity called for immediate dissolution of all groups with a separate platform on penalty of expulsion from the party. See "Preliminary Draft Resolution of the Tenth Congress of the R.C.P. on Party Unity," in V. I. Lenin, *Collected Works*, Vol. 32 (Moscow: Progress Publishers, 1965), pp. 241–244.

[3] I. Pomelov, "Common Principles and National Characteristics in the Development of Socialism," *Pravda*, August 14, 1968; *CDSP* Vol. XX, No. 33 (September 4, 1968), pp. 3–5.

DOCUMENT 43

KSČ DRAFT STATUTES

Complete Text

[*Rudé právo* supplement, August 10, 1968]

❦

[The following passage is printed as an introduction.] The party Central Committee Presidium is presenting the draft of the new statutes of the Czechoslovak Communist Party for internal party discussion. The draft was drawn up by a working committee under the leadership of Comrade Dr. M. Havlíček, deputy head of the Department of Political Theory and Political Work at the Klement Gottwald Military Political Academy.

It has been reviewed stage by stage at two meetings of the commission for drafting the statutes that was set up by the Czechoslovak Communist Party Central Committee plenum. A working variant was discussed by the Czechoslovak Communist Party Central Committee Presidium and the political commission for preparations for the extraordinary 14th congress of the Czechoslovak Communist Party.

After these discussions the working committee presented the amended draft for final review by the Czechoslovak Communist Party Central Committee Presidium, which discussed it in great detail and unanimously approved the text which is being presented for internal party discussion.

A basic prerequisite for high-quality discussion of the draft at the August membership meetings is that each individual be acquainted with its content. The membership meetings will express their views on the draft. Concrete proposals and comments will be conveyed in writing to the party Central Committee by the basic organizations through the Czechoslovak Communist Party district committees.

With regard to the pressure of time and the effort to process all comments, we ask the basic organizations that comments and proposals on individual articles or paragraphs of the party statutes be listed separately on individual sheets of paper with reference to the number of the article.

The basic railroad transport organizations will pass on their suggestions to the party Central Committee through the party committees of the political section of Czechoslovak State Railroads.

The basic organizations of the party in the Czechoslovak Army will proceed in a similar way, according to the instructions of the main political directorate.

The basic party organizations will send their standpoints, proposals, and suggestions to the party district committees by August 25, 1968, at the very latest. [end of introduction]

The Czechoslovak Communist Party is a voluntary union of progressive, politically active members of all social classes who have come together to implement in their country the programmatic aims of socialism and communism and thus create conditions for the full emancipation of man.

The party regards the fulfillment of material, cultural, and ethical needs of people and the development of opportunities for the all-round assertion of human individuality as the humanistic and democratic character of a socialist society.

The activity of the Czechoslovak Communist Party evolves from the scientific theory and method of Marxism-Leninism. The party strives to creatively apply and develop Marxism-Leninism on the basis of the latest information obtained from social science and in association with social practice. Proceeding from the fact that class antagonism exists between the forces of socialism and capitalism in the world, the party is carrying on a thorough struggle against all forms of bourgeois ideology.

The Czechoslovak Communist Party is linked with the national, democratic, and revolutionary traditions of our people and the progressive tradition of the revolutionary workers' movement. The party has led the working people to overthrow the exploiting classes and to build a socialist society. The party has consistently guarded the fundamental values of socialism. In its effort to promote the development of socialist society, the party proceeds from concrete conditions in the life of our nations and nationalities and fosters in them an awareness of belonging to a socialist fatherland. It is an integral part of the international Communist and revolutionary movement. Creatively, and under the specific conditions of our country, the party makes use of the experiences of Communist and Workers' parties, especially of the CPSU. On the basis of the principle of proletarian internationalism and socialist patriotism, the party consolidates the fraternal relations and collaboration of the Czechoslovak people with the Soviet people, peoples of the socialist states, and workers of all countries. It supports socialist, revolutionary, national liberation and peace movements in the struggle against imperialism.

The aim the Communist party has set for itself is to express in a socialist society the progressive, long term interests of all classes and strata of society. The party proceeds from the fact that under socialism, during the process of the scientific and technical revolution, the working class is the main social force whose historic mission and most natural interest is the Communist arrangement of society. The working class, in firm alliance with the farmers and the intelligentsia, therefore provides necessary support for the entire social development of socialism toward a Communist society. At the same time, since the extinction of class antagonisms the party itself has been changing, as have the forms it uses to carry out its social roles. The working class cannot be replaced in this historic role.

In its activity the Communist party relies for support on the progressive forces of all social classes and young people.

On the basis of scientific analysis the party, as the leading and unifying force in the complex of political and social relations, is elaborating the program and concept of the development of a socialist society and organizing the workers to carry out this program.

The party supports the democratic principles of the activity of the representative organs and their responsibility to all people, and endeavors to ensure that they be true representatives of the people, safeguard the people's socialist achievements and strictly adhere to socialist law.

The party considers the National Front, which is based on joint participation and responsibility for carrying out the socialist program agreed upon, as the foundation for cooperation with social organizations of workers and with the other political parties. The Czechoslovak Communist Party is continually renewing its leading political role in the National Front on the basis of continuous ideological political initiative and political organizational activity. It is aware that its strength lies in close communication with the people, with their lives and needs. Therefore, by its activity it is continually soliciting their trust and voluntary support, and is subordinate to their control.

At the present time, the party is striving for the development of socialism as a society devoid of class antagonisms, founded on unity and the diversity of social interests; a free, democratically organized society; deeply international, socially just, and giving rewards according to competence and results of work; an industrially mature society, having at its disposal a flexible economic system and intensively developing production forces; a society that by the richness of its resources makes possible a worthy cultural life and comradely, cooperative relations between people, stage by stage extending the scope for the development of human individuality. The definitive aim of the party is to build a classless Communist society. Therefore, the party is mindful of the continuous development and consolidation of socialist production and social relations. It is striving for the development of socialist democracy and the fulfillment of the program of Communist humanism.

The Czechoslovak Communist Party is a deeply humanistic party. As the grandfather of the progressive revolutionary and national traditions, it is striving for a better future for Czechs and Slovaks. As the unifying agent of society it is striving for full equality and development of the Czech and Slovak nations and of all nationalities in Czechoslovak socialist society. Simultaneously, it is struggling against nationalism and, on the basis of socialist internationalism, is strengthening fraternal ties between the workers of our nations and nationalities.

The party wants to preserve its vanguard mission in the struggle of our nations for socialism, democracy, human justice, freedom, and the humanistic ideals of communism in our country. It sees its main mission in the service of the people and of progress.

I. Fundamental Principles of the Party's Internal Life and Activities

1. The Czechoslovak Communist Party develops its activities on the basis of democratic centralism.

Democratic centralism means:

The democratic creation of a party program and political line resulting from creative Marxist-Leninist activity, which is based on the most up-to-date scientific information;

A confrontation of views and evaluations of various suggestions from Communists and non-Communists;

Participation of party members and the lowest links of the organizational structure in the creation and implementation of party policy and the continual verification of their correctness in practice;

An equal opportunity for all party members to express their standpoints on party policy, defend their views in party organizations, put forward proposals, and criticize any member, organization, and organ;

The whole system of party executive and control organs is created democratically by election, evaluation, and the control of officials from below;

Party organs regularly present accounts of, and give reports on, their activity to the organizations that elected them, and by this means to all members. The lower organizations and organs report on their activities and on how they fulfill the party decrees to the higher organs; and

Programmatic documents as well as the decrees of the higher organs are binding for the lower organizations and organs and for every party member.

2. Decisions in party organizations and organs are passed after collective discussion by a simple majority of votes of the members present. Annual membership meetings, plenary sessions of organs, conferences, and congresses can adopt resolutions, provided more than half the members or regularly elected delegates are present.

The organ's method of voting determines its order of proceedings.

Before passing important decisions the Czechoslovak Communist Party or the central committees of the national territorial organizations organize internal party discussions or internal party inquiries. They report to the party public on their results.

3. In the spirit of democratic centralism, the minority is subordinate to the majority and carries out the decrees that have been passed. The minority has the right:

a. To formulate its standpoints and request that they be recorded; and

b. To persist in its view and to request from the relevant party organization or organ a reevaluation of its standpoints on the basis of new information and the examination of a decree that has been accepted into practice. It is admissible to use purely ideological means in relation to supporters of the minority view, as long as they are not in fundamental conflict with the program and statutes of the party.

It is inadmissible to organize minority supporters outside the framework of the statutes or to set up groupings of party members with their own fraction discipline.

4. Voluntary and conscious discipline is a prerequisite for the capacity for action of the whole party and its individual organizations and organs. It stems from a deep understanding of Marxism-Leninism, the aims and needs of the party, and the loyalty of Communists to the cause of socialism.

5. The activity of party organizations and organs is governed by the program, statutes, and decrees of the higher organs, and these are binding on them. The higher organs are required to create conditions for the development of the initiative and independence of the lower organs. Decisions on political and organizational questions in their own sphere of action are made inde-

pendently by the organizations and organs. In cases of a difference of opinion they have the right to refer to a higher organ, the control and auditing commission, or a conference or congress.

6. In the specific sphere of party social activity party members, organizations, and organs, with the agreement of higher party organs, can arrange joint talks to coordinate their activity or to elaborate standpoints or alternative proposals for the party organizations and organs.

7. Party members set up basic organizations according to their place of work or place of residence. Basic organizations in localities, cities, factories, and enterprises consolidate into local, municipal, factorywide, and enterprise organizations. The organization that operates over a certain area is as a rule the leading one for all party organizations operating in parts of this area.

A chairman is elected to the head of the organ at all levels.

The party congress acts in the name of the party as a whole. In the period between congresses action is taken by the Central Committee, or in individual cases by delegations and organs empowered by the Central Committee. The remaining organizations and organs act in their own name.

8. All party organs are elected by a secret ballot. Communists are chosen for office who, on the basis of their political, professional, and moral qualities and experience in party and public activity, have personal authority and the confidence of the workers.

In order to ensure these principles the Czechoslovak Communist Party Central Committee approves a uniform voting procedure.

9. Organizations and organs at all levels depend on the voluntary active groups of members and officials and develop practical democratic forms for the participation of party members in management. With this aim in view, they set up standing or interim commissions and working committees from among the members of the organizations and organs and from among other experienced and enterprising officials and specialists.

Together with their proposals, the commissions and working committees present the results of their activity to the organization or organ which sets them up and which discusses them (the proposals and results) with their (the commissions and working committees) participation.

10. To fulfill their political and organizational tasks the party organs set up an apparatus that is subordinate to them and controlled by them.

The apparatus cannot take over the authority of the party organizations, organs, and Communists in state, economic, and social organizations and institutions. It takes an active part in the preparation and implementation of decrees. Party members who are experienced and politically and professionally competent will be received into the party apparatus.

11. A prerequisite of ideological unification and internal party democracy is an identification and information system that includes: the unity of scientific knowledge and the pooling of the experience of party members and all workers; the mutual exchange of internal party information from the top down and from the bottom up; the accessibility of information and documents of party organizations and organs to their members; an exchange of views and

information between the party and the public at large by means of the communication media; and the systematic use of specialist expertise and scientific research in decision-making and propaganda.

The party press is an important part of the identification and information system. Every party paper is governed by the organ that publishes it.

12. The following principles are valid for cadre work:

a. Cadre questions are resolved exclusively by organizations and elected organs;

b. Party organizations and organs make every effort to develop the capabilities and activity of every party member;

c. Cadre selection is carried out with the participation of the party public at large;

d. It is customary, when discussing cadre proposals, to present further alternative proposals;

e. Quality is the only valid criterion in choosing and recommending candidates and applicants for party, public, and economic functions;

f. Organizations and organs give all officials conditions for executing their function and regularly evaluate them.

13. In order to avoid excessive concentration of power in one pair of hands, to overcome stagnation, and to ensure an influx of new forces into the party organs, the following principles are valid in selection and election:

a. Not to amalgamate leading party, state, and public functions which, if joined, could lead to the privileged position of an individual and would weaken control over this individual;

b. To create conditions to prevent several important party functions from being concentrated in one person;

c. With the exception of the basic organizations, officials can be elected to the same organ no more than three times in succession for a two-year election period and twice in succession for a four-year election period; in exceptional cases membership in the organs can be prolonged by one functional period. The exceptions must be approved by a two-thirds majority of delegates to a conference or congress.

14. A party control system will verify whether party activities are meeting the programmatic aims, whether its policy is reacting to the needs of a socialist society, how the party statutes are being carried out, and what methods of party work are being used by the organizations and organs.

The control will be realized:

a. By self-control of members, organizations, and organs of the party at all levels, above all, in the development of criticism and self-criticism;

b. By the independent system of the control and auditing commissions; and

c. By public control of society.

II. Party Membership

15. Party membership is open to every citizen of the Czechoslovak Socialist Republic over 18 years of age who agrees with the party program and statutes, wants to commit himself to party and public work and share in the develop-

ment of a socialist society, and is resolved to work actively in one of the party organizations and to pay the membership dues.

16. A citizen voluntarily joins the party and can leave it of his own free will.

17. Party members are united by the ideas of Marxism-Leninism, the struggle for joint tasks and aims, comradely cooperation, conscious discipline, and mutual trust and criticism.

The party member is a decisive active agent of the party organism. He is organized in one of the basic organizations and actively takes part in political work under its leadership or under the leadership of a higher organ of which he is a member. Communists engaged in the working process are organized in principle in the basic organization at their place of work. The basic organization can agree to the party member's being enrolled in an organization at his place of residence and, with the agreement of the Czechoslovak Communist Party district committee, in another basic organization as well.

18. The acceptance of new members into the party is carried out according to the following principles:

a. An applicant for party membership presents the relevant basic organization with his application and curriculum vitae, together with the recommendation of two party members who know him personally and have been party members for more than three years;

b. A membership meeting of the basic organization discusses and decides individually by open ballot the acceptance of each member; he becomes a party member if he receives an absolute majority of the votes of those present;

c. The acceptance of those who have foreign state nationality and the method of including members of other Communist and Workers' parties is determined by guidance from the Czechoslovak Communist Party Central Committee;

d. The district committee issues the new member a membership card and enrolls him; loss of the membership card should be reported to the basic organization committee by the party member.

19. All members have equal status in the party without regard to sex, race, nationality, social origin, education, office, or social position. Any sort of racial, social, or nationality discrimination and the extension of these views and ideologies is incompatible with party membership; no privileges or advantages for the member result from membership. Awareness of party discipline is equally valid for all Communists, irrespective of their merit and function.

The party member has the right:

a. To share in the creation and realization of the party program, statutes, political line, and tactics;

b. To elect and be elected to party organs and to hand in his resignation;

c. To be informed on all basic questions of party policy and on the work of party organs and their members; to request any sort of information and documents on the activity of the organizations and organs of which he is a member;

d. To express openly and critically at party meetings and in the party press his opinion on the activity of the party and of all its organs and members irrespective of the office that they hold;

e. While respecting and fulfilling the will of the majority, to persist in his view and to request from the relevant party organization or organ a reevaluation of his standpoints on the basis of new information and the examination of a decree that has been accepted into practice;

f. To present questions, comments, and proposals to the party organs up to the congress of the Czechoslovak Communist Party; and

g. To take part in meetings of party organizations and organs at which his work is evaluated and at which decisions are made concerning him; to know the views and suggestions raised with regard to his activity and conduct; and to assert his standpoints on them. In party affairs, he has the right to appeal to the party organs up to the congress of the Czechoslovak Communist Party.

The party member is bound:

a. To take an active part in political work in party and other organizations, to carry out party policy, and to win citizens over to it;

b. To keep party statutes, to fulfill party decrees, and to take part in membership meetings;

c. To strive for the development of critical comradely relations in the party and society and to defend the democratic rights and freedom of all workers;

d.. To act truthfully and honestly in the party and in everyday life;

e. To deepen his knowledge of Marxism-Leninism and to use it on behalf of the development of a socialist society;

f. To strengthen the authority and capacity for action of the party by developing specialized knowledge and qualifications and by fulfilling his duties as a party member, citizen and worker in an exemplary way;

g. To pay the fixed membership dues; and

h. To inform his basic organization of every change of place of work or residence.

20. If the party member, despite repeated warnings from the committee and personal discussion, does not unceasingly fulfill the basic membership obligations or is delinquent in some other way, the decision can be taken by the membership meeting to strike him off the list of party members.

21. Party membership expires with resignation from the party, deletion from the list of members, expulsion, or death.

At the termination of membership the membership card is to be given to the basic organization committee.

III. Party Organizational Structure

Basic Party Organizations

22. Communists join together in basic organizations, which are the primary link in the organizational structure and form the basis of party activity. Communists can set up basic organizations with the agreement of the district committees where there are more than five party members.

23. Basic organizations carry on an open policy toward all citizens, consult them, respect and make use of their views and suggestions, and verify through them the effectiveness of their own work.

Basic organizations work in all sectors of social life. By their ideas and proposals, they share in creating the general party line and ensure that it is carried out in its sphere of operation. On the basis of knowledge of the local situation, they create and implement an independent policy in harmony with the general party line.

They clarify the political aims and intentions of the party; by means of attractive ideological and political organizational work under local conditions, they win over citizens to solve individual problems in their sphere of operation and to participate in the development of a socialist society. They win over the most active citizens, especially the young people, as party members.

They direct Communists on national committees and in social, autonomous, and special interest organizations in the active fulfillment of the tasks and particular mission of these organs and organizations, and afford them the necessary information.

They organize the Marxist-Leninist education of party members and non-party members, objectively reporting and communicating to them information on important social problems and events.

For party members, they create the conditions necessary for the fulfillment of aims resulting from the decrees of the higher organs and for the tasks that the organization itself imposes; they assert the personal and social responsibility of Communists.

They report to the higher party organs on their activity.

They administer the financial resources and the property of the party organization.

24. The highest organ of the basic organizations is the membership meeting. The membership meeting:

a. Reviews the political activity of the organization; on the basis of an analysis of the situation passes decrees, imposes tasks on all members, and checks that they are being fulfilled;

b. Evaluates the activity of the committee, of individual party groups, and of all officials and members; changes the composition of the committee;

c. Takes a stand on the work of the higher party organs, especially of the district committee, and on the policy of the entire party;

d. Accepts new party members;

e. Elects a chairman, committee members, a control and auditing commission or management auditors to a 2-year functional period, and elects delegates to conferences;

f. Approves Communist candidates for deputies on national committees; evaluates their work and the work of Communists in social organizations; discusses their suggestions and proposals; and

g. Makes decisions on the introduction of a disciplinary system; establishes subcommittees to carry out party investigation of complaints and charges against party members; imposes party punishment.

Meetings can approve certain concessions for invalids and elderly members in fulfilling party tasks or in other serious cases.

The committee convenes meetings as often as the need arises to ensure the continual active political work of the party organization, at least once every 2 months.

The committee is further obliged to convene meetings at the request of:

a. One of the party subcommittees;

b. A third of the members;

c. On the basis of a decision of the higher party organ.

25. In order to discuss important problems concerning the majority of workers, the committee convenes a meeting of its members and invites the interested groups of non-Communists or convenes a public meeting of the party.

At these meetings Communists are dutybound to create an atmosphere in which citizens have the opportunity to put forward their standpoints, suggestions, and critical proposals.

26. The basic organization committee provides incentive for the political activity of members of the organization. It organizes the fulfillment of the decrees of the meetings, governs the work of the party subcommittees, and works individually with Communists between meetings. It gives regular reports on its activity to the meetings.

27. According to specific conditions of individual places of work or localities, basic organizations set up party subcommittees that elect their subcommittee head. By means of the party subcommittees, the committee organizes the fulfillment of party tasks between meetings, encourages Communists to take on active work, and makes use of their suggestions and proposals.

Party subcommittees work in close collaboration with all workers and consult them about procedure in resolving local problems or problems at places of work.

28. All factory and local organizations within the framework of a city or community operate as a whole and create a municipal or local organization.

In large factories, places of work, or other establishments where there are a number of basic organizations, factory-wide or enterprise committees are set up.

Municipal, local, factorywide and enterprise committees, and control and auditing commissions are elected at conferences or general plenary annual membership meetings for a term of 2 years.

With the development of the independence of the basic organizations, the municipal, local, enterprise, and factory-wide committees determine a unified procedure in solving political, economic, ideological, and cultural problems in their sphere of action, thus uniting the efforts of Communists and basic organizations at the given place of work or locality. Together with them the committees organize mass political and ideological activity.

They propose Communist candidates as deputies to the municipal and local national committee and to trade union, enterprise, and autonomous organs. In the course of the election period the committees work with them systematically.

They direct Communists on national committees, in social, autonomous, and special interest organizations in the active fulfillment of the tasks and special mission of these organizations and organs. They afford them the necessary information, evaluate their work, and discuss their suggestions and proposals.

National territorial central committees can grant selected municipal, enterprise, and factory-wide committees the partial or full rights of the district committee.

District Party Organization

29. Party organizations on the territory of a district form the district organization of the party.

30. The highest organ of the district organization is the district conference, which is formed of delegates with a full vote who are elected in the basic organizations and delegates with an advisory vote who are previous members and alternate members of the district committees and members of the district control and auditing commission, provided they have not been elected as delegates with a full vote.

The district conference:

a. Reviews the political work of the district organization for the past period and determines the targets for its further activity;

b. Discusses reports on the activity of the district committee and the district control and auditing commission;

c. Elects the district committee, and the district control and auditing commission;

d. Elects delegates to congresses of the national territorial organizations and delegates to the congress of the Czechoslovak Communist Party;

e. Makes decisions on the requests, complaints, and appeals of party members;

f. Discusses and formulates standpoints of the district organization on the work of the higher party organs and on party policy; and

g. Discusses and recommends proposals of the district organization to members of the Central Committees.

The district committee convenes the district conference once every two years. The district committee makes known the date and program of the meeting at least two months before it is held.

31. The district committee convenes an extraordinary district conference:

a. On the basis of the decision of a two-thirds majority of the plenary session of the district committee;

b. At the request of one-third of the members of the district organization;

c. At the request of the district control and auditing commission, approved by a four-fifths majority of its members;

d. On the decision of the higher party organ.

Party members and basic organizations put forward requests to convene an extraordinary district conference to the district committee and the district control and auditing commission. These organs are obliged to inform the party public on the number of requests that have been raised.

The extraordinary conference is held at the very latest one month after the announcement that it will be convened.

32. The highest organ of the district conference in the period between conferences is the party district committee.

The district committee of the party:

a. By consistently engaging in fact-finding activities in harmony with the party program and the decrees of the higher organs stipulates independent procedure to solve the political, economic, and social problems of the district;

b. Participates in the creation of political decisions taken by the higher party organs and the whole party, and ensures that these decisions are realized in the district;

c. Governs the work of the lower party organizations and organs, while respecting their independence in resolving local questions, and helps them in their work; dissolves basic organizations in which the number of members has fallen below the prescribed number;

d. Governs ideological work in the district organization; sets up party schools and units for the promotion of the work of officials;

e. Elects the presidium, chairman, and secretaries of the district committee;

f. Elects commissions of the district committee and their chairman;

g. Renders accounts of its activity to the district conference and party organizations and reports to the higher party organs;

h. Approves Communist candidates as deputies of the district national committee and approves its own representatives to the district organs of the national front; works consistently with the Communist deputies and with Communists in the district organs of the National Front and in the social and special interest organizations and creates conditions for their successful activity; makes use of their knowledge and consults with them on its decisions;

i. Establishes and governs the press organs of the district committee and approves the chief editors;

j. Approves its budget and controls the implementation of this budget; manages financial resources and party property that have been entrusted to it;

k. Checks and evaluates the work of the apparatus of the district committee.

The district committee meets according to the needs stemming from the political situation and the tasks of the district organization at least once every three months.

The Presidium convenes a meeting of the district committee:

a. On its own decision;

b. According to the working plan of the plenum or on the decision of the plenum;

c. At the request of one-third of the members of the district committee;

d. At the request of the district control and auditing commission;

e. At the request of one-third of the basic organizations;

f. On the decision of the higher party organ.

33. The Presidium is the executive organ of the district committee that in the period between the meetings of the district committee ensures the implementation of the tasks arising from the decrees of the district conference

and the district committee. It governs and controls the work of the apparatus and carries out the work that has been entrusted to it by the district committee. The Presidium is responsible to the district committee and regularly gives it reports on its activity.

34. Communist deputies of the district national committee form an association of Communist deputies that works under the leadership of the plenum of the district committee and in accordance with its resolutions.

35. In the municipal organizations that have been placed on a level with the district organizations by the central committee of the national territorial organization it is possible to set up city-zone committees working with the same rights as the local party committees.

According to need, the district committees of national territorial organizations can set up other party organizations and afford them some of the rights of the district committees or place them on a level with the district organizations.

36. Party municipal organizations in Prague, Bratislava, and other large statutory cities have a special position. They set up municipal committees that govern city-zone and other organizations with the rights of district organizations, uniting the efforts of Communists in the creation and realization of a city-wide policy.

37. The activity of regional committees is governed in principle by decrees valid for the district organizations that are located in the area of the regional committee's responsibility and by the decrees of the central committees of the national territorial organizations. Upon agreement with the Czechoslovak Communist Party Central Committee, central committees of the national territorial organizations can establish certain institutions to help the district organizations.

IV. National Territorial Organizations of the Communist Party of Czechoslovakia in the Czech Lands and Slovakia

38. The Communist Party of the Czech Lands and the Communist Party of Slovakia are national territorial organizations of the united international Communist Party of Czechoslovakia. They are guided by its program and its statutes, and its members have uniform membership cards.

39. The supreme organ of the national territorial organization is the congress of the Communist Party of the Czech Lands and the Communist Party of Slovakia. The congress is composed of delegates, each with a full vote, elected at district conferences, and delegates, each with a consultative vote, who are the current members and alternate members of the Central Committee of the Communist Party of the Czech Lands and the Communist Party of Slovakia, and members of the Control and Auditing Commission, provided they have not been elected as delegates with full votes.

The congress of the national territorial organization:

a. Reviews political, economic, ideological, cultural, and social problems of the national territorial organization, studies their solutions in the past period, and lays down the course of further activity;

b. Discusses the report on the activity of the central committee and the Control and Auditing Commission of the national territorial organization;

c. Elects the central committee and the Control and Auditing Commission — only persons who have been party members for at least five years can be elected as members or alternate members of the central committee and the Control and Auditing Commission;

d. Decides on petitions, complaints, and appeals of party members and organizations; and

e. Discusses and formulates standpoints of the national territorial organization toward the work of the Central Committee of the Communist Party of Czechoslovakia and toward party policy.

The congress of the national territorial organization is convened by its central committee at least once every four years. The date and the agenda of the congress shall be announced by the central committee at least four months before the congress takes place.

40. An extraordinary congress is convened by the central committee of the national territorial organization:

a. At the decision of a two-thirds majority of members of the central committee;

b. At the request of one-third of its members;

c. At the request of the Control and Auditing Commission of the national territorial organization, approved by a four-fifths majority;

d. At the decision of the Central Committee of the Communist Party of Czechoslovakia.

Requests for convening an extraordinary congress are submitted by members, primary organizations, district committees, or district conferences to the central committee and the Control and Auditing Commission of the national territorial organization. These organs are obliged to inform the party public about the number of requests submitted.

An extraordinary congress takes place no more than three months from the time of the announcement of its convocation.

41. The supreme organ of the national territorial organization between congresses is the central committee of the national territorial organization.

The central committee of the national territorial organization:

a. Independently solves political, ideological, cultural, economic, and social problems of the national territorial entity on the basis of systematic fact-finding activity and in harmony with the program of the Communist Party of Czechoslovakia;

b. Shares in the forming of political decisions of the Central Committee of the Communist Party of Czechoslovakia and ensures their finalization and implementation within the sphere of its activity;

c. Directs the work of lower party organizations and organs, while respecting their independence in solving questions within the sphere of their activities and helping them in their activities;

d. Elects a presidium, secretariat, a chairman, and secretaries;

e. Elects commissions and their chairmen;

f. Renders accounts of its activities to the congress, lower party organizations and organs, and keeps the Central Committee of the Czechoslovak Communist Party informed;

g. Approves both Communist candidates for posts as deputies to the Czech National Council and the Slovak National Council and its representatives to national governments and organs of the National Front; systematically works with Communist deputies of the National Council, Communist functionaries of the national government, organs of the National Front, social and special interest organizations; and creates conditions for their successful work, uses their findings and suggestions, and consults them about its decisions;

h. Sets up and directs press organs of the national territorial organization and approves their editors-in-chief;

i. Establishes party enterprises and institutions and approves their heads; and

j. Approves its own budget and the budget of its institutions, controls their implementation, and manages the funds and party property entrusted to it.

The Central Committee meets according to the needs arising from the political situation and the tasks of the national territorial organization at least once every three months. A plenary meeting of the Central Committee is convened by the Presidium:

a. According to the working plan of the Central Committee of the national territorial organization;

b. At the decision of the plenary meeting or the Presidium;

c. At the request of one-third of the members of the Central Committee;

d. At the request of one-third of the district committees;

e. At the request of the national territorial Control and Auditing Commission;

f. At the request of the Central Committee of the Czechoslovak Communist Party.

Central committees of national territorial organizations can meet at a joint meeting to consult on concurrent problems, agree on their solution, and work out opposing standpoints, proposals, and ideas for the Central Committee of the Czechoslovak Communist Party. They will notify the Central Committee of the Czechoslovak Communist Party about this intention.

42. The Presidium is the executive organ of the Central Committee of the national territorial organization, which in the periods between its meetings and with the help of commissions of work groups studies problems of a conceptual character, secures the implementation of tasks emanating from the resolutions of the congress or the Central Committee and carries on activities entrusted to it by the Central Committee of the national territorial organizations.

The Presidium is responsible to the Central Committee of the national territorial organization, to which it reports regularly about its activity.

43. The Secretariat ensures the operative implementation of tasks emanating from resolutions of the Central Committee and its Presidium and organizes and directs the day-to-day activities of the apparatus and party machinery.

The Secretariat is responsible to the Central Committee of the national territorial organization to which it reports regularly about its activity.

44. Communist deputies of the Czech National Council and the Slovak National Council form an association of Communist deputies that works under the leadership of the Central Committee of the national territorial organization and in accordance with its resolution.

Supreme Organs of the Communist Party of Czechoslovakia:

45. National territorial organizations form the united international Communist Party of Czechoslovakia, which respects their equality of rights and integrates the interests of both nations, the nationalities, and the entire society.

46. The supreme organ of the Communist Party of Czechoslovakia is the party congress. The congress is composed of delegates, each with a full vote, elected at congresses of national territorial organizations, and delegates, each with a consultative vote, who are the current members and alternate members of the Central Committee and members of the Central Control and Auditing Commission, provided they have not been elected as delegates with full votes.

The congress of the Communist Party of Czechoslovakia:

a. Approves the party program and statutes;

b. Evaluates the realization of the programmatic aims of the party and lays down a set of concepts and tactics for the party in internal and foreign policy;

c. Discusses the report on the activity of the Central Committee and the Central Control and Auditing Commission;

d. Elects the party Central Committee and the Central Control and Auditing Commission — only persons who have been party members at least five years can be members or alternate members of the Central Committee or the Central Control and Auditing Commission; and

e. Decides about petitions, complaints, and appeals of party members and organizations.

A party congress is convened by the Central Committee of the Communist Party of Czechoslovakia at least once every four years. The convening of the congress and the agenda are announced by the Central Committee at least six months before the congress takes place.

47. An extraordinary congress is convened by the Central Committee of the Communist Party of Czechoslovakia:

a. On the basis of a two-thirds majority of members of the Central Committee;

b. At the request of one-third of its members;

c. At the request of the Central Control and Auditing Commission, approved by a four-fifths majority of its members;

d. If it is requested by one of the congresses of the national territorial organization.

Requests for the convocation of an extraordinary congress are submitted by members, primary organizations, district committees, central committees, or congresses of national territorial organizations to the Central Committee of the Communist Party of Czechoslovakia and the Central Control and Auditing Commission. These organs are obliged to inform the party public about the number of requests for the convocation of an extraordinary congress.

An extraordinary congress takes place no more than three months from the announcement of its convocation.

48. The supreme organ of the Communist Party of Czechoslovakia in the period between congresses is the Central Committee of the Communist Party of Czechoslovakia.

The Central Committee of the Communist Party of Czechoslovakia:

a. Adopts standpoints toward the internal and foreign policies and unites the activities of the whole party in order to carry through the political line of the congress;

b. Lays down the course of action in solving political, economic, ideological, cultural, and social problems on the basis of systematic fact-finding activities and in harmony with the party program;

c. Directs national territorial organizations and party organs and organizations in institutions of state-wide character which do not form a part of the national territorial organization, while respecting their rights and supporting their initiative;

d. Elects the Presidium, Secretariat, chairman, and secretaries of the party Central Committee;

e. Elects commissions of the Central Committee and their chairmen;

f. Approves Communist candidates for deputy of the National Assembly and party representative to the government organs and organs of the National Front. It works systematically with Communists in central, state, and legislative organs, in organs of the National Front and social organizations, creates conditions for their activity, uses their findings and suggestions, and consults them about its decisions;

g. Renders accounts of its activity to the congress and the lower organizations and organs;

h. Sets up and directs central press organs of the party and approves appointments of editors-in-chief;

i. Establishes enterprises and institutions of the central committee and approves appointments of their heads; and

j. Approves its budget and the budget of its institutions and controls their implementation; lays down principles for the administration of party finances, rates of membership contributions, and the determination of financial resources needed for the party activity and approves their allocations.

The Central Committee and delegations authorized by it represent the party in dealing with Communist and Workers' parties of other countries.

The Central Committee meets in accordance with needs emanating from the internal and international situation and the party tasks, but it must meet at least three times a year. The plenary meeting of the Central Committee is convened by the Presidium:

a. According to a working plan of the Central Committee;

b. At the decision of the plenary meeting or the Presidium;

c. At the request of one third of the members of the Central Committee;

d. At the request of the Central Committee of the national territorial organization;

e. At the request of the Central Control and Auditing Commission.

49. The decisions of the Central Committee of the Communist Party of Czechoslovakia touching upon questions of the international Communist movement and international relations, the work of Communists in organs and institutions of a statewide character, cadre questions of these organs and institutions, questions of party work in the armed forces including the people's militias, the central press organs of the Communist Party of Czechoslovakia, and the central party archive fall within its exclusive jurisdiction and are resolved in accordance with the principles of democratic centralism.

The Central Committee of the Communist Party of Czechoslovakia has full access to all information about the activity of national territorial organs and organizations.

In all questions, as far as they concern existence, sovereignty, or national or territorial interests, the decision of the Central Committee of the Communist Party of Czechoslovakia is final, provided an absolute majority of representatives of both national territorial organizations have voted in favor of it in a separate voting.

This method of voting is applicable at the suggestion of an absolute majority of representatives of several of the national territorial organizations.

The Central Committee of the Communist Party of Czechoslovakia approaches the discussion of such questions on the basis of familiarity with the standpoint of the central committee of the relevant national territorial organization. It can convene a joint meeting of central committees of national territorial organizations for the purpose of reaching a political agreement on the settlement of problems. Joint meetings of central committees of national territorial organizations do not make binding resolutions.

50. The Presidium is the executive organ of the Central Committee of the Communist Party of Czechoslovakia, which in the periods between its meetings and with the assistance of commissions and work groups studies questions of a conceptual character, secures the implementation of tasks emanating from the resolutions of the congress and the Central Committee, and carries on activities entrusted to it by the Central Committee.

The Presidium is responsible to the Central Committee, to which it submits regular reports about its activity.

51. The Secretariat ensures the operative implementation of talks emanating from resolutions of the Central Committee and its Presidium and organizes and directs the day-to-day activities of the apparatus and the party machinery.

The Secretariat is responsible to the Central Committee, to which it regularly submits reports about its activity.

52. Communist deputies of the national assembly form an association of Communist deputies that works under the leadership of the Central Com-

mittee of the Communist Party of Czechoslovakia and in accordance with its resolutions.

Control and Auditing Commissions of the Communist Party of Czechoslovakia:

53. Control and auditing commissions of the Communist Party of Czechoslovakia are objective control organs independent of directing organs. They form within the framework of party organs a relatively independent system of effective self-control and are a necessary prerequisite for the healthy running and development of the party organism. They are elected by congresses, conferences, plenary sessions, or annual party members' meetings, and they are responsible only to them for carrying out their functions. Principles for their activity are approved by the congress of the Communist Party of Czechoslovakia.

The position of the commissions and their functions exclude them from any direct link with the decision-making and executive activity, nor can they be entrusted with such activity by the directing organs. They do not replace the responsibility of directing and executive organs, nor do they direct commissions at lower levels of the organizational structure with which they methodically work.

54. A control and auditing commission elects a chairman and vice chairmen of the commission who are responsible to the plenum for carrying out the operative work.

The plenum of the commissions approves the setup of its executive apparatus and the appointment and dismissal of its own officials. It approves its own budget and controls its implementation.

55. Control and auditing commissions carry out the following basic functions:

a. The political control function, including control of the creation, elaboration, and implementation of the line of the congress, the resolutions of conferences, and plenary meetings of party organs; control of the activity of executive organs and officials of the apparatus in the observance of democratic principles in party activity and in the development of internal party relations; and the examination and evaluation of the level and effectiveness of the control work of party organs;

b. The verification and appeal function, in which the task is to observe whether organs and members of the party are acting in accordance with party statutes, especially how organs are creating conditions for the implementation of their members' rights, whether suggestions and recommendations are used, and whether complaints of members and other citizens, organizations, and organs which are sent to directing organs are dealt with; to settle appeals of members, organizations, and organs against party punishments and other decisions of directing organs; to consider and settle disputes between party members by conciliatory party proceedings; and to provide effective protection of the rights of members, organizations, or minority groups.

c. The auditing function which consists of ensuring reasonable expenditures of funds in accordance with political tasks, examining the party economy and finances and keeping order in the administration of organizations and organs. They also observe at higher levels the regional setup of administrative works and the use of modern working methods and equipment.

The cadre composition and facilities of control and auditing commissions should be such as to enable them to carry out these demanding functions. Membership in a control and auditing commission is incompatible with membership in directing and executive organs at the same level.

56. Control and auditing commissions submit their findings, suggestions, and recommendations to directing and executive organs, which are obliged to deal with them and communicate to the commission their standpoint or decision within no more than three months.

Control and auditing commissions acquire the necessary information independently, provide each other with information and enjoy the right to use fully the party information system, having access to all party materials and documents.

57. The chairman, or if need be the vice chairman, of a control and auditing commission attends the plenary meetings of directing organs and proceedings of executive organs. Other members attend on the basis of authorization by the plenum of the commission. Control and auditing commissions at all levels have the right to ask for the convening of the plenary meeting of the directing organ, an extraordinary conference, or a congress.

Joint meetings of directing organs and control and auditing commissions take place for the purpose of discussing important political and internal party problems or suggestions and standpoints which the commission submits to the plenum. Each organ decides separately about resolutions that are being proposed. If these organs do not agree, their dispute is resolved at a joint meeting of higher organs. When the highest organs are involved, the congress of the Communist Party of Czechoslovakia makes the decision.

The press organs of the party are obliged to publish without alterations the full texts of the standpoints and resolutions of the plenum of a control and auditing commission, once the commission has decided it is to be published.

V. Party Organizations and Organs in the Armed Forces and Federal Organs of Security.

58. Communists in the army and in organs of federal security form party organizations in accordance with the structural organization of the armed forces. They are guided in their activity by the program, party statutes, and resolutions of the higher party organs. In case of war, they work in accordance with special directives of the Central Committee of the Czechoslovak Communist Party.

Party work in the armed forces is directed by the Central Committee of the Czechoslovak Communist Party through democratically elected organs.

Party organizations and organs of the armed forces closely cooperate with the territorial party organizations and organs. They support the public and political activity of their members.

VI. Party Investigations and Punishments

59. Party organizations and organs are obliged to discuss protests and complaints of Communists and other citizens concerning acts and behavior of their members. The organ sets up a special commission for each investigation, the task of which is to prove whether the complaint is valid or unfounded. A member has the right to propose his own representative as a member of the commission. The commission is obliged to discuss its conclusions in the presence of the member concerned. The investigation is closed at a meeting or in the plenum of the organ either by a rejection of the accusation or with the use of educational processes, and, in graver cases, by instituting disciplinary proceedings.

60. Disciplinary proceedings involving a member can be instituted if he does not carry out his duties, if he does not act in accordance with the party statutes, or if he otherwise harms the party's name in public. If the accusation is not proved, disciplinary proceedings will be stopped. If the accusation is proved, then one of the following educational means is applied depending on the magnitude of the case and with consideration for the personality of the guilty party member: reasoning, rebuke, and instruction to the member to mend his ways, comradely criticism at a members meeting or at a meeting of the organ or public criticism. If these means are insufficient, party punishment is applied, which includes: admonition, reprimand, deprivation of party functions, or reprimand with warning. If the wrong-doing of the member is such that his membership in the party ranks unduly harms the party, he is expelled from the party by the party collective. The results of the disciplinary proceeding are discussed and approved by the members meeting or by the plenum of the relevant organ.

It is not permissible to impose party punishment for differences of views, provided the party member's activity which is in contradiction with the party program and statutes does not emanate from such views.

61. The decision to impose party punishment and expel a member from the party is made by secret vote at a meeting of the basic organization. The decision to impose party punishment is carried by a simple majority. Expulsion from the party becomes valid if at least two-thirds of the members present have voted in favor of it. The expelled member is obliged to surrender his membership card to the committee of the basic organization.

62. Decisions regarding party punishment of members and alternate members of district committees, central committees of national territorial organizations, and the Central Committee of the Communist Party of Czechoslovakia and members of control and auditing commissions are made by basic organizations with the cognizance of the appropriate party organ, when the reason for the punishment originated within their field of activity. The decision is valid if it is confirmed by the organ of which the punished person is a member. If the reason for punishment results from the implementation of a function of a higher organ, the decision to punish is made by the appropriate organ in agreement with the basic organization.

Removing from his post a member or alternate member of the district committee, the central committee of a national territorial organization, the Central Committee of the Communist Party of Czechoslovakia or control and auditing commissions is the right of the plenum of the appropriate organ, by a two-thirds majority of its members. The decision is confirmed by the appropriate conference or congress.

The expulsion of a member of a higher party organ from the party is discussed by the basic organization with the cognizance of that organ. The decision of the basic organization to expel a member from the party is valid in such cases if it is confirmed by the party organ of which the punished person is a member by a two-thirds majority of its members. In cases where the party basic organization refuses to expel a member from the party in spite of serious breaches of the program and statutes, the decision on his expulsion can be made by a higher party organ. Higher party organs can in exceptional cases propose to basic organizations and lower organs the imposition of disciplinary proceedings upon a member and invoke their standpoints and conclusions.

63. In cases where a party member violates the law and a court proceeding is started against him, the party organization or organ of which he is a member can suspend his membership in the party pending the decision of the court. The party's proceedings are instituted following the court verdict.

64. A party member who has had party punishment imposed upon him, who has been expelled from the party, or whose request for the annulment of his party punishment has been refused is entitled to appeal within one month following the decision from lower party organs to the congress of the Communist Party of Czechoslovakia, which finally decides on the appeal.

Party organizations and organs, whose decision has been changed by a superior organ, have the same right of appeal from lower party organs to the congress of the Communist Party of Czechoslovakia.

Party punishment remains valid until countermanded by a higher party organ, which is obliged to deal with a member's petition within no more than two months.

If there has been a revision of an unsubstantiated punishment and if the member involved demands it, the appropriate party organ is obliged to announce this in the party press.

65. The organ which imposed the punishment is obliged to help the member to overcome and correct his shortcomings and to assess the activity of the member after a period of six months to a year from the time of the imposition of the punishment depending upon the nature of the offense and the degree of punishment. If the reasons for which the punishment was imposed no longer exist or the member has overcome his shortcomings, the appropriate party organ or meeting decides, at the request of the member or on its own initiative, to rescind the party punishment by a simple majority.

66. If the basic organization or if a lower party organ commits a serious breach of the program and statutes, the appropriate central committee of the national territorial organization can, in an extreme case, dissolve the party

organization or organ concerned and decide at the same time how to re-apportion the members of this organization. The decision regarding the dis-solution of organs and organizations is adopted by a two-thirds majority.

67. More detailed procedures concerning party investigation, disciplinary proceedings, and the imposition of party punishment are specified by direc-tives adopted by the plenum of the Central Committee of the Communist Party of Czechoslovakia.

VII. Party Financing

68. Financial resources of the party are accrued from members' fees, money yielded by party enterprises, and other income. Party organs keep the party membership informed as to the administration of funds.

Party organizations, organs, institutions, and enterprises can acquire rights and incur liability in property matters in their own name within the latitude set forth by principles approved by the Central Committee of the Communist Party of Czechoslovakia.

VIII. Concluding Provisions

69. The statutes of the Communist Party of Czechoslovakia contain funda-mental, binding provisions concerning the party's internal life. No directives or resolutions of party organizations and organs may be at variance with these statutes.

The basis for the interpretation of the statutes and their individual articles, besides the text of the statutes itself, is the preamble to the statutes as approved by the extraordinary 14th Congress of the Communist Party of Czechoslovakia.

In disputed cases, interpretation is the responsibility of the plenum of the Central Committee of the Communist Party of Czechoslovakia upon con-sultation with the Central Control and Auditing Commission.

70. The right to change the party statutes belongs exclusively to the congress of the Communist Party of Czechoslovakia.

IV. Invasion of Czechoslovakia and Split in World Communism

"Workers of all countries unite—or I'll shoot!"

Literární listy, special edition, August 28, 1968.

SOVIET POLEMICS BEGIN AGAIN

DURING THE BRIEF LULL following Bratislava, the Dubček regime worked furiously to consolidate support. Tito arrived in Czechoslovakia on August 9,[1] a Rumanian delegation led by Ceauşescu on August 15. Both leaders were warmly welcomed in Prague. Tito's press conference and the new "Czechoslovak-Rumanian Treaty of Friendship, Cooperation and Mutual Aid" signed during Ceauşescu's visit[2] each stressed the principle of noninterference in one another's internal affairs, a principle pointedly missing in the Bratislava Statement. Moreover, Ulbricht's almost simultaneous journey to Karlovy Vary netted only a vague agreement that both sides would continue to oppose the rise of Nazism in West Germany.[3]

Moscow understandably suspected that a "Communist Little Entente" directed against Soviet hegemony was forming in Eastern Europe. Indeed the Soviet press returned to polemical attack while Ceauşescu was still in Prague.[4]

[1] Interestingly enough, U.S. Senator Mike Mansfield was also in Prague August 9 visiting Czechoslovak National Assembly Chairman Josef Smrkovský (ČTK International Service in English, August 9, 1968; *The New York Times*, August 10, 1968).

[2] The Soviet-Rumanian treaty that came up for renewal February 4, 1968, remained conspicuously unsigned. In April 1969 pressure on Bucharest was mounting in this respect. Rumanian Foreign Minister Manescu visited Moscow, and reportedly Soviet leaders were scheduled to go to Rumania for the signing of a new treaty (*The Washington Post*, April 10, 1969).

[3] For communiqué see *Neues Deutschland*, August 14, 1968; summarized in *Pravda*, August 14, 1968. Candidate member of the SED Politburo and Secretary of the Central Committee Hermann Axen later accused the Dubček regime of consciously sabotaging the Čierná and Bratislava accords by "fiercely" opposing any formulation relating to the struggle against bourgeois ideology at Karlovy Vary. See Hermann Axen, "Proletarischer Internationalismus in unserer Zeit," in *Einheit*, No. 10 (September 18, 1968), p. 1207.

[4] Yuri Zhukov, *Pravda*, August 16, 1968. Simultaneously, final arrangements for the military attack must have been taken care of, for Soviet Defense Minister Grechko, Head of the Warsaw Pact Joint Forces Yakubovsky, and Director of the Political Administration Yepishev conferred first with the East German Defense Minister H. Hoffmann August 16 and then went to "Southwest Poland," where they were joined by the new Warsaw Pact Chief of Staff S. M. Shtemenko for talks with Polish Deputy Minister of National Defense B. Hocha that included "Division General Tadeusz Tuczapski, Deputy Minister of National Defense and Chief Inspector for Combat Readiness of Polish Troops" (*Pravda*, August 17 and 18). Also on the 17th, *Pravda* reprinted a long article from the Hungarian *Nepszábadság* detailing the horrors of the Hungarian counterrevolution in 1956.

I. Alexandrov ("Insolent Attacks by Reactionaries," Document 44) set the stage for invasion with descriptions of hooligans attacking the KSČ Central Committee building and honest workers, who had published a letter in *Pravda* July 30, being subjected to "frenzied persecutions."

DOCUMENT 44

"INSOLENT ATTACKS BY REACTIONARIES"
I. Alexandrov
August 18, 1968
Complete Text

[*Pravda,* August 18, 1968, quoted from *CDSP,* Vol. XX, No. 33 (September 4, 1968), pp. 10–11]

Recently an intensification of subversive activities aimed by antisocialist forces against the Czechoslovak Communist Party and the foundations of the socialist system in Czechoslovakia has again been observable in Prague.

On Aug. 17 Rude Pravo, the organ of the C.C.P. Central Committee, published a report that the Presidium of the C.C.P. Central Committee and the editors of Rude Pravo had received letters requesting coverage of details of the Aug. 13 meeting of the Presidium of the C.C.P. Central Committee, which analyzed the outrageous shenanigans of certain groups in Prague in the last few days. The actions of these groups, the newspaper writes, harbor a danger to the efforts of honest people to revive democracy in our society and constitute a threat to the society itself.

This is absolutely true of, for example, the incident that took place on Aug. 8 at the C.C.P. Central Committee building, where at about 9:00 P.M. some 300 people gathered, primarily young people who had come there from Stare Mesto Square. They yelled hooligan slogans and demanded that a speaker be dispatched to Stare Mesto Square; one of the youths declared: "If we give the word to the crowd, it will smash everything here." Those assembled did not disperse and at 10:00 P.M. began shouting: "Come on out of there!", "We'll show you!", "Swine, get out of there!" The group rushed at the doors, pounded on them and threw rocks. With the same sort of shouts the crowd then set off for Stare Mesto Square, where the rally resumed.

The Presidium of the C.C.P. Central Committee rightly denounced these shenanigans, in which the disputes only served as excuses for some individuals to commit outrages and act like hooligans.

The slander campaign by reactionary elements against the people's militia has also intensified. The armed detachments of the working class, created in 1948 at Czechoslovakia's enterprises to defend its socialist gains, are under fierce attack by the enemies of socialism. For example, small groups of provocateurs have appeared on the streets of Prague to gather signatures demanding the dissolution of the people's militia. Furthermore, it turned out that these demands were written in two Western European languages in addition to Czech. The provocational onslaught aroused indignation and alarm among the working people. Despite the fact that the provocateurs' actions were denounced by the Presidium of the C.C.P. Central Committee, they have not subsided.

Reactionary forces have launched a frenzied campaign of persecution against the 99 workers at the Auto-Praha Plant whose letter was published in Pravda on July 30. As is known, in this letter workers expressed both profound patriotic concern for the fate of socialism in their country and sentiments of fraternal friendship for the Soviet people and their armed forces. Certain newspapers pounced on the workers for this; on Aug. 9 one of them — Svobodne Slovo — printed a letter from a certain M. Jodl, who wrote that "the 99 persons who as working people of the Auto-Praha Plant signed the perfidious letter later printed in the Soviet Pravda are traitors, they have excluded themselves from our society and should go where they seek support and where they get a response."

The workers who authored the letter found themselves in an atmosphere of moral terrorism; at the plant meetings were called one after another, and at the meetings those workers were subjected to abusive accusations of antipatriotism. The baiting and persecution of the workers did not cease even after the newspaper Rude Pravo came to their defense and the Presidium of the C.C.P. Central Committee condemned, in the words of the press announcement, "the undemocratic forms of the campaign unleashed over this letter."

The results of the meeting between the Politburo of the C.P.S.U. Central Committee and the Presidium of the C.C.P. Central Committee in Cierna-on-Tisa and the Bratislava conference of representatives of the Communist and Workers' Parties of the socialist countries met with a profound response and approval among Communists and the masses of Czechoslovak working people. The working people of the Czechoslovak Socialist Republic see the consolidation and further development of socialism in Czechoslovakia and the strengthening of friendship and brotherhood with the Soviet Union and the other socialist countries as a guarantee of successful advancement along the chosen path.

It was this that aroused fierce new efforts by right-wing, reactionary forces, encouraged from abroad by imperialist reaction, to undermine the foundations of socialism, discredit the leading role of the working class and its party and cut Czechoslovakia off from the socialist commonwealth. The by now completely insolent reactionaries even dare to make crude attacks on the decisions adopted at the meeting in Cierna-on-Tisa and at the Bratislava conference, using for this purpose press organs such as Literarni Listy, Prace, Mlada Fronta and some others. The enemies of socialism dream of restoring the old bourgeois order in Czechoslovakia, and their efforts are directed toward this end.

But the enemies' schemes are doomed to failure. The working people of Czechoslovakia, leaning on the international solidarity and support of the fraternal socialist countries as clearly and profoundly expressed in the Bratislava statement, are fully resolved to rebuff the schemes of internal and external reaction and to uphold and strengthen their socialist gains.

INVASION

THERE REMAINED only last-minute political maneuvering. Kádár, who was probably still trying to promote a compromise,[1] met with Dubček August 17. On August 19, Premier Kosygin informed President Johnson that he was ready for the summit meeting Johnson desired and suggested August 21,[2] the day of invasion. At the same time the CPSU Politburo sent a strongly worded warning to the KSČ Presidium that in Moscow's view Prague's implementation of the Čierná and Bratislava agreements had not gone far enough.[3]

As with Hungary in 1956, Moscow claimed to have been invited. TASS stated that unidentified "party and government leaders" in Czechoslovakia had requested urgent assistance.[4] An appeal — ostensibly by a group of members of the Czechoslovak Central Committee, government, and National Assembly — calling on the people of Czechoslovakia to give all possible support to the allied military units (Document 45) duly appeared, as did an exhaustive editorial defense of Moscow's position ("Defense of Socialism Is the Highest International Duty," Document 46). Here for the first and only time, Dubček was attacked by name as leading a "right-wing, opportunist minority" in the KSČ Presidium.

Within Czechoslovakia, the "honest comrades" which the Soviet and East European troops had come to assist did not materialize, but only because 72-year-old President Svoboda absolutely refused to appoint the puppet regime proposed to him by Alois Indra, who reportedly was to have been the new Prime Minister.[5] Thus, even though the Soviet military plan had gone into

---

[1] Richard Lowenthal, "The Sparrow in the Cage," *Problems of Communism*, Vol. XVII, No. 6 (November–December 1968), pp. 20–22, indicates that Kádár may have first met with Soviet leaders vacationing in Yalta to try to persuade them against invasion.

[2] *The New York Times*, August 23, 1968. The coincidence of date was hardly an accident. Indeed, Moscow had been careful to equalize pressure against Prague with conciliatory gestures toward Washington. For example, Gromyko indicated that the Soviets were ready to negotiate limitation of the arms race in long-range missiles and ABMs July 1 just after Vaculík's "2000-Word Statement" and during a period when Prague was refusing multilateral negotiations prior to the Warsaw Letter.

[3] Unofficial translation in *Wochenpresse* (February 26, 1969).

[4] *Pravda*, August 21, 1968.

[5] *Frankfurter Allgemeine Zeitung*, September 23, 1968, and *Der Spiegel*, October 21, 1968, p. 147.

flawless operation, miscalculation of Svoboda had prevented the Kádár solution Moscow desired.[6]

DOCUMENT 45

APPEAL BY GROUP OF MEMBERS OF CCP CENTRAL COMMITTEE
AND CSR GOVERNMENT AND NATIONAL ASSEMBLY
August 22, 1968
Complete Text

[*Pravda,* August 22, 1968, *CDSP,* Vol. XX, No. 34 (September 11, 1968), pp. 3–5]

❦

Citizens of Czechoslovakia, workers, peasants, representatives of the working intelligentsia, men, women and young people!

At this moment, when the country's fate is being decided, at a moment that will forever be crucial in our history and our further socialist and democratic development, at a moment when for us it is a matter of the values won by our 20 years of effort, by our sacrifices and by our labor, at a moment when we have staked our all, we appeal to everyone to whom our socialist homeland is dear and for whom it really is the homeland, we appeal to all of you, regardless of political affiliation, nationality, religion or social position.

We appeal to you at a time when the results of our socialist system have been jeopardized by forces that are abusing the progressive steps initiated by the party itself at the January plenary session of the C.C.P. Central Committee and sincerely carried out by the party since then in the interests of achieving genuine democracy and genuine humanism — ideals dear to all decent citizens of our homeland.

On the party's initiative we embarked in January on the path of seeking and finding a new outline of socialism that would be consonant with our people's way of life and thinking and that would involve all prospects of society and individuality. It resolutely dissociated itself from the period of the regime of personal power, which had really deformed the humane and democratic nature of socialism. With the active participation and support of all honest-minded patriots it resolutely entered on a new period with the most honest intentions of correcting the errors of the past and of creating the conditions for a full, rich and happy life for our homeland.

[6] Subsequently the Soviets somewhat indirectly admitted that the invasion was denounced by the Czechoslovak leadership as a violation of sovereignty. See *Za rubezhom* (January 10–16, 1969), p. 20. For an excellent analysis of the reasoning that may well have gone into the Soviet decision to invade see Fritz Ermarth, *Internationalism, Security, and Legitimacy: The Challenge to Soviet Interests in East Europe 1964–1968* (RAND Memorandum RM-5909-PR, March 1969).

Basic civil rights, which had always been fundamentally connected with our people's conceptions of democracy and humanism, were again restored in the ideas and progressive spirit of the action program, a long-term platform for our socialist advance, a program that was given unprecedented mass support by our people.

First and foremost, this unanimous support confirmed the correctness, strength and attractiveness of our new path. This fact proved especially that despite all the shortcomings of the pre-January period, the ideas of socialism had taken deep root among our people and that our people regard socialism as their natural milieu; our people's profound desire for law and justice was effectively expressed precisely in the progressive ideas outlined by the January plenary session. With the aid of these ideas, society was removed from a state of unhealthy indifference, and in this way the gates were fully opened to a powerful current of healthy, unutilized initiative. Our people stood up to this historic test brilliantly and once again proved their high level of maturity.

Unfortunately, forces that for many years had been awaiting such a favorable moment in order to discredit the party and contest its political and moral right to lead society abused this period of our society's quest and transformation to accomplish their own purposes and to make an active entrance into the political arena. In fact, certain forces within the party and in party bodies met these right-wing forces halfway, and they thereby found themselves in contradiction to the party's principles and goals and to the ideas of proletarian internationalism. Together they directed their forces at systematic violation of the constitutional nature of our political reform and concentrated these forces on a struggle against positive efforts by party and state bodies to implement the January goals. They organized a filthy campaign for the purposes of compromising individual functionaries, including those in the new C.C.P. leadership who had the courage to call public attention to the impending danger and to see the real situation in all its complexity. They violated public order and activated base nationalist passions; they did not even hesitate to slander our Czechoslovak socialist homeland and the honest labor of our people, our party, the army and the security agencies; and they demanded changes in our foreign policy. Their filthy campaign even went so far as to attack the alliance with the Soviet Union, especially in connection with the staff training exercises of the Warsaw Pact armed forces, as well as to attack the friendship with socialist countries. They thereby created an atmosphere that was absolutely unacceptable to the socialist countries.

The C.C.P., the government of the republic and the National Front remained exceptionally patient and understanding.

But more than once, especially at the May plenary session, it was therefore emphasized that the paramount task is to foil the plans of the right-wing anti-socialist forces; to refrain from any erroneous step that would jeopardize implementation of the action program; to ensure that the question of the party's future line would be decided not by advocates of extremist views, but by the healthy, progressive nucleus of the party; to give complete support publicly to the party and state machinery, the army, security, the prosecutor's office, the courts, the people's militia — in short, to consolidate the situation.

However, extremist right-wing forces, which saw this magnanimity and patience and the party's truly democratic method of deciding a serious political question as a weakness of the party rather than a strength, intensified their activities still further. In Prague, as is known, during spontaneous mass meetings matters reached the point of crude indecencies when various elements attacked the party and insulted its representatives, whom they themselves often forced to take part in these meetings. In the center of the city a public campaign was started to collect signatures in favor of liquidating the people's militia. Communists who spoke from their own point of view in the discussions at these spontaneous street rallies were crudely silenced, and on several occasions physical force was used against them. Many of the people who signed the letter at the Auto-Praha Plant were subjected to shameful persecutions, including dismissal from their jobs. The defamation of leading functionaries by other, more subtle means continues in the press, although indirectly, and this organized subversive activity recently culminated in a completely overt attack by a group of right-wing extremists on the building of the C.C.P. Central Committee Secretariat in Prague. Thus, the extremist forces have not heeded the party's appeals and in trying at all costs to cause conflict in our country are stepping up their subversive activities even more. Thus a situation has arisen wherein the obligations stemming from the Bratislava declaration of the six fraternal Communist and Workers' Parties, which was also signed by representatives of our party, are being publicly and systematically violated.

Citizens! Today everything that our working people have created in the past 20 years is at stake; all the gains of socialism are at stake. Not only the path of socialist democracy on which we embarked in January, but also the very foundation of socialism and our republic are in jeopardy.

Aware of a lofty responsibility to our people, filled with a sense of real patriotism and international socialist solidarity and aware of our international obligations, we have taken on ourselves the initiative of rallying all patriotic forces in the name of our socialist future and our homeland. The danger of a fratricidal struggle, which reaction has prepared and which would be a tragic repetition of Lipany [meaning the battle of Lipany in 1434. — Ed.], has confronted us with the necessity of making the historic decision to appeal to the Soviet Union and other fraternal socialist countries for assistance. Our allies have granted us this assistance as they did in 1945, when it was a matter of whether or not we were to survive.

We call on all citizens to give all possible support to the military units of our allies. After liquidation of the danger of a reactionary coup, the allied troops will leave the territory of Czechoslovakia. All foreigners who are now in Czechoslovakia can continue to enjoy our hospitality, and their safety and immunity will be fully guaranteed if they abide by our laws.

Guided by a sense of the deepest responsibility to our people, our working class, the peoples of our country, the international working class and the world Communist movement, we appeal to you at this grave moment, citizens of the republic, to rally around the realistic-minded nucleus of the party, to whom the cause of socialism, progress and the new post-January path is dear, to whom the cause of friendship with the peoples of the Soviet Union and the other socialist countries is dear.

With firm faith in your reasonableness, maturity and political awareness, we call on you, all honest citizens of our homeland, workers, peasants, representatives of the intelligentsia, men, women, young people, healthy forces of the National Front, military servicemen, security agency personnel, Communists and non-Communists — all honest people — to prevent by your concrete deeds and concrete actions a further attack by any reactionary forces, whether from outside or within the party. Do not permit spontaneous outbursts, devastation and anarchy; remain calm and orderly.

We reject the practice of the pre-January policy. We will not tolerate any sign of a return to the compromised pre-January methods, which were resolutely rebuffed by the overwhelming majority of our people and which jeopardized the party's leadership role and the socialist gains of our working people and helped to create a situation truly fraught with conflict involving the use of force. On the contrary, we want to defend and carry through to completion the progressive January ideas, which are leading us to the creation of a socialist society that is truly contemporary, reborn and humane, the kind of society intended by the founders of Marxism-Leninism and those who began to make it a reality after the victory of October.

We are and will remain completely loyal to our progressive national traditions connected with the 50th anniversary of the beginning of the republic, with the precepts of antifascist struggle, with national and democratic values, with the traditions of the Slovak national uprising, the Prague uprising of May, 1945, and with the revolutionary appeal of February, 1948 — "Forward, not one step backward!" We shall guard as the apple of our eye our fraternal ties of alliance and friendship with the Soviet Union, its people, the peoples of all the countries in the world socialist commonwealth and with all the forces of peace, democracy, progress and socialism — these are the values that guarantee us our autonomy, independence and national and state sovereignty, without which we would again be faced with the threat of a new Munich and with those who organized it in 1938. Czechoslovakia can develop only as a socialist country and as an inseparable component of the socialist commonwealth; its strength and stability create the bases for the future prospects of the international revolutionary movement; any weakening and disruption of the socialist camp would cause a harm difficult to imagine to the cause of revolutionary progress and socialism in the world.

We appeal to you, esteemed citizens, with full confidence that through common actions we shall create barriers against the impending danger, that through common efforts we shall overcome the present grave situation and shall ensure a happy present and future for our homeland, for our generation and for future generations.

We appeal to all of you — from the Sumava Mountains on the border to Cierna-on-Tisa, from the Krkonose to the banks of the Danube — to understand the awesome and grave nature of these days, when for us it is a matter of everything we associate with the concepts of "democracy" and "socialism," to realize your responsibility and to preserve the unity and mutual trust with which we must act in the days ahead.

Our guiding principles are and will continue to be farsightedness, order, progress, truth, the future of socialism, state sovereignty and united solidarity.

May democratic socialist Czechoslovakia live and flourish!

DOCUMENT 46
"DEFENSE OF SOCIALISM IS THE HIGHEST INTERNATIONALIST DUTY"

August 22, 1968

Complete Text

[Editorial, *Pravda,* August 22, 1968, quoted from *CDSP,* Vol. XX, No. 34 (September 11, 1968), pp. 5–14]

Party and state leaders of the Czechoslovak Socialist Republic have requested the Soviet Union and other allied states to give the fraternal Czechoslovak people immediate assistance, including assistance with armed forces.

The reason for this appeal is the threat posed to the socialist system existing in Czechoslovakia and to the constitutionally established state system by counterrevolutionary forces that have entered into collusion with external forces hostile to socialism.

The necessity of adopting the historic decision to request assistance from the Soviet Union and other fraternal socialist countries is fully substantiated in the appeal by a group of members of the C.C.P. Central Committee, the government and the C.S.R. National Assembly, which is published today in Pravda. This necessity arose because of the danger of a fratricidal struggle being prepared by the reactionaries in the C.S.R.

In accordance with the commitments undertaken at the conference of Communist and Workers' Parties in Bratislava and proceeding on principles of indissoluble friendship and cooperation and in accordance with existing treaty obligations, the governments of the U.S.S.R. and other allied countries have decided to meet the above-mentioned request to give the fraternal Czechoslovak people the necessary assistance. The fraternal socialist countries are fulfilling their common international duty.

Relations with Czechoslovakia and its Communist Party have always occupied an important place in the policy of the C.P.S.U. and the Soviet government and in the minds and hearts of Soviet Communists and all Soviet people. And this is not by chance. The centuries-old traditions of Slavic community have long since been augmented by the indestructible bonds of the joint struggle for the freedom, independence and social progress of our peoples.

Our parties and our peoples fought hand in hand against the danger of enslavement, against the Hitlerian invaders. More than 20,000,000 Soviet people gave their lives in mortal combat with fascism for the freedom and independence of the first socialist country and for the liberation of other enslaved peoples; the graves of more than 100,000 Soviet soldiers are scattered over Czechoslovak territory. Together with the heroic Czechoslovak patriots, together with the glorious corps of Ludvik Svoboda, these people battled to liberate Czechoslovakia from Hitlerian fascism. It was in those grim years that the sturdy foundations were laid for unity and brotherhood.

After the rout of the Hitlerites the Czechoslovak people chose the path to socialism. This still further consolidated the bonds of friendship between our peoples. The years of joint advance along the path of building socialism and communism have raised our friendship to a new level.

The fraternal friendship and military alliance between the Soviet Union and Czechoslovakia were sealed by the Treaty on Friendship, Mutual Aid and Postwar Cooperation, which was signed back in 1943 and renewed in 1963. True to this treaty, our states, our parties and peoples are obligated to come to each other's aid in the event of a threat to the security of our borders and a threat to the cause of socialism.

In response to the creation of the aggressive NATO bloc, which includes revanchist West Germany, a number of socialist countries in Europe united in the Warsaw Pact, which became an insuperable barrier to all those who would try to encroach upon peace and the socialist gains of our peoples.

For two decades the fraternal relations between the U.S.S.R. and Czechoslovakia developed successfully in all areas: in politics, in economics, in culture. Nothing clouded our friendship. The successes of the Czechoslovak people were our successes, and the working people of Czechoslovakia took the achievements of the Soviet peoples as their own.

During the period when Soviet people were marking the 50th anniversary of Soviet rule and were summarizing the results of the path traversed under the leadership of Lenin's Communist Party, the C.C.P. and the Czechoslovak people rejoiced together with us at the glorious results of October's victorious march.

Our peoples are linked by sincere and heartfelt bonds of friendship, respect and love. For every Soviet person the words "Czech" and "Slovak" have become synonymous with the concepts of "friend" and "brother." The Communists of the U.S.S.R. and the C.S.R. are united by a sense of duty as comrades-in-arms and like-minded people who are moving under one banner and have chosen for themselves one road for life — the road of communism. Soviet Communists have always felt profound respect for the Czechoslovak Communist Party as a reliable, steadfast, militant detachment of the world Commu-

nist movement, unshakable in its fidelity to Marxist-Leninist ideas and the
noble banner of proletarian internationalism.

Our party and the Soviet people are convinced that to this moment Czechoslovakia's working class, peasantry and honest intelligentsia have not changed
their attitude toward our common cause — the construction of a new society —
and that they are faithful in their friendly feelings for our people and for the
cause of socialism in the C.S.R. The 240,000,000 Soviet people who are building
a Communist society have also not changed their attitude toward Czechoslovakia and the Czechoslovak people. We, too, are faithful to the friendship our
parties have been strengthening throughout the postwar period.

I. — Our party took an understanding attitude toward the decisions of the
January, 1968, plenary session of the C.C.P. Central Committee. At the same
time it was already evident then that the situation that had taken shape could
lead to a weakening of the party of Czechoslovak Communists and to the
growth of sentiments dangerous to socialism among certain circles of Czechoslovak society that were under the influence of bourgeois views and imperialist
propaganda.

In the talks between C.P.S.U. leaders and Czechoslovak leaders held in
Moscow in January and in Prague in February, these apprehensions were
voiced openly, in a party spirit. At the same time it was stated in no uncertain
terms that the choice of paths of building socialism and the choice of forms
and methods of Party guidance of social processes were within the full and
exclusive competence of the C.C.P. Central Committee and that our party had
and could have no intention of imposing on the C.C.P. any recommendations
concerning these questions. Simultaneously, the attention of the C.C.P. Central
Committee leadership was directed to the already increased activity of right-
wing, revisionist elements, who were trying to exploit the situation that had
taken shape in the country for purposes far removed from the interests of socialism.

During this period the C.C.P. leaders stated that they were aware of the
tense political situation in the country and that they would take the necessary
measures to stabilize the situation. However, time passed, and with growing
anxiety our party became convinced that the actual course of events was starting
to differ increasingly from the predictions the Czechoslovak leaders had made.
Events showed that an atmosphere of disorder, vacillations and uncertainty was
beginning to take shape within the C.C.P. itself. Reactionary, antisocialist
forces supported by world imperialism were rearing their heads.

All this alarmed not only our party. The fraternal parties of Bulgaria, Hungary, the G.D.R. and Poland were as seriously disturbed as we were by the
course of events in Czechoslovakia. It became necessary to hold a collective
meeting and exchange opinions with the leaders of the C.C.P. and the C.S.R.
By mutual consent, this meeting was held on March 23 in Dresden.

At the Dresden meeting the Czechoslovak comrades did not deny that some
negative processes were developing in the country, that the radio, television
and press had broken away from party control and were in fact in the hands of

antisocialist elements and that right-wing forces were consolidating themselves. At the same time the Czechoslovak representatives stated that on the whole the party was in control of the situation and that there was no cause for serious alarm.

The Soviet representatives and all the delegations of the other fraternal parties noted with complete candor that they saw the picture in a different light. They pointed out the real danger in the situation that had taken shape. They concluded from all the facts that there was evidence of developments that could lead to a counterrevolutionary coup. The C.P.S.U. delegation, as well as the delegations of the Bulgarian Communist Party, the Hungarian Socialist Workers' Party, the Polish United Workers' Party and the Socialist Unity Party of Germany, stated that they supported the C.C.P. leadership and supported the positive substance of the January plenary session's decisions and that their whole stand was aimed at helping the Czechoslovak comrades to rebuff insolent antisocialist elements and to strengthen the positions of socialism in Czechoslovakia.

The course of events in the subsequent period confirmed the fraternal parties' conclusions and, unfortunately, failed to justify the optimism of the C.C.P. leaders. The March–April plenary session of the C.C.P. Central Committee was unable to stabilize the situation. Moreover, as life has shown, a number of propositions in the C.C.P. action program adopted at that plenary session were in fact used by the rightists as a sort of legal platform for further attacks on the Communist Party, the foundations of socialism and the friendship of the Czechoslovak and Soviet peoples.

Anxiety increased still further when, patently under the influence of rightist, antisocialist forces, a wide-scale campaign was launched in the country to discredit all the previous activity of the C.C.P.; when a process of mass replacement of party and state personnel developed on a wide scale, shattering the stability of the social system; when a clearly instigated wave of anti-Soviet propaganda rose in the press, radio and television; and when all sorts of organizations opposed to the Communist Party began to emerge and legalize their activities in the C.S.R. In this atmosphere the C.P.S.U. Central Committee deemed it necessary to take new steps to reemphasize its fears for the fate of socialism in Czechoslovakia. At the same time, needless to say, there was understanding both for the objective complexity of the situation and for the complexity of the position of the C.C.P. leadership itself. This was why the C.P.S.U. Central Committee, while continuing to abstain from making any public appraisals and statements, again proposed that a bilateral meeting be held. At this meeting, which was held in Moscow on May 4, the C.C.P. leaders themselves spoke of the seriousness of the situation in the country. Moreover, they said that the negative aspects of the internal political development in Czechoslovakia "exceed the bounds of purely internal affairs of ours and affect the fraternal countries, for example, the Soviet Union and Poland." It was impossible to disagree with this.

The Czechoslovak leaders also said they were ready to take the necessary measures to control the situation. At that time they said the following, word for word: "The enemy is acting. He wants to turn events in the interests of counterrevolution."

They admitted that the enemy was seeking primarily to discredit the Communist Party and weaken its influence on the masses, that increased demands were being made for creating a legal political opposition to the C.C.P. that by nature could only be an antisocialist opposition, and that "if firm steps are not taken, it could develop into a counterrevolutionary situation." They said they knew the specific people responsible for this and asserted that they had evidence of their connection with imperialist circles and that an end would be put to it.

At the May plenary session of the C.C.P. Central Committee it was admitted that the chief danger to the cause of socialism in Czechoslovakia comes from the right. This seemed to give grounds for hoping that the leaders of the C.C.P. Central Committee would pass from words to deeds. The readiness to undertake resolute defense of socialist gains was voiced at conferences of party committee secretaries, in the statewide *aktiv* of the workers' militia and at numerous meetings of plants and factory party organizations.

Unfortunately, the hopes of the healthy forces in the party and the country and the hopes of all the friends of the Czechoslovak people were not justified. The decisions of the May plenary session were not carried out. Antisocialist elements launched an offensive against the line of the May plenary session of the C.C.P. Central Committee. The manifestations of anti-Soviet elements became still sharper. The wave of the antisocialist forces' offensive rose still higher in late June, when the counterrevolutionary forces published in the press the statement "2,000 Words," which contained an open call for struggle against the C.C.P. and against constitutional rule.

The leadership of our party called A. Dubcek's attention to the danger of this document as a platform for further intensification of counterrevolutionary actions. He replied that the Presidium of the Central Committee was discussing this question and that the severest appraisal of the statement would be given and the most resolute measures taken. But aside from a liberal verbal denunciation, no practical measures really followed.

All this compelled the C.P.S.U. and the other fraternal parties to raise the question of another meeting with the C.C.P. leaders. The C.P.S.U. and the other fraternal parties made a proposal to the C.C.P. Central Committee to this effect, but, unfortunately, the Central Committee leaders declined to take part in the conference in Warsaw.

Thus, during the past seven months the Soviet and Czechoslovak leaders and the leaders of the other fraternal parties have had numerous and varied types of contacts, in the course of which the C.P.S.U. Central Committee has steadfastly taken a consistent and clear stand.

What, in brief, is the gist of this stand?

First, the C.P.S.U. Central Committee from the very beginning took an understanding attitude toward the decisions of the C.C.P. Central Committee aimed at correcting errors and shortcomings, perfecting party guidance of every sphere of public life and developing socialist democracy. We regarded and continue to regard these decisions as the exclusive internal affair of the Czechoslovak Communists and all the working people in the C.S.R.

Second, the C.P.S.U. Central Committee has constantly emphasized that successful implementation of the decisions adopted can be guaranteed only through realization of the party's leading role and preservation of full party control over developments. In this connection attention was repeatedly called to the fact that a weakening of party leadership creates favorable conditions for the increased activity of rightists and even overtly counterrevolutionary forces, which make it their task to discredit the Czechoslovak Communist Party and remove it from power, to wrest the C.S.R. from the socialist commonwealth and ultimately to change the social system in Czechoslovakia.

Third, the C.P.S.U. Central Committee contended and still contends that fate of the Czechoslovak people's socialist gains and of Czechoslovakia as a socialist state linked by alliance commitments to our country and the other fraternal countries is not merely the C.C.P.'s internal affair. It is the common affair of the entire commonwealth of socialist countries and the entire Communist movement. This is why the C.P.S.U. Central Committee believes its international duty lies in taking every measure to promote the strengthening of the C.C.P., the preservation and consolidation of socialism in the C.S.R. and the defense of Czechoslovakia against imperialism's intrigues. It is our international duty and the international duty of all the fraternal parties to do so, and we would cease to be Communists if we refused to discharge it.

Such is the principled stand of the Communist Party of the Soviet Union — a stand based on the principles of Marxism-Leninism and proletarian internationalism.

II. — The first and foremost point arousing serious alarm and concern is the position in which the Czechoslovak Communist Party has found itself — especially because without strengthening the Communist Party and without materially ensuring its leadership role in all spheres of public life, any talk of "perfecting" socialism inevitably becomes fraudulent.

In past months the counterrevolutionary forces in Czechoslovakia have been steadfastly waging a campaign to discredit the Communist Party. As a result, a real threat has been created that it will lose its leading position in society. The activation of anti-Communist forces was promoted by the incorrect stand taken by a segment of the C.C.P. leadership and its deviation in a number of questions from Marxist-Leninist principles. It was precisely the repeated calls by certain C.C.P. leaders "to put an end to the Communists' monopoly on power," "to separate the party from the government" and to establish "equality" between the C.C.P. and other political parties, calls to repudiate party leadership of the state, the economy, culture, etc., that served as the original impetus for the unbridled campaign against the Czechoslovak Communist Party, a campaign led by forces seeking to wreck the C.C.P. and deprive it of its leading role in society.

As is known, the attacks on the party began under the guise of talk, by some C.C.P. leaders among others, about the necessity to put an end to "outmoded" methods of work and adapt it to the demands of the present day. It is clear that the party is a living organism developing as the whole society develops and that the forms and methods of party work and party leadership can and must change in accordance with the changes taking place in society. But in the case under discussion this was not the point. The point was that this talk in fact led to the undermining of the fundamental principles of the work done by the political organization these leaders were called upon to lead and strengthen.

Only this can account for the fact that in Czechoslovakia both the self-criticism necessary in every party and critical assessments of certain measures quickly developed into an unrestrained and dangerous campaign to discredit the party's entire work. Taking advantage of the indecisive, vacillating position of the C.C.P. Central Committee, the revisionists and rightist forces engaged in wholesale smearing of the C.C.P.'s entire work over the past 20 years, thereby denying its right to lead society and the state.

The following facts show how far matters have gone.

An article by one Liehm, printed on June 13, 1968, in the weekly Literarni Listy, said: "The C.C.P. bears the responsibility for all the mistakes of the 20 years since February, 1948, for all the diseases and crimes in society." He went on to say: "The C.C.P. is performing its leadership role although it has neither the moral nor the political right to do so."

·Meanwhile, Hanzelka, an active spokesman for the antiparty forces, alleged in the June 9 issue of the newspaper Mlada Fronta that 1,500,000 C.C.P. members had become fanatics who were supposedly exploited by a few party "despots" in the interests of their own personal power.

At a rally of the Klub Mlodych in Semily, a certain Temicek wailed hysterically: "The Czechoslovak Communist Party must be regarded as the criminal organization it really was and it must be thrown out of public life." And these wails were immediately published in Literarni Listy.

Tens, if not hundreds, of statements with similar content could be cited. And this whole stream of hysterical wails openly hostile to communism and socialism has bombarded the working people every day.

Unfortunately, some leaders of the C.C.P. Central Committee did not draw the necessary conclusions from the fact that the country was being swept by a fierce anti-Communist campaign organized by counterrevolutionary forces and patently inspired by imperialist propaganda. Instead of resolutely obstructing efforts to wreck the party, they continue to lead matters to the point of transforming the C.C.P. into an amorphous, incompetent organization, a kind of discussion club.

The chief Leninist principles of the organization of party life — the principles of democratic centralism and the party's ideological-organizational unity — have begun, in effect, to be violated in the C.C.P. The party has found itself on the threshold of legalizing factional groupings and disintegrating into "autonomous," weakly connected organizations.

Everyone who has studied the history of the Communist movement and who is familiar with V. I. Lenin's theoretical legacy knows well that only a Marxist party all of whose organizations and members are guided by the principle of democratic centralism can be viable. Disregard for either side of this principle — democracy or centralism — inevitably leads to the weakening of the party and its leading role and to the transformation of the party into either a bureaucratic organization or some kind of enlightenment society.

It was evident from press reports that the revisionist elements in the party were hatching a plan to create a situation within the C.C.P. that would turn it into a loose and formless organization deprived of Leninist party norms, party discipline and responsibility.

Proposals began to be made on introducing some sort of principle of autonomy for party bodies and organizations, i.e., in the new party situation to reinforce their right to take their own stands with regard to decisions by higher bodies. Moreover, it was proposed that certain components of the party not be linked by community of discipline; it was proposed that they be voluntarily linked by "associative ties" "as cooperatively unified organizations formed from below." This would mean turning the party into some sort of "association" whose members are free to join as the fancy takes them. This thesis can be regarded as nothing other than a call for breaking up the party.

The attack on the unity of party ranks was also waged along other lines. Representatives of rightist forces persistently sought to reinforce in the Statutes "the right of minority and group views," i.e., the right to oppose party decisions after they have already been adopted.

All these aspirations are in striking opposition to Leninist principles of party organization. Let us recall Lenin's formulation of the question of party unity in the resolution that Lenin proposed to the Tenth Congress of the Russian Communist Party (Bolsheviks) and that was adopted by the Congress. It stated: "It is imperative that all politically conscious workers clearly realize the harmful and inadmissible nature of any factionalism whatever, which inevitably leads in fact to the enfeeblement of harmonious work and to intensified and repeated attempts by the ruling party's enemies in its own camp to deepen the division and exploit it for purposes of counterrevolution."

Unfortunately, even among members of the Presidium of the C.C.P. Central Committee there were those who in essence openly opposed the Leninist principles of party construction. The particular reference here is to public statements on these questions made by J. Spacek, a member of the Presidium of the C.C.P. Central Committee.

It is well known that the world's reactionaries have not ceased their efforts to take advantage of any weakening in the unity of Communist Party ranks to intensify attacks on Communists and on socialism. In these conditions to undermine the unity of the party is to help our class enemies.

III. — The mass campaign that was being carried out in the country to quash party cadres also resulted in undermining the C.C.P.'s leadership role. Criticism of individual leaders who had made certain mistakes grew into an indiscriminate demand for the mass elimination of party executives. In the center and the localities many experienced people were dismissed who were devoted to the cause of the party and the working class, who fought courageously against fascism during the Hitlerian occupation and who took active part in the construction of socialism in Czechoslovakia. The atmosphere of a real pogrom, a "moral execution" of cadres, was created.

A definite political line could be clearly traced — that of the removal from active political life of Communists who were the most ideologically and politically tempered and who were taking resolute stands against the right-wing opposition. There is no other way to evaluate, for example, the statement by C. Cisar, Secretary of the C.C.P. Central Committee, who urged that between 200,000 and 300,000 young people be admitted to the C.C.P., so as to give a "shot in the arm" to the "aging" party, as he put it, while ignoring the class aspect of this important question.

The policy of the mass rout of executive personnel affected not only the party apparatus. It was also extended to important links in the state apparatus, to trade unions and to the youth league. Most of the members of the government were replaced. Among those dismissed were quite a few officials whom the C.C.P. leaders had characterized even after the January plenary session as reliable and steadfast Communists.

It was publicly announced that the Communists who were expelled from leading party and state bodies had in the past made mistakes in their work. But to what extent was it right on these grounds to raise the question of political mistrust of thousands of officials and to exclude people from political life in effect only because they had taken active part in the life of the party and the country before the January plenary session?

It could be hoped that the Presidium of the C.C.P. Central Committee would use the preparations for the 14th Extraordinary Party Congress, scheduled for Sept. 9, to put an end to the defamation of cadres. But this did not happen. On the contrary, the preparations for the congress were used by the rightist forces to increase their thrusts against the healthy forces in the party, plant their people in district and province party organizations and impose their policy on the party.

The press, which was controlled by the rightists, openly meddled in the election of delegates to party conferences and the congress and even published "recommendations" on who should or should not be elected to the future C.C.P. Central Committee — an obvious attempt to exert intolerable pressure on the delegates to the future congress.

This was how matters stood. The party is not an abstract concept. The party is the people and principles that ensure the unity of action of Communists. And when the principles of party life were being discarded, when party cadres were being defamed, it was valid to conclude that the Czechoslovak Communist Party was in danger.

Equally dangerous to the cause of socialism in Czechoslovakia was the fact that, in addition to the sharp weakening of organizational-political work, the C.C.P. leadership in effect yielded control over the means of ideological influence on the masses to rightist, antisocialist forces. Many newspapers and radio and television in Czechoslovakia were essentially at the disposal of certain groupings that were pursuing patently antisocialist objectives. The facts provide irrefutable proof that these groupings were acting with the clear purpose of seeking to discredit the C.C.P. and socialism.

Publications such as Literarni Listy, Mlada Fronta, Prace, Lidova Demokracie, Svobodne Slovo, Zemedelske Noviny, The Student and The Reporter conducted the most unbridled antisocialist propaganda.

The Czechoslovak working people stated outright that the mass propaganda media were being used not in the interests of the Czechoslovak people but to their detriment. For example, participants in the nationwide meeting of the Czechoslovak *aktiv* of the workers' militia pointed out that party leadership and the propaganda organs were not taking measures against the action of reactionary elements. The workers adopted a resolution, and it was no accident that they deemed it necessary to take this resolution to the Soviet Embassy and ask that it be transmitted to Moscow. However, such a significant meeting of workers' representatives failed to receive the proper coverage in the Czechoslovak press, and the message sent by this meeting to the Soviet people was long concealed from Czechoslovakia's working people.

Many Czechoslovak comrades made attempts to take up this question in the press, but they were not allowed to do so. Comrade Jodas, an old underground Communist, only with difficulty found an opportunity to publish his protest against the actions of the rightist, antisocialist forces that were trying to monopolize the mass news media. Here are his words: "At present a certain reactionary group in the party, well organized and with all the news media in its possession, is waging the most flagrant attack on the party over television and radio and in the press. For five months this group, in which various reactionary elements actively operate, has been waging this campaign, which must inevitably lead to the destruction of party unity. This group must be resolutely and openly opposed, after branding it and unmasking its intentions before the eyes of the public."

The situation that had taken shape in the news organs aroused legitimate concern among the working people of the C.S.R. The workers at the Auto-Praha Plant wrote in their July 18 letter: "We categorically oppose the fact that an acrimonious atmosphere against the U.S.S.R., the socialist countries and the party has been created on radio, in the press and on television. We [too] are chilled with fear for our country's future."

In short, a situation had been created in Czechoslovakia wherein the rightists could openly make antisocialist statements in the press and hold demonstrations and rallies under their counterrevolutionary slogans, while statements assessing the situation in the country from a Marxist-Leninist standpoint were silenced, and their authors persecuted.

It can be said that the baiting of honest Communists, the discrediting of the party, and the attacks on Marxism-Leninism, proletarian internationalism and the fraternal friendship between the Soviet and Czechoslovak peoples were carried out under the eyes of the C.C.P. Central Committee.

The denigration of the Communist Party, particularly its activities in the past 20 years, the beatings of cadres, the placement of mass news media at the disposal of elements attacking the party and the violation of the principle of democratic centralism — all this demoralized the broad masses of Communists, caused them to lose hope and confidence, produced confusion in party bodies and at the same time promoted intensification of the rightists' influence and the increased activity of counterrevolutionary forces.

IV. — The reactionaries' effort to wreck the Communist Party and weaken the positions of socialism in Czechoslovakia was accompanied by a large-scale offensive against Marxist-Leninist ideology. Methodicalness and purposefulness are clearly discernible in the actions undertaken by the enemies of socialism. They acted from different positions, but they were pursuing the same objective — to undermine the Communists' ideological-theoretical base and to replace scientific socialism with different ideological concepts.

The pages of the Czechoslovak press were eagerly made available for the publication of creations by overt opponents of Marxism-Leninism. Suffice it to recall that many Czechoslovak newspapers and magazines carried articles by the not unknown Trotskyite Isaac Deutscher and excerpts from his book.

But the antisocialist forces in Czechoslovakia did not stop here.

One may recall the so-called "Memorandum From the People of Czechoslovakia," composed by the organizational committee of the "Party of Czechoslovak Fair Socialists," as they have dubbed themselves, which was mentioned on June 14 in the newspaper Mlada Fronta. With overt insolence the authors of this diatribe proclaimed: "The law we adopt must ban all Communist activity in Czechoslovakia. We shall ban C.C.P. activity and disband the C.C.P." The authors urged that the classics of Marxism-Leninism be destroyed.

The Hitlerites who burned Marxist books in the squares of German cities would have eagerly signed these demands.

With natural anxiety Deputy Turosek asked the following question on this point in the National Assembly: "When and how will the struggle begin in our country against such manifestations reviling the Communist Party and Communists?"

Certain figures in the Czechoslovak Communist Party were among those who took part in the offensive against Marxism-Leninism being waged in the C.S.R.

An overtly revisionist speech that C. Cisar, Secretary of the C.C.P. Central Committee, delivered at a ceremonial meeting in Prague devoted to the 150th anniversary of Karl Marx's death was widely publicized throughout the country. To expose the essence of this speech, it boils down to a repudiation of Leninism, a denial of its international significance and a denial of the premise that Leninism is a guide to action in present-day conditions.

Unfortunately, some C.C.P. leaders did not pluck up the courage to criticize this speech and defend the ideological foundations of the Communist movement in Czechoslovakia. Moreover, a widespread campaign was launched in Czechoslovakia attacking the Soviet press for voicing protests against the latest subverters of Marxism-Leninism.

Incidentally, C. Cisar's speech was far from the only attack on Leninism. Similar assertions could be found in other publications that have recently appeared in Czechoslovakia.

And this is not surprising, for an atmosphere was created in Czechoslovakia that made it fashionable and advantageous to assail Marxism-Leninism and dangerous to uphold the fundamental propositions of Communist doctrine.

What is the explanation for this? The lack of theoretical discrimination on the part of certain leaders or deliberate indulgence toward those who would like to deprive the party of its theoretical weapons, who would like to demolish the base of the C.C.P.'s ideological solidarity with the other detachments of the world Communist movement?

We are well aware of how essential it is constantly to develop Marxist-Leninist theory and generalize and analyze the new processes and phenomena of life. Marxism-Leninism would be dead if in every historical era it did not develop through the collective efforts of its theorists and followers. However, it is perfectly clear that the above-mentioned statements were aimed not at developing Marxism but at revising and subverting it.

Yet the C.C.P. leaders did nothing to defend the ideological positions of the Communist Party.

Unquestionably the erosion of these positions was also promoted by the phenomenon of the uncritical, nonclass approach taken to some pages of the country's history, an approach that was becoming increasingly widespread in Czechoslovakia.

After all, it is a fact that there has been a recent revival of the cult of Masaryk, who was always a sworn enemy of the Communist movement and was an instigator of the intervention against Soviet Russia. It is a strange development when even some Communists in Czechoslovakia laud a bourgeois figure at whose instructions the Czechoslovak Communist Party was persecuted and warrants were issued for the arrest of its leaders, including Klement Gottwald. Benes, who led the country to Munich, is also being made a hero again.

Is it with this history, is it with these figures that a socialist country's press should be concerned, the press of a party with its own glorious revolutionary history full of heroism, valor and courage displayed in the struggle for the people's freedom and the independence of the homeland? It is difficult to comprehend why the Czechoslovak press recently has left virtually unmentioned the outstanding leaders and organizers of the Communist Party, the internationalists, the heroes of the workers' and Communist movement who gave their lives in the struggle against the Hitlerian occupiers, in the struggle for socialism and for strengthening the friendship between our peoples.

On the other hand, articles have appeared that have been monstrous in their political cynicism, such as the article by one Mlynirek in the Aug. 15 issue of Literarni Listy; the article attempts to denigrate the entire history of the C.C.P., especially after the socialist revolution in Czechoslovakia, and to slander Klement Gottwald and entire generations of heroic fighters in the Czechoslovak Communist Party.

And one more circumstance. Considerable efforts have been made lately in Czechoslovakia to inflame sentiments among the people that can only be called nationalistic. This was precisely the point of a vociferous propaganda campaign artificially organized in late July to support the stand of the Presidium of the C.C.P. Central Committee at the forthcoming talks with the Politburo of the C.P.S.U. Central Committee. The message published in the Czechoslovak press, in this connection to the C.C.P. delegation, which was en route to the meeting, served to inflame just such base nationalistic passions.

Certain leaders of the C.C.P. Central Committee did everything possible to popularize this document. It was discussed in addresses on television, its authors were received with special warmth, and leading functionaries demonstratively appeared on the streets, where signatures were being collected to sign the text of the message. Can this be considered a normal method of preparing for talks with a friendly fraternal party?

The most serious point is that the mass campaign whipped up in Czechoslovakia by these contrived methods was directed not against the class enemies of Czechoslovakia's working people, not against those who really threatened the republic's security, not against the imperialists. It was directed, monstrous as it may seem, against the closest friends of socialist Czechoslovakia, against the Soviet Union and other fraternal socialist countries.

In this connection the following question arises: If the C.S.R.'s leaders did not want to take into account the ideas of their friends, if they did not want to heed their voices, if they did not want to travel a common road with them, then toward whom did they intend to orient themselves, with whom did they want to travel? And where did they want to seek a guarantee of the Czechoslovak people's security, sovereignty and socialist gains against attacks by imperialism?

Incidentally, in the aforementioned message, around which a noisy campaign was launched, something else deserves attention, and one cannot help attaching great importance to it: The text of the message, which lists the historical stages of Czechoslovakia's development, completely ignores February, 1948, when Czechoslovakia turned to socialism. To those who have at all been following developments in the country in recent months, it is perfectly clear that this omission was not fortuitous and that it reflects a definite political concept.

Apparently some C.C.P. leaders assumed that by stirring up nationalistic passions it would be possible to gain wider support for their position from broad strata of the population, including rightists and including opponents of socialism. But this is a very dangerous path. Dangerous primarily because it led them farther and farther away from those who are the natural allies and real friends of the C.C.P. and the Czechoslovak people.

V. — The opponents of Soviet-Czechoslovak friendship made wide use in their arguments of one other theme, which must be dealt with. The ideas ran persistently through numerous press articles and radio and television statements that all Czechoslovakia's "woes" were related to the circumstance that until recently it was guided in its development by what someone called "the Soviet model of socialism."

It is hardly necessary to explain that this allegation is pure invention.

It is well known that the U.S.S.R. and Czechoslovakia have different state structures, that the forms of solving the national question differ in many ways, and that the systems of national-economic management are not the same. Many other questions of our peoples' political, economic and cultural life are also solved in different ways.

Czechoslovakia's development as a socialist state, the development of its state system, its economy and culture and the development of its Communist Party have proceeded and continue to proceed in forms that reflect the country's characteristics, traditions and specific attributes in all respects. Talk of the "imposition" of some kind of "Soviet model of socialism" on the Czechs and Slovaks is nothing but a malevolent and provocative lie spread by hostile elements for the purpose of undermining the fraternal friendship that links our countries, our parties and our peoples.

The forces that attempted to undermine the C.C.P.'s positions are seeking in every possible way to denigrate the economic cooperation between the Soviet Union and Czechoslovakia. They did everything possible to present the matter as if the economic ties that have taken shape between our countries are disadvantageous and, moreover, burdensome to Czechoslovakia. It is perfectly obvious what such statements are designed to do. They all serve one purpose: to prepare the groundwork for reorienting the C.S.R.'s economic development toward the West. But in order to do so they had to convince the Czechoslovak public that the C.S.R. cannot solve its problems by developing cooperation with the Soviet Union and other socialist countries and that this cooperation supposedly fails to meet its national interests.

In reality the experience of socialist construction indicates that the socialist countries' economic relations are relations of a new type and that their development contributes to the economic and social progress of each country individually and to the strengthening of the world socialist system as a whole.

On the basis of the principles of proletarian internationalism, the socialist countries for the first time in history accomplished a transition to comprehensive cooperation and mutual aid, participating in this process as completely sovereign and equal states. Now no one can ever again put the yoke of imperialist exploitation around their necks. This is an enormous achievement of our socialist commonwealth, and at the same time it has been the basis on which it proved possible to effect rapid development of the socialist states' economies.

In the 17 years between 1950 and 1967, the volume of industrial output produced by the C.M.E.A. [Council for Mutual Economic Aid] countries as a whole increased 440% and reached almost one-third of world industrial output. In the past seven years alone the increase in the C.M.E.A. countries' industrial output has totaled 76%, while it has not exceeded 45% in the developed capitalist countries.

The wide-scale development of economic cooperation and the intensification of the international division of labor within the framework of the world socialist system were conditioned not only by the economic needs of individual socialist countries but also by the nature of the international situation and the conditions of the struggle between the two world systems.

Nevertheless, a number of statesmen in Czechoslovakia, including O. Sik, vice-chairman of the government, and some others, have criticized Czecho-slovakia's economic development and its cooperation with other socialist countries. Criticism, of course, is a necessary thing. But it must satisfy two criteria: It must be scientific and objective and it must meet the interests of the working people and the interests of socialism. Yet O. Sik criticized Czecho-slovakia's economy as backward and in a state of crisis. The whole path of Czechoslovakia's economic development during the period of socialism was crossed out and smeared with black paint.

At the same time the Czechoslovak press tried to make the working class and the whole population of Czechoslovakia believe that the allegedly incorrect economic policy pursued by the C.C.P. afforded no possibilities of increasing the people's well-being and that it is better to live in the capitalist countries.

However, it is well known that in output of electric power, steel, cement, fabrics, footwear, meat and meat products, Czechoslovakia is ahead of the developed capitalist countries of Europe, including Britain, West Germany and others. Czechoslovakia has developed a machine-building industry and is among the world's leaders in per capita machine production.

The press indirectly, and sometimes even directly, linked the exaggerated shortcomings in Czechoslovak economic development to Czechoslovakia's economic relations with the Soviet Union. The trade between the C.S.R. and the U.S.S.R. was pictured in a disadvantageous light.

Let us take some figures on the foreign trade between the Soviet Union and Czechoslovakia in the 1956–1968 period, i.e., over the past 12 years. During this period the Soviet Union delivered to Czechoslovakia 17,000,000 tons of grain, almost 700,000 tons of cotton, about 70,000 tons of wool, 51,000,000 tons of petroleum, 80,000,000 tons of ore, about 2,000,000 tons of pig iron, about 2,500,000 tons of rolled metal, 285,000 tons of copper, more than 200,000 tons of aluminum, more than 200,000 tons of lead, almost 3,500,000 tons of apatite concentrate, 170,000 tons of zinc, more than 200,000 tons of asbestos, almost 5,000,000 cubic meters of milled lumber and almost 1,200,000,000 rubles' worth of machinery and equipment. If Czechoslovakia had had to purchase all these commodities for free currency, it would have been forced to spend about $3,500,000,000.

At the same time, Czechoslovakia is a major supplier to the Soviet Union of machinery and consumer goods, such as footwear, fabrics, clothing, haber-dashery items and other commodities.

Needless to say, if the Soviet Union switched over to a purely commercial basis in its trade with Czechoslovakia — which is in effect what O. Sik was urging — this obviously would not benefit Czechoslovakia's economy and would create many difficulties in the national economy.

In Czechoslovakia criticism was unleashed of the entire international experience of socialist construction provided by the Soviet Union's half-century of practice, as well as the long practice of socialist states. They tried to oppose to this experience a new "model of socialism," which exists only in arguments, and some people who made a lot of noise about sovereignty and noninterference would like to pass off this model as an example for universal imitation.

Our party cannot ignore the campaign conducted in the Czechoslovak press to discredit the Soviet Union's socialist national economy.

The development of the socialist economy is one of the most important tasks constantly occupying the center of attention for our party, as well as for other fraternal parties. In maintaining close ties with the economies of other socialist countries, the Soviet Union takes the necessary measures to see that the U.S.S.R.'s economic development simultaneously meets the national-economic needs of our friends and allies and provides opportunities for their economic development with the least possible dependence on capitalist countries or dangers of any sort proceeding from imperialism.

History has evolved in such a way that the Soviet Union bears enormous responsibility for the security of the socialist camp. Therefore it is natural that, in developing our economy, we are always compelled to allocate enormous investments to the defense industry, which is needed not only by the Soviet Union but also by all the socialist countries and which today makes it possible to repulse the imperialist aggression against Vietnam and against the Arab states.

We know that other fraternal countries are also making their contributions to the cause of defending the peoples' socialist gains. We all see this as our internationalist duty.

Our party constantly perfects the style, forms and methods of party and state construction.

This same work is also being done in other socialist countries. It is being done peacefully, proceeding from the bases of the socialist system.

Unfortunately, in Czechoslovakia the discussion of questions of economic reform proceeded on a different basis. In the center of this discussion were, on the one hand, sweeping criticism of the entire previous development of the socialist economy, and on the other, proposals for replacing principles of planning with unregulated market relations, giving private capital broad scope for activity. The economic debate in the C.S.R. was used by revisionist and counterrevolutionary elements for the clear purpose of turning the country's economy onto the capitalist path.

VI. — Some C.S.R. leaders began to revise a number of important foreign-policy principles and C.S.R. commitments adopted in accordance with the Warsaw Pact and the bilateral treaty with the Soviet Union.

Under the Soviet-Czechoslovak treaty our countries committed themselves to unite their efforts and cooperate closely in safeguarding their security and the security of the other states of the socialist commonwealth. These commitments, together with the commitments of the other socialist states made under bilateral treaties and the Warsaw Pact, constitute a sturdy foundation that reliably safeguards the security of each of the pact members.

The Warsaw Pact countries mutually undertook a solemn commitment — to stand up in defense of the gains of socialism, in defense of their borders and in defense of peace in Europe.

The Soviet Union has contended and continues to contend that these commitments must be fulfilled as sacred by all the participants in the treaties, and that only thus can the security of each be guaranteed. Hitherto, the U.S.S.R. thought that Czechoslovakia took the same attitude toward its commitments under these treaties.

However, certain tendencies have recently manifested themselves in the area of Czechoslovakia's foreign policy — especially in European affairs — that are cause for serious apprehensions. These tendencies have manifested themselves not only in Czechoslovak press articles and in radio and television broadcasts, but also in the speeches of some officials. In particular, they were demonstrated quite definitely in statements made by Foreign Minister J. Hajek. Those involved more frequent calls for revising Czechoslovak foreign policy.

Definite attempts were made to deal a blow to the Warsaw Pact and impair this pact. V. Prchlik, a responsible representative of the C.C.P. Central Committee, made a public statement to journalists in Prague in which he lashed out at the Warsaw Pact and said it was necessary to revise its structure. He went on to defame the activities of the Warsaw Pact states' Political Consultative Committee, whose work, as is known, is conducted on the level of party and government leaders. It was to be expected that these actions would be condemned by the leadership of the C.C.P. Central Committee, but this did not happen.

This is our common question, the question of the participants in the Warsaw Treaty Organization. It is impossible to tolerate a breach in this organization. Such a line contradicts the vital interests of all the member countries of the Warsaw Treaty Organization, including the vital interests of the U.S.S.R.

The commitments the socialist states undertook in the treaties among them demand that the parties to these treaties ensure the vigorous protection of their borders. What is the situation here with respect to Czechoslovakia's western borders? On the Czechoslovak side these borders are, in effect, open.

A situation has been created where saboteurs and spies, sent in from Western countries by imperialist intelligence services, have been flooding Czechoslovakia. Imperialist agents have had a chance to transport weapons into Czechoslovakia secretly.

Serious concern has been aroused by the statements made in the course of recent events by some figures in Czechoslovakia on the question of Czechoslovakia's relations with West Germany.

The Czechoslovak leaders are aware that West Germany does not recognize and does not intend to recognize the borders established in Europe, including those between the G.D.R. and the F.R.G., that it continues to demand recognition of its right to speak "on behalf of all Germans," that it still makes claims on West Berlin and has been organizing all sorts of provocations there and that the F.R.G. government has still not declared that it completely renounces access to nuclear weapons and has still not declared that the Munich Pact was invalid from the very outset.

Nevertheless, statements have been made in Czechoslovakia that were aimed at a rapprochement with West Germany and at strengthening ties with it.

Matters reached the point where it was officially stated on behalf of the Czecho-slovak government that the C.S.R.'s policy in European affairs must be largely determined by the fact that Czechoslovakia is situated between the Soviet Un-ion and West Germany.

But such an approach is completely devoid of class content, contradicts the whole of historical experience and is inconsonant with the interests of the se-curity of the socialist countries and Czechoslovakia itself.

Some figures in Czechoslovakia urged that its foreign policy be reoriented toward the West and that it be made "more independent" of the policies of the Soviet Union and the other socialist countries. It is not difficult to discern that behind the word "independence" they wanted to conceal the desire to wrest Czechoslovakia's foreign policy from the unified policy of the countries in the socialist commonwealth.

Unfortunately, such declarations failed to receive the proper rebuff in the C.S.R.

Our common interests, including the interests of fraternal Czechoslovakia, are met not by weakening but by strengthening the Warsaw Pact members' cooperation in questions of European security and international policy in gen-eral. This obligates the pact members to deal a resolute rebuff to any provo-cational attempts to demand that the Warsaw Pact be broken up.

Attention is called to instances of an inadmissible attitude toward Czecho-slovakia's Warsaw Pact commitments in connection with the Warsaw Pact countries' staff exercises recently held on Czechoslovak territory. A hostile campaign was launched against the presence in Czechoslovakia of the socialist countries' military units that had been brought in for the period of the staff exercises. The presence of Soviet troop contingents was depicted by antiso-cialist and rightist forces as an occupation of Czechoslovak territory. Now, does this look like respect for the alliance commitments under the Warsaw Pact? No. It looks more like an effort to hamper the practical functioning of the Warsaw Treaty Organization's military mechanism. A side that takes into consideration the alliance commitments it has assumed cannot do this. A side that disregards these commitments can act this way. The Warsaw Pact mem-bers could not help drawing the appropriate conclusions from this.

Recent developments show that anti-Soviet propaganda and anti-Soviet mani-festations have clearly been on the increase in Czechoslovakia. One may recall the provocational assemblage on May 2 in Stare Mesto [Old Town] Square, where some speakers made anti-Soviet statements. One may recall the insult-ing speeches by Prochazka, Hanzelka and a number of other people of that ilk. One may recall the numerous press, radio and television statements whose authors did everything in their power to denigrate friendly Soviet-Czechoslovak relations. In recent years even the capitalist states have rarely delivered attacks and insults such as those that have emanated from Czechoslovakia. The ene-mies used any pretext — be it the Sejna case or the speculation surrounding the circumstances of Jan Masaryk's death, or the maneuvers of the Warsaw Pact army — to pour oil on the flames of anti-Soviet sentiments. Instances occurred where anti-Soviet leaflets were circulated in the cities and the Soviet flag was desecrated. Needless to say, such acts could not be conducive to an improvement in our relations.

Whose interests were served by sowing the seeds of hostility toward the Soviet Union? Solely the interests of those who want to eradicate from the Czechoslovak people's memory our joint struggle against Hitlerism, those to whom the Czech and Slovak peoples' socialist gains are not dear, those who would like to liquidate the achievements of world socialism. As has always been true, anti-Sovietism and anti-Communism go hand in hand and supplement each other.

The C.S.R. leaders have more than once made statements about the firmness of Czechoslovak-Soviet friendship. Sincere alarm for the state of our relations was voiced at the May plenary session of the C.C.P. Central Committee. But no effective measures were taken to combat the bourgeois-nationalist wave and anti-Soviet manifestations in Czechoslovakia. Of course, fine words can be said about friendship and solidarity and about fidelity to an ally's duty; however, what is important is not the words but what lies behind them, what is important is the concrete actions that follow the declarations.

There is no question that the inspirers of the hostile anti-Soviet campaign will fail to obliterate the truth that Czechoslovakia can preserve its independence and sovereignty only as a socialist country, as a member of the socialist commonwealth.

Reactionary forces, in seeking to undermine the C.S.R.'s relations with the U.S.S.R. and the other socialist countries, were thereby preparing for the Czechoslovak people the destiny of slavery in the imperialist yoke.

VII. — Counterrevolutionary, antisocialist organizations recently have become established and have started to operate actively in Czechoslovakia; they have a definite social base, they rest on support from abroad, and they make increasingly open claims to power. In effect a political opposition took shape in the country that was called upon to restore the capitalist order in Czechoslovakia.

For 20 years non-Communist parties belonging to the National Front have existed in the C.S.R. The leaderships of these parties pursued a policy of building socialism, and through their activities they promoted the enlistment in constructive work of certain non-Communist forces in the country. However, in the past seven months radical changes have occurred in the policies of these parties. The leaderships of the People's and Socialist Parties changed their courses drastically and, in effect, although still covering up by using slogans of cooperation with the C.C.P. within the framework of the National Front, brought matters to the point of creating a legal opposition. In provisional program documents the leaderships of both non-Communist parties voiced claims to equal participation with the Communist Party in the exercise of power. But that was in the spring, while as early as July it was no longer concealed that something else was involved — ousting the Communist Party from power and creating a new, non-Communist leadership of the country.

The role the Czechoslovak Social Democratic Party played in the past is common knowledge. In splitting the ranks of the working class, the right-wing leadership of the C.S.D.P. rendered extremely vigorous support to the reactionaries in their struggle against the Communists and served as a reliable bulwark for the bourgeois system.

In 1948, when honest revolutionary elements in the Social Democratic Party united with the Communists, the C.S.D.P. ceased to exist. However, this year, despite the fact that the National Front and the C.C.P. Central Committee adopted a decision banning the creation of a Social Democratic Party, such a party began in fact to be reconstituted.

On June 12 a document was widely circulated in Prague under the title "The Position of the City Preparatory Committee of the Czechoslovak Social Democratic Party on the Present Political Situation." The document stated that the Social Democratic Party was returning to political life after a 20-year hiatus and that it allegedly had not ceased to exist either from the legal standpoint or as "an expression of a certain concrete political concept." The merger with the C.C.P. in June, 1948, was declared "invalid."

On June 21, 1968, in Prague the preparatory committee of the Czechoslovak Social Democratic Party held a meeting in which representatives of the Social Democrats from individual provinces in Bohemia and Moravia took part. Subsequently, province and district committees and hundreds of primary organizations of the Social Democratic Party were created. The party began to operate, and to operate against the Czechoslovak Communist Party.

In the past seven months many varied groups and organizations with antisocialist tendencies have sprung up in Czechoslovakia. These organizations have claimed the role of centers of opposition and have done less and less to hide the fact that their goal has been to liquidate the socialist system.

The 231 Club, for example, was an overt counterrevolutionary organization; the club was headed by such people as the old fascist Brodsky; the former bourgeois general Palecek; the imperialist intelligence agents Rambousek and Cech, who were once convicted of espionage; and others. All of them are experienced, vicious enemies of socialism.

The Club of Non-Party Activists was another patently antisocialist organization; it operated with exceptional vigor and sought to enlist the intelligentsia, workers and servicemen in its ranks. Ivan Svitak, who in the past was expelled from the C.C.P., became the ideological leader of the club. He devised the organization's strategy and tactics. In his lengthy statement published in the magazine Reporter, Svitak painted a whole picture of the step-by-step elimination of Communists from power and the anti-Communists' advent to power through the device of special parliamentary elections.

The 231 Club and the Club of Non-Party Activists are far from the only organizations with antisocialist tendencies, and, moreover, they have been working actively.

The antisocialist organizations in the C.S.R. have had very extensive ties with foreign counterrevolutionary émigré centers and with foreign bourgeois parties and circles.

The C.S.R. leaders stated that legal measures would be taken with respect to the opposition organizations. But nothing has been done.

The seriousness of the situation that had taken shape in the country and the necessity of urgent measures to stop the activity of hostile forces were illustrated especially vividly by the publication and wide propaganda of an overtly counterrevolutionary platform — the "2,000 Words" appeal. This document, aimed directly against the C.C.P., contains an open call for struggle against constitutional rule. It was widely used to unite all those dissatisfied with the socialist system and served as a program of action for them. It is impossible to disregard the fact that the authors of this hostile platform threatened to use arms to defend their position. The open statement of these forces — the "2,000 Words" appeal — constituted good reason for taking resolute actions against them with support from the forces of the party and the working class. But nothing ensued that could be called a rebuff to the counterrevolutionary forces.

This opened the floodgates for other such statements, and they were not long in coming. The facts show that in recent weeks and days the reactionaries and antisocialist organizations intensified their subversive activities against the Communist Party and the people's rule. The baiting of honest Communists devoted to the cause of socialism assumed an even more overt and unbridled character.

Under the slogan of "removing the conservatives from the bodies of state rule," increasingly vigorous demands began to be made for holding elections to the National Assembly ahead of schedule. The representatives of right-wing organizations took matters to the point of seeking to defeat the Communist Party in the elections. In other words, what was involved was an open attempt to stage a counterrevolutionary coup.

The counterrevolutionaries sought to win power peacefully, without an armed conflict, but they also foresaw other possibilities. The well-known instances of the discovery of hidden weapons indicate that the reactionaries did not rule out an armed conflict against the supporters of socialism. An alliance of officers in the former Benes army was created — the Association of Fighting Men Abroad. Across the borders of Czechoslovakia and in direct proximity to it, large groups of counterrevolutionaries met and united, and some of them, with weapons in their possession, filtered into Czechoslovakia. At an assembly at Prague University Svitak stated outright that in the interests of carrying the principle of democratization to the point of achieving "absolute freedom," even the path of civil war was possible.

VIII. — As a result of the actions of right-wing, antisocialist and counterrevolutionary forces, a real threat arose in Czechoslovakia of a counterrevolutionary coup and the loss of the gains of socialism. It was precisely this that was the chief cause for the concern shown by the C.P.S.U. and the other fraternal parties about the political processes under way in Czechoslovakia and the direction in which they were developing.

It is well known that the Central Committees of the Bulgarian Communist Party, the Hungarian Socialist Workers' Party, the Socialist Unity Party of Germany, the Polish United Workers' Party and the Communist Party of the Soviet Union for their part did everything they could, in accordance with their rights as friends, to help the C.C.P. and the peoples of Czechoslovakia to overcome the dangerous crisis and through political means to defeat the forces of the mounting counterrevolution.

After the May meetings in Moscow of the representatives of the C.P.S.U. and the C.C.P., the C.P.S.U. Central Committee repeatedly proposed that another bilateral meeting be held with the C.C.P. leadership to discuss the situation that had taken shape. However, the leaders of the C.C.P. Central Committee declined every time, citing various reasons.

True to the principles of internationalism and motivated by a sense of solidarity with fraternal Czechoslovakia and responsibility for the fate of socialism on our continent, the leaders of several fraternal Warsaw Pact countries decided to meet with the C.S.R. leaders in order to discuss the situation in a comradely manner, find a solution to it and offer the C.S.R. leaders their assistance. Unfortunately, the leaders of the C.C.P. Central Committee rejected this proposal and declined to meet in Warsaw. Yet the situation was such that there was every political and moral reason to hold this meeting of fraternal parties.

The meeting in Warsaw demonstrated the total unity of the five Communist and Workers' parties, their unshakable solidarity and their determination to rebuff the intrigues of the counterrevolutionary forces.

Analysis of the counterrevolutionary antisocialist manifestations that took place in Czechoslovakia convincingly demonstrates that they were not spontaneous but highly organized. The moments for action were precisely determined, as were the directions and targets of the attacks by antisocialist forces, the sequence of the manifestations and the coordination of the actions of all the forces — right-wing revisionists within the C.C.P., antisocialists and overt counterrevolutionaries inside the country and their support from outside.

All this indicates that the events were directed by organized counterrevolutionary forces that had extensive ties within the country, supervised the actions of the antisocialist forces in the mass news organs and maintained contact with various clubs and with other parties. The counterrevolutionary forces also struck blows at the most important agencies for defending the state. The people carrying out the counterrevolutionary objectives were connected with foreign intelligence services and with foreign imperialist circles. At the same time, until recently some of the organizers of the counterrevolutionary forces attempted to remain in the shadows. The rightist forces had their people in C.C.P. executive bodies and were kept informed of these bodies' actions. This made the developments under way more dangerous and required a resolute struggle by the whole party against the counterrevolution and, above all, vigorous action by the Presidium of the C.C.P. Central Committee and each of its members and the members of the C.S.R. government. Nevertheless, certain members of the Presidium of the C.C.P. Central Committee and government leaders were frequently observed acting counter to the policy defined by the Presidium of the C.C.P. Central Committee on fundamental questions. Thus, F. Kriegel, a member of the Presidium of the C.C.P. Central Committee, not only failed to rebuff the antisocialist elements, but essentially sided with the authors of outright counterrevolutionary statements, as he did, for example, in his television interview with the authors of "The 2,000 Words."

The C.P.S.U. and the other fraternal parties of socialist countries repeatedly called the C.C.P. leadership's attention to this. Our experience and the experience of the political struggles of other fraternal parties and socialist countries teach that one cannot turn away from a counterrevolutionary danger and close one's eyes to it. A conciliatory approach, deliberate minimization of the danger and, especially, flirtation with the forces of counterrevolution give reactionaries the opportunity to carry matters to the point of destroying socialism. On the basis of analyzing the incidents and phenomena occurring in the C.S.R., the fraternal parties emphasized that socialism was the target of a broad offensive being waged in Czechoslovakia and in which the forces of counterrevolution were playing the most active role. External imperialist forces, the forces of counterrevolution and right-wing revisionist elements in the Czechoslovak Communist Party had objectively joined in implementing this antisocialist offensive.

The Communist and Workers' Parties of the socialist countries, seeking to support their brother Communists and all the working people in the C.S.R. and to prevent a dangerous turn of events in Czechoslovakia, did everything they could toward this end. This objective was served by the meeting in Cierna-on-Tisa of the Politburo of the C.P.S.U. Central Committee and the Presidium of the C.C.P. Central Committee, and then by the Bratislava conference of representatives of six Communist and Workers' Parties of the Socialist Countries. The leaders of the C.C.P. Central Committee gave assurances at these meetings that they would take immediate concrete measures to stabilize the situation in the country and to strengthen and defend the socialist gains. However, after the meeting in Cierna and the conference in Bratislava the C.S.R.'s leading bodies did nothing to repulse the counterrevolution, while right-wing, antisocialist forces became still more active. These forces set themselves well-defined goals: to deprive the C.C.P. of its leadership role in the development of socialist society — toward this end they launched a broad offensive against the party's authority and organized a vicious campaign of slander and lies against it; to disorganize and jolt Czechoslovakia's Communist Party and socialist society from the ideological platform of scientific communism onto the path of reformism and Social Democracy — for this reason they launched attacks on Marxism-Leninism as an integrated, creative doctrine and attacks on Leninism; and to change the political essence of the Czechoslovak Socialist Republic — to switch it from a socialist platform along the rails of social democratism to a bourgeois republic.

The accomplishment of these objectives would be wholly in the interests of the imperialists. It is for precisely this reason and for no other — not because of a suddenly conceived love for socialism and democracy and for Czechoslovakia's working people — that imperialist propaganda so actively supported the alarming developments in Czechoslovakia.

After the Cierna meeting and the Bratislava conference the right-wing coun-

terrevolutionary forces became still more active. Antisocialist elements organized campaigns to collect signatures supporting demands for the dissolution of
the workers' militia. These campaigns were accompanied by rallies and demonstrations of an antisocialist nature. Communists who spoke at these rallies were
rudely silenced, and physical force was even used against them. Frenzied antisocialist hysteria has again been launched in the press. It is common knowledge
that the reactionaries have rabidly persecuted the 99 workers at the Auto-Praha
Plant just for boldly taking up the defense of the working class socialist gains
and the friendship between the peoples of Czechoslovakia and the Soviet Union. In recent days the organized subversive activities culminated in an open
assault on the building of the C.C.P. Central Committee's Secretariat in Prague.

A demarcation of forces within the Presidium of the C.C.P. Central Committee became evident in the course of the meeting in Cierna-on-Tisa. While
a minority of Presidium members, headed by A. Dubcek, took overtly right-
wing opportunist stands, the majority adopted a principled line and affirmed
the necessity of waging a resolute struggle against the reactionary antisocialist
forces and against connivance with the reactionaries.

However, right-wing revisionist elements among the leadership of the Communist Party and the government of Czechoslovakia thwarted fulfillment of
the understanding reached in Cierna-on-Tisa and Bratislava with respect to
defending the positions of socialism in Czechoslovakia, combating antisocialist
forces and repulsing imperialism's intrigues. These people, in declaring as a
cover-up their desire to defend socialism, were in reality attempting only to
gain time, while pandering to counterrevolution. As a result of their perfidious,
treacherous actions, a real threat arose to the socialist gains of Czechoslovakia.
Inveterate reactionaries emerged in the arena of Czechoslovakia's political life.

"Extremist forces," the appeal by a group of members of the C.C.P. Central
Committee, the government and the C.S.R. National Assembly stressed, "thus
failed to heed the party's calls and have increased their subversive activities
even more, seeking to cause a conflict in our country at any cost." Everything
the working people of the C.S.R. have created in the past 20 years and all the
gains of socialism are at stake. Not only the path of socialist democracy along
which the people of the C.S.R. embarked in January but also the very foundations of socialism and the republic itself have been jeopardized.

An atmosphere was created that was absolutely unacceptable to the socialist
countries. In this situation it was necessary to act, and act purposefully and
resolutely, without losing time. It was precisely for this reason that the Soviet
Union and other socialist states decided to satisfy the request by C.S.R. party
and state figures to render the fraternal Czechoslovak people urgent assistance,
including assistance with armed forces.

The fate of socialist Czechoslovakia is near and dear to the peoples of all
socialist countries. They cannot acquiesce when our common enemies jolt
Czechoslovakia from the path of socialism and create a threat that it will break
away from the socialist commonwealth. The peoples of our countries have made
too many painful sacrifices and shed too much blood in the savage battle of
the last war and in the struggle for social and national liberation to allow the

counterrevolutionaries to wrest Czechoslovakia from the family of socialist states.

The defense of socialism in Czechoslovakia is not only the internal affair of that country's people but also a problem of defending the positions of world socialism. It is for this reason that we are rendering support to the people of Czechoslovakia in defense of the gains of socialism. In giving fraternal internationalist support to our Czechoslovak Communist comrades and the entire Czechoslovak people, we are discharging our internationalist duty to them and to the international Communist, workers' and national-liberation movement. For us this duty is the highest of all.

INTERNATIONAL COMMUNIST REACTION

THE SOVIET INVASION of Czechoslovakia left the slowly fading myth of international Communist unity in shambles. Among the major parties, it was almost blanketly condemned. However, grounds for attack varied. Initially, the Chinese line amounted to a plague on both houses. Not unexpectedly, Peking (Document 47) dismissed the TASS statement that fraternal socialist troops had been invited to Prague as a ridiculous fig-leaf, denounced Moscow as fascist and imperialist, and condemned Dubček for failing to lead the Czechoslovak people in armed struggle.[1] Albania, fearing Soviet invasion, went a step further to denounce the Warsaw Pact as a Treaty of Enslavement (Document 48).[2] The extent of Albanian anxiety expressed itself in an unprecedented, if temporary, drop in her hostility toward Yugoslavia, following Belgrade's condemnation of Moscow for invading Czechoslovakia.[3]

In Western Europe, support for Moscow was limited to the Communist parties of Luxemburg, West Germany, and West Berlin (the latter subordinate to the SED), Greece (a pro-Soviet group in exile), and Portugal (in exile in Moscow). The Italians (Document 49) considered the decision to intervene

---

[1] See also Chou En-lai's speech at the Rumanian National Day Reception, Supplement to *Peking Review*, Vol. 11, No. 34 (August 23, 1968). For analysis, see "Asia and the Crisis in Czechoslovakia," *Asian Analyst* (September 1968), pp. 10–12. Although Peking continued to treat the Czechoslovak leaders as ineffectual revisionists, later assessments focused on attacking Moscow. The theme of Soviet-U.S. collaboration was elaborated by Chou En-lai in his September 2 speech on the twenty-third anniversary of North Vietnam (*Peking Review*, Vol. 11, No. 36 [September 6, 1968], pp. 6–7).

[2] Subsequently, Albania formally withdrew from the Warsaw Treaty Organization, a move that Hoxha had been reluctant to take previously despite Albanian absence from Pact meetings since 1961 (*Zëri i Popullit*, September 13, 1968, and Paul Yankovitch in *Le Monde*, September 14, 1968).

[3] Although Chinese attacks on the Yugoslavs had ceased at the end of June 1968, the Albanians continued polemicizing against Belgrade in July and August. With the occupation of Czechoslovakia, Tirana moved closer to the Chinese. Indeed, when Albania returned to denouncing the Yugoslavs (*Zëri i Popullit*, November 5, 1968), care was taken to show that the move was consistent with Peking's position by reprinting the Chinese congratulations on the founding of the Albanian Party of Labor that condemned the Tito clique's long-standing territorial designs on Albanian territory (*Zëri i Popullit*, November 9, 1968). An interesting account of the initial results for Albanian-Yugoslav relations is Peter R. Prifti, "Albania Gets the Jitters," *East Europe*, Vol. 18, No. 1 (January 1969), pp. 9–14.

on the heels of the Čierná and Bratislava agreements incomprehensible and incompatible with Communist principles. Secretary General of the PCI Luigi Longo, who had been in Moscow when Soviet troops invaded Czechoslovakia, condemned the move and then flew to Paris to exchange views with the French Communist leaders.

Longo's claim that he found similar opinions in Paris[4] was true only to a limited extent. Like the Italian party, the PCF officially disapproved—pointing out that safeguarding socialism in Czechoslovakia was the job of the Czechoslovak rather than Soviet Communists (Document 50). Yet the French were particularly anxious to preserve friendly ties with Moscow, and party leader Waldeck Rochet made it quite clear that despite disapproval the French party would not join in anti-Soviet attacks.[5] Differences of opinion split the PCF leadership. Roger Garaudy, a leading ideologist in the Politburo, accused the Soviets of a return to Stalinism, while the widow of former Secretary General Maurice Thorez, Mme. Thorez-Vermeersch, attempted to justify the intervention and then resigned from the Central Committee and the Politburo in protest. Officially, the party rejected both positions and maneuvered to find a middle road.[6]

The British deplored the use of troops as completely unjustified, while C. H. Hermansson, Chairman of the Swedish party, said on Swedish television August 22 that the Soviet government was "a disgrace to socialism" and should resign. However, none of the European parties' condemnations quite equalled the biting tone of Cuban approval. Castro (Document 51) joined the other Latin American Communist parties in endorsing the invasion, after first pointing out that it had no justification in international law. But his support did not come without a price. The Cuban leader took advantage of the occasion to launch a massive attack on the softening of revolutionary fiber among European Communists. He castigated Moscow and the East European regimes for not fulfilling their international duty with respect to aid for less developed socialist countries and for guerrilla warfare in Latin America, and he raised the crucial question of consistency: Would Warsaw Pact divisions be sent to Korea, if need be, to Vietnam, to Cuba? [7]

[4] *L'Unità*, August 23, 1968; Henry Tanner, *The New York Times*, August 22, 1968.

[5] *L'Humanité*, August 27, 1968. Prior to the invasion, the PCF, realizing that its own political difficulties would only be aggravated if Moscow resorted to force against Dubček, had suggested a conference of European Communist parties to take some of the heat out of the situation (*L'Humanité*, July 18, 1968). French and Italian delegations traveled to Prague and Moscow only to see the idea dropped due to Soviet lack of enthusiasm.

[6] Garaudy was condemned in a Politburo Statement for going beyond the PCF stand (*L'Humanité*, August 28, 1968). The French Party's Central Committee meeting October 20–21 accepted Mme. Thorez-Vermeersch's resignation, rejected her views, and reprimanded Garaudy (*L'Humanité*, October 22, 1968). For analysis, see Kevin Devlin, "The New Crisis in European Communism," *Problems of Communism*, Vol. XVII, No. 6 (November–December 1968), pp. 57–68 and Heinz Brahm, "Das Echo in Weltkommunismus auf die Okkupation der Tschechoslowakei," *Europa Archiv*, Vol. 23, No. 20 (October 25, 1968), pp. 744–753.

[7] See Claude Julien, *Le Monde*, September 5, 1968, and Ernst Halperin, "The Cuban Revolution in 1968," *Current History*, Vol. 56, No. 329 (January 1969), pp. 42–46.

DOCUMENT 47

"TOTAL BANKRUPTCY OF SOVIET MODERN REVISIONISM"

Jen-min Jih-pao, Commentator

August 23, 1968

Complete Text

[*Jen-min Jih-pao,* August 23, 1968, quoted from *Peking Review,* Vol. 11, No. 34 (August 23, 1968)]

The Soviet revisionist renegade clique, at a time when the masses of the people are being hoodwinked, deployed late on the night of August 20 large numbers of aircraft, tanks and ground forces and, in a surprise attack, carried out a military occupation of Czechoslovakia. This act of naked armed intervention has brought out to the full the grisly fascist features of the Soviet revisionist renegade clique, fully revealed its extreme weakness, and proclaimed the total bankruptcy of Soviet modern revisionism.

That the Soviet revisionist renegade clique has flagrantly set in motion its armed forces is the outcome of the extremely acute contradictions within the whole modern revisionist bloc. It is the result of the extremely acute contradictions between U.S. imperialism and Soviet modern revisionism in their struggle for control of Eastern Europe. It is the outcome of the collaboration between the United States and the Soviet Union in their vain attempt to redivide the world. For a long time, there have existed profound contradictions and bitter strife between the Soviet revisionist renegade clique and the revisionist cliques of the Eastern European countries. The Khrushchev revisionist renegade clique, ever since it rose to power, has most shamefully made one dirty deal after another with U.S. imperialism. Emulating the example of the Soviet revisionists, the Czechoslovak revisionist renegade clique wants to follow in their footsteps, throwing themselves into the lap of U.S. imperialism. However, the Soviet revisionists regard Eastern Europe as their own sphere of influence and forbid the Czechoslovak revisionists to have direct collaboration with U.S. imperialism. As the difficulties besetting the Soviet revisionist clique both at home and abroad are growing from day to day, the trend of disintegration within the modern revisionist bloc is coming to the surface more and more. An outstanding manifestation of this trend of development is the recent rise to power of the Dubček revisionist clique in Czechoslovakia. In order to force the Dubček clique into submission and bring Czechoslovakia back under the continued control of the Soviet revisionists, the Soviet revisionist ruling clique has resorted to all sorts of tough and soft tactics against the Dubček clique. At times they used threats of force by staging military maneuvers; at other times they arranged conferences with honey on their lips and murder in their hearts in an attempt to make the Czechoslovak revisionist leaders fall into their trap. But as the Czechoslovak revisionist renegade clique was hell-bent on establishing direct links with U.S. imperialism (and also with West Germany), all the threats and cajolery of the Soviet revisionist renegade clique failed one after another. At the end of its rope, the Soviet revisionist clique was compelled to throw away its mask and, mustering the revisionist cliques of Gomułka, Ulbricht, Kádár and Zhivkov, resorted to armed force. Thus the melodramatic dogfight within the modern revisionist bloc is being acted out on the world stage.

The day after it sent its troops into Czechoslovakia, the Soviet revisionist renegade clique issued a statement through TASS. The statement is a ridiculous fig leaf used by the Soviet revisionist clique in an attempt to cover up its disgusting features.

The Soviet revisionist renegade clique claims that it sent troops into Czechoslovakia in order to "defend" the "socialist gains." What amazing gall! Who, after all, has capitulated to U.S. imperialism and ruined the socialist gains of the Soviet Union? Who has peddled Soviet modern revisionism in Eastern Europe and ruined the socialist gains of a number of European countries? You are the guilty ones, you, the worst renegades in history! It is completely useless for you to put up such a phony signboard in a vain attempt to deceive the people of Czechoslovakia, the people of the Soviet Union and of the rest of the world.

The Soviet revisionist renegade clique claims that it sent troops into Czechoslovakia out of "concern for the consolidation of peace" and to preserve "the mainstays of European peace." This is sheer gangster logic of the imperialists. Is it not true that both Hitler's occupation of the Sudeten region of Czechoslovakia in the past and U.S. imperialism's present aggression against Vietnam were carried out under the flag of "defending peace"? The apprentices have learnt from their teachers. This claptrap spread by the Soviet revisionist clique is merely a cover-up in its struggle with U.S. imperialism for control of Czechoslovakia. It is nothing but putrid junk picked up from the imperialists' garbage pails.

The Soviet revisionist renegade clique also claims that its action was taken for the "unbreakable solidarity" of the "fraternal countries" and in "the interests of the security of the states of the socialist community." In that miserable mishmash of your revisionist bloc, where is your "unbreakable solidarity"? It is clearly a case of each trying to cheat and outwit the other and each going his own way. You do not really want to build any "socialist community." What you really want is to found a colonial empire with the Soviet revisionist clique as the overlord, and redivide the world in collaboration with U.S. imperialism. All those countries who are part of your "community" have to put themselves at your disposal and at your mercy, or else they will meet with disaster.

The Soviet revisionist renegade clique has long ago degenerated into a gang of social-imperialists. The relations between it and the U.S. imperialists, just like the relations among all the imperialist countries, are relations of mutual collaboration and struggle. In spite of the fact that they have conflicts of interest of one kind or another, they are at one with each other in their stand against communism, against the people and against revolution. No sooner had the Soviet revisionist renegade clique ordered the troops into Czechoslovakia than it reported this action to Johnson. This gives a vivid picture of the relations between them.

At a time when U.S. imperialism is having a very hard time, this action of the Soviet revisionist renegade clique in Czechoslovakia has actually done a great service to the Johnson government.

Our great teacher Chairman Mao pointed out long ago: "The people of all countries, the masses of the people who comprise more than 90 percent of the entire population, invariably want revolution and will invariably support Marxism-Leninism. They will not support revisionism. Though some people may support revisionism for a while, they will eventually cast it aside. They are bound to awaken step by step; they are bound to oppose imperialism and the reactionaries of all countries; they are bound to oppose revisionism."

U.S. imperialism is a paper tiger, so are the Soviet revisionist renegade clique and the reactionaries of all countries. The ugly performance by the Soviet revisionist renegade clique at this time has further educated the Soviet people, the Czechoslovak people and the revolutionary peoples all over the world. It has helped them to see more clearly the counterrevolutionary features of the Soviet revisionist clique and its pawns, and has given an impetus to their awakening and their revolutionary struggle.

The 700 million Chinese people, armed with Mao Tse-tung's thought, firmly stand on the side of the revolutionary people of the Soviet Union, of the revolutionary people of Czechoslovakia and of all the revolutionary peoples in the world who oppose imperialism, modern revisionism and the reactionaries of all countries. The Chinese people resolutely support the struggle of the peoples the world over against U.S. imperialism and Soviet modern revisionism. The Chinese people resolutely support the proletariat and all the revolutionary people in the Soviet Union, in Czechoslovakia and in the other countries under the rule of the modern revisionist cliques to rise and overthrow the modern revisionist reactionary regimes and take back the state power, so that their homelands will return to the road of the dictatorship of the proletariat and socialism. We are deeply convinced that such a day is bound to come!

DOCUMENT 48
"DECLARATION OF THE CENTRAL COMMITTEE OF APL AND
THE COUNCIL OF MINISTERS OF APR ON THE AGGRESSION
OF THE SOVIET REVISIONISTS AND THEIR SATELLITES AGAINST
THE CZECHOSLOVAK SOCIALIST REPUBLIC AND
THE CZECHOSLOVAK PEOPLE."
August 22, 1968
Complete Text
[*Zëri i Popullit,* August 23, 1968]

The Central Committee of the Albanian Party of Labor and the Council of
Ministers of the People's Republic of Albania issued on August 22 a solemn
statement on the armed intervention and aggression unleashed by the Soviet
revisionist renegade clique against Czechoslovakia. The full text of the statement follows:

On the night of August 20–21 of 1968, the military forces of the Soviet
Union, the People's Republic of Poland, the German Democratic Republic,
the People's Republic of Hungary and the People's Republic of Bulgaria, in
flagrant contravention of all norms governing the relations between states,
committed brutal aggression against the Czechoslovak Socialist Republic
and the Czechoslovak people in a surprising, perfidious and fascist manner,
occupying by force the whole territory of Czechoslovakia.

While the occupation troops attacked and invaded Czechoslovak territory
from many directions simultaneously, the traitorous Czechoslovak revisionist
leadership headed by Alexander Dubček, which was hell-bent on the road
of betrayal of the interests of the Czechoslovak people and was terrified by
the force of the oppressors, capitulated in the most shameful way, calling on
the Czechoslovak people and their army not to put up any resistance at all
in defense of their homeland and against the invading foreign troops.

The Central Committee of the Albanian Party of Labor and the Government of the People's Republic of Albania most resolutely condemn and denounce the barbarous aggression by the Soviet revisionists and their servants
against the Czechoslovak Socialist Republic and the Czechoslovak people, as
well as the betrayal and capitulation by the Czechoslovak revisionist leadership.

The Central Committee of the Albanian Party of Labor and the Government of the People's Republic of Albania consider that the Czechoslovak
tragedy originates from the 20th Congress of the Communist Party of the
Soviet Union, which threw the Marxist-Leninist line of the Communist Party
of the Soviet Union of Lenin-Stalin overboard, replacing it with the Khrushchev reactionary revisionist line, which led to the revival of the revisionist
forces in Czechoslovakia as well, led to disastrous consequences in the Soviet
Union itself, and brought difficulty to the whole international Communist

movement. The military occupation of Czechoslovakia by the Soviet revisionists and their servants is a product of the global strategy of the Soviet revisionist treacherous leadership's collaboration with U.S. imperialism.

The aggression against Czechoslovakia by the Soviet revisionists and their servants is a fascist-type aggression and constitutes the most flagrant violation of the principle of the freedom and sovereignty of the peoples. This shameful aggression committed by the Brezhnev-Kosygin-Khrushchevite revisionist clique has brought the greatest disgrace to the honor and prestige of the Soviet Union and the Soviet people. After this base aggression, no one in the world can have the slightest faith in the Soviet revisionist leadership. This is the greatest warning to the Soviet people, to the peoples of the socialist countries and of the countries which are ruled by the revisionist cliques, to the peoples of Europe and of the whole world about the danger posed by the counter-revolutionary revisionist clique which is ruling today in the Soviet Union and about its imperialist and fascist aims and methods for the domination of the peoples by relying on its collaboration with U.S. imperialism.

The revisionists' aggression against the Czechoslovak Socialist Republic, which was committed in the name of the Warsaw Treaty, once more confirms what has long been declared by the Albanian Party of Labor and the Government of the People's Republic of Albania: the Warsaw Treaty has ceased to be a pact protecting the socialist countries which are signatories to it from imperialist aggression and West German revanchism. From a peace treaty, the Warsaw Treaty has been turned into a treaty of war for enslavement. From a treaty of defense against imperialist aggression, it has been turned into an aggressive treaty against the socialist countries themselves. Therefore, the Albanian Party of Labor, the Government of the People's Republic of Albania, and the Albanian people condemn with disgust this aggressive treaty and solemnly declare that whoever dares to touch the sacred frontiers of the People's Republic of Albania, even if he is a member of the Warsaw Treaty, will receive the merited response and find certain death at the hands of the Albanian people who are united as one around their party and government.

In these tragic moments for the Czechoslovak people, the Albanian Party of Labor, the Government of the People's Republic of Albania, and the Albanian people express to the fraternal Czechoslovak people their most determined internationalist solidarity and support. They have faith in the revolutionary and freedom-loving spirit of the Czechoslovak people. They consider that for the Czechoslovak people the only way of salvation and to regain their freedom is the road of uncompromising struggle through to the end against the foreign invaders, the Soviet, German, Polish, Hungarian, and Bulgarian revisionists, against U.S. imperialism and German revanchism, and against all the local revisionists and reactionaries. This struggle will be a difficult and protracted one, but it is the only correct and possible road for the salvation of Czechoslovakia, for the defense of freedom and socialism. The Albanian people have followed this road; that is why they are today free and sovereign and have thwarted the imperialist-revisionist plans.

The Albanian people are convinced by their own experience and age-old history that freedom is not bestowed but is gained through blood and sacrifice. Therefore, the Albanian Party of Labor, the Albanian Government, and people call on the genuine Czechoslovak revolutionary Communists and freedom-loving Czechoslovak people to rise up in uncompromising struggle through to the end against the revisionist invaders and against the internal enemies; and they can be sure that they are not alone, that all the freedom-loving peoples of the world support their struggle, and that siding with them are also the real revolutionary Communists and the peoples of the Soviet Union, of the German Democratic Republic, Poland, Hungary and Bulgaria, who are suffering under the yoke of the revisionist cliques which organized the barbarous aggression against Czechoslovakia. The Albanian Communists and the Albanian people will always side with the Czechoslovak people in their struggle for freedom. The Czechoslovak people will surely win in this liberation struggle.

The Albanian Party of Labor, the Government of the People's Republic of Albania, and the Albanian people have faith in and call on the genuine Soviet Bolsheviks and the Soviet people to rise up in struggle against the revisionist-fascist clique which is oppressing them, to re-enact the great October Revolution by burying once and for all the ill-famed 20th Congress and its tragic consequences on a national and international scale by overthrowing the Brezhnev-Kosygin revisionist clique and by causing the invading Soviet forces to leave Czechoslovakia and all other countries where these forces have been stationed for domination.

The Albanian Party of Labor, the Government of the People's Republic of Albania, and the Albanian people call on all revolutionary Communists and all freedom-loving peoples in the world to support the sacred cause of freedom of the Czechoslovak people, to condemn this barbarous aggression by the Soviet revisionists and their servants, and to frustrate the big Soviet-American plot for world domination, a plot which is becoming the basis of the revival of fascist methods in oppressing the peoples and in depriving them of their freedom.

DOCUMENT 49

COMMUNIQUÉ OF THE POLITBURO OF THE COMMUNIST PARTY OF ITALY

August 22, 1968

Complete Text

[*L'Unità,* August 22, 1968]

The Politburo of the PCI met this morning, with the participation of the members of the Directorate present in Rome, to discuss the grave situation that has unexpectedly arisen as a result of the intervention of Soviet troops and of troops from other Warsaw Pact countries in Czechoslovakia.

The Čierná-nad-Tisou and Bratislava discussions and agreements were greeted by the leading PCI organs with great satisfaction, as they were considered to be fully consistent with their demands for a political solution of the problems that had arisen in Czechoslovakia and with regard to the relations between Czechoslovakia and other socialist countries — a solution that was to be realized with all due respect for the autonomy of every party and country, following the line of development of socialist democracy in the spirit of solidarity with the revival process taking place in Czechoslovakia and in a manner that would effectively strengthen the unity of the international Communist and workers' movement.

In these conditions and given the facts, it is hard to understand how a decision for military intervention could have been taken.

The PCI Politburo therefore considers this decision to be unjustified and incompatible with the principles of the autonomy and independence of every Communist party and socialist state and with the need to defend the unity of the international Communist and workers' movement. In the firmest and most convinced spirit of proletarian internationalism and reaffirming once again the profound, fraternal, and genuine relations that unite the Italian Communists with the Soviet Union and the CPSU, the PCI Politburo considers it to be its duty to immediately express its strong dissent and to reserve the party directorate's right to make a more profound evaluation of the situation and its further developments; to make itself the spokesman of the emotion and deepest concern felt by the workers' movement at this moment; and to reaffirm its solidarity with the action of renovation undertaken by the Czechoslovak Communist Party.

The PCI Politburo expresses its hope that all Italian democratic forces will be able to assume a responsible position and to steer clear of emotionalism; it also commits all Communist organizations to hold to the positions of the party's leading organs and to be firmly vigilant against all anti-Communist speculation and provocation.

DOCUMENT 50

COMMUNIQUÉ OF THE CENTRAL COMMITTEE OF THE
COMMUNIST PARTY OF FRANCE

August 22, 1968
Complete Text
[*L'Humanité,* August 23, 1968]

The Central Committee of the French Communist Party, in a special session held on August 22, 1968, has examined the situation created by the military intervention in Czechoslovakia on the part of the Soviet Union, Bulgaria, Poland, Hungary, and the Democratic Republic of Germany.

It approves the report presented by Comrade Waldeck Rochet in the name of the Politburo.

Of late our party has made no secret of its concern with regard to certain aspects of the situation in Czechoslovakia. Taking advantage of the correct efforts of the Communist Party of Czechoslovakia to develop socialist democracy and to modify the working style and method of the party and state, forces hostile to socialism have been carrying out their activities. The actions of these elements did not meet with the full political and ideological response necessary. World reaction, in particular the leading circles of the revanchist and expansionist state of West Germany, did not conceal their expectation of a weakening of the alliance that binds Czechoslovakia to the other countries in the socialist community, an alliance which constitutes the guarantee of security of the Czechoslovak people, the socialist countries, and European peace.

Our party expressed its concern at the Central Committee meeting of April 19 and to the fraternal party of Czechoslovakia itself, in particular during the conversations of the Secretary General of the French Communist Party with the leadership of the Communist Party of Czechoslovakia.

It greeted the positive conclusions of the Čierná and Bratislava meetings with lively satisfaction. It hailed the understanding reached by the Communist Parties of the Soviet Union, Czechoslovakia, Poland, Bulgaria, Hungary, and the Democratic Republic of Germany on current problems in the struggle against imperialism and for socialism. The Bratislava meeting created favorable conditions for strengthening cooperation between the socialist countries on the basis of equality, national independence, mutual assistance, and solidarity as well as the recent success of these countries in constructing a new, prosperous, and democratic society.

As it has steadfastly continued to do, our party considers that the problems arising between Communist parties must be examined and resolved by fraternal discussion in bilateral and multilateral meetings. At the same time, this must be done with respect for sovereignty of each country, the free determination of each party, and in the spirit of proletarian internationalism.

Our party is resolutely attached to the principle according to which each Communist party must determine its policy, its forms of action, and its methods of struggle in complete independence on the basis of Marxism-Leninism, at the same time taking into account the particular conditions under which it wages its struggle, the interests of the working class and its own people, and the interests of the world democratic and revolutionary movement.

Consequently, our party declares itself against all interference in the internal affairs of a brother country.

Based on these principles, which were defined by the Declaration of the 81 Communist and Workers' Parties in 1960, the French Communist Party has taken a series of initiatives: talks with the leaders of the Communist Party of the Soviet Union and the Communist Party of Czechoslovakia and a proposal for a meeting of the European Communist and Workers' parties. It has made its opposition to all external military intervention clearly known to the parties concerned.

This is why the Central Committee, adopting the Politburo Declaration of August 21, 1968, disapproves of the military intervention in Czechoslovakia. It belongs to the Communist Party of Czechoslovakia, keeping in mind its international obligations, to find within itself, in the working class and people of Czechoslovakia, and in the support of the socialist countries and the body of fraternal parties the forces necessary to safeguard and develop socialism in Czechoslovakia.

The French Communist Party will not relinquish its efforts in behalf of the unity of the international Communist movement and the strengthening of the bonds of solidarity and cooperation with all Communist and Workers' parties, and especially the ties of fraternal friendship which have always united it with the Communist Party of the Soviet Union.

At the same time, the French Communist Party will resolutely pursue its struggle for a national policy of peace, independence, democracy, and socialism, the objectives, methods, and conditions for which have been defined at its congresses — in particular the 18th Congress.

It calls upon all Communists, workers, and democrats to combat the anti-Communist and anti-Soviet speculations and provocations to which the enemies of socialism in France and around the world, taking advantage of the events, will not hesitate to apply themselves.

DOCUMENT 51

FIDEL CASTRO SPEECH ON CZECHOSLOVAK SITUATION

August 23, 1968

Excerpts

[*Granma,* August 24, 1968]

. . . First of all I wish to state that we considered Czechoslovakia to be heading toward a counterrevolutionary situation, toward capitalism, and into the arms of imperialism.

Thus, this is the operative concept in our first position toward the action carried out by a group of socialist countries. That is, we consider that it was necessary to prevent it from happening at any cost, in one way or another. Let us not become impatient, because we propose to analyze this in line with our ideas.

Discussing the form is not really the most fundamental thing. The essential thing, whether we accept it or not, is whether or not the socialist bloc could permit the development of a political situation which would lead to the breakdown of a socialist country and its fall into the arms of imperialism. From our viewpoint, it is not permissible, and the socialist bloc has the right to prevent it in one way or another. We first wish to begin by establishing what our opinion is about this essential fact.

Now, it is not enough to accept simply that Czechoslovakia was heading toward a counterrevolutionary situation and that it had to be stopped. It is not enough to conclude simply that the only alternative was to prevent it and nothing more. We must analyze the causes and determine the factors which made possible and necessary such a dramatic, drastic, and painful remedy. Those are the factors which required a step unquestionably involving a violation of legal principles and of international standards, which have often served as shields for peoples against injustices and are highly regarded in the world.

What is not appropriate here is to say that in the case of Czechoslovakia the sovereignty of the Czechoslovak state was not violated. That would be fiction and a lie. The violation was flagrant.

And this is what we will concentrate on: sovereignty and our ideas of legal and political principles. From the legal viewpoint, it cannot be justified. This is quite clear. In our judgment, the decision on Czechoslovakia can be explained only from the political viewpoint and not from a legal viewpoint. Frankly, it has absolutely not one appearance of legality.

What are the circumstances that have permitted a remedy of this nature, a remedy which places in a difficult situation the entire world revolutionary movement, a remedy which constitutes a really traumatic situation for an entire people — as is the present case in Czechoslovakia — a remedy which implies that an entire nation has to pass through the most unpleasant circumstances of seeing the country occupied by armies of other countries, although they are armies of the socialist countries. How did a situation come about in which millions of citizens have to see themselves today in the tragic circumstances of choosing either to be passive toward these circumstances and this event — which so much brings to mind previous episodes — or to struggle in comradeship with pro-Yankee agents and spies, in comradeship with the enemies of socialism, in comradeship with the agents of West Germany, and all that fascist and reactionary rabble that in the heat of these circumstances will try to present themselves as champions of the sovereignty, patriotism, and freedom of Czechoslovakia?

Logically, for the Czechoslovak people this experience and this fact constitute a bitter and tragic situation. Therefore, it is not enough simply to conclude that it has arisen as an inexorable necessity and even, if you wish, as an unquestionable obligation of the socialist countries to prevent such events from happening. [One must inquire] what are the cases, the factors, and the circumstances that made it possible — after twenty years of communism in Czechoslovakia — that a group of persons whose names do not even appear anywhere would have to request other countries of the socialist camp, asking them to send their armies to prevent the triumph of the counterrevolution in Czechoslovakia and the triumph of the intrigues and conspiracies of the imperialist countries interested in tearing Czechoslovakia from the community of socialist countries.

Could it be imagined, gentlemen, that at the end of twenty years of communism in our country — of Communist revolution, of socialist revolution — that under any circumstances it could happen that a group of honest revolutionaries in this country, terrified at the prospects of an advance or, better said, of a retrogression toward counterrevolutionary positions and imperialism, would be forced to ask the aid of friendly armies to prevent such a situation from occurring? What would have remained of the Communist consciousness of this people? What would have remained of the revolutionary consciousness of this people, of the dignity of this people, of the revolutionary morale of this people? What would have remained of all those things that mean for us the essence of the revolution if such circumstances should one day arise?

Of course, no circumstances of that kind will ever occur in our country. First, because we believe that it is a fundamental duty and fundamental responsibility of those who direct a revolution to prevent deformations of such a nature that might make possible such circumstances. Second, gentlemen — for an unquestionably practical reason and not only an elemental moral reason — because would it be worth the trouble if, after twenty years, in order to survive, a revolution had to resort to such procedures. And also, for a very simple practical reason: who would the false personalities of this country ask to send armies? The only armies that we have in our vicinity are the Yankee army and the armies of the puppets allied with the Yankee imperialists, and because we are too alone in this part of the world for there ever to exist the most remote possibility of saving this revolution by asking aid of allied armies. And it must be said that I do not know anyone capable of going through such shame if they had the need and opportunity to do it. Because what kind of Communists would we be and what kind of Communist revolution would this be if at the end of twenty years we found ourselves having to do such a thing to save it?

Whatever we have thought about foreign aid, we have never had another idea than foreign aid for fighting against the imperialist soldiers and against the imperialist armies.

I simply analyze these facts because I know that, logically, our people are concerned with the enlightenment of these concepts.

Such things are not in our idea of the revolution.

I do not think that the appeal of high-ranking persons could be a justification because the justification can only be the political fact in itself — that Czechoslovakia was marching toward a counterrevolutionary situation and this was seriously affecting the entire socialist community.

And besides, there is no need for fig leaves of any kind. It is the political fact in itself, with all its consequences and all its importance. We are asking whether simply recognizing that and nothing else is enough. Or whether it is obligatory, it is elementary to draw from this most bitter experience all the political conclusions. And how are, we repeat, these circumstances possible? An analysis must be made of all the factors. For the Communist movement, there is the unavoidable duty of investigating deeply the causes leading to such a situation. A situation inconceivable for us, the Cuban revolutionaries, a situation impossible for us, the Cuban revolutionaries — we who saw the necessity of carrying out as we have this revolution ninety miles from the imperialists. We know that we cannot fall into these circumstances because it would mean the very end of the revolution and falling into the worst situation of slavery by our enemies, full of hatred.

But of course these are not the circumstances for making or trying to make this profound analysis. . . .

A series of opinions, ideas, and practices which we do not understand have really contributed to the relaxation and softening up of revolutionary spirit in the socialist countries; to ignoring the problems of the underdeveloped world; to ignoring the ghastly poverty which exists; to tendencies to maintaining trade practices with the underdeveloped world that are the same trade practices followed by the capitalist, bourgeois, developed world. This does not prevail in all countries, but it does in several countries.

Technical aid. Gentlemen, as you know, our country is a country that has great need for technicians, great need for technicians. However, when we render some technical assistance, we do not think of sending anyone a bill. We think that the least that a developed country, a socialist and revolutionary country can do, the least way in which it can help the underdeveloped world is with technology. It does not enter our mind to send anyone a bill for arms that we give or to send anyone a bill for technical assistance. It does not even enter our minds to mention it. If we give aid and mention it every day, what we are going to do is constantly humiliate those to whom we are giving aid. I believe that one should not talk about it too much.

But that is the way we are. And it is no virtue; one cannot claim it as a virtue. It is a basic thing. The day we have thousands or tens of thousands of technicians, surely, gentlemen, the most basic of our duties is to contribute at least with technical aid to all the countries that achieve their liberation after us or that need our assistance.

All these ideas have never been brought up. All these problems that have a great bearing on Communist awareness, internationalist awareness, and which are not given the place they should have in the education of the masses in the socialist camp, have much to do with the terrible softening up which explains these situations.

We all know that the leadership that Czechoslovakia generally had for twenty years was a leadership saturated with many vices, dogmatism, bureaucracy, and in sum, many things which cannot be considered a model of a truly revolutionary leadership.

When we here present our views on the pseudo-liberal nature of the group which has been praised too much by imperialism, it does not at all mean that we are expressing our support for that [former] leadership. We must keep in mind that that leadership, with which we maintained relations from the very beginning, sold us, at good price, many arms that were war booty captured from the Nazis; and we have been paying and are still paying for weapons that belonged to the Hitlerite troops that occupied Czechoslovakia. Naturally, I am not referring to the weapons which a country has to manufacture as an industrial and commercial product, especially if it is a country with a limited economy. We do not pretend to say: Give away the arms you manufacture in your industry as part of the social production and trade exchange to a country with relatively few resources. But they sold to us many weapons that belonged to the Nazi armies, and we have to pay for them and we are still paying for them.

That is a reality. It is the same as if any country that liberated itself from imperialism needed the rifles that we took from Batista, and instead of rushing to give them away we were to charge it for them — a country ridden with poverty, with many needs, an underdeveloped country. It is as if any country liberated itself tomorrow and it asked us to send it some weapons and we sent them — the San Cristobal carbines, the Springfield rifles, and all such things belonging to Batista's army — and we charged for them as if it were a great trade transaction.

Does there exist doubt that this deviates from the most basic concept regarding the duty of a revolutionary country toward other countries? On many occasions, they sold us industries whose technology was very backward. We have seen the results of many of the economic ideas about trade transactions carried out in desperation to sell any scrap iron. It is necessary to say that such practices led to circumstances under which a country that has carried out a revolution and needs to develop was sold scrap iron of backward technology. I am not going to say that this was always the case. However, all the concepts about self-financing, benefits, profits, lucres, and material incentives that were applied to foreign trade organizations led to desperation to sell an underdeveloped country any scrap iron. And this, naturally, leads to discontent, disgust, misunderstandings, and a deterioration of relations with the underdeveloped world.

These are truths, and if today we have to say bitter truths and to admit some bitter truths, we are going to take advantage of the occasion, not as an opportunity, but as a need to explain to ourselves some of the things that otherwise would be inexplicable.

It would be very unfair if I did not say that we have known, and our country has known, many technicians from various countries, many Czechoslovak technicians, many good men, who have worked in this country loyally and enthusiastically. I am not referring to men but to institutions, and especially the institutions that deform men. Even though there are institutions that deform men, many times we have seen men who have not been deformed by institutions. . . .

Our people have been developing that spirit of struggle, that spirit of combat, that willingness to challenge any danger that they have always had. And naturally, all those factors have contributed to the development of our revolutionary awareness.

For surely — from the point of view of socialist ideas, from the point of view of revolutionary ideas — not a justification, but rather an explanation,

an analysis of why such circumstances might arise in a country like Czechoslovakia is required.

And they did indeed occur, and the need did indeed arise. Once the need
arises, it is undeniable that there was only one alternative — to prevent it. But
to prevent it, of course, the price that has to be paid is a very high price.

For a people such as ours, with such a historical, revolutionary tradition,
who for many years had to face the problems of intervention, and struggled
against all of Yankee imperialism's policies, it is logical that there be an
emotional reaction from many people, in the face of the fact that armies from
outside a country's borders have had to enter in order to prevent a catastrophe.

And since logically, for different reasons, awareness and concepts repudiating
those actions have been formed, only the development of our people's political
awareness can give the ability to analyze when it [the entry of foreign armies]
becomes necessary. And even when — it is also necessary to admit this —
even when it [the action] violates rights such as the right of sovereignty, that
right in this case, in our judgment, has to give way to the more important
interest — the rights of the world revolutionary movement and of the people's
struggle against imperialism, which is, in our judgment, the fundamental
question. And without any doubt, the tearing away of Czechoslovakia and its
fall into the arms of imperialism would have constituted a very hard blow —
harder still — to the interests of the world revolutionary movement.

And we must learn to analyze these realities, and [learn] when one interest
must give way to another interest in order that romantic and idealistic positions that do not fit in with these realities may be avoided.

We were against all those bourgeois liberal reforms within Czechoslovakia.
But we are also against the liberal economic reforms that were taking place
in Czechoslovakia and that have also been taking place in other socialist camp
countries.

Of course, we have the criterion that we should not tell them how they
should realize the building of socialism. But when faced with the facts, we
must analyze them. A whole series of reforms were tending more and more to
accentuate mercantile relations within the socialist society — profits, benefits,
and all those things.

In an article published in the newspaper *Pravda* regarding Czechoslovakia,
the following fact is pointed out. "The CPSU is constantly perfecting the
style, the form and the method of the building of the party of the state
— stresses *Pravda* — and this same task is being effected in other socialist countries. It is being effected with tranquility, based on the fundamentals of the
socialist system." This observation is very interesting. *Pravda* says: "Unfortunately, it was on another basis that discussion of the matter of economic
reform in Czechoslovakia developed. During that discussion, on the one hand
over-all criticism of the entire earlier development of the socialist economy was
presented, and on the other hand replacement of the principles of planning
with spontaneous mercantile relations, leaving a wide margin for action to
private capital, was proposed."

Does this mean that in the Soviet Union they are also going to brake certain trends that in the economic field advocate putting the accent more and more on mercantile relations and on the effects of spontaneity in those relations, on those criteria that have been defending even the existence of the market and the beneficial effect of that market's prices? Does this mean that the Soviet Union is becoming aware of the need to brake those trends, for more than one imperialist press article speaks jubilantly of those trends, that have also appeared within the Soviet Union. On reading these statements, we ask ourselves if this means that an awareness of the problem has been reached.

In any case, we find it very interesting that this was noted in the *Pravda* editorial. There are a series of matters worrying us. We are concerned that up to now, in the statements of the countries that sent their divisions to Czechoslovakia and in the explanation of that action no direct accusation of Yankee imperialism has been made. There has been exhaustive talk about all the antecedents, of all the circumstances, of all the deviations, of the rightist group, of the liberal group — there has been talk about everything they did. The activities of the imperialists, the intrigues of the imperialists are known, and we are nevertheless worried that neither the Communist party nor the Soviet government, nor the governments of the other countries that sent their troops to Czechoslovakia, have made any direct accusation of Yankee imperialism for its responsibility for events in Czechoslovakia.

Certain vague references to world imperialism, to imperialist circles of the world, have been made, and certain more concrete references to West German imperialist circles. But who can fail to know that West Germany is simply a pawn of Yankee imperialism in Europe — the most aggressive, the most committed, the CIA's pawn, the Pentagon's pawn, and the pawn of the imperialist government of the United States? We certainly wish to express our concern that none of the statements has made a direct accusation of Yankee imperialism, the main cause of the machinations and the world-wide conspiracy against the socialist camp. It is only elementary that we express this concern.

The events in Czechoslovakia serve only to confirm to us the correctness of the positions and the theses that our revolution and our party have been maintaining — our position at the Tricontinental Conference, our positions in the OLAS, and our positions regarding all international problems. There are a series of facts that confirm this point of view.

It is known, for example, that one of the factors that we have explained — which has been a constant element of irritation in our relations with many countries of the socialist camp and with many Communist parties — is the problem of Yugoslavia. Some people must have asked themselves the reason for that attitude — why Cuba is always emphasizing the role that the Yugoslav League of Communists Party plays in the world. What is the role that that party plays as an instrument of imperialism in the world?

Now, in relation to the events in Czechoslovakia, the main promoter of all that bourgeois liberal policy — the main defender, the main promoter — was the organization of the so-called Yugoslav Communists. They applauded with both hands all those liberal reforms — that whole concept of the party ceasing to be the instrument of revolutionary power, of power ceasing to be a function of the party — because this is very closely linked to the entire thought of the Yugoslav League of Communists. All those criteria of political nature that completely deviate from Marxism, those criteria of an economic nature, are intimately linked with the ideology of the Yugoslav League of Communists. Our country has been a continual accuser of that organization. However, you know that recently many Communist parties, including the Communist parties of the Warsaw Pact, have begun quite to forget the role and nature of the Yugoslav League of Communists.

They began to call Yugoslavia a Communist country, they began to call it a Communist party, to invite the Yugoslav League of Communists to meetings of the socialist countries, to meetings of mass organizations of the Communist parties; and this evoked our constant opposition, our constant disagreement, our constant disagreement expressed on various occasions. And here we have the facts.

It was this organization that was one of the principal promoters of the deformations of the political process in Czechoslovakia as the agent — that is what this organization is — of the imperialists. Some will say that I exaggerate but I am going to demonstrate it with at least one fact. Tito was received as a hero in Prague a few weeks ago. This was the result of what? Of the ideological weakening, of the political weakness in the consciousness of the masses.

And we were saying to ourselves, how this can be? And to what extremes are we going, when this element — known to be revisionist, condemned historically by the revolutionary movement, which has taken the role of an agent of imperialism — could be received by a nation practically as a hero? Now, of course, Tito is one of those most scandalized by this event of the participation of Warsaw Pact countries in Czechoslovakia. . . .

And we wonder whether, perhaps, this bitter experience with Czechoslovakia will not lead to a rectification of these errors, and whether the party of the League of Yugoslav Communists will cease to be accepted as a Communist party, as a revolutionary party, and will cease to be invited to mass meetings and the political organizations of the socialist camp. We are seeing many interesting things as a result of these events.

It is explained that the countries of the Warsaw Pact sent armies to put down an imperialist plot and the development of counterrevolution in Czechoslovakia. However, it has caused us to disagree and be discontented and to protest over the fact that these same countries have been fomenting relations and a rapprochement of an economic, cultural, and political nature with the oligarchical governments of Latin America, which are not simply reactionary governments, exploiters of their peoples, but are shameless accomplices in the imperialist aggressions against Cuba and shameless accomplices in the economic blockade against Cuba. And these countries have seen themselves stimulated and encouraged by the fact that our friends, our natural allies, have forgotten this base role, this traitorous role, that these governments carry out against a socialist country — the blockade policy which those countries carry out against a socialist country.

And when we see that there is explained the necessity for an internationalist spirit and for giving aid, even with troops, to a brother country against the intrigues of the imperialists, we ask ourselves whether perhaps this policy of economic, political, and cultural rapprochement with these oligarchical governments, these accomplices of the imperialist blockade against Cuba, is not going to cease. It is well to see now how those countries react to this situation.

They say all the Latin American bloc expressed, in the forum of the nations of the world, their unanimous repudiation of this Russian intervention in Czechoslovakia. A spokesman for the group said that "we all receive this intervention with sadness and we feel sympathy with the Czechs."

"The political result of this Soviet intrusion into Czechoslovak internal affairs will strengthen the anti-Soviet tendency in Latin America," said the informant, and so on. . . .

The same occurs with the Communist parties of Europe that at this time have fallen prey to vacillation. We ask if perhaps in the future the relations with Communist parties will be based on their principles or will continue to be governed by their degree of submissiveness, satellitism, and lackeyism, and if only those who unconditionally accept everything and are unable to express absolutely no disagreement with anything will be considered friends.

Look at those who have criticized us many times, how under these circumstances they have now fallen confused in the midst of the greatest hesitations.

Our party did not hesitate to help the Venezuelan guerrillas when a rightist and traitorous leadership, deviating from the revolutionary line, abandoned the guerrillas and entered into shameful connivance with the regime. At that time we analyzed who was right — the group committed to maneuvering and political chicanery, which betrayed the fighters, which betrayed the dead, or those who continued to uphold the banner of rebelliousness. We did not take into account the numbers involved in the rightist group; we took into consideration who was right. We did not take into account how many members of the Central Committee or Politburo were involved because right has nothing to do with numbers.

At that time, the revolutionaries remained in the minority, keeping the banner of guerrilla warfare flying. We were loyal to the same positions that we hold today when we supported the guerrillas over and above the rightist leadership in Venezuela, when for the same reason we supported the Guatemalan guerrillas over and above the maneuvers and betrayals of the rightist leadership in Guatemala, and when we supported the Bolivian guerrillas over and above the maneuvers and betrayal of the rightist leadership in Bolivia. However, we were accused of being adventurers, of intervening in the affairs of other countries and in the affairs of other parties.

I ask myself in the light of the facts and in the light of the bitter reality which led the Warsaw Pact countries to send their forces to crush the counter-revolution in Czechoslovakia and to support a minority there — yes, it is said — against a majority with rightist positions; I ask if they will cease supporting also in Latin America those rightist, reformist, traitorous, and conciliatory leaderships, enemies of revolutionary armed struggle who are opposed to the people's liberation struggle.

In the face of this example, in the face of this bitter experience, I ask myself if the parties of those countries will keep themselves in line with the decision made in Czechoslovakia and will cease supporting those rightist groups which are betraying the revolutionary movement in Latin America. Surely we do not believe in the possibilities of improving relations of the socialist camp with imperialism under present conditions, and really under no conditions so long as such imperialism exists. We do not and cannot believe in the possibilities of improvement between the socialist camp and the imperialist U.S. Government so long as that country represents the role of international gendarme, an enemy of the revolution throughout the world, an aggressor against the peoples, and a systematic opponent of revolution throughout the entire world. And much less do we believe in that improvement in the midst of such a criminal and cowardly aggression as the aggression against Vietnam.

Certainly our position on this is very clear: either one faces the reality of the world, either one is really internationalist and really and resolutely supports the revolutionary movement in the world — and relations then with the imperialist U.S. Government cannot be improved — or relations with the imperialist U.S. Government are improved, but only at the expense of ceasing to loyally support the world revolutionary movement. This is our thesis, this is our position.

Here is a press dispatch from Washington 22 August — " 'The Soviet intervention in Czechoslovakia hinders any rapprochement between the East and West,' U.S. Secretary of State Dean Rusk stated here publicly today."

"The situation created can compromise ratification of the nonproliferation treaty by the U.S. Senate," he added. The chief of the U.S. diplomatic corps issued this press statement upon leaving a cabinet meeting at the White House, a meeting devoted to "the Czechoslovak problem and the Vietnam situation."

We can only express our happiness over this. Our people are aware of the position assumed by the Cuban delegation toward this famous nonproliferation treaty, a treaty which amounted to a permanent concession of monopoly of the nuclear weapons and of the technology of a power source which will be essential to the future of mankind. We were especially concerned over the fact that this meant that many countries of the world would accept an imperialist U.S. Government monopoly over those weapons, which could be used at any time against any nation, since, in addition, that draft treaty was accompanied by an astounding declaration in defense of the countries signing the treaty which were threatened by nuclear arms. Such countries as Vietnam and Cuba, if they desired to differ and not agree with that type of treaty and even less to sign it under circumstances in which the aggression against Vietnam was being carried out in the sharpest manner, were deprived of any protection. Theoretically the imperialists could even have the right to attack us with nuclear weapons. Of course, all are aware of our position.

In the light of events, in the face of an imperialism that is always plotting, always conspiring against the socialist camp, we ask if we should continue maintaining idyllic hopes for an improvement in relations with the imperialist government of the United States. We ask whether, in line with the events in Czechoslovakia — in the relations with Yankee imperialism — a position will not be adopted that will imply the renunciation of such idyllic hopes. And it is said here that this will make rapprochement more difficult, and that the new ratification is endangered. In our opinion, the best thing that can happen is for it not to be ratified. Now, in our judgment, the two most important questions.

The statement by TASS explaining the decision of the governments of the Warsaw Pact says in its final paragraph: "The brother nations firmly and resolutely oppose their unbreakable solidarity against any threat from abroad. They will never permit anyone to snatch away even a single link of the socialist community." We ask: Does this statement include Vietnam? Does this statement include Korea? Does this statement include Cuba? Does it consider Vietnam, Korea, and Cuba as links in the socialist camp that cannot be snatched away by the imperialists or not?

On the basis of this declaration, Warsaw Pact divisions were sent to Czechoslovakia. And we ask: Will Warsaw Pact divisions be sent to Vietnam also if the imperialists increase their aggression against that country and the people of Vietnam ask for this aid? Will Warsaw Pact divisions be sent to the Korean Democratic Republic if the Yankee imperialists attack that country? Will Warsaw Pact divisions be sent to Cuba if the Yankee imperialists attack our country, or simply if, in the face of the threat of an attack by the Yankee imperialists, our country requests it?

We accept the bitter necessity which demanded the sending of troops to Czechoslovakia. We do not condemn the socialist countries that adopted this decision; but we, as revolutionaries, and on the basis of principles, have the right to demand that a consistent policy will be adopted in all the other questions that affect the revolutionary movement in the world. . . .

ITALIAN IDEOLOGICAL OFFENSIVE

FROM THE FIRST, the Prague spring had appealed strongly to Italian Communists. PCI Secretary General Luigi Longo had called the creation of an advanced socialist democracy in Czechoslovakia an incentive to all Communist and socialist forces in Western Europe.[1] His visit to Prague in early May attempted to strengthen Dubček in the midst of a concerted Soviet, Polish, and East German press campaign against the Czechoslovak experiment.[2] As the situation deteriorated further, French and Italian Communists joined forces to promote a compromise. Giancarlo Pajetta and Carlo Galuzzi went with PCF Secretary General Waldeck Rochet to Moscow in mid-July. Longo himself was vacationing in Moscow when the invading troops entered Czechoslovakia.

The invasion came as a bitter shock to the PCI. Presented with a *fait accompli,* the Italians made clear that they would resist other long-standing Soviet objectives within the international Communist movement in response to the invasion. Longo (Document 52) explicitly rejected Moscow's bid for a world Communist conference until the situation in Czechoslovakia had been "normalized" and foreign troops withdrawn. Describing the invasion as a "tragic error," he then questioned not only the effects on relations among Communist countries but the underlying, "incorrect" Soviet assumption concerning the balance of power in Europe.

The Soviets had undoubtedly calculated that their conference plans would be set back by the use of force to achieve their objectives in Czechoslovakia. The November 25 meeting was postponed until May with another preparatory session set for March 17 in Moscow.[3] It is less sure that Soviet leaders realized they would be coping with a sustained Italian ideological offensive as a result. For the issue of Czechoslovakia set off a series of PCI polemics with Mos-

---

[1] *L'Unità,* March 29, 1968.

[2] *L'Unità,* May 8, 1968; for analysis, see Kevin Devlin, "Italian CP Attacks 'Unjustified' Invasion," RFE Research Analysis, August 22, 1968.

[3] Subsequently, the March 1969 Sino-Soviet border clash meant still another delay. The conference was postponed to June 5, 1969 with another meeting of the preparatory commission scheduled for May 23 (*The New York Times,* March 23, 1969).

cow that extended to Soviet East European supporters and went far beyond the events themselves.[4]

DOCUMENT 52

"DEVELOPMENTS IN, LESSONS LEARNED FROM CZECH CRISIS"

September 8, 1968

Complete Text

[Interview granted by Luigi Longo to *L'Astrolabio,* in *L'Unità,* September 8, 1968; revised from *JPRS* 46515, Translations on Western Europe, September 24, 1968]

L'Astrolabio: Following the disagreements between the Communist parties of the Soviet Union, Poland, the German Democratic Republic, Hungary, and Bulgaria on the one hand and the Communist party of Czechoslovakia on the other over the "new course" undertaken in Czechoslovakia, there was in May an understood truce with Kosygin's trip to Karlovy Vary; this was followed by the formal accords reached at Čierná and Bratislava. Then came the unexpected military intervention. Why? What do you think of the arguments presented to justify this intervention?

Longo: I do not believe, as I have repeatedly stated in recent months, that the Czechoslovak Communist Party (CCP) was in danger, with the "new course," of falling into the hands of the reformists and that socialist Czechoslovakia could have been overturned by the counterrevolution even if it had tried to attack.

In my opinion, twenty-three years of existence and construction of socialism in Czechoslovakia had already sent down, despite shortcomings and errors, such solid roots throughout Czechoslovak economic, social and political life that the country was in the position of facing with security and tranquility any destructive attacks by rightist domestic forces and imperialist and counter-revolutionary foreign forces.

On the other hand, the "new course" adopted by the Czechoslovak Communist Party proposed precisely to consolidate socialism in Czechoslovakia by overcoming the errors and delays of the past, activating democratic life within the party and the country, and adapting relations between party and

---

[4] For example, the Italian Communist Party bimonthly ideological organ, *Critica Marxista,* Vol. VI, Nos. 4 and 5 (July and October 1968), was largely devoted to articles by leading PCI spokesmen analyzing the questions raised by developments in Czechoslovakia, Soviet military intervention, and the consequences for West European communism. In particular, see Enrico Berlinguer's reply to East German criticism, "Autonomy and Diversity, Conditions for Genuine Internationalism," *Rinascita,* October 25, 1968; JPRS No. 46896, Translations on Western Europe, No. 15, November 18, 1968.

state and their relations with the working classes, the popular masses, and public opinion to new requirements.

Moreover, the decisions adopted by the Central Committee in January and April, decisions that inaugurated the "new course," were also welcomed by the responsible organs of the CPSU. It is true that the new CCP leadership was subsequently accused of having inadequately reacted to the social-democratic and counterrevolutionary attacks that were directed against the Communist party itself, the socialist foundations, and the international position of Czechoslovakia.

It is equally true that in that period the CCP was deeply divided, with its foreign activity almost halted, by the divergencies of the past and the disagreements over domestic organizational and leadership problems. But it was to unite again on these matters and rally around the new leaders including Dubček, especially after the encounters at Čierná and Bratislava. It therefore had broad opportunities to defeat rightist and antisocialist forces.

It is my opinion that, following those encounters, there were no facts to indicate that the counterrevolution posed an imminent and inevitable threat and that socialist power was about to disintegrate. I therefore do not believe that military intervention to ward off a hypothetical catastrophe was warranted. And even less do I believe that the situation in Czechoslovakia was such that it warranted that "painful necessity" with which the intervention in Hungary in 1956 had been justified.

Because of this, we immediately expressed our disagreement and disapproval as soon as we heard about the military intervention in Czechoslovakia by the five socialist states, which had sent jointly the so-called July "Warsaw letter." And we expressed our disagreement and disapproval not only for the aforesaid reasons of fact but also for the more general reasons of principle.

In fact, we consider the following reasons of principle to be inviolable: the autonomy, independence, and national sovereignty of every state and the autonomy and sovereignty of every Communist party. We hold that the fate and future of socialism in a country are of interest not only to Communists, democrats, and people of the given country but also to the Communists, democrats, and peoples of all countries. However, this principle, in our view, cannot be understood in any way as the right of intervening militarily in the internal life of another Communist party and another country.

Moreover, this principle was solemnly stated by the government of the Soviet Union itself in a resolution of October 1956 following the Hungarian events. This resolution affirmed clearly that "the countries of the great commonwealth of socialist nations can establish their relations only on positions of complete equality, respect for territorial integrity, state independence, and sovereignty, and noninterference in the affairs of others." The resolution also mentioned that "the Twentieth CPSU Congress has condemned with maximum resolution violations and errors and has posed the task of consistent application by the Soviet Union in its relations with the other socialist countries, of the Leninist principles of equality among peoples."

The same resolution specified in a very concrete way how the Leninist principles of equality among peoples were to be consistently applied. "The deployment of troops of this or that signatory state of the Warsaw Pact on the territory of another signatory country of the Warsaw Pact is effected in agreement with all the signatory states and only with the concurrence of that state on whose territory, through its request, these military units are deployed or are to be deployed."

L'Astrolabio: Specifically, how do you evaluate the military intervention itself, and what do you believe the Soviet leaders could have done without violating such frequently stated positions of principle and political attitudes?

Longo: I consider the military intervention in Czechoslovakia a tragic error, even in the light of the decisions of the Twentieth CPSU Congress.

These decisions were proposed to correct the errors made in the Stalin period and to overcome the political and doctrinaire bottlenecks that were harming, after the heroic efforts to construct socialism and the victories achieved in the struggle against Nazism and fascism and for the freedom and independence of peoples, the prestige and influence of the world of socialism and the Soviet Union.

The results of the new course inaugurated by the Twentieth Congress were, within the Soviet Union and on the international level, of great importance and significance irrespective of all the limitations and uncertainties under which the new course was advanced and the disagreements it provoked.

Those decisions were the expression of a profound trust in the class, anticapitalist consciousness of the workers and in the activation of socialist ideas on the part of the broad masses of the people. These decisions were open to the new possibilities that were ripening in the world, possibilities such as attracting new countries and new peoples to the liberation and anticapitalist struggles. There is no doubt that these decisions contributed greatly to the development of the Communist and workers' movement in the world and to the national liberation struggles that brought the great majority of the colonial peoples to national independence and some onto the path leading to socialism.

It is true that many socialist countries have solved only a few or none of the problems posed by the Twentieth Congress. And these problems have become complicated and made more difficult by the presence of forces that resist and oppose the socialist option. The drive in this direction is observed primarily in the new socialist countries and comes not only from the still extant remainder of the old social groups but also from new strata that were formed in the very process of the development of socialist society. Consequently, there persist on a large or small scale paternalistic and bureaucratic forms in which socialist regimes express themselves in various fields of political, economic, social, and cultural activity. It is a contradiction of this type that is at the basis of the Czechoslovak events and that the initiators of the "new course" proposed to overcome.

The new course, in fact, was born of the long period of stagnation of Czechoslovak society, of the twelve years of delay in activating the shift sought by the renovating impulse of the Twentieth Congress. This delay led to a gap, to a conflict between the political structure and civil society, and a certain political direction was thereby transformed into an obstacle to the complete flourishing of all the creative capacity of socialism.

The responsibility for having allowed this situation to develop devolves on the former CCP leaders. The error of the Soviet comrades is their lack of faith in the desire and the ability of the new Czechoslovak leaders to bring the new course to completion by bringing the party and the state back to a correct democratic life and adjusting their relations with the country, without compromising the fate of socialism and the authority of the party.

It has been said in our Central Committee that the military intervention stemmed from a conception that sees in the manifestation of erroneous, agitational, or liquidational opinions an immediate danger to the socialist regime and in a new articulation of social and political life an attempt to undermine the leading role of the Communist party. This conception subordinates the same principles of national independence and party autonomy to a military judgment that it is necessary to defend the frontiers of the socialist countries.

But there were, it is said, speculations and threats from rightists and imperialism. To be sure there were and are.

Nobody denies that reaction and imperialism are conducting in every field, in every situation, and in every way a destructive campaign against socialist society, increasing above all "ideological pressure."

They were doing this under the conditions created by the initiation of the "new course," and they continue to do so under current conditions. The question is one of how to battle efficiently all forms of this destructive action in whatever form or way it is conducted and [how] to rally the great majority of the people around the Communist party in this struggle by overcoming the errors and shortcomings of the past and returning to socialism all its social, humane, and democratic concomitants. In short, I do not believe that the best way of responding to capitalist and imperialist "ideological pressure" is to use our arms as a political and ideological reply, thereby relying primarily on authoritative and administrative pressure.

L'Astrolabio: With your position on the Czechoslovak events and especially with the manifestation of "disagreement" and "disapproval" of the military intervention, you have assumed a position in complete opposition to the Kremlin's judgment and especially to its action in Czechoslovakia. What elements underlie this choice?

Longo: Our disagreement and disapproval are not based on moralistic or democratic motives, but on political reasons and on principle.

I say this not because I want to refer to our conception of the "Italian path to socialism." We have never aspired and we do not aspire to impose our socialist prospect as a model valid for the Soviet Union, the socialist countries, or any other party or country. I well know that the past, the evolution, and the actual situation not only condition the development of every society but also and to a greater extent condition the development of the existing socialist societies, particularly their economic systems and their social and political structures.

But I also think that the socialist countries, precisely because of the development attained, the problems posed by this development and by modern technology and science, and the weight assumed by the national momentum of every country in the process of socialist construction, cannot avoid the requirements of facing, in a manner adapted to the different conditions and in complete autonomy, the problems connected with the appropriate and profound democratization of their respective economic, political, social, and cultural systems.

But, getting back to the case of Czechoslovakia which is what interests us, I can say that our positions on this matter were taken on the basis of our party's position in the international Communist and workers' movement and the current world situation, in which converge the existence of the socialist countries, the liberation and profound wretchedness of the colonial peoples, and the continuing strength and at the same time crisis of capitalism and imperialism.

Because of this, I believe that the interests of socialism must also be considered beyond the frontiers of the extant socialist states. In fact, our conception of the development of the Communist and workers' movement hinges on the respect and autonomy of every Communist party and the independence of every state and, along with this, on the exigencies of the consequent development of socialist democracy.

I have told our Central Committee that the recognition, respect, and practice of these principles in the socialist countries and in relations between socialist states are indispensable for consolidating and extending the prestige and influence of the Soviet Union, raising the attraction potential of socialist ideals, and promoting the advance toward socialism — in an atmosphere of peaceful coexistence — of new countries and new peoples.

Therefore, we were also influenced, in assuming our position on the Czechoslovak events, by our preoccupation with the interests and prospects of the international Communist and workers' movement, because the peaceful competition between the two systems must manifest fully the political and ideological superiority of socialism, its democratic potentiality, and a conception of relations between socialist states based on equality and the complete independence of the nations.

Because of this, I believe that any restrictive conception of problems, articulation of political and civil life, and comparison and clash between opinions does not contribute, just as every tendency to intervene in the internal matters of another party and state does not, to the spread of socialist ideas in the world and to the cause of unity and solidarity among the Communist and workers' parties and to their influence on other popular and democratic forces.

L'Astrolabio: However, as the days pass, one has the impression that the intervention in Czechoslovakia was determined not only through a mistaken evaluation of the developments and the new course in that country but also and to a large extent by a precise choice of a strategic nature on the ways to deal with the centrifugal forces that today are being manifested within the

Warsaw Pact by the socialist countries, just as other centrifugal forces are being manifested within the Atlantic alliance.

A series of articles published by the organs of the USSR and the other four countries that intervened in Czechoslovakia seem to be rigidly based on that "logic of blocs" that, you affirmed in your report to the Central Committee, was to have operated within the socialist camp. Could all this, along with the attacks on the Rumanian and Yugoslav leaders, mean that there is a danger, although bearing in mind the diverse international positions of Rumania and Yugoslavia, that such intervention will be repeated?

Longo: We have followed and are following with great attention these articles to which you have referred also because they tend or seem to tend toward a "theorization" of the intervention in Czechoslovakia. It is in this direction that a recent article in *Pravda* seemed to move, while newspapers of the German Democratic Republic have affirmed that the intervention in Czechoslovakia "is a decision of international and strategic significance."

Underlying these affirmations are analyses according to which the imperialist threat to the European socialist countries is not expressed in the current phase through military pressure, but through a policy of infiltration into the socialist countries — a policy carried out with slogans aimed at objectives of ideological, political, and cultural "liberalization" — and through a policy directed at creating differences between the various socialist countries. According to these analyses, "this is the European variant of the global strategy that is expressed in Vietnam with the tactic of limited war and in the Middle East with that of representative war."

It is even possible to agree with the general judgment underlying these analyses in the sense that today the threat of war in Europe does not exist and that the struggle between capitalism and socialism is being waged in other fields: political, ideological, cultural, and economic. But it seems to us that from this analysis, provided it is accepted, one must draw conclusions that are quite different from those that have been drawn from the intervention in Czechoslovakia.

The problem for the socialist countries is to place themselves in a position of waging this struggle in the best possible way. The affirmation that imperialism aims at the creation of differences among the socialist countries and at a "liberalization" should not result in equating all those who within the socialist countries and their Communist parties speak out for the necessary renovation of socialist society, with agents, conscious or unconscious, of imperialism.

If one takes this path he, in our opinion, retreats and does not advance. To continue along this path means the inevitable hardening of the internal life of these countries and the postponement of solutions to the problems discussed — problems that are even acknowledged by the parties of these countries and require solution. This path, in the final analysis, does not lead to the consolidation of a single socialist country, nor does it lead to the consolidation of the system of socialist states.

The current clash between ideologies and ideas must be waged with ideological and ideal weapons, with initiative, with an ideological and political offensive, and not with administrative measures that lead to an extreme solution, to a military intervention such as that effected in Czechoslovakia.

These convictions of ours we have expressed, and we shall express them in the clearest possible way both publicly and privately.

It is also our impression that underlying these theorizations of the intervention in Czechoslovakia is an incorrect consideration of the balance of power: the European socialist states seem to be made out to be some kind of fortress under siege. Reality, instead, is the opposite of this. Conceptions of this kind lead, *inter alia,* to an underestimation of the contradictions within the Western camp; the profound tensions within the Western countries; the new drives manifested in various fields, including the overcoming of the unequal relations that have been created between the United States and the other countries of the Atlantic alliance.

As to our most direct concern as Italian Communists, it is quite evident that we cannot share the conception (which in Italy is La Malfa's) whereby the consolidation of the existing bloc is, in the final analysis, the condition enabling us to move along the path toward *détente.* According to this conception, we are face to face with a bipolar world, which means that we should consider only the existence of the two leading states. We recognize neither a leading state nor a leading party. The conception of a bipolar world is ever surely being disproved by facts, although one cannot but recognize the special positions of the two greatest powers.

The promotion of *détente* and coexistence necessitate, in our view, that every country, including Italy which is our most direct concern, make an original, autonomous contribution both to the establishment of new relations on the international level and to the attainment of the most advanced political equilibrium on the domestic level. It is within this context that national paths to socialism constitute a reality of the present era. A reality that is at times stubbornly opposed. But an unrenounceable reality. A reality that will make headway along this path despite the difficulties encountered and the obstacles thrown up by conservatives.

L'Astrolabio: What is your judgment of the compromise reached in Moscow between the Czechoslovak and Soviet delegations? Do you think that it is possible, on the basis of this compromise, to start Czechoslovakia toward an internal arrangement that will avoid great splits in the party and nation?

Longo: It is not easy to appraise the compromise, given the way it was reached — under conditions of grave uneasiness and the "state of necessity," — which was brought about by the presence of foreign troops in Czechoslovakia.

At this time I believe it is possible to say that the compromise avoided a catastrophe and that it can be a first step toward the normalization of the situation in Czechoslovakia and the relations between the socialist countries. I think that the establishment of a normal situation alone — and this implies the withdrawal of foreign troops — will help avoid a further, dramatic aggravation of the situation and deeper lacerations in the international workers', Communist, and democratic movement.

I hope that the conclusions reached at the Moscow conference will allow the people and the Communist Party of Czechoslovakia to promote in complete autonomy, despite all that has happened, the process of democratic renewal and the consolidation of the socialist society, which was inaugurated with the Central Committee decisions of January and the CCP programmatic declaration of April. The problem now is that of fully reestablishing and developing, on the basis of reciprocal trust, relations of collaboration and solidarity between the socialist countries.

The Moscow compromise was also reached thanks to the strength and unity demonstrated by the Communist party and the people of Czechoslovakia who, with foreign troops in their country, gave proof of unprecedented dignity and discipline and loyalty to the ideas of a democratic and humanist socialism and who were able to avoid errors and ill-advised gestures that might have had irreparable consequences.

The fundamental task of the CCP at this time is the preservation of the trust that the party has gained in recent days among all the people. Only a united party headed by Dubček, Černík, and others is in the position of having Czechoslovakia overcome the current situation and guaranteeing the continuation of the policy undertaken after the January plenum.

As to our party, I think that it must do whatever it can so that the government and Communist Party of Czechoslovakia will attain complete autonomy. I think we would be very much remiss if we were to superimpose our position on that very dignified and firm position of the party and government of Czechoslovakia. We shall continue, however, even under the new conditions to promote our solidarity with the CCP and its renovating activity.

We must do nothing that may weaken or disturb the activity of Svoboda and Dubček or weaken the unity of the Communist party and the Czechoslovak people around the leaders who directed the Moscow negotiations. Conversely, we must do our utmost to help the CCP leadership group to overcome the grave and difficult situation, obtain the restoration of every guarantee of independence, sovereignty, and freedom, eliminate everything that weakens the government and humiliates the party, and avoid provocations that weaken Svoboda's and Dubček's calls for calmness and tranquility.

L'Astrolabio: The Czechoslovak events are reposing with dramatic urgency two great problems: the problem of national paths to socialism and that of the unity of the international Communist and workers' movement. What can you say on this matter?

Longo: We reject the idea proposed only by our adversaries and the enemies of the unity of the Communist and workers' movement, namely, that the Czechoslovak events may indicate the end of the strategy of national paths to socialism and every form of international unity and collaboration among the workers' and Communist, popular, democratic, and progressive forces.

As to us, we hold more clearly and consistently than ever to our concept of the Italian path to socialism, and we believe, precisely with respect to the Czechoslovak events, that we have once again given indisputable proof of our complete autonomy — and precisely with respect to an extremely important and significant instance of policy and international action of the Soviet Union.

On the other hand, we have always stated that autonomy and national particularities must not in any way constitute, and for us they do not constitute, a provincial isolation. We have always regarded and we regard ourselves as an integral and active component of the great international Communist and workers' movement, of which the socialist countries, primarily the Soviet Union, are so great a part.

It is true that the Czechoslovak crisis confronts the Communist movement with profound problems that must be adequately worked out on a theoretical level as well. It is up to us to learn from those events the necessary lessons. But we must continue to work for the establishment of relations based on the understanding and collaboration of all the Communist, democratic, and progressive forces. It is up to us to further the critical and theoretical search, via debates and comparisons, for solutions to problems connected with the renewal and expansion of socialist democracy, with the causes and the nature of the serious resistance, isolation, and delay that are encountered in this field, and with the new forms of the unity of the Communist and workers' movement that we must and can attain — all this we must do without diminishing the diversity of the experiences and the variety of the contributions, without foregoing the necessary respect for the autonomy of every party and the independence of every state.

L'Astrolabio: The concepts of autonomy and unity obviously have contradictory elements. How do you reconcile them?

Longo: For us, the two concepts have the following meaning: the former requires openly comparing the positions that each party can and must independently assume on the basis of the situations in which it operates and the problems that confront it. These positions can never exactly coincide because of the uneven development of the world and the diversity of capitalist and imperialist characteristics prevailing in different situations and the class relations deriving from this diversity. The latter necessitates finding, despite the particularities and differences of situations and conditions, what is common in the reasons for and the objectives of struggle. And what is common must, in our opinion, establish the basis for agreement, collaboration, and unity in struggle so that the impetus and power of the various components will be strengthened and their success and general advance will thus be promoted.

Insofar as one discusses global strategy and global contradiction, he can never disregard considerations relative to the variety and multiplicity of the contributions that can be made to this strategy and this contradiction. And the only penalty here is the reduction of many pompous expressions to empty declamations. I would say that every dispute is the more "global" the more it involves the capitalist and imperialist system in its totality. But this is also true in the following respect: the more the effort expended to bring forces into the dispute, the larger the number of forces that can strengthen and expand it.

We are struggling for unity in diversity while aware that the frontiers of socialism do not coincide with the frontiers of the socialist countries. They are much wider and include all the world's forces struggling against capitalism and imperialism under very diverse conditions and with objectives that converge only in the general prospect of socialism.

The conditions and objectives of the socialist struggle in the countries where the initial phase of socialist construction has triumphed obviously are very different from those in the countries where advanced capitalism holds sway. Here the struggle, because of all kinds of difficulties, still aims solely at creating the requisite conditions for the transition from capitalism to socialism. In this diversity of conditions and objectives, to aspire to reduce the socialist struggle to a single common denominator and to determine a tactic and strategy valid for one and make it valid for another is simply illusory and absurd.

It has been said with reason in our Central Committee that in this case the first internationalist requirement is that each do his work within the borders of the country in which he is located, without ever forgetting the camp as a whole, the various exigencies of struggle, and the necessity of ties and collaboration among the various fronts. Such is our unity in diversity.

As to our party — one in an advanced capitalist country — it has also been said with reason that we must not expect liberation from either the countryside of the world or the action of the socialist states. The successes of the socialist struggles in one and the other camp can also be of great assistance to our struggle, but the proletariat, Communists, and democrats of the advanced socialist countries have their own task to carry out in the general struggle for peace, for freedom, for the advancement of man along the path toward socialism.

We shall assist the other fronts of the socialist struggle, including the Czechoslovak new course, making our contribution toward forcing the imperialist and revanchist forces to withdraw from the positions that they occupy in Europe, so that conditions will be created to overcome the blocs.

L'Astrolabio: Have you thought about the feasibility and possibility of having conferences and discussions with the other Communist parties on the Czechoslovak events? Following the disagreements that have surfaced in this regard, what will be the fate of the World Conference of Communist and Workers' Parties that is supposed to be held in Moscow next November?

Longo: I believe that a comparison and an exchange of ideas on the Czechoslovak events and related political and theoretical problems with the other Communist countries would be worthwhile. Moreover, during these events we maintained continuing contacts not only with the parties of the countries most directly involved but also with the representatives of other Communist parties, primarily European.

Various proposals made by different Communist parties on broader meetings of the Communist and workers' parties, above all from capitalist Europe, are under consideration. In these countries the problems of the struggle against speculation and imperialist and Atlantic intrigues and threats, against the policy of rearmament and the division of Europe into antagonistic military blocs, which under the pretext of the Czechoslovak events has gained a new impetus, necessitate in my view not only an exchange of information and a comparison of experience but also the exact determination of attitude and the coordination of initiative and action, with a view above all to the unity of all the worker, democratic, and progressive forces that intend to resist and react against the threats of the dangerous steps taken behind the shield of *détente,* disarmament, nuclear-free zones, and peaceful coexistence.

In my opinion it is necessary to find, on the basis of the principle of the autonomy and independence of each party, the ways and forms that will give to the Communist and workers' movement of capitalist Europe common grounds and objectives for a joint struggle. And this must be done in a way that will strengthen the resistance to and the struggle against the dangers of a reactionary involution and a consequent threat of war.

As I have said to our Central Committee, I think, broadly speaking, that the essential condition for making every meeting at any level useful and politically productive is that one group of parties refrain from opposing others. A meeting must permit a frank comparison of opinions and an open examination of facts and experience for the purpose of realizing an effective search for positive solutions directed at the restoration of the most trustful collaboration among all the Communist and workers' parties.

It seems to me that what is hopeful in this regard, at least with respect to the Communist and workers' parties of capitalist Europe, is that during the dramatic situation created by the Czechoslovak events, they gave new indications of vitality and initiative. I allude to the joint and convergent action of the PCI and the French Communist Party before and after the military intervention and to the positions of the Communist parties of Spain, Finland, England, Austria, Belgium, Switzerland, and other countries.

This convergence and unity of positions and the autonomous initiatives of the Communist parties of capitalist Europe demonstrates that autonomy corresponds to a capacity for initiative that is manifested with a lively internationalist feeling. It is my opinion that, with the conditions created by the Czechoslovak events, it is the duty of every Communist party to refrain from isolating itself, and from fostering the formation of groups of opposed parties, and to make every effort to avoid new splits, opposing, therefore, anathemas and illegitimate interferences.

As to the World Conference of Communist and Workers' Parties, I can say that the preparatory work has greatly advanced. But I think that until the situation created by the Czechoslovak events is definitively and satisfactorily normalized, it will be neither opportune nor useful nor perhaps even possible to conclude this work.

RUMANIA AND YUGOSLAVIA
SUPPORT PRAGUE

RUMANIA AND YUGOSLAVIA (Documents 53 and 55) flatly rejected Moscow's interpretation of the invasion. Both countries combined their attack on the occupation of Czechoslovakia as a violation of socialist principles with practical measures to ensure their own borders. Bucharest (Document 54) warned that Rumania would not permit any violation of its territory and reactivated the People's Militia. Tito said that the Yugoslavs knew how to defend themselves.[1] Yugoslav soldiers on leave were recalled and preparations were made for resistance. The two leaders conferred August 24 in the Yugoslav border town of Vršac.

Moscow countered by accusing the Yugoslavs and Rumanians of taking phrases from the mouths of imperialists (see V. Kudryavtsev, "Counterrevolution Disguised as 'Regeneration,'" Document 56). Rumors of Soviet troops on Rumanian borders persisted.[2] Soviet Ambassador to Bucharest Alexander V. Basov called President Ceauşescu from a Central Committee meeting to express Moscow's displeasure and reportedly pressed for Warsaw Pact maneuvers on Rumanian territory.[3] Bucharest sidestepped but did not back down — the tone of criticism softened, it was not retracted.[4] Belgrade remained in-

[1] Paul Yankovitch in *Le Monde*, August 26, 1968.

[2] *Washington Post*, August 26, 1968; Paul Hoffman, *The New York Times*, August 27, 1968. In response to intelligence reports apparently confirming such rumors, Washington publicly stated that it would view any Soviet military intervention in Yugoslavia or Rumania with the utmost seriousness (*The New York Times*, August 31, 1968), providing a marked contrast to American response to intensive Soviet pressure on Prague at the time of the Čierná meeting. See Tom Wicker in *The New York Times*, August 1, 1968. For an increasingly sharp denunciation of the Rumanian position ridiculing such speculation as Western fabrications, see N. Gribachev, *Pravda*, September 4, 1968.

[3] If the demand for such maneuvers took place, by the spring of 1969 it had been effectively (although perhaps temporarily) avoided by the Rumanian leadership. At the end of March, Bucharest participated in Warsaw Pact exercises held in Bulgaria (*Scînteia*, April 2, 1969). For analysis, *The New York Times*, April 2, 1969.

[4] Speeches by Ceauşescu August 26 and September 9 emphasized that Rumania would never betray socialist friends. For analysis of Bucharest's maneuvering, see Philippe Ben in *Le Monde*, September 9, 10, 12, and 14, 1968.

transigent, setting off an anti-Yugoslav propaganda war reminiscent of Cominform polemics in 1948.[5]

DOCUMENT 53

OFFICIAL RUMANIAN COMMUNIQUÉ ON THE MILITARY OCCUPATION OF CZECHOSLOVAKIA

August 21, 1968

Complete Text

[*Scînteia*, August 22, 1968]

On August 21, 1968, a joint session of the Rumanian Communist Party Central Committee, of the State Council, and of the government of the Rumanian Socialist Republic was held. In addition to the members of the Central Committee, the State Council, and the government of the Rumanian Socialist Republic, the plenary session was attended by the leaders of the trade unions, youth organization, and other civic organizations, representatives of the press, and activists with responsible state and party jobs.

Comrade Nicolae Ceaușescu reported about the particularly grave situation created as a consequence of the penetration of the armed forces of some socialist countries into the Czechoslovak Socialist Republic and presented the conclusions which were reached by the Executive Committee of the party Central Committee and by the Presidium of the Central Committee in this connection.

The Central Committee, the State Council, and the Council of Ministers have unanimously expressed their profound concern in connection with this act, stressing that it represents a flagrant violation of the national sovereignty of a fraternal, socialist, free, and independent state, of the principles on which the relations between socialist countries are based, of the unanimously recognized norms of international law.

Nothing can justify this armed action — the occupation of Czechoslovakia by the troops of these countries. The interference in the internal affairs of the Czechoslovak people and of their Communist party, the armed intervention against Czechoslovakia, represents a grave blow for the interests of the unity of the world socialist system, for the international Communist and workers' movement, for the prestige of socialism throughout the world, and for the cause of peace. The party and government, all our people, express their conviction that the only road for the liquidation of the grave consequences created by the armed intervention in Czechoslovakia is the speedy withdrawal of the troops of the five countries and the ensuring of conditions for the Czecho-

---

[5] *Borba*, August 31, 1968, makes the comparison explicit. See also the *Komunist*, September 12, 1968, polemic and the *Trybuna ludu*, August 31, 1968, attack on Yugoslav leaders. For specific condemnations of Tito, see Paul Yankovitch, *Le Monde*, September 19, 1968.

slovak people to solve for themselves their internal affairs without any outside interference. The party and government, all our people, manifest on this occasion, too, all their solidarity with the fraternal Czechoslovak people and with their Communist party and express their conviction that the Czechoslovak workers' class, the Czechoslovak intelligentsia, peasantry, the Communist party, and its leadership elected by the party, the legal bodies of leadership of the Czechoslovak state will successfully solve all the problems connected with the march forward of socialist building in the fraternal Czechoslovak republic.

The party Central Committee, the State Council, and the government of the Rumanian Socialist Republic have unanimously approved the activity of the Presidium and of the Executive Committee of the party Central Committee directed toward the promotion of the principles of independence, sovereignty, noninterference in internal affairs, and mutual respect, the strengthening on this basis of the unity of the socialist countries, of the Communist and workers' parties, and of all anti-imperialist forces.

The measures proposed by the Executive Committee to ensure the peaceful creative work of the Rumanian people, builders of socialism, the independence, and sovereignty of our fatherland, were also approved unanimously.

It has been decided to convoke for tomorrow, 22 August, the Grand National Assembly of the Rumanian Socialist Republic in extraordinary session.

DOCUMENT 54

BALCONY SPEECH BY NICOLAE CEAUSESCU ON
CZECHOSLOVAKIA

August 21, 1968
Complete Text

[*Scînteia,* August 22, 1968]

❦

Dear comrades, citizens of Rumania. In this difficult moment for the situation in Europe and for the fraternal Czechoslovak people, in the name of the Central Committee, of the State Council, and of the government, I wish to address myself to you and express myself to you and express our confidence in our people, who are aspiring to ensure the peaceful construction of socialism.

We know, comrades, that the entry of the forces of the five socialist countries into Czechoslovakia is a great error and a serious danger to peace in Europe and to the fate of socialism in the world. It is inconceivable in today's world, when the peoples are rising to the struggle to defend their national independence and for equality in rights, that a socialist state, that socialist states, should violate the freedom and the independence of another state. There is no justification whatsoever, and there can be no excuse for accepting even for a moment the idea of military intervention in the affairs of a fraternal socialist state.

Our party-state delegation which last week visited Czechoslovakia convinced itself that the Czechoslovak people, the Czechoslovak Communist Party, and the Czechoslovak workers' class, old people, women, and young people, unanimously support the party and state leadership in order to put right the negative state of affairs in Czechoslovakia inherited from the past, in order to ensure the triumph of socialism in Czechoslovakia.

The problem of choosing the ways of socialist construction is a problem of each party, of each state, and of every people, and nobody can set himself up as an adviser and guide for the way in which socialism must be built. It is the affair of every people, and we deem that, in order to place the relations between socialist countries and Communist parties on a truly Marxist-Leninist basis, it is necessary to put an end once and for all to interference in the affairs of other states and other parties.

The measures which the Central Committee, the Council of Ministers, and the State Council have decided to adopt aim at submitting to the Grand National Assembly a declaration in which we would set out clearly the relations we mean to build, our relations with the socialist countries and with all the countries of the world, based on respect for independence and national sovereignty, full equality in rights, and noninterference in internal affairs, and to base these relations on a truly Marxist-Leninist collaboration which would contribute to the triumph of the ideas of Marx, Engels, and Lenin, to the triumph of communism, and to restoring the authority of and confidence in Marxist-Leninist ideas.

We have today decided to set up armed patriotic guards made up of workers, peasants, and intellectuals: defenders of the independence of our socialist fatherland. We want our people to have their armed units in order to defend their revolutionary achievements and in order to ensure their peaceful work and the independence and the sovereignty of our socialist fatherland.

In our activity, we proceed from the responsibility we have toward the people, toward all the working people regardless of nationality — Rumanians, Hungarians, Germans, and other nationalities; we all — Rumanians, Hungarians, Germans, people of other nationalities — have the same destiny and the same aspiration: the forging of communism in our fatherland. We are determined that in complete unity we shall ensure the attainment of our ideals.

It has been said that in Czechoslovakia there was danger of counterrevolution; perhaps tomorrow they will say that our meeting has mirrored counterrevolutionary tendencies. If so, we answer to all that all the Rumanian people will not permit anybody to violate the territory of our fatherland. Look comrades: Our whole Central Committee, the State Council, and the Government are here. We are all determined to faithfully serve the people in socialist construction and in the defense of the revolutionary achievements and its independence. Many of those who are here are Communists and antifascists who have faced prisons and death but have not betrayed the interests of the workers' class and our people. Be sure, comrades, be sure, citizens of Rumania, that we shall never betray our fatherland, that we shall not betray our people's interests.

We are confident that the Communist and workers' parties will know how to find the way to put the speediest end to this shameful event in the history of the revolutionary movements. We are convinced that no Communist can be found who can accept this military action in Czechoslovakia, that all the Communists would raise their voices to ensure the triumph of freedom, the triumph of the Marxist-Leninist principles, so that Czechoslovak people, so that the peoples, may be able to build socialist society as they themselves want it.

We are determined to act with all our force and with all our responsibility in order to contribute to the finding of ways for the speediest solution of this situation created by the entry of foreign forces into Czechoslovakia, and so that the Czechoslovak people can carry out their activity in tranquility. We are firmly determined to act so that together with the other socialist countries and with the other Communist and workers' parties we shall contribute to the elimination of the divergencies and to the strengthening of the unity of the socialist countries and of the Communist parties because we are convinced that only in this way are we serving the interests of the people and the interests of socialism in the whole world.

We ask the citizens of our fatherland that, having complete confidence in the leadership of the party and the state and in our Communist party, they should give proof of complete unity and act calmly and firmly, with everyone at his place of work, to increase his efforts to ensure the implementation of the program for the development of our socialist society, and to be ready, comrades, at any moment to defend our socialist fatherland, Rumania.

I thank you, all the citizens of the capital and all the citizens of our fatherland for your confidence, for this warm manifestation, and for the attention with which you are watching our party's policy; and we wish you comrades good health and success in your activity for the triumph of socialism in our fatherland.

We request you, comrades, that you return to your work and have confidence that we shall keep you informed regarding the unfolding of events. Good-bye.

DOCUMENT 55

RESOLUTION ADOPTED BY THE CENTRAL COMMITTEE OF THE LEAGUE OF COMMUNISTS OF YUGOSLAVIA

August 23, 1968
Complete Text

[*Borba*, August 26, 1968; revised from the unofficial translation by the Yugoslav Information Center, September 25, 1968]

❦

The Communists and other citizens of Yugoslavia have in recent days overwhelmingly expressed their deep indignation and protest against the occupation of Czechoslovakia. They have given full support to the people of Czechoslovakia who under difficult conditions of occupation rallied around their party and state leadership, so unanimously and courageously fighting for the independence and free socialist development of their country.

In endorsing the policy of the League of Communists of Yugoslavia (LCY), our people have once again declared themselves ready to defend uncompromisingly their independence, their right to determine their own way of internal socialist development and to act freely in international relations. They have taken this stand in line with their internationalist responsibility and in solidarity with socialist and all anti-imperialist and democratic forces in the world, in the interests of peace, independence, and the equality of peoples in the interests of socialism. In the stand taken by our people, the LCY sees an inexhaustible source of strength and encouragement for further efforts in the struggle for the development of socialist, democratic, and humane relations among people and for the resolute support to all the forces fighting for the liberation of man and nations from all forms of repression and hegemony.

Together with all the people of socialist Yugoslavia, the Central Committee (CC) of the LCY has once again expressed its protest against a violent action, the method and aims of which are directly opposed to the essence and interests of socialism.

The CC condemns the policy which attempts to shirk responsibility to the working class and peoples of the whole world, to the interests of peace, progress and socialism. No matter what arguments are used to justify the occupation of Czechoslovakia, the fact remains that the governments of the five Warsaw Treaty countries, by applying brute force, have perpetrated an attack against the independence of a socialist country in order to hinder its independent socialist development and to subject it to their will.

The peoples of our country, led by the LCY, once again raise their voice in protest, as they have been doing in the matters of American aggression in Vietnam, threats to the independence and independent internal development of Cuba, Israeli aggression against Arab countries, or imperialist violence and intervention in various countries of Africa, Asia, and Latin America. Viewed historically, the action against Czechoslovakia is all the more grave and far-reaching in its harmful effect on progress, peace, and freedom for having been undertaken by socialist countries ostensibly to protect socialism.

Striking at the working class and the Communist Party of Czechoslovakia (KSČ), the forces which alone can ensure the progress of socialism, the intervention against the Czechoslovak Socialist Republic (ČSSR) can in no way be described as protection of socialism nor as directed against counterrevolution. Neither can the intervention be justified by any strategic interests of the struggle against imperialism because, by weakening the position of the socialist countries and socialism, it is, on the contrary, strengthening the positions of the imperialist forces. Finally, this action can least of all be justified by ideological reasons and arguments drawn from the theory of Marxism-Leninism, because it is flagrantly at odds with the ideas of Marx, Engels, and Lenin.

The occupation of Czechoslovakia has also dealt a hard blow to the interests of the struggle of workers' and anti-imperialist movements in the world. That is why the large majority of the Communist and workers' parties and anti-imperialist forces are resolutely resisting such a policy. The indignation in the workers', national liberation and other anti-imperialist movements is all the greater as the blow against the elementary interests of their struggle came from a source from which they expected only support and help. Thus the organizers of the occupation of Czechoslovakia, by this action, have deepened the rift in the international workers' movement and the Communist movement in particular.

The encouraging fact in all this is that never in the history of socialism has an act of hegemony and bureaucratic arrogance stood so isolated and bare vis-à-vis the historical interests of the working class and anti-imperialist forces.

The events connected with Czechoslovakia clearly show that socialism has now reached a crucial historical point. These events concern not only Czechoslovakia but also the development of socialism in the world. The occupation of the ČSSR is not an accident, but is the consequence of an obstinate endeavor to resolve the contradictions and conflicts within socialism — which are focused on the essence, character, and perspectives for the development of socialist relations, and on the policy of socialist and anti-imperialist forces at the international level — by the increasing application of force in order to preserve obsolete relationships and institutions, instead of by the further emancipation of labor and man and by the greater development of socialist and human relationships among men.

Socialism has become a world practice, the strength and influence of which are leaving an imprint on contemporary social development. The ideas of socialism have conquered the minds of the large majority of mankind. The inexorable advance and the constant strengthening of the forces of socialism are reflected in the socialist revolutions, from the October Revolution, the Chinese and the Yugoslav revolutions, to the revolutions in a number of other countries which have embarked on the road of socialism, in the powerful strengthening of the role and influence of the working class in Europe and the rest of the world, in the victory of the anticolonial revolution and in the other social changes which constitute a part of the socialist transformation of the contemporary world. That is why subjective socialist forces, today more than ever, bear responsibility for the fate of the world, not only in the anti-imperialist struggle, but first and foremost through their own practice and their critical attitude toward that practice.

The ways and forms of the development of socialism are different, at times even contradictory. Socialism could not develop nor could it reveal to mankind new ways of social progress and freedom if it were uniform, if its forms were determined in one center.

The progress of socialism is being opposed by the forces of bureaucratic statism which are hindering the emancipation of labor and of man's personality, and seek to identify socialism with statist authoritarianism and monopoly of centers of economic and political power acting independently of the working class and society, which lead to the confinement of socialism within the narrow boundaries of camps and to its isolation from the rest of the world. Such a conception and practice reduce the prospects for the development of socialism, reflect a lack of confidence in man and peoples, hobble the creativeness of the working class, of the younger generation, of intellectuals — of all the forces of labor and knowledge — and lead to the strengthening of dogmatism and compromise the idea of socialism.

Such concepts are inevitably followed by the big power hegemonic policy of monopolism and national inequality, which is directly opposed to socialism. Such a policy seeks allies in chauvinism and other forces and ghosts of the past, as was seen in connection with the events in Czechoslovakia. The peoples of Yugoslavia cannot help regarding the chauvinist campaign conducted in Bulgaria against socialist Yugoslavia and particularly against the Socialist Republic of Macedonia, as part and parcel of such a policy.

The inexorable growth of the internal forces of socialism has constantly opposed the forces of stagnation and conservatism. This struggle imbues the contemporary history of the workers' movement of all countries; it has been a source of constant encouragement to the further development of socialism. This struggle is reflected in the long years of resistance to Stalinism in the USSR and in the decisions of the Twentieth Congress of the Communist Party of the Soviet Union; it is reflected in the broad revival process in the Communist and workers' movement; in the creative effort of the Communist and other revolutionary parties to find their own way of socialist development, including the present struggle of the CP of Czechoslovakia for its own renaissance; in the stronger trends toward unity of action among the workers' parties and progressive public opinion; and in the more resolute raising of the question of equality in relations among socialist countries and Communist parties. In view of such progressive changes in socialism, the present situation, conditions and the balance of forces are essentially different from those of 1948. This is best demonstrated by the broad support given by Communist and workers' parties and progressive public opinion in the world to the Czechoslovak peoples in their struggle for independent and free socialist development. It is also demonstrated by the fact that Communist parties are developing an independent critical attitude toward their own activity and toward policies and practice in the socialist countries.

Socialist Yugoslavia has made its own contribution to this.

It was not by accident that the CP of Czechoslovakia resolutely proceeded to resolve the accumulated contradictions and problems in the social development of its country. This reflects the needs of a developed society and the impossibility of pursuing the interests of peoples and socialism within the framework of bureaucratic-statist relationships. In this the leadership of the CP has obtained the full support of its members, the working class, and the people of the Czechoslovak Socialist Republic. Antisocialist currents in Czechoslovakia have never been able to obtain support among the people and have remained only a by-product of the process, precisely because the socially conscious forces, led by the Communists, have been successfully performing their historical role. Hence the blow dealt to the CP, its leadership and the working class of Czechoslovakia, which are the only standard-bearers and the sole guarantee of progress and socialism, represents not help to socialism but hindrance to its development.

In the struggle for the transformation of the contemporary world, there is an increasingly dominant trend toward the liberation of peoples, toward national independence and toward democratic cooperation and unification on the basis of equality and against any hegemony and exploitation, against any form of monopoly in economic, political, and other power. Both ideologically and in practice, Communists must be in the front ranks of this struggle.

The intervention by the five Warsaw Treaty countries in Czechoslovakia is indeed in contradiction with these elementary demands and once again confirms the thesis that the policy of blocs cannot provide either a just peace or independence. Insistence on the bloc division of the world necessarily encourages the creation of spheres of interest among the big powers, and puts pressure on the small countries to opt in favor of the big powers, rather than for the policy of transcending hegemony, violence, interference in the internal affairs of other peoples, and establishing equitable cooperation among nations and states. It also leads to growing militarization, with increasing independence for military power and its escape from political control. Peace and lasting stability in the world cannot be preserved on such a basis.

The struggle to overcome bloc divisions in the world is therefore an important component of the struggle against imperialism, hegemony and war. The policy of nonalignment is an expression of resistance, by peoples who feel threatened by such practices in international relations, and is becoming one of the most significant factors in the struggle for peace and equality of peoples.

In developing a socialist society in Yugoslavia we face the same or similar laws of development, contradictions, and phenomena. The Yugoslav Communists, together with all the creative forces of our society, have always endeavored to find answers and solutions which open up prospects for the further advancement of socialism.

We are striving for the emancipation of labor and of man's personality, and against bureaucratic statism, by developing self-government and direct socialist democracy.

We are coordinating the interests of the working class and those of the various peoples and nationalities of our country by developing conditions conducive to the independent material and cultural development of these peoples, on the basis of equality, and to the promotion of their solidarity and unity.

By ensuring the independence of our country we have created conditions for our own free and unhindered socialist development and consequently for active participation in the struggle for democratic relations among peoples and for the socialist transformation of the world.

Through reorganization and democratization of the LCY we are striving to help the Yugoslav Communists successfully resist the influence of statist bureaucracy and to exercise a leading ideological-political role in conformity with the present needs of the development of self-governing socialist relationships.

We oppose the policy of might, hegemony, and pressure in international relations by striving for equal relations and cooperation among peoples and states, for the policy of nonalignment, for active and peaceful coexistence among countries having different social systems, and for the broadest possible cooperation and solidarity with all the anti-imperialist and democratic forces in the world.

We have had both successes and failures along our socialist path. The LCY and our society continually reexamine their own socialist practice. The acquired experience has convinced our working class and our people that only the promotion of self-management and direct social democracy can provide them with material welfare, cultural advancement, and the development of a society in which the working man can become the master of his own labor and his own destiny. Any other way would lead to stagnation and political and economic subordination.

The stability and strength of our socialist community and its international status depend on the outcome of this struggle for the implementation of the goals contained in the Program of the LCY.

Broad and dynamic social action to study and implement the stands contained in the Guidelines of the CC LCY marked the beginning of a new offensive by the LCY and all progressive forces in society, designed to bring about the consolidation and further development of socialist self-government.

The CC LCY believes that a period of deterioration in international relations is imminent, along with an arms race and pressure on the freedom and independence of peoples.

In this situation, the CC LCY emphatically declares that:

1. The LCY does not recognize the right of anyone willfully to interfere in the internal development and affairs of an independent country by recourse to military intervention or any other form of pressure.

2. The LCY rejects as completely unacceptable all the arguments submitted by the governments of the five Warsaw Treaty countries designed to justify the invasion of Czechoslovakia. The LCY offers full support to the CP, the working class, and the peoples of Czechoslovakia in their struggle for the independence of their country and free socialist development.

3. The LCY demands the immediate termination of the occupation of Czechoslovakia and release of the democratically elected representatives and leaders of the people of the ČSSR and the KSČ, and the creation of all the conditions necessary for the socialist development of Czechoslovakia, unhampered by outside interference.

4. The LCY and Socialist Yugoslavia will continue to strive for the broadest possible cooperation with socialist and all other anti-imperialist and democratic forces and movements in the struggle for freedom, peace, and social progress, for equality among states and nations, for full respect for the right to independent development for each country and party, and for noninterference in their policies and internal development.

In developing our relations with socialist countries and Communist and workers' parties, we consistently adhere to and strive for implementation of the principles expressed in the Belgrade and Moscow Declarations of the Governments and Parties of Yugoslavia and the USSR in 1955 and 1956.

5. The LCY and Socialist Yugoslavia do not recognize any agreements, open or tacit, regarding spheres of interest which transform the small nations into pawns of power politics. Just as we opposed the Yalta Agreement, which carved out spheres of interest for the great powers, so do we today oppose any such arrangements at the expense of other peoples. Historical practice has shown that the policy of division into spheres of interest and of hegemony by the big powers is not only a disaster for the peoples concerned but also a constant threat to world peace.

6. Today, as before, we are resolved to use all our forces and means to defend our independence, revolution, and our own way of socialist development. We shall strive to strengthen the defensive power and security of our country. This is a matter that concerns all the peoples of our socialist community. Created and educated in the revolution, the Yugoslav national army is ready unwaveringly to do its duty in defending the country.

7. By increasing political vigilance and by energetic, uncompromising action, we must oppose all attempts to undermine the foundations of our system, to hinder our independent democratic socialist development, and to strike at the unity of our peoples and our workers. We must also oppose any provocative action geared toward weakening the strength of our resistance, and interference from any quarter whatever.

The CC LCY addresses itself particularly to the young people from the cities and countryside to take part in sociopolitical activities and to join the ranks of the LCY in order to strengthen its striking force and creative power in the further development of our socialist society.

The CC LCY invites all citizens, all sociopolitical organizations, and particularly the Socialist Alliance of the Working People of Yugoslavia, the Federation of Trade Unions of Yugoslavia, youth organizations, and all Communists steadfastly to continue their creative work and to go on fighting for the broadest possible political mobilization and for the unity of the working class, peasants, intelligentsia, all the peoples and nationalities of Yugoslavia in the struggle for the implementation of the adopted policy.

DOCUMENT 56

"COUNTERREVOLUTION DISGUISED AS 'REGENERATION'"

V. Kudryavtsev

August 25, 1968

Condensed Text

[*Izvestia*, August 25, 1968, revised from *CDSP*, Vol. XX, No. 35, September 18, 1968, pp. 7–8]

The fraternal socialist countries' performance of their highest internationalist duty in defending socialism in Czechoslovakia has called forth a frenzied anti-communist campaign in the capitalist countries. . . . It is precisely those in Czechoslovakia who cry heartrendingly that they seek to "regenerate" social-ism who are being defended by the American and other imperialists. The imperialists in the role of "defenders" of socialism! Is this not a sight for the gods? Should this not put on guard all those who, deluded or failing to un-derstand the essence of the matter, furnish a pretext to raise their voices in the antisocialist chorus?

One cannot help recalling 1938. At that time Czechoslovakia was bourgeois and headed by Benes, a man now being made a hero by people who in words are expressing concern for the regeneration of socialism but in deeds are drag-ging the country backward to the time when the capitalist system prevailed in Czechoslovakia and the imperialists regarded it as their outpost in Eastern Europe. So even then the capitalist West betrayed bourgeois Czechoslovakia and handed it over to Hitler fascism. Why is imperialism, which betrayed bourgeois Czechoslovakia, suddenly acting as the "defender" of socialist Czecho-slovakia?

There can be only one answer: What changed is not imperialism (it merely changes its tactics depending on the situation), but those in Czechoslovakia who under the disguise of "regenerating" socialism really advocate reviving the capitalist system in Czechoslovakia and including that country in the system of the imperialist world. It is precisely for this reason that the impe-rialist reactionaries are coming to these people's defense. It is precisely for this reason that the whole NATO apparatus has been mobilized to defend them.

When the imperialists call the fulfillment of the socialist countries' interna-tionalist duty "intervention," it shows why they are imperialists. But it is strange, to say the least, to hear exactly the same phrases from the mouths of the Rumanian and Yugoslav leaders. Don't they know that the Warsaw Pact was concluded not only to defend the signatory states' national borders and territories? It was concluded in order to defend socialism in response to the creation of the aggressive NATO military bloc, which is openly aimed against the socialist states for the purpose of counteracting communism. And those who now attempt to interpret the Warsaw Pact in narrowly nationalistic terms ("it's none of my business") contribute to the imperialists' frenzied anti-socialist campaign. The defense of socialism in Czechoslovakia is not only the internal affair of that country's people, but also a problem of defending the positions of world socialism.

In this connection it should be noted that some people have taken the absolutely correct thesis that each country chooses its own path of building socialism and moved it so far from the principles common to all socialist countries that they are objectively assisting the Czechoslovak counterrevolution in its efforts to wrest Czechoslovakia from the socialist commonwealth. In justification of this position the thesis has been advanced that, as N. Ceausescu said, "no one can act as an adviser or instructor on how and by what method socialism should be built." But for some reason it is the supporters of this thesis who are giving advice left and right to the Soviet Union, subjecting not only its foreign policy, but occasionally its domestic policy as well, to unsubstantiated criticism. The Yugoslav press has been specializing in just this. Yet at the same time Belgrade is very sensitive to any criticism in the other direction.

Statements made by some of our friends seem to reproach the Soviet Union and other socialist countries for bringing their armed forces into Czechoslovakia to defend socialism despite the fact that the Czechoslovak leaders had given assurances in Cierna-on-Tisa and Bratislava that they would take measures to curb the antisocialist forces. But this is the whole point: The C.C.P. leadership and the Czechoslovak government did not keep their word, and the counterrevolutionaries launched their activity at full blast. . . .

It might be asked what sort of policy an opposition party will pursue if it comes to power after ousting the Communist Party, whose program provides for the construction of socialism. If it is going to be the same policy as was pursued by the Communist Party, then why make all that fuss? Would it not be better, would it not be more advisable, to correct the mistakes and improve the methods of leadership through common efforts and continue to construct socialism under the Communist Party's leadership? But the "regenerators" had something entirely different in mind.

This is not difficult to guess if one considers the thirst of the supporters of "regeneration" for the bourgeois democracy of Masaryk and Benes. After all, it is not fortuitous that these bourgeois figures are praised to the skies, and it is not by chance that they see in their policies almost the very image of that to which the "revolution of revival" must lead. The paper *Zemedelske Noviny* even reached the absurd conclusion that socialist democracy can only satisfy Russia, and particularly the Soviet Asian republics, insofar as they had absolutely no idea of democracy before the October Revolution. As far as Czechoslovakia is concerned, it appears from what this paper says that it saw the "peak" of its democracy during Masaryk's and Benes' time and therefore does not need socialist democracy, but a certain kind of "democratic socialism" which, in fact, turns out to be bourgeois democracy. . . .

What could justify the introduction of a multiparty system in Czechoslovakia on the bourgeois-democratic model if its leaders had given assurances that the country would not retreat from socialism and that socialism had become rooted so deeply that there could not even be talk of repudiating it? Nothing, were it not for the fact that the adherents of "regeneration" are contemplating a gradual retreat from socialism. Otherwise, it becomes pointless to raise the question. Parties that disagree with the Communist Party and its guiding role can appear only in a socialist country that antisocialist elements are dragging backward toward a bourgeois-democratic system. . . .

The transformation of yesterday's supporters of "regeneration" into out-and-out degenerates was crowned by the underground assemblage that passed itself off as an "extraordinary congress of the C.C.P." Brought together in conceal-ment not only from the people of the country but also from Communist Party members, the assemblage set as its goal the seizure of party leadership by the right-wing revisionists in order to conceal behind the name Communist the degenerate, right-wing revisionist organization generated by this assemblage. . . . People are being dug up for leading roles who hitherto hid in the shad-ows, awaiting the proper moment to raise their revisionist voices. These "re-servists" include one Venta Silhan, "Acting First Secretary of the C.C.P. Cen-tral Committee."

Silhan's first words were to call for the "neutralization" of Czechoslovakia, involving withdrawal from the Warsaw Treaty Organization. Yet the ink was scarcely dry on the C.C.P. representatives' signatures to the statement of the Communist and Workers' Parties of the socialist countries adopted in Brati-slava. This statement, as everyone well remembers, reemphasized the particular importance of the Warsaw Pact and contained a pledge to strengthen political and military cooperation in this organization. And then supporters of the Czechoslovak degenerates in Yugoslavia and Rumania extol the sanctity of the Czechoslovak leaders' signatures and call on the other socialist countries to sit back quietly while the degenerates drag the country into the bosom of the capitalist world. No thanks, spare us that! Consistent fighters for socialism will not be confused by degenerates disguised as "true socialists." The under-ground assemblage has torn off even this fig leaf, which covered up the anti-socialist essence of a group daring to assert that it was authorized to speak in the name of the Czechoslovak people. No one will believe them now! . . .

In analyzing the situation that has taken shape, one must not lose sight of the substantial difference between the status of Communist Parties in capitalist states and their status in socialist states. For the Communist Parties in capitalist countries the temporary loss of a position is an episode in the convolutions of the class struggle, which naturally does not develop along a straight line. For Communist Parties in the socialist countries, where they occupy the domi-nant, leading position — without which the construction of a socialist society is unthinkable — losing a position is tantamount to letting the class enemy into the house. Progressive forces in the capitalist countries must beware when their criticism at all coincides with statements directed by the class enemies against the socialist countries that are performing their internationalist duty in defense of the socialist system in Czechoslovakia.

While using one hand to sign the statement at the conference of Communist and Workers' Parties in Bratislava, which involved principles of building socialism that are common to all countries, the Czechoslovak leaders used the other hand to argue that the other socialist countries supposedly have poor knowledge of the "psychology" of the Czechoslovak people and the special features of the country's historical development and that therefore the other socialist countries find it difficult to understand that the C.S.R. needs its own, "Czechoslovak socialism." This nationalist point of view has its defenders in Rumania and Yugoslavia.

Well, all right, this is nothing new, and the world has now become very familiar with such "national socialisms," which in fact prove to be out-and-out nationalism in a socialist casing, used because socialism has become such a popular doctrine that nationalism has become simply inedible without socialist camouflage. And wherever nationalism flourishes, bourgeois ideology should be sought. It is to be found in the glorification of the bourgeois figures Masaryk and Benes, whose ideas, wrapped in a socialist casing, have been presented to the Czechoslovak people in the guise of a "revitalization of socialism."

No, this constitutes not a "regeneration" of socialism, but overt attempts to achieve its degeneration. . . .

V. Normalization

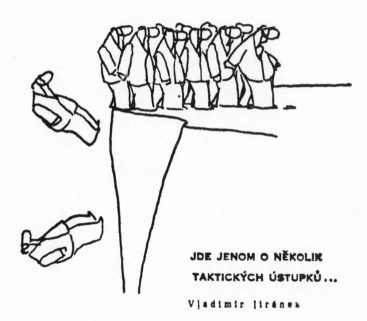

JDE JENOM O NĚKOLIK
TAKTICKÝCH ÚSTUPKŮ...

Vladimír Jiránek

"It is only a matter of a few tactical steps back."

Listy, No. 4, January 30, 1969.

SOVIET-CZECHOSLOVAK COMMUNIQUÉ
OF AUGUST 28

REALIZING THAT none of the Soviet representatives in Prague had power to negotiate, President Svoboda requested to go to Moscow. He left on August 23 with a delegation including the conservatives Alois Indra and Vasil Bil'ak. Yet progress toward replacing the Dubček regime with pro-Soviet collaborators was no greater in Moscow than in Prague. It soon became clear that Svoboda would not cooperate unless Dubček and the other arrested leaders joined the Czechoslovak delegation. Since the Soviets were unwilling to resort to the Hungarian solution of simply arresting the negotiators,[1] in the end the circle had completed itself. Moscow reinstated the Czechoslovak leadership that had been arrested by Soviet troops a few days before. The Soviet-Czechoslovak Communiqué of August 28 (Document 57) euphemistically dismissed the invasion as a temporary entry of troops that would be withdrawn when the situation was "normalized." It was as if, in a Kafkaesque fashion, everyone had agreed to wait before a door that could not open. If the Moscow Protocol (Document 58) is, in fact, a secret counterpart of the published communiqué, Soviet expectations become less ambiguous.[2]

Nonetheless, Svoboda's courageous stand had succeeded to the extent that it did due to the remarkable passive resistance of the Czechoslovak population.[3] Within hours of the invasion, clandestine radio stations operated in and outside of Prague.[4] Street names were removed or made illegible. Swastikas

[1] Paul E. Zinner, *Revolution in Hungary* (New York, Columbia University Press, 1962), p. 317.

[2] Although not acknowledged by either the Soviet or Czechoslovak leadership, there is reason to think that the Moscow Protocol was agreed upon before Svoboda and Dubček returned to Prague after the forced August negotiations. Not only do the fifteen points fit the pattern of subsequent Soviet demands, but Dubček's speech of September 13 (Document 61) mentions an otherwise unidentified "Moscow Protocol" while the October Treaty (Document 67) refers to the *documents* of the August Moscow meeting — a strong indication that the agreement included more than the published communiqué. For analysis see Pavel Tigrid, *Le Monde*, March 23, 25, and 26, 1969.

[3] Michel Tatu, *Le Monde*, August 26, 1968.

[4] Sláva Volný, "The Saga of Czechoslovak Broadcasting," *East Europe*, Vol. 17, No. 12 (December 1968), pp. 10–16 and Joseph Wechsberg, *The Voices* (New York: Doubleday, 1969). For the strategic implications of such passive resistance, see Hans-Joachim Winkler, "Die 'Soziale Verteidigung' der Tschechoslowaken," *Gegenwartskunde*, No. 4 (1968).

were painted on Soviet tanks. Moreover, governmental activity continued. The National Assembly met and issued a statement condemning occupation of Czechoslovakia as a violation of the Warsaw Pact (Document 59). The extraordinary 14th Congress defiantly reelected Dubček as First Secretary. Under pressure, the Communist Party of Czechoslovakia had become a genuinely popular government[5] and recognized itself as such, a fact eloquently underlined by President of the National Assembly Smrkovský's speech when he returned from Moscow (Document 60) — "We realized that our decision could be regarded by the Czechoslovak people and by history as a wise solution or as treason."

DOCUMENT 57

COMMUNIQUÉ ON SOVIET-CZECHOSLOVAK TALKS

August 28, 1968

Complete Text

[*Pravda*, August 28, 1968, quoted from *CDSP*, Vol. XX, No. 35 (September 18, 1968), p. 3]

Soviet-Czechoslovak talks were held in Moscow from Aug. 23 to 26, 1968. The participants were:

for the Soviet side — Comrade L. I. Brezhnev, General Secretary of the C.P.S.U. Central Committee; Comrade A. N. Kosygin, Chairman of the U.S.S.R. Council of Ministers and member of the Politburo of the C.P.S.U. Central Committee; Comrade N. V. Podgorny, Chairman of the Presidium of the U.S.S.R. Supreme Soviet and member of the Politburo of the C.P.S.U. Central Committee; Comrade G. I. Voronov, member of the Politburo of the C.P.S.U. Central Committee and Chairman of the Russian Republic Council of Ministers; Comrade A. P. Kirilenko, member of the Politburo of the C.P.S.U. Central Committee and Secretary of the Central Committee; Comrade D. S. Polyansky, member of the Politburo of the C.P.S.U. Central Committee and First Vice-Chairman of the U.S.S.R. Council of Ministers; Comrade M. A. Suslov, member of the Politburo and Secretary of the C.P.S.U. Central Committee; Comrade A. N. Shelepin, member of the Politburo of the C.P.S.U. Central Committee and Chairman of the Central Council of Trade Unions; Comrade P. Ye. Shelest, member of the Politburo of the C.P.S.U. Central Committee and First Secretary of the Ukraine Communist Party Central Committee; Comrade K. F. Katushev, Secretary of the C.P.S.U. Central Committee; Comrade B. N. Ponomarev, Secretary of the C.P.S.U. Central Committee; Comrade A. A.

---

[5] Returning to Prague, President Svoboda said simply, "It was a difficult time for us and for you. Our thoughts were with you all the time" (Moscow TASS International Service in English 1907 GMT, August 27, 1968; not reprinted in *Pravda* version of August 28, 1968).

Grechko, U.S.S.R. Minister of Defense; and Comrade A. A. Gromyko, U.S.S.R. Foreign Minister;

for the Czechoslovak side — Comrade L. Svoboda, President of the C.S.R.; Comrade A. Dubcek, First Secretary of the Central Committee of the Czechoslovak Communist Party; Comrade J. Smrkovsky, Chairman of the C.S.R. National Assembly and member of the Presidium of the C.C.P. Central Committee; Comrade O. Cernik, Chairman of the C.S.R. Government and member of the Presidium of the C.C.P. Central Committee; Comrade V. Bilak, member of the Presidium of the C.C.P. Central Committee and First Secretary of the Slovak Communist Party Central Committee; Comrade F. Barbirek, member of the Presidium of the C.C.P. Central Committee and Vice-Chairman of the Slovak National Council; Comrade J. Piller, member of the Presidium of the C.C.P. Central Committee; Comrade E. Rigo, member of the Presidium of the C.C.P. Central Committee; Comrade J. Spacek, member of the Presidium of the C.C.P. Central Committee; Comrade O. Svestka, member of the Presidium of the C.C.P. Central Committee; Comrade M. Jakes, Chairman of the C.C.P. Central Control and Inspection Commission; Comrade J. Lenart, candidate member of the Presidium and Secretary of the C.C.P. Central Committee; Comrade B. Simon, candidate member of the Presidium of the C.C.P. Central Committee; Comrade G. Husak, Vice-Chairman of the C.S.R. Government; Comrade A. Indra, Secretary of the C.C.P. Central Committee; Comrade Z. Mlynar, Secretary of the C.C.P. Central Committee; Comrade Lieut. Gen. M. Dzur, C.S.R. Minister of National Defense; Comrade B. Kucera, C.S.R. Minister of Justice; Comrade V. Koucky, C.S.R. Ambassador to the U.S.S.R.

In the course of the talks there was discussion, which proceeded in frank, comradely debate, of questions related to the present development of the international situation, to the intensification of imperialism's schemes against the socialist countries, to the recent situation in Czechoslovakia and to the temporary entry of the five socialist countries' troops into C.S.R. territory.

The sides expressed firm mutual conviction that the most important point in the current situation is to implement the joint decisions made in Cierna-on-Tisa and the propositions and principles formulated by the Bratislava conference, and also to carry out consistently the practical steps stemming from the understanding reached during the talks.

The Soviet side affirmed its understanding and support for the stand of the C.C.P. and C.S.R. leadership, which intends to proceed on the basis of the decisions made by the January and May plenary sessions of the C.C.P. Central Committee for perfecting the methods of guiding society, developing socialist democracy and strengthening the socialist system on the foundation of Marxism-Leninism.

An understanding was reached on measures aimed at the swiftest possible normalization of the situation in the C.S.R. The Czechoslovak leaders described the immediate measures they have outlined and are carrying out toward this end.

The Czechoslovak side declared that the entire work of party and state bodies through all channels of influence will be aimed at providing effective measures to serve socialist rule, the guiding role of the working class and the Communist Party and the interests of developing and strengthening friendly relations with the peoples of the Soviet Union and the entire socialist commonwealth.

The Soviet leaders, in expressing the unanimous desire of the U.S.S.R.'s peoples for friendship and brotherhood with socialist Czechoslovakia's peoples, confirmed their readiness for the broadest and sincerest cooperation on the bases of mutual respect, equality, territorial integrity, independence and socialist solidarity.

The allied countries' troops that temporarily entered Czechoslovak territory will not interfere in the internal affairs of the Czechoslovak Socialist Republic. Agreement was reached on conditions for the withdrawal of these troops from C.S.R. territory as the situation there is normalized.

The Czechoslovak side announced that the supreme commander-in-chief of the Czechoslovak armed forces had given the appropriate orders for preventing incidents and clashes that could cause a breach of the peace and public order. He also directed the C.S.R. military command to maintain contact with the command of the allied troops.

In connection with the discussion in the U.N. Security Council of the so-called question of the Czechoslovak situation, the C.S.R. representatives stated that the Czechoslovak side had both not requested the Security Council to consider this question and demanded its removal from the agenda.

The C.P.S.U. leaders and the C.C.P. leaders confirmed their determination steadfastly to implement in the international arena a policy in the interests of strengthening the solidarity of the socialist commonwealth and upholding the cause of peace and international security.

The Soviet Union and Czechoslovakia will continue to deal a resolute rebuff to militarist, revanchist and neo-Nazi forces seeking to revise the results of the second world war and to breach the inviolability of the borders existing in Europe. The determination was reaffirmed to fulfill unswervingly all the commitments they have assumed under the multilateral and bilateral treaties signed among the socialist states, strengthen the defense might of the socialist commonwealth and enhance the effectiveness of the defensive Warsaw Pact.

The talks proceeded in an atmosphere of frankness, comradeship and friendship.

DOCUMENT 58

THE MOSCOW PROTOCOL

[Svědectví, Vol. IX, Nos. 34, 35, 36 (Winter 1969), pp. 228–231]

1. During the course of the talks problems were discussed concerning the defense of socialist achievements in the situation which has arisen in Czechoslovakia as well as the most essential measures dictated by the situation and by the stationing of allied troops in the ČSSR. Both sides acted according to all the generally acknowledged norms for relations among fraternal parties and countries and according to the principles affirmed in the documents of the Čierná-nad-Tisou and Bratislava conferences. There was an affirmation of allegiance to the compacts of the socialist countries for the support, consolidation and defense of socialism and the implacable struggle with counterrevolutionary forces, which is a common international obligation of all socialist countries. Both sides likewise affirmed the strong conviction that in the present situation the most important task is to put into practice the principles and tasks of the conference in Bratislava, from the agreement at the negotiations in Čierná-nad-Tisou and their concrete realization.

2. The Presidium of the CC KSČ announced that the so-called 14th Congress of the KSČ, opened August 22, 1968, without the agreement of the CC, violated party statutes. Without the participation of the members of the Presidium, secretaries, secretaries of the CC KSS, most of the delegates from the army and many other organizations, it is invalid. All measures pertinent to this problem will be taken by the Presidium of the CC KSČ upon its return to the ČSSR. A special meeting will be called after the situation has been normalized within the party and the country.

3. The KSČ delegation reported that a plenum of the CC KSČ would be held within the next six to ten days with the participation of the party's control and revision commission. It will review problems of the normalization of the situation within the country, measures for improving the work of party and state organs, economic problems and problems of living standard, measures for consolidating all links of party and state rule, and it will discharge from their posts those individuals whose further activities would not conform to the needs of consolidating the leading role of the working class and the Communist party. It will carry out the resolution of the 1968 January and May plenums of the CC KSČ concerning consolidation of the positions of socialism within the country and further development of relations between the ČSSR and countries of the socialist community.

4. The KSČ representatives declared the necessity for the speedy implementation of a number of measures fostering the consolidation of socialism and a workers' government with top priority to measures for controlling the communications media so that they will serve the cause of socialism fully by preventing antisocialist statements on radio and television, putting an end to the

activities of various organizations with antisocialist positions, and banning the activities of the anti-Marxist social democratic party. Suitable and effective measures will be taken in the interest of accomplishing these tasks. The party and state organs will remedy the situation in the press, radio and television by means of new laws and measures. In this unusual situation it will be essential, if these tasks are to be accomplished, to take several temporary measures so that the government can have firm control over the ways and means of opposing antisocialist individuals or collectives. Essential personnel changes will be carried out in the leadership of the press and radio and television stations. Here, as at the meeting in Čierná-nad-Tisou, the representatives of the CPSU expressed full solidarity with these measures, which also conform to the basic interests of the socialist community, its security and unity.

5. Both delegations discussed problems connected with the presence of troops of the five socialist countries and agreed that the troops will not interfere with the internal affairs of the ČSSR. As soon as the threat to socialism in the ČSSR and to the security of the countries in the socialist community has passed, allied troops will be removed from the territory of the ČSSR in stages. The command of the allied troops and the command of the Czechoslovak Army will immediately begin discussions concerning the removal and change in position of military units from cities and villages where local organs are able to establish order. Repositioning of the troops is to be effected in barracks, exercise grounds and other military areas. The problem of the security of the Czechoslovak border with the German Federal Republic will be reviewed. The number of troops, their organization and repositioning will be effected in cooperation with representatives of the Czechoslovak Army. Material, technical, medical and other forms of security for the troops temporarily stationed in the ČSSR will be determined by special agreement at the level of the Ministry of National Defense and the Ministry of Foreign Affairs. Problems involving matters of principle will be dealt with by the governments of both countries. A treaty concerning the conditions of the stay and complete removal of allied troops will be concluded between the government of the ČSSR and the other governments.

6. The Presidium of the CC KSČ and the government will adopt measures in the press, radio, and television to exclude the possibility of conflicts between the troops and citizens on ČSSR territory.

7. The KSČ representatives announced that they would not tolerate that party workers and officials who struggled for the consolidation of socialist positions against antisocialist forces and for friendly relations with the USSR be dismissed from their posts or suffer reprisals.

8. An agreement was reached regarding the establishment in the near future of negotiations on a number of economic problems with an eye to expanding and intensifying economic and technical cooperation between the USSR and the ČSSR, especially as concerns the needs for further development of the economy of the ČSSR in the interest of fulfilling the plan for the development of the national economy with respect to the CC KSČ resolution.

9. There is full agreement that the development of the international situa-

tion and the treacherous activities of imperialism, working against peace, the security of nations and socialism, necessitate the further consolidation and increase in effectiveness of the defense system of the Warsaw Pact as well as of other existing organs and forms of cooperation among socialist countries.

10. The leading representatives of the CPSU and KSČ affirmed their resolve to scrupulously maintain the principle of coordinated action in international relations fostering the consolidation of unity in the socialist community and of peace and international security. Concerning European problems the USSR and the ČSSR will follow as before a scrupulous policy in conformity with the common interests of the socialist countries and the interests of each of them, interests of European security and offer strong resistance to militaristic, anti-Soviet and neonationalistic forces, which follow a policy of revising the results of the Second World War in Europe and existing European borders. Both sides announced that they will scrupulously fulfill all the obligations resulting from the multilateral and bilateral treaties among socialist countries. In close cooperation with the rest of the countries in the socialist community they will continue in the future to struggle against imperialism's treacherous activities, support the national liberation movement, and work toward the easing of international tension.

11. In connection with the discussion of the so-called ČSSR problem in the United Nations Security Council, the leading KSČ and government representatives announced that the ČSSR did not request the Security Council to discuss this matter. The KSČ representatives reported that the Czechoslovak representative in New York had been instructed by the government of the Republic to lodge a categorical protest against the discussion of the ČSSR problem in the Security Council or in any other United Nations organ and make a categorical request for the deletion of this issue from the proceedings.

12. The CC KSČ Presidium and the government announced that it would review the activities of those members of the government who were outside the country and made statements in the name of the government of the ČSSR concerning internal and foreign policy, especially with regard to the maintenance of the policy of the KSČ and the government of the Republic. Suitable conclusions will be drawn from this review. In this connection the representatives of the CC KSČ consider it necessary to carry out several further personnel changes in party and state organs and organizations in the interest of ensuring complete consolidation within the party and the country. These problems will be considered from all points of view upon the representatives' return to their country. The activities of the Ministry of the Interior will also be examined, and measures will be taken to consolidate its leadership on the basis of the results.

13. An agreement was reached to set up negotiations of party and state delegations within a short period of time to further deepen attempts at reviewing and resolving the problems which arise in relations with one another and discussions of contemporary international problems.

14. The delegations agreed in the interest of both communist parties and friendship between the ČSSR and the USSR to regard the contacts between

the representatives of the KSČ and the representatives of the CPSU as strictly confidential in the period following 20 August 1968, which therefore holds for talks just concluded.

15. Both sides pledged in the name of their parties and governments to promote all efforts of the CPSU and KSČ and the governments of these countries to intensify the traditional friendship between the peoples of both countries and their fraternal friendship for time everlasting.

DOCUMENT 59

DECLARATION OF THE CZECHOSLOVAK NATIONAL ASSEMBLY

August 21, 1968

Complete Text

[Text as Issued in English by the Czechoslovak Embassy in London]

The deputies of the National Assembly have met and unanimously agreed on the following declaration at a time when the government and other organs cannot carry out their functions:

1. We fully agree with the declaration of the Central Committee of the Communist Party of Czechoslovakia and the Presidium of the National Assembly protesting against the occupation of Czechoslovakia by the armies of the five countries — members of the Warsaw Treaty — and considering it a violation of international law, the provisions of the Warsaw Treaty and the principles of equal relations among nations.

2. We demand the release from detention of our constitutional representatives, namely President of the Republic Ludvík Svoboda, Prime Minister Oldřich Černík, President of the National Assembly Josef Smrkovský and First Secretary of the Central Committee of the Communist Party of Czechoslovakia Alexander Dubček, Chairman of the Central Committee of the National Front Dr. František Kriegel, Chairman of the Czech National Council Čestmír Císař, and others in order that they can carry out their constitutional functions entrusted to them by the sovereign people of the country.

The delegation which we have sent to the Soviet Embassy this morning has not yet returned. We protest against the fact that the National Assembly, the government and all bodies of the National Front are prevented from carrying out their legal rights and the freedoms of movement and assembly.

3. We categorically demand immediate withdrawal of the armies of the five states — members of the Warsaw Treaty — and full respect of the state sovereignty of the Czechoslovak Socialist Republic. We call on the parliaments of all countries and the world public opinion to support our legal demands.

4. We empower a delegation of the National Assembly composed of Marie Miková, Josef Macek, Josef Valló, Pavol Peos, Josef Pospíchal and Václav

Kučera to enter into contact with the President of the National Assembly Josef Smrkovský, the President of the Republic Ludvík Svoboda, and the Prime Minister O. Černík, in order to inform them about the above decision and agree with them on further procedure. The delegation will immediately inform the Czechoslovak people about the result of their negotiations.

5. We call on all the people not to take any violent action against the occupation armies and not let themselves be provoked by various forces which want to gather proof for the justification of the intervention and use the situation for self-appointed actions.

Working people, citizens, remain in your workshops and offices and safeguard your factories and enterprises. Use all democratic methods for further development of socialism in Czechoslovakia! If necessary you will surely be able to resist by general strike. We believe that we will come out of these difficult moments with raised head and firm backbones.

At the above meeting, the Deputy President of the National Assembly Josef Vallo has likewise informed the deputies about his discussion with the President of the Republic in which President Ludvík Svoboda expressed his approval of the calling of the plenary session of the Assembly.

6. In view of the fact that the government is primarily aware of the political consequences of the occupation and at the same time of its responsibility for the proper management of the national economy, it turns to all workers, peasants and intelligentsia to constantly guard the line contained in the declaration of the Presidium of the Central Committee of the Communist Party of Czechoslovakia adopted at today's session and simultaneously turn their attention to the safeguarding of the industrial production, agriculture, transport and supplies in order to prevent a disruption of the national economy.

7. The government particularly calls on the young people — the hope of our nation — that especially they face the situation which has arisen with a dignified and self-conscious calmness and in no case give any pretext for useless sacrifices.

8. We call on all people to refute the arguments about the necessity of military action from abroad by securing proper management of production and maintenance of calmness and sound reason. The government appreciates the support of all international progressive forces all over the world which has been given to our socialist republic in today's difficult situation.

DOCUMENT 60

AN ADDRESS BY JOSEF SMRKOVSKÝ, PRESIDENT OF THE
CZECHOSLOVAK NATIONAL ASSEMBLY

August 29, 1968
Excerpts
[*The New York Times,* August 30, 1968]

❦

This is not the moment to look back, to draw up the balance sheet of developments since January. The events of the last few days have proved that, so far,
we have not paid sufficient attention to certain factors that have considerable
influence on the evolution of our country, in particular the external and international factor that brought about the biggest and most difficult complications
in our undertaking.

You know that our party's policy was gradually becoming the object of
criticisms and pressures on the part of neighboring socialist countries, pressures that on Aug. 21, or more exactly on the night of Aug. 20–21, took on immeasurable proportions. Our country was suddenly submerged by a gigantic
storm that it was impossible and hopeless for us to face with the same means.

Alas, alas, alas, such a situation is neither new nor unprecedented in our
past. It has happened a number of times in the history of the Czechs and
Slovaks, and for the second time in our century.

Tragedy of Small Nation

It is the tragedy of a small nation whose country is located in a particularly
sensitive region of our continent. It is also the tragedy of an effort toward
social renewal, the tragedy of those who seek to go ahead, the tragedy of peoples
whose efforts aim at great and noble goals.

Such efforts are never easy and are much more difficult when they involve
small nations, because they are even more doomed to failure or misunderstanding.

I think that we were aware of this risk, that we suspected that we would
have to pay for all that, but — and I want to emphasize this — we never
thought we would have to pay the price we paid the night of Aug. 20–21.

Starting then, not only all our efforts since January but also everything that
we cherished — namely the state and its sovereignty, liberty, the evolution of
our internal affairs, even the existence and security of each citizen — have been
threatened with a mortal danger

Negotiations Described

Our negotiations in Moscow were held under conditions that were hardly
normal. You know that we did not arrive there together and you know the

circumstances under which some of us and others went there and negotiated.

I do not think I have to go into details that still are too painful and sad for myself as well as for Comrade Dubček and the others.

To make decisions under such conditions was, as each of you can imagine, extremely problematical.

Our communications with the country were restricted. At the beginning we had little information, not to say no information at all, and we had to rely more on our faith in the country's attitude than on any information on actual facts.

On the other hand, the position of our interlocutors was put to us clearly, but we suspected that the armed invasion had given them some political problems. We knew the world sympathized with us but that the big powers would accept a compromise rather than anything else. In these conditions we found ourselves in a dilemma with no way out.

Choice of Attitudes

We could have refused any compromise and allowed matters to develop to the point where an occupation regime would have been installed with all the consequences for the state's sovereignty, political rights, economy, including possible loss of life, that such a development would undoubtedly have implied.

I must say that we did not forget the possibility that at a given moment there might be no alternative but to refuse any arrangement and to have recourse to bayonets and expel the troops from our territory so as to safeguard the nation's character.

But after consideration we concluded that we had not arrived at such a critical stage and that despite all that had happened, there remained another possibility that, as statesmen, we could not leave unexploited. This is why we subsequently tried to seek a way out consisting of an acceptable compromise.

But equally, in this case, we took into account the moral and historic consequences such a solution would entail. I beg you to believe that at those moments our personal fate was put in the background despite the fact that this was not a matter of indifference to us, as is natural for a human being.

The decisive consideration was the question of whether it was still possible to try to get the Czechoslovak state and people out of the crisis into which they had been plunged through no fault of their own.

Such a possibility became apparent when the clear and unanimous position of the Czech and Slovak peoples was demonstrated, and this influenced the attitude of our interlocutors and our personal situation.

We then decided to choose the second way, that of compromise making it possible to hope that it would be possible to continue along the path indicated by the January plenary session. This was accepted by the other party as the basis of a possible solution.

Our subsequent decisions were not easier to make, and we spent a day and a night before reaching them. We realized that our decision could be regarded by the Czechoslovak people and by history as a wise solution or as treason.

We were aware that our mandate was problematical and limited.

Clashed with Russians

I beg you to believe that we were not silent, that we clashed hard not only with our interlocutors but among ourselves, and that we made use of every argument within our reach.

From all this came the solution whose main terms you know, particularly from the mouth of President Svoboda, the First Secretary and the Premier, who, unlike the communiqué, spoke a more understandable language and a language closer to ourselves.

Terms of Accord

As most of you know the main points of the Moscow agreement were the following:

¶Our internal life, as defined by the January plenary session, will continue.

¶Our political life will not be directed by an imposed government, but by all the legitimately elected bodies, and the National Assembly will assume all the functions that devolve upon it under the Constitution.

¶Czechoslovakia's foreign policy will follow the course it followed previously.

¶The Warsaw Pact troops have undertaken, as the communiqué said, a temporary occupation, will not interfere in the internal affairs of our country and will leave again after a normal situation returns.

It will certainly be asked what are the guarantees on this agreement. I say openly that despite the aid of all our friends, of whom we have a great many at present and whom I thank sincerely, our country must not rely in the present world situation on any other real guarantee than her own wisdom, and especially her unity.

Smrkovský Urges Calm

After the first reaction of pain and indignation, I ask you to reflect with calm and coolness. The Warsaw Pact troops must stay here for a certain time and the Czechoslovak Government is opening discussions concerning their departure.

We shall have to take special measures in the field of radio, television and the press to prevent writings against the foreign policy requirements and the interests of the republic.

In the domain of liberty of association, the required measures will lead to the dissolution of political clubs and to a ban on the formation of new political parties. For this the Government will avail itself of certain special powers. All these arrangements will be discussed by the National Assembly in the days to come.

We are aware that these measures will slow down and make more difficult the process of evolution towards democratic socialism. We are sure that you will understand why this must be so and that you will not impute wrong intentions to the party and state leadership. We are sure that you will see in all this an essential measure aimed at a return to a normal situation, the departure of foreign troops and a renewal of the trend towards socialist democratization.

TWO INTERPRETATIONS:
DUBČEK AND KOSÍK

A STRONG SENSE of identification with the Czechoslovak nation permeated Dubček's speech of September 14 (Document 61). He spoke at a time of great uncertainty. There was confusion as to just what had been agreed to in Moscow.[1] Details of the "normalization" required before occupying troops would leave Czechoslovakia were still being negotiated.[2] And the gaps between Soviet demands, pressure from the Czechoslovak people, and liberal hopes as expressed by the philosopher Karel Kosík's[3] conclusion that "in politics you may even make an alliance with the devil to achieve your goal, but you must

[1] At the beginning of September, the new First Secretary of the Slovak Communist Party, Gustav Husák, indicated that repudiation of the extraordinary 14th KSČ Congress, elected during the first days of occupation, had been a part of the August Moscow agreement (Radio Czechoslovakia in Slovak 1815 GMT 5 September 1968, and *Pravda*, September 7, 1968). The most detailed official account from Prague was the television speech of Zdeněk Mlynář, member of the party Presidium, reassuring the nation that the question of what was or was not antistate activity would be decided by Czechoslovak laws and "not by the journalists or police organs of any other country" (Bratislava Television Service in Czech 1835 GMT 13 September 1968). At the time of the November 1968 KSČ CC Plenum, Mlynář resigned his party posts reportedly after his apartment had been searched by Soviet KBG agents (*Der Spiegel*, December 16, 1968). For an unofficial translation of notes taken by a party member briefed at closed meetings, see *The New York Times*, September 8, 1968. If these notes are accurate, even the unpublished Moscow Protocol (Document 58) represented considerable compromise on such issues as the existence of counterrevolution in Czechoslovakia.

[2] Soviet First Deputy Foreign Minister Vasili Kuznetsov arrived in Prague September 6 for a series of intensive discussions (Henri Pierre in *Le Monde*, September 9 and 13, 1968). For an unofficial report of Kuznetsov's conversation with Smrkovský see *Der Spiegel*, October 14, 1968. In Moscow, Czechoslovak Premier Oldřich Černík concluded an economic agreement with only vague reference to elaborating the political questions raised by the August Protocol [Communiqué in *Pravda*, September 11, 1968; *CDSP*, Vol. XX, No. 37 (October 2, 1968), p. 5; for commentary, Michel Tatu in *Le Monde*, September 10, 11, 12, 1968].

[3] One of Czechoslovakia's most respected contemporary philosophers, Karel Kosík is best known as the author of *Dialectic of the Concrete: A Study on the Problematics of Man and the World* [*Dialektika konkrétního: studie o problematice člověka a světa* (2nd ed. Nakladatelství Československe akademie věd: Prague, 1965)].

be certain that you will outwit him, not that he will outwit you" (Document 62) were potentially unbridgeable by the party leadership.

Domestically, the political clubs so objectionable to Moscow were being phased out.[4] Censorship had been "temporarily" reinstated.[5] Resignations and dismissals of unacceptable officials had begun: František Kriegel and Čestmír Císař were dropped from the Presidium and Secretariat respectively.[6] Nor was the First Secretary's speech encouraging despite its tone. Amid pledges not to return to pre-January conditions, Dubček warned against extremists, antisocialist forces, and irresponsible elements — unfavorable phenomena that would not be permitted to occur "even when the situation becomes normal."

DOCUMENT 61

"NORMALIZING THE SITUATION BY FULFILLING THE MOSCOW PROTOCOLS — CONSISTENT CONTINUATION OF POST-JANUARY POLICY AS A BASIS FOR UNITY IN OUR SOCIETY"

Dubček Speech to Czechoslovak Citizens
September 14, 1968
Excerpts
[*Rudé právo,* September 15, 1968]

Dear citizens and comrades: I am addressing you again with observations that concern the lives of all of us. I tell you frankly that I feel better in my work when I can share with you the worries which occupy us all wherever we work; we are all faced with the same worries. I am all right when I feel that I am among you and that you understand me.

In the recent radio speeches after the resumption of work by party and state organs, we acquainted you with the complex political situation in our country, with the difficult tasks we are expected to fulfill in the next period, and with the ways we intend to resolve the situation that has arisen. We begged you for understanding, help, and unity in order to be able to fulfill

[4] On September 5, the Ministry of the Interior refused to approve the statutes of Club K-231 and the Club of Committed Non-Party Members (KAN).

[5] Prague ČTK International Service, 2017 GMT 13 September 1968; *The New York Times,* September 14, 1968.

[6] Subsequently, Deputy Premier Ota Šik, the architect of Prague's economic reform, and Foreign Minister Jiří Hájek also resigned. At least initially, these resignations were balanced by a reshuffling of conservatives suspected of collaborating with the invaders. Thus Drahomír Kolder lost his Presidium seat to become Commercial Councilor to the Czechoslovak Embassy in Sofia (reported to Yugoslav News Agency Tanyug, September 18, 1968), and Oldřich Švestka was shifted out of the Presidium and from his position as editor-in-chief of *Rudé právo* to director of the CC weekly *Tribuna.*

with dignity the mission we have taken upon ourselves in the political guidance of our country and implementation of the conclusions of the Moscow protocols.

I know very well that it was not easy for you to accept our statements which frankly expressed the reality which we all have encountered, that it was not easy to accept the only possible way out which we who represented you in Moscow arrived at unanimously according to our best conscience and after long deliberations. Today I wish to thank you for the wisdom with which you grasped the meaning of the situation and for the confidence which you have again expressed in us these days.

I greatly appreciate the fact that courage, drive, and voluntary discipline have been preserved, that no one has let himself be led astray by provocateurs or instigators, by those who would like to misuse grave times in the life of the nation for their personal or other aims. If we preserve these qualities, which have become important political reality, then we can be optimists and trust that our socialist nations will be able to pass every test, even through this complex period from which we all must jointly find a way out.

The guarantee for this must be the work of all Communists wherever they work, in the central organs or in the primary organizations. In brief, a great deal today depends on each individual. In order to preserve the unity of our people, which everything today depends upon, we must fulfill consistently, even if more slowly, the principles of the post-January policy. Abandoning this policy would mean the disintegration of the political unity of our society and — I do not hesitate to say — tragic clashes between political forces, all of which would in turn make the fulfillment of the Moscow protocol impossible. We regard the Moscow protocol as a reality which opens wide the possibility of developing still further the work of our party and our country and gives us a certain leeway to find a way out of the present situation. In fact, the failure to fulfill the points of the Moscow protocol would also spell danger for the post-January policy. This is why there is today no other way out but to fulfill the Moscow protocols.

We have started in on the difficult tasks laid down at the latest session of the Czechoslovak Communist Party Central Committee; we have started to fulfill the Moscow conclusions. We shall fulfill them consistently without avoiding even those provisions which are difficult and complex for us.

For us, this is a matter of political honor and Communist morality. You know that the new post-January leadership of the party and the state has always spoken frankly to our people and that we have never broken the pledge we gave to our people and our partners. This is how we proceed today, too. We shall cope with this task no matter what the price, and we shall do so successfully. There is no trickery in this, nor do we have any underhanded intentions. We have rejected once and for all any behind-closed-doors policy toward our people, and this is what we Communists must keep in mind during this period of solving the grave problems of our party work and socialist construction. That is why we shall fulfill with the greatest strictness all commitments stemming from Moscow. This will entitle us to discuss with our partners the fulfillment of the commitments of the other side, which include the departure of the troops from our territory.

People ask us in many letters whether it is really possible to combine the tasks set by the Moscow protocol with the aims of our domestic policy. I am convinced that there is no contradiction here. On the contrary. This is the way of resolving the present situation. Our standpoints are well known and have been expressed in pertinent statements by party and state organs.

The Moscow protocols speak of their understanding for the road of socialist progress started in the Czechoslovak Socialist Republic after January, but only under the new, changed conditions and provided that no mistakes are made, that the reality of the presence of the troops of the five countries is taken into account.

We see the way out in the firm unity of the working people on the basis of translating the principles of the post-January policy of socialist progress into reality, and in the thorough fulfillment of the Moscow protocol which, I beg of you, should be regarded by our entire public as our own. This is the result of the decision and the directive of the latest and very important plenum of the Czechoslovak Communist Party Central Committee.

If you approach these tasks in unity and with the determination and tenacity shown thus far, we shall find, under the leadership of our party, the way out of this complex situation.

The fundamental question for us today is the normalization and consolidation of conditions and the departure of the troops of the five countries from our republic.

This is what the Moscow protocol says.

How are we to understand the term "normalization"? A variety of comments and all sorts of speculations are today being spread by various quarters about this question. Normalization certainly includes fully restoring the economic, political, and cultural life of the country. It includes developing the activities of the legally and democratically elected organs of our working people, the further unequivocal socialist development in the country, and enhancing the leading role of the party and working class.

We are also taking into consideration that in our future development we must avoid all extreme standpoints that could complicate and hamper our future development. We must work in such a way as not to allow scope for any forces that would like to misuse the present complex period for working in the direction of antisocialist tendencies and ideas. And the decisive point is this:

The main and the determining factor in our development has been the positive, prosocialist content which our working people call the post-January policy — everything that has been prosocialist and new and that we were trying to resolve in the period of the post-January policy, all that our people, both Communists and non-Communists, our youth, view as the task of making good the mistakes and shortcomings, the deformations of the past pre-January period, everything we have termed as building socialism with a humane face.

And I believe that in the period to come much will be gained by a stick-to-it-ive attitude toward work and life.

It is necessary, dear friends, to take it as a fact that some features of the post-January development caused apprehension in the five socialist countries and that these countries lost confidence in our policy, in particular with regard to the fact that the elimination of some negative tendencies was not consistently ensured, tendencies which we ourselves had referred to, especially at the May plenary session of the Czechoslovak Communist Party Central Committee. We have never concealed these mistakes and shortcomings. In fact, we pointed them out ourselves because we saw in them a brake and obstacle to the realization of our post-January policy. We must, therefore, in the spirit of the Moscow protocol uncompromisingly and without any underhanded intentions remove from political and social life everything that caused this distrust and seek to convince our partners in the course of our socialist construction of the profound socialist substance of our policy. Above all, it is imperative to prevent even more thoroughly the vestiges of antisocialist forces from taking an active part in politics.

Our work, the work of Communists and other working people, will certainly continue to be marked in the coming period by the determination to refuse to allow those antisocialist forces any leeway in the realization of the conclusions of the action program and of all that we call post-January policy. You well know that the party has acted in the past against such manifestations and has sought to solve these problems by ideological and political struggle and by the preparation of legislation which we planned to complete by the end of August at the session of the Czechoslovak Communist Party Central Committee and at the scheduled session of the National Assembly.

The endeavors for speedy consolidation make it imperative these days to take swift administrative measures, and, in this connection, the government has adopted the well-known measures in the spheres of the right of association, the press, political organizations, the National Front, and so forth so that legislation is enacted in this regard and so that the measures we have taken in party organs are expressed in legal norms. In no instance will we allow anyone to carry out antisocialist activities, which would be at variance with our post-January policy.

I am convinced that all honest citizens will not see in these measures an attack on their endeavors for social involvement and that they will help with all their might to solve the current political problems. After all that we have had to go through, I can say that the overwhelming majority of our citizens seek unity on the basis of socialist development, that is, not just any unity, but unity on the basis of socialism, unity on the basis of the socialist evolution of our society, unity of socialist forces around the Communist party and isolation of the forces that would take a stand against socialism or that would even attempt to endanger it. It is on this basis that our nations have united since January, and it is on this position that they stand unequivocally. . . .

There are individuals who carry a share of the responsibility for the damage caused to socialism and the party by the former, discredited pre-January leadership and its methods, who have subsequently learned nothing and have not really identified themselves with the policy of the party after January and have seen in it nothing but mistakes and shortcomings. Yet these individuals are trying to make use of the situation and turn history back to pre-January conditions and replace only the *people* of the pre-January regime. To these people we must say clearly and unambiguously: No, this time is over, far behind us. And not only the party but also our people will not allow any variation of a return to pre-January conditions.

In the course of rapid development along untrodden paths there have, of course, also been some unfavorable phenomena which we have pointed out many times. The solution of many problems demands time for the elimination of these tendencies. Some people have often acted rashly, and there have been confused opinions. In the nervous atmosphere, there has been an unwarranted blackening of the work that has been done and of some honest comrades.

There have been attempts of some individuals to misuse some clubs, even to renew social democracy and the like. We have always seen in these tendencies to recreate social democracy an undesirable policy which would seriously violate the unity of the Marxist Communist party, the unity of the working class.

We have pointed out these problems openly and clearly in public discussions and speeches. We have, therefore, dashed all these attempts not only ideologically and politically but also organizationally. The rest was left to legal provisions which we expected to enact in the National Assembly by the end of August. We also opposed these symptoms in our action program as well as in the plenums of the Czechoslovak Communist Party Central Committee and on other occasions.

We have deep faith in truth, in the persuasiveness of the ideas of socialism, in their strength, and hence in our ability to defeat any antisocialist campaign. I think we can say that the past has shown that our people will not easily accept anything that could be at variance with the socialist character of the social order in our Czechoslovak Socialist Republic.

I tell you frankly that in the future we must not permit similar unfavorable phenomena, even when the situation in our country becomes normal, when the sovereignty of our organs and our state is fully restored. At present, of course, the remnants of antisocialist forces can harm our development and the fulfillment of the Moscow agreements. They would surely receive appropriate support for this from the imperialist forces, which have never favored the democratization process in our republic or the consolidation of socialism in our country.

There is a special need to warn against the danger of provocations, against clashes between our citizens and military units, against such foolhardy steps which could lead to undesirable bloodshed. This must be avoided always and under all circumstances. Irresponsible elements could try to play upon the people's nerves by causing panic and thus lead them upon a road of political adventurism. I beg you all not to allow yourselves to be so misused. . . .

I am fully aware of the fact that our nations are socialist nations, and it is only natural that we Communists, as internationalists, must look on our policy not only from the viewpoint of today but also of tomorrow. It is quite clear to us that from the strategic point of view our republic will live in the community of the nations of the other socialist countries. It is important that we keep this in mind in these days. We must not think only of today but also of tomorrow.

We have been and will continue to be internationalists. Our place is and will most certainly remain in the future within the socialist community, in cooperation with the people of the socialist countries, and in unity with Communist parties and the revolutionary Communist movement. The principles of internationalism are close to our people — the widest possible and sincere cooperation among nations on the basis of mutual respect, equality, territorial integrity, independence, and socialist solidarity.

In this sense, our foreign political orientation has been clearly determined by the action program precisely in this direction. We must continue to fulfill this policy consistently even though conditions now are substantially more complicated and the minds of our people have been subjected to a tremendous shock.

We must today also think, as I have mentioned, of the strategic aim of our foreign policy, which is the international consciousness that we belong to the community of nations of the socialist countries. There is not and cannot be any other choice for our republic.

The process of consolidation is by and large proceeding successfully, though I do not want to create unnecessary illusions. In this strategic policy, in this strategic aim, however, one must also see an element of the consolidation of our conditions. If this process of consolidation is by and large proceeding successfully, this is thanks to you, thanks to the fact that our citizens are acting in accordance with their common sense and conscience and with the suggestions of the Central Committee and the government of the Republic, and are paying close attention to the words of the president of our republic, Comrade Svoboda.

Dear friends, what should we regard as decisive? The starting point is primarily the unity of the party and the unity of the people under the leadership of the party. This unity cannot be understood in any other way than as an attitude toward socialism, toward our republic, toward our international principles, toward the united effort to safeguard the conclusions of the latest plenum of the Czechoslovak Communist Party Central Committee, which approved the actions of the Presidium of the Czechoslovak Communist Party Central Committee at the Moscow negotiations and which with its specific tasks is uniting Communists in this complicated period.

The Central Committee has closed its ranks, and the reconstruction of its organs has increased the authority and unity of the party leadership. We know that the unity of the party and the people will have to go through further tests.

The complex situations we are going through and the tremendous pressures on the consciousness of the people can very definitely give rise to various extremes and cause personal and group interests to be put above the interests of the whole society. This could disturb unity and lead to passivity and even a certain resignation by many people; it could cause frequent squabbles and intolerance as well as petit-bourgeois adventurism or the revival of conservative attitudes.

I say openly that anyone who attempts to violate the unity of the party and the people by such extremism bears a heavy moral responsibility not only before the party but before our entire nation. People everywhere must try to prevent the most tragic thing that could happen: the disintegration of the party's unity, of the unity of party and state, and the emergence of discord within our society; they must oppose anything that could cause disunity within the ranks of our party.

We must also carefully guard the firm unity of our state, of the Czechs and Slovaks and the other nationalities of our state, which showed up so impressively during the past period. Let us keep in mind that it would be a great mistake to allow these relations and our joint basic interests to be affected by anything that could disrupt unity and mutual confidence. As part of the consolidation of our present situation, we are strengthening and deepening this unity as we proceed with implementing the federal system in the state and the party. This we always have interpreted as a means to strengthen the coexistence of our nations and the unity of our homeland, the Czechoslovak Socialist Republic.

The implementation of the decisions of the Czechoslovak Communist Party Central Committee includes developing the activities of state organs right down to the lowest components: national committees in towns and villages. All these organs are responsible to our people for the maintenance of law and order of this socialist country.

The Moscow protocol and the communiqué contain the pledge that the military and other organs of the five states will not interfere in our internal affairs. In recent negotiations we have again received assurances in this matter from our Soviet comrades. Hence, leading representatives of the party and government have publicly and with full responsibility made statements regarding anxieties about the possibility of reprisals.

I am reiterating this because I consider it a very important factor for consolidation to assure the Czechoslovak citizen that he is really at home in his homeland, that he enjoys the protection of the law and all the guarantees based on the laws and constitution of this country. This is a basic question of sovereignty upon which we shall firmly insist. There can be no alternative nor must there under any circumstances be a repetition of the fifties.

Proceeding from this principle, I repeat that every patriot who has the Czechoslovak Republic and the building of socialism with humanistic and democratic features at heart should participate in its implementation here at home, in his country. Here in the Czechoslovak Socialist Republic, on his native soil, is the place for everyone who was honest in accepting our socialism, our post-January policy, who honestly and sincerely cares about the implementation of socialism in our country and truly cares for our Czechoslovak Socialist Republic. . . .

In recent weeks and days you have expressed unprecedented confidence in us. The challenge "We think of you, think of us" has come from you. In this mutual confidence is the foundation of truly human social relations. It was confidence which has created the great and unshakeable unity of our society. Protect this socialist, national, and state unity as you would your own life. Do not allow it to fall apart.

We have sworn to each other that we shall live through good and bad times, and I believe that all of us — workers, peasants, intelligentsia, young and old — will hold out in the battleline of socialist attempts to implement our post-January policy.

To all of you who think in the same way, who are filled with the same conviction and resolution, I thank you from this rostrum from the bottom of my heart and in the name of the entire leadership of our party. Thank you.

DOCUMENT 62
"ILLUSION VERSUS REALISM"
Karel Kosík
Complete Text
[*Listy*, November 7, 1968]

The following statement could never have originated in Bohemia: "In politics you may even make alliance with the devil to achieve your goal, but you must be certain that you will outwit him, not that he will outwit you." Modern Czech politics has been characterized since its beginnings by childish gullibility. It has fallen prey to false illusions even when it seems realistic and attempts to be cold and calculating. Founders of the modern Czech program have gone so far in this self-deception as to identify political illusion with realism and sobriety.

Since the nineteenth century, realism in our country has worn a mask of naïveté and folly. Havlíček* based his Austrian-Slavic concept on three assumptions: "First of all, we Slavs must adhere faithfully to democracy and freedom; second, we must be loyally united with the dynasty; and third, the dynasty must also stand firmly behind democracy and freedom." That third assumption is the hereditary sin of Czech politics. When and where has a "dynasty" ever been liberal and democratic? How can we assume that a reactionary force will be progressive?

The permanent wretched state and crises of Czech politics in the nineteenth

* Nineteenth-century Czech liberal. Translator.

century stemmed from futile efforts to solve the unsolvable and from waiting for a miracle to turn reactionary into progressive. This illusionism confined Czech politics to a vicious circle. The assumption was that the Czechs *should* be democratic and liberal, but the conclusion was that in point of fact they *could not* be too liberal or democratic, because that would antagonize their only powerful and influential ally — the "dynasty." This principle was defended by words to the effect that Czechs should carry out their *own* policy, but practice followed the rule that they could not proceed otherwise than in harmony with the interests of the "dynasty."

The very foundations of modern Czech politics contain an ambiguity which became a source of vacillation and pragmatism. The founders stated correctly that in the current of world centralization and between the two colossi of expansionist Germany and Tsarist Russia, the Czechs could not maintain themselves as a free and political nation without strong and influential allies. However, this finding led them to a false conclusion: They looked for an ally in the Habsburg monarchy. They gave Czech politics a well-motivated foundation, while burdening it for decades with an ideological façade which made it impossible to distinguish between true allies and imaginary ones.

Ideological façades are the reason why Czech politics is losing the struggle against time. Instead of anticipating situations, instead of seeing through its opponent's intentions in time to organize its forces to play its own game, it allows itself to be surprised by events and fall into traps. Reason always gets into politics *post festum,* after the events have been decided, and consequently misses out on taking a creative part. Instead it comes as a delayed commentary on things which have already happened, deliberating afterward about what should have been done before. An ideological façade is the opposite of the sober observation of reality. To see reality as it is primarily means destroying myths and illusions which force us to look at ourselves, things, and situations through alien eyes.

Politics as a game for and with power is always a struggle in which one side tries to force the other to accept its view of the reality and its interpretation of the events. The distinctive dialectics between master and slave is executed in such a way that the victor forces the vanquished to accept not only his way of looking at the world and himself but also the formulas he prescribes as to how the vanquished should perform his capitulation. To be more exact, in this game the vanquished *becomes* the one who lets the other force his view on himself and judges himself, his actions, and his behavior through the eyes of his opponent. This element is not appreciated enough in the traditional way of understanding the "Czech question," which is why we overlook the fact that there is a basic difference between regarding the Czech question as a problem of a small nation living between the East and the West or a political nation in central Europe.

In the first case we want to know how we can survive as a small nation, while in the second case we ask about the relationship between central Europe and a political nation. Central Europe is not a geographic concept; it is a historical reality. We are a political nation only to the extent that we participate in the creation of central Europe. Central Europe exists only to the extent that the nation continues to exist as a historical subject which can not only put up with the tension of various currents and influences, but convert them into an independent political, cultural, and spiritual synthesis. If the nation does not hold its own under onslaught and conflict, it ceases to be a historical subject and sinks to the level of a mere object of pressures and forces; it decomposes as a political nation and is converted into a Czech-speaking populace. In the metamorphosis from political nation to Czech-speaking or Slovak-speaking producers of steel and grains, Central Europe disappears as a historical reality and is transformed into a mere strategic space or colonized territory. And at the same time a sovereign country becomes a province.

The Czech question is a dispute about the meaning of the existence of a political nation in Central Europe. The nation exists, is renewed and consolidated in this conflict, in which noble is separated from base, dignified from humiliating. In this conflict the nation lives in the constant danger that through its own fault it may fall or be hurled by others into a lower, subordinated, dependent position.

And so the "Czech question" is a historical struggle to determine whether the political nation will be converted into mere populace, whether the country will sink to the level of province, whether democracy will give way to fascism and humanism to barbarism. At the same time the Czech question is an attempt at settling the argument of whether a political nation in central Europe can exist as a progressive and sovereign nation.

We have grown accustomed to saying that the Czech question is a worldwide question. Yet this habit obviously deprives us of the courage to face today's world. Palacký* set the Czech question against the background of world events, which tend to centralize humanity and make the existence of small states in Europe difficult. How is the Czech question related to world events today?

Was not and is not our crisis part of the European and world crisis? Has not our crisis become a privileged element revealing the foundations of the European crisis? Modern politics is characterized by the manipulation of masses in an atmosphere of fear and hysteria. Political manipulation as a manifestation of technical rationality in human relations is based on an artificially created atmosphere of irrationality; manipulation techniques assume and require permanent hysteria, fear, and hope. Politics as manipulation of the masses can exist only in a system where everything can be manipulated.

Before politics can become mass manipulator, before people can be converted into controllable masses, an epoch-making change must reduce the world to wide open spaces, nature, and sources of raw materials and energy. Truth must be reduced to correctness, and man to a subject assigned to the appropriate object. Not until such a momentous change takes place can there appear a system of general manipulability in which people and nature, the living and the dead, and ideas and feelings will be handled as if they were manipulable objects.

* Nineteenth-century Czech historian. Translator.

In the days of Palacký, the nation was threatened by world centralization. In our times the nation is endangered by a system of general manipulability. Parts of this system are the predominance of a false consciousness in social life and the individual's decreasing ability and diminishing interest to distinguish between truth and falsity, between good and evil. In a system of general manipulability, truth is permeated by lies, goodness by evil; and this lack of differentiation, this indifference and aloofness go to make up the prevailing atmosphere of everyday life. As a result, in a system of general manipulability there is more danger of a political nation turning into a mass of indifferent people, that is, an agglomeration of inhabitants who have lost the capacity and interest to distinguish by their actions, thought, and way of life between what is true and what is false, what is good and what is evil, between what is noble and what is base.

The Czech question is presently a world question only to the extent that we realize that our present crisis can be solved only as a world crisis, that is, by surmounting the foundations from which the crisis stems. The Czech question today is a world question only to the extent that we know that to overcome our crisis means abolishing the system of general manipulability. The liberating and revolutionary alternative to the system of general manipulability in all its forms, varieties, and manifestations is based on an entirely different concept of man and history, nature and time, being and truth, and therefore also requires a new concept of politics. This is why searching out and implementing new foundations of politics basically different from those used by political manipulation are important aspects of the Czech question.

Former ruling strata and classes set forth certain characteristics and features of their deformed existence as basic virtues of politics. As a result it seems as if the basic elements of politics are shrewdness and cunning, cruelty and dullness, violence and arrogance. But are these traditional, tried and true qualities of politics compatible with the mission of the working class and working strata in the modern world? Can the working class take them over and use them to carry out its own policy, or does it and must it create new qualities? Is it not true that the basic and revolutionary contribution of the working class is and will be that it makes a distinction in politics between wisdom and shrewdness, between clarity of vision and astuteness, between courage and arrogance, but also between cautiousness and childish gullibility, between careful deliberation and illusion, between true and false realism?

In this sense, we can say that the Czech question will not measure up to the level of the times or become truly a world question until it overcomes in politics the domination of ideological façades and the ambiguity and weaknesses of the magnificent beginnings of its founders, Palacký and Havlíček. The more deeply Czech politics dredges out the meaning of the following statement by Marx, the sooner it will rid itself of these shortcomings: "In politics you may even make alliance with the devil to achieve your goal, but you must be certain that you will outwit him, not that he will outwit you."

THE "WHITE" AND "BLACK" BOOKS

MOSCOW'S ATTEMPTS to justify the invasion culminated in a Soviet "White Book" (*On Events in Czechoslovakia: Facts, Documents, Press Reports and Eyewitness Accounts*, Document 63) written by "a group of Soviet journalists." The "White Book" drew together conspiracy theories tying the Club of Committed Non-Party Members (KAN) to anti-Communist activities in West Germany, the British Intelligence Service, and "an international Zionist organization." Apart from its sensationalism, the "book" primarily served as a check list for the charges raised more formally by the Warsaw Letter (Document 34) and the *Pravda* August 22 editorial on the Defense of Socialism (Document 46). It infuriated scholars in Prague, who responded with a mammoth "Black Book" (*Seven Days in Prague*, Document 64) attacking the Soviet explanation as "lies," "inventions," and "distortions of Marxist-Leninist thought." [1] Compiled by the Institute of History of the Czechoslovak Academy of Sciences, the "Black Book" was not published in Czechoslovakia but circulated in photo-offset copies, some of which reached the West.[2]

DOCUMENT 63
SOVIET "WHITE BOOK" ON CZECHOSLOVAKIA
by a group of Soviet journalists
Excerpts
[*On Events in Czechoslovakia: Facts, Documents, Press Reports and Eye-witness Accounts* (Moscow, 1968), pp. 75–83 and 108–115]

. . . The policy pursued by reactionary elements was to organizationally secure the seizure of power. Therefore a major role was assigned to the oppo-

---

[1] Tad Szulc in *The New York Times*, October 24, 1968.
[2] Robert Littell, ed. *The Czech Black Book* (New York: Praeger, 1969).

sition which openly sought to change the people's views on the destiny of Czechoslovakia.

Who tackled this dirty job?

The same people who with renewed force are now continuing the line of opposition to the Communist Party of Czechoslovakia and to the legitimate Government of Czechoslovakia which are implementing the resolutions of the Cierna-nad-Tisou and Bratislava conferences and the Moscow talks.

These forces rallied round different flags and came out under the signboards of various clubs, circles, associations and even parties: "Club-231," "Club of Non-Party Activists", "Circle of Independent Writers", "Club of Critically-Minded Individuals", "Organization for the Defence of Human Rights", "Preparatory Central Committee of Social-Democratic Party", etc.

Naturally these bodies set about obtaining legal status as soon as possible. By mid-June 1968, the Ministry of the Interior had received a total of 70 applications from new organizations and associations. Representatives of 31 organizations submitted their Rules, while representatives of 39 organizations came to the Ministry for "consultation" about their legal status, to ask for information, etc.

"Club-231" had over forty thousand members, many of whom were recruited from among ex-felons and those who had committed crimes against the state. The Rude Pravo pointed out that among the members of this club were former nazis, Henlein fascists, ministers of the puppet, so-called Slovak State set up by the nazis, and representatives of the reactionary clergy.

These people have murdered a large number of guiltless Communists and honest Czechoslovak citizens.

"Club-231" * was founded on March 31, 1968, at a meeting in Prague, though the Ministry of the Interior never officially authorized its existence. The press gave the names of some of its leaders.

Who are they? Radovan Prochazka became Head of the Information Department of the Central Committee of "Club-231", Vaclav Palecek, a former bourgeois general, was among the members of the Central Committee, Otakar Rambousek was appointed Chairman of the Documentation Commission, and Jaromir Brodsky became General Secretary of the Club in Prague.

Earlier, Radovan Prochazka and Otakar Rambousek had been exposed as American intelligence agents. Vaclav Palecek maintained close contact with the British Embassy. Jaromir Brodsky had long been notorious for his fascist views.

That the Club is the meeting place of the most rabid reactionaries is borne out also by statements by some rightly rehabilitated political figures.

Here is what they wrote:

"Among the members of the club are collaborators of the nazi occupation period, thieves and murderers who have been and remain enemies of our

* After the rout of reaction in February 1948 antistate and counter-revolutionary activity was punished in socialist Czechoslovakia on the basis of Article 231 of the Constitutional Act on the Defence of the Republic.

people and of all honest men and women. People, who in the period of the 1948 Revolution and after it, fought against the progressive forces in our country and committed political murders and other acts of violence, have also insinuated themselves into the club."

Here is an example of Brodsky's views:

At a gathering of the Club members, seething with malice and hatred for Communists, he said:

"The best Communist is a dead Communist, and if he is alive, his legs should be torn off."

The Club chairman in Prague-I district, a certain Hruby, did not conceal what he thought, too. He declared that the "situation in the country is ripe for overthrowing the socialist system."

"Club-231" set up a ramified network of provincial committees. Branches of the Club appeared even in the United States of America and Canada where Czechoslovak émigrés from among political criminals, turncoats and traitors were recruited and money was collected for the Club. In Czechoslovakia the Club held illegal meetings and conferences.

Rude Pravo recently published an open letter to Srom, a secretary of "Club-231". The author of the letter, A. Cerny, exposes this profiteer and traitor.

According to this letter — and its charges were confirmed by documents and quotations from an autobiography written by Srom — the latter had been the owner of a large private enterprise. After the liberation of Czechoslovakia he went in for managerial work. In 1944, 1948 and 1950 he was brought to court for profiteering and black market dealings. Later he began to work as a paid agent of the American intelligence service and, as he himself admitted, provided it with secret intelligence data.

The "documentation commission of 'Club-231'" headed by Otakar Rambousek was entrusted with "collecting materials for the prosecution by law of those guilty of unlawful activity." In the Rules, this task was formulated in this vague manner in order to give the "commission members" a free hand for arbitrary rule.

Rambousek himself, as we see from an article in Rude Pravo of May 28, was in 1949 sentenced to life imprisonment for hostile activities against the state. In 1964 he was released on probation till 1971.

Another member of "Club-231", Frantisek Poull, maintained constant ties with Pechacek, editor of the émigré magazine Svedetctvi published in Paris and an agent of the US Central Intelligence Agency, as well as with employees of the "Free Europe" broadcasting station which hinted broadly that it was ready to render the Club all possible assistance.

An active member of the Club, Jaromir Nebesky of Prague, established contact with the representative of the Pan-American Airways which liberally promised to donate 10,000 dollars to the Club.

In early May, Prague was visited by Stanislav Jencik, a CIA agent, who demonstratively joined "Club-231" and offered it "disinterested" financial aid in dollars.

A prominent functionary of "Club-231", Hruby, is the son of a former minister of the Bohemia and Moravia Protectorate. Among the leaders of the Club there is the terrorist Kebl and a certain Slavik whose father is at the head of the reactionary "Free Czechoslovakia Council" in the USA today.

Prasek, another leading figure at "Club-231", not bothering to conceal his hatred for the people's state, demanded that Czechoslovak workers be removed from power in the country, while a certain Siska requested no more and no less than the complete elimination of the Communist Party of Czechoslovakia.

"Club-231" activists travelled unhindered to the cities and villages of Czechoslovakia, where they called upon people not to elect Communists to government bodies and, at the same time, collected in the various localities information on Communist Party members so as to "settle scores with them when the hour strikes."

Taking advantage of the complex political situation in the country and complete impunity, and proclaiming itself a "nation-wide political organization," "Club-231" requested that it be granted the right to have its own faction in the CSSR National Assembly.

Inspired by the West, the leaders of the club worked out plans to capture key positions in all political, governmental and economic spheres in the CSSR. Their men penetrated to leading positions in political organizations, at enterprises and in offices.

"Club-231" set up secret "four-men teams" instructed to spread various false rumours, defame and terrorize honest citizens.

The bosses of "Club-231" put their own, special meaning into the conception of the "democratization process" and demanded that the process be brought "to conclusion." . . .

The Club of Non-Party Activists (KAN) which claimed to be practically the biggest mass-scale political organization in the country, did not lag behind the others in counter-revolutionary activity.

On April 5 in Prague, a gathering attended by 144 persons announced the setting up of the "Club of Non-Party Activists." It is revealing that this took place at precisely the time when the press, radio and television controlled by reactionary forces launched a large-scale campaign against the Communist Party of Czechoslovakia.

Leadership of the Club was in the hands of I. Svitak, a rabid reactionary working at the CSSR Academy of Sciences. He had earlier been expelled from the Communist Party. Rybacek, Musil and Klementjev — agents of the international Zionist organization — became his assistants.

In mid-May the Club published its programme openly opposing the Communist Party of Czechoslovakia.

The journal Reporter published a long statement by I. Svitak, containing a plan for the phased removal of Communists from power and for the transfer of state power into the hands of antisocialist forces.

The agitation and propaganda activity of the club (its "activists" held meetings and rallies every week in Prague and other cities) was entirely designed to discredit the Communist Party of Czechoslovakia and the socialist system, opposing to them "other versions of political organization," for instance, a bourgeois republic.

The club leaders tried to recruit supporters not only from among the professionals, but also from among workers and servicemen.

With this purpose they set up club branches at enterprises and in various organizations. They named these branches "Societies for the Freedom of Speech and the Press," which was a popular catch cry in Czechoslovakia this summer.

The chief aim of these "societies" was defence of the "right" of individuals who attacked the Communist Party of Czechoslovakia and all the progressive forces in the country to publish what they wanted in the press and make broadcasts over the radio and TV.

Answering a question put by the West German magazine "Der Spiegel" about what audience the "Club" intended to appeal to, I. Svitak said:

"To a force with a fantastical potential: to 6 million people of electoral age who are politically unorganized in our country. It is easy to imagine that these people will play a more active part — they were only manipulated before."

"Der Spiegel" asked:

"Do you consider that this may be a reserve for a new political group, a new party which, if not today, then possibly tomorrow or the day after, might appear next to the Communist Party?"

I. Svitak answered:

"Yes, the trend is developing in that direction."

The ultimate aim of the leaders of that club differed very little from the aims set by the leaders of "Club-231."

They were doing their best to get high posts in various government bodies and to establish themselves in the foreground of the country's political life. The "Club of Non-Party Activists" demanded full participation in the government and the "right" for its active members to occupy leading positions.

"Philosopher" I. Svitak championed similar ideas in other newspapers, too.

In the weekly "Student" (No. 16) he appealed to intellectuals and students to prevent the election of any of the present deputies to the National Assembly in the coming elections. He called upon them to "break through the wall that partitions Czechoslovakia from Europe by propagating corresponding ideas."

I. Svitak was even more outspoken in the "Manifesto of the 'Club of Non-Party Activists'" which said:

" 'The club of Non-Party Activists' must act the way a mongoose does when fighting a huge snake twice as strong as he. The mongoose is manoeuvring all the time, he often retreats, then attacks and again assumes the defensive. He is waiting for the moment when the snake could be seized by its most vulnerable spot and then gives it the fatal strike."

It is worth noting that in his counter-revolutionary activity I. Svitak made contacts with the anti-Soviet NTS organization.

I. Svitak is no novice on FRG TV screens and on the pages of the West German press. He has been shamelessly smearing socialist practice in Czechoslovakia and jeering at the memory of Soviet soldiers who fell in battle for the liberation of Czechoslovakia.

I. Svitak declares that in the interest of the democratization process, the way of civil war is possible, too, to gain "absolute freedom."

The leaders of the "Club of Non-Party Activists" in Prague took steps to build up its provincial branches. For instance on June 4, Jan Stepanek spoke as a representative of the centre at an organizational meeting of the Club's preparatory committee in the small town of Ricany. In his speech he called for a "purge" of the Communist Party, army and security bodies.

Though barely founded, the "Club of Non-Party Activists" proved to have broad and well organized links with some foreign anti-Communist organizations and parties, first and foremost, in West Germany. . . .

All was grist to the mill in their subversive activities. They set up illegal party committees at enterprises, and actively proclaimed their plans to abolish the Communist Party of Czechoslovakia. Their leaders did not shun cooperation with Western intelligence services, with reactionary Czechoslovak emigrants, and with the leaders of the so-called Socialist international. They established close contacts with Vilim, a former leader of the Czechoslovak Social-Democratic Party and an agent of the British Intelligence Service, now residing in London. . . .

Manfred von Kont, correspondent for the Munich paper Suddeutsche Zeitung in Vienna (who is also an agent of the West-German Secret Service) had contact with the counter-revolutionary underground and actively engaged in subversive activities in Czechoslovakia.

Amazing details of a talk between Heipertz, head of the Bonn trade mission in Prague, and Turnwald, an expert on the "new Eastern policy" in the West German Ministry of Foreign Affairs, became known in the Bonn journalist circles.

Heipertz told Turnwald that events in Czechoslovakia developed more quickly than he had expected, that pressures exerted by certain pro-Western circles, particularly certain intellectuals who disagreed with the leading role of the working class and its Party, had increased appreciably, and that these circles were conspiring to tear the Czechoslovak Socialist Republic away from the Soviet Union and the other socialist countries.

Heipertz quoted in his report the writer Prochazka, who had told him at a dinner at the Dutch Diplomatic Mission that events in Czechoslovakia could be further accelerated if not for the allied commitments undertaken by the Czechoslovak Socialist Republic with regard to the Soviet Union and the other Warsaw Treaty countries.

The hundreds of correspondents representing capitalist papers were followed into the country by so-called financial and economic experts, bankers and even such outright emissaries of imperialism, as, for instance, Blessing, President of the West German Federal Bank; Scheel, Chairman of the West German Party of Free Democrats; Epler, Deputy to the Bundestag from the Social Democratic Party and Zbigniew Brzezinski, a rabid anti-Communist "soviet-ologist" from the United States.

For many years a consultant and employee of the Planning Board of the US State Department, Brzezinski, who headed the institute "on problems of communism", stressed in his book "An Alternative to a Split" (1965) that in the East European socialist countries "the most desirable form of transformation must start with liberalization inside the country. This," he wrote, "applies above all to Czechoslovakia."

On June 14, Czechoslovak counter-revolutionaries invited Brzezinski to deliver lectures in Prague. There Brzezinski expounded his "liberalization" strategy. He called for the destruction of the Communist Party of Czechoslovakia and the disbandment of the people's militia and the security forces. He said the following at a closed meeting at the Institute of Foreign Politics in Prague on June 14, 1968:

"My basic thesis is that Leninism in an advanced modern society has become outdated." He also said he fully supported the "interesting Czechoslovak experiment."

Commenting on the increasing activity of these emissaries from the West in Czechoslovakia, the Berliner Zeitung wrote:

"Now, they are carrying out in practice what previously they propounded in theory: Johnson's bridge-building policy and Kiesinger and Brandt's new Eastern policy, whose aims are to do everything possible to pull the socialist countries out of the common front one by one."

Situated between the Oder and the Danube, stretching from the Sudetic Mts. to the Carpathians, Czechoslovakia has always attracted the greedy eyes of the German imperialists. "He who controls Bohemia, holds the keys to Europe in his hands," Bismarck used to say.

The people of Czechoslovakia tasted the bitter pill of the Munich treason. The Western powers sacrificed Czechoslovakia to Hitler's Drang nach Osten plans. For many years Czechoslovakia ceased to exist as an independent state. And only the victory of the Soviet people over Hitlerism brought freedom to the Czechs and Slovaks.

The West German militarists have always connected their revenge-seeking plans with the liquidation of the socialist system in Czechoslovakia. . . .

What "European integration" means for the Bonn ultras was stated with utmost clarity by the leader of the CSU, Minister Strauss, in his latest book.

"Communist regimes must be totally liquidated: the way and standard of life in East Europe must be adapted to the way of life in West Europe. We must encourage and support this process . . ."

In other words, what is meant is the complete re-shaping of the political map of Europe.

World imperialism and its stooges in Czechoslovakia considered the attacks against socialism and the Communist Party to be the first, important step in carrying out their plans against all the European socialist countries.

Characteristic in this respect is the reaction of West German ruling circles and the press to the events in Czechoslovakia. Rejoicing loudly each time an anti-socialist trend appeared, the West German press at the same time published a great deal of "friendly" advice and recommendations to the Czech counter-revolutionaries.

In March 1968 Strauss stated during a talk with high-ranking CDU functionaries that beginning with 1966 the US and Federal Germany governments had done a great deal to compromise the leaderships of the Communist Party of Czechoslovakia before the Czechoslovak public.

According to Strauss the Western world must subtly and ably employ all ideological and economic channels to further undermine the role of the Communist Party of Czechoslovakia in the state and political life of the country and gradually to tear Czechoslovakia away from the USSR. Towards this end a broad propaganda campaign was planned in order to remove from leading posts Communists devoted to the cause of socialism.

It was proposed to allot up to 260 million marks for bribing Czechoslovak citizens who were going to Western countries in delegations or as tourists and for other kinds of "economic aid." It was considered necessary in carrying out these steps to exercise great caution and circumspection so as to avoid bringing the situation in the country to a climax and provoking the Soviet Union to bring in its troops.

Back in March 31, 1968 the West Berlin newspaper *Tagespiegel* advised the Czechoslovak counter-revolutionaries to display caution and not to disclose their intentions before the time was ripe.

The ink had not dried on the recently adopted Emergency Laws in Bonn, when Bonn suddenly became a zealous supporter of the "democratization process" in Czechoslovakia.

The well-known anti-Communist Klaus Mehnert, commenting on the events in Czechoslovakia over West German television was quite frank concerning Bonn's plans:

> "In my opinion, this is a stimulus for Germany's Eastern policy. I think we should continue it. If Czechoslovakia, if other East European countries go towards social-democracy, then it will undoubtedly be much easier for us to talk with a social-democratic, although formally, possibly still a communist Czechoslovakia . . . Besides it is necessary to isolate still more East Berlin."

The newspaper *Die Zeit,* which is close to Bonn official circles, carried recommendations on how to "guarantee the unity" of the socialist camp on the basis of a "national multiplicity."

In May 1968 the FRG press debated with gusto the readiness of the FRG government to grant Czechoslovakia 700 million marks in financial aid. The press was of the opinion that such a measure would seriously aggravate relations between Czechoslovakia and the USSR.

The appeals for rapprochement with Federal Germany, made through the press, radio and TV and also in speeches delivered by some leading figures in Czechoslovakia, directly undermined the national interests of the people of Czechoslovakia. This did not end only with statements.

Czechoslovakia's western borders were actually open and, together with the usual influx of tourists, came numerous sabotage specialists and spies from the Western countries and, of course, mainly from West Germany. . . .

DOCUMENT 64

THE CZECHOSLOVAK "BLACK BOOK"

October 1968

Excerpts

[Robert Littell, ed. *The Czech Black Book,* prepared by the Institute of History of the Czechoslovak Academy of Sciences (New York, Praeger, 1969), pp. 208–212 and 285–286]

. . . *Commentary of the Day from* Reportér, *No. 35, August 26, 1968*

It is impossible, in the long run, to call things by words other than those that really describe them. Terms cannot be confused or mixed up for long. This is also true about "liberation," which is the label they have tried to put on their aggression against our country, on the occupation of Czechoslovakia.

A country that does not need to be saved from anything or freed from anything, that is not asking for it and is actually rejecting it for weeks in advance as an absurdity — such a country cannot be "liberated." Such a country can only be occupied — unlawfully, brutally, recklessly. Not liberation but aggression, not rescue but occupation.

These are unpleasant truths, and one cannot be surprised that the occupiers do not want to read them on the asphalt of the roads, on the walls of houses, on the locomotives on the rails, on the sides of trucks, on millions of posters throughout the country or even — in not a few instances — on their own vehicles and other facilities. But they cannot do away with these truths, least of all by driving the "natives" into the streets under their automatics and forcing them to tear down the posters.

True, there is something peculiar in this case, something they cannot admit to themselves, something they have to mask and deny before each other. Are they not acting "in the interests of socialism," have they not come as "class brethren" performing their "noble internationalist duty"? It is totally inconceivable to them that they should be compared with those who subjugated this country in an equally brutal manner three decades ago. It is totally unacceptable for them to be compared, for instance, with the Americans in Vietnam.

They find it unacceptable, they protest violently. They spew out miles of magnetic tape of pitiful self-justifications and tons of paper printed over with high-sounding phrases, but they cannot change matters one bit. They did not come to liberate socialist Czechoslovakia on the twenty-first of August, but to trample it down; they did not come to save the Czechs and Slovaks, but to enslave them.

Let us recapitulate — bluntly and briefly: Stealthily, not like a government of a decent country, but like medieval conspirators, behind the backs of all the legal organs of this country, they joined in a compact with a handful of discredited political corpses and stool pigeons who feared punishment for their participation in the crimes of the 1950's and while still pretending to conduct a dialog in their formal contacts, they forcibly invaded the country. Like gangsters, they abducted the Premier of the legal government of a sovereign country, the Chairman of the legal parliament of that country, the First Secretary of the leading political party, and they restricted the freedom of movement and action of the head of state, the President of the Republic, a bearer of the highest medals of their own country.*

They trampled upon all agreements that had bound them with that country, and yet they had enough arrogance to claim that they were doing so precisely on the basis of those agreements.

They brutally surrounded the parliament of that country with their tanks and machine guns. They surrounded the residence of the head of the state and the seat of the government. They invaded the offices of leading cultural and other institutions. Within three days, they flooded that small country with twenty-six military divisions and a half-million soldiers, with thousands of tanks and even rocket weapons, which they aimed against our capital city. They drove the voices of this country, its press, radio, and television, underground, and they tried to replace them with their disgusting prattle disseminated out of [East] Berlin in an insulting distortion of our language. Although they are formally joined with us by ties of alliance, they placed their tanks around our military barracks and facilities of our armed forces, and they aimed their gun barrels against those who had until then been their allies.

They employed the methods of military and police terror. They were shooting at children and crushing people under the treads of their tanks, destroying roadways and homes, not sparing even the most precious cultural monuments, as witnessed by the disfigured front of the National Museum.

Encountering the calm of the people, a country that fails to offer a single proof in support of their nonsensical pretext for aggression, they started a futile barrage from all their weapons in the middle of the night — perhaps to be able to pretend to themselves that there is, after all, a need to fight.

They have brought in some selected cutthroats of their secret police in order to imprison the political and cultural elite of our nation and make it easier to install new collaborationists of the Moravec type.†

---

* Svoboda is one of the very few foreigners to have received the Soviet Union's highest military decoration, Hero of the Soviet Union.

† A cabinet minister who urged cooperation with the "protectorate" set up by the Nazis in Bohemia and Moravia during World War II.

Can all this be called a rescue, can all this be called a liberation? How does it actually differ from the fifteenth of March, 1939? Is this not a replica of all that we already went through once? Of *Wehrmacht* and Gestapo, of blood and iron? Of injustice and arrogance, cruelty and recklessness?

Is anything changed by the fact that all this is being perpetrated not by enemies but by "friends," not by recognized aggressors but by allies, not by those of whom we might have expected it but by those whom we would never have thought capable of it?

Can they expect of us that, in condemning this crime, we, its very victims, shall be less resolute, less eloquent than the whole civilized world, which is condemning them?

We want to honestly differentiate between those who bear the main responsibility for this criminal decision and those whose task it is to implement it, many of whom did not even know where they were, where they were going, what they were doing. But it is not easy to maintain such distinctions for long in situations such as ours after the twenty-first of August. More than twenty years ago, the International Court of Justice established the collective responsibility of the German people, and it still remains true that "the most honorable duty of a soldier is to disobey a criminal order."

After five days of occupation, it is clear that the moral victory is ours. The short-sighted stage direction of the aggression has failed shamefully. The aggressors have encountered such a single-minded resistance by the two nations of our country that there is no precedent for it in history. Enraged, but to no avail, they are desperately seeking some authoritative collaborationists to provide a semblance of "legality" to the aggression after the fact. There simply are none. The occupation army is totally isolated, helpless, completely rejected. Throughout the country, orientation signs, street names, house numbers, name plates on doors have disappeared; the country is anonymous and mute. Arrest warrants and lists of victims have become worthless. The occupiers have seized our printing houses, but newspapers keep appearing several times a day with full freedom of expression. They have seized the radio, but the broadcasts go on in freedom. They have seized the television but failed to silence it, too. Already in these first days, the occupation has been politically defeated, defeated morally and psychologically, defeated and rendered ridiculous before the eyes of the whole world. The central expression of this defeat is the fact, above all, that, in spite of all the fabrications about a counterrevolution and a collapse of the socialist order in Czechoslovakia, it is precisely the Communist Party that has demonstrated its tremendous viability and, in accordance with the will of the people of the entire country, has again assumed its position at the head of the national resistance in this fateful hour, at the head of the struggle for socialism and for state and national sovereignty.

We can hardly hope, given the treachery and brutality shown by this aggressor on the twenty-first of August, that there will soon arrive a favorable turn of events. But the adventurist, antisocialist, aggressive policy of the Brezhnev clique at the head of the Soviet Communist Party has no future. It is deeply contrary to the objective interests of the Soviet Union itself and of the Soviet people, and this contradiction is bound to engulf it sooner or later. Until then, we must persevere, we must overcome this grave crisis, we must defend our truth with minimum sacrifices and with maximum determination. A compromise is impossible: We cannot lose more than we have already lost or offer more than they have already stolen from us. The sympathies of the entire civilized world are on our side. Truth and justice are on our side. The future is on our side.

. . . From the archives of the Institute of History of the Czechoslovak Academy of Sciences

Dear Fellow Citizens:

Having heard the communiqué on the Moscow negotiations and the speeches by the President of the Republic and the First Secretary of the Communist Party, the entire personnel of the Institute of History of the Czechoslovak Academy of Sciences, which has been speaking to you during the past seven days on behalf of Prague historians, states the following:*

For us, for our nation, for the entire Czechoslovak people, there is no way back. We promised each other in that unforgettable message that we would never leave the road upon which we had started. These seven days, which can never be erased from our minds, have only strengthened our determination and irrevocable decision to follow our own path.

The most precious result of the united struggle of the entire nation against the occupation is the fact that the people of this country have taken their fate into their own hands. This sovereign people, determined to defend its freedom and independence, must be able to express its position on any agreement that may be deciding its fate, possibly for a whole generation, and it must be respected by anyone who wants to have its confidence.

We stand without reservation behind all decisions of the Extraordinary Fourteenth Party Congress and behind the Central Committee elected at that Congress. Without a recognition of the results of the Extraordinary Fourteenth Party Congress, there can be no Party unity. This is the feeling of those of us who live among the people as rank-and-file members of the nation, and it must be clear as well to the politicians who speak on the nation's behalf and ask for its confidence.

We are in favor of calm and prudence. We are not adventurists; we do not want nonsensical sacrifices. But both the old and the recent historical experiences tell us: Any concession in matters of principle in dealing with force is a step along a steep incline, a step on a road whose end cannot be seen. What may today appear merely as an inevitable act of realistic policy will tomorrow turn out to be the beginning of capitulation.

We continue to stand behind the workers of the legal Czechoslovak Radio stations. We express our confidence in them.

There is no reconciliation with the occupiers. A free people cannot live on its knees.

* Telephoned to Czechoslovak Radio at 7:30 P.M., August 27, 1968, but not broadcast.

BREZHNEV DOCTRINE

KNOWN AS THE Brezhnev Doctrine, the Soviet theoretical justification was first formulated as a *Pravda* article (Document 65). This doctrine put forth the concept of limited sovereignty within the socialist commonwealth.[1] The sovereignty of socialist states, in the author's view, could not be understood abstractly. Rather, among these states international law must be subordinated to the laws of class struggle — i.e., Moscow reserved the right to intervene militarily or otherwise if developments in any given socialist country inflicted damage on (1) socialism within that country or (2) the basic interests of other socialist countries. The idea was hardly new. It could equally as well have been articulated by Zhdanov in conjunction with the "two-camp theory" at the founding of the Cominform in 1947.

For Albania, Yugoslavia, and Rumania, the implications were ominous. Of the three, Bucharest was the most vulnerable due to the potential leverage of Rumanian membership in the Warsaw Pact. Consequently, Rumania became less publicly critical, appeared more cooperative on the issue of a world Communist conference,[2] and seemingly gave assurances of Bucharest's willingness to fulfill Warsaw Pact obligations.[3] Yet despite this tactical retreat, Ceauşescu

---

[1] For analysis, see Christian Duevel, "*Pravda* Proclaims 'Doctrine of Intervention' in Socialist Countries," Radio Liberty Research Bulletin, No. 41 (October 2, 1968) and "Czechoslovakia and the Brezhnev Doctrine," prepared by the Subcommittee on National Security and International Operations, U.S. Senate, 91st Congress (Washington, D.C.: U.S. Government Printing Office, 1969).

[2] During late September, a Rumanian delegation attended the working group in Budapest that agreed to postpone the November 25 conference date in favor of another preliminary meeting on November 17, 1968. When the long-delayed conference convened in June 1969, Rumania participated. However, Bucharest had far from acquiesced to Soviet goals. See Ceauşescu's attack on the Paraguayan delegate's criticism of China (*Scînteia*, June 6, 1969; *The New York Times*, June 7, 1969).

[3] Rumania's Defense Minister Ionita attended a session of Warsaw Pact ministers in Moscow, October 29–30, 1968 (*Pravda*, October 31, 1968). However, when the Warsaw Pact chiefs-of-staff met in Bucharest November 26–29, the issue of joint maneuvers on Rumanian territory remained unresolved. The communiqué, in *Pravda*, November 30, 1968, mentioned only strengthening of defensive capacity, while an interview with Ceauşescu in *The Times* (London), December 9, 1968, indicated the matter had not come up.

adamantly rejected the Brezhnev Doctrine as a return to old methods incompatible with the interests of individual parties and the international movement as a whole.[4] The Yugoslavs refused to back down at all and passed a new defense bill making it possible to mobilize the entire population in case of attack.[5]

DOCUMENT 65

"SOVEREIGNTY AND THE INTERNATIONAL OBLIGATIONS OF SOCIALIST COUNTRIES"

S. Kovalev
September 26, 1968
Complete Text

[*Pravda,* September 26, 1968, quoted from *CDSP,* Vol. XX, No. 39 (October 16, 1968), pp. 10–12]

In connection with the events in Czechoslovakia the question of the relationship and interconnection between the socialist countries' national interests and their internationalist obligations has assumed particular urgency and sharpness. The measures taken jointly by the Soviet Union and other socialist countries to defend the socialist gains of the Czechoslovak people are of enormous significance for strengthening the socialist commonwealth, which is the main achievement of the international working class.

At the same time it is impossible to ignore the allegations being heard in some places that the actions of the five socialist countries contradict the Marxist-Leninist principle of sovereignty and the right of nations to self-determination.

Such arguments are untenable primarily because they are based on an abstract, nonclass approach to the question of sovereignty and the right of nations to self-determination.

There is no doubt that the peoples of the socialist countries and the Communist Parties have and must have freedom to determine their country's path of development. However, any decision of theirs must damage neither socialism in their own country nor the fundamental interests of the other socialist countries nor the worldwide workers' movement, which is waging a struggle for socialism. This means that every Communist Party is responsible not only to its own people but also to all the socialist countries and to the entire Communist movement. Whoever forgets this in placing sole emphasis on the autonomy and

---

[4] Ceauşescu speech to the Rumanian National Assembly, *Scînteia,* November 30, 1968; for analysis, *Neue Zürcher Zeitung,* December 7, 1968.

[5] *Borba,* November 8, 1968.

independence of Communist Parties lapses into one-sidedness, shirking his internationalist obligations.

The Marxist dialectic opposes one-sidedness; it requires that every phenomenon be examined in terms of both its specific nature and its overall connection with other phenomena and processes. Just as, in V. I. Lenin's words, someone living in a society cannot be free of that society, so a socialist state that is in a system of other states constituting a socialist commonwealth cannot be free of the common interests of that commonwealth.

The sovereignty of individual socialist countries cannot be counterposed to the interests of world socialism and the world revolutionary movement. V. I. Lenin demanded that all Communists "struggle *against* petty national narrowness, exclusivity and isolation, and for taking into account the whole, the overall situation, for subordinating the interests of the particular to the interests of the general" ("Complete Collected Works" [in Russian], Vol. XXX, p. 45).

Socialist states have respect for the democratic norms of international law. More than once they have proved this in practice by resolutely opposing imperialism's attempts to trample the sovereignty and independence of peoples. From this same standpoint they reject left-wing, adventurist notions of "exporting revolution" and "bringing bliss" to other peoples. However, in the Marxist conception the norms of law, including the norms governing relations among socialist countries, cannot be interpreted in a narrowly formal way, outside the general context of the class struggle in the present-day world. Socialist countries resolutely oppose the export and import of counterrevolution.

Each Communist Party is free in applying the principles of Marxism-Leninism and socialism in its own country, but it cannot deviate from these principles (if, of course, it remains a Communist Party). In concrete terms this means primarily that every Communist Party cannot fail to take into account in its activities such a decisive fact of our time as the struggle between the two antithetical social systems — capitalism and socialism. This struggle is an objective fact that does not depend on the will of people and is conditioned by the division of the world into two antithetical social systems. "Every person," V. I. Lenin said, "must take either this, our, side or the other side. All attempts to avoid taking sides end in failure and disgrace" (Vol. XLI, p. 401).

It should be stressed that even if a socialist country seeks to take an "extra-bloc" position, it in fact retains its national independence thanks precisely to the power of the socialist commonwealth — and primarily to its chief force, the Soviet Union — and the might of its armed forces. The weakening of any link in the world socialist system has a direct effect on all the socialist countries, which cannot be indifferent to this. Thus, the antisocialist forces in Czechoslovakia were in essence using talk about the right to self-determination to cover up demands for so-called neutrality and the C.S.R.'s withdrawal from the socialist commonwealth. But implementation of such "self-determination," i.e., Czechoslovakia's separation from the socialist commonwealth, would run counter to Czechoslovakia's fundamental interests and would harm the other socialist countries. Such "self-determination," as a result of which NATO troops might approach Soviet borders and the commonwealth of European socialist countries would be dismembered, in fact infringes on the vital interests of these countries' peoples, and fundamentally contradicts the right of these peoples to socialist self-determination. The Soviet Union and other socialist states, in fulfilling their internationalist duty to the fraternal peoples of Czechoslovakia and defending their own socialist gains, had to act and did act in resolute opposition to the antisocialist forces in Czechoslovakia.

Comrade W. Gomulka, First Secretary of the Central Committee of the Polish United Workers' Party, used a metaphor to illustrate this point: "To those friends and comrades of ours from other countries who believe they are defending the just cause of socialism and the sovereignty of peoples by denouncing and protesting the introduction of our troops in Czechoslovakia, we reply: If the enemy plants dynamite under our house, under the commonwealth of socialist states, our patriotic, national and internationalist duty is to prevent this by using any means that are necessary."

People who "disapprove" of the actions taken by the allied socialist countries ignore the decisive fact that these countries are defending the interests of worldwide socialism and the worldwide revolutionary movement. The socialist system exists in concrete form in individual countries that have their own well-defined state boundaries and develops with regard for the specific attributes of each such country. And no one interferes with concrete measures to perfect the socialist system in various socialist countries. But matters change radically when a danger to socialism itself arises in a country. World socialism as a social system is the common achievement of the working people of all countries, it is indivisible, and its defense is the common cause of all Communists and all progressive people on earth, first and foremost the working people of the socialist countries.

The Bratislava statement of the Communist and Workers' Parties on socialist gains says that "it is the common internationalist duty of all socialist countries to support, strengthen and defend these gains, which were achieved at the cost of every people's heroic efforts and selfless labor."

What the right-wing, antisocialist forces were seeking to achieve in Czechoslovakia in recent months was not a matter of developing socialism in an original way or of applying the principles of Marxism-Leninism to specific conditions in that country, but was an encroachment on the foundations of socialism and the fundamental principles of Marxism-Leninism. This is the "nuance" that is still incomprehensible to people who trusted in the hypocritical cant of the antisocialist and revisionist elements. Under the guise of "democratization" these elements were shattering the socialist state step by step; they sought to demoralize the Communist Party and dull the minds of the masses; they were gradually preparing for a counterrevolutionary coup and at the same time were not being properly rebuffed inside the country.

The Communists of the fraternal countries naturally could not allow the socialist states to remain idle in the name of abstract sovereignty while the country was endangered by antisocialist degeneration.

The five allied socialist countries' actions in Czechoslovakia are consonant with the fundamental interests of the Czechoslovak people themselves. Obviously it is precisely socialism that, by liberating a nation from the fetters of an exploitative system, ensures the solution of fundamental problems of national development in any country that takes the socialist path. And by encroaching on the foundations of socialism, the counterrevolutionary elements in Czechoslovakia were thereby undermining the basis of the country's independence and sovereignty.

The formal observance of freedom of self-determination in the specific situation that had taken shape in Czechoslovakia would signify freedom of "self-determination" not for the people's masses and the working people, but for their enemies. The antisocialist path, the "neutrality" to which the Czechoslovak people were being prodded, would lead the C.S.R. straight into the jaws of the West German revanchists and would lead to the loss of its national independence. World imperialism, for its part, was trying to export counterrevolution to Czechoslovakia by supporting the antisocialist forces there.

The assistance given to the working people of the C.S.R. by the other socialist countries, which prevented the export of counterrevolution from the outside, is in fact a struggle for the Czechoslovak Socialist Republic's sovereignty against those who would like to deprive it of this sovereignty by delivering the country to the imperialists.

Over a long period of time and with utmost restraint and patience, the fraternal Communist Parties of the socialist countries took political measures to help the Czechoslovak people to halt the antisocialist forces' offensive in Czechoslovakia. And only after exhausting all such measures did they undertake to bring in armed forces.

The allied socialist countries' soldiers who are in Czechoslovakia are proving in deeds that they have no task other than to defend the socialist gains in that country. They are not interfering in the country's internal affairs, and they are waging a struggle not in words but in deeds for the principles of self-determination of Czechoslovakia's peoples, for their inalienable right to decide their destiny themselves after profound and careful consideration, without intimidation by counterrevolutionaries, without revisionist and nationalist demagoguery.

Those who speak of the "illegality" of the allied socialist countries' actions in Czechoslovakia forget that in a class society there is and can be no such thing as nonclass law. Laws and the norms of law are subordinated to the laws of the class struggle and the laws of social development. These laws are clearly formulated in the documents jointly adopted by the Communist and Workers' Parties.

The class approach to the matter cannot be discarded in the name of legalistic considerations. Whoever does so and forfeits the only correct, class-oriented criterion for evaluating legal norms begins to measure events with the yardsticks of bourgeois law. Such an approach to the question of sovereignty means, for example, that the world's progressive forces could not oppose the revival of neo-Nazism in the F.R.G., the butcheries of Franco and Salazar or the reactionary outrages of the "black colonels" in Greece, since these are the "internal affairs" of "sovereign states." It is typical that both the Saigon puppets and their American protectors concur completely in the notion that sovereignty forbids supporting the struggle of the progressive forces. After all, they shout from the housetops that the socialist states that are giving aid to the Vietnamese people in their struggle for independence and freedom are violating Vietnam's sovereignty. Genuine revolutionaries, as internationalists, cannot fail to support progressive forces in all countries in their just struggle for national and social liberation.

The interests of the socialist commonwealth and the entire revolutionary movement and the interests of socialism in Czechoslovakia demand full exposure and political isolation of the reactionary forces in that country, consolidation of the working people and consistent fulfillment of the Moscow agreement between the Soviet and Czechoslovak leaders.

There is no doubt that the actions taken in Czechoslovakia by the five allied socialist countries in Czechoslovakia, actions aimed at defending the fundamental interests of the socialist commonwealth and primarily at defending Czechoslovakia's independence and sovereignty as a socialist state, will be increasingly supported by all who really value the interests of the present-day revolutionary movement, the peace and security of peoples, democracy and socialism.

OCTOBER TREATY

IN EFFECT, the treaty "temporarily" stationing Soviet troops in Czechoslovakia (Document 67) ratified Brezhnev's doctrine of limited sovereignty[1] within the socialist commonwealth, despite its claim that Soviet troops would not interfere in Czechoslovak internal affairs.[2] Although ostensibly directed against the rise of revanchist forces in West Germany, the circumstances indicated that Moscow was at least as interested in containing liberalism in Prague. While a Czechoslovak delegation including Dubček, Černík, and Husák was agreeing to such a treaty in principle (Document 66),[3] Soviet Foreign Minister Andrei Gromyko warned the United Nations 23rd General Assembly against "imperialist intrigues designed to roll back the socialist commonwealth or snatch one link from it." [4]

---

[1] In presenting the treaty to the Czechoslovak National Assembly, Premier Černík explicitly conceded that in the present world sovereignty could not be realized in an absolute sense or the national interests of individual socialist countries separated from common interests of the socialist community (*Rudé právo,* October 19, 1968; *The New York Times,* October 19, 1968). Publication of *Zprávy* was discontinued in May 1969 after Gustav Husák replaced Dubček as First Secretary of the KSČ.

[2] The incident of the philosophy student Jan Palach who set fire to himself January 16, 1969— partially as a protest at the continued distribution of *Zprávy,* a Soviet occupation news sheet featuring bitter attacks on Czechoslovak reformers — provided a tragic index of how meaningless that pledge was in practice. Not only did circulation of *Zprávy* violate Czechoslovak publishing laws but no such publication appeared in other East European countries where Soviet troops are stationed (Eric Bourne, *The Christian Science Monitor,* January 23, 1968).

[3] The best running coverage of these negotiations is given by Eric Bourne in *The Christian Science Monitor,* October 5, 7, 10, 1968; also Michel Tatu in *Le Monde,* October 7, 1968. At this time, rumors appeared that Dubček had strongly opposed the conditions and was considering resigning (Bourne, *The Christian Science Monitor,* October 10, 1968). Altogether his lack of enthusiasm for "the new reality" that he described to party officials in Prague, October 11, 1968 was clear (Prague Domestic Service in Slovak, 1800 GMT, October 11, 1968 [excerpts]; *Pravda,* October 14, 1968 [excerpts]; *CDSP,* Vol. XX, No. 41 [October 30, 1968], pp. 9–10).

[4] *The New York Times,* October 4, 1968. An interesting example of East German prodding of Soviet policy can be seen in a *Neues Deutschland* editorial's reference to Gromyko's statement in which the Soviet Foreign Minister's pledge that Moscow would not allow "one link to be snatched" from the socialist commonwealth was hardened by the addition of "never and nowhere," *Neues Deutschland,* October 10, 1968. See also Melvin Croan,

The terms of the treaty were harsh. In return for a staged withdrawal of the bulk of an estimated 600,000 Soviet and East European troops occupying the country, Czechoslovakia had legalized stationing of an unspecified number of Soviet troops for an indefinite time. Indeed, even after the Hungarian "counter-revolution," Budapest had gotten a better deal. Similar treaties "temporarily" stationing Soviet troops in Poland (1956) and Hungary (1957) required agreement of the host government for troop movement outside their normal garrisons. There was no such provision in the Soviet-Czechoslovak Treaty of 1968. Nor did the Treaty provide any compensation for damages inflicted during the invasion. Step by step, Dubček was being forced back.

DOCUMENT 66

COMMUNIQUÉ ON SOVIET-CZECHOSLOVAK TALKS IN MOSCOW
October 3–4, 1968
Complete Text

[*Pravda,* October 5, 1968, quoted from *CDSP,* Vol. XX, No. 40 (October 23, 1968), pp. 7–8]

Soviet-Czechoslovak talks were held in Moscow on Oct. 3 and 4, 1968.

The following participated in the talks for the Soviet side: Comrade L. I. Brezhnev, General Secretary of the C.P.S.U. Central Committee; Comrade A. N. Kosygin, member of the Politburo of the C.P.S.U. Central Committee and Chairman of the U.S.S.R. Council of Ministers; and Comrade N. V. Podgorny, member of the C.P.S.U. Central Committee Politburo and Chairman of the Presidium of the U.S.S.R. Supreme Soviet.

The following participated for the Czechoslovak side: Comrade A. Dubček, First Secretary of the Czechoslovak Communist Party Central Committee; Comrade O. Černík, Chairman of the C.S.R. Government and member of the Presidium of the C.C.P. Central Committee; and Comrade G. Husák, First Secretary of the Slovak Communist Party Central Committee and member of the Presidium of the C.C.P. Central Committee.

The two sides examined questions of the development of relations between the U.S.S.R. and the C.S.R. Special attention was paid to the fulfillment of the understanding and measures worked out in Moscow between Aug. 23 and 26, 1968, by the U.S.S.R. and C.S.R. delegations on the basis of the principles set forth in the summarizing documents of the meeting in Cierna-on-Tisa and the Bratislava conference. It was reaffirmed that these measures constitute the basis for achieving normalization of social and political life in the C.S.R. and for

---

"Czechoslovakia, Ulbricht, and the German Problem," *Problems of Communism,* Vol. XVIII, No. 1 (January–February 1969), pp. 1–8.

Czechoslovakia's development of friendly relations with the Soviet Union and the other countries of the socialist commonwealth.

The Czechoslovak delegation informed the C.P.S.U. Central Committee delegation about the concrete measures that are being taken in Czechoslovakia to implement the above-mentioned understanding and also about their ideas on further work in this direction.

The Czechoslovak delegation stated that the C.C.P. Central Committee and the C.S.R. government would take every measure to ensure fulfillment of the Moscow understanding. They will increase efforts to raise the Communist Party's leading role, will intensify the struggle against the antisocialist forces, will take the necessary measures to place the mass news media wholly at the service of socialism and will reinforce party and state bodies with people who stand firmly on positions of Marxism-Leninism and proletarian internationalism.

The C.P.S.U. Central Committee delegation confirmed its readiness to give the Czechoslovak comrades all possible assistance in carrying out their plans to normalize the situation in the country and the party in the spirit of the Moscow understanding.

During the talks the question of the allied troops' stay on C.S.R. territory was discussed. The sides agreed that the governments would consider and sign a treaty on the temporary stationing of allied troops in Czechoslovakia. Step-by-step withdrawal of the rest of the troops will be conducted in accordance with the documents of the Moscow talks held on Aug. 23–26, 1968.

The delegations of the Soviet Union and Czechoslovakia discussed the tasks of consolidating the fraternal alliance and the indestructible friendship between the peoples of the two countries, of developing comprehensive and fruitful cooperation between them in the economic, political, cultural and other areas and of strengthening the relations between the cities and provinces that maintain traditional, friendly ties.

Extremely important problems of safeguarding international peace and security were also discussed. The two sides confirmed their determination to follow steadfastly the foreign-policy course jointly elaborated in the interests of strengthening the socialist commonwealth and waging a successful struggle against the polices of the imperialist powers. The delegations consider a paramount task here to be the implementation of measures to create a reliable barrier to the intensified revanchist aspirations of the West German militarist forces, to give effective aid to the people of struggling Vietnam and to curb imperialist aggression in the area of the Near East.

The talks proceeded in a spirit of comradeship, business-like cooperation and frankness.

DOCUMENT 67

TREATY BETWEEN USSR GOVERNMENT AND THE CSR GOVERNMENT
ON THE CONDITIONS FOR THE TEMPORARY STATIONING OF
SOVIET TROOPS ON CSR TERRITORY

October 16, 1968

Complete Text

[*Pravda,* October 19, 1968, quoted from *CDSP,* Vol. XX, No. 42 (November 6, 1968), pp. 3-4]

The government of the Union of Soviet Socialist Republics and the government of the Czechoslovak Socialist Republic,

Fully resolved to make every effort to strengthen friendship and cooperation between the Union of Soviet Socialist Republics and Czechoslovakia, as well as among all the countries of the socialist commonwealth, and to defend the gains of socialism and consolidate peace and security in Europe and throughout the world, in accordance with the statement of the Bratislava conference of Aug. 3, 1968,

Taking into account the Treaty on Friendship, Mutual Aid and Postwar Cooperation of Dec. 12, 1943, and extended by the Protocol of Nov. 27, 1963,

in accordance with the understanding reached during the Soviet-Czechoslovak talks held in Moscow on Aug. 23-26 and Oct. 3 and 4, 1968,

have decided to conclude this treaty and have agreed on the following:

Art. 1. — The government of the Union of Soviet Socialist Republics, acting with the assent of the governments of the People's Republic of Bulgaria, the Hungarian People's Republic, the German Democratic Republic and the Polish People's Republic, and the government of the Czechoslovak Socialist Republic have agreed that part of the Soviet troops in the Czechoslovak Socialist Republic will remain temporarily on C.S.R. territory for the purpose of safeguarding the security of the countries of the socialist commonwealth against the mounting revanchist ambitions of West German militarist forces.

The rest of the U.S.S.R.'s troops, as well as the troops of the People's Republic of Bulgaria, the Hungarian People's Republic, the German Democratic Republic and the Polish People's Republic, in accordance with the documents of the Moscow talks of Aug. 23-26 and Oct. 3 and 4, 1968, will be withdrawn from Czechoslovak territory. The withdrawal of these troops will begin after both sides ratify this treaty, and it will be carried out by stages over a period of two months.

The number and places of deployment of the Soviet troops that are remaining temporarily on C.S.R. territory will be determined by agreement between the U.S.S.R. and C.S.R. governments.

The Soviet troops being stationed temporarily on C.S.R. territory remain under the jurisdiction of the Soviet Military Command.

Art. 2. — 1. The temporary presence of Soviet troops on C.S.R. territory does not violate its sovereignty. Soviet troops are not interfering in the internal affairs of the Czechoslovak Socialist Republic.

2. Soviet troops, persons serving with them and members of the families of such persons who are in the C.S.R. will observe the legislation in effect in the Czechoslovak Socialist Republic.

Art. 3. — 1. The Soviet side will bear the expenses for maintaining Soviet troops on C.S.R. territory.

2. The C.S.R. government will provide Soviet troops, persons serving with them and members of the families of such persons, during the period of their temporary stay in the C.S.R., with barracks and housing at military settlements; offices, warehouses and other premises; airfields with fixed installations and equipment; means of communication and transportation from the state-owned network, electric power; and other services.

Proving grounds and firing and training ranges will be used jointly with the Czechoslovak People's Army.

The procedure and terms for using the above-mentioned facilities, as well as communal, trade and other services, will be determined by agreement between the contracting sides.

Art. 4. — Soviet troops, persons serving with them and members of the families of such persons may travel to the places of Soviet troop deployment in the C.S.R. and from the C.S.R. either in direct trains and coaches belonging to the Soviet Union or by changing from coaches of one country to those of the other country, as well as by car and air.

Persons serving with Soviet troops and members of their families are exempted from passport and visa control when entering, staying in and leaving the C.S.R.

The points and procedure for crossing the Soviet-Czechoslovak border and the methods of control, as well as the types and forms of the appropriate documents, will be determined by agreement between the contracting sides.

Art. 5. — The Czechoslovak side agrees to allow the following to cross the C.S.R.'s state borders without collecting duties and without customs or border inspection:

— Soviet troops and persons serving with them who are traveling with military units, elements and crews;

— all military cargo, including cargo intended for commercial and everyday services for Soviet troops;

— persons serving with Soviet troops who are traveling to the C.S.R. or leaving the C.S.R. alone or together with members of their families, with their personal belongings, upon showing customs officials documents certifying their right to cross the C.S.R.'s state borders.

The property, equipment and materiel brought into the C.S.R. by the Soviet side may be taken back to the U.S.S.R. without paying duty.

Art. 6. — 1. Trade and everyday services for Soviet troop personnel temporarily stationed on C.S.R. territory and members of the families of persons serving with Soviet troops will be provided through Soviet trade and service enterprises.

2. The Czechoslovak side will provide the Soviet trade and service enterprises with goods, within the limits agreed upon by the competent U.S.S.R. and C.S.R. trade organizations, at the state retail prices prevailing in the C.S.R. and with the same trade discount as that granted to corresponding C.S.R. trade enterprises.

Payments for deliveries are made in the currency of the C.S.R.

3. Under the contracts concluded between the appropriate Soviet and Czechoslovak foreign-trade organizations, the Czechoslovak side will deliver foodstuffs and industrial goods, including fuel (coal, coke and firewood), in agreed amounts for the planned supply of Soviet troops and at the prices prevailing in the trade relations between the U.S.S.R. and the C.S.R.

Art. 7. — The C.S.R. government will provide the U.S.S.R. government with the necessary sums in Czechoslovak crowns for expenses related to the temporary stationing of Soviet troops on C.S.R. territory. The amount of these sums will be established by agreement between the competent agencies of the contracting parties.

Art. 8. — The procedure of payment for the services stipulated by Art. 3 and for the Czechoslovak koruny to be supplied in accordance with Art. 7 of this treaty will be established by an additional agreement between the contracting parties within a month and a half after this treaty goes into effect. The above-mentioned sums in Czechoslovak koruny will be translated into transfer rubles based on the relationship between domestic prices and charges in the C.S.R. on the one hand and foreign-trade prices on the other.

Art. 9. — Jurisdictional questions related to the temporary stationing of Soviet troops on C.S.R. territory will be settled in the following manner:

1. In cases of crimes and misdemeanors committed by persons serving with Soviet troops or by members of their families on C.S.R. territory, Czechoslovak legislation will apply, and the cases will be handled by the Czechoslovak courts, prosecutors' offices and other Czechoslovak agencies competent to prosecute punishable offenses.

Cases of crimes committed by Soviet servicemen will be investigated by the military prosecutor's office and will be investigated by the C.S.R.'s military judicial bodies.

2. The provisions of Point 1 of this article will not apply:

(a) to crimes or misdemeanors committed by persons serving with Soviet troops or by members of their families only against the Soviet Union or against persons serving with Soviet troops or members of their families;

(b) to crimes or misdemeanors committed by persons serving with Soviet troops in the performance of their duties in areas where the military units are deployed.

The cases specified in (a) and (b) are within the competence of Soviet courts, prosecutors' offices and other agencies operating on the basis of Soviet legislation.

3. The persons guilty of committing punishable offenses against Soviet troops temporarily stationed on C.S.R. territory or against persons serving with them will bear the same responsibility as for committing punishable offenses against the C.S.R.'s armed forces and persons serving with them.

4. Competent Soviet and Czechoslovak agencies may request one another reciprocally to transfer or accept jurisdiction in individual cases stipulated in Points 1 and 2 of this article. Such requests will be treated favorably.

5. Competent Soviet and Czechoslovak agencies will render one another legal and any other kind of assistance in prosecuting the punishable offenses indicated in Points 1, 2 and 3 of this article.

Art. 10. — 1. The U.S.S.R. government agrees to compensate the C.S.R. government for material damage that might be done to the Czechoslovak state through the actions or negligence of Soviet military units or by persons serving with them, and also for harm that might be done by Soviet military units or persons serving with them in the performance of their duties to Czechoslovak citizens, institutions or citizens of third states who are on C.S.R. territory — in both cases in amounts set (on the basis of stated charges and taking into account the provisions of Czechoslovak legislation) by the Representatives for the Affairs of the Temporary Stationing of Soviet Troops in the C.S.R., to be appointed in accordance with Art. 13 of this treaty.

Disputes that might arise from the obligations of Soviet military units are subject to examination on the same grounds.

2. The U.S.S.R. government also agrees to compensate the C.S.R. government for harm that might be done to Czechoslovak institutions and citizens, as well as to citizens of third states who are on C.S.R. territory, as a result of the actions or negligence of persons serving with Soviet troops that are not committed in the performance of their duties, and also as a result of the actions or negligence of members of the families of persons serving with Soviet troops — in both cases in amounts set by a competent Czechoslovak court, on the basis of the charges brought against the persons who inflicted the harm.

Art. 11. — 1. The C.S.R. government agrees to compensate the U.S.S.R. government for harm that might be done to the property of Soviet military units temporarily stationed on C.S.R. territory or to persons serving with Soviet troops through the actions or negligence of Czechoslovak state institutions — in amounts set by the Representatives for the Affairs of the Temporary Stationing of Soviet Troops in the C.S.R., on the basis of stated charges and taking into account Czechoslovak legislation.

Disputes that might arise from the obligations of Czechoslovak state institutions to Soviet military units are subject to examination on the same grounds.

2. The C.S.R. government also agrees to compensate the U.S.S.R. government for harm that might be done to Soviet military units temporarily stationed on C.S.R. territory, to persons serving with Soviet troops or to members of the families of such persons as a result of the actions or negligence of

Czechoslovak citizens — in amounts set by a Czechoslovak court on the basis of charges brought against the persons who inflicted the harm.

Art. 12. — Compensation for the damage specified in Arts. 10 and 11 will be paid by the sides within three months from the day a decision is adopted by the Representatives for the Affairs of the Temporary Stationing of Soviet Troops in the C.S.R. or a court decision goes into effect.

The sums due the victimized persons, units and institutions will be paid out by the competent agencies of the sides: in the cases provided for in Art. 10, by Czechoslovak agencies, and Art. 11, by Soviet agencies.

Art. 13. — For the purpose of properly settling current questions connected with the temporary stationing of Soviet troops in the C.S.R., the U.S.S.R. government and the C.S.R. government will appoint their Representatives for the Affairs of the Temporary Stationing of Soviet Troops in the C.S.R.

Art. 14. — 1. In this treaty, "Soviet troops and persons serving with them" include:

(a) servicemen of the Soviet Army;

(b) civilians who are Soviet citizens and are working in Soviet troop units temporarily stationed in the C.S.R.

2. "Members of the families of Soviet troops and persons serving with them" are:

(a) spouses;

(b) unmarried children;

(c) close relatives who are dependents of these personnel.

3. "Place of development" is the territory made available by the C.S.R. government or by local authorities to Soviet troops, including the places of encampment of military units.

Art. 15. — This treaty will go into force after it is ratified by both sides and will be in effect for the duration of the temporary stationing of Soviet troops on C.S.R. territory.

The treaty may be changed with the assent of the contracting parties.

Concluded in the city of Prague on Oct. 16, 1968, in two authentic copies, each in Russian and Czech, and both texts have equal force.

> A. KOSYGIN, Chairman,
> U.S.S.R. Council of Ministers.
> O. ČERNÍK, Chairman,
> C.S.R. Government.

NOVEMBER: THE NEW REALISM

GOMUŁKA'S REWORKING of the Brezhnev Doctrine (Document 68) bared the emptiness of Soviet, or for that matter Polish or East German, statements about noninterference in Czechoslovak internal affairs. The Polish leader explained in the bluntest possible terms the threat of liberalization in Prague. In his view, Dubček's brand of inner-party democracy was organically linked to West German *Ostpolitik* designed to wrest Czechoslovakia from the Warsaw Pact. If Czechoslovakia fell away, there was the danger of the community of socialist nations turning into a collection of Yugoslavias — each going its own way, an obvious target for all kinds of "imperialist and reactionary intervention, pressures, and chaos." The balance of power in Europe would have tipped in favor of imperialism.[1]

The extent of political retreat forced upon Prague can be seen in the KSČ Central Committee November Plenum Resolution (Document 69). Not only was the Plenum a time of self-criticism for the post-January regime but pitifully little was left of the August KSČ Draft Statutes. Once again members of the working class were put forward as the core of the party. There was no mention of the rights of the minority. Rather party organs were encouraged to "part without hesitation with persons unwilling to follow the party line." The role of national territorial bodies was to be clearly defined [2] and "uniform control" established over regional committees. Workers in press, radio, and television were reminded that such mass information media must be primarily instruments for implementing party and state policy.

First Secretary of the Slovak Communist Party, Gustav Husák, soon emerged as one of the most forceful proponents of the "new realism," based on the

[1] Gomułka also took the occasion to attack strongly the position of Western Communist parties on the "allied" invasion of Czechoslovakia. For analysis see Anatole Shub in the *Washington Post*, November 12, 1968. Also see Adam Bromke, "Poland's Political Crisis," *The World Today*, February 1969.

[2] The territorial question is extremely complex. Although the constitutional bill officially turning Czechoslovakia into a federation was signed October 30, 1968, the Communist Party of Czechoslovakia remains subject to principles of democratic centralism and undivided. So far only a Bureau of the KSČ CC has been set up for the direction of party work in Czech lands. (Decision of Presidium October 22. Prague Domestic Service, 2000 GMT, 22 October 1968.)

assumption of no alternative.[3] His address to the Slovak Central Committee at the close of the November Plenum (Document 70) rewrote the history of post-January developments. Husák went much further than the November Resolution, in blaming the difficulties with controlling communications media on weak party leadership. He characterized the path for Slovakia as a middle road, eschewing conservative trends and struggling against rightist, opportunist extremes. No one wanted to resort to political trials; yet the arbitrary actions of small groups must not lead to anarchy. The warning was clear.

DOCUMENT 68

REPORT BY W. GOMUŁKA TO THE FIFTH CONGRESS OF
THE POLISH UNITED WORKERS' PARTY
November 11, 1968
Excerpts
[*Trybuna ludu,* November 12, 1968]

. . . In its Eastern policy, the present government of the German Federal Republic is also guided by this program, but it has chosen different tactics in order to implement it. The Eastern policy of the previous West German governments was based on the illusory hopes that with the help of the aggressive NATO bloc they would be able to force the Soviet Union to agree to the so-called unification of Germany in accordance with Bonn's prescription. But Bonn's Eastern policy born out of this concept was a fiasco; it found itself in a cul-de-sac. For this reason the Kiesinger-Brandt coalition government created in 1966 initiated a maneuver of leading its policy out of this cul-de-sac to the so-called new road, while retaining its old goals.

The essence of this maneuver lies in the tactics of splitting the unity of the socialist states, the tendency toward isolating the GDR and the creation of conditions which promise success for the paramount strategic goal of the West German bourgeoisie, that is the liquidation of the socialist German state, the GDR. . . .

The events in Czechoslovakia have once again shown how far they [West German leaders] had deviated from this basic principle of peaceful coexistence. Their new Eastern policy occupies the leading place in the subversive policy of world imperialism, which is aimed at undermining, splitting, and disintegrating the community of socialist states embraced by the Warsaw Pact.

Peaceful coexistence is a political concept designed to reduce international

[3] Just before the November Plenum, Husák strongly attacked antisocialist forces for sabotaging reforms (Speech to a Slovak *aktiv* of the People's Militia, Radio Bratislava, November 13, 1968).

tensions, to create a system of collective security, to bar the way to wars, to prevent a nuclear catastrophe. The coexistence of states irrespective of their social structure does not change the essence of socialism and capitalism one iota. Sociopolitical systems can coexist and cooperate, especially in the economic and scientific fields, but they can never penetrate each other; they can never converge. Coexistence can never give birth to something that is neither socialism nor capitalism.

The Western invented abstract, revisionist theory of a so-called convergence is only imperialist subversion. The class struggle inevitably accompanying the birth and development of socialism is waged not only within the individual socialist countries; its worldwide scope stems from the fact of division of the world into two social systems. Therefore, even the complete liquidation of antagonistic classes does not bring about an end to the class struggle in individual socialist countries.

The building of socialism in every country is a manifestation of the class struggle against the capitalism on the world scale. The liquidation of the old economic and material basis of capitalism by no means eliminates the remnants of influence of bourgeois ideology on society's consciousness. This makes it easier for the enemy to carry out its subversive activities. Therefore, even in those socialist countries in which antagonistic class contradictions no longer exist, the socialist system can, in definite conditions, be endangered.

An open attack against the socioeconomic foundations of socialism, by means of classical counterrevolution in the form of armed action by reactionary forces supported by external intervention, has no chance of success in our European conditions. In such a situation the strategists of imperialism have laid the main stress on ideological subversion, as a result of which the socialist structure would be deformed in a bourgeois direction and the given country would find itself economically and politically dependent upon the capitalist states. Revisionism has become the first ally of imperialism and reaction in this strategy.

In the political crisis in Czechoslovakia revisionism, attacking the basic theoretical premises and principles of the party's practical activity evolving from Marxism-Leninism, played the main role in preparing the ground for an offensive by openly rightist and counterrevolutionary forces. These forces, acting in fact in a united front with the revisionist forces, were, with increasing determination, pushing Czechoslovakia onto a road of retreat from Marxism-Leninism and proletarian internationalism, to a road of wresting this state from the community of socialist states of the Warsaw Pact. This would have changed the balance of power in Europe in favor of imperialism. This process had entered a dangerous phase and might have become irreversible had it not been stopped in time.

The fraternal parties and governments of the socialist states could not remain indifferent in view of this threat not only to one of the socialist states, but to their common and vital interests. The entry into Czechoslovakia of troops of the five socialist countries with a view to thwarting the imperialist plans and removing the danger threatening the Czechoslovak link of the socialist camp was, in the circumstances, a necessity dictated by our internationalist duty and our national *raison d'état,* the interests of peace and security.

In fact, the steps taken on August 21 by the five socialist states constituted a preventive move in defense of peace and security in Europe, and thus were in the interest of all nations. There could have been no greater encouragement for the forces of aggression, war, and anticommunism to try to reshape the frontiers and the sociopolitical order in Europe anew than the disintegration of the Warsaw Pact and the acceptance of a so-called independent policy by the states of this pact.

Yugoslavia, while maintaining a policy of so-called nonalignment, can maintain it only in the shadow of the unity of the Warsaw Pact states. If other socialist states should follow the steps of Yugoslavia, then, in a situation in which Europe did not have any collective security mechanism, each of these countries would represent an open gate to all kinds of imperialist and reactionary intervention, pressures, and chaos. . . .

In view of this objectively existing situation, the education of the party ranks both in the socialist and in the capitalist countries in the spirit of proletarian internationalism, in the spirit of understanding the fundamental community of aims and unity of action of all units of the international workers movement in the struggle for peace, democracy, and freedom of nations, is all the more important. At the same time, the Communists must carry out a realistic policy that takes into consideration the realities of the struggle between the two systems. They must combine their national objectives with the striving for victory on an international scale.

The nationalist tendencies apparent in the international Communist and workers' movement, as well as the revisionist and leftist tendencies, weaken this unity; and thus the might and effectiveness of action of the Communist and workers' parties are also weakened. All these disintegrating tendencies are being skillfully stimulated and exploited by imperialism and its agencies. The animation of opportunism of all ilk, both right wing and left wing, puts definite pressure on the Communist and workers' movement. A Marxist-Leninist analysis of the sources of these phenomena cannot be confined to superficial causes, which are temporary and subjective in nature. It should focus its attention on the conditions stemming from the existing balance of forces and the present stage in the struggle between the two systems.

Revisionism, like any kind of opportunism, is primarily a result of bending under the pressure of obstacles and difficulties encountered in the struggle for socialism, a result of losing the revolutionary perspective of socialism's inevitable victory over capitalism. When the Communists lose that perspective and try to find answers to the difficult contemporary problems somewhere else, suitable conditions are created for opportunism and, first of all, for revisionist tendencies. No one can forecast when and how the historical victory of socialism over capitalism on a world scale will come about. Most likely the struggle between the two systems which will bring about that victory will go on for a long time yet, but the outcome of that struggle is already today indisputable. The victory will belong to socialism.

On the road to that victory the revolutionary workers' movement must still overcome many an obstacle, tread many a new path, and solve problems which the classics of Marxism could not even have foreseen. Only creative Marxist thinking, free of dogmatism, can cope with this historical task and light the way for the development of socialist revolution in our era.

We do not deny that the conditions of the developed capitalist countries in which a struggle is being waged by the brotherly Communist parties may be quite specific; we do not negate the premises designed to exploit parliaments and other institutions of bourgeois democracy; to build a broad alliance between Communists and various anti-imperialist, democratic, and peace-loving forces. The roads to socialism not only can but must differ. But there is only one socialism; its fundamental essence is rule by the working masses under the hegemony of the working class, and a planned management of socialized means of production.

Roads mapped out by one party and appropriate to one of the countries building socialism cannot be imposed on other parties and countries, but they can and should be a source of experience for every party struggling for power or building the new system. These experiences cannot be ignored or rejected without harming individual parties and the entire working movement, the international struggle for socialism.

Every one of the Communist parties in capitalist countries is directed by a definite strategy and tactics arising from conditions in which it operates. But they cannot demand from the fraternal parties, which hold power and carry a direct responsibility for the development and strength of their countries and of the entire socialist system, that they adapt their political line to the actual policy of Communist parties in Western countries, to their tactics in the struggle against the bourgeoisie, the struggle to take their countries onto the road of socialist changes.

This is neither possible nor correct. The extension of the scope of the rights and liberties of the working class and laboring masses within the framework of the bourgeois democracy, the curbing and expropriating of the capitalist monopolies and similar postulates for which the Western Communist parties are struggling, lies, surely, in the line of the struggle for socialism. But the grafting of the content of bourgeois democracy onto the organism of socialist democracy would amount to a revisionist deformation of socialism, to opening a way to capitalist transformations in socialist countries.

The power of the entire socialist movement and the power of each party comprising it is inseparable from the development and unity of socialist countries. The international position of the socialist camp exerts a direct influence on the power and action of every Communist party. He who, disregarding this, attacks the socialist countries without regard for the subjective motives of that stance, weakens his own party's and the entire Communist movement's position.

Quite properly then, the workers of many capitalist countries are against the attacks on the Soviet Union and other countries of our camp, no matter from what position those attacks are undertaken. The attitude of every Communist and workers' party toward the Soviet Union and other socialist countries should be defined by the ongoing struggle between two systems, and should give expression to the internationalist understanding of what that struggle demands. . . .

DOCUMENT 69

"THE PARTY'S MAIN TASKS FOR THE NEAR FUTURE"

November Resolution of Central Committee
of the Czechoslovak Communist Party
Excerpts
[*Rudé právo*, November 19, 1968]

. . . The fundamental reasons for the complicated development following January were the long-drawn-out refusal to solve overdue problems within the party and society, the misevaluation of their causes, and the suppression of elements within the party which made legitimate suggestions as to their solution. This refusal contributed to the extraordinary tension accompaning the sudden discovery of all the long-hidden and unsolved problems within such a short period of time and to criticism of the party as a whole, its entire apparatus, and all its active members — criticism which would have been justified had it been directed against those primarily responsible for the errors.

Antisocialist and anti-Soviet forces, which ostensibly followed the positive course of post-January party policy, exploited this situation with an eye to misusing criticism and self-criticism advanced by the party. These forces were assisted by rightist elements and opportunist trends within the party itself. . . .

Using the [post-January] situation to their own advantage, certain forces aimed at discrediting the KSČ, undermining and even disintegrating its leading position in society, sapping individual decision-making components of the socialist state, and finally weakening the party's and the country's international ties within the framework of the community of socialist countries.

They made primary use of one-sided and often distorted appraisals, intentional misinformation, and the tactic of piling up more and more new problems regardless of the ability of the party and society to find immediate and correct solutions. All this was exploited by rightist, opportunist elements as well as antisocialist forces which succeeded in penetrating some of the mass communication media and misusing their extraordinary influence. The Central Committee of the KSČ is aware that a large part of the workers and collectives in the communications media supported reasonably and responsibly the truly positive values of the post-January policy and respected the tasks and the tactical course adopted by the party and expressed in the decisions of the KSČ Central Committee.

Neither the Presidium of the KSČ CC nor the government had prepared a system for the control of the press, radio, and television. Censorship was abolished, but the impact of the negative activities of the communication media was not analyzed or evaluated; there was no accurate distinction made between what was correct in their work and what complicated the process which was taking place, was harmful to it, and had a negative effect upon its development. Their work was often viewed with an insufficiently critical eye.

Mass communication media gradually began to assume an uncontrollable power. Moreover, inadequate thought was given to methods of providing systematic guidance for Communists working in mass communication media and to improving their influence on editorial boards in accordance with the over-all party line.

As a result of all these influences — particularly in February, March, and the beginning of April — there was a rise in pressures from all sides and considerable confusion of opinion in the party and among the public, this criticism often being directed against the whole party instead of the real culprits. At the same time, unjust blanket accusations made against the party and state apparatus and organs of power — particularly against the security forces and judiciary — for the encroachments of the fifties, affected the honor of the overwhelming majority of honest workers who had nothing in common with these deformations and upset the work of these important political and authoritative bodies.

Particularly in the initial phase of post-January development, it became necessary to face up to the serious resistance shown by dogmatic and conservative forces.

In some instances, even the unity of the party itself and its leading role in society was jeopardized. It is natural enough that, both before the January Plenum and after it, developments in the party and society did not proceed at an equal rate throughout the republic and that antisocialist forces and tendencies did not manifest themselves with equal vigor.

The conclusions of the April Plenum, the Party Action Program, was the first integrated step toward the party's future course. The Action Program naturally could not and did not give an immediate answer to all questions, and a number of questions could not be given a complete and absolutely exact answer. . . .

. . . Due to petit-bourgeois impatience and adventurism and the accumulation of more and more problems proper attention was not paid to the Action Program. It did not become the basis for the process of unification in the party and in society. The future activity of the party was notably clarified by the May session of the party's Central Committee, which commented on the growing danger of antisocialist forces. The Central Committee correctly stressed that while it would not allow a return to the pre-January conditions, it would not accept the slightest retreat from the achievements of socialism and that in the case of a threat to socialism in Czechoslovakia the party and the state would resort to forceful expedients to defend socialism.

An integrated and complex evaluation of the positive and negative aspects of post-January developments, particularly of the individual stages, together with an elucidation of the role played by objective causes and subjective short-comings will take much time to prepare.

The main thing now, however, — and this the Central Committee wants to stress — is that we adopt a standpoint on the main developmental features of that complicated period, but particularly that we show the whole party a positive starting point for further work, for unifying the party on Marxist-Leninist principles and for strengthening the links joining the party and the working people in building a socialist society. . . .

Developments inside the party itself were very complicated and contradictory. The basic feature of the situation was and is a profound difference of opinion which of course did not wait to spring into being until after the January session of the Central Committee; it existed long before it. In the post-January development, however, these differences greatly increased on a qualitatively different level which was difficult to control in the short period of time.

The decisive element among party officials and members took its stand on the platform formulated by the Central Committee, actively participated in the creation of new policy, and made efforts to implement it, even though it naturally required further elaboration. It set the pace of the post-January political development and was the main guarantee of further socialist development in Czechoslovakia. It presented correctly the interests and standpoints of the workers, thereby providing the main guarantee of ties between the party and the public and gradually winning back confidence in the policy of the party which had been shaken in the past. It was also a guarantee of the consolidation and further development of friendly relations with the socialist countries, especially with the Soviet Union, based on healthy principles of mutual understanding, confidence, and respect.

The complicated developments in the party were caused by right-wing forces and opportunistic tendencies which confused legitimate criticism of the distorted application of the principle of the party's leading role with "partnership" in the sense of a free play of political forces and regarded the use of power instruments in the present stage of political struggle as unacceptable. Under the false slogan of absolute democracy they overlooked the class aspects of socialist democracy, tolerated and actually supported an unhealthy atomization of the political system and social organizations, and onesidedly emphasized the independence of the individual parts of the political system from the KSČ and its policy. They underrated the dangers generated by antisocialist forces, took an unsympathetic view of the development of an ideological fight against them, and held subjective views which minimized the foreign political aspects of the development of socialism in Czechoslovakia — for instance, on the influence of the class struggle carried out on the international scale, on imperialist efforts to misuse the process taking place in Czechoslovakia, and on the international interests of the world socialist community of which Czechoslovakia is an inseparable part.

These views were given disproportionate publicity, thus giving rise to the impression that they represented the official policy of the KSČ, which played into the hands of the antisocialist forces and disoriented part of the party membership and public.

Coupled with this was the decreasing attention paid by the mass communication media to positive features of post-January policy.

At the same time sectarian-dogmatic tendencies prevailed in the party. These were and are forces and standpoints which are unable to grasp the new developmental needs of socialist society, the new content and forms of expression of the interests of the working class and other working people, forces which persist in evaluating social situations and thus also political standpoints which were valid under other historical circumstances. Such a policy never was and is not now able to convince and win over the majority of Communists, the working class, and other working people.

Such standpoints can only belittle the party in the eyes of the broad masses who pinned their hopes on a post-January policy capable of eliminating sectarian and dogmatic methods of work. Thus attempts to revive sectarian and dogmatic approaches rendered the whole situation more difficult and, in fact, played to a certain extent into the hands of anti-Communist sympathizers.

However, it must be also said quite truthfully that in many cases, a wholesale denunciation of sectarianism was aimed at silencing and discrediting honest Communists who stood up bravely against rightist approaches. . . .

The nucleus of the antisocialist forces consisted of some of the people who had been victimized by the force of the revolution and some former rightist party officials who after January 1968, began to believe that the time had come when they would be able to reenter the political arena and even seize the leadership of the other parties. At the same time, the effect of the foreign propaganda should not be underrated, stimulating, as it did, false illusions about capitalism and bourgeois democracy.

The antisocialist forces concentrated mainly on discrediting and repudiating socialism, idealizing bourgeois democracy, and attempting to introduce some of its elements into our political system; they interpreted socialist democracy as fully open to the "free play" of all political forces, even those opposed to the socialist platform of the entire National Front, and to the leading role of the party. They attempted to undermine the party and the state, and offered opportunity for attacks against the alliance with the Soviet Union and the other socialist countries, for attacks against the Warsaw Pact and against economic cooperation with the socialist countries.

To attain their aims, antisocialist forces attempted to create gradually for themselves an organizational platform. They misused, therefore, the valid ideas of the Action Program concerning the democratization of political life, rehabilitation of unjustly prosecuted citizens, and inclusion of the broad non-Communist masses into political life. From the beginning, they aimed at establishing and dominating such organizations as K-231 and KAN and especially at reviving the rightist anti-Marxist Social Democratic Party in order to break up the unity of the workers' class and weaken thereby the position of the KSČ in society. They also attempted to misuse politically the "opus of council revival." The KSČ CC also regards as irresponsible the extreme attacks launched against the People's Militias in total disregard of the clear standpoint as to their role and mission stated on several occasions by the party.

Although opposition to these clearly antisocialist and anti-Soviet trends and their supporters was growing both within the party and among the public, the mass communications media gave them systematic and disproportionate publicity.

Regular space was intentionally alloted to direct attacks against socialism on the pages of the periodical *Student,* whose aims, however, did not express the views of the vast majority of students. Both in this periodical, and in other forms of public communication, antisocialist ideas were on the increase. The KSČ CC called attention to this danger from the right as being the chief danger and now, in evaluating post-January development as a whole, it confirms its standpoint. . . .

At all its post-January meetings, the Central Committee analyzed the complicated situation that had evolved, and evaluated its positive and negative aspects. Despite the complexity of developments, the party retained its decisive influence on the political situation. The overwhelming majority of the people supported and still support socialism because of the honorable and honest efforts of the Communists both to rectify the wrongs of the past and seek positive ways for the further development of socialism in Czechoslovakia. However, activities of antisocialist forces which frustrated the party's post-January policy have seriously complicated the internal political situation and our relations to the allies.

The Central Committee, by submitting our post-January development to a critical evaluation, even though it is aware that it does not thereby exhaust the entire problem and that this is merely the first over-all attempt to judge the various aspects of the post-January development, is primarily motivated by the aim of making the whole party understand the nature of the positive content of post-January policy. Only in this way will it be possible to judge in a uniform way what was — and what remains — the principal meaning behind our actions and goals, what we must dissassociate ourselves from, and what was not only divorced from the post-January policy of the party but even damaged and opposed it.

The sincere and consistent fulfillment of the Bratislava agreement and the Moscow protocol of August 26, 1968, is of exceptional importance for the course of action and policy decisions taken by the party after the August events. It is the only realistic way to normalize conditions within Czechoslovakia and relations between Czechoslovakia and the five countries of the Warsaw Treaty.

The question of the temporary stationing of Soviet troops on the territory of Czechoslovakia has now been solved by the treaty signed between the governments of the Czechoslovak Socialist Republic and the Union of Soviet Socialist Republics and ratified by the National Assembly on October 18, 1968.

The KSČ Central Committee stresses to all regional and district committees of the KSČ the basic organizations of the KSČ and the Communist Party of Slovakia, and to all Communists working in state, social, and economic bodies the need to fulfill the letter of all these documents thoroughly.

The KSČ Central Committee stresses once again that the basic postulates of the policy of our party stem from the principles of Marxism-Leninism and proletarian internationalism. Our party will consistently comply with its international obligations and defend our alliance with the Soviet Union and the other socialist countries.

In the building of socialism, the KSČ and its agencies will proceed from the general principles of the building of socialism and at the same time respect the specific conditions of the building of socialism in Czechoslovakia.

Our party is now faced with a very important task. In the interests of strengthening socialism in our republic, in the interests of our people and the future of our country it must develop all positive aspects of socialism, ensure the development of socialist economy, and socialist democracy, strengthen the leading role of the party, develop socialist patriotism, and deepen and defend the principles of proletarian internationalism. In the same spirit it must likewise develop and strengthen our friendship with the Soviet Union and the other socialist countries, remain consistently loyal to democratic centralism and internal party democracy, conduct a concentrated ideological struggle against right-wing opportunistic forces and a general struggle against anti-socialist and anti-Soviet forces and bourgeois ideology. It must use these principles to unify all healthy forces in the party and support them by passing and executing political-organizational and cadre measures.

The KSČ Central Committee, proceeding from the fundamental principles of the construction of socialism, aware of the necessity for a uniform and coordinated stand by the whole party, all its bodies and organizations, and attempting to orient the whole party clearly and unambiguously to an offensive which utilizes all positive elements of post-January development, lays down the following main tasks for the forthcoming period:

A. *Strengthening Party Unity in Ideology and Action and Developing Internal Party Democracy and Democratic Centralism*

. . . An important condition of conscious discipline and activity for Communists is the full development of internal party democracy. This entails creating in each organization conditions enabling all Communists to participate in discussing all questions of party policy, criticism and self-criticism, comradely relations of equality in rights and duties, preventing the incrimination of Communists, taking consistent action on their remarks, ideas, and proposals. It is urgently necessary to build up an integrated internal party information system and thus to alleviate the problem of inadequate information within the party.

Collective leadership must be further developed and must not be merely regarded as the collective decision-making of agencies regarding all basic questions, but also as a style of work relying on the broadest possible base of active party members in formulating and carrying out the policies of the party which ensure the correct relationship between the plenums and their executive bodies and between the higher and lower agencies of the party. It is necessary to ensure that every agency member is kept fully informed on all fundamental questions and participates in formulating party policies, instead of merely attending meetings of his agency, that the principles of democratic centralism and internal party discipline are strictly observed, and that lower agencies strictly adhere to the decrees of higher agencies, while at the same time higher agencies pay heed to the observations, proposals, and recommendations of the lower agencies.

At all levels, it is necessary to increase the role of elected party bodies, particularly their plenums, in the formulation and execution of party policy.

The KSČ Central Committee is resolved energetically to confront all attempts to disturb the unity of the party, although the party cannot underestimate the influence of dogmatic-sectarian tendencies.

The Central Committee will also energetically confront all attempts to interfere with this decisive stand by suppressing factually justified criticism and the rights of a party member to express freely and openly at party meetings his views on party policy and the activities of all party bodies from top to bottom.

Differences of opinion as to how questions within the party are to be judged or settled must not, however, lead to a disruption of the united stand of the Communists when decisions which have been adopted are to be effected.

Cadre work is of exceptional importance for strengthening the party's unity and ability to act. Its basic task is to see to it that all party functions are occupied by comrades who have won the confidence of the party and the rest of the public and are determined consistently to implement the Marxist-Leninist policy of the party and resolved to carry out party resolutions consistently.

In this work the ability to judge the problems which the agency concerned has to settle and explain the policies of the party to win over for it not only Communists, but also other citizens, must be the principal aspect.

Seen in this light, cadre selection and training techniques must be perfected.

The Central Committee and its agencies will also combat all attempts to discredit upright comrades who honorably enforce the principles of party policy against all harassment on the basis of our open internationalist relation to the Soviet Union. The KSČ CC stresses that the decisive points in judging party members will be the honesty, devotion, and discipline with which they fulfill the tasks demanded by the party's political line.

In the interest of the maximal unity of its membership, the party must safeguard the principle that no party member be persecuted for his past or present views, unless they involve antiparty activity or activities conflicting with the law.

The work of the Central Committee itself must be improved. The role of the plenum must be enhanced in the spirit of the decision of the January CC Plenum and the Action Program; the relations between the plenum and its executive agencies must be set right. The Presidium of the Central Committee must deal with all the fundamental tasks stemming from the resolutions of the KSČ CC and must exert efficient control in this respect. The CC Secretariat must concentrate primarily on CC administration. It must make sure that the CC apparatus consistently enforces the policy of the Central Committee of the party.

All the most active party members must participate in determining and executing party policy and make good use of work teams and *ad hoc* committees with the assistance of both theoreticians and practicians.

The role of the national territorial bodies must be clearly defined, uniform control of regional committees must be consolidated and their leading members summoned more frequently to joint meetings. Similar measures must be taken in the regions and districts. Group work with members of individual regional central committees must be promoted.

Increased attention must be paid to strengthening the ranks of the party by including the most progressive citizens. Our goal must be to place Communists capable of safeguarding party policy in all spheres of social activity and life of our society. New party members must be acquired from all social classes, strata and groups, i.e., the most progressive workers, cooperative farmers, members of the intelligentsia, and other working people.

In future, too, members of the workers' class must form the core of the party. Increased attention must be paid to the winning over of the collective farmers, the new socialist class, and above all youth, whose role in the party is completely inadequate.

Party agencies and organizations must have the courage to part without hesitation with those who are unwilling to follow the party line and thereby impair the unity of the party and its state of preparedness.

It is exceptionally important at present to increase the role of the working class, the leading force of our society, in the development of our policy and its participation in the formulation and execution of our policy and in strengthening the socialist unity of our people. As they go about their day-to-day affairs, party agencies must work at developing the workers' initiative, turning it toward the most urgent tasks in the development of our society and overcoming individual problems and local interests.

All party functionaries must pay increased attention to working-class party organizations. Party bodies must factually, clearly and completely openly inform workers about the home situation and the intentions of the party, take counsel with them on the main problems of our life, and systematically explain to them the party's standpoints. The opinions of the workers find a more important place in the system of party work as a whole and in the mass means of communication. Together with the most able Communists in the theoretical field, officials from all levels of managing bodies and the natural spokesmen of the workers, farmers, and intelligentsia, who have authority and are able to support party policy actively, must be included among party activists. . . .

It must be clear in the work of the whole party that the current criticism of extremist tendencies and forces must not mean restoration of the old sectarian, bureaucratic methods. Otherwise, the party would not be able to maintain its ties with the people, strengthen the unity of all socialist forces of the society, or reinforce its leading role, which we consider to be a basic condition for the further development of socialism in our country and simultaneously a guarantee of the prevention of the influence of all forces wanting a reversal to pre-January conditions, a guarantee of political isolation and liquidation of anti-socialist forces.

B. Developing Socialist Democracy and Strengthening the Leading Role of the Communist Party in Society

The Central Committee stresses again that it considers the strengthening of the leading role of the party to be the most important prerequisite for correctly reinforcing the whole political system.

The party safeguards its leading role by:

1. Working out a political line for social development;

2. Unifying and coordinating state, economic, and social organizations in the spirit of the political line;

3. Carrying out day-to-day political, organizational, and control activities, and ensuring their execution through purposefully developed cadre work;

4. Developing ideological activity to produce an increased socialist consciousness, ensuring education on the principles of Marxism-Leninism, and striving to overcome influences alien and hostile to socialism;

5. Taking care that the public is given complete, truthful information about the plans of the party and the reasons for its decisions.

The Central Committee regards it as necessary to stress the validity of the following principles:

1. The cooperation between party agencies and Communists in state agencies in elected representative bodies and in the governmental and other executive apparatus, as well as in the armed forces of the Ministry of the Interior and of the army, in the judiciary, etc., must be deepened. In particular, it is important that:

   a. The Communists always inform relevant party agencies about the situation and about the course they have adopted in basic questions of a political nature and consult with the party agencies about major problems before making decisions on these problems. At the same time party agencies and the party apparat must not act instead of the state and other agencies and assume their responsibilities. The purpose of party guidance is the early political preparation of a united attitude on the part of Communists in all sectors and effective control of the fulfillment of party decisions;

   b. The correct principles governing the placement of cadres in the state apparat be strictly adhered to;

2. Coordination with Communists in the social organizations of the National Front must be ensured, the work of party groups in elected bodies of social organizations activized, and their work (as well as the work of the basic organizations of the party and the apparat of these social organizations and of the National Front) consistently guided;

3. Systematic cooperation — in accordance with the same principles — is also essential with Communists in the mass information media, which form an inseparable part of the political system and exert a decisive influence on the forming of public opinion. In particular, special care must be taken of the party organization in publishing enterprises and editorial offices and the work and the responsibility of Communists in editorial offices and in the organization of the Union of Journalists must be actively influenced;

4. In the development of socialist democracy the policy of the National Front — in which the KSČ is the leading force — must be actively pursued. The leading role of the party must also be ensured through the nomination by the party of capable members for posts in the National Front and in individual social organizations.

Communists must actively support the internal democratic development and unity of social organizations so that their members recognize them as real spokesmen of their interests, and so that they will be able — through them and through the National Front — to participate fully in making and implementing policy in the state.

Increased attention must be paid not only to the development of the trade union organization but also to newly forming organizations such as the Union of Cooperative Farmers, the Union of Czechoslovak Women, youth organizations, and those of the intelligentsia.

The Central Committee of the Communist Party of Czechoslovakia regards a clear elaboration of the principles of the KSČ's trade union policy and its policy toward the younger generation as a particularly important political task. This is necessary in support of measures ensuring the needs both of justified special-interest differentiation and the necessary degree of unity of these organizations.

5. The constitutional solution of the relations of Czechs and Slovaks on a federative basis and the democratic solution of the legal status of other nationalities in Czechoslovakia by a special constitutional law in harmony with the Action Program is regarded by the KSČ Central Committee as one of the basic positive steps in the implementation of post-January policy.

Accordingly the CC thinks it necessary to speed up the settlement of outstanding questions in the entire federative political system. In doing this care must be taken that the entire directing system is put on a rationalized and economical footing;

6. The National Front, the government, and the National Assembly are to continue their preparation of election laws dealing with election to the National Assembly, the Czech and Slovak National Councils, and the national committees;

7. The press, radio, and television are exceptionally important means for exerting political influence and they must actively clarify the policies of party and state, with the aim of unifying and organizing the citizens for the purpose of carrying out these policies.

Responsible workers in mass information media must orient the work of the press toward helping to bring about unity of opinion on matters of principle among socialist forces, take a principled stand against all signs of bourgeois ideology, and counter extreme alien and hostile viewpoints which might impair socialist development in Czechoslovakia. It is an urgent task of the mass information media to contribute actively to an understanding of the contexts of world development, the struggle between socialism and imperialism, and the firm integration of our nations into the socialist system.

The press, radio, and television are primarily an instrument for the implementation of the policy of the party and state. They carry out exchanges of suggestions and views between the bodies of the party, state, National Front, and public, which must be regarded as part of the correct implementation of the leading role of the party and at the same time one of the democratic forms of citizens' participation in the management and administration of the state.

Political work through the medium of the mass information media is one of the decisive tasks of party and state bodies social organizations and the National Front as a whole. Communist journalists working in the mass information media form an important element among the party activists, and the rights and duties of party activists fully relate to them.

The party will ensure that they are sufficiently informed about its intentions and goals and that they can understand them correctly and implement party policy with a sense of responsibility. All workers in the mass information media, regardless of party affiliation, are responsible for the protection of state interests, the fulfillment of the political program of elected state bodies, the government and the National Front. They are responsible for the mass information media working in an exclusively socialist spirit.

The publishers bear the main responsibility for a correct orientation of the contents of what they publish in accordance with the requirements of the development of socialism. In cases in which the workers in the information media do not respect the fundamental interests of the state and of socialism and the policy of their organizations, the appropriate organizational cadre conclusions must be resolutely drawn.

The KSČ CC is aware of the exceptional importance of the information media in supporting the policies of the party and the state, and it will therefore pay close attention to their orientation. It will establish political and cadre conditions which favor this end.

A special role falls to the party press, which is responsible to elected party bodies at each level. These bodies must pay increased attention to it, orientate its contents and use it as a real tribune of party policy which expounds that policy to party members and the whole public. In this respect *Rudé právo* and *Pravda* (the organ of the CC of the Communist Party of Slovakia) have an exceptionally important mission.

It is necessary to bear in mind that direct statements made by political and state leaders on the pages of the press, on the radio and television, along with a maximum use of the mass information media's opportunities to communicate the opinions of the workers, farmers, and intelligentsia, can effectively provide political help in forming public opinion;

8. The KSČ CC will devote increased attention to strengthening the defense system of the state and the security of the republic and all its citizens.

The KSČ CC must face major tasks in strengthening and consolidating the people's army. It is necessary to boost further the political and moral state and the battle-readiness of the army, to complete and implement a uniform system of direction of the party agencies and organizations in the army, to tackle resolutely the problems which arise for members of the army in connection with the deployment of their units. Preconditions must be established which permit the further reinforcement of the defense system of our homeland which we understand to consist in inseparable cohesion with the Warsaw Pact. A National Security Council must be established to direct defense policies.

All components of the Ministry of the Interior, the judiciary, and the Prosecutor's offices have an important role to play in society. They must be vigilant guardians of socialist legality and generally ensure the security of the socialist republic, the protection of socialist property, public order, and the laws and legitimate interests of the citizens. It is the duty of Communists in this sphere to support these institutions in every possible way in their responsible work.

The KSČ Central Committee again stresses the role and significance of the people's militia, which it regards as one of the guarantees of the socialist development of our society. The people's militia is irreplaceable in the defense system of the socialist state. The main task at present is to strengthen the unity of opinions of members of the people's militia on the basis of the policy and resolutions of the KSČ CC, to increase its militant and political preparedness and capacity for action, and, in harmony with the elaboration of the conception of the state's defense system, to work out the place and role of the people's militia in the present period and to incorporate it into a decree. . . .

Basic Questions of International Policy

. . . In harmony with the Action Program, the points of departure of our policy in this field are the principles of proletarian internationalism, treaties with the socialist countries, and the documents of international meetings of Communist parties, as well as the conclusions of the meetings in Čierná and Bratislava and the Moscow protocol.

1. We shall continue to develop all-round cooperation and friendship with the Soviet Union and other socialist countries. As always in the past, we confirm the inviolability of our ties with all the socialist countries and our fidelity to the obligations we have taken upon ourselves. No alternative has ever existed for us but to belong to the socialist system, to the Warsaw Treaty, and to participate actively in the Council of Mutual Economic Assistance. Therefore, we intend to do everything we can to further these activities, to increase the effectiveness of the work of all organizations of the socialist countries and, in particular, of Comecon and the organizations of the Warsaw Pact. Any endeavor to weaken our cooperation with the socialist countries, as well as any irresponsible attempts on the part of individuals to propagate the slogan of neutrality, will face the determined resistance of the party.

2. Together with the other socialist countries we shall carry out a coordinated policy corresponding to the common interests of the socialist countries; we shall unrelentingly and systematically face up to aggressive imperialist actions, particularly attempts to change the setup in Europe that resulted from the Second World War — which, primarily, militaristic and revanchist circles in West Germany are making efforts to do. We shall actively contribute to the creation of a system of collective European security, struggle to achieve recognition of the invalidity of the Munich pact since its inception, strengthen the international status of the German Democratic Republic, and support West German Communists and all forces which in West Germany are consistently struggling against militarism and revanchism for democratic progress.

We shall continue to give full support to the just struggle of the Vietnamese people. Within the limits of her ability, Czechoslovakia will contribute to the rapid implementation of the Security Council resolution on the situation in the Middle East and particularly the withdrawal of Israeli troops from the occupied Arab countries. Within the limits of our ability we shall continue to strengthen international solidarity with nations fighting for national liberation and political and economic independence and provide them with aid.

3. In keeping with the Action Program and the Bratislava Declaration we shall carry out, in cooperation and mutual coordination with the other socialist countries, an active foreign policy vis-à-vis countries with different social systems; in essence a policy of peaceful coexistence, a policy of the development of mutually beneficial relations leading to understanding and confidence among nations, a policy that can be an effective instrument against the efforts of the aggressive circles of imperialism to whip up again an atmosphere of cold war and to create new opportunities for attacks against socialism.

We shall persevere in our policy of establishing and strengthening relations with all democratic, progressive, and revolutionary forces in the interest of the common struggle against imperialism and for peace and social progress.

4. As laid down in the Action Program and in the Bratislava Declaration, we shall continue to foster bilateral and multilateral relations with the Communist and workers' parties of socialist and other countries, exchange experiences, confront convictions and opinions on various questions, clarify confused issues, and coordinate our course with theirs in the settlement of important political and ideological problems and in the struggle against imperialism and for the progress of socialism. Accordingly, our party will contribute actively to the convocation of and preparations for an international conference of Communist and workers' parties, which we regard as an important step toward gradually overcoming current difficulties in the international Communist movement and toward strengthening its unity and increasing its readiness for action. . . .

DOCUMENT 70
"INCREASE ACTIVITY AND COMMITMENT AMONG COMMUNISTS"
Speech by First Secretary of the KSS CC Gustav Husák
November 19, 1968
Excerpts
[Bratislava *Pravda,* November 20, 1968]

. . . This [the post-January period] was a great historic opportunity for Czechoslovak Communists to purify our theory and practice, strengthen the humanistic content of our doctrine, consolidate democratic and human methods of work and government in our country, and establish new relations between various social strata and between our party and the nonparty population. It was a great historic opportunity for our economically, politically, and culturally mature state and peoples. We will continue to have faith in the post-January policy, which is concretely described in both the report of Comrade Dubček and the resolution adopted at the party Central Committee session. We also place our faith in the Marxist-Leninist nucleus of post-January policy and the elimination of all deformations from our social life. We wish to regard this content, this interpretation of post-January policy as a permanent component part of our policy and to actively implement it into all areas of life.

Another extreme lay in the extensive boundless interpretation of post-January policy that deprived it of its Marxist positions and allowed no criticism. Among both party members and other citizens, it is still unclear exactly why this great upsurge, which was supported by millions of our people, resulted in such shocks and even tragedies. As a Marxist party, it is our duty to make strict and self-critical examinations of the shortcomings and mistakes in our work. We are obliged to set them forth and learn from them, as it is said in the report of Comrade Dubček and in the resolution of the Czechoslovak Communist Party Central Committee.

Concurrently with the elimination of the personal power regime of Novotný and his guard, more and more leeway opened up for antisocialist forces. It would be naive to believe that such forces and trends did not exist in our society. They did exist, and when they got enough leeway, they began to fight in the political arena — diffidently at first, but then more openly. Along came the forces which had been defeated in 1948, the leftover bourgeois and petit bourgeois with their ideological and political views. Nor was Western propaganda without influence. The way was prepared for petit bourgeois radicalism.

Each such dynamic period we experienced after January in our country is very accessible to a radical escalation of demands — what was radical today is not sufficient for some groups tomorrow. Thus, demands are stepped up beyond all proportion to society's political and economic possibilities, and crisis situations then emerge. You will find a great number of examples of this in history. The way was prepared for petit bourgeois radicalism.

Rightist-opportunist forces and groups formed inside the party. They explained Marxism and the doctrine, aims, and principles of our party so broadly that there was almost nothing left of socialism and Marxism. . . .

In practice this became evident in several areas. First of all, our party and state leadership underrated the role of the mass communications media, of the press, radio, and television. Although roughly one half or perhaps more of the workers in these areas are party members, they failed to come to the aid of the party leadership or give adequate promotion to the line and tasks which the party leadership regarded as correct at the given stage. In fact, they opened up their gates to rightist-opportunist and radical or even antisocialist forces and trends.

This daily influence of the mass communications media, of the press, radio, and television, on millions of our people challenged all the principles which Marxist-Leninist doctrine stipulates with respect to society and the position of the party. It introduced various radical slogans into the people's heads and thus caused ideological and political confusion thereby weakening the line laid down by the party.

These media actually tried to become an independent power. Although they were state media or periodicals published by the party or the trade union movement or other social organizations, their content and line were determined by groups of people.

When the press came under criticism, several journalists said to me that it seemed as if we were looking for a scapegoat for the difficulties of the past months and that we had found it among the workers of these mass communications media. This is not so. We are not seeking a scapegoat and even less among journalists.

That this situation should prevail in a majority of the mass communications media — though there were certainly very many exceptions — is not only a question of the guilt or innocence of journalists. It was caused by weaknesses in a party leadership which was unable to lead or deal with the cadre question in these media in such a way as to enforce and assert its leading role in a new — that is, democratic — way in these media. This is more a question of criticism and self-criticism of the party and the party leadership — that is, the leading party organs — than a question of the criticism of journalists or other workers in these sectors. This criticism is carried on because we have come to realize the enormous power of these media, the influence they have on people's thinking and how extremely important it is for all party work, who controls these media, who influences them politically and ideologically, and what purposes and aims they are serving. This is how we must understand our attitude to this issue.

Other negative features of our approach are reflected in the weakening of state power and of the working class and the working people in our country. The attempt to purify our security agencies — which was absolutely necessary — of people who had compromised themselves in the past and deserved to be eliminated went so far that several branches ceased to carry out their functions.

This pressure began to manifest itself in the army and in other sectors of state power, thus crippling this important component of political power of the working class and consequently the position of the party in the state. . . .

In post-January developments rightist-opportunist forces and various anti-socialist tendencies damaged our international position. There were growing anti-Soviet tendencies, criticism of the Soviet Union and our mutual relations.

When our party leadership tried to restrain these tendencies and the growing nationalist approach toward these problems, it was not always very successful. The lesson our party and work must derive from all this is that in solving internal party and state problems small nations like ours cannot ignore international implications. Party leadership and the Czechoslovak Communist Party Central Committee have fully confirmed this. They base their international policies on the principles of the Bratislava Declaration of the summer of this year, the Moscow agreement of the end of August 1968, and on the agreement on the temporary stay of troops in our territory and the departure of other troops. This is a line of international cooperation between our parties and states, a line of military, political, and economic alliance and friendship. . . .

Conservative elements gradually became a target for criticism among both our party and nonparty public. After January a middle trend has been taking shape and growing in Slovak society and particularly in our party. Characteristic of Slovakia as distinct from the Czech Lands is their preference for a middle way which criticizes conservative trends in our party but also struggles against rightist and opportunist extremes. These trends have been supported at our party's district and regional conferences, where there was criticism of the conservative elements of our party life in the higher organs, too. At the same time, we polemicize with the rightist extremes, with the rightist-opportunist trends. I believe that this middle trend was gradually becoming the characteristic of our party — a perspective for the work of our party — and was gradually winning the majority to its side. . . .

It must be stressed that after August a new situation emerged. Our party had to take it as a basis and seek possibilities for the free development of our nations, the free development of our state within its framework. Future developments will show that the firm course we have taken at this congress and which we are carrying out today, even if it has been sometimes criticized, was the only possible, the only correct one. People frequently express suspicions — especially when unpopular measures have to be taken — that this is a return to the fifties. We discussed this at the congress, at the last session of the Central Committee, and we speak about it again today. We want to remedy the deformations of the fifties. We have condemned these deformations of Marxist theory and especially practice and we are firmly resolved not to permit them to enter our life, our party and public life, even under today's difficult conditions. We are firmly resolved to maintain all that is positive in the post-January developments, all that is creative, as mentioned in the Czechoslovak Communist Party Central Committee resolution. We must rid our work of extremes, of the conservative elements which still abound in many places in our organizations and agencies, we must lead a political struggle against opportunist-rightist trends which have gained a place even in our party and above all against the antisocialist forces which operate outside our party but have the power to influence many Communists.

After this August our party had to resort to certain restrictions. There was the law on censorship, restricting the press, television, and mass communications, there were certain other measures affecting the right of assembly or the recent measures regarding certain temporary restrictions on our borders, etc. We have our critics who compare what our leaders said after January with what they are doing now. They will point out, for example, that Husák said on such and such occasion that our border did not need barbed-wire, whereas today border crossings are restricted. This type of argument only seems effective; it actually balks all logic. When a situation undergoes a basic change, any reasonable person takes it into account. Although we have not given up the principles which we spoke of prior to January we are now dutybound to make certain concessions and restrictions in the interests of the state, in the interests of its domestic and foreign consolidation, in the realization that its scope will expand to the extent to which its entire consolidation will continue on a domestic and international scale. It is a firm principle of the Czechoslovak Communist Party and the Slovak Communist Party leadership to renew legal order and the safety of our citizens, to its full extent, guarantee the people their civic rights granted them by law, and not permit any violations of laws by organs of state power.

Two and a half months have passed since the August events. And you can all witness whether legality with regard to citizens is being violated in our country in these difficult times. We have maintained socialist legality and will adhere to it permanently so that every citizen knows he is protected by law and that there is no organ which can violate his personal or civil rights without being punished.

Another aspect of this matter is adherence to law. Since January discipline has slackened greatly in this respect. We have stressed merely one aspect of the law, as far as it suited the citizens. And at the same time, in various sectors law has been violated, not adhered to. Even organs of state power did not devote any great attention to this. We will insist on adherence to and respect for law and the legal regulations by everybody, by every citizen.

If somebody violates these laws, whether individually or in various mass disturbances, street demonstrations, or elsewhere, he must reckon with the law being applied in his case. This is the case in every civilized state, and thus we cannot permit the willfulness of small groups and trends to lead to anarchy. We wish to state very clearly at this CC session that the leadership of the KSČ and KSS are strongly resolved to stand firm against any pressures or ultimatums submitted to them by student groups or any other type of organization.

None of us in this leadership wants to resort to political trials, political reprisals, or the like. Although other opinions exist elsewhere, we want to struggle against them politically, we want to explain, we want to win over the people. True, wherever the law is violated, the situation becomes different; then we no longer have an ideological problem.

I would also like to mention here mass communications media so that we can go a step further than the discussions or criticisms of mutual suspicion. The resolution of the Czechoslovak Communist Party Central Committee states very clearly that in this sphere, which is of extreme importance for forming the people's minds and orienting them on basic issues, the party cannot renounce its decisive influence and the implementation of its leading role. This theoretical principle must be transferred to the practical sphere. Of course we do not want to do these things insensitively. We do not want to make the journalists and workers in these fields robots or executors of some illiterate orders or commands. We want to reach an agreement with this entire large front of mature workers on how to transfer this line given by the Czechoslovak Communist Party Central Committee and Central Committee to every aspect of work. We want to seek methods of cooperation, creation, agreement; it is in this form that we want to implement the party's leading role. However, wherever we do not find goodwill, wherever there is no readiness to support this line, we will have to take cadre measures and use other forms of ensuring the party's leading role.

"BY WINTER WE SHALL
KNOW EVERYTHING"

BY DECEMBER, Dubček, squeezed between Soviet demands and popular pressures to resist implementing them, personally attacked "anarchistic elements" for suggesting that any realistic alternatives existed to the November Plenum Resolution (Speech to Slovak CP CC Plenum, Document 71). Accusing those who held a "harmful biased view" of post-January developments of isolating the party leadership from the people, he implied that, if necessary, force would be used to cut off dissent.[1] "Inevitable measures" would be taken, enforced by "other politicians" — i.e., Dubček himself would resign.

This dismal prophecy was fulfilled April 18, 1969. Alexander Dubček was replaced as the First Secretary of the KSČ by Gustav Husák. Despite Czechoslovakia's refusal to act like an occupied country,[2] anti-Soviet violence following the second Czechoslovak ice-hockey victory over the USSR in the World Championship competition in Stockholm provided the excuse for Moscow to crack down.[3] The future remained unclear. Yet Vaculík's prediction — "The spring is now ended and never will return. By winter we will know everything" [4] — appeared only too accurate.

[1] A similar threat had been made a month before by Central Committee Secretary Lubomír Štrougal in a polemic against "direct expression of non-Marxist opinions by Communists" and "adventurism" in the communications media. For analysis see Harry Schwartz, *The New York Times*, December 23, 1968.

[2] Protests had continued. See, for example, the reports of public reaction to pressure for the resignation of Josef Smrkovský, Chairman of the National Assembly (*The New York Times*, December 24 and 25, 1968). When the new federal Assembly was created in late January, Smrkovský was shifted to a second-ranking post as chairman of the houses (*The New York Times*, January 31, 1968). The press had continued to be openly critical of the regime. See M. Lakatoš, "Information! Information! Information!", *Zítřek*, No. 10 (December 11, 1968); RFE Czechoslovak Press Survey, No. 2164 (January 14, 1968); and Jiří Hochman, "A Lame Cuckoo Clock," *Reportér*, No. 45 (December 13–20, 1968); RFE Czechoslovak Press Survey No. 2164 (January 2, 1968).

[3] *The New York Times*, April 6, 1969.

[4] Ludvík Vaculík, "2,000 Words Statement," Document 29.

DOCUMENT 71

"CONCERNING THE PRESENT ECONOMIC SITUATION AND THE PARTY'S TASKS IN SLOVAKIA"

Speech to KSS CC December Plenum

A. Dubček

December 21, 1968

Excerpts

[*Rudé právo,* December 22, 1968]

❧

. . . The party's policy and fundamental tasks are damaged by all tendencies and speeches which in one way or another disagree with the tasks stipulated by the November plenum.

This could greatly impair concern for the December tasks and especially for positive points of departure for the following period.

I am referring to viewpoints which persist in opposing the post-January policy and ignoring the concrete tasks necessary for further development, as laid down by the Czechoslovak Communist Party Central Committee and the government of the Republic. The party is not helped by these various rumors and fabrications which cause tension and uncertainty. Nor is it helped by illusions or tough gestures which accuse the leadership of making undue compromises and create the impression that a different and realistic alternative might exist to the course of action chosen by the Czechoslovak Communist Party Central Committee as concerns the preservation of the positive results of the post-January development. . . .

The problems which have arisen in connection with the application of the November resolution are in substance of a political nature. Hence, we shall solve them primarily by political means. . . .

We want to, we must return to a thorough implementation of the tasks and ideas of January; but we do not desire a repetition of those phenomena which diverted us from their implementation, held us back, and very much complicated our efforts. The present situation, too, will be successfully mastered if the substance of the post-January policy is put into practice. On the other hand, society's new excitement, the new confrontations, the attempts to find an outlet in extremes which deviate from the conclusions and policy of the Communist Party of Czechoslovakia Central Committee — these are the chief dangers which can in the present situation throw us far back and nullify our efforts.

An uncritical approach to deficiencies which accompanied and obstructed the activities of the Communist Party of Czechoslovakia Central Committee on the one hand, and the very harmful biased view of the post-January development are clear-cut and very serious signs of this. The first provides leeway for trends which can still create mistrust of established jobs and methods and consequently cripple the party's ability to execute an active policy. The second ignores the views of the broadest party and nonparty masses, driving the party and its leadership into isolation from them and, hence, leads to unforeseeable consequences.

Just as the Action Program was ignored by the press after it was approved in April, so now the advantages of the November resolution, backed by the basic postulates of the Action Program, are being ignored. And quite often resolutions contain demands and problems which have already been included. Who benefits from this?

A variety of campaigns undertaken against the conclusions of the November Czechoslovak Communist Party Central Committee Plenum have caused the party and society as a whole immeasurable damage. They contain demands which in the present situation or within the time limit demanded cannot be accomplished by the leadership of the party, the government, the National Assembly, or the president of the republic, or which embody a course of action that exerts undue pressure on these agencies and their representatives from the right and left, making it impossible for them to foster active work oriented toward the future and discrediting them in the eyes of the public. Their aim is to force the leadership to adopt more and more undesirable measures, and then exploit it from a rightist position as proof of its having compromised itself and deviated from the post-January policy. Quite frequently this is done under the slogan of defending the post-January policy.

To prevent this from having tragic consequences for both our party and the entire society, everything must be done to achieve a united course of action among Communists in safeguarding the tasks of the November and December Czechoslovak Communist Party Central Committee Plenums. If the developments of recent days, resulting from the above-mentioned tendencies, continue to interfere with a positive solution in this situation, the leadership of the party, government, state, and National Assembly will turn to the party and people with inevitable measures. It is possible that these measures will appear to be undemocratic, but they will be in the interest of democracy; they will be in the interest of preventing anarchist elements and their initiators from pushing this republic much further back than the pre-January point. I think this is now sufficiently clear. Of course, politicians other than us would enforce these policies. You may think that these are harsh words, but I am convinced that this is the truth and that it is therefore our duty to state it frankly. . . .

DOCUMENT 72

HUSÁK SPEECH TO KSČ CC APRIL 1969 PLENUM

April 17, 1969
Excerpts

[*Rudé právo,* April 19, 1969]

. . . During the discussion several comrades requested me to make a program declaration. There is no tradition in our party of one person making his own personal program declaration, and no collective organ has had time to draw up such a document. Therefore this is not possible. As early in May as possible we would like to convene the Central Committee to prepare a Central Committee Presidium statement concerning the political situation, prepare a statement on economic questions — at least on those which can now be solved with regard to future plans — and give the Central Committee an opportunity to consider the problems involved in all their breadth and to make suitable decisions.

Although I cannot make a program declaration on behalf of any organ or even on my own behalf, I would like to express my positions on some issues which coincide with those of the Presidium.

There has already been some discussion about the crisis situation in our state and party. The crisis has grown deeper and deeper for the past year and has reached such intensity that our entire society has reached the brink of extraordinary danger. Comrade Černík has expressed the view that our party has not been in such a crisis since 1929. I, too, believe that our party has never experienced such a deep crisis and such divided views. The discussion at this plenum has pointed up the great differences among the views of members of the highest party organ. These are grave matters and we must reflect on them. We will not settle them all today, but we must seek a solution, an honest Communist solution.

We are a government party, and what is happening internally is not unimportant. We are responsible for the fate of 14 million people, their lives, their economic and social situation. I am not sure whether it is not reckless to put off issues as important to our people as economic issues, but this is a question of the over-all political atmosphere. Such crisis situations have grown in intensity. The latest events, such as those of March 28 and 29, have resulted in actions which not only bordered on illegality, provoked an international scandal, and greatly aggravated international relations but also in some places were of a pronounced counterrevolutionary nature. I do not fear to use this term.

It is particularly worth considering how some officials and members of the party — and even members of this body — have been trying to belittle the issues. Why should everyone be punished for something done by a bunch of hooligans, they ask. This is what I have read from monitor reports and heard from foreign radio stations. Fed by various other streams, it has also been making the rounds here at home. On that night half a million people were out in the streets. Did these events not have an anti-Soviet character? Is this sort of demonstration compatible with the honor of our peoples? Let me recall one document. The university students' organization in Prague which deals with all Communists at universities has sent a letter to the Presidium saying: "The events of March 28 were not just an expression of our people's joy over sports. They reflected the feelings of our people regarding August." This is the unambiguous way the university students' organization explains the demonstrations. The true state of affairs could be confirmed by the Ministry of the Interior and the Ministry of National Defense. The university students' committee says in its resolution: "Hold out. That's the nation's position." Now is that a bunch of hooligans talking?

Another question. Why do tens of thousands of people think this way? Take, for instance, our numerous periodicals. Let me remind you of one: the literary journal *Listy*. In almost every issue before these events it carried intensive anti-Soviet propaganda (for example, many articles on the self-immolation of Zajíc). Or let us take *Zítřek*: systematic anti-Soviet propaganda. And what did other newspapers do? If this sort of thing is being drummed into our people, what are the possible results? Is it not an intentionally organized affair? Are there really only a few hooligans? We must learn to call a spade a spade. We must camouflage nothing, to ourselves or to the public. I do not want to accuse anybody, but given the fierce propaganda which started long before August and ended the way it did, let no one say that all we have to do to put things right is to lock up a few hooligans. I am surprised that people whom I otherwise respect hold such opinions.

We are constantly driven into crises. The statement of the Central Committee Presidium of April 2 this year had many fine, reasonable things to say in this respect and also warned how we would have to continue. For all intents and purposes the party and our state organs cannot put their positive program into practice. We are constantly drawn away from concrete work and all of us, wherever we work, must tone down certain operations; we must make constant efforts to bring people over to our way of thinking; we must take steps against certain forces. As soon as the party and state organs eliminate the crisis of one week, the next week brings a new one.

All this leads to aggravations in our relations with other nations. What state can afford that? You well know that such matters can have all sorts of repercussions. You know what the situation in the party looks like. You know to what extent it is capable of acting, to what extent it is unified and how this affects the state's power, the economy, party discipline, working morale, etc. The disintegration process is continuing and bringing us to a very dangerous point.

The causes of this development were well defined in the Central Committee resolution of November last year. We have allowed various forces — which we generally call antisocialist and which objectively oppose the socialist order and endeavor to replace it with something else — to enter the political arena. They act legally and in many cases terrorize Communists. We receive letters about how badly Communists are being treated everywhere.

Rightist tendencies undermine the party's unity and ability to act. There are many links with foreign propaganda. Reading broadcasts monitored from Radio Free Europe, one finds the same sort of talk, the same style and often the same phraseology as used by some of our journalists. Where can this lead, if our Central Committee and our central organs keep silent and do not interfere? What can be the aim? Civil war. Or should we wait until somebody provokes the Soviet armies on our territories to such an extent that they undertake some action in defense? Who has an interest in this sort of catastrophic situation?

Anyone who mingles with the people knows that our party masses and our people have come to realize that it is no longer possible to go on this way and that in some basic issues we must restore order within the party, within our society, that we must limit the activity of various disruptive forces and tendencies and create conditions for fruitful, positive work in the party and among all the citizens of our country.

The documents which we approved are fundamentally good. What then is bad? Our approach to putting the documents into practice. We need only cite the fate of the November resolution. What good is a cause if the organ involved merely outlines it, if there is no struggle for it, if a fight is not organized for its implementation? How can it be seen through?

We do not want to change our way of looking at politics. We do not want to change the political line. But we must make a very definite change in the approach to this line, its realization and organization, and the fight for its implementation. All these issues are part of the political struggle. The problem is not one of the various views of one or another comrade. Different views inside the party have existed before, and in a certain sense they must exist. After all, the exchange of views, the sifting of views is necessary for seeking out the best solution. But it is another thing when decisions are reached once discussion has run its course. There must be a unified solution and a united struggle for its implementation. Otherwise there would be no sense in accepting the solution, if we don't want to deceive ourselves or anyone else, if we don't just want to play at finding solutions.

The same holds true for those various forces, whatever we may call them. I am not pointing a finger at anyone, but let us not permit the tension and unrest in our society which these forces deliberately increase. We must wage an organized political struggle against them, whether inside or outside the party. I expressly say political struggle, as long as it is in the framework permitted by law, as long as it does not infringe any laws. But the struggle must be waged. It must be waged primarily by the party leadership, the members of the Central Committee, and other organs.

Some of our comrades, for instance, are very committed to freedom. They are for freedom, while we, the others, are probably the executioners of freedom. They are the bearers of the torch of freedom and democracy, while we are a den of reactionaries out to smother the press. Yet I do not know one single bourgeois democracy in the West which would permit what has been happening here lately without any repercussions.

But these are large differences. What is going to be new in our work? If we accept the solution of the November resolution, we must organize a political struggle for it; we must implement it.

Permit me to bring up our foreign political relations, relations with the Soviet Union. Opposition currents, antisocialist currents, right-wing currents, are hiding behind patriotism, be it Czech or Slovak, behind Czechoslovak patriotism, and are spreading anti-Soviet ideas — literally bordering on hatred — by all legal means. Before this Central Committee session a comrade from Ostrava showed me a book of photographs from an exhibition which had been held there. One after the other was provocatively anti-Soviet, and that exhibition was paid for by state funds. Today we happened to discuss another such "document." Do you know what the *Black Book* is? Do you know what political damage it has caused us? It was put together by the Institute of History of the Czechoslovak Academy of Sciences, and apparently at the time the authors were paid a fee of 30,000 crowns. Now, the funds of the Academy are not private funds, and fees cannot be paid for something which has been condemned by party and government. In this situation anti-Soviet feeling is the main weapon of the opposition forces, and I will say it outright, of anti-party currents, even when they exist inside the party.

I am not going to recall here the history of how or under what conditions we gained freedom in 1945, that more than 100,000 Soviet people died here. Those who took part in the resistance struggle during those years know what this means. How else can we safeguard the freedom of our two nations, of our people, in this divided world, in a divided Europe? It seems that only a very weak brew of our principles has survived in practice. How can anyone concerned about the internal security of our state permit and tolerate anti-Soviet feelings or spread such hate through the legal state means, on television and radio, and in the press. Where can this lead?

One comrade here has said that anti-Soviet feelings had one meaning before August and another after August. Before August we had to take a stand against it, but after August it became a matter of patriotism.

We will have to make these things clear. Anti-Soviet feelings are incompatible with the ideology of the Czechoslovak Communist Party and stand in sharp contradiction to the policy of this state. We cannot tolerate it in public life.

I know it will be said that a new Novotný era awaits us. But people will judge our activity and our work. A policy popular enough to put one on good terms with everybody does not exist. We are not going to pursue a course designed to please everyone; we must wage a merciless struggle for issues we agree to solve and do the jobs given us by the Central Committee.

This holds for the leading role of the party in society. Let me give you a significant example: the role of the Revolutionary Trade Union Movement.

A large percentage of the officials in the organs of the Revolutionary Trade Union Movement are members of the party — Communists. Many Communists work honorably and devotedly in the trade unions, but do some of them feel any responsibility or duty toward the party? How do they interpret the leading role of the party? If the party does not apply these principles in all other organs — in economic organs — how can it be responsible for the entirety of life and for all problems? Our tolerance went so far that people in the apparatus can do what they please; in some places they work, and in some places they do no work at all! This is a complete desertion of all principles upon which the socialist state is being constructed. Thus, for example, we received information that a conference of students and workers in Prague is being held without the knowledge of the appropriate organs. What are they up to? Planning strikes perhaps? There are also Communists among them. But we ask ourselves: Is what they wanted to do with this republic at this given moment only their affair? Or is it a matter for the entire party and all state organs? Will they continue to play with the fate of 14 million people indefinitely? Everything has its limits, our tolerance not excepted. Otherwise we will all be called to account. We will all be rightly condemned if we are unable to prevent the operations of irresponsible elements. . . .

This certainly also applies to mass communications, of which we have already spoken. If the party does not secure decisive ideological influence over television, radio, and the press, it cannot fulfill its role in this state. The duty of all Communists in these areas is to help the party in an honorable way. We shall not beseech those who do not wish to. Nothing can be done. We must adopt cadre and other measures. There is no other way. There is talk about a limitation of freedom of the press. Can one group of people, however, control a great part of the press, which, with circulations in the millions, influences the entire public? To whom are they responsible?

In this connection there is also talk about freedom. The problem of freedom and democracy is for us a class problem. There can be no freedom for people who in crisis situations such as today's, such as the one through which we are now living, abuse freedom and democracy against the interests of the state and socialism. . . .

And now very briefly about our prospects. Our first task, essential for all further development, is the consolidation of our party, society, and relations with the Soviet Union and the socialist countries. The sooner we attain this aim, the sooner we shall create political conditions for further advances. At the next plenary session we will speed up the beginning of the solution of economic problems and thereby acquire the necessary leeway for developing foreign relations. I am convinced that if we pursue a comradely policy toward the Soviet Union and the socialist countries, there is no question upon which we will be not able to reach an agreement. This also applies to those questions which cause tension and on which our success depends in keeping things at home in our own hands. As soon as we have achieved political consolidation, we will be able to settle the issues which the public expects from us: democratic elections in all sectors and the congress. Given concentrated efforts, I believe we can advance very far within one year, but this requires a firm line in running our internal affairs. . . .

We are not frightened, however, by these difficulties. I want to say on my own behalf that as far as the fundamental questions are concerned I will not retreat. I will not give up one centimeter of the Marxist positions and the fundamental issues which are decisive for the life of these peoples. We cannot make concessions to any hostile forces, any right-wing elements. We shall pick up the gauntlet which has been flung down in the political struggle.

VI. Epilogue

Vladimír Renčín

„Seřezal mě jako psa, jako psa, pane! Ale já jsem se nedal, já mu
to vpálil – pravda zvítězí, holenku! To jsem mu řekl..."

"He beat me like a dog. Like a dog, I tell you. But I didn't give in.
I let him have it. 'The truth will prevail,' I told him."

Dikobraz, January 1, 1969.

A Prayer for Tonight

❦

O God who created this beautiful country, you see our pain and frustration. We do not have to tell you how we feel nor that our heads are bowed. But they are not bowed in shame. Even though fate is beating us with an iron rod, we have no reason to feel shame. We have not been defeated. We have not been found wanting in courage. Our nation has lost none of its honor; it has merely lost a part of its body. We are like a man caught in a cogwheel for whom excruciating pain is a sign of life. Our nation lives, and in our excruciating pain we feel how excruciatingly, how intensely we live.

O God who created this nation, we do not have to tell you anything. It is for our own selves that our lips and our hearts try to formulate something we must never lose: our faith. Faith in ourselves and faith in your history. We believe that we have stood for what is right in history and we will continue to do so. We believe our side and our efforts will lead to a more fruitful future than violence and transitory power. Truth is more than power because it is everlasting. But even now in these difficult times we must commit ourselves; we must not sit and wait for the future with our hands in our laps. We must work harder than we ever did before for our nation and for its inner strength and unity. The better people we make of our nation, the more we will do for history's better side.

Our fate is an integral part of world events, which follow one another with great and glorious necessity. We have nothing to fear from the way the world develops. On the contrary. Violence cannot hold out against mankind's need for freedom, peace, and equality among peoples and nations. We still have very much to accomplish and we must do it ourselves. We must love our nation more. We must love each other more. We believe our great mission on earth is to make ourselves into a nation fully capable of building a better future than the present, temporarily bleak episode in European history.

O God, we do not ask you to avenge us. We do ask you, though, to breathe a spirit of faith into each of us and let no one despair when he should be seeking ways to make himself useful in the future tasks of our undying nation. We do not need defeatists. We need faith. We need internal strength. We need love enough to multiply us ten times over. No nation will ever be small as long as its faith in a better future, in working toward a better future, remains unshaken.

Karel Čapek
Lidové noviny, September 9, 1938

SELECTED BIBLIOGRAPHY

Brahm, Heinz, "Die sowjetisch-tschechoslowakische Konfrontation," *Berichte des Bundesinstituts für ostwissenschaftliche und internationale Studien*, No. 1 (January–August 1968), 1969.
A detailed survey, the first of two parts.

————, "Das Echo im Weltkommunismus auf die Okkupation der CSSR," *Europa Archiv*, Vol. 23, No. 20 (October 25, 1968).

Bromke, Adam, John C. Campbell, and Alastair Buchan, "Lessons of Czechoslovakia," Occasional Papers, No. 3, 1968, Carleton University School of International Affairs, reprinted in the *Canadian Slavonic Papers*, Vol. 10, No. 4 (1968) and Vol. 11, No. 1 (1969).

Brown, J. F., *The New Eastern Europe* (New York: Praeger, 1966).
The most recent standard survey.

Burks, R. V., "The Decline of Communism in Czechoslovakia," *Studies in Comparative Communism*, Vol. 2, No. 1 (January 1969).

Conquest, Robert, "Czechoslovakia: The Soviet Outlook," *Studies in Comparative Communism*, Vol. 1, Nos. 1 and 2 (July/October 1968).

Croan, Melvin, "Czechoslovakia, Ulbricht, and the German Problem," *Problems of Communism*, Vol. XVIII, No. 1 (January–February 1969).

ČSSR: The Road to Democratic Socialism: Facts from January to May 1968 (Prague: Prago Press, 1968).
Excellent, detailed chronology. Particularly good on changes in leadership.

Devlin, Kevin, "The New Crisis in European Communism," *Problems of Communism*, Vol. XVII, No. 6 (November–December 1968).
Excellent analysis of impact of Czechoslovakia on European Communist parties.

Ebert, Theodor, "Der zivile Widerstand in der Tschechoslowakei," *Europa Archiv*, Vol. 23, No. 33 (December 10, 1968), pp. 865–874.

Elliáš, Zdeněk and Jaromír Netík, "Czechoslovakia" in William E. Griffith, ed., *Communism in Europe*, Vol. 2 (Cambridge, Mass.: The M.I.T. Press, 1966).
Background, through 1965.

Ello, Paul, ed., *Czechoslovakia's Blueprint for "Freedom"* (Washington, D.C.: Acropolis Books, 1968).
An inadequate documentary volume.

Ermarth, Fritz, *Internationalism, Security, and Legitimacy: The Challenge to Soviet Interests in East Europe, 1964–1968*. RAND Memorandum RM-5909-PR (March 1969).
The best recent analysis of Soviet policy in Eastern Europe.

Fejtö, François, "Moscow and Its Allies," *Problems of Communism*, Vol. XVII, No. 6 (November–December 1968).

Fischer-Galati, Stephen, *The Socialist Republic of Rumania* (Baltimore, Md.: Johns Hopkins Press, 1969).
    Analyzes implications of the invasion of Czechoslovakia for Rumania.

Gamarnikow, Michael, *Economic Reforms in Eastern Europe* (Detroit, Mich.: Wayne State University Press, 1968).
    The most recent good survey.

Garaudy, Roger, *La liberté en sursis: Prague 1968* (Paris: Fayard, 1968).
    A documentary volume with an introduction by a PCF Politburo member criticized by the leadership for his support of the Czechoslovak position.

Griffith, William E., *Eastern Europe After the Invasion of Czechoslovakia*, RAND P-3983, October 9, 1968.
    A country-by-country survey.

Holešovský, Václav, "Prague's Economic Model," *East Europe*, Vol. XVI, No. 2 (February 1967).

————, "The Revolution Begins in Czechoslovakia," *Dissent* (May–June 1968).

Leonhard, Wolfgang, "Differenzierung des Ostblocks — Ausmass und Grenzen," *Osteuropa*, Vol. 18, No. 12 (December 1968), pp. 851–870.
    An excellent analysis, by a leading expert on the U.S.S.R.

Littell, Robert, ed., *The Czech Black Book* (New York: Praeger, 1969).
    A collection of documents and eyewitness accounts of the invasion of Czechoslovakia prepared by the Czechoslovak Academy of Sciences under the title *Seven Days in Prague*. Contains detailed information on the activities of the invaders, the population, and the Czechoslovak political élite.

Lowenthal, Richard, "The Sparrow in the Cage," *Problems of Communism*, Vol. XVII, No. 6 (November–December 1968).
    An excellent analysis of Soviet policy and the Czechoslovak crisis.

Montias, John Michael, "A Plan for All Seasons," *Survey*, No. 51 (April 1964).
    The key analysis of the causes and significance of the Czechoslovak economic crisis.

Remington, Robin Alison, "Czechoslovakia and the Warsaw Pact," *East European Quarterly*, Vol. 3, No. 3, September 1969.

Riveles, Stanley, "Slovakia: Catalyst of Crisis," *Problems of Communism*, Vol. XVII, No. 3 (May–June 1968).
    The best analysis of the Slovak factor.

Robinson, William F., "Czechoslovakia and Its Allies," *Studies in Comparative Communism*, Vol. 1, Nos. 1 and 2 (July/October 1968).

Schwartz, Harry, *Prague's 200 Days* (New York: Praeger, 1969).

Schwartz, Morton, "Czechoslovakia's New Political Model: A Design for Renewal," *Journal of Politics*, Vol. 30, No. 4 (November 1968).
    Czech and Slovak interest group theories.

————, "Czechoslovakia: Toward One-Party Pluralism?", *Problems of Communism*, Vol. XVII, No. 3 (May–June 1968).

Šik, Ota, *Plan and Market Under Socialism* (New York: International Arts and Sciences Press, Inc., 1969).
    By the leading Czech economic reformer.

Skilling, H. Gordon, "Crisis and Change in Czechoslovakia," *International Journal*, Vol. XXIII, No. 3 (Summer 1968).
    An excellent, brief analysis.

————, "Interest Groups and Communist Politics," *World Politics*, Vol. XVIII, No. 3 (April 1966).

Spender, Stephen, *The Year of the Young Rebels* (London: Weidenfeld and Nicolson, 1969). See section "Czechoslovakia and Western Students," pp. 59–81.

Suda, Zdeněk, *The Czechoslovak Socialist Republic* (Baltimore, Md.: Johns Hopkins Press, 1969).
Focuses on the 1960's; historical background for recent events in Czechoslovakia.

Táborský, Edward, "The New Era in Czechoslovakia," *East Europe*, Vol. 17, No. 11 (November 1968).

Tatu, Michel, *L'hérésie impossible: chronique du drame tchéchoslovaque* (Paris: Bernard Grasset, 1967–1968).
A collection of dispatches to *Le Monde* by their Vienna correspondent; the ablest journalistic coverage of the events.

Tigrid, Pavel, *Le printemps de Prague* (Paris: Seuil, 1968).
The best book-length survey of the pre-invasion period, based on the author's running analyses in *Svědectví*.

Toma, Peter A., "Czech-Slovak Question Under Communism," *East European Quarterly*, Vol. 3, No. 1, March 1969.

United States Senate Committee on Government Operations, "Czechoslovakia and the Brezhnev Doctrine," prepared by the Subcommittee on National Security and International Operations, 91st Congress, 1st Session, Washington, D.C., 1969.

Urban, G. R., "Eastern Europe After Czechoslovakia," *Studies in Comparative Communism*, Vol. 2, No. 1 (January 1969).

Wechsberg, Joseph, *The Voices* (Garden City, N.Y.: Doubleday, 1969).
A brief, sensitive account of the "underground radios," by the Central European correspondent of *The New Yorker*.

Windsor, Philip and Adam Roberts, *Czechoslovakia, 1968: Reform, Repression and Resistance* (London: Institute for Strategic Studies Paperback, 1969).
Excellent analyses, with 10 documents.

Zeman, A. A. B., *Prague Spring: A Report on Czechoslovakia, 1968* (Middlesex, England: Penguin Books, 1969).
Brief, penetrating analysis of events leading up to August 1968 invasion.

ADDITIONAL BIBLIOGRAPHY

Devlin, Kevin, "Austrian Communism After Czechoslovakia," *Survey*, No. 73 (Autumn 1969).

James, Robert Rhodes, ed., *The Czechoslovak Crisis of 1968* (London: Weidenfeld and Nicholson, 1969).

Kipály, Béla and Tamas Aczel, "From Budapest to Prague," *Problems of Communism*, Vol. XVIII, No. 4–5 (July-October 1969).

Klokočka, Vladimír, *Demokratischer Sozialismus* (Hamburg: Konkret, 1968). An analysis of socialist pluralism. Author a constitutional lawyer who participated in the reforms.

Liehm, Antonín, *Gespräch an der Moldau: Das Ringen um die Freiheit der Tschechoslowakei* (Vienna: Molden, 1968).
An editor of *Literární listy* describes conversations among intellectuals, many of them prior to 1968. A good indicator of unrest among the intelligentsia.

Löbl, Eugen and Leopold Grünwald, *Die intellektuelle Revolution: Hintergründe und Auswirkungen des "Prager Frühlings"* (Düsseldorf: Econ, 1969). An original interpretation of the events in 1968 as a "new phase" in the Czechoslovak socialist revolution.

Loebl, Eugen, *Stalinism in Prague: The Loebl Story* (New York: Grove Press, 1969).
Memoirs of a high-ranking Slovak Communist who was one of the major victims of
the Slánský trials who lived to write about them.

London, Artur, *L'aveu: Dans l'engrenage du procès de Prague* (Paris: Gallimard, 1968).
Memoirs of the Stalinist purges in Czechoslovakia.

Ludz, Peter and J. H. Huizinga, "Doctrinal Myths and Realities," *Problems of Communism*,
Vol. XVIII, No. 4–5 (July-October 1969).

Provazník, Jan, "The Politics of Retrenchment," *Problems of Communism*, Vol. XVIII, No.
4–5 (July-October 1969).

Šik, Ota, *La verité sur l'économie tchécoslovaque* (Paris: Fayard, 1969). Six television
broadcasts dealing with the plight of the economy in summer 1968.

Skilling, H. Gordon, "Thaw and Freeze-Up: Prague 1968," *International Journal*, Vol. XXV,
No. 1 (Winter 1969-1970).
An excellent review article of books published on the 1968 invasion of Czechoslovakia.

Sviták, Ivan, *Verbotene Horizonte, Prag zwischen zwei Wintern* (Freiburg im Breisgau:
Rombach, 1969).
Collection of articles of the Czech philosopher, who himself was prominent in the fer-
ment leading up to August 1968.

Škvorecký, Josef, ed., *Nachrichten aus der ČSSR* (Frankfurt: Suhrkamp, 1968).
Articles on the changing nature of Czechoslovak political theory and practice during
1968, translated from the journal of the Writers' Union *Literární listy*.

Slánská, Josefa, *Report on My Husband* (London: Hutchinson, 1969). Account by Rudolph
Slánský's widow of the purges in the 1950's.

Tigrid, Pavel, "Czechoslovakia: A Post-Mortem," *Survey*, No. 73 (Autumn 1969).

——————, *La chute irrésistible d'Alexandre Dubček* (Paris: Calmann-Lévy, 1969).
An excellent post invasion analysis.

Ulč, Otto, "The Vagaries of Law," *Problems of Communism*, Vol. XVIII, No. 4–5 (July-
October 1969).

Viney, Deryck, "Rewriting History in Czechoslovakia," *Studies in Comparative Communism*, Vol. 3, No. 1 (January 1970).

INDEX